The Successful Medical School Department Chair: A Guide to Good Institutional Practice

A Manual for Medical School Deans, Teaching Hospital CEOs, Department Chairs, Search Committees, and Chair-Candidates.

The Successful Medical School Department Chair offers helpful advice, details good practice, and provides a wealth of sample documents and policies that can be adapted for local use. Each of the three modules is devoted to a different time period in the total career life of the medical school department chair.

Module 1: Search, Selection, Appointment, Transition
$50 Member
$75 Non-Member Non-Profit
$100 Non-Member For-Profit
(Product ID CHAIR1)

Module 2: Characteristics, Responsibilities, Expectations, Skill Sets
$50 Member
$75 Non-Member Non-Profit
$100 Non-Member For-Profit
(Product ID CHAIR2)

Module 3: Performance, Evaluation, Rewards, Mentorship
$50 Member
$75 Non-Member Non-Profit
$100 Non-Member For-Profit
(Product ID CHAIR3)

For a full listing of publications that are for sale and those that are free, please visit our Web site, **www.aamc.org/publications**.

AAMC President and CEO
Darrell G. Kirch, M.D.

Project Coordinators
Sara Halperin
Joanna Ouellette

2012

Directory of American Medical Education

Acknowledgements

The association wishes to express appreciation to its staff members and to the deans of the medical schools and their representatives for their assistance in revising the information for this edition of the AAMC directory.

The entries appearing in this edition were updated in fall 2011 for the 2012 academic year.

Orders

To order additional copies of this publication, please contact:

Association of American Medical Colleges
Section for Publication Orders
2450 N Street, NW
Washington, DC 20037

Phone: 202-828-0416
Fax: 202-828-1123

Price: $85, plus shipping
(Item Code: DAME12)

AAMC Members: $25, plus shipping
(Item Code: DAME12)

AAMC Members (Additional copies after the first copy): $10
(Item Code: DAME12)

See order form in this publication for ordering instructions.

ISBN 978-1-57754-109-7

Handbook of Academic Medicine: How Medical Schools and Teaching Hospitals Work 2nd Edition
$35 Member/Non-Member
(Product ID HANDBOOK2)

Medical schools and teaching hospitals can be complex, intimidating organizations, surely to those new to the enterprise, even to those who have made their careers within its walls. The Handbook of Academic Medicine describes this world of academic medicine, explaining what medical schools and teaching hospitals are, how they work and interrelate, and what prominent issues they face. The Handbook is a comprehensive reference source on the fundamentals of academic medicine.

The Handbook is essential reading for medical school and teaching hospital leaders, governing board members, university officials, members of the media, national and state legislators and staff members, Federal agency staff, and anyone who wants to know more about medical schools and teaching hospitals, their structure, financing, interrelationships, and programs - and the issues they and society face in preserving and enhancing their unique contributions to the national well-being.

Human Embryonic Stem Cell Research: Regulatory and Administrative Challenges
2006
$25 Member/Non-Member
(Product ID STEMCELL06)

The Bush Administration has limited the federal funding of human embryonic stem (hES) cell research to those successful applications that utilize one or more of the 22 lines currently listed on the NIH Human Embryonic Stem Cell Registry. The derivation and use of hES cell lines developed after the Administration's August 9, 2001 policy declaration remains legal and there is no pending legislative or regulatory effort to prohibit their use. The AAMC sponsored a workshop on April 27, 2006 to discuss policy and administrative issues on how best to organize, monitor, document, and allocate costs for laboratories that utilize stem cell lines both listed and not listed on the NIH stem cell registry. This monograph summarizes the workshop discussions and provides additional background information on the topics considered.

AAMC Data Book: Medical Schools and Teaching Hospitals by the Numbers
April 2011
$74 Member
$130 Non-Member Non-Profit
$188 Non-Member For-Profit
(Product ID DATABOOK11)

The *AAMC Data Book*, a statistical abstract of U.S. medical schools and teaching hospitals, includes current and historical data on a comprehensive list of topics including: Applicants and Students, Faculty, Medical School Revenue, Tuition and Financial Aid, Graduate Medical Education, Teaching Hospitals, Faculty Compensation, Physicians, Biomedical Research, and reference data such as Price Indices.

Report on Medical School Faculty Salaries 2010-2011
2012
$128 Member
$238 Non-Member Non-Profit
$409 Non-Member For-Profit)
(Product ID FACSAL12)

The Report on Medical School Faculty Salaries contains 33 tables that present the total income attributable to teaching, patient care, or research for full-time medical school faculty. The total income is broken out in a number of ways, such as by discipline, degree, region, and school ownership. The tables provide the 25th percentile and 75th percentile as well as the mean and median for each combination of faculty rank and faculty department/specialty. The number of faculty in each total income statistic is given also.

Minority Student Opportunities in United States Medical Schools
2009
$15 Member/Non-Member
(Product ID MSOUSMS09)

The information in this book is supplied by individual medical schools in response to a questionnaire from the AAMC's Division of Diversity Policy and Programs about minority student opportunities.

Medicaid Direct and Indirect Graduate Medical Education Payments: A 50 State Survey 2010
May 2010
$10 Member
$25 Non-Member Non-Profit
$50 Non-Member For-Profit
(Product ID MEDIGME10)

The AAMC, working jointly with the Society for Simulation in Healthcare (SSH), the Association for Standardized Patient Educators (ASPE), and the American Association of Colleges of Nursing (AACN) developed a survey in 2010 to better understand how medical schools and teaching hospitals are using simulation for education and assessment and determine the operational impact of simulation at AAMC-member institutions.

Regional Medical Campuses: Bridging Communities, Enhancing Mission, Expanding Medical Education
November 2006
$25 Member
$50 Non-Member
(Product ID BRIDGING06)

Regional Medical Campuses: Bridging Communities, Enhancing Mission, Expanding Medical Education is a reprinting of the 2003 AAMC monograph, the first comprehensive study of regional campuses at medical schools in the United States. This book examines the distinct educational benefits for medical students offered by regional clinical campuses. It also investigates the structure, organization, governance, leadership, and strengths and weaknesses of regional campuses.

Finding Top Talent: How to Search for Leaders in Academic Medicine
October 2009
$50 Member
$100 Non-Member
(Product ID TOPTALENT)

Integrative leadership teams are key to the future of every academic medical center. *Finding Top Talent* presents innovative ideas and promising practices to help medical schools and teaching hospitals recruit the best leaders for the future. The premise of this book is that process is the key to every successful search.

Teaching Hospitals and Health Systems: Serving the Nation Through Education, Research and Patient Care 2008
June 2008
$20 Member
$75 Non-Member
(Product ID COTHSERV)

This report provides an overview of the characteristics that uniquely distinguish teaching hospitals from other teaching and nonteaching hospitals. It includes charts and tables that compare Council of Teaching Hospitals and Health Systems (COTH) hospitals to other teaching and nonteaching hospitals in three categories (short-term, general, nonfederal hospitals; VA hospitals; and Children's hospitals).

Publication Order Form

Association of American Medical Colleges
2450 N Street, N.W., Washington, D.C. 20037-1127
T 202 828 0400 **F** 202 828 1125
www.aamc.org

Item Code	Title	Quantity	Unit Price	Total

*Shipping/Handling

Shipping not included. Please call or email for quotes.

	Subtotal	
	*Shipping/Handling	
	Total Amount Enclosed	

NAME

TITLE

INSTITUTION

ADDRESS

CITY   **STATE**   **ZIP**

PHONE   **E-MAIL ADDRESS**

PAYMENT

All orders must be accompanied by payment. Please make checks payable to AAMC. All payments must be in U.S. dollars, drawn on a U.S. bank. Prices are subject to change without notice.

❏ Check   ❏ Money Order   ❏ Mastercard   ❏ Visa   ❏ American Express

NAME OF CARD HOLDER_____

CARD NUMBER_____   **EXPIRATION DATE**_____

SIGNATURE_____

ORDER ONLINE	**ORDER BY MAIL**	**ORDER BY PHONE**
www.aamc.org	Customer Service & Order Fulfillment AAMC 2450 N Street, NW Washington, DC 20037	202-828-0416
		ORDER BY FAX
		202-828-1123

Questions? Call us at the number noted above, or email publications@aamc.org.

Contents

Alphabetical Listing of Medical Schools

MEDICAL SCHOOL MEMBERS
**(Accredited by the Liaison Committee on Medical Education [LCME].
Preliminary and provisional accreditation are sufficient for eligibility.)**

MEDICAL SCHOOL MEMBERS (Continued)

PROVISIONAL MEDICAL SCHOOL MEMBERS

AFFILIATE MEDICAL SCHOOL MEMBERS
(Jointly accredited by the LCME and the Committee on Accreditation of Canadian Medical Schools [CACMS])

Geographical Listing of Medical Schools

UNITED STATES

Geographical Listing of Medical Schools

Geographical Listing of Medical Schools

CANADA

Association Organizational Structure and Activities

2012

About the AAMC

Founded in 1876, the AAMC is a not-for-profit association representing all 137 accredited U.S. and 17 accredited Canadian medical schools; nearly 400 major teaching hospitals and health systems, including 62 Department of Veterans Affairs medical centers; and nearly 90 academic and scientific societies. Through these institutions and organizations, the AAMC represents 128,000 faculty members, 75,000 medical students, and 110,000 resident physicians.

What We Do

The AAMC serves and leads the academic medicine community to improve the health of all. To fulfill this mission, the association focuses on nine strategic priorities:

- Serve as the voice and advocate for academic medicine on medical education, research, and health care
- Lead innovation along the continuum of medical education to meet the health needs of the public
- Facilitate development of a health system that meets the needs of all for access, safety, and quality of care
- Strengthen the national commitment to discovery that promotes health and enhances the treatment of disease and disability
- Lead efforts to increase diversity in medicine
- Be a valued and reliable resource for data, information, and services
- Help our members identify, implement, and sustain organizational performance improvement
- Provide outstanding leadership and professional development to meet the most critical needs of our members
- Nurture a culture at the AAMC that promotes excellence in service to our members and the public good.

Medical Education

Each year, more than 17,000 students graduate with an M.D. degree from AAMC-member medical schools, and over 110,000 resident physicians continue their training at teaching hospitals and associated community sites across the United States. The AAMC works to ensure that the medical education and advanced preparation of these new doctors meet the highest standards and keep pace with the changing needs of patients and the nation's health care system.

The Liaison Committee on Medical Education (LCME) is the U.S. Department of Education-recognized accrediting body for U.S. medical education programs leading to the M.D. degree. It also accredits M.D. programs in Canada, in cooperation with the Committee on Accreditation of Canadian Medical Schools. The LCME is jointly sponsored by the AAMC with the American Medical Association.

Medical schools and teaching hospitals, as well as the future physicians and medical scientists they train, rely on AAMC service programs, such as the admission test to medical school (the MCAT® examination) and Web-based applications for medical school (AMCAS®) and residency programs (ERAS®).

Information and Data

The AAMC also provides leaders of medical schools and teaching hospitals with an extensive array of data to support their missions, including the Medical School Profile System, a source of information about medical school revenues, expenditures, enrollments, faculty counts, and other operations; the Faculty Roster and FAMOUS (Faculty Administrative Management Online User System) interface, an online database of full-time, part-time, volunteer, and emeritus faculty appointments at U.S. medical schools; GME Track®, an online graduate medical education resource; clinical productivity benchmarking tools for faculty practice plans; and annual surveys of teaching hospitals and residents' and fellows' stipends.

Advocacy

As the leading voice of the academic medical community, the AAMC represents the interests of the nation's medical schools and teaching hospitals before Congress, federal regulatory agencies, and the executive branch on a wide range of issues, including Medicare and Medicaid funding; graduate medical education (GME); federal support for medical research and public health; federal student loan programs; health professions education funding; and veterans' medical care and biomedical research.

Through various programs and communications, the AAMC also educates the public to build awareness of and support for the unique missions of the nation's medical schools and teaching hospitals.

About the AAMC

Organization and Governance

The association is governed by a 17-member board of directors, composed of the chair and chair-elect of each of the AAMC's three member councils, as well as seven at-large members who include a medical student, a resident, and a public member.

The AAMC has five member councils and organizations:

The Council of Deans (COD) represents the leaders of America's medical schools, providing medical school deans with a forum to discuss important issues, and offering services, information, and programs that advance their efforts.

The Council of Teaching Hospitals and Health Systems (COTH®) comprises the leaders of America's major teaching hospitals and health systems. Participation in COTH is recognized throughout the world as a benchmark for excellence in patient care, research, and medical education.

The Council of Academic Societies (CAS) provides a forum for discussing and exchanging information of interest to medical school faculty and scientists involved in life sciences research, research training, and medical education.

The Organization of Student Representatives (OSR) represents the interests of students enrolled in the nation's medical schools.

The Organization of Resident Representatives (ORR) provides a venue for discussing issues of interest to resident physicians, and offers leadership opportunities for those interested in academic medical careers.

AAMC Services

Following is a list of major services the AAMC provides.

Advisor Information System (AIS)—an online reporting tool that assists health professions advisors by providing them AMCAS® application and MCAT® examination data about medical school applicants.

American Medical College Application Service (AMCAS®)—a not-for-profit, Internet-based application processing service for first-year applicants to U.S. medical schools.

AspiringDocs.org—a Web site and outreach campaign to increase diversity in medicine by encouraging well-prepared African American, Latino/a, and Native American students to apply to and enroll in medical school.

Careers in Medicine®—a print and Web-based career planning program that helps medical students understand options in choosing a specialty and identifying residency programs that meet individual career objectives.

Electronic Residency Application Service (ERAS®)—an Internet-based service that enables medical students and graduates to transmit applications, transcripts, recommendations, and other supporting credentials to U.S. residency program directors.

FindAResident®—a year-round Web-based service that allows residents and residency programs to search for, and fill, open residency and fellowship positions.

FIRST for Medical Education—a program that offers a full range of Financial Information Resources, Services, and Tools for applicants, medical students, residents, advisors, and financial aid officers.

Medical College Admission Test (MCAT®)—the national standardized test used to assess medical school applicants' science knowledge, reasoning, and communications skills.

MedEdPORTAL®—an online resource designed to help faculty publish and share educational resources—focusing exclusively on the continuum of medical education and addressing the unique needs of medical educators.

Student Records System (SRS)—houses secure, centralized enrollment information on national medical school population and tracks student progress from matriculation to graduation.

Visiting Student Application Service (VSAS®)—an AAMC application designed to make it easier for medical students to apply for senior electives at other U.S. medical schools.

For more information about these and other AAMC service programs, go to www.aamc.org/services.

AAMC Data

Key informational resources provided by the AAMC include:

COTH Data Tool—provides benchmark and data book reports, operating statement and financial ratio data, trend data, and custom analyses on data collected through the annual COTH Financial Survey.

Curriculum Reports—an interactive online resource of information and data on medical school curricula.

GME Track®—a Web-based graduate medical education resource and resident and program database, jointly conducted with the American Medical Association.

Faculty Roster—a comprehensive collection of information on the characteristics of paid faculty members at accredited U.S. medical schools.

Medical School Profile System (MSPS)—information on U.S. medical school revenues and expenditures, faculty counts, curricula, student enrollment, and student financial aid.

For more information about these and other AAMC data resources, go to www.aamc.org/data.

Professional Development

The AAMC's 16 professional development groups offer individuals at member institutions opportunities for information sharing, professional growth, and leadership. The groups include:

Chief Medical Officers Group (CMOG)
Government Relations Representatives (GRR)
Graduate Research, Education, and Training Group (GREAT)
Group on Business Affairs (GBA)
Group on Diversity and Inclusion (GDI)
Group on Educational Affairs (GEA)
Group on Faculty Affairs (GFA)
Group on Faculty Practice (GFP)
Group on Information Resources (GIR)
Group on Institutional Advancement (GIA)
Group on Institutional Planning (GIP)
Group on Regional Medical Campuses (GRMC)
Group on Research Advancement and Development (GRAND)
Group on Resident Affairs (GRA)
Group on Student Affairs (GSA)
Group on Women in Medicine and Science (GWIMS)

For links to these groups and additional information, go to www.aamc.org/members.

Other member communities include:
Compliance Officers' Forum (COF)
Forum on Conflict of Interest in Academe (FOCI Academe)

Publications

The AAMC publishes a range of books, journals, reports, and other print and electronic resources, including the following:

Academic Medicine®, the monthly journal of the AAMC, publishes articles on the most pressing challenges facing the leaders of medical schools and teaching hospitals today. www.academicmedicine.org

Directory of American Medical Education (DAME), a directory of all AAMC members and their key staff in U.S. and Canadian medical schools, teaching hospitals, and academic societies, along with a description of the AAMC organizational structure and a listing of key staff contacts.

Medical School Admissions Requirements (MSAR), a comprehensive guide featuring the most up-to-date information about medical school entrance requirements, curriculum features, first-year expenses, financial aid, and application procedures. www.aamc.org/msar

Reporter, the AAMC's monthly news publication, covers major programs and initiatives at the AAMC and member institutions, as well as broader issues that affect the nation's medical schools and teaching hospitals. www.aamc.org/newsroom/reporter

STAT (Short, Topical, and Timely), a weekly electronic newsletter featuring brief and immediate news bites about AAMC activities, as well as policy developments, initiatives, and data important to the academic medicine community. www.aamc.org/newsroom/aamcstat

Washington Highlights, a weekly electronic newsletter focusing on key federal legislative and regulatory developments. www.aamc.org/advocacy/washhigh

On the Web

The AAMC Web site provides a rich source of data, information, and services, along with the latest association news, publications, and events. To learn more about the association and its initiatives, visit www.aamc.org.

The AAMC also maintains a presence on Facebook (www.facebook.com/aamctoday) and in a Twitter feed updated daily (www.twitter.com/aamctoday).

AAMC Board of Directors, 2011-2012

Chair
Mark R. Laret
University of California,
San Francisco Medical Center

Chair-elect
Valerie N. Williams, Ph.D.,
M.P.A.
University of Oklahoma
Health Sciences Center

Immediate Past Chair
Thomas J. Lawley, M.D.
Emory University
School of Medicine

President and CEO
Darrell G. Kirch, M.D.
Association of American
Medical Colleges

Members
Marna P. Borgstrom
Yale-New Haven Hospital

Sheila P. Burke, R.N., M.P.A.
Baker, Donelson, Bearman,
Caldwell & Berkowitz

Ruth-Marie (Rhee) E. Fincher,
M.D.
Medical College of Georgia at
Georgia Health Sciences
University

Rosemarie L. Fisher, M.D.
Yale University
School of Medicine

J. Lloyd Michener, M.D.
Duke University
Medical Center

Kathleen G. Nelson, M.D.
University of Alabama
School of Medicine

Lois Margaret Nora, M.D.,
J. D., M.B.A.
The Commonwealth Medical
College

Harold L. Paz, M.D.
Pennsylvania State University

Claire Pomeroy, M.D.,
M.B.A.
University of California, Davis

David J. Skorton, M.D.
Cornell University

Peter L. Slavin, M.D.
Massachusetts General
Hospital

Catherine (Katie) Spina
Boston University

Javeed Sukhera, M.D.
University of Rochester
Department of Psychiatry

AAMC

2450 N Street, N.W. • Washington, D.C. 20037
Phone: 202-828-0400 • Fax: 202-828-1125

Office of the President

President and CEO
Darrell G. Kirch, M.D.
828-0460
dgkirch@aamc.org

Chief of Staff
Jennifer M. Schlener
828-0466
jmschlener@aamc.org

Academic Affairs

Chief Academic Officer
John E. Prescott, M.D.
828-0533
jprescott@aamc.org

Senior Director, Accreditation Services & LCME
Dan Hunt, Ph.D.
828-0596
dhunt@aamc.org

Director, Careers in Medicine
George V. Richard
828-6223
grichard@aamc.org

Senior Director, Continuing Education and Performance Improvement
David A. Davis, M.D.
862-6275
ddavis@aamc.org

Director, Council of Deans
Ann Steinecke, Ph.D.
828-0475
asteinecke@aamc.org

Director, LCME Surveys and Team Training
Robert F. Sabalis, Ph.D.
828-0556
rsabalis@aamc.org

Senior Director, Leadership and Talent Development
Kevin Grigsby, D.S.W.
822-0575
kgrigsby@aamc.org

Senior Director, Medical School Financial and Administrative Affairs
Jack Y. Krakower, Ph.D.
828-0654
jykrakower@aamc.org

Senior Director, Student Affairs and Programs
Geoffrey Young
741-6466
gyoung@aamc.org

Director, Student/Resident Debt Management
Julie Fresne
828-0511
jfresne@aamc.org

Communications

Chief Communications and Marketing Officer
Elisa K. Siegel
828-0459
esiegel@aamc.org

Director and Managing Editor, *Academic Medicine*
Anne Farmakidis
828-0593
afarmakidis@aamc.org

Senior Director, Marketing and Institutional Advancement
Chris Tucker
828-0989
ctucker@aamc.org

Senior Director, Print and Electronic Publishing
Eric Weissman
828-0044
eweissman@aamc.org

Senior Director, Strategic Communications
Susan Beach
828-0983
sbeach@aamc.org

Diversity Policy and Programs

Chief Diversity Officer
Mark A. Nivet, Ed.D.
862-6105
mnivet@aamc.org

Senior Director, DPP & Organizational Capacity Building Portfolio
Laura Castillo-Page, Ph.D.
828-0579
lcastillopage@aamc.org

Director, Human Capital Portfolio
Norma Poll-Hunter
862-6115
npoll@aamc.org

Finance and Administration

Chief Financial and Administration Officer
Bernard K. Jarvis, M.B.A., C.P.A.
828-0404
bjarvis@aamc.org

Controller
Daniel Berringer
862-6295
dberringer@aamc.org

Senior Director, Human Resources
Roby Hunt
741-5484
rhunt@aamc.org

Senior Director, Membership & Constituent Services
Heather Brinton-Parker
828-0427
hbrinton@aamc.org

AAMC Senior Staff

Director of Membership & Meetings
Kirsten Olean
828-0479
kolean@aamc.org

Health Care Affairs

Chief Health Care Officer
Joanne M. Conroy, M.D.
828-0584
jconroy@aamc.org

Director, Center for Workforce Studies
Clese E. Erikson
828-0587
cerikson@aamc.org

Director & Regulatory Counsel
Ivy S. Baer, J.D.
828-0499
ibaer@aamc.org

Director, Health Care Affairs
David E. Longnecker, M.D.
862-6113
dlongnecker@aamc.org

Director, Health Care Affairs
Sunny G. Yoder
828-0497
syoder@aamc.org

Information Technology

Chief Information Officer
Jeanne L. Mella
862-6173
jmella@aamc.org

Senior Director, Enterprise Architecture
Uwe Vielle
828-0964
uvielle@aamc.org

Senior Director, Enterprise Information & Information Architecture
Kirke B. Lawton
828-0974
klawton@aamc.org

Senior Director, Enterprise Technology
Lee Leiber
862-6247
lleiber@aamc.org

Senior Director, IT Service Delivery
Greg Haywood
862-6172
ghaywood@aamc.org

Legal

Chief Legal Officer
Frank L. Trinity, J.D.
828-0540
ftrinity@aamc.org

Medical Education

Chief Medical Education Officer
Carol A. Aschenbrener, M.D.
828-0665
caschenbrener@aamc.org

Senior Director, Competency-Based Medical Education
Robert Englander
828-0255
renglander@aamc.org

Director, Educational Affairs
Katherine McOwen
478-9345
cmcowen@aamc.org

Senior Director, Medical Education Projects
Harry Sondheimer, M.D.
828-0648
hsondheimer@aamc.org

Director, MedEdPORTAL
Robby Reynolds
828-0962
rreynolds@aamc.org

Operations and Services

Chief Operating Officer
Robert F. Jones, Ph.D.
828-0520
rfjones@aamc.org

Director, AMCAS
Kelly Begatto
862-6003
kbegatto@aamc.org

Senior Director, Admissions Testing Service
Karen J. Mitchell, Ph.D.
828-0500
kmitchell@aamc.org

Senior Director, Application Services
Stephen J. Fitzpatrick
828-0621
sfitzpatrick@aamc.org

Senior Director, Business Strategy and Development
Gabrielle Campbell
828-0643
gcampbell@aamc.org

Senior Director, Data Resources and Studies
Susan J. Bodilly
862-6019
sbodilly@aamc.org

Director, MCAT Development and Research
Scott H. Oppler, Ph.D.
862-6073
soppler@aamc.org

Director, Medical School and Faculty
Hershel Alexander
828-0649
halexander@aamc.org

AAMC Senior Staff

Senior Director, Special Studies
Paul Jolly Jr., Ph.D.
828-0257
pjolly@aamc.org

Public Policy and Strategic Relations

Chief Public Policy Officer
Atul Grover, M.D., Ph.D.
828-0666
agrover@aamc.org

Senior Director, Government Relations
David B. Moore
828-0525
dbmoore@aamc.org

Senior Director, Strategy and Innovation Development
William T. Mallon, Ed.D.
828-0424
wmallon@aamc.org

Scientific Affairs

Chief Scientific Officer
Ann C. Bonham, Ph.D.
828-0509
abonham@aamc.org

Senior Research Director, Implementation Science
Mildred Z. Solomon
828-0543
msolomon@aamc.org

Senior Research Director, Implementation Science
Anthony J. Mazzachi
828-0509
tmazzaschi@aamc.org

Senior Director, Science Policy and Regulatory Counsel
Heather H. Pierce
478-9926
hpierce@aamc.org

AAMC Subject Listing

A

AAMC Data Book
Susannah Rowe
828-0653
srowe@aamc.org

AAMC Reference Center and Mary H. Littlemeyer Archives
Marian Taliaferro
828-0433
mtaliaferro@aamc.org

AAMC Reporter
Eric Weissman
828-0044
eweissman@aamc.org

AAMC STAT
Lesley Ward
828-0655
lward@aamc.org

Academic Affairs
John E. Prescott, M.D.
828-0533
jprescott@aamc.org

Academic Medical Center Organization and Governance
Joanne Conroy, M.D.
828-0584
jconroy@aamc.org

Academic Medicine
   Editorial
   Anne Farmakidis
   828-0593
   afarmakidis@aamc.org

   Subscriptions/Renewals
   Complimentary
   Subscriptions
   Member Services
   862-6239
   memberservices@aamc.org

   Paid Subscriptions
   Lippincott Williams &
   Wilkins
   Customer Service
   800-638-3030
   www.lww.com/customerservice

Accounting
Daniel Berringer
862-6295
dberringer@aamc.org

Accreditation of Continuing Medical Education
David Davis, M.D.
862-6275
ddavis@aamc.org

Accreditation of Medical Schools
Dan Hunt, M.D.
828-0505
dhunt@aamc.org

Robert F. Sabalis, Ph.D.
828-0556
rsabalis@aamc.org

Accreditation of Residencies (ACGME)
Sunny G. Yoder
828-0497
syoder@aamc.org

Ad Hoc Group for Medical Research
David Moore
828-0525
dbmoore@aamc.org

Tannaz Rasouli
828-0057
trasouli@aamc.org

Admission Policies and Procedures
Geoffrey H. Young, Ph.D.
741-6466
gyoung@aamc.org

Holistic Review
Geoffrey H. Young, Ph.D.
741-6466
gyoung@aamc.org

Admission Traffic Rules
Geoffrey H. Young, Ph.D.
741-6466
gyoung@aamc.org

Advisor Information Service (AIS)
Kelly Begatto
862-6003
kbegatto@aamc.org

Advisory Panel on Health Care
Joanne M. Conroy, M.D.
828-0584
jconroy@aamc.org

Advisory Panel on Medical Education
Carol A. Aschenbrener, M.D.
828-0988
caschenbrener@aamc.org

Advisory Panel on Research
Ann C. Bonham, Ph.D.
828-0509
abonham@aamc.org

AIDS/HIV
Henry M. Sondheimer, M.D.
828-0684
hsondheimer@aamc.org

American Board of Medical Specialties (ABMS)
Carol A. Aschenbrener, M.D.
828-0988
caschenbrener@aamc.org

AMCAS (American Medical College Application Service) Policies, Procedures
Kelly Begatto
862-6003
kbegatto@aamc.org

AAMC Subject Listing

AMCAS General Information
828-0600
amcas@aamc.org

Analysis in Brief
Sarah Bunton, Ph.D.
862-6225
sbunton@aamc.org

Animals in Education and Research
Anthony J. Mazzaschi
828-0059
tmazzaschi@aamc.org

Legislation
Tannaz Rasouli
828-0057
trasouli@aamc.org

Annual Meeting
Heather Brinton Parker
828-0427
hbrinton@aamc.org

Annual Meeting Exhibits (Commercial, nonprofit, and Innovations in Medical Education)
Rachael Bradshaw
862-6070
rbradshaw@aamc.org

Applicant/Acceptance and Matriculation Data
Collins Mikesell
862-6080
cmikesell@aamc.org

Archives
Molly Alexander
862-6261
malexander@aamc.org

AspiringDocs.org
Tami Levin
862-6084
mlawtlevin@aamc.org

Awards
Alpha Omega Alpha
Geoffrey H. Young, Ph. D.
741-6466
gyoung@aamc.org

Award for Distinguished Research
Sandra D. Gordon
828-0472
sgordon@aamc.org

Caring for Community
Ally Anderson
828-0682
aanderson@aamc.org

David E. Rogers Award
Sandra D. Gordon
828-0472
sgordon@aamc.org

Flexner Award for Distinguished Service
Sandra D. Gordon
828-0472
sgordon@aamc.org

Gold Foundation Humanism in Medicine Award
Ally Anderson
828-0682
aanderson@aamc.org

Monique Mauge
862-6006
mmauge@aamc.org

Herbert W. Nickens Award
Angela R. Moses
862-6203
amoses@aamc.org

Herbert W. Nickens Faculty Fellowship
Angela R. Moses
862-6203
amoses@aamc.org

Herbert W. Nickens Medical Student Scholarships
Angela R. Moses
862-6203
amoses@aamc.org

Spencer Foreman Award for Outstanding Community Service
Sandra D. Gordon
828-0472
sgordon@aamc.org

B

Biosecurity Issues
Stephen J. Heinig
828-0488
sheinig@aamc.org

Biotechnology Regulation
Stephen J. Heinig
828-0488
sheinig@aamc.org

Bioterrorism Preparedness Legislation
Tannaz Rasouli
828-0057
trasouli@aamc.org

Board of Directors
Jennifer M. Schlener
828-0466
jmschlener@aamc.org

Budget and Appropriations
David Moore
828-0525
dbmoore@aamc.org

Tannaz Rasouli
828-0057
trasouli@aamc.org

Business Development
Gabrielle Campbell
828-0643
gcampbell@aamc.org

C

Career Advising for Medical Students
George V. Richard, Ph.D.
862-6223
grichard@aamc.org

CareerConnect
Pia Aladdin
828-0524
paladdin@aamc.org

Careers in Medicine Program
George V. Richard, Ph.D.
862-6223
grichard@aamc.org

Centers for Medicare and Medicaid Services (CMS)
Regulations, Teaching Hospitals
Ivy S. Baer, J.D.
828-0499
ibaer@aamc.org

Hospitals
Lori Michalich-Levin
828-0599
lmlevin@aamc.org

Regulations, Physicians
Mary Patton-Wheatley
862-6297
mwheatley@aamc.org

Legislation
Christiane A. Mitchell
828-0526
cmitchell@aamc.org

Leonard Marquez
862-6281
lmarquez@aamc.org

Children's Health Insurance Programs (CHIP)
Christiane A. Mitchell
828-0526
cmitchell@aamc.org

Clinical Research
Ann Bonham, Ph.D.
828-0509
abonham@aamc.org

Legislation
David Moore
828-0525
dbmoore@aamc.org

COD Fellowship Program (on hiatus)
John E. Prescott, M.D.
828-0533
jprescott@aamc.org

Communications and Marketing
Elisa K. Siegel
828-0459
esiegel@aamc.org

Community Benefit
Regulations
Ivy S. Baer, J.D.
828-0499
ibaer@aamc.org

Legislation
Christiane A. Mitchell
828-0526
cmitchell@aamc.org

Comparative Effectiveness Research
Millie Solomon, Ph. D.
828-0543
msolomon@aamc.org

Compliance Officer Forum
Ivy S. Baer, J.D.
828-0499
ibaer@aaamc.org

Conflict of Interest in Research
Heather Pierce, J.D.
478-9926
hpierce@aamc.org

Congress, U.S.
Dave Moore
828-0559
dbmoore@aamc.org

Continuing Medical Education
David Davis, M.D.
862-6275
ddavis@aamc.org

Contracts
Frank R. Trinity, J.D.
828-0540
ftrinity@aamc.org

Councils at the AAMC
Academic Societies (CAS)
Anthony J. Mazzaschi
828-0059
tmazzaschi@aamc.org

Deans (COD)
John E. Prescott, M.D.
828-0533
jprescott@aamc.org

Ann Steinecke, Ph.D.
828-0475
asteinecke@aamc.org

Teaching Hospitals and Health Systems (COTH)
Joanne M. Conroy, M.D.
828-0584
jconroy@aamc.org

Criminal Background Checks
Kelly Begatto
862-6003
kbegatto@aamc.org

Centralized Service for Medical Schools
Stephen Fitzpatrick
862-0621
sfitzpatrick@aamc.org

AAMC Subject Listing

Cultural Competence
Norma Poll, Ph.D.
862-6115
npoll@aamc.org

Curriculum Management & Information Tool (CurrMIT)
CurrMIT Helpline
helpcurrmit@aamc.org

D

Databases on Medical Education

Data Warehouse
Kirke Lawton
828-0974
klawton@aamc.org

Dean's Letter (Medical Student Performance Evaluation)
Geoffrey H. Young, Ph.D.
741-6466
gyoung@aamc.org

Development Survey
Chris Tucker
828-0989
ctucker@aamc.org

Directory of American Medical Education
Eric Weissman
828-0044
eweissman@aamc.org

Disability/ADA
Medical Schools
Geoffrey H. Young, Ph.D.
741-6466
gyoung@aamc.org

Medical College Admission Test
Karen Mitchell, Ph.D.
828-0500
kmitchell@aamc.org

Diversity
Marc A. Nivet, Ed.D.
862-6022
mnivet@aamc.org

Diversity and Health Equity Legislation
Tannaz Rasouli
828-0057
trasouli@aamc.org

Alex Khalife
828-0418
akhalife@aamc.org

Diversity Research Forum
Laura Castillo-Page, Ph.D.
828-0579
lcastillopage@aamc.org

E

Education Programs
Katherine McOwen
487-9345
kmcowen@aamc.org

Electronic Residency Application Service (ERAS)
B. Renee Overton
828-0508
broverton@aamc.org

Emergency Preparedness (Medical Schools)
John E. Prescott, M.D.
828-0533
jprescott@aamc.org

ERAS General Information
828-0413
ERASHelp@aamc.org

Enrollment/Graduation Data
Hershel Alexander, Ph.D.
828-0649
halexander@aamc.org

Executive Development Seminars for Deans
Ann Steinecke, Ph.D.
828-0475
asteinecke@aamc.org

Executive Development Seminars for Associate Deans and Chairs
Kevin Grigsby, D.S.W.
828-0575
kgrigsby@aamc.org

F

Facilities at the AAMC
Mark Wood
828-0450
mwood@aamc.org

Facilities at Medical Schools
Heather Sacks
862-6220
hsacks@aamc.org

Facts & Figures Data Series
Laura Castillo-Page, Ph.D.
828-0579
lcastillopage@aamc.org

Faculty Forward Program
Shannon Fox, Ph.D.
862-6162
sfox@aamc.org

Faculty Policies (Promotion and Tenure)
Kevin Grigsby, D.S.W.
828-0575
kgrigsby@aamc.org

Sarah Bunton, Ph.D.
862-6225
sbunton@aamc.org

Faculty Practice Plan Survey
Mary Patton-Wheatley
862-6297
mwheatley@aamc.org

Faculty Practice Plans
Ivy S. Baer, J.D.
828-0499
ibaer@aamc.org

Faculty Practice Solutions Center
Mary Patton-Wheatley
862-6297
mwheatley@aamc.org

Faculty Roster
Hershel Alexander, Ph.D.
828-0649
halexander@aamc.org

Faculty Salary Survey
Stefanie Wisniewski
862-6101
swisniewski@aamc.org

Federal Budget
David Moore
828-0559
dbmoore@aamc.org

Fee Assistance Program (FAP)
Kelly Begatto
862-6003
kbegatto@aamc.org

Financial Aid
Legislation
J. Matthew Shick
862-6116
jmshick@aamc.org

Policies/Procedures and Indebtedness
Shelley J. Yerman
828-0539
syerman@aamc.org

Julie Fresne
828-0511
jfresne@aamc.org

FindAResident Service
findaresident@aamc.org

FIRST for Medical Education
Julie Fresne
828-0511
jfresne@aamc.org

Fogarty International Clinical Research Scholars Support Center
Tanya Smith
828-0481
tsmith@aamc.org

Forum on Conflict of Interest in Academe (FOCI Academe)
Heather Pierce, J.D.
478-9926
hpierce@aamc.org

Fraud and Misconduct in Research
Anthony J. Mazzaschi
828-0059
amazzaschi@aamc.org

G

Genetics Research
Stephen J. Heinig
828-0488
sheinig@aamc.org

GME Track
Hershel Alexander, Ph.D.
828-0649
halexander@aamc.org

Governance of AAMC
Jennifer M. Schlener
828-0466
jmschlener@aamc.org

Government Relations
David Moore
828-0559
dbmoore@aamc.org

Graduate Medical Education
Administration
Sunny G. Yoder
828-0497
syoder@aamc.org

Accreditation
Carol A. Aschenbrener, M.D.
828-0665
caschenbrener@aamc.org

Curriculum
Alexis L. Ruffin
828-0439
alruffin@aamc.org

Financing
Lori Mihalich-Levin
828-0599
lmlevin@aamc.org

Immigration
Sunny G. Yoder
828-0497
syoder@aamc.org

Legislation
Leonard Marquez
862-6281
lmarquez@aamc.org

Christiane A. Mitchell
828-0526
cmitchell@aamc.org

Regulatory Payments
Lori Mihalich-Levin
828-0599
lmlevin@aamc.org

Grants Administration
Leslye Fulwider
828-0646
lfulwider@aamc.org

AAMC Subject Listing

Groups at the AAMC

Chief Medical Officers (CMO)
David Longnecker, M.D.
828-0490
dlongnecker@aamc.org

Government Relations Representatives (GRR)
Christiane A. Mitchell
828-0526
cmitchell@aamc.org

Graduate Research, Education, and Training Group (GREAT)
Jodi B. Lubetsky, Ph.D.
828-0485
jlubetsky@aamc.org

Group on Business Affairs (GBA)
Heather Sacks
862-6220
hsacks@aamc.org

Group on Diversity and Inclusion (GDI)
Juan Amador
862-6149
jamador@aamc.org

Group on Educational Affairs (GEA)
Katherine McOwen
487-9345
kmcowen@aamc.org

Group on Faculty Affairs (GFA)
Valarie Clark
828-0586
vclark@amc.org

Group on Faculty Practice (GFP)
Ivy S. Baer, J.D.
828-0499
ibaer@aaamc.org

Group on Information Resources (GIR)
Morgan Passiment
828-0476
mpassiment@aamc.org

Group on Institutional Advancement (GIA)
Chris Tucker
828-0989
ctucker@aamc.org

Group on Institutional Planning (GIP)
Heather Sacks
862-6220
hsacks@aamc.org

Group on Regional Medical Campuses (GRMC)
Katherine McOwen
478-9345
kmcowen@aamc.org

Group on Research Advancement and Development (GRAND)
Stephen J. Heinig
828-0488
sheinig@aamc.org

Group on Resident Affairs (GRA)
Sunny G. Yoder
828-0497
syoder@aamc.org

Group on Student Affairs (GSA)
Geoffrey H. Young, Ph.D.
741-6466
gyoung@aamc.org

Group on Woman in Medicine and Science (GWIMS)
Liz Coakley
862-6235
ecoakley@aamc.org

H

Health Care Affairs
Joanne Conroy, M.D.
828-0584
jconroy@aamc.org

Health Care Delivery
Leonard Marquez
862-6281
lmarquez@aamc.org

Christine A. Mitchell
828-0526
cmitchell@aamc.org

David Moore
828-0559
dbmoore@aamc.org

Health Care Disparities
Laura Castillo-Page, Ph.D.
828-0579
lcastillopage@aamc.org

Legislation
Tannaz Rasouli
828-0057
trasouli@aamc.org

Alex Khalife
828-0418
akhalife@aamc.org

Health Care Innovation
Joanne M. Conroy, M.D.
828-0584
jconroy@aamc.org

Health Care Reform
Atul Grover, M.D., Ph.D.
828-0666
agrover@aamc.org

Health Information Technology Legislation
Leonard Marquez
862-6281
lmarquez@aamc.org

Christiane A. Mitchell
828-0526
cmitchell@aamc.org

Policy
Lori Mihalich-Levin
828-0599
lmlevin@aamc.org

Health Privacy Legislation
Tannaz Rasouli
828-0057
trasouli@aamc.org

Policy
Ivy S. Baer, J.D.
828-0499
ibaer@aamc.org

Health Profession and Nursing Education Coalition (HPNEC)
Tannaz Rasouli
828-0057
trasouli@aamc.org

Alex Khalife
828-0418
akhalife@aamc.org

Health Professions Education Funding
Tannaz Rasouli
828-0057
trasouli@aamc.org

Alex Khalife
828-0418
akhalife@aamc.org

Health Services Research (HSR)
  Legislation
  Tannaz Rasouli
  828-0057
  trasouli@aamc.org

Healthcare Innovation Zones (HIZs)
Joanne M. Conroy, M.D.
828-0584
jconroy@aamc.org

HHS Office of Inspector General
Ivy S. Baer, J.D.
828-0499
ibaer@aamc.org

HIPAA
Ivy S. Baer, J.D.
828-0499
ibaer@aamc.org

Morgan Passiment
828-0476
mpassiment@aamc.org

Holistic Review
Henry M. Sondheimer, M.D.
828-0684
hsondheimer@aamc.org

Hospital Operations and Financial Data
LaTonya Ford
862-6192
lford@aamc.org

Hospital Payment
  Legislation
  Leonard Marquez
  862-6281
  lmarquez@aamc.org

  Regulatory (CMS)
  Ivy S. Baer, J.D.
  828-0499
  ibaer@aamc.org

Hospital Quality Alliance
Jennifer Faerberg
862-6221
jfaerberg@aamc.org

House Staff Salary and Benefits Survey and Data
LaTonya Ford
862-6192
lford@aamc.org

Human Resources (AAMC)
Roby Hunt
828-0446
rhunt@aamc.org

I

Implementation Science
Mildred Solomon, Ph.D.
828-0543
msolomon@aamc.org

Industry/Academia/Government Relations
Stephen J. Heinig
828-0488
sheinig@aamc.org

Information Technology
Jeanne L. Mella
862-6173
jmella@aamc.org

Intellectual Property (AAMC)
Gabrielle Campbell
828-0643
gcampbell@aamc.org

Intellectual Property (and Public Policy)
Stephen J. Heinig
828-0488
sheinig@aamc.org

International Accreditation Issues
Carol A. Aschenbrener, M.D.
828-0988
caschenbrener@aamc.org

Interprofessional Issues
Carol A. Aschenbrener, M.D.
828-0988
caschenbrener@aamc.org

AAMC Subject Listing

J

Journal
Academic Medicine
Anne Farmakidis
828-0593
afarmakidis@aamc.org

L

Leader to Leader
Kelly Mahon
828-0551
kmahon@aamc.org

Leadership and Talent Development
Kevin Grigsby, D.S.W.
828-0575
kgrigsby@aamc.org

Leadership Training and Development Program for Associate Deans and Chairs
Kevin Grigsby, D.S.W.
828-0575
kgrigsby@aamc.org

Legal Counsel
Frank R. Trinity, J.D.
828-0540
ftrinity@aamc.org

Liaison Committee on Medical Education (LCME)
Dan Hunt, M.D.
828-0505
dhunt@aamc.org

Robert F. Sabalis, Ph.D.
828-0556
rsabalis@aamc.org

Librarian
Marian Taliaferro
828-0433
mtaliaferro@aamc.org

Loan Repayment Programs
Shelley J. Yerman
828-0539
syerman@aamc.org

Legislation
J. Matthew Shick
862-6116
jmshick@aamc.org

Log-in
Member Services
accounthelp@aamc.org

M

MACPAC
Christiane A. Mitchell
828-0526
cmitchell@aamc.org

Mailing Labels
Membership Services
862-6239
memberservice@aamc.org

Matriculating Student Questionnaire (MSQ)
Hershel Alexander, Ph.D.
828-0649
halexander@aamc.org

David Matthew, Ph.D.
862-6151
dmatthew@aamc.org

MedEdPORTAL
Robby Reynolds
828-0962
rreynolds@aamc.org

Media Relations
Susan Beach
828-0983
sbeach@aamc.org

Medicaid
Legislation
Christiane A. Mitchell
828-0526
cmitchell@aamc.org

Regulatory
Scott Wetzel
828-0495
swetzel@aamc.org

Medical Center Leaders Caucus
Jennifer M. Schlener
828-0466
jschlener@aamc.org

Medical College Admission Test (MCAT)
General Information
828-0690
mcat@aamc.org

Policy Research
Karen Mitchell, Ph.D.
828-0500
kmitchell@aamc.org

Scott Oppler, Ph.D.
862-6073
soppler@aamc.org

Test Administration
Judith Byrne
828-0603
jbyrne@aamc.org

Medical Education
Carol Aschenbrener, M.D.
828-0988
caschenbrener@aamc.org

Legislation
J. Matthew Shick
862-6116
mshick@aamc.org

Medical Liability Reform
Christiane A. Mitchell
828-0526
cmitchell@aamc.org

Medical Minority Applicant Registry (Med-MAR)
Lily May Johnson
828-0573
lmjohnson@aamc.org

Angela R. Moses
862-6203
amoses@aamc.org

Medical Records Confidentiality
Legislative
David Moore
828-0559
dbmoore@aamc.org

Tannaz Rasouli
828-0057
trasouli@aamc.org

Regulations
Ivy S. Baer, J.D.
828-0499
ibaer@aamc.org

Medical Research Issues
Stephen J. Heinig
828-0488
sheinig@aamc.org

Legislative
David Moore
828-0559
dbmoore@aamc.org

Tannaz Rasouli
828-0057
trasouli@aamc.org

Medical School Admission Requirements (MSAR)
Tami Levin
862-6084
tlevin@aamc.org

Medical School Admissions
Geoffrey H. Young, Ph.D.
741-6466
gyoung@aamc.org

Medical School Application, Acceptance, and Matriculation Data
Collins Mikesell
862-6080
cmikesell@aamc.org

Medical School Finances
Jack Krakower, Ph.D.
828-0654
jvkrakower@aamc.org

Medical School Graduation Questionnaire
Henry Sondheimer, M.D.
828-0684
hsondheimer@aamc.org

Medical School Objective Project (MSOP)
Alexis L. Ruffin
828-0439
aruffin@aamc.org

Medical School Profile System
Katherine Brandenburg
862-6158
kbrandenburg@aamc.org

Medical Schools
John E. Prescott, M.D.
828-0533
jprescott@aamc.org

Medical Student Education Costs
Medical Schools
Jack Krakower, Ph.D.
828-0654
jvkrakower@aamc.org

Students
Julie Fresne
828-0511
jfresne@aamc.org

Medical Students
Career Counseling, Health Services, Insurance, Disability
Geoffrey H. Young, Ph.D.
741-6466
gyoung@aamc.org

George V. Richard, Ph.D.
862-6223
grichard@aamc.org

Medical Student Performance Evaluation (Dean's Letter)
Geoffrey H. Young, Ph.D.
741-6466
gyoung@aamc.org

Medicare
Compliance
Ivy S. Baer, J.D.
828-0490
ibaer@aamc.org

Hospital Legislation
Leonard Marquez
862-6281
agrover@aamc.org

Christiane A. Mitchell
828-0526
cmitchell@aamc.org

Hospital Payments
Ivy S. Baer, J.D.
828-0499
ibaer@aamc.org

Medicare Payment Advisory Commission (MedPAC)
Christiane A. Mitchell
828-0526
cmitchell@aamc.org

Physician Legislation
Leonard Marquez
862-6281
agrover@aamc.org

AAMC Subject Listing

Christiane A. Mitchell
828-0526
cmitchell@aamc.org

Physicians Payment
Ivy S. Baer, J.D.
828-0499
ibaer@aaamc.org

Meeting Planning
Kirsten Olean
828-0479
kolean@aamc.org

Meeting Registration
Nathalie Tavel
862-6227
ntavel@aamc.org

Membership and Constituent Services
Heather Brinton Parker
828-0427
hbrinton@aamc.org

Member Database Update and Questions
Member Services
862-6239
memberservices@aamc.org

Minority Faculty Development
Lily May Johnson
828-0573
lmjohnson@aamc.org

Laura Castillo-Page, Ph.D.
828-0579
lcastillopage@aamc.org

Minority Physician Database
Kehua Zhang, Ph.D.
828-0578
kzhang@aamc.org

Minority Student Data
Kehua Zhang, Ph.D.
828-0578
kzhang@aamc.org

Minority Student Medical Career Awareness Workshops and Recruitment Fair
Juan Amador
862-6149
jamador@aamc.org

Angela R. Moses
862-6203
amoses@aamc.org

Minority Student Opportunities in U.S. Medical Schools
Lily May Johnson
828-0573
lmjohnson@aamc.org

N

National Health Service Corps (NHSC)
J. Matthew Shick
862-6116
mshick@aamc.org

National Institutes of Health Legislation
David Moore
828-0559
dbmoore@aamc.org

New and Developing Medical Schools Consortium
Henry M. Sondheimer, M.D.
828-0684
hsondheimer@aamc.org

O

Operations and Services
Robert Jones
828-0520
rfjones@aamc.org

Organization of Resident Representatives (ORR)
Alexis L. Ruffin
828-0439
aruffin@aamc.org

Organization of Student Representatives (OSR)
Ally Anderson
828-0682
aanderson@aamc.org

Monique Mauge
862-6006
mmauge@aamc.org

P

Patents and Licensing
Stephen J. Heinig
828-0488
sheinig@aamc.org

Patient Safety Legislation
Christiane A. Mitchell
828-0526
cmitchell@aamc.org

Ph.D. and Postdoctoral Training
Jodi B. Lubetsky, Ph.D.
828-0485
jlubetsky@aamc.org

Physician Workforce
Research
Scott Shipman, M.D., M.P.H.
828-0979
sshipman@aamc.org

Clese Erikson
828-0587
cerikson@aamc.org

Legislation
Christiane A. Mitchell
828-0526
cmitchell@aamc.org

Physicians Payment
Legislation
Leonard Marquez
862-6281
lmarquez@aamc.org

Christiane A. Mitchell
828-0526
cmitchell@aamc.org

Regulatory
Ivy S. Baer, J.D.
828-0499
ibaer@aaamc.org

Physicians and Teaching Hospitals (PATH)
Ivy S. Baer, J.D.
828-0490
ibaer@aamc.org

Premedical Advising
Henry M. Sondheimer, M.D.
828-0684
hsondheimer@aamc.org

Premedical Student Questionnaire (PMQ)
Hershel Alexander, Ph.D.
828-0684
halexander@aamc.org

Privacy Officer
Frank R. Trinity, J.D.
828-0540
ftrinity@aamc.org

Program Integrity and Compliance
Ivy Baer
828-0499
ibaer@aamc.org

Project Medical Education (PME)
Chris Tucker
828-0989
ctucker@aamc.org

Public Health Service
Tannaz Rasouli
828-0057
trasouli@aamc.org

Shannon Curtis
828-0558
scurtis@aamc.org

Public Opinion Research
Susan Beach
828-0983
sbeach@aamc.org

Publication Orders
Publications
828-0416
publications@aamc.org

Public Policy & Strategic Relations
Atul Grover, M.D., Ph.D.
828-0666
agrover@aamc.org

R

Research and Research Training
Legislation
David Moore
828-0559
dbmoore@aamc.org

Tannaz Rasouli
828-0057
trasouli@aamc.org

Research in Medical Education (RIME)
Katherine McOwen
478-9345
kmcowen@aamc.org

Caroline Ford Coleman
828-0412
ccoleman@aamc.org

Research Funding
Anthony J. Mazzaschi
828-0059
tmazzaschi@aamc.org

Legislation
David Moore
828-0559
dbmoore@aamc.org

Research Infrastructure and Instrumentation
Legislation
David Moore
828-0559
dbmoore@aamc.org

Regulation and Policy
Stephen J. Heinig
828-0488
sheinig@aamc.org

Research Means Hope
Susan Beach
828-0983
sbeach@aamc.org

Residency Applications
Electronic Residency Application Service (ERAS)
B. Renee Overton
828-0504
broverton@aamc.org

National Resident Matching Program (NRMP)
Mona Signer
828-0629
msigner@aamc.org

Resident Education
Alexis L. Ruffin
828-0439
alruffin@aamc.org

Sunny Yoder
828-0497
syoder@aamc.org

AAMC Subject Listing

S

Scientific Affairs
Ann Bonham, Ph.D.
828-0509
abonham@aamc.org

STAT (Short, Topical, and Timely)
Lesley Ward
828-0655
lward@aamc.org

Stem Cell Research Legislation
David Moore
828-0559
dbmoore@aamc.org

Stem Cell Research Policy
Anthony J. Mazzaschi
828-0059
tmazzaschi@aamc.org

Student Affairs
Geoffrey H. Young, Ph.D.
741-6466
gyoung@aamc.org

Student Records
Geoffrey H. Young, Ph.D.
741-6466
gyoung@aamc.org

Vickie Lindsey
828-0680
vlindsey@aamc.org

Student Records System
Hershel Alexander, Ph.D.
828-0684
halexander@aamc.org

Subscriptions
Member Services
862-6239
memberservices@aamc.org

Summer Medical and Dental Education Program (SMDEP)
Norma Poll, Ph.D.
862-6115
npoll@aamc.org

T

Teaching Hospitals
Joanne M. Conroy, M.D.
828-0584
jconroy@aamc.org

Legislation
Christiane A. Mitchell
828-0526
cmitchell@aamc.org

Leonard Marquez
862-6281
lmarquez@aamc.org

Clark Thomason
471-0748
cthomason@aamc.org

Teaching Physicians
Christiane A. Mitchell
828-0526
cmitchell@aamc.org

Leonard Marquez
862-6281
lmarquez@aamc.org

Clark Thomason
471-0748
cthomason@aamc.org

Technology Transfer
Stephen J. Heinig
828-0488
sheinig@aamc.org

Title VII Health Professions
Tannaz Rasouli
828-0057
trasouli@aamc.org

Tool for Assessing Cultural Competence Training (TACCT)
Norma Poll, Ph.D.
862-6115
npoll@aamc.org

U

"Underrepresented in Medicine" Definition
Amy Addams
828-0531
aaddams@aamc.org

V

Veterans Affairs Issues
Legislation
J. Matthew Shick
862-6116
jmshick@aamc.org

Research Policy
Stephen J. Heinig
828-0488
sheinig@aamc.org

Visiting Student Application Service (VSAS)
Melissa Donner
862-6002
mdonner@aamc.org

W

Washington Highlights
David Moore
828-0559
dbmoore@aamc.org

www.aamc.org
Eric Weissman
828-0044
eweissman@aamc.org

AAMC Elected Leaders

Past Presidents

1876-79 J. B. Biddle
1879-81 Samuel D. Gross
1881-82 J. M. Bodine
1882-83 W. W. Seely
1890   Aaron Friedenwald
1890-94 Nathan S. Davis
1894-95 E. Fletcher Ingals
1895-96 William Osler
1896-97 J. M. Bodine
1897-98 James W. Holland
1898-99 Henry O. Walker
1899-00 Parks Ritchie
1900-01 Albert R. Baker
1901-02 Victor C. Vaughan
1902-03 William L. Rodman
1903-04 James R. Guthrie
1904-06 Samuel C. James
1906-07 George M. Kober
1907-08 Henry B. Ward
1908-09 Eli H. Long
1909-10 George H. Hoxie
1910-11 John A. Witherspoon
1911-12 William P. Harlow
1912-13 Egbert LeFevre
1913-14 E. P. Lyon
1914-15 Isadore Dyer
1915-16 Charles R. Bardeen
1916-17 John L. Heffron
1917-18 W. S. Carter
1918-19 William J. Means
1919-20 George Blumer
1920-21 William Pepper
1921-22 Theodore Hough
1922-23 Charles P. Emerson
1923-24 Irving S. Cutter
1924-25 Ray Lyman Wilbur
1925-26 Hugh Cabot
1926-27 Charles F. Martin
1927-28 Walter L. Niles
1928-29 Burton D. Myers
1929-30 William Darrach
1930-31 Maurice H. Rees
1931-33 Louis B. Wilson
1933-35 Ross V. Patterson
1935-36 John Wyckoff
1936-37 E. Stanley Ryerson
1937-38 Alan M. Chesney
1938-39 Willard C. Rappleye
1939-40 Russell H.
        Oppenheimer
1940-41 C. W. M. Poynter
1941-42 Loren R. Chandler
1942-43 Waller S. Leathers
1943-44 E. M. MacEwen
1944-45 Albert C. Furstenberg

1945-46 John Walker Moore
1946-47 William S. McEllroy
1947-48 Waller A. Bloedom
1948-49 J. Roscoe Miller
1949-50 Joseph C. Hinsey
1950-51 Arthur C. Bachmeyer
1951-52 George Packer Berry
1952-53 Ward Darley
1953-54 Stanley E. Dorst
1954-55 Vernon W. Lippard
1955-56 Robert A. Moore
1956-57 John B. Youmans
1957-58 Lowell T. Coggeshall
1958-59 John McK. Mitchell
1959-60 Thomas H. Hunter
1960-61 George N. Aagaard
1961-62 Donald G. Anderson
1962-63 John E. Deitrick
1963-64 Robert C. Berson
1964-65 George A. Wolf, Jr.
1965-66 Thomas B. Turner
1966-67 William N.
        Hubbard, Jr.
1967-68 John Parks

Past Chairs

1968-69 Robert J. Glaser
1969-70 Robert B. Howard
1970-71 William G. Anlyan
1971-72 Russell A. Nelson
1972-73 Charles C. Sprague
1973-74 Daniel C. Tosteson
1974-75 Sherman M.
        Mellinkoff
1975-76 Leonard W.
        Cronkhite, Jr.
1976-77 Ivan L. Bennett, Jr.
1977-78 Robert G. Petersdorf
1978-79 John A. Gronvall
1979-80 Charles B. Womer
1980-81 Julius R. Krevans
1981-82 Thomas K. Oliver, Jr.
1982-83 Steven C. Beering
1983-84 Robert M. Heyssel
1984-85 Richard Janeway
1985-86 Virginia V. Weldon
1986-87 Edward J. Stemmler
1987-88 John W. Colloton
1988-89 D. Kay Clawson
1989-90 David H. Cohen
1990-91 William T. Butler
1991-92 J. Robert Buchanan
1992-93 Spencer Foreman
1993-94 Stuart Bondurant
1994-95 Kenneth I. Berns
1995-96 Herbert Pardes
1996-97 Mitchell T. Rabkin
1997-98 Robert O. Kelley
1998-99 William A. Peck
1999-00 Ralph W. Muller
2000-01 George F. Sheldon
2001-02 Ralph Snyderman
2002-03 Theresa Bischoff
2003-04 Donald E. Wilson
2004-05 N. Lynn Eckhert
2005-06 Thomas M. Priselac
2006-07 Richard D. Krugman
2007-08 Robert J. Desnick
2008-09 Elliot J. Sussman
2009-10 Deborah G. Powell
2010-11 Thomas J. Lawley
2011-2012 Mark R. Laret

Annual Awards and Lectures

Abraham Flexner Award for Distinguished Service to Medical Education

The Abraham Flexner Award for Distinguished Service to Medical Education was established in 1958 to recognize extraordinary individual contributions to medical schools and to the medical educational community as a whole. Recipients of this award have been:

1958	Joseph C. Hinsey	1977	Paul B. Beeson	1995	Saul J. Farber
1959	Alfred N. Richards	1978	Ivan L. Bennett, Jr.	1996	Arthur C. Guyton
1960	Herman G. Weiskotten	1979	Julius H. Comroe, Jr.	1997	Edmund D. Pellegrino
1961	Willard C. Rappleye	1980	William G. Anlyan	1998	Joseph S. Gonnella
1962	George Packer Berry	1981	Sherman M. Mellinkoff	1999	Joseph B. Martin
1963	Lowell T. Coggeshall	1982	Robert H. Ebert	2000	Howard S. Barrows
1964	Ward Darley	1983	Julius R. Krevans	2001	Daniel D. Federman
1965	Jospeh T. Wearn	1984	Robert J. Glaser	2002	Kelley M. Skeff
1966	James A. Shannon	1985	John A. D. Cooper	2003	Kenneth M. Ludmerer
1967	Stanley E. Dorst	1986	David E. Rogers	2004	Haile T. Debas
1968	Lister Hill	1987	Frederick C. Robbins	2005	Georges Bordage
1969	John M. Russell	1988	Thomas H. Hunter	2006	Jordan J. Cohen
1970	Eugene A. Stead	1989	Lloyd H. Smith, Jr.	2007	David C. Leach
1971	Carl V. Moore	1990	James A. Pittman, Jr.	2008	Donald E. Wilson
1972	William R. Willard	1991	Daniel C. Tosteson	2009	Arthur H. Rubenstein
1973	George T. Harrell, Jr.	1991	Daniel C. Tosteson	2010	John A. Benson Jr.
1974	John L. Caughey, Jr.	1992	August G. Swanson		Harry R. Kimball
1975	Thomas Hale Ham	1993	Robert G. Petersdorf	2011	David M. Irby
1976	Franz J. Ingelfinger	1994	Richard S. Ross		

Alpha Omega Alpha Distinguished Teacher Awards

The Alpha Omega Alpha Distinguished Teacher Awards were initiated by AOA in the spring of 1988. The name of the award was changed in 1997 to the Alpha Omega Alpha Robert J. Glaser Distinguished Teacher Awards, in honor of Robert J. Glaser, M.D., long-time Executive Secretary of AOA. The establishment of these awards by AOA emphasizes the importance of recognizing those who devote their time and energy to the accomplishment of the educational mission of the medical schools. The selection committees for the awards are jointly appointed by the AOA and the Association of American Medical Colleges. Each U.S. and Canadian school of medicine may make one nomination annually. The purpose of these awards is to provide national recognition to faculty members who have distinguished themselves in medical student education. Recipients of this award have been:

1988	W. Proctor Harvey; Carson D. Schneck	2002	Lewis R. First; Faith T. Fitzgerald;
1989	Jerome P. Kassirer; Cornelius Rosse		Aviad Haramati; Ralph F. Jozefowicz
1990	Thomas H. Kent; David L. Sackett	2003	Joel M. Felner; Barry D. Mann;
1991	John P. Atkinson; William K. Metcalf		Gabriel Virella; Lawrence Wood
1992	David C. Sabiston; Robert L. Trelstad	2004	Linda S. Costanzo; Arthur F. Dalley:
1993	Kelley M. Skeff; Parker A. Small		Steven L. Galetta; Charles H. Griffith
1994	Jane F. Desforge; William E. Erkonen;	2005	Paul F. Aravich; David E. Golan;
	Jose Ignacio; Guido Majno		Louis N. Pangaro; Robert T. Watson
1995	Pamela C. Champe; Phyllis A. Guze	2006	Carmine D. Clemente; Molly Cooke;
1996	Ruth-Marie E. Fincher; Edward C. Klatt;		Helen Davies; Jeffrey Wiese
	Steven R. McGee	2007	Robert M. Klein; John Nolte;
1997	George Libman Engel;		Richard M. Schwartzstein; James L. Sebastian
	William H. Frishman; Carlos Pestana;	2008	Peter G. Anderson, Daniel W. Foster,
	Michael S. Wilkes		David W. Nierenberg, Paul L. Rogers
1998	Bruce M. Koeppen; Daniel H. Lowenstein;	2009	Ronald A. Arky, David A. Asch,
	Hugo R. Seibel; Mark H. Swartz		Eugene C. Corbett Jr., Erika A. Goldstein
1999	Susan Billings; L.D. Britt;	2010	James R. Stallworth, John W. Pelley,
	W. Patrick Duff; John T. Hansen		Duane E. Haines, Gary L. Dunnington
2000	Frank M. Calia; Cyril M. Grum;	2011	Gerald D. Abrams, Dennis H. Novack,
	Ronald J. Markert; Jeanette J. Norden		Mark T. O'Connell, LuAnn Wilkerson
2001	Walter J. Bo; J. John Cohen;		
	Douglas S. Paauw; Steven E. Weinberger		

Annual Awards and Lectures

Award for Distinguished Research in the Biomedical Sciences

The AAMC Award for Distinguished Research in the Biomedical Sciences was established in 1981, continuing a tradition of honoring high caliber research begun in 1946 with the Borden Award. The award recognizes outstanding clinical or laboratory research conducted by a member of the faculty of a medical school, which is a member of the Association of American Medical Colleges. Recipients of this award have been:

1981	J. Michael Bishop	1991	Sheldon M. Wolff	2001	C. David Allis
1982	Raymond L. Erikson	1992	Bruce M. Alberts	2002	Stanley Korsmeyer
1983	Philip Leder	1993	Bert Vogelstein	2003	Aaron J. Shatkin
1984	Michael S. Brown	1994	Francis S. Collins	2004	Cynthia Kenyon
	Joseph L. Goldstein	1995	Solomon H. Snyder	2005	Stuart H. Orkin
1985	Eric R. Kandel	1996	Stanley B. Prusiner	2006	François M. Abboud
1986	Paul C. Lauterbur	1997	David M. Livingston	2007	Seymour J. Klebanoff
1987	Joseph Larner	1998	Mario R. Capecchi	2008	Max D. Cooper
1988	Alfred G. Gilman		Oliver Smithies	2009	Robert C. Gallo
1989	Sanford L. Palay	1999	Elizabeth H. Blackburn	2010	David Ginsburg
1990	Robert J. Lefkowitz	2000	Ferid Murad	2011	William S. Sly

David E. Rogers Award

The David E. Rogers Award sponsored jointly by the AAMC and the Robert Wood Johnson Foundation was established in 1995. The award is granted annually to a medical school faculty member who has made major contributions to improving the health and health care of the American people. Recipients of this award have been:

1995	Diane M. Becker	2001	Barbara Barlow	2006	Eugene Braunwald
1996	Robert G. Newman	2002	David A. Kessler	2007	Robert H. Brook
1997	Julius B. Richmond	2003	Frank E. Speizer;	2008	Steven A. Schroeder
1998	Philip R. Lee		Walter C. Willett	2009	Jerome P. Kassirer
1999	William N. Kelley	2004	Michael DeBakey	2010	Patricia A. Gabow
2000	Jeremiah Stamler	2005	C. Everett Koop	2011	Paul A. Offit

Spencer Foreman Award for Outstanding Community Service

The AAMC Spencer Foreman Award for Outstanding Community Service was first granted in 1993 to recognize the extraordinary contributions that medical schools and teaching hospitals make to their communities. The award recipient must have a broad-based, continuing commitment to community service as reflected in a variety of programs and initiatives that are responsive to community and social needs and show evidence of a true partnership with the community.

1993	University of Miami School of Medicine
1994	University of Medicine and Dentistry of New Jersey New Jersey Medical School
1995	Boston University School of Medicine
1996	Montefiore Medical Center
1997	Wright State University School of Medicine
1998	University of California, Los Angeles, School of Medicine, with
	Charles R. Drew University of Medicine and Science
1999	Morehouse School of Medicine
2000	University of Colorado School of Medicine
2001	Medical University of South Carolina
2002	University of Washington School of Medicine
2003	Creighton University School of Medicine; University of Nebraska College of Medicine
2004	University of Rochester Medical Center
2005	Medical College of Wisconsin; University of California Davis Health System
2006	West Virginia University School of Medicine
2007	St. Joseph's Hospital and Medical Center
2008	University of New Mexico School of Medicine
2009	Mount Sinai School of Medicine
2010	Tulane University School of Medicine
2011	Massachusettts General Hospital

Arnold P. Gold Foundation Humanism in Medicine Award

The Arnold P. Gold Foundation Humanism in Medicine Award recognizes a physician faculty member who exemplifies the qualities of a caring and compassionate mentor in the teaching and advising of medical students and possesses the personal qualities necessary to the practice of patient-centered medicine.

1999	Andrew Hsi	2006	Robert J. Paeglow
2000	Richard P. Usatine	2007	Yasmin S. Meah
2001	Coleen H. Kivlahan	2008	Yolanda Wimberly
2002	Edward F. Bell	2009	Jonathan Woodson
2003	Samuel LeBaron	2010	George R. Buchanan
2004	Sharad Jain	2011	Henri R. Ford
2005	Melissa A. Warfield		

Herbert W. Nickens Award

The Herbert W. Nickens Award was established by the AAMC in 2000 to honor the late Dr. Nickens and his lifelong concerns about the educational, societal, and health care needs of minorities. This award is given to an individual who has made outstanding contributions to promoting justice in medical education and health care. The recipients of this award have been:

2000	Donald E. Wilson	2006	Spero M. Manson
2001	Lee C. Bollinger	2007	M. Roy Wilson
2002	David Satcher	2008	Vivian W. Pinn
2003	Anna Cherrie Epps	2009	Jeanne C. Sinkford
2004	Michael V. Drake	2010	Alvin F. Poussaint
2005	Joan Y. Reede	2011	Elijah Saunders

Herbert W. Nickens Faculty Fellowship

The Herbert W. Nickens Faculty Fellowship was established by the AAMC in 2000. The award recognizes an outstanding junior faculty member who has demonstrated leadership in the United States in addressing inequities in medical education and health care; demonstrated efforts in addressing educational, societal, and health care needs of minorities; and is committed to a career in academic medicine. The recipients of this award have been:

2000	Charles E. Moore	2006	Alfredo Quiñones-Hinojosa
2001	Vanessa B. Sheppard	2007	Thomas D. Sequist
2002	Janice C. Blanchard	2008	Marcella Nunez-Smith
2003	Monica J. Mitchell	2009	Elizabeth Miller
2004	Katherine J. Mathews	2010	Carmen Peralta
2005	Ugo A. Ezenkwele	2011	Tumaini Coker

Annual Awards and Lectures

Herbert W. Nickens Medical Student Fellowship

The Herbert W. Nickens Medical Student Scholarships were established by the AAMC in 2000. These awards consist of five scholarships given to outstanding students entering their third year of medical school who have shown leadership efforts to eliminate inequities in medical education and health care and have demonstrated leadership efforts in addressing educational, societal, and health care needs of minorities in the United States. The recipients of these awards have been:

2000	Opeolu M. Adeoye; Diana I. Bojorquez; Jim F. Hammel; Yolandra Hancock; Sonia Lomeli
2001	Alberto Mendivil; Constance M. Mobley; Chukwuka C. Okafor; Sheneika M. Walker; Melanie M. Watkins
2002	Aimalohi A. Ahonkhai; Lukejohn W. Day; Tarayn A. Grizzard; Alejandrina I. Rincón; David T. Robles
2003	Cedric K. Dark; Francine E. Garrett; David E. Montgomery; Johnnie J. Orozco; Nicholas J. Smith
2004	Nicolas L. Cuttriss; Joy Hsu; Angela Chia-Mei Huang; Risha R. Irby; Richard M. Vidal
2005	Erik S. Cabral; Christopher T. Erb; Harlan B. Harvey; Osita I. Onugha; Sloane L. York
2006	Nehkonti Adams; Dora Cristina Castañeda; Luis Isaac Garcia; AeuMuro Gashaw Lake; Katherine Leila Neuhausen
2007	Christain A. Corbit; Cheri Cerella Cross; Maria-Esteli Garcia; Marlana M. Li; Danielle Ku`ulei Potter
2008	Aretha Delight Davis, Nereida Esparza, Tamika E. Smith, Jorge A. Uribe, Brtant Cameron Webb
2009	Olatokundo M. Famakinwa, Yohko Murakami, Lisa M. Ochoa-Frongia, Blayne A. Sayed, Lloyd A. Webster Jr.
2010	Noemi LeFranc, Shazia Mehmood, Marizabel Orellana, Jaime W. Peterson, Kara Toles
2011	Monique Chambers, Toussaint Mears-Clarke, Teresa Schiff, LaShon Sturgis, Martha Tesfalul

Alan Gregg Memorial Lecture

Named in honor of the late Alan Gregg, American physician, educator, and philanthropist, this lecture was presented for the first time at the 1958 annual meeting of the Association of American Medical Colleges. Lectures have been given by:

1958	James B. Conant	1977	Donald W. Seldin	1994	W. French Anderson
1959	Warren Weaver	1978	Lewis Thomas	1995	Stanley Chodorow
1960	Joseph T. Wearn	1979	David E. Rogers	1996	Andrew G. Wallace
1961	Wilder G. Penfield	1980	Daniel C. Tosteson	1997	David Satcher
1962	C. Sidney Burwell	1981	David M. Kipnis	1998	Richard L. Cruess
1963	Willard C. Rappleye	1982	Sherman M.	1999	Molly Corbett Broad
1964	Robert S. Morison		Mellinkoff	2000	Donald M. Berwick
1965	Ward Darley	1983	Robert G. Petersdorf	2001	Steven A. Schroeder
1966	James A. Shannon	1984	Lloyd H. Smith, Jr.	2002	Deborah Prothrow-Stith
1967	Colin M. MacLeod	1985	Harold T. Shapiro	2003	Harvey V. Fineberg
1968	John M. Russell	1986	Thomas F. Eagleton	2004	Christine K. Cassell
1969	Kingman Brewster, Jr.	1987	Alvin R. Tarlov	2005	M. Roy Schwarz
1970	Lincoln Gordon	1988	C. Everett Koop	2006	Charles L. Rice
1971	Alexander Heard	1989	Louis W. Sullivan	2007	Carolyn Clancy
1972	Clark Kerr	1990	James D. Watson	2008	Fitzhugh Mullan
1973	John R. Evans	1991	Daniel Callahan	2009	Stanley Fish
1974	Terry Sanford	1992	Robert M. Heyssel	2010	David M. Walker
1975	William B. Castle	1993	Samuel Thier	2011	Javeed Sukhera
1976	William B. Bean				

Annual Awards and Lectures

John A.D. Cooper Lecture

Named in honor of John A.D. Cooper, president of the Association of American Medical Colleges from 1969 to 1986, this lecture was presented for the first time at the 1985 annual meeting of the AAMC. The lecture was originally endowed by the American Hospital Supply Corporation Foundation. Lectures have been given by:

1985	John A. D. Cooper	1997	David Stern	2002	David M. Lawrence
1986	Paul B. Beeson	1998	Barbara A. DeBuono	2003	Edward H. Wagner
1987	Uwe E. Reinhardt	1999	Christopher J.L. Murray	2004	Clayton Christensen
1988	Henry G. Cisneros	2000	Ruth Rothstein	2005	David J. Brailer
1989	Lauro F. Cavazos	2001	Robert L. Marier	2006	John E. Wenneberg
1990	John F. Sherman		(moderator);	2007	Sara Rosenbaum
1991	Margaret Catley-Carlson		Valerie Florance,	2008	Karen Davis
1992	Leroy Hood		Edward D. Miller,	2009	Herbert Pardes
1993	Bruce M. Alberts		Daniel R. Masys,	2010	Rita Charon
1994	Merwyn R. Greenlick		Suzanne S. Stensaas	2011	Prathibha Varkey
1995	Sherif S. Abdelhak		(panelists)		
1996	Judith Feder				

Robert G. Petersdorf Lecture

Named in honor of Robert G. Petersdorf, president of the Association of American Medical Colleges from 1986 to 1994, this lecture was presented for the first time at the 1994 annual meeting of the AAMC.

1994	Christine K. Cassel	2001	Michael E. Whitcomb;	2005	Daniel R. Masys
1995	Joseph L. Goldstein		Donald O. Nutter;	2006	Elizabeth G. Nabel
1996	Francis S. Collins		Steven W. Weinberger	2007	Thomas R. Cech
1997	Judith Rodin		(panelists)	2008	Alan I. Leshner
1998	Gilbert S. Omenn	2002	Anthony Fauci	2009	Harold E. Varmus
1999	David Satcher	2003	Risa Lavizzo-Mourey	2010	Steven Kanter
2000	Uwe E. Reinhardt	2004	Julie Gerberding	2011	Patricia A. Gabow

Jordan J. Cohen Leadership in Health Care Lecture

Named in honor of Jordan J. Cohen, president of the Association of American Medical Colleges from 1994 to 2006, this lecture was presented for the first time at the 2006 annual meeting of the AAMC.

2006	William M. Sulivan	2008	Madeline H. Schmitt	2010	Jim Yong Kim
2007	Daniel D. Federman	2009	Abraham Verghese	2011	Francis S. Collins

Institutional Members

2012

University of Alabama School of Medicine

University of Alabama at Birmingham
1530 3rd Avenue South, FOT 12th Floor
Birmingham, Alabama 35294-3412
205-934-4011 (general information); 205-934-1111 (dean's office); 205-934-0333 (fax);
205-934-2330 (medical student affairs)
Web site: www.uab.edu/uasom

The University of Alabama School of Medicine is a continuation of medical training begun in Mobile more than 150 years ago. The medical school was moved from the Tuscaloosa campus to Birmingham in 1945 and expanded from a two-year to a four-year school. Clinical campuses are located in Tuscaloosa, Huntsville, and Birmingham.

Type: public
2011 total enrollment: 700
Clinical facilities: Chauncey Sparks Center for Developmental and Learning Disorders, University of Alabama Hospitals, Children's Hospital, Spain Rehabilitation Center, the Kirklin Clinic, Veterans Administration Hospital, Center for Psychiatric Medicine, Callahan Eye Foundation Hospital, L. B. Wallace Tumor Institute, Druid City Hospital (Tuscaloosa), Huntsville Hospital, Family Medicine Centers (Birmingham, Huntsville, and Tuscaloosa), UAB Highlands.

University Officials

Chancellor	Malcolm Portera, Ph.D.
President, University of Alabama at Birmingham	Carol Z. Garrison, Ph.D.
Provost	Linda C. Lucas, Ph.D. (Interim)
Chief Executive Officer, Health System	Will Ferniany, Ph.D.
Associate Vice President for Marketing and Public Relations	Dale G. Turnbough

Medical School Administrative Staff

Senior Vice President and Dean	Ray L. Watts, M.D.
Senior Associate Dean for Administration and Finance	S. Dawn Bulgarella
Senior Associate Dean for Research	Robert P. Kimberly, M.D.
Senior Associate Dean for Academic Affairs	Hughes Evans, M.D.
Senior Associate Dean for Faculty Development	Kathleen G. Nelson, M.D.
Associate Dean, Huntsville Program	Robert M. Centor, M.D.
Associate Dean, Tuscaloosa Program	Thaddeus Ulzen, M.D. (Interim)
Associate Dean for Student Services	Vacant
Associate Dean for Veteran Affairs	Doug Reifler
Associate Dean for Rural Programs and Primary Care	William A. Curry, M.D.
Associate Dean for Undergraduate Medical Education	Craig J. Hoesley, M.D.
Assistant Dean for Graduate Medical Education	Gustavo Heudebert, M.D.
Assistant Dean for Admissions	Nathan B. Smith, M.D.
Assistant Dean, Continuing Medical Education	Monika Safford, M.D.
Registrar	Deborah Blackstone

Department and Division or Section Chairs

Basic Sciences

Biochemistry	Tim M. Townes, Ph.D.
Cell Biology	Etty Benveniste, Ph.D.
Microbiology	David D. Chaplin, M.D., Ph.D.
Neurobiology	David Sweatt, Ph.D.
Nutrition Sciences	W. Timothy Garvey, M.D.
Pathology	Kevin A. Roth, M.D., Ph.D.
Anatomic Pathology	Gene P. Siegal, M.D.
Forensic	Robert M. Brissie, M.D.
Informatics	Jonas Almeida, Ph.D.
Laboratory Medicine	John A. Smith, M.D., Ph.D.
Molecular and Cellular Pathology	Victor Darley-Usmar, Ph.D. (Interim)
Neuropathology	Steven Carroll, M.D., Ph.D.
Pharmacology	Mary-Ann Bjornsti, Ph.D.

Physiology and Biophysics . . . . Kevin L. Kirk, Ph.D. (Interim)

Clinical Sciences

Anesthesiology. . . . . Keith A. Jones, M.D.
Dermatology . . . . Craig A. Elmets, M.D.
Emergency Medicine . . . . Janyce Sanford, M.D.
Family Medicine . . . . T. Michael Harrington, M.D.
Genetics . . . . Bruce R. Korf, M.D., Ph.D.
Medicine. . . . . Anupam Agarwal, M.D. (Interim)
  Cardiovascular Disease . . . . Sumanth Prabhu, M.D.
  Endocrinology and Metabolism. . . . . Stuart Frank, M.D.
  Gastroenterology and Hepatology. . . . . Charles M. Wilcox, M.D.
  General Internal Medicine . . . . Carlos Estrada, M.D.
  Gerontology, Geriatrics, and Palliative Care. . . . . Richard M. Allman, M.D.
  Hematology and Oncology. . . . . Boris Pasche, M.D., Ph.D.
  Infectious Diseases . . . . Michael Saag, M.D.
  Nephrology . . . . Anupam Agarwal, M.D.
  Preventive Medicine . . . . Mona Fouad, M.D., Ph.D.
  Pulmonary, Allergy, and Critical Care . . . . Victor Thannickal, M.D.
  Rheumatology . . . . Lou Bridges, M.D., Ph.D.
Neurology . . . . David G. Standaert, M.D., Ph.D.
Obstetrics and Gynecology. . . . . William W. Andrews, M.D.
Ophthalmology . . . . Christopher Girkin, M.D. (Interim)
Pediatrics . . . . Sergio B. Stagno, M.D.
Physical Medicine and Rehabilitation . . . . Amie B. Jackson, M.D.
Psychiatry . . . . James Meador-Woodruff, M.D.
Radiation Oncology. . . . . James A. Bonner, M.D.
Radiology . . . . Cheri L. Canon, M.D. (Interim)
  Advanced Medical Imaging Research . . . . Kurt R. Zinn, D.V.M., Ph.D.
  Diagnosic Radiology. . . . . Cheri L. Canon, M.D.
  Nuclear Medicine. . . . . Janis P. O'Malley, M.D.
  Physics and Engineering. . . . . Michael V. Yester, Ph.D.
Surgery . . . . Kirby I. Bland, M.D.
  Cardiothoracic Surgery. . . . . James Kirklin, M.D.
  General Surgery. . . . . Kirby I. Bland, M.D.
  Neurosurgery. . . . . James Markert, M.D.
  Orthopedic Surgery . . . . Thomas R. Hunt III, M.D.
  Otolaryngology. . . . . Glenn E. Peters, M.D.
  Pediatric Surgery . . . . Keith E. Georgeson, M.D.
  Plastic Surgery . . . . Luis O. Vasconez, M.D.
  Transplantation . . . . Devin E. Eckhoff, M.D.
  Urology . . . . L. Keith Lloyd, M.D. (Interim)

University-wide Interdisciplinary Research Centers

Center for Aging. . . . . Richard M. Allman, M.D.
Center for AIDS Research . . . . Michael S. Saag, M.D.
Center for Cardiovascular Biology . . . . Steven Pogwizd, Ph.D.
Center for Clinical and Translational Science . . . . Lisa Guay-Woodford, M.D.
Center for Emerging Infections and Emergency Preparedness. . . . . Richard Whitley, M.D.
Center for Free Radical Biology . . . . Victor Darley-Usmar, Ph.D.
Center for Outcomes and Effectiveness Research and Education . . . . Kenneth Saag, M.D.
Civitan International Research Center . . . . Harald Sontheimer, Ph.D.
Comprehensive Arthritis and Musculoskeletal Disease Center . . . . Robert P. Kimberly, M.D.
Comprehensive Cancer Center. . . . . Edward Partridge, M.D.
Comprehensive Neuroscience Center . . . . David Standaert, M.D., Ph.D.
Cystic Fibrosis Research Center . . . . Eric J. Sorscher, M.D.
Gregory Fleming James Cystic Fibrosis Research Center . . . . Eric J. Sorscher, M.D.
Minority Health and Health Disparities Research Center. . . . . Mona N. Fouad, M.D.

University of South Alabama College of Medicine
307 University Boulevard
Mobile, Alabama 36688
251-460-7176 (admissions); 251-460-6278 (fax)
Web site: www.southalabama.edu/com

On August 19, 1969, the state legislature passed a resolution that a second medical school should be established in Alabama under the auspices of the University of South Alabama. On January 3, 1973, the charter class entered the University of South Alabama College of Medicine. The Basic Medical Sciences Building is located on the main university campus. Clinical teaching is conducted at the University of South Alabama Hospitals, the Infirmary Health Systems-affiliated hospitals, and numerous ambulatory facilities.

Type: public
2011 total enrollment: 256
Clinical facilities: University of South Alabama Medical Center, University of South Alabama, Children's & Women's Hospital, Infirmary Medical Center, Infirmary West and Alta Pointe Health System.

University Officials

President. . . . . V. Gordon Moulton
Vice President for Health Sciences . . . . Ronald D. Franks, M.D.

Medical School Administrative Staff

Vice President for USA Health System . . . . Stanley K. Hammack
Dean. . . . . Samuel J. Strada, Ph.D.
Associate Dean for Student Affairs and
   Continuing Medical Education . . . . Margaret O'Brien, J.D., M.D.
Associate Dean for Medical Education . . . . Susan LeDoux, Ph.D.
Assistant Dean, Student Affairs and Educational Enrichment. . . . . Hattie M. Myles, Ph.D.
Assistant Dean for Faculty Affairs . . . . Mary I. Townsley, Ph.D.
Assistant Dean for Graduate Medical Education . . . . Carole Boudreaux, M.D.
Coordinator, Graduate Medical Education . . . . Judy Getty
Assistant Vice President for Medical/Financial Affairs . . . . John Pannelli
Director, Health Sciences Finance and Administration . . . . Susan Sansing
Director, Biomedical Library . . . . Judith F. Burnham
Director of Admissions. . . . . D. Mark Scott
Director, Office of Student Records . . . . Rhonda Smith
Director of Public Relations . . . . Paul Taylor
Chief Executive Officer, Health Services Foundation. . . . . Becky Tate

University of South Alabama College of Medicine: ALABAMA

Department and Division or Section Chairs

Basic Sciences

Biochemistry and Molecular Biology........................ William T. Gerthoffer, Ph.D.
Comparative Medicine................................... Jonathan G. Scammell, Ph.D.
Microbiology and Immunology............................... David O. Wood, Ph.D.
Pharmacology.. Mark N. Gillespie, Ph.D.
Physiology.. Thomas M. Lincoln, Ph.D.
Cell Biology and Neuroscience............................. Glenn L. Wilson, Ph.D.

Clinical Sciences

Emergency Medicine..................................... Frank S. Pettyjohn, M.D.
Family Medicine .... R. Allen Perkins, M.D.
Internal Medicine .... Errol Crook, M.D.
Neurological Surgery................................ Anthony Martino, M.D. (Acting)
Neurology.. Dean Naritoku, M.D.
Obstetrics and Gynecology................................ David F. Lewis, M.D.
Orthopedic Surgery.................................... Frederick N. Meyer, M.D.
Pathology .... J. Allan Tucker, M.D.
Pediatrics .... Charles Hamm, M.D. (Interim)
Psychiatry .... Ronald D. Franks, M.D. (Acting)
Radiology .... Jeffrey Brandon, M.D.
Surgery .... William O. Richards, M.D.

University of Arizona College of Medicine
P.O. Box 245017
Tucson, Arizona 85724-5017
520-626-6214 (Tucson admissions); 520-626-6337 (Tucson dean's office);
602-827-2005 (Phoenix admissions); 602-827-2066 (Phoenix dean's office)
Web site: www.medicine.arizona.edu

In 1961, the Arizona board of regents authorized the University of Arizona to establish a four-year college of medicine on its Tucson campus. In 1963, the state legislature appropriated funding, and planning began in 1964. The first class was admitted in fall 1967 and graduated in June 1971. The Phoenix campus has trained third- and fourth-year students since 1992. It has been a four-year campus the last five years, matriculating 24 students its first year and 48 students the following years.

Type: public
2011 total enrollment: 656
Clinical facilities: Tucson: Tucson Med. Ctr.; Tucson VA Med. Ctr.; University Med. Ctr.; University Physicians Hospital **Phoenix:** Carl T. Hayden VA Med. Ctr.; Banner Good Samaritan Med. Ctr.; Hospice of the Valley; Maricopa Integrated Health System; Mayo Clinic/Scottsdale; Phoenix Baptist Hospital and Med. Ctr.; Phoenix Children's Hospital; Scottsdale Health Care; St. Joseph's Hospital and Med. Ctr.; Barrow Neurological Institute; Translational Genomics Research Institute.

University Officials
President. . . . . Eugene G. Sander, Ph.D.
Executive Vice President and Provost . . . . Meredith Hay, Ph.D.
Vice President for Health Sciences. . . . . William M. Crist, M.D.
Vice President for Research . . . . Leslie P. Tolbert, Ph.D.

Medical School Administrative Staff
Dean. . . . . Steve Goldschmid, M.D.
Dean, Phoenix. . . . . Stuart D. Flynn, M.D.
Vice Dean/Deputy Dean, Clinical Affairs . . . . Bruce M. Coull, M.D.
Vice Dean, Academic Affairs, Phoenix . . . . Jacqueline A. Chadwick, M.D.
Deputy Dean, Education . . . . Kevin F. Moynahan, M.D.
Deputy Dean, Finance, Administration, Chief of Staff . . . . Sarah M. Hiteman
Deputy Dean, Research Affairs . . . . Anne E. Cress, Ph.D.
Senior Associate Dean, Evaluation . . . . Nancy A. Koff, Ph.D.
Senior Associate Dean, Faculty Affairs. . . . . Anne L. Wright, Ph.D.
Associate Dean, Graduate Medical Education . . . . Conrad J. Clemens, M.D. (Interim)
Associate Dean, Graduate Medical Education, Phoenix . . . . Michael Grossman, M.D.
Associate Dean, Info. Resources and Edu. Tech., Phoenix . . . . Howard D. Silverman, M.D.
Associate Dean, Outreach and Multicultural Affairs. . . . . Ana Maria Lopez, M.D.
Associate Dean, Outreach and Multicultural Affairs, Phoenix. . . . . Michael H. Trujillo, M.D.
Associate Dean, Planning and Facilities, Phoenix . . . . Nancy H. Tierney
Associate Dean, Research Affairs, Phoenix . . . . Joan R. Shapiro, Ph.D.
Associate Dean, Student Affairs . . . . James P. Kerwin, M.D. (Interim)
Associate Dean, Student Affairs, Phoenix . . . . Cheryl J. Pagel, M.D.
Assistant Dean, Curricular Affairs, Phoenix. . . . . Paul R. Standley, Ph.D
Assistant Dean, Educational and Student Affairs . . . . Linda K. Don
Assistant Dean, Graduate Medical Education. . . . . Victoria E. Murrain, M.D.
Assistant Dean, Medical Student Education. . . . . Carol Q. Galper
Assistant Dean, Planning and Facilities . . . . Angela M. Souza
Special Assistant to Dean, Finance and Administration, Phoenix . . . . Gail Barker, Ph.D.
Director, Arizona Arthritis Center . . . . Eric P. Gall, M.D. (Interim)
Director, Arizona Cancer Center . . . . David S. Alberts, M.D.
Co-Dir, AZ Center on Aging. . . . . . Mindy J. Fain, M.D., and Janko Nikolich-Zugich, M.D., Ph.D.
Director, Applied NanoBioScience & Medicine Center, Phx. . . . . Frederic Zenhausern, Ph.D.
Executive Director, Arizona Center for Integrative Medicine . . . . Victoria H. Maizes, M.D.
Director, Arizona Emergency Medicine Research Center. . . . . Harvey W. Meislin, M.D.
Director, Arizona Hispanic Center of Excellence. . . . . Ana Maria Lopez, M.D.
Director, Arizona Respiratory Center . . . . Fernando D. Martinez, M.D.
Director, Sarver Heart Center . . . . Gordon A. Ewy, M.D.
Director, Steele Memorial Children's Research Center . . . . Fayez K. Ghishan, M.D.
Director, Valley Fever Center of Excellence . . . . John N. Galgiani, M.D.
Director, Arizona Health Sciences Library. . . . . Gary A. Freiburger

Department Heads and Section Chiefs
Basic Sciences
Basic Medical Sciences, Phoenix. . . . . Paul E. Boehmer, Ph.D.

Biochemistry and Molecular Biophysics. . . . . Vicki H. Wysocki, Ph.D.
Cellular and Molecular Medicine . . . . Carol C. Gregorio, Ph.D.
Immunobiology . . . . Janko Nikolich-Zugich, M.D., Ph.D.
Pharmacology . . . . Todd W. Vanderah, Ph.D. (Interim)
Physiology . . . . Nicholas A. Delamere, Ph.D.

Clinical Sciences

Anesthesiology. . . . . Steven J. Barker, Ph.D., M.D.
Child Health . . . . Murray M. Pollack, M.D.
Emergency Medicine . . . . Samuel M. Keim, M.D. (Interim)
Family and Community Medicine. . . . . Tamsen L. Bassford, M.D.
Medicine. . . . . Thomas D. Boyer, M.D.
  Cardiology. . . . . Karl B. Kern, M.D.
  Dermatology . . . . James E. Sligh, Jr., Ph.D., M.D.
  Endocrinology . . . . Craig S. Stump, Ph.D., M.D.
  Gastroenterology . . . . Bhaskar Banerjee, M.D.
  General Medicine and Palliative Care Medicine. . . . . Mindy J. Fain, M.D.
  Hematology and Oncology . . . . Michael A. Bookman, M.D.
  Infectious Diseases . . . . Stephen A. Klotz, M.D.
  Inpatient Medicine. . . . . Tejo Vemulapalli, M.D. (Interim)
  Nephrology . . . . Bruce Kaplan, M.D.
  Pulmonary. . . . . Kenneth S. Knox, M.D.
  Rheumatology . . . . Jeffrey R. Lisse, M.D.
Neurology . . . . David M. Labiner, M.D.
Obstetrics and Gynecology. . . . . Kathryn L. Reed, M.D.
  Female Pelvic Medicine and Reconstructive Surgery. . . . . Kenneth D. Hatch, M.D.
  General Obstetrics and Gynecology. . . . . Ilana B. Addis, M.D.
  Gynecologic Oncology . . . . Setsuko K. Chambers, M.D.
  Maternal and Fetal Medicine . . . . Karen B. Lesser, M.D.
Ophthalmology and Vision Science . . . . Joseph M. Miller, M.D.
Orthopaedic Surgery . . . . John T. Ruth, M.D.
Pathology . . . . Achyut S. Bhattacharyya, M.D.
Pediatrics . . . . Fayez K. Ghishan, M.D.
  Cardiology. . . . . Ricardo A. Samson, M.D.
  Critical Care. . . . . Andreas A. Theodorou, M.D.
  Endocrinology . . . . Mark D. Wheeler, M.D.
  Gastroenterology and Nutrition . . . . Hassan H. Hassan, M.D.
  General Pediatrics and Adolescent Medicine . . . . Kimberly D. Gerhart, M.D.
  Hematology and Oncology. . . . . Emmanuel Katsanis, M.D.
  Hospitalist . . . . Cleo K. Hardin, M.D.
  Infectious Diseases . . . . Ziad M. Shehab, M.D.
  Medical and Molecular Genetics . . . . Christopher M. Cunniff, M.D.
  Neonatology and Developmental Biology. Alan D. Bedrick, M.D.
  Nephrology . . . . Emmanuel Apostol, M.D.
  Pulmonary, Allergy, and Immunology . . . . Wayne J. Morgan, M.D.
Psychiatry . . . . Fransiscs A. Moreno, M.D. (Interim)
Radiation Oncology. . . . . Baldassarre D. Stea, Ph.D., M.D.
Radiology . . . . Diego R. Martin, M.D., Ph.D.
  Chest. . . . . Veronica A. Arteaga, M.D.
  Cross-Sectional Imaging . . . . Bobby Kalb, M.D.
  Mammography. . . . . Marisa H. Borders, M.D., and Kimberly A. Fitzpatrick, M.D.
  Musculoskeletal . . . . Mihra S. Taljanovic, M.D.
  Neuroradiology . . . . Raymond F. Carmody, M.D.
  Nuclear Medicine. . . . . Phillip H. Kuo, M.D., Ph.D.
  Pediatric Medicine . . . . Dorothy Gilbertson-Dahdal, M.D.
  Research . . . . Elizabeth A. Krupinski, Ph.D.
  Vascular and Interventional . . . . Stephen H. Smyth, M.D.
Surgery. . . . . Rainer W. G. Gruessner, M.D.
  Abdominal Transplantation . . . . Rainer W. G. Gruessner, M.D.
  Cardiovascular and Thoracic. . . . . Robert S. Poston, M.D.
  General Surgery. . . . . John B. Kettelle, M.D.
  Neurosurgery . . . . G. Michael Lemole, Jr., M.D.
  Otolaryngology. . . . . Alexander G. Chiu, M.D.
  Reconstructive Surgery . . . . Warren G. Breidenbach,. III, M.D.
  Surgical Oncology . . . . James A. Warneke, M.D.
  Trauma, Critical Care & Emergency Surgery . . . . Peter M. Rhee, M.D.
  Urology. . . . . Mitchell H. Sokoloff, M.D.
  Vascular Surgery. . . . . Joseph L. Mills, Sr., M.D.

University of Arkansas for Medical Sciences College of Medicine
4301 West Markham Street
Little Rock, Arkansas 72205
501-686-5000; 501-686-5350 (dean's office); 501-686-8160 (dean's office fax)
Web site: www.uams.edu

The college of medicine is part of the University of Arkansas for Medical Sciences, one of the 18 campuses of the University system. The college was founded in 1879. Eight area health education centers operate in the larger cities of the state as satellite centers of medical education. The college opened a branch campus in Fayetteville, AR, in July 2009.

Type: public
2011 total enrollment: 622
Clinical facilities: University Hospital of Arkansas, John L. McClellan Memorial Veterans Administration Hospital, North Little Rock Veterans Administration Hospital, Arkansas State Hospital, Arkansas Children's Hospital, Baptist Rehabilitation Institute of Arkansas, St. Vincent Infirmary Medical Center, Baptist Medical Center, Central Arkansas Radiation Therapy Institute, Sparks Regional Medical Center, St. Edwards Mercy Medical Center, St. Bernards Regional Medical Center, Jefferson Regional Medical Center, Washington Regional Medical Center Fayetteville City Hospital, Northwest Medical Center, Veterans Administration Medical Center (Fayetteville), Baxter Regional Medical Center, Medical Center of South Arkansas, St. Michael Hospital, Wadley Regional Medical Center, White River Medical Center, Helena Regional Medical Center, NEA Baptist Memorial Hospital, Christus St. Michael Hospital.

University Officials

President. . . . . Donald R. Bobbitt
Chancellor, University of Arkansas for Medical Sciences . . . . Daniel W. Rahn, M.D.
Vice Chancellor for Academic Affairs . . . . Jeanne K. Heard, Ph.D.
Vice Chancellor for Administration and Fiscal Affairs . . . . Melony Goodhand
Vice Chancellor for Development and Alumni Relations . . . . Lance Burchett
Executive Director of Clinical Programs . . . . Richard A. Pierson
Director, Library . . . . Mary Ryan
Assistant Hospital Director for CIS . . . . David Miller
Assistant Vice Chancellor for Diversity . . . . Billy Thomas, M.D.

Medical School Administrative Staff

Dean. . . . . Debra H. Fiser, M.D.
Associate Dean, Finance and Administration. . . . . Susan B. Leon
Executive Associate Dean, Clinical Affairs . . . . Charles W. Smith, Jr., M.D.
Executive Associate Dean, Academic Affairs . . . . Richard P. Wheeler, M.D.
Executive Associate Dean, Medical Research . . . . Larry Cornett, Ph.D.
Associate Dean, AHEC Programs . . . . Mark B. Mengel, M.D.
Associate Dean, Cancer Programs. . . . . Peter Emanuel, M.D.
Associate Dean, Continuing Medical Education
  and Faculty Affairs . . . . Jeannette M. Shorey II, M.D.
Associate Dean, Children's Affairs . . . . William R. Morrow, M.D.
Associate Dean for Translational Research . . . . Aubrey J. Hough, Jr., M.D.
Associate Dean, Veterans Administration Affairs . . . . Margie Scott, M.D.
Assistant Dean, Research, Arkansas Children's Research Institute. . . . . Richard Jacobs, M.D.
Associate Dean, Undergraduate Medical Education. . . . . James Graham, M.D.
Associate Dean, Graduate Medical Education . . . . James A. Clardy, M.D.
Chief Operating Officer, Faculty Group Practice. . . . . Paula M. White
Director, Communications . . . . Leslie Taylor
Director, Faculty Group Practice Billing Operations (UAMS) . . . . Beth Wheeler
Director, Faculty Group Practice Billing Operations (ACH). . . . . Gayle Fiser
Director, Lab Animal Medicine . . . . Mildred Randolph, D.V.M.
Assistant Dean for Housestaff Affairs and Registrar . . . . Dwana McKay
Executive Director of Alumni Affairs . . . . Judith K. McClain
Assistant Dean for Medical Student Admissions. . . . . Tom G. South
Director of Development for College of Medicine. . . . . Renie P. Rule, and Chasse Conque

University of Arkansas for Medical Sciences College of Medicine: ARKANSAS

Department and Division or Section Chairs

Basic Sciences

Neurobiology and Developmental Sciences . . . . Gwen V. Childs, Ph.D.
Biochemistry and Molecular Biology . . . . Kevin Raney, Ph.D.
Biostatistics . . . . Paula Roberson, Ph.D.
Microbiology and Immunology . . . . Richard Morrison, Ph.D.
Pathology . . . . Jennifer Hunt, M.D.
Pharmacology and Interdisciplinary Toxicology . . . . Nancy Rusch, Ph.D.
Physiology and Biophysics . . . . Michael Jennings, Ph.D.

Clinical Sciences

Anesthesiology . . . . Carmelita Pablo, M.D.
Dermatology . . . . Cheryl A. Armstrong, M.D.
Emergency Medicine . . . . Marvin Leibovich, M.D.
Family and Preventive Medicine . . . . Daniel A. Knight, M.D.
Geriatrics . . . . Jeanne Wei, M.D.
Internal Medicine . . . . James Marsh, M.D.
  Cardiology . . . . David L. Rutlen, M.D.
  Endocrinology and Metabolism . . . . Stavros C. Manolagas, M.D., Ph.D.
  Gastroenterology . . . . Jonathan Dranoff, M.D.
  General Medicine . . . . Jo Ann Wood, M.D.
  Hematology and Oncology . . . . Laura Hutchins, M.D.
  Infectious Diseases . . . . Robert W. Bradsher, Jr., M.D.
  Nephrology . . . . Sudhir V. Shah, M.D.
  Pulmonary . . . . Larry Johnson, M.D.
  Rheumatology . . . . Robert A. Ortmann, M.D.
Medical Humanities . . . . Micah Hester, Ph.D.
Neurology . . . . John Greenfield, M.D., Ph.D.
Neurosurgery . . . . J.D. Day, M.D.
Obstetrics and Gynecology . . . . Curtis Lowery, M.D.
Ophthalmology . . . . Christopher Westfall, M.D.
Orthopaedic Surgery . . . . Richard Nicholas, M.D.
Otolaryngology and Head and Neck Surgery . . . . James Y. Suen, M.D.
Pediatrics . . . . Richard F. Jacobs, M.D.
Psychiatry and Behavioral Sciences . . . . G. Richard Smith, M.D.
  Child and Adolescent Psychiatry . . . . Jody Brown, M.D. (Interim)
  University Hospital . . . . G. Richard Smith, M.D.
  VA Hospitals . . . . Tina McClain, M.D.
Radiation Oncology . . . . Vaneerat Ratanatharathorn, M.D.
Radiology . . . . Philip Kenney, M.D.
Rehabilitation Medicine . . . . Kevin Means, M.D.
Surgery . . . . Richard H. Turnage, M.D.
Urology . . . . Richard H. Turnage, M.D. (Interim)

David Geffen School of Medicine at UCLA
10833 Le Conte Avenue
Los Angeles, California 90095
310-825-9111; 310-825-6373 (dean's office); 310-206-5046 (fax)
Web site: http://dgsom.healthsciences.ucla.edu/

The UCLA School of Medicine was established in 1951. It is the second oldest of the five medical schools of the University of California (UC). In 1999, it became the David Geffen School of Medicine. The school is on the UCLA campus, part of a complex including the other health science schools of dentistry, nursing, and public health. In 2008, the state-of-the-art Ronald Reagan Medical Center opened. The medical school has two partners jointly admitting 24 students yearly to each program. The Charles Drew University of Medicine and Science is a private, minority-serving medical and health science institution serving California since the 1960s. Its mission is to help society's poorest communities. The UCLA/Drew medical student program was established in 1970. Students do their first two years at UCLA and clinical work through the Drew program. The University of California at Riverside (UCR) is in the Inland Empire region in southern California and has one of the most diverse student bodies of the UC system. In 1966, the UCLA/UCR medical student program was established. It is a four-year medical program with students doing the first two years of medical school at UCR and transferring to UCLA for the clinical years. The PRIME UCLA Program takes 18 students yearly to a combined M.D./Masters program for students who will be leaders in addressing issues of the underserved. Finally, UCLA has an M.D./Ph.D. program for future academic physician scientists.

Type: public
2011 total enrollment: 748
Clinical facilities: Ronald Reagan UCLA Medical Center; UCLA Neuropsychiatric Hospital; Brentwood, Sepulveda, and West L.A. VA medical centers; Cedars-Sinai Medical Center; L.A. County hospitals: Harbor-UCLA Medical Center; Olive View Medical Center; St. Mary Medical Center; Kaiser Foundation hospitals: Panorama City, Sunset Boulevard, West Los Angeles; Woodland Hills; Kern (County) Medical Center; Northridge Hospital Foundation; Santa Monica UCLA Medical Center and Orthopaedic Hospital; Shriners Hospital for Crippled Children; Venice Family Clinic; Ventura County General Hospital; Kern Medical Center, Riverside General Research Center.

Medical School Administrative Staff

Dean and Vice Chancellor, Health Sciences . . . . A. Eugene Washington, M.D.
Vice Dean for Faculty. . . . . Jonathan R. Hiatt, M.D.
Executive Vice Dean and Associate Vice Chancellor . . . . John Mazziotta, M.D., Ph.D.
Associate Vice Chancellor for Finance and
    Senior Associate Dean, Finance &
    Administration . . . . Judith E. Rothman
Senior Associate Dean, Translational Research . . . . Steven Dubinett, M.D.
Senior Associate Dean, Student Affairs and
    Graduate Medical Education . . . . Neil H. Parker, M.D.
Senior Associate Dean, Research . . . . Leonard H. Rome, Ph.D.
Senior Associate Dean, Graduate Studies . . . . Ren Sun, Ph.D.
Senior Associate Dean, Medical Education . . . . LuAnn Wilkerson, Ed.D.
Associate Dean, Diversity Affairs. . . . . Lynn K. Gordon, M.D., Ph.D.
Associate Dean, UCLA, and Dean, Charles R.
    Drew University of Medicine and Science . . . . Richard S. Baker, M.D.
Associate Dean, Harbor-UCLA Medical Center . . . . Gail Anderson, M.D.
Associate Dean, UCR-UCLA Biomedical Sciences Program . . . . Craig Byus, Ph.D.
Associate Dean, Cedars-Sinai Medical Center . . . . Shlomo Melmed, M.D.
Assistant Dean, Biomedical Library. . . . . Judith Consales
Associate Dean, Olive View Medical Center. . . . . Rima Matevosian, M.D.
Assistant Deans, Student Affairs . . . . Theodore Hall, Josephine Isabel-Jones, M.D.,
                                                          and Daphne Calmes, M.D.

Department and Division or Section Chairs

Basic Sciences

Biological Chemistry . . . . Kelsey Martin, M.D., Ph.D.
Biomathematics. . . . . Elliot Landaw, M.D., Ph.D.
Human Genetics . . . . Kenneth Lange, Ph.D.
Microbiology, Immunology, and Molecular Genetics . . . . Jeffery F. Miller, Ph.D.

Molecular and Medical Pharmacology .... Michael Phelps, Ph.D.
Neurobiology................................. Marie Francoise Chesselet, M.D., Ph.D.
Physiology .... Kenneth Philipson, Ph.D.

Clinical Science

Anesthesiology... Patricia A. Kapur, M.D.
    Olive View Medical Center .... Selma Calmes, M.D.
Family Medicine .... Patrick Dowling, M.D.
Head and Neck Surgery...................................... Gerald S. Berke, M.D.
Medicine.. Alan Fogelman, M.D.
    Cedars-Sinai Medical Center...................... Glenn Braunstein, M.D.
    Harbor-UCLA Medical Center........................ William Stringer, M.D.
    Kern Medical Center .... Royce Johnson, M.D.
    Olive View Medical Center .... Dennis Cope, M.D.
    Sepulveda VA Medical Center........................ Michael Golub, M.D.
    West LA VA Medical Center .... Gregory Brent, M.D.
Neurology....................................... John Mazziotta, M.D., Ph.D.
    Harbor-UCLA Medical Center....................... Mark A. Goldberg, M.D.
    Olive View Medical Center .... Alan Shewman, M.D.
    Sepulveda VA Medical Center.................... Claude G. Wasterlain, M.D.
Neurosurgery... Neil Martin, M.D.
Obstetrics and Gynecology.................... Gautam Chaudhuri, M.D., Ph.D.
    Cedars-Sinai Medical Center....................... Sarah Kilpatrick, M.D.
    Harbor-UCLA Medical Center....................... Michael Ross, M.D.
    Olive View Medical Center .... Dominic Muzsnai, M.D.
Ophthalmology... Bartly Mondino, M.D.
    Harbor-UCLA Medical Center....................... Sherwin J. Isenberg, M.D.
    Olive View Medical Center .... Robert Engstrom, M.D.
    Sepulveda VA Medical Center........................... John McCann, M.D.
    VA Greater Los Angeles Healthcare System .... Lynn Gordon, M.D.
Orthopaedic Surgery .... Jeffrey Eckardt, M.D.
Pathology and Laboratory Medicine...................... Jonathan Braun, M.D., Ph.D.
    Cedars-Sinai Medical Center....................... Stephen Geller, M.D.
    Harbor-UCLA Medical Center........................ Robert Morin, M.D.
    Olive View Medical Center .... Paul Liu, M.D.
    West LA VA Medical Center .... Joan Howanitz, M.D.
Pediatrics .... Sherin Devaskar, M.D.
    Cedars-Sinai Medical Center.................... Charles Simmons, Jr., M.D.
    Harbor-UCLA Medical Center........................ Adam Jonas, M.D.
    Olive View Medical Center .... Mohammed Malekzader, M.D.
Psychiatry and Biobehavioral Sciences........................ Peter C. Whybrow, M.D.
    Cedars Sinai Medical Center....................... Mark Rapaport, M.D.
    VA Greater Los Angeles Healthcare System .... Andrew Shaner, M.D.
    Harbor-UCLA Medical Center........................ Milton H. Miller, M.D.
    Olive View Medical Center .... Albert Ketannis, M.D.
    Sepulveda VA Medical Center.................... Daniel Auerbach, M.D.
Radiation Oncology.................................... Michael L. Steinberg, M.D.
Radiological Sciences..................................... Dieter Enzmann, M.D.
    Harbor-UCLA Medical Center....................... Mark Mehinger, M.D.
    Olive View Medical Center .... Ramesh Verma, M.D.
    West LA VA Medical Center .... Scott Goodwin, M.D.
Surgery .... Ronald Busuttil, M.D.
    Cedars-Sinai Medical Center...................... Achilles Demetriou, M.D.
    Harbor-UCLA Medical Center....................... Bruce E. Stabile, M.D.
    Olive View Medical Center .... Jessie E. Thompson, M.D.
    West LA VA Medical Center .... Mathias Stelzner, M.D.
Urology.. Mark S. Litwin, M.D.
    Harbour-UCLA Medical Center........................ Jacob Rajfer, M.D.
    Olive View Medical Center .... William Aronson, M.D.
    West LA VA Medical Center .... Carol Bennett, M.D.

Keck School of Medicine of the University of Southern California

1975 Zonal Avenue, KAM 500
Los Angeles, California 90033
323-442-1900 (dean's office); 323-442-2724 (fax)
E-mail: deanksom@usc.edu
Web site: www.usc.edu/keck

The University of Southern California (USC) was founded in 1880, and its school of medicine was established in 1885 as the region's first medical school. In 1952, the medical school moved to land adjoining the Los Angeles County LAC†USC Medical Center, seven miles from the main university campus. In 1999, the school was renamed the Keck School of Medicine of USC.

Type: private
2011 total enrollment: 680
Clinical facilities: Barlow Hospital, California Hospital Medical Center, Children's Hospital Los Angeles, Doheny Eye Institute, Queen of Angels/Hollywood Presbyterian Medical Center, Hospital of the Good Samaritan, The Doctors of USC Beverly Hills, The Doctors of USC LaCanada, The Doctors of USC Pasadena, Westside Center for Diabetes, House Ear Institute, Huntington Memorial Hospital, USC/Norris Comprehensive Cancer Center and Hospital, LAC†USC Medical Center, Presbyterian Intercommunity Hospital, Rancho Los Amigos National Rehabilitation Center, Edward R. Roybal Comprehensive Health Center, El Monte Comprehensive Health Center, H. Claude Hudson Comprehensive Health Center, USC University Hospital, Westside Center for Diabetes, White Memorial Medical Center, Veterans Administration Outpatient Clinic.

University Officials

President. . . . . C.L. Max Nikias, Ph.D.
Provost and Senior Vice President for Academic Affairs. . . . . Elizabeth Garrett, J.D.
Dean. . . . . Carmen A. Puliafito, M.D., M.B.A.

Medical School Administrative Staff

Chief Operating Officer. . . . . Coreen A. Rodgers
Vice Dean for Faculty Affairs . . . . Judy A. Garner, Ph.D.
Vice Dean for Educational Affairs. . . . . Henri Ford, M.D.
Vice Dean for Research . . . . M. Elizabeth Fini, Ph.D.
Associate Vice President, Public Relations. . . . . Jane Brust
Associate Dean for Curriculum. . . . . Allan V. Abbott, M.D.
Associate Dean for Graduate Medical Education . . . . Lawrence M. Opas, M.D.
Associate Dean for Continuing Medical Education . . . . Allan V. Abbott, M.D.
Associate Dean of Undergraduate, Master's, and
  Professional Degree Programs . . . . Elahe Nezami, Ph.D.
Associate Dean for Graduate Programs. . . . . Deborah L. Johnson, Ph.D.
Associate Dean for Student Affairs . . . . Donna D. Elliott, M.D., Ed.D.
Associate Dean for Educational Affairs . . . . Raquel Arias, M.D.
Associate Dean for Admissions . . . . Raquel Arias, M.D. (Interim)
Associate Dean for Clinical Innovation . . . . Inderbir Gill, M.D.
Associate Dean for Clinical Research . . . . Thomas A. Buchanan, M.D.
Assistant Dean for Clinical Research Studies . . . . Darcy Spicer, M.D.
Associate Dean for Clinical Administration (LAC † USC) . . . . Glenn T. Ault, M.D.
Assistant Dean for Diversity . . . . Althea Alexander
Assistant Dean for Student Affairs. . . . . Sajjad A. Yacoob, M.D.
Assistant Dean for Curriculum . . . . Pamela B. Schaff, M.D.
Assistant Dean for Faculty Development . . . . Frank Sinatra, M.D.
Assistant Dean for Research Integrity . . . . Stanley P. Azen, Ph.D.
Vice Dean for Clinical Affairs (CHLA) . . . . D. Brent Polk, M.D.
Assistant Dean for Educational Affairs . . . . Joyce Richey, Ph.D.
Assistant Dean for Global Relations . . . . David Baron, M.D.

Department and Division or Section Chairs

Anesthesiology. . . . . Philip D. Lumb, M.B., B.S., FCCM
Biochemistry and Molecular Biology. . . . . Michael R. Stallcup, Ph.D.
Cell and Neurobiology. . . . . Pat R. Levitt, Ph.D.
Dermatology . . . . David T. Woodley, M.D.
Emergency Medicine . . . . Edward J. Newton, M.D.
Family Medicine . . . . Jerry D. Gates, Ph.D.

12

Medicine . . . . Edward D. Crandall, Ph.D., M.D.
    Oncology* . . . . Darcy Spicer, M.D.
    Cardiovascular Medicine* . . . . Leslie A. Saxon, M.D.
    Diabetes and Endocrinology* . . . . Thomas A. Buchanan, M.D.
    Gastrointestinal and Liver Diseases* . . . . Neil Kaplowitz, M.D.
    Geriatric, Hospital, Palliative, and General Internal Medicine* . . . . David Goldstein, M.D.
    Hematology . . . . Preet Chaudhary, M.D., Ph.D.
    Infectious Diseases* . . . . Fred R. Sattler, M.D.
    Nephrology* . . . . Vito M. Campese, M.D.
    Pulmonary, Critical Care, and Sleep Medicine* . . . . Zea Borok, M.D.
    Rheumatology* . . . . William Stohl, M.D.
Molecular Microbiology and Immunology. . . . . Jae Jung, Ph.D.
Neurological Surgery . . . . Steven L. Giannotta, M.D.
Neurology . . . . Helena Chui, M.D.
Obstetrics and Gynecology . . . . Laila I. Muderspach, M.D.
    Family Planning* . . . . Daniel R. Mishell, Jr., M.D.
    Female Pelvic Medicine and Reconstructive Surgery* . . . . Begum Ozël, M.D.
    Gynecologic Oncology* . . . . Lynda D. Roman, M.D.
    Maternal and Fetal Medicine* . . . . Joseph Ouzounian, M.D.
    Reproductive Endocrinology/Infertility* . . . . Richard Paulson, M.D.
Ophthalmology . . . . Ronald E. Smith, M.D.
Orthopaedics. . . . . Michael J. Patzakis, M.D.
Otolaryngology . . . . Dale H. Rice, M.D.
Pathology . . . . Michael E. Selsted, M.D., Ph.D.
Pediatrics . . . . D. Brent Polk, M.D.
    Adolescent Medicine . . . . Marvin E. Belzer, M.D.
    Allergy and Clinical Immunology . . . . Joseph Church, M.D.
    Anesthesiology and Critical Care Medicine . . . . Randall Wetzel, M.D.
    Bone Marrow Transplant and Hematology . . . . Ami Shah, M.D.
    Cardiology . . . . Michael Silka, M.D.
    Emergency Medicine . . . . Alan Nager, M.D.
    Endocrinology and Metabolism. . . . . Mitch Geffner, M.D.
    Gastroenterology . . . . Danny Thomas, M.D.
    General Pediatrics/UAP . . . . Robert Jacobs, M.D.
    Hematology and Oncology . . . . Stuart Siegel, M.D.
Hospital Medicine . . . . Michael Bryant, M.D.
    Infectious Diseases . . . . Jill Hoffman, M.D.
    Medical Genetics . . . . Linda M. Randolph, M.D. (Interim)
    Neonatology. . . . . Istvan Seri, M.D., Ph.D.
    Nephrology . . . . Carl Grushkin, M.D.
    Neurology . . . . Wendy G. Mitchell, M.D.
    Pediatric Pulmonary . . . . Sally Davidson Ward, M.D.
    Psychiatry. . . . . Susan Turkel, M.D.
    Rehabilitation. . . . . Kevin Craig, M.D.
    Research on Children, Youth, and Families . . . . Michele Kipke, Ph.D.
    Rheumatology . . . . Andreas Reiff, M.D.
Student Health . . . . Lawrence Neinstein, M.D.
Physiology and Biophysics . . . . Berislav V. Zlokovic, M.D.
Preventive Medicine. . . . . Jonathan M. Samet, M.D.
Psychiatry and the Behavioral Sciences . . . . Carlos N. Pato, M.D.
Radiation Oncology. . . . . Eric L. Chang, M.D.
Radiology . . . . Edward G. Grant, M.D.
Surgery . . . . Vaughn A. Starnes, M.D.
    General Surgery* . . . . Namir Katkhouda, M.D.
    Pediatric Surgery* . . . . Henri Ford, M.D.
    Plastic and Reconstructive Surgery*. . . . . Mark M. Urata, M.D.
    Breast/Surgical Oncology. . . . . Stephen Sener, M.D.
    Cardiothoracic Surgery. . . . . Robbin Cohen, M.D.
    Colorectal Surgery . . . . Anthony Senagore, M.D.
    Hepato/Pancreas and Abdominal Organ Transplant Surgery . . . . Rick Selby, M.D.
    Thoracic and Foregut Surgery. . . . . Jeffrey A. Hagen, M.D.
    Transplant Institute . . . . Cynthia Herrington, M.D.
    Trauma and Critical Care Surgery. . . . . Demetrios Demetriades, M.D.
    Tumor and Endocrine Surgery . . . . Steven Sener, M.D.
    Vascular Surgery. . . . . Fred A. Weaver, M.D.
Urology. . . . . Inderbir Gill, M.D.

*Specialty without organizational autonomy.

Loma Linda University School of Medicine

11175 Campus Street, Suite A1108
Loma Linda, California 92350
909-558-4462 (general information); 909-558-4481 (dean's office); 909-558-0292 (fax)
E-mail: bleno@llu.edu
Web site: www.llu.edu/medicine/

The medical school was founded in 1909 and was known as the College of Medical Evangelists until 1961, when it was renamed Loma Linda University. For 100 years, the school of medicine has held to its founding mission of clinical excellence, whole person care, and global partnerships. A curriculum in whole person care is designed to make the students competent in managing the patients' physical, mental, and spiritual well-being. Our global partnerships throughout the world provide a broad spectrum of service learning opportunities. Approximately one out of nine Loma Linda graduates will serve at least one year in an underserved population throughout the developing world.

Type: private
2011 total enrollment: 685
Clinical facilities: Loma Linda University Medical Center, Loma Linda University Children's Hospital, Loma Linda University Behavioral Medicine Center, Jerry L. Pettis Veterans Medical Center, Riverside County Regional Medical Center, White Memorial Medical Center, Arrowhead Regional Medical Center, Glendale Adventist Medical Center, Kettering Medical Center, Portland Adventist Hospital, Riverside Community Hospital, Redlands Community Hospital, Eisenhower Medical Center, The Betty Ford Center at Eisenhower, Florida Hospital, Hinsdale Hospital.

University Officials

President and Chief Executive Officer . . . . Richard H. Hart, M.D., DR.PH
Provost . . . . Ronald L. Carter, Ph.D.
Vice President and Chief Financial Officer . . . . Kevin J. Lang
Senior Vice President, Financial Affairs. . . . . Rodney D. Neal
Vice President, Community Partnerships and Diversity . . . . Vacant
Vice President, Research Affairs . . . . Vacant

Medical School Administrative Staff

Dean. . . . . H. Roger Hadley, M.D.
Senior Associate Dean, Medical Student Education . . . . Leonard S. Werner, M.D.
Associate Dean, Basic Science and Translational
  Research . . . . Penelope J. Duerksen-Hughes, Ph.D.
Associate Dean, Clinical Faculty . . . . Ricardo L. Peverini, M.D.
Associate Dean, Faculty Practice Affairs. . . . . David G. Wren
Associate Dean, Clinical Education. . . . . Tamara M. Shankel, M.D.
Associate Dean, Graduate Medical Education . . . . Daniel W. Giang, M.D.
Associate Dean, Recruitment and Admissions . . . . Stephen A. Nyirady, Ph.D.
Associate Dean, Los Angeles Programs . . . . Leroy A. Reese, M.D.
Associate Dean, Faculty Development . . . . Tamara L. Thomas, M.D.
Associate Dean, Quality and Patient Safety . . . . James M. Pappas, M.D.
Assistant Dean, Continuing Medical Education . . . . Lawerence K. Loo, M.D.
Associate Dean, Student Affairs . . . . Henry H. Lamberton, Psy.D.
Assistant Dean, Admissions. . . . . Lenoa Edwards
Assistant Dean, Career Advisement. . . . . M. Daniel Wongworawat, M.D.
Assistant Dean, Clinical Site Recruitment . . . . Lynda Daniel-Underwood, M.D.
Assistant Dean, Development . . . . Treva C. Webster
Assistant Dean, Graduate Student Affairs . . . . Penelope J. Duerksen-Hughes, Ph.D.
Assistant Dean, Veterans Affairs . . . . Dwight C. Evans, M.D.
Assistant Dean, Program Development and Evaluation . . . . Loretta B. Johns, Ph.D.
Assistant Dean, Residency Curriculum . . . . Martie E. Parsley, Ph.D.
Assistant to the Dean for Basic Science Education. . . . . Resa L. Chase, M.D.
Assistant to the Dean for Diversity . . . . Daisy D. De Leon, Ph.D.

Department and Division or Section Chairs

Basic Sciences

Pathology and Human Anatomy. . . . . Brian S. Bull, M.D.
  Human Anatomy . . . . P. Ben Nava, Ph.D.
  Pathology. . . . . Darryl G. Heustis, M.D.
Basic Sciences . . . . Penelope J. Duerksen-Hughes, Ph.D. (Interim)
  Biochemistry . . . . Penelope J. Duerksen-Hughes, Ph.D.

Microbiology . . . . Hansel M. Fletcher, Ph.D.
Pharmacology. . . . . John N. Buchholz, Ph.D.
Physiology . . . . John H. Zhang, M.D., Ph.D.

Centers

Center for Molecular Medicine and Health Disparities . . . . Marino A. De Leon, Ph.D.
Center for Perinatal Biology. . . . . Lawrence D. Longo, M.D.
Neurosurgery Center for Research, Training, and Education. . . . . Wolff M. Kirsch, M.D.

Clinical Sciences

Anesthesiology. . . . . Robert D. Martin, M.D.
  Critical Care*. . . . . Gary R. Stier, M.D.
Cardiovascular and Thoracic Surgery . . . . Anees J. Razzouk, M.D.
  Cardiothoracic . . . . Anees J. Razzouk, M.D.
  Vascular. . . . . Ahmed M. Abou-Zamzam, M.D.
Dermatology . . . . Abel Torres, M.D.
Emergency Medicine . . . . Kathleen J. Clem, M.D.
  General Emergency Medicine . . . . Robert Steele, M.D.
  Pediatric Emergency Medicine* . . . . Lance A. Brown, M.D.
Family Medicine . . . . John K. Testerman, M.D., Ph.D.
Surgery . . . . Carlos A. Garberoglio, M.D.
  General . . . . Vacant
  Pediatric . . . . Donald C. Moores, M.D.
  Trauma . . . . Richard D. Catalano, M.D.
Gynecology and Obstetrics. . . . . Ron E. Swensen, M.D.
Medicine. . . . . Douglas R. Hegstad, M.D.
  Cardiology. . . . . Kenneth R. Jutzy, M.D.
  Endocrinology* . . . . J. Lamont Murdoch, M.D.
  Gastroenterology and Nutrition . . . . Terence D. Lewis, M.B.B.S.
  General Internal Medicine and Geriatric Medicine . . . . Raymond Wong, M.D.
  Hematology and Oncology* . . . . Chien-Shing Chen, M.D., Ph.D.
  Hospitalist Medicine. . . . . Debra D. Craig, M.D.
  Infectious Disease* . . . . James J. Couperus, M.D.
  Nephrology* . . . . Siegmund Teichman, M.D.
  Pulmonary and Critical Care. . . . . Philip M. Gold, M.D.
  Regenerative Medicine . . . . David J. Baylink, M.D.
  Rheumatology and Immunology . . . . Keith K. Colburn, M.D.
Neurology. . . . . Bryan E. Tsao, M.D.
Neurosurgery. . . . . Austin R.T. Colohan, M.D.
Ophthalmology . . . . Howard V. Gimbel, M.D.
Orthopedic Surgery. . . . . Gary D. Botimer, M.D.
Otolaryngology: Head and Neck Surgery . . . . Alfred A. Simental, M.D.
Pediatrics . . . . Richard E. Chinnock, M.D.
  Allergy and Immunology*. . . . . Yvonne F. Fanous, M.D.
  Cardiology* . . . . Michael A. Kuhn, M.D.
  Endocrinology* . . . . Eba H. Hathout, M.B.B.S.
  Gastroenterology* . . . . Manoj C. Shah, M.D.
  General Pediatrics*. . . . . Ravindra Rao, M.B.B.S.
  Genetics*. . . . . Robin D. Clark, M.D.
  Hematology and Oncology* . . . . Antranik A. Bedros, M.D.
  Infectious Disease*. . . . . Jane N. Bork, M.D.
  Neonatology*. . . . . Ricardo L. Peverini, M.D.
  Nephrology* . . . . Shobha Sahney, M.B.B.S.
  Neurology* . . . . Stephen Ashwal, M.D.
  Pediatric Critical Care Medicine* . . . . Shamel A. Abd-Allah, M.D.
  Pulmonary* . . . . Yvonne F. Fanous, M.D.
  Rheumatology* . . . . Wendy L. De la Pena, M.D.
Physical Medicine and Rehabilitation . . . . Murray E. Brandstater, M.B.B.S., Ph.D.
Plastic and Reconstructive Surgery . . . . Subhas C. Gupta, M.D., Ph.D.
Preventive Medicine. . . . . Wayne S. Dysinger, M.D.
Psychiatry . . . . William G. Murdoch, Jr., M.D.
Radiation Medicine . . . . Jerry D. Slater, M.D.
Radiology . . . . David B. Hinshaw, Jr., M.D.
Urology. . . . . Herbert C. Ruckle, M.D.

*Specialty without organizational autonomy.

Stanford University School of Medicine
300 Pasteur Drive, Alway Building, Room M121
Stanford, California 94305-5119
650-725-3900 (dean's office); 650-725-7368 (dean's office fax)
Web site: www.med.stanford.edu

The school of medicine was established in 1908 when the properties and equipment of Cooper Medical College were transferred to Stanford. The medical school is part of the Stanford University Medical Center.

Type: private
2011 total enrollment: 462
Clinical facilities: Stanford University Hospital and Clinics (SHC); Lucile Salter Packard Children's Hospital at Stanford (LPCH); Palo Alto Veterans Administration Medical Center; Santa Clara Valley Medical Center.

University Officials

President . . . . John L. Hennessy, Ph.D.
Provost . . . . John W. Etchemendy, Ph.D.

Medical School Administrative Staff

Dean, School of Medicine . . . . Philip A. Pizzo, M.D.
Vice Dean and Senior Associate Dean for Academic Affairs . . . . David K. Stevenson, M.D.
Senior Associate Dean for Adult Clinical Affairs . . . . Norman W. Rizk, M.D.
Senior Associate Dean for Pediatric and Obstetric Clinical Affairs . . . . Kenneth L. Cox, M.D.
Senior Associate Dean for Diversity and Leadership . . . . . . Hannah A. Valantine, M.D., M.R.C.P.
Senior Associate Dean for Finance and Administration . . . . Marcia Cohen
Senior Associate Dean for Information Resources and Technology . . . . Henry J. Lowe, M.D.
Director of Lane Library, Associate Dean . . . . Heidi Heileman
Senior Associate Dean for Research and Training . . . . Daria Mochly-Rosen, Ph.D.,
and Harry B. Greenberg, M.D.
Managing Assistant Vice President of Medical Development . . . . Barbara Clemons
Senior Associate Dean for Medical Student Education . . . . Charles Prober, M.D.
Associate Dean for Medical Admissions . . . . Gabriel Garcia, M.D.
Associate Dean for Alumni Affairs . . . . Linda Hawes Clever, M.D.
Senior Associate Dean for Graduate Education
and Postdoctoral Affairs . . . . Daniel Herschlag, Ph.D.
Associate Dean for Minority Advising and Programs . . . . Fernando S. Mendoza, M.D.
Assistant Dean for Postdoctoral Affairs . . . . Rania Sanford, Ed.D.
Assistant Dean for Graduate Education . . . . John Bray, and Melanie Bocanegra
Assistant Dean for Minority Affairs . . . . Ronald D. Garcia, Ph.D.
Assistant Dean for Student Affairs . . . . Charlene C. Hamada
Associate Dean for Medical Student Advising . . . . Neil Gesundheit, M.D.
Associate Dean for Veterans Affairs . . . . Lawrence Leung, M.D.
Executive Director, Office of Communication and Public Affairs . . . . Paul Costello
Senior Associate Dean for Global Health . . . . Michele Barry, M.D.
Senior Associate Vice President for Development . . . . Michele Schiele

Department and Division or Section Chairs

Basic Sciences

Biochemistry . . . . Mark Krasnow, Ph.D.
Bioengineering . . . . Russ Altman, M.D., Ph.D.
Developmental Biology . . . . Roeland Nusse, Ph.D.
Genetics . . . . Michael Snyder, Ph.D.
Health Research and Policy . . . . Philip W. Lavori, Ph.D.
Microbiology and Immunology . . . . Peter Sarrow, Ph.D.
Molecular and Cellular Physiology . . . . Brian Kobilka, M.D.
Chemical and Systems Biology . . . . Tobias Meyer, Ph.D.
Neurobiology . . . . Ben Barres, Ph.D.

Structural Biology . . . . Joseph D. Puglisi, Ph.D.

Clinical Sciences

Anesthesia . . . . Ronald G. Pearl, M.D.
Cardiothoracic Surgery . . . . Robert C. Robbins, M.D.
Comparative Medicine . . . . Sherril Green, M.D.
Dermatology . . . . Paul Khavari, M.D.
Medicine . . . . Linda Boxer, M.D.
    Bone Marrow Transplant . . . . Robert Negrin, M.D.
    Cardiovascular Medicine . . . . Thomas Quertermous, M.D. (Co-Chief),
                                                and Alan C. Yeung, M.D. (Co-Chief)
    Endocrinology, Gerontology, and Metabolism . . . . Frederic B. Kraemer, M.D.
    Gastroenterology and Hepatology . . . . Pankay J. Pasricha, M.D.
    General Internal Medicine and Family Community Medicine . . . . Mark Cullen, M.D.
    Hematology . . . . Linda M. Boxer, M.D.
    Immunology and Rheumatology . . . . C. Garrison Fathman, M.D.
    Infectious Diseases . . . . Upinder Singh, M.D.
    Nephrology . . . . Timothy Meyer, M.D.
    Oncology . . . . Ronald Levy, M.D.
    Primary Care and Outcomes Research . . . . Alan M. Garber, M.D., Ph.D.
    Pulmonary and Critical Care Medicine . . . . Mark Nicolls, M.D., and Steve Ruoss, M.D.
    Stanford Prevention Research Center . . . . Stephen P. Fortmann, M.D.
    Stanford Medical Informatics . . . . Mark A. Musen, M.D., Ph.D.
Neurology and Neurological Sciences . . . . Frank M. Longo, M.D., Ph.D.
Neurosurgery . . . . Gary K. Steinberg, M.D., Ph.D.
Obstetrics and Gynecology . . . . Jonathan Berek, M.D.
Opthalmology . . . . Mark S. Blumenkranz, M.D.
Orthopedic Surgery . . . . William J. Maloney, M.D.
    Sports Medicine . . . . Gordon O. Matheson, M.D.
Otolaryngology . . . . Robert K. Jackler, M.D.
Pathology . . . . Stephen J. Galli, M.D.
Pediatrics . . . . Hugh O'Brodovich, M.D.
    Adolescent Medicine . . . . Neville Golden, M.D.
    Cancer Biology . . . . Michael Cleary, M.D.
    Cardiology . . . . Daniel Bernstein, M.D.
    Endocrinology . . . . Darrell M. Wilson, M.D.
    Gastroenterology . . . . Kenneth L. Cox, M.D.
    General Pediatrics . . . . Fernando S. Mendoza, M.D.
    Genetics . . . . Louanne Hudgins, M.D.
    Hematology and Oncology . . . . Michael P. Link, M.D.
    Immunology . . . . Alan Krensky, M.D.
    Infectious Diseases . . . . Yvonne Maldonado, M.D.
    Neonatology . . . . William Benitz, M.D.
    Nephrology . . . . Steven R. Alexander, M.D.
    Pulmonary, Allergy, and Critical Care . . . . David Cornfield, M.D.
    Rheumatology . . . . Christy L. Sandborg, M.D.
    Stem Cell Transplantation (BMT) . . . . Kenneth Weinberg, M.D.
Psychiatry and Behavioral Sciences . . . . Laura Roberts, M.D.
Radiation Oncology . . . . Quynh Le, M.D.
Radiology . . . . Sanjir Sam Gambhir, M.D., Ph.D.
Surgery . . . . Thomas M. Krummel, M.D.
    Anatomy . . . . John Gosling, M.D., and Ian Whitmore, M.D.
    Emergency Medicine . . . . Robert L. Norris, M.D.
    General Surgery . . . . Jeff Norton, M.D.
    Pediatric Surgery . . . . Craig T. Albanese, M.D.
    Plastic and Reconstructive Surgery . . . . James Chang, M.D.
    Vascular Surgery . . . . Ronald L. Dalman, M.D.
    Multi-Organ Transplantation . . . . Carlos O. Esquivel, M.D., Ph.D.
Urology . . . . Joe Presti, M.D.

University of California, Davis, School of Medicine
4610 X Street, Suite 3101
Saramento, California 95817
916-734-7131 (dean's office); 916-734-7055 (fax)
Web site: www.ucdmc.ucdavis.edu/medschool

The Regents of the University of California authorized the development of a medical school on the Davis campus near Sacramento in 1963, and legislative funds were made available for planning and development in 1966. The school admitted an entering class of 48 students in 1968. By fall 1971, the size of the entering class had more than doubled. Currently, the school admits a first-year class of 105 students who train at the Sacramento and Davis campuses of University of California, Davis, and at affiliated sites.

Type: public
2011 total enrollment: 436
Clinical facilities: University of California, Davis, Medical Center (Sacramento); Veterans' Affairs Northern California System of Clinics (Mather); David Grant Medical Center (Travis Air Force Base); Kaiser Permanente Medical Centers (Sacramento); Mercy Healthcare (Sacramento); Sutter Community Hospitals (Sacramento); San Joaquin General Hospital (Stockton); Merced Community Medical Center; Contra Costa Medical Services (Martinez); Stanislaus Medical Center (Modesto); Mercy General Hospital (Redding); Shriners Children Hospital (Sacramento).

University Officials

President. . . . . Mark G. Yudof, L.L.B.
Chancellor, Davis Campus . . . . Linda Katehi, Ph.D.
Provost and Executive Vice Chancellor, Davis Campus . . . . Ralph J. Hexter, Ph.D.
Vice Chancellor, Human Health Sciences. . . . . Claire Pomeroy, M.D.

Medical School Administrative Staff

Dean. . . . . Claire Pomeroy, M.D.
Executive Associate Dean. . . . . Frederick J. Meyers, M.D.
Associate Vice Chancellor Strategic Technologies and Alliances. . . . . Thomas Nesbitt, M.D.
Associate Dean, Academic Personnel . . . . Edward Callahan, Ph.D.
Associate Dean, Admissions . . . . Mark Henderson, M.D.
Associate Dean, Cancer Programs. . . . . Ralph deVere White, M.D.
Director, Practice Management Group, and
    Associate Dean, Clinical Affairs . . . . James Goodnight, M.D., Ph.D.
Senior Associate Dean, Research . . . . Lars Berglund, M.D., Ph.D.
Assistant Dean, Continuing Medical Education . . . . Gibbe Parsons, M.D.
Senior Associate Dean, Medical Education . . . . Mark Servis, M.D.
Associate Dean, Student Affairs . . . . Leon Jones, M.D.
Associate Dean, Graduate Medical Education . . . . James Nuovo, M.D.
Associate Dean, Veterans' Affairs . . . . William Cahill, M.D.
Assistant Dean, Administration. . . . . Michael Condrin, M.B.A.
Executive Director, Facilities Planning and Construction. . . . . Michael W. Boyd
Controller. . . . . Vacant
Assistant Vice Chancellor, Health Sciences Advancement. . . . . Vacant
Executive Director, Human Resources . . . . Stephen Chilcott
Assistant Dean, Interprofessional Programs. . . . . Jana Katz-Bell, M.P.H.
Chief Medical Officer, Medical Center . . . . Allan D. Siefkin, M.D.
Chief Financial Officer. . . . . Timothy Maurice
Chief Executive Officer, Medical Center. . . . . Ann Madden Rice
Chief Operating Officer, Medical Center . . . . Vincent Johnson, M.B.A.
Chief Patient Care Services Officer, Medical Center . . . . Carol Robinson
Chief Information Officer . . . . Michael Minear
Associate Vice Chancellor, Diversity and
    Inclusion and Chief External Affairs Officer . . . . Shelton Duruisseau, Ph.D.
Assistant Director, Public Affairs. . . . . Bonnie Hyatt
Coordinator, Alumni Association . . . . Beth Abad

University of California, Davis, School of Medicine: CALIFORNIA

Department and Division or Section Chairs

Basic Sciences

Biochemistry and Molecular Medicine .... Kit Lam, M.D., Ph.D.
Cell Biology and Human Anatomy .... Paul Fitzgerald, Ph.D.
Medical Microbiology and Immunology .... Satya Dandekar, Ph.D.
Medical Pharmacology and Toxicology.......................... Donald M. Bers, Ph.D.
Physiology and Membrane Biology.............................. Peter M. Cala, Ph.D.

Clinical Sciences

Anesthesiology and Pain Medicine .... Peter Moore, M.D.
Dermatology .... Fu-Tong Liu, M.D., Ph.D.
Emergency Medicine .... Nathan Kupperman, M.D., Ph.D.
Family and Community Medicine........................... Klea D. Bertakis, M.D.
Internal Medicine .... Timothy Albertson, M.D. (Acting)
Medical Pathology and Laboratory Medicine...................... Lydia Howell, M.D.
Neurological Surgery..................................... J. Paul Muizelaar, M.D.
Neurology.. Michael Rogawski, M.D., Ph.D.
Obstetrics and Gynecology................................. Mitchell Creinin, M.D.
Ophthalmology .... Mark Mannis, M.D.
Orthopaedic Surgery .... Richard Marder, M.D. (Acting)
Otolaryngology .... Hilary Brodie, M.D., Ph.D.
Pediatrics .... Anthony Philipps, M.D.
Physical Medicine and Rehabilitation .... Craig McDonald, M.D.
Psychiatry and Behavioral Sciences........................... Robert E. Hales, M.D.
Public Health Sciences... Ellen Gold, Ph.D.
Radiation Oncology....................................... Richard Valicenti, M.D.
Radiology .... Raymond Dougherty, M.D.
Surgery .... Diana Farmer, M.D.
Urology.. Chris Evans, M.D.

University of California, Irvine, School of Medicine

Irvine, California 92697-3950
949-824-6119; 949-824-5926 (dean's office); 949-824-2676 (fax)
Web site: www.som.uci.edu

Founded in 1898, the California College of Medicine became part of the University of California, Irvine (UCI), one of nine campuses in the University of California System, in 1965. The college officially moved from Los Angeles to a 122-acre site on the Irvine campus in 1968. Today, the UCI School of Medicine provides teaching, research, and patient care facilities at the health sciences complex on the Irvine campus and at UCI Medical Center, the school's principal clinical facility, located in Orange.

Type: public
2011 total enrollment: 428
Clinical facilities: University of California, Irvine, Medical Center (Orange); Veterans Administration Medical Center (Long Beach); Memorial Hospital Medical Center (Long Beach); Family Health Care Center (Santa Ana); Family Health Center (Anaheim); Gottschalk Medical Plaza (Irvine).

University Officials

Chancellor . . . . Michael Drake, M.D.
Executive Vice Chancellor and Provost . . . . Michael R. Gottfredson, Ph.D.

Medical School Administrative Staff

Dean, School of Medicine . . . . Ralph V. Clayman, M.D.
Chief Executive Officer, Medical Center . . . . Terry A. Belmont
Senior Associate Dean, Academic Affairs . . . . F. Allan Hubbell, M.D.
Senior Associate Dean, Educational Affairs . . . . Gerald Maguire, M.D.
Senior Associate Dean, Clinical Affairs/President/CEO-UPS . . . . John Heydt, M.D.
Associate Dean, Faculty Affairs and Development . . . . Lari Wenzel, Ph.D.
Senior Associate Dean, Research and Graduate Studies . . . . Paolo Casali, M.D.
Corporate Compliance and Privacy Officer . . . . Marion Mallory
Associate Dean, Clinical Policy and Health Sciences Research . . . . Sherrie Kaplan, Ph.D.
Associate Dean, Clinical Translational Science . . . . Dan Cooper, M.D.
Associate Dean, Student Affairs . . . . Michael D. Prislin, M.D.
Associate Dean, Continuing and Simulation Education . . . . Elspeth McDougall, M.D.
Associate Dean, Curricular Affairs, Clinical . . . . Shahram Lotfipour, M.D.
Associate Dean, Curricular Affairs, Basic Science . . . . Harry Haigler, M.D.
Associate Dean, Admissions . . . . Ellena Peterson, Ph.D.
Associate Dean, Graduate Studies . . . . Alan L. Goldin, M.D.
Associate Dean, Graduate Medical Education . . . . Russell Williams, M.D.
Associate Dean, Clinical Operations . . . . Zeev Kain, M.D.
Associate Dean, Research Administration and Development . . . . William Bunney, M.D.
Associate Dean, Finance . . . . Ginger Osman
Assistant Dean, Administration . . . . Rebecca Brusuelas
Chief of Staff, VA Medical Center, Long Beach . . . . Sandor Szabo, M.D.
Director, Office of Technology Alliances . . . . Ronnie Hanecak

Department and Division or Section Chairs

Basic Sciences

Anatomy and Neurobiology . . . . Ivan Soltesz, Ph.D.
Biological Chemistry . . . . Eva Lee, Ph.D.
Microbiology and Molecular Genetics . . . . Rozanne Sandri-Goldin, Ph.D.
Pharmacology . . . . Olivier Civelli, Ph.D.
Physiology and Biophysics . . . . Michael Cahalan, Ph.D.

Clinical Sciences

Anesthesiology and Perioperative Care . . . . Zeev N. Kain, M.D.
Dermatology . . . . Christopher Zachary, M.D.
Emergency Medicine . . . . Mark Langdorf, M.D.

Epidemiology . . . . Hoda Anton-Culver, Ph.D.
Family Medicine . . . . Laura Mosqueda, M.D.
Medicine . . . . Alpesh N. Amin, M.D.
  Basic and Clinical Immunology . . . . Sudhir Gupta, M.D.
  Cardiology . . . . Jagat Narula, M.D.
  Endocrinology . . . . Ellis Levin, M.D.
  Gastroenterology . . . . Kenneth Chang, M.D.
  General Internal Medicine . . . . Alpesh Amin, M.D.
  Hematology and Oncology . . . . Edward Nelson, M.D.
  Infectious Diseases . . . . Donald Forthal, M.D.
  Nephrology . . . . Nosratola D. Vaziri, M.D.
  Occupational Medicine . . . . Dean Baker, M.D.
  Pulmonary Diseases and Critical Care Medicine . . . . Matthew Brenner, M.D.
  Rheumatology . . . . George Lawry, M.D.
Neurological Surgery . . . . Johnny Delashaw, M.D.
Neurology . . . . Steven Small, M.D.
Obstetrics and Gynecology . . . . Manual Porto, M.D.
Ophthalmology . . . . Roger F. Steinert, M.D.
Orthopedic Surgery . . . . Ranjan Gupta, M.D.
Otolaryngology . . . . William Armstrong, M.D.
Pathology . . . . Fritz Lin, M.D.
Pediatrics . . . . Dan Cooper, M.D.
  Cardiology . . . . Nafiz Kiciman, M.D.
  Child Development . . . . Tim Wigal, Ph.D.
  Critical Care . . . . Mehrdad Jalili, M.D.
  Developmental/Behavioral Pediatrics . . . . Marc Lerner, M.D.
  Endocrinology . . . . Ajanta Naidu, M.D.
  General Pediatrics . . . . Melitza Cobuam-Browne, M.D.
  Human Genetics . . . . Virginia Kimonis, M.D.
  Infectious Disease . . . . Behnoosh Afghani, M.D.
  Neonatal and Perinatal Medicine . . . . Cherry Uy, M.D.
  Nephrology . . . . Deepak Rajpoot, M.D.
  Neurology . . . . Ira Lott, M.D.
  Pulmonary . . . . Dan Cooper, M.D.
Physical Medicine and Rehabilitation . . . . Jen Yu, M.D., Ph.D.
Psychiatry and Human Behavior . . . . Barry Chaitin, M.D.
Radiation Oncology . . . . Nilam Ramsinghani, M.D.
Radiological Sciences . . . . Scott Goodwin, M.D.
  Cardiothoracic Radiology . . . . Mayil Krishnam, M.D.
  ER Radiology . . . . Duane Vajgrt, M.D.
  General Imaging and CT . . . . Chandana Lall, M.D.
  Magnetic Resonance Imaging . . . . Fred Greensite, M.D.
  Mammography . . . . Stephen Feig, M.D.
  Musculoskeletal . . . . Hiroshi Yoshioka, M.D., Ph.D.
  Molecular Imaging . . . . Tatiana Kain, M.D.
  Neuro Endovascular Radiology . . . . Shuichi Suzuki, M.D., Ph.D.
  Neuroradiology . . . . Anton Hasso, M.D.
  Pediatric Radiology . . . . Liliane Gibbs, M.D.
  Ultrasound . . . . Mohammad Helmy, M.D.
  Vascular and Interventional . . . . Laura Findeiss, M.D.
  Women's Imaging . . . . Joan Campbell, M.D.
Surgery . . . . Michael Stamos, M.D.
  Colorectal Surgery . . . . Steven Mills, M.D.
  Gastrointestinal . . . . Ninh Nguyen, M.D.
  Hepatobiliary . . . . David Imagawa, M.D.
  Oncology . . . . John Butler, M.D.
  Plastic Surgery . . . . Gregory Evans, M.D.
  Thoracic Surgery . . . . Jeffrey Milliken, M.D.
  Transplantation . . . . Clarence Foster, M.D.
  Trauma and Critical Care . . . . Michael Lekawa, M.D.
  Vascular Surgery . . . . Roy Fujitani, M.D.
Urology . . . . Jaime Landman, M.D.

University of California, San Diego, School of Medicine

La Jolla, California 92093
858-534-0830; 858-534-1501 (dean's office); 858-534-6573 (fax)
Web site: http://som.ucsd.edu

The University of California Regents voted to establish a school of medicine on the University of California, San Diego (UCSD), campus in 1962. The first medical school class matriculated in fall 1968. Today, the entering class size is 125 new students, including 8-10 M.D./Ph.D. students each year. The school's La Jolla campus complex has grown to encompass the Biomedical Sciences Building, Stein Clinical Research Building, Leichtag Biomedical Research Building, Cellular and Molecular Medicine buildings, and the Center for Neural Circuits and Behavior. UCSD's Skaggs School of Pharmacy facility is also located on this complex, and pharmacy students join medical students in several common classes. The primary teaching hospital is located 13 miles south of the campus in Hillcrest. A newer medical center complex with a hospital and specialty centers is located on UCSD campus property east of the school of medicine. Both complexes also have ambulatory care facilities.

Type: public
2011 total enrollment: 469
Clinical facilities: UC San Diego Health System includes UC San Diego Medical Center Hospital, La Jolla and Thornton, Hillcrest (complex includes three ambulatory care centers); Rebecca and John Moores Cancer Center, Sulpisio Cardiovascular Center, Donald and Darlene Shiley Eye Center, Perlman Ambulatory Care Center on UCSD's east campus in La Jolla. **Partner Institutions:** VA San Diego Healthcare System, Rady Children's Hospital San Diego. Joint Bone Marrow Program with Sharp Hospital. Teaching and service agreements with Scripps Hospitals, Sharp Hospitals, Kaiser Foundation Hospital, Community Clinics, Alvarado Hospital.

University Officials

President. . . . . Mark G. Yudof, L.L.B.
Chancellor, San Diego Campus . . . . Marye Anne Fox, Ph.D.

Medical School Administrative Staff

Vice Chancellor and Dean, School of Medicine . . . . David A. Brenner, M.D.
Associate Vice Chancellor, Academic Affairs . . . . Andy Ries, M.D.
Dean, Clinical Affairs. . . . . Thomas McAfee, M.D.
Associate Vice Chancellor, Scientific Affairs . . . . Vacant
Associate Dean, Scientific Affairs . . . . Jerrold M. Olefsky, M.D.
Associate Vice Chancellor and Chief Executive Officer . . . . Thomas E. Jackiewicz
Assistant Vice Chancellor, Resource Strategy and Planning . . . . Shawn Sheffield
Associate Vice Chancellor, Development. . . . . Pat Carew
Associate Vice Chancellor, Translational Medicine . . . . Gary Firestein, M.D.
Assistant Dean, Global Health . . . . Steffanie A. Strathdee, Ph.D.
Associate Dean, Admissions and Student Life . . . . Carolyn Kelly, M.D.
Associate Dean, Continuing Education . . . . Terence M. Davidson, M.D.
Associate Dean, Graduate Medical Education . . . . Stephen Hayden, M.D.
Dean for Medical Education. . . . . Maria C. Savoia, M.D.
Assistant Dean, Diversity and Community Partnerships . . . . Lindia Willies-Jacobo, M.D.
Director, Animal Care Program . . . . Phillip Richter, D.V.M., Ph.D.
Chief, Health Sciences Marketing and Communications Officer . . . . Kim Kennedy
Assistant Vice Chancellor, Business and Fiscal Affairs . . . . Ron Espiritu
Assistant Vice Chancellor, Health Affairs. . . . . Tony Perez, Esq.
Assistant Vice Chancellor, Faculty Affiars . . . . Vivian Reznik, M.D.

Department Chairs and Division or Section Heads

Anesthesiology. . . . . Gerard Manecke, M.D.
Cellular and Molecular Medicine . . . . Don W. Cleveland, Ph.D.
Emergency Medicine Department. . . . . David Guss, M.D.
Family and Preventive Medicine. . . . . Bess Marcus, Ph.D.
   Division of Biostatistics and Bioinformatics . . . . Charles Berry, M.D.
   Epidemiology. . . . . Elizabeth Barrett-Connor, M.D.
   Family Medicine. . . . . Gene (Rusty) Kallenberg, M.D.
   Health Care Sciences . . . . Richard G. Kronick, Ph.D.
   Preventive Medicine. . . . . Michael Criqui, M.D.
Medicine. . . . . Wolf Dillmann, M.D.
   Division of Biomedical Informatics . . . . Lucila Ohno-Machado, Ph.D.

Division of Genetics . . . . Trey Ideker, Ph.D.
Division of Geriatrics . . . . Laura Dugan, M.D.
Allergy, Rheumatology, and Immunology . . . . Robert Terkeltaub, M.D.
Cardiology . . . . Kirk Knowlton, M.D.
Dermatology . . . . Richard Gallo, M.D., Ph.D.
Endocrinology and Metabolism . . . . Nick Webster, M.D.
General Internal Medicine . . . . Joe W. Ramsdell, M.D.
Gastroenterology . . . . William J. Sandborn, M.D.
Hematology and Oncology . . . . Sanford Shattil, M.D.
Infectious Disease . . . . Robert Schooley, M.D.
Nephrology . . . . Roland C. Blantz, M.D.
Physiology . . . . Peter D. Wagner, M.D.
Pulmonary . . . . Vacant
Neurosciences . . . . William C. Mobley, M.D.
Pediatric Neurology . . . . Doris A. Trauner, M.D.
Ophthalmology . . . . Robert N. Weinreb, M.D.
Orthopaedics . . . . Steven R. Garfin, M.D.
Pathology . . . . Steve Gonias, M.D.
Neuropathology . . . . Scott VandenBerg, M.D., Ph.D.
Pediatrics . . . . Gabriel Haddad, M.D.
Division of Genome Information Sciences . . . . Kelly Frazer, Ph.D.
Division of Genetics . . . . Albert R. La Spada, M.D., Ph.D.
Allergy and Immunology . . . . Jane Burns, M.D.
Cardiology . . . . John Moore, M.D., Ph.D.
Dysmorphology . . . . Kenneth Lyons Jones, M.D.
Endocrinology . . . . Michael E. Gottschalk, M.D., Ph.D.
Hematology and Oncology . . . . Donald Durden, M.D., Ph.D.
Infectious Diseases . . . . Stephen A. Spector, M.D.
Neonatology and Perinatology . . . . Neil Finer, M.D.
Nephrology and Renal Medicine . . . . Robert Mak, M.D., Ph.D.
Neurology . . . . Doris A. Trauner, M.D.
Pharmacology and Drug Discovery . . . . Victor Nizet, M.D.
Pulmonary Medicine . . . . Mark S. Pian, M.D.
Pharmacology . . . . Joan Heller Brown, Ph.D.
Psychiatry . . . . Lewis L. Judd, M.D.
Child Psychiatry . . . . Saul Levine, M.D.
Clinical Psychology Doctoral Program . . . . Robert K. Heaton, Ph.D.
Geropsychiatry . . . . Dilip Jeste, M.D.
Radiology . . . . William Bradley, M.D., Ph.D.
Diagnostic Radiology . . . . John Renner, M.D.
Nuclear Medicine . . . . Carl K. Hoh, M.D.
Vascular and Interventional . . . . Anne C. Roberts, M.D.
Radiation Oncology . . . . Stephen Seagren, M.D.
Reproductive Medicine . . . . Thomas R. Moore, M.D.
Gynecologic Oncology . . . . Steven Plaxe, M.D.
Reproductive Endocrinology . . . . R. Jeffrey Chang, M.D.
Surgery . . . . Mark Talamini, M.D.
Anatomy . . . . Mark C. Whitehead, Ph.D.
Cardiothoracic Surgery . . . . Stuart W. Jamieson, M.D.
General Surgery . . . . Mark Talamini, M.D.
Minimally Invasive Surgery . . . . Santiago Horgan, M.D.
Neurosurgery . . . . Robert Carter, M.D.
Otolaryngology-Head and Neck Surgery . . . . Jeffrey P. Harris, M.D., Ph.D.
Plastic Surgery . . . . Ann Wallace, M.D.
Trauma-Burn . . . . Raul Colmbra, M.D.
Urology . . . . Christopher Kane, M.D.

Organized Research Units

Rebecca and John Moores Cancer Center . . . . Thomas Kipps, M.D. (Interim)
Stein Institute for Research on Aging . . . . Dilip Jeste, M.D.
ARI - AIDS Research Institute . . . . Douglas Richman, M.D.
GRTC - Glycobiology Research and Training Center . . . . Ajit Varki, M.D.
CARTA - Center for Academic Research and Training in Anthropogeny . . . . Ajit Varki, M.D.
CTRI - Clinical and Translational Research Institute . . . . Gary S. Firestein, M.D.

University of California, San Francisco, School of Medicine

513 Parnassus Avenue
Room S-224
San Francisco, California 94143-0410
415-476-1000; 415-476-2342 (dean's office); 415-476-0689 (fax)
Web site: www.medschool.ucsf.edu

The school of medicine at the University of California, San Francisco, dates from 1864 when it was founded as the Toland Medical College. In 1873, it was formally transferred to the Regents of the University of California.

Type: public
2011 total enrollment: 600
Clinical facilities: UCSF Medical Center; Langley Porter Psychiatric Institute; San Francisco General Hospital Medical Center; San Francisco Veterans Affairs Medical Center; and major teaching hospitals associated with the UCSF/Fresno Medical Education Program.

University Officials

President. . . . . Mark G. Yudof
Vice President, Health Sciences and Services . . . . John D. Stobo, M.D.
Chancellor, San Francisco Campus. . . . . Susan Desmond-Hellmann, M.D., M.P.H.

Medical School Administrative Staff

Dean. . . . . Samuel Hawgood, M.B.,B.S.
 Associate Dean, Cancer Center. . . . . Frank McCormick, Ph.D.
 Associate Dean, Mount Zion Medical Center. Jeffrey M. Pearl, M.D.
 Associate Dean, San Francisco General Hospital . . . . Amanda S. Carlisle, M.D., Ph.D.
 Associate Dean, San Francisco Veterans Affairs
  Medical Center . . . . C. Diana Nicoll, M.D., Ph.D.
Vice Dean, Academic Affairs . . . . Neal Cohen, M.D. (Interim)
 Associate Deans, Academic Affairs. . . . . Renee L. Binder, M.D.
Vice Dean, Administration, Finance, and Clinical Programs. . . . . Michael Hindery
Vice Dean, Education . . . . Catherine R. Lucey, M.D.
 Associate Dean, Admissions. . . . . David Wofsy, M.D.
 Associate Dean, Curricular Affairs. . . . . Susan Masters, Ph.D.
 Associate Dean, Student Affairs. . . . . Maxine A. Papadakis, M.D.
 Associate Dean, Graduate Medical Education,
  and Associate Dean, Continuing Medical
  Education . . . . Robert B. Baron, M.D.
 Associate Dean, Fresno Medical Education Program . . . . Joan L. Voris, M.D.
 Associate Dean, School of Medicine . . . . Peter R. Carroll, M.D., M.P.H.
Executive Vice Dean . . . . Keith R. Yamamoto, Ph.D.
Vice Deans, School of Medicine. . . . . Neal H. Cohen, M.D., Nancy Milliken, M.D.,
and Bruce U. Wintroub, M.D.

Department and Division or Section Chairs

Basic Sciences

Anatomy. . . . . Allan I. Basbaum, Ph.D.
Anthropology, History, and Social Medicine . . . . Nancy Milliken, M.D. (Acting)
Biochemistry and Biophysics. . . . . Graeme W. Davis, Ph.D.
Bioengineering and Therapeutic Sciences. . . . . Kathy Giacomini, Ph.D., and Sarah Nelson, Ph.D.
Cellular and Molecular Pharmacology . . . . Kevin Shokat, Ph.D.
Epidemiology and Biostatistics . . . . Robert A. Hiatt, M.D., Ph.D.
Microbiology and Immunology. . . . . Lewis L. Lanier, Ph.D.
Pathology . . . . Abul K. Abbas, M.D.
Physiology. . . . . David J. Julius, Ph.D.

University of California, San Francisco, School of Medicine: CALIFORNIA

Clinical Sciences

Anesthesia and Perioperative Care . . . . Mervyn Maze, M.B., Ch.B.
Dermatology . . . . Bruce U. Wintroub, M.D.
Emergency Medicine . . . . Michael L. Callaham, M.D.
Family and Community Medicine . . . . Kevin Grumbach, M.D.
Laboratory Medicine . . . . Clifford A. Lowell, M.D., Ph.D.
Medicine . . . . Talmadge E. King, Jr., M.D.
Neurological Surgery . . . . Mitchel S. Berger, M.D.
Neurology . . . . Stephen L. Hauser, M.D.
Obstetrics, Gynecology, and Reproductive Sciences . . . . Linda C. Giudice, M.D., Ph.D.
Ophthalmology . . . . Stephen D. McLeod, M.D.
Orthopaedic Surgery . . . . Thomas P. Vail, M.D.
Otolaryngology . . . . David W. Eisele, M.D.
Pediatrics . . . . Donna Ferriero, M.D.
Physical Therapy and Rehabilitation Sciences . . . . Kimberly S. Topp, Ph.D.
Psychiatry . . . . Lowell Tong, M.D. (Interim)
Radiation Oncology . . . . Mack Roach III, M.D.
Radiology and Biomedical Imaging . . . . Ronald L. Arenson, M.D.
Surgery . . . . Nancy L. Ascher, M.D., Ph.D.
Urology . . . . Peter R. Carroll, M.D.

University of Colorado School of Medicine

13001 East 17th Place
Campus Box C290
Aurora, Colorado 80045
720-848-0000 (general information); 303-724-8025 (admissions);
303-724-0882 (dean's office); 303-724-6070 (fax)
E-mail: SOMdean@ucdenver.edu
Web site: www.Medschool.ucdenver.edu

The University of Colorado School of Medicine was opened on the main campus in Boulder in 1883. The school was moved to downtown Denver in 1911 to be merged with the Denver and Gross College of Medicine. In 1922, a facility was built on a 17-acre site in a residential section of east Denver (which later grew to 45 acres), and the school of medicine moved there in 1925. The school completed its move six miles east to the Anschutz Medical Campus in Aurora, site of the former Fitzsimons Army Medical Hospital. The new 227-acre Anschutz Medical Campus is adjacent to a 160-acre bioscience park.

Type: public
2011 total enrollment: 635
Clinical facilities: The Children's Hospital Colorado, University of Colorado Hospital, Denver Health, National Jewish Health, and the Veterans Affairs Medical Center, which is a dean's committee VA center.

University Officials

President. . . . . Bruce Benson
Chancellor, University of Colorado Denver. . . . . Jerry Wartgow, Ph.D.
Vice President for Health Affairs, Executive Vice Chancellor AMC. . . . . Lilly Marks
Vice Chancellor for Academic and Student Affairs . . . . Roderick Nairn, Ph.D.
Vice Chancellor for Administration and Finance. . . . . Jeff Parker
Vice Chancellor for Health Affairs and Dean,
    School of Medicine . . . . Richard D. Krugman, M.D.
Vice Chancellor for Research Affairs. . . . . Richard Traystman, Ph.D.

Medical School Administrative Staff

Dean. . . . . Richard D. Krugman, M.D.
Senior Associate Dean for Academic Affairs . . . . E. Chester Ridgway, M.D.
Senior Associate Dean for Administration and Finance . . . . Jane Schumaker
Senior Associate Dean for Clinical Affairs. . . . . M. Douglas Jones, Jr., M.D.
Senior Associate Dean for Education . . . . Celia Kaye, M.D., Ph.D.
Associate Dean for Admissions. . . . . Robert A. Winn, M.D.
Associate Dean for Continuing Medical Education . . . . Ronald S. Gibbs, M.D.
Associate Dean for Diversity and Inclusion . . . . Ann-Christine Nyquist, M.D.
Associate Dean for Faculty Affairs. . . . . Steven R. Lowenstein, M.D.
Associate Dean for Graduate Medical Education . . . . Carol M. Rumack, M.D.
Associate Dean for Research Affairs . . . . John W. Moorhead, Ph.D.
Associate Dean for Research Development . . . . Richard B. Johnston, Jr., M.D.
Associate Dean for Rural Affairs. . . . . John M. Westfall, M.D.
Associate Dean for Student Advocacy . . . . John E. Repine, M.D.
Associate Dean for Student Affairs . . . . Maureen Garrity, Ph.D.
Associate Dean for Physical Therapy. . . . . Margaret L. Schenkman, Ph.D., P.T.
Associate Dean for CHAPA . . . . Anita Glicken, M.S.W.
Associate Dean for Research Education . . . . Nancy R. Zahniser, Ph.D.
Associate Dean Administration and Finance, and Chief of Staff. . . . . Terri C. Carrothers

Department and Division or Section Chairs

Basic Sciences

Biochemistry and Molecular Genetics. . . . . Mark Johnston, Ph.D.
Cell and Developmental Biology. . . . . Wendy Macklin, Ph.D.
Immunology. . . . . John C. Cambier, Ph.D.
Microbiology. . . . . Randall K. Holmes, M.D., Ph.D.
Pathology . . . . Ann D. Thor, M.D.

Pharmacology . . . . Andrew Thorburn, Ph.D.
Physiology and Biophysics . . . . William Betz, Ph.D.

Clinical Sciences

Anesthesiology. . . . . Thomas K. Henthorn, M.D.
Dermatology . . . . David A. Norris, M.D.
Emergency Medicine . . . . Richard D. Zane, M.D.
Family Medicine . . . . Frank deGruy, M.D.
Medicine. . . . . David Schwartz, M.D.
  Allergy and Clinical Immunology . . . . Andrew Fontenot, M.D.
  Cardiology. . . . . Peter Buttrick, M.D.
  Clinical Pharmacology and Toxicology . . . . Curt Freed, M.D.
  CVP Research. . . . . Kurt Stenmark, M.D.
  Endocrinology, Metabolism, and Diabetes . . . . Bryan Haugen, M.D.
  Gastroenterology . . . . Hugo Rosen, M.D.
  General Internal Medicine . . . . Jean Kutner, M.D.
  Geriatrics . . . . Robert S. Schwartz, M.D.
  Health Care Policy and Research . . . . Eric Coleman, M.D.
  Hematology . . . . Robert H. Allen, M.D., and Sally P. Stabler, M.D. (Co-Head)
  Infectious Diseases . . . . Thomas Campbell, M.D. (Interim)
  Medical Oncology . . . . S. Gail Eckhardt, M.D.
  Pulmonary Sciences and Critical Care Medicine . . . . Mark Geraci, M.D.
  Renal Diseases and Hypertension . . . . Richard Johnson, M.D.
  Rheumatology . . . . V. Michael Holers, M.D.
Neurology. . . . . Kenneth L. Tyler, M.D.
Neurosurgery. . . . . Kevin Lillehei, M.D.
Obstetrics and Gynecology. . . . . Nanette F. Santoro, M.D.
Ophthalmology . . . . Naresh Mandava, M.D.
Orthopaedics. . . . . Robert D. D'Ambrosia, M.D.
Otolaryngology . . . . Herman A. Jenkins, M.D.
Pediatrics . . . . Stephen R. Daniels, M.D., Ph.D.
Physical Medicine and Rehabilitation . . . . Dennis Matthews, M.D.
Psychiatry . . . . Robert Freedman, M.D.
  Adult Psychiatry . . . . Robert E. Feinstein, M.D.
  Child Psychiatry . . . . Marianne Z. Wamboldt, M.D.
  Depression Center . . . . Marshall Thomas, M.D.
  Medical Student Education. . . . . Michael Weissberg, M.D.
  Neuro Behavioral Disorders . . . . David Arciniegas, M.D.
  Psychology . . . . Josette Harris, Ph.D.
  Residency Education. . . . . Alexis Giese, M.D.
  Schizophrenia Research Center. . . . . Robert Freedman, M.D.
  Substance Dependence. . . . . Paula D. Riggs, M.D.
Radiation Oncology. . . . . Laurie Gaspar, M.D.
Radiology . . . . Gerald D. Dodd, M.D.
  Abdominal Imaging . . . . Thomas Suby-Long, M.D.
  Breast Imaging . . . . Lara Hardesty, M.D.
  Interventional Radiology. . . . . Charles Ray, M.D.
  Musculoskeletal . . . . Brian Petersen, M.D.
  Neuroradiology . . . . Jody Tanabe, M.D.
  Nuclear Medicine. . . . . William (Bill) Klingensmith, M.D.
  Radiological Sciences . . . . Ann Scherzinger, Ph.D.
  Thoracic Imaging. . . . . Peter Sachs, M.D.
Surgery. . . . . Frederick L. Grover, M.D.
  Cardiothoracic Surgery. . . . . David Fullerton, M.D.
  Gastrointestinal, Tumor, and Endocrine Surgery . . . . Greg Stiegmann, M.D.
  Pediatric Surgery* . . . . Frederick Karrer, M.D.
  Plastic and Reconstructive Surgery . . . . Michael Gordon, M.D.
  Transplant Surgery. . . . . Igal Kam, M.D.
  Trauma . . . . Ernest E. Moore, M.D.
  Urology . . . . Randall B. Mcacham, M.D.
  Vascular Surgery and Podiatry. . . . . Mark R. Nehler, M.D.

*Specialty without organizational autonomy.

University of Connecticut School of Medicine

263 Farmington Avenue
Farmington, Connecticut 06030
860-679-2000; 860-679-2594 (dean's office); 860-679-1255 (fax)
Web site: http://medicine.uchc.edu/

The University of Connecticut School of Medicine appointed its first faculty members in 1963 and admitted its first class in 1968. The University of Connecticut Health Center, 35 miles from the main university campus, includes the school of medicine, school of dental medicine, ambulatory services, and John Dempsey Hospital.

Type: public
2011 total enrollment: 353
Clinical facilities: John Dempsey Hospital, Connecticut Children's Medical Center, Veterans Administration Medical Center (Newington). Bristol Hospital, Hartford Hospital, the Institute of Living, Middlesex Hospital, The Hospital for Special Care, Saint Francis Hospital and Medical Center, the Hebrew Home and Hospital, The Hospital of Central Connecticut.

University Officials

President	Susan Herbst
Vice President, Health Affairs	Philip E. Austin (Interim)
Chief Financial Officer	John Biancamano
Chief Information Officer	Sandra Armstrong
Associate Vice President, Facilities Management	Thomas P. Trutter, A.I.A.
Associate Vice President, Research Administration and Finance	Jeff Small
Associate Vice President, Human Resources	Jeff Chitester
Director of Communications	Maureen McGuire
Associate Vice President, Budget	Lisa Danville
Chief Executive Officer, John Dempsey Hospital	Mike Summerer, M.D.
Medical Director, UConn Medical Group	Denis Lafrenire, M.D. (Interim)

Medical School Administrative Staff

Dean	Bruce T. Liang, M.D. (Interim)
Senior Associate Dean, Education	Suzanne Rose, M.D.
Senior Associate Dean, Research Planning and Coordination	Marc E. Lalande, Ph.D.
Senior Associate Dean, Faculty Affairs	Mary Casey Jacob, Ph.D.
Director of Finance and Administration	Donna McKenty
Associate Dean, Clinical Affairs	Denis Lafreniere, M.D. (Interim)
Associate Dean for Continuing and Community Education	Leighton Huey, M.D.
Associate Dean of the Graduate School	Barbara Kream, Ph.D.
Associate Dean, Graduate Medical Education	Jacqueline Nissen, M.D.
Associate Dean, Health Career Opportunity Program	Marja Hurley, M.D.
Associate Dean for Postdoctoral and External Affairs	Gerald D. Maxwell, Ph.D.
Associate Dean, Primary Care	Bruce Gould, M.D.
Associate Dean, Student Affairs	David Henderson, M.D.
Assistant Dean, Clinical Affairs	Jane Grant-Kels, M.D.
Assistant Dean, Health Career Opportunity Program	Granville E. Wrensford, Ph.D.
Assistant Dean, Research, Planning, and Coordination	Lawrence Klobutcher, Ph.D.
Assistant Dean, Student Affairs	Richard Zeff, M.D.

Department and Division or Section Chairs

Basic Sciences

Cell Biology	Laurinda A. Jaffe, Ph.D.
Community Medicine and Health Care	Thomas Babor, Ph.D.
Genetics and Developmental Biology	Marc Lalande, Ph.D.
Division of Genetics	Vacant
Immunology	Leo Lefrancois, Ph.D.
Molecular, Microbial, and Structural Biology	Sandra K. Weller, Ph.D.
Neuroscience	Richard Mains, Ph.D.

Clinical Sciences

Anesthesiology	Jeffrey B. Gross, M.D.
Dermatology	Jane Grant-Kels, M.D.
Diagnostic Imaging and Therapeutics	Douglas Fellows, M.D.
Radiation Oncology	Robert Dowsett, M.D.
Radiology	Douglas Fellows, M.D.
Nuclear Medicine	John Vento, M.D.
Family Medicine	Robert A. Cushman, M.D.

University of Connecticut School of Medicine: CONNECTICUT

Medicine. . . . . Paul Skolnik, M.D.
  Cardiology. . . . . Bruce T. Liang, M.D.
  Endocrinology. . . . . Andrew Arnold, M.D.
  Gastroenterology . . . . John Birk, M.D.
  General Medicine. . . . . Jacqueline Nissen, M.D. (Interim)
  Geriatrics . . . . George Kuchel, M.D.
  Hematology and Oncology. . . . . Jeffrey Wasser, M.D. (Interim)
  Hypertension . . . . William B. White, M.D.
  Infectious Diseases . . . . Kevin Dieckhaus, M.D.
  Nephrology . . . . Nancy Adams, M.D.
  Public Health and Population Sciences. . . . . Robert Trestman, M.D., Ph.D.
  Pulmonary and Critical Care Medicine . . . . Daniel McNally, M.D.
  Rheumatology . . . . Micha Abeles, M.D. (Interim)
Neurology. . . . . Leslie Wolfson, M.D.
Obstetrics and Gynecology. . . . . Winston Campbell, M.D. (Interim)
  Gynecological Oncology* . . . . Molly A. Brewer, M.D.
  Maternal Fetal Medicine*. . . . . Winston A. Campbell, M.D.
  Reproductive Endocrinology and Infertility* . . . . John C. Nulsen, M.D.
  Urogynecology. . . . . Vacant
  Generalist . . . . Joseph Walsh, M.D.
Orthopaedic Surgery. . . . . Jay Lieberman, M.D.
Pathology and Laboratory Medicine. . . . . M. Melinda Sanders, M.D.
Pediatrics . . . . Paul Dworkin, M.D.
  Adolescent Medicine*. . . . . Aric Schichor, M.D.
  Developmental and Behavioral* . . . . Ann Milanese, M.D.
  Cardiology* . . . . Harris Leopold, M.D.
  Child and Family Studies* . . . . Mary Beth Bruder, Ph.D.
  Community Pediatrics*. . . . . Douglas MacGilpin, M.D., and Larry Scherzer, M.D.
  Critical Care*. . . . . Aaron Zucker, M.D.
  Endocrinology* . . . . Karen R. Rubin, M.D.
  Education and Residency Program* . . . . Edwin L. Zalneraitis, M.D.
  Gastroenterology* . . . . Jeffrey S. Hyams, M.D.
  General Pediatrics*. . . . . Catherine C. Wiley, M.D. (Interim)
  Hematology and Oncology* . . . . Nathan Hagstrom, M.D.
  Hospital Medicine . . . . Anand Sekaram, M.D.
  Infectious Diseases* . . . . Juan C. Salazar, M.D.
  Neonatology and Perinatal Medicine. . . . . Victor C. Herson, M.D. (Interim)
  Nephrology* . . . . Lawrence Zemel, M.D.
  Neurology* . . . . Gyula Acsadi, M.D.
  Pain and Palliative Medicine. . . . . William Zempsky, M.D.
  Allergy and Immunology*. . . . . Louis Mendelson, M.D.
  Emergency Medicine . . . . John Peng, M.D. (Interim)
  Dermatology . . . . Vacant
  Pathology*. . . . . Fabiola Balarezo, M.D.
  Pathology*. . . . . Vijay Joshi, M.D.
  Psychiatry*. . . . . Robert Sahl, M.D.
  Radiology*. . . . . Timothy Brown, M.D.
  Pediatric Rehabilitative Medicine*. . . . . Vacant
  Research* . . . . Georgine S. Burke, Ph.D.
  Rheumatology* . . . . Lawrence Zemel, M.D.
  Pulmonary Medicine*. . . . . Craig Schramm, M.D.
Psychiatry . . . . Victor Hesselbrock, M.D. (Interim)
Surgery. . . . . David McFadden, M.D.
  Cardiothoracic Surgery. . . . . Stephen J. Lahey, M.D.
  General Surgery. . . . . Denis Lafreniere, M.D. (Interim)
  Neurosurgery. . . . . Hilary Onyiuke, M.D.
  Ophthalmology and Clinical . . . . Jeanine Suchecki, M.D.
  Otorhinolaryngology. . . . . Denis Lafreniere, M.D.
  Plastic Surgery . . . . Rajiv Y. Chandawarkar, M.D.
  Surgery Research . . . . Mansoor Sarfarazi, Ph.D.
  Urology. . . . . Peter Albertsen, M.D.
Traumatology and Emergency Medicine. Lenworth Jacobs, M.D.

*Specialty without organizational autonomy.

Yale University School of Medicine

333 Cedar Street; P.O. Box 208055
New Haven, Connecticut 06520-8055
203-785-4672 (dean's office); 203-785-7437 (fax)
Web site: http://medicine.yale.edu

The Medical Institution of Yale College was chartered in 1810, opened in 1813, and has been in continuous operation since that date. Yale College became Yale University in 1887; the current designation of the school was adopted in 1918.

Type: private
2011 total enrollment: 805
Clinical facilities: Yale-New Haven Hospital, Veterans Administration Hospital (West Haven), Connecticut Mental Health Center, Hill Health Center, Yale Child Study Center, Bridgeport Hospital, Danbury Hospital, Greenwich Hospital, Griffin Hospital, Lawrence and Memorial Hospitals, Norwalk Hospital, St. Mary's Hospital, Hospital of St. Raphael, Waterbury Hospital, Yale Health Center.

University Officials

President. . . . . Richard C. Levin, Ph.D.
Provost . . . . Peter Salovey, Ph.D.
Deputy Provost for Health Affairs and Academic Integrity. . . . . Stephanie S. Spangler, M.D.

Medical School Administrative Staff

Dean. . . . . Robert J. Alpern, M.D.
Dean, Yale School of Public Health . . . . Paul D. Cleary, Ph.D.
Deputy Dean for Academic and Scientific Affairs . . . . Carolyn W. Slayman, Ph.D.
Deputy Dean for Education . . . . Richard Belitsky, M.D.
Deputy Dean for Finance and Administration. . . . . Cynthia Walker
Deputy Dean for Clinical Affairs. . . . . David J. Leffell, M.D.
Special Advisor to the Dean. . . . . Linda C. Mayes, M.D.
Dean's Special Advisor for Research. . . . . Richard Lifton, M.D., Ph.D.
Director, Office of Admissions . . . . Richard A. Silverman
Registrar for Student Affairs. . . . . Terri L. Tolson
Associate Dean for Student Affairs . . . . Nancy Angoff, M.D.
Associate Dean for Student Progress. . . . . James P. Comer, M.D., M.P.H.
Associate Dean for Faculty Affairs. . . . . Carolyn M. Mazure, Ph.D.
Associate Dean for Graduate Medical Education. . . . . Rosemarie L. Fisher, M.D.
Associate Dean for Admissions and Financial Aid . . . . Laura Ment, M.D.
Associate Dean for Clinical Affairs . . . . Ronald J. Vender, M.D.
Associate Dean and Ombudsperson, Title IX Coordinator. . . . . Merle Waxman, M.A.
Associate Dean for Veterans' Affairs . . . . Michael Ebert, M.D.
Associate Dean for Scientific Affairs . . . . Sara Rockwell, Ph.D.
Acting Director, Physician Associate Program . . . . David Brissette, M.S., P.A.-C.
Assistant Dean for Multicultural Affairs. . . . . Forrester A. Lee, M.D.
Director, Division of Animal Care. . . . . James D. Macy, D.V.M.
Director, Medical Library. . . . . Regina K. Marone, M.L.S.
Director, Program in Biological and Biomedical Sciences . . . . Lynn Cooley, Ph.D.
Director, Office of Student Research . . . . John N. Forrest, Jr., M.D.
Director, Faculty Development and Equity . . . . Linda Bockenstedt, M.D.

Department, Section, or Center Chairs
Basic Sciences

Cell Biology. . . . . James E. Rothman, M.D., Ph.D.
Cellular and Molecular Physiology . . . . Michael J. Caplan, M.D.
Center for Molecular Medicine . . . . Vincent T. Marchesi, M.D., Ph.D.
Comparative Medicine*. . . . . Tamas Horvath, D.V.M., Ph.D.
History of Medicine. . . . . John H. Warner, Ph.D.
Immunobiology. . . . . Richard A. Flavell, Ph.D.
Microbial Pathogenesis*. . . . . Jorge E. Galan, Ph.D.
Molecular Biophysics and Biochemistry. . . . . Patrick Sung, Ph.D.
Neurobiology. . . . . Pasko Rakic, M.D., Sc.D.
Pharmacology . . . . Joseph Schlessinger, Ph.D.

Clinical Sciences

Anesthesiology. . . . . Roberta L. Hines, M.D.
Child Study Center† . . . . Fred Volkmar, M.D.
Comprehensive Cancer Center. . . . . Thomas Lynch, M.D.
Dermatology . . . . Richard L. Edelson, M.D.

Yale University School of Medicine: CONNECTICUT

Diagnostic Radiology . . . . James A. Brink, M.D.
Emergency Medicine . . . . Gail D'Onofrio, M.D.
Epidemiology and Public Health . . . . Paul D. Cleary, Ph.D.
   Biostatistics . . . . Hongyu Zhao, Ph.D.
   Chronic Disease Epidemiology . . . . Susan T. Mayne, Ph.D.
   Environmental Health Sciences. . . . . Tongzhang Zheng, Ph.D.
   Epidemiology of Microbial Diseases. . . . . Albert Ko, M.D.
   Health Policy and Administration . . . . Jody Sindelar, Ph.D.
Genetics . . . . Richard Lifton, M.D., Ph.D.
Internal Medicine . . . . Jack A. Elias, M.D.
   Allergy and Immunology . . . . Fred Kantor, M.D. (Interim)
   Cardiology. . . . . Michael Simons, M.D.
   Digestive Diseases. . . . . Michael Nathanson, M.D.
   Endocrine and Metabolism. . . . . Robert Sherwin, M.D.
   General Medicine. . . . . Patrick O'Connor, M.D.
   Geriatric Medicine . . . . Mary E. Tinetti, M.D.
   Hematology. . . . . Madhav V. Dhodapkar, M.D.
   Infectious Diseases . . . . Erol Fikrig, M.D.
   Nephrology . . . . Stefan Somlo, M.D.
   Oncology. . . . . Roy Herbst, M.D.
   Pulmonary and Critical Care. . . . . Patty Lee, M.D. (Interim)
   Rheumatology . . . . Joseph E. Craft, M.D.
Laboratory Medicine . . . . Brian R. Smith, M.D.
Neurology. . . . . David Hafler, M.D.
Neurosurgery. . . . . Dennis D. Spencer, M.D.
Obstetrics and Gynecology. . . . . Peter Schwartz, M.D. (Interim)
Ophthalmology and Visual Sciences . . . . James C. Tsai, M.D.
Orthopedics and Rehabilitation . . . . Gary E. Friedlaender, M.D.
Pathology . . . . Jon S. Morrow, M.D., Ph.D.
Pediatrics . . . . Clifford W. Bogue, M.D. (Interim)
   Adolescent Medicine . . . . Sheryl Ryan, M.D.
   Cardiology . . . . William Hellenbrand, M.D.
   Critical Care. . . . . Clifford W. Bogue, M.D.
   Emergency Medicine . . . . Karen Santucci, M.D.
   Endocrinology . . . . William Tamborlane, M.D.
   Gastroenterology/Hepatology. . . . . Pramod Mistry, M.D.
   General Pediatrics . . . . Paul McCarthy, M.D.
   Hematology/Oncology. . . . . Gary Kupfer, M.D.
   Immunology. . . . . Fred Kantor, M.D. (Interim)
   Infectious Diseases . . . . I. George Miller, M.D.
   Nephrology . . . . Alda Tufro, M.D.
   Neurology . . . . Bennett A. Shaywitz, M.D.
   Perinatal Medicine/Neonatology. . . . . Ian Gross, M.D.
   Respiratory Medicine . . . . Alia Bazzy Asaad, M.D.
Psychiatry . . . . John H. Krystal, M.D.
Surgery. . . . . Robert Udelsman, M.D.
   Anatomy and Experimental Surgery . . . . William B. Stewart, Ph.D.
   Cardiac . . . . David Yuh, M.D.
   Dentistry* . . . . Suher Baker, D.M.D. (Acting)
   Endocrine Surgery . . . . Sanziana Roman, M.D.
   Gross Anatomy. . . . . William B. Stewart, Ph.D.
   Organ Transplantation and Immunology. . . . . Sukru H. Emre, M.D., F.A.C.S.
   Neuropathology. . . . . Laura Manuelidis, M.D.
   Otolaryngology. . . . . Clarence T. Sasaki, M.D.
   Pediatric . . . . William Caty, M.D.
   Plastic and Reconstructive. . . . . John A. Persing, M.D.
   Surgical Gastroenterology. . . . . Walter E. Longo, M.D.
   Surgical Oncology . . . . Ronald Salem, M.D.
   Thoracic Surgery . . . . Frank Detterbeck, M.D.
   Trauma and Surgical Critical Care . . . . Kimberly Davis, M.D.
   Vascular. . . . . Bauer Sumpio, M.D.
Therapeutic Radiology. . . . . Peter M. Glazer, M.D.
Urology. . . . . Peter G. Schulam, M.D., Ph.D.

*Autonomous section.
†Autonomous study center.

The George Washington University
School of Medicine and Health Sciences
2300 Eye Street, N.W.
Washington, D.C. 20037
202-994-1000 (university operator); 202-994-2987 (dean's office); 202-994-0926 (fax)
Web site: www.gwumc.edu/smhs/

The school of medicine was founded in 1821 as the Medical Department of the Columbian College. In 1974, the name was changed to the school of medicine and health sciences. The Walter G. Ross Hall of Health Sciences, Paul Himmelfarb Health Sciences Library, University Hospital, Burns Memorial Building and Ambulatory Care Center (Medical Faculty Associates, Inc.), and Warwick Building are situated on the main campus and constitute the George Washington University Medical Center.

Type: private
2011 total enrollment: 725
Clinical facilities: The George Washington University Hospital, Anne Arundel Medical Center, Children's National Medical Center, Fairfax Hospital, Holy Cross Hospital, Kaiser Permanente-D.C., National Institutes of Health, National Rehabilitation Hospital, Northern Virginia Mental Health Institute, Prince George's Hospital Center, Providence Hospital, Psychiatric Institute of Washington, St. Elizabeth's Hospital, Suburban Hospital, Sibley Memorial Hospital, Veterans Administration Hospitals (Washington, D.C.), Walter Reed Army Medical Center, Washington Hospital Center.

University Officials

President. . . . . Steven Knapp, Ph.D.
Provost and Executive Vice President for Academic Affairs . . . . Steven Lerman, Ph.D.
Interim Vice Provost & Vice President for Health Affairs. . . . . Jeffery S. Akman, M.D.

Medical School Administrative Staff

Dean. . . . . Jeffery S. Akman, M.D.
Interim Associate Dean & Associate Vice Provost
   for Health Affairs . . . . Vincent Chiappinelli, Ph.D.
Associate Dean for Administration . . . . W. Scott Schroth, M.D.
Senior Associate Dean for Education . . . . Alex Stagnaro-Green, M.D.
Interim Senior Associate Dean for Health Sciences . . . . Margaret Plack, P.T., Ed.D.
Associate Dean for Academic Affairs at CNMC . . . . Mark L. Batshaw, M.D.
Associate Dean for Graduate Medical Education . . . . Nancy Gaba, M.D.
Associate Dean for Graduate Studies . . . . Linda Werling, Ph.D.
Associate Dean for Clinical and Translational Research. . . . . Jill Joseph, M.D., Ph.D.
Associate Dean for Health Sciences . . . . Sylvia Silver, D.A.
Associate Dean for Student Affairs and Education. . . . . Rhonda M. Goldberg
Assistant Dean for Admissions . . . . Diane P. McQuail
Assistant Dean for Community-based Partnerships. . . . . Lisa Alexander, Ed.D.
Associate Dean for Student and Curricular Affairs. . . . . Yolanda C. Haywood, M.D.
Associate Vice President for Health Research . . . . Anne N. Hirshfield, Ph.D.

Department and Division or Section Chairs

Basic Sciences

Anatomy and Regenerative Biology. . . . . Robert G. Hawley, Ph.D.
Biochemistry and Molecular Biology. . . . . Rakesh Kumar, Ph.D.
Integrative Systems Biology . . . . Eric Hoffman, Ph.D.
Interim Microbiology, Immunology, and Tropical Medicine . . . . Michael I. Bukrinsky, Ph.D.
Pathology . . . . Donald S. Karcher, M.D.
   Anatomical and Surgical Pathology. . . . . Sana O. Tabbara, M.D.
   Clinical Pathology . . . . Louis A. DePalma, M.D.
Pharmacology and Physiology. . . . . Vincent A. Chiappinelli, Ph.D.

Clinical Sciences

Anesthesiology. . . . . Michael J. Berrigan, M.D., Ph.D.
   Intensive Care Medicine . . . . Michael G. Seneff, M.D.
Emergency Medicine . . . . Robert F. Shesser, M.D.

Medicine . . . . Alan G. Wasserman, M.D.
  Allergy . . . . Daniel Ein, M.D.
  Cardiology . . . . Richard J. Katz, M.D.
  Dermatology . . . . Gary L. Simon, M.D. (Acting)
  Endocrinology . . . . Kenneth L. Becker, M.D., Ph.D.
  Gastroenterology and Liver Diseases . . . . Marie Borum, M.D.
  General Internal Medicine . . . . April Barbour, M.D.
  Hematology and Oncology . . . . Robert S. Siegel, M.D.
  Hospital Medicine . . . . Sian L. Spurney, M.D. (Acting)
  Infectious Diseases . . . . Gary L. Simon, M.D., Ph.D.
  Pulmonary, Critical Care, and Sleep Disorders Medicine . . . . Guillermo Gutierrez, M.D., Ph.D.
  Renal Diseases and Hypertension . . . . Dominic S. Raj, M.D.
  Rheumatology . . . . James Katz, M.D.
Neurological Surgery . . . . Anthony Caputy, M.D.
Neurology . . . . Henry J. Kaminski, M.D.
Obstetrics and Gynecology . . . . John W. Larsen, M.D.
Ophthalmology . . . . Craig E. Geist, M.D.
Orthopaedic Surgery . . . . Robert J. Neviaser, M.D.
Pediatrics . . . . Mark L. Batshaw, M.D.
  Adolescent Medicine . . . . Lawrence D'Angelo, M.D.
  Allergy, Pulmonary, and Sleep Medicine . . . . Anastassios Koumbourlis, M.D.
  Anesthesiology . . . . Richard Kaplan, M.D.
  Cardiology . . . . Gerard Martin, M.D.
  Cardiovascular Surgery . . . . Richard Jonas, M.D.
  Critical Care Medicine . . . . David Wessel, M.D.
  Dermatology . . . . Roselyn Epps, M.D.
  Diagnostic Imaging and Radiology . . . . Raymond Sze, M.D.
  Emergency Medicine . . . . Jim Chamberlain, M.D.
  Endocrinology . . . . Paul Kaplowitz, M.D.
  Gastroenterology . . . . John Snyder, M.D.
  General and Community Pediatrics . . . . Denice Cora-Bramble, M.D.
  Hearing and Speech . . . . Sheela Stuart, Ph.D.
  Hematology and Oncology . . . . Max Coppes, M.D.
  Infectious Disease . . . . Nalini Singh, M.D.
  Laboratory Medicine . . . . Naomi Luban, M.D.
  Medical Genetics and Metabolism . . . . Marshall Summar, M.D.
  Neonatology . . . . Billie Lou Short, M.D.
  Nephrology . . . . Kanwal Kher, M.D.
  Neurology . . . . Roger Packer, M.D.
  Neurosurgery . . . . Robert Keating, M.D.
  Ophthalmology . . . . Mohamad Jaafar, M.D.
  Orthopedics . . . . Laurel Blakemore, M.D.
  Otolaryngology . . . . George Zalzal, M.D.
  Pathology . . . . D. Ashley Hill, M.D.
  Pediatric Surgery . . . . Anthony Sandler, M.D.
  Physical Medicine and Rehabilitation . . . . Sally Evans, M.D.
  Psychiatry . . . . Paramjit Joshi, M.D.
  Urology . . . . H. Gil Rushton, M.D.
Psychiatry and Behavioral Sciences . . . . James Griffith, M.D.
Radiology . . . . Robert K. Zeman, M.D.
  Breast Imaging and Intervention . . . . Rachel F. Brem, M.D.
  Diagnostic Radiology . . . . Robert K. Zeman, M.D.
  Nuclear Medicine . . . . Esma A. Akin, M.D.
  Radiation Oncology and Biophysics . . . . Howard Griffith, Ph.D.
Surgery . . . . Anton Sidawy, M.D.,MPH
  Breast Care Center . . . . Christine B. Teal, M.D.
  Colon and Rectal . . . . Vincent Obias, M.D.
  General . . . . Paul Lin, M.D.
  Otolaryngology . . . . Steven Bielamowicz, M.D.
  Plastic . . . . Michael Olding, M.D.
  Vascular . . . . Rienard Neville, M.D.
Urology . . . . Thomas Jarrett, M.D.

Georgetown University School of Medicine

3900 Reservoir Road, N.W.
Washington, D.C. 20007
202-687-3922 (dean's office); 202-687-2792 (fax); 202-697-5055 (general information)
Web site: http://som.georgetown.edu/

Georgetown University was founded in 1789, and its school of medicine was established in 1849 with the first class graduating in 1851. The school of medicine is part of the Georgetown University Medical Center (GUMC) and is one of four operational units, including the school of nursing and health studies, the Lombardi Comprehensive Cancer Center, and the Biomedical Research Organization and its Clinical Translational Science Award. GUMC is managed through a partnership with MedStar Health, a not-for-profit organization of nine hospitals in the Baltimore-Washington region. In 2005 the school of medicine opened its Integrated Learning Center, which supports the school of medicine's emphasis on a patient-centered, competence-based curriculum and provides the latest methods of clinical teaching and evaluation. In 2009, medical center research and teaching projects brought in $125.6 million in sponsored research funding.

Type: private
2011 total enrollment: 803
Clinical facilities: Georgetown University Hospital, Virginia Hospital Center-Arlington, Washington Hospital Center, Walter Reed Army Medical Center, Providence Hospital, Inova Fairfax Hospital, Inova Loudoun Hospital, Veterans Affairs Hospital, and Holy Cross Hospital.

University Officials

President . . . . John J. DeGioia, Ph.D.
Executive Vice President for Health Sciences
and Executive Dean . . . . Howard J. Federoff, M.D., Ph.D.

Medical School Administrative Staff

Dean for Medical Education. . . . . Stephen Ray Mitchell, M.D.
Senior Associate Dean for Clinical Education
and Medical Director of Georgetown
University Hospital . . . . Stephen R.T. Evans, M.D.
Associate Vice President Regulatory Affairs . . . . Sheila Zimmet, J.D.
Senior Associate Dean for Faculty Affairs . . . . Herbert Herscowitz, Ph.D.
Senior Associate Dean for Students . . . . Princy Kumar, M.D.
Senior Associate Dean for Admissions and Student Services. . . . . Russell Wall, M.D.
Associate Dean for Finance and Administration . . . . Diana Kassar
Associate Dean for Curriculum and Assessment . . . . Shyrl Sistrunk, M.D.
Associate Dean for Clinical Education . . . . James Duffy, M.D., S.J.
Senior Associate Dean for Students and Special Programs. . . . . Joy Williams
Associate Dean for Graduate Medical Education . . . . Jamie Padmore, MHA
Associate Dean for Graduate Education . . . . Barbara Bayer, Ph.D.
Assistant Dean of Admissions . . . . Brandon C. Schneider
Assistant Dean for Financial Planning. . . . . David Pollock
Assistant Dean for Community Service and Advocacy . . . . Eileen Moore, M.D.
Associate Dean for Knowledge Management and Librarian . . . . Jett McCann
Senior Associate Dean for International Programs. . . . . Irma Frank, D.D.S.
Associate Dean for Faculty Development. . . . . Bonnie Green, Ph.D.
Associate Dean for Clinical Informatics. . . . . Steven Schwartz, M.D.
Assistant Dean for Student Affairs. . . . . Cameron Jones, MSC
Associate Dean for Medical Education, VA
Hospital Center, Arlington . . . . Robert Holman, M.D.
Assistant Dean for Medical Education, INOVA Fairfax. . . . . Craig Cheifetz, M.D.
Assistant Dean for Medical Education, Washington Hospital Center. . . . . . Deborah Topol, M.D.
Associate Dean for Evaluation and Assessment . . . . Peggy Weissinger, Ed.D.
Assistant Dean for Student Learning. . . . . David Taylor
Assistant Dean for Curriculum Management. . . . . Linda Gwinn
Assistant Dean for Student Research. . . . . Joseph Timpone, M.D.
Medical School Registrar . . . . John Hammett
Director for Student Affairs . . . . Valerie Johnson

Georgetown University School of Medicine: DISTRICT OF COLUMBIA

Department and Division or Section Chairs

Basic Sciences

Biostatistics, Bioinformatics, and Biomathematics . . . . Christopher Loffredo, Ph.D.
Biochemistry and Molecular and Cell Biology . . . . Elliott Crooke, Ph.D.
Clinical Pathology . . . . Norio Azumi, M.D.
Microbiology and Immunology . . . . Richard A. Calderone, Ph.D.
Neuroscience . . . . Barbara M. Bayer, Ph.D.
Oncology . . . . Louis M. Weiner, M.D.
Pathology . . . . Richard Schlegel, M.D., Ph.D.
Pharmacology . . . . Kenneth L. Dretchen, Ph.D.
Physiology and Biophysics . . . . Elliott Crooke, Ph.D. (Interim)

Clinical Sciences

Anesthesia . . . . Young D. Kim, M.D.
Emergency Medicine . . . . Mark Smith, M.D.
Family Medicine . . . . James C. Welsh, M.D.
Medicine . . . . Bruce Luxon, M.D.
  Cardiology . . . . Richard Morrisey, M.D.
  Dermatology . . . . Alan Moshell, M.D.
  Endocrinology and Metabolic Diseases . . . . Joseph Verbalis, M.D.
  Gastroenterology . . . . Stanley B. Benjamin, M.D.
  Hematology and Oncology . . . . John L. Marshall, M.D.
  Infectious Diseases . . . . Princy Kumar, M.D.
  Internal Medicine . . . . Dennis R. Murphy, M.D.
  Lombardi Cancer Center . . . . Louis M. Weiner, M.D.
  Nephrology . . . . Christopher S. Wilcox, M.D., Ph.D.
  Pulmonary Disease . . . . Anne O'Donnell, M.D.
  Rheumatology, Immunology, and Allergy . . . . Thomas R. Cupps, M.D.
Neurology . . . . Edward Healton, M.D.
Neurosurgery . . . . Kevin McGrail, M.D.
Obstetrics and Gynecology . . . . Helain Dicker Landy, M.D.
Ophthalmology . . . . Jay Lustbader, M.D.
Orthopedics . . . . Sam W. Wiesel, M.D.
Otolaryngology and Head and Neck Surgery . . . . Bruce Davidson, M.D.
Pediatrics . . . . David B. Nelson, M.D.
Physical Medicine and Rehabilitation . . . . Edward B. Healton, M.D.
Psychiatry . . . . Steven A. Epstein, M.D.
Radiation Medicine . . . . Anatoly Dritschillo, M.D.
Radiology . . . . James B. Spies, M.D.
Surgery . . . . Lynt B. Johnson, M.D.
Plastic Surgery . . . . Scott Spear, M.D.
Urology . . . . John H. Lynch, M.D.

Howard University College of Medicine
520 W Street, N.W.
Washington, D.C. 20059
202-806-6270 (dean's office); 202-806-7934 (fax)
Web site: http://medicine.howard.edu

The college of medicine had its beginning as the medical department of Howard University when it was chartered by the Congress of the United States on March 2, 1867. Instruction in the department began on November 9, 1868. In 1882, instruction in dentistry and pharmacy was sufficiently formalized to warrant the division of the medical department into the medical, dental, and pharmaceutical colleges. The name of the department was changed to the school of medicine in 1907, and its component parts were named the college of medicine, college of dentistry, and college of pharmacy. The colleges of medicine and dentistry are now autonomous units within the Howard University Center for the Health Sciences, which also encompasses the college of pharmacy, nursing, and allied health sciences, Howard University Hospital, the Louis Stokes Health Sciences Library, and the student health center.

Type: private
2011 total enrollment: 452
Clinical facilities: Howard University Hospital, Inova Fairfax Hospital, Providence Hospital, St. Elizabeths Hospital, Washington Veterans Affairs Medical Center, Prince George's Hospital Center, Washington Hospital Center, Children's National Medical Center.

University Officials

President. . . . . Sidney A. Ribeau, Ph.D.
Interim Senior Vice President for Health Sciences . . . . LaSalle D. Leffall, Jr., M.D.
Deputy Senior Vice President for Health Services . . . . Wayne A.I. Frederick, M.D.
Associate Senior Vice President for Clinical
   Affairs and Quality and Designated
   Institutional Official . . . . Robin C. Newton, M.D.
Assistant Vice President for Health Sciences . . . . Celia J. Maxwell, M.D.

Medical School Administrative Staff

Dean. . . . . Mark S. Johnson, M.D.
Senior Associate Dean for Academic Affairs . . . . Sheik N. Hassan, M.D.
Associate Dean for Clinical and Translational Research. . . . . Thomas A. Mellman, M.D.
Associate Dean for Student Affairs and Admissions . . . . Walter P. Bland, M.D.
Assistant Dean for Medical Education. Pamela L. Carter-Nolan, Ph.D.
Director, Curriculum Office. . . . . Scott M. Satterlund, Ph.D.
Director of Development . . . . Karine A. Sewell
Director, Veterinary Services . . . . Doris E. Hughes, D.V.M.
Director, Office of Continuing Medical Education . . . . Debra White-Coleman, M.D.
Director, Office of Faculty Development. . . . . Renee R. Jenkins, M.D.
Director, Academic Support Services . . . . Bonnie S. Cobbs
Financial Aid Manager. . . . . Rozanna J. Aitcheson
Director of Admissions. . . . . Judith M. Walk
Director of Finance and Grant Affairs. . . . . Donnell H. Scott
Executive Director and Chief Administrative Officer, Faculty Practice Plan. . . . . . . Jeanette Gibbs
Director, Clinical Skills and Simulation Center . . . . Tamara L. Owens
Director, Informatics and Biomedical Communications. . . . . Stephen G. Whetstone
Director, Data Analysis Center . . . . Diane Williams
Director, Administrative Services . . . . Royette Leatham Stewart

Howard University College of Medicine: DISTRICT OF COLUMBIA

Department and Division or Section Chairs

Basic Sciences

Anatomy . . . . Thomas Heinbockel, Ph.D. (Interim)
Biochemistry and Molecular Biology . . . . Matthew George, Jr., Ph.D.
Microbiology . . . . Agnes A. Day, Ph.D.
Pathology . . . . Edward L. Lee, M.D.
Pharmacology . . . . Robert E. Taylor, M.D.
Physiology and Biophysics . . . . Werner M. Graf, M.D., Ph.D.

Clinical Sciences

Anesthesiology . . . . John T. Herbert, M.D.
Cancer Center . . . . Wayne A. I. Frederick, M.D.
Community and Family Medicine . . . . Babafemi B. Adenuga, M.D. (Interim)
Dermatology . . . . Rebat M. Halder, M.D.
Medicine . . . . Shelly R. McDonald-Pinkett, M.D. (Interim)
  Allergy/Immunology . . . . Elena R. G. Reece, M.D.
  Cardiology . . . . Steven N. Singh, M.D.
  Clinical Pharmacology . . . . Clifford L. Ferguson, M.D.
  Critical Care and Medical Intensive Care Unit . . . . R. George Adams, M.D.
  Endocrinology . . . . Gail L. Nunlee-Bland, M.D.
  Gastroenterology . . . . Andrew K. Sanderson II, M.D.
  General Internal Medicine . . . . Shelly R. McDonald-Pinkett, M.D.
  Geriatrics . . . . Thomas O. Obesisan, M.D.
  Hematology and Medical Oncology . . . . Sara Horton, M.D. (Interim)
  Infectious Diseases . . . . Faria Farhat, M.D.
  Nephrology . . . . Constance Mere, M.D.
  Pulmonary Diseases . . . . Alvin V. Thomas, Jr., M.D.
  Rheumatology . . . . Gail S. Kerr, M.D.
Neurology . . . . Annapurni Jayam-Trouth, M.D.
Obstetrics and Gynecology . . . . Kerry M. Lewis, M.D. (Interim)
Ophthalmology . . . . Robert A. Copeland, Jr., M.D.
Orthopaedic Surgery . . . . Terry L. Thompson, M.D.
Pediatrics and Child Health . . . . Michal A. Young, M.D.
  Adolescent Medicine . . . . Esther E. Forrester, M.D.
  Allergy and Immunology . . . . Elena R. G. Reece, M.D.
  Ambulatory Pediatrics . . . . Habiballah Shariat, M.D.
  Cardiology . . . . Vacant
  Child Development . . . . Edwin W. Powell, Ph.D.
  Endocrinology . . . . Gail L. Nunlee-Bland, M.D.
  Genetics . . . . Verle E. Headings, M.D., Ph.D.
  Hematology . . . . Sohail R. Rana, M.D.
  Neonatology . . . . Michal A. Young, M.D.
Physical Medicine and Rehabilitation . . . . Janaki Kalyanam, M.D.
Psychiatry and Behavioral Sciences . . . . William B. Lawson, M.D., Ph.D.
Radiation Oncology . . . . Oscar E. Streeter, Jr., M.D.
Radiology . . . . Andre J. Duerinckx, M.D., Ph.D.
Sickle Cell Disease Center . . . . Sergei Nekhai, Ph.D.
Surgery . . . . Edward E. Cornwell III, M.D.
  General Surgery . . . . Wayne A. I. Frederick, M.D.
  Neurosurgery . . . . Damirez T. Fossett, M.D.
  Otolaryngology . . . . Ernest M. Myers, M.D.
  Outcomes Research . . . . Edward E. Cornwell III, M.D. (Interim)
  Plastic and Reconstructive Surgery . . . . Henry Paul, M.D.
  Podiatry . . . . Kirk Geter, D.P.M.
  Thoracic and Cardiovascular . . . . Arthur N. Mcunu, M.D.
  Transplant . . . . Clive O. Callender, M.D.
  Urology . . . . Chiledum A. Ahaghotu, M.D.
  Trauma and Critical Care . . . . Suryanarayana M. Siram, M.D.
  Vascular Surgery . . . . David A. Rose, M.D.

University of Florida College of Medicine
Box 100215, JHMHC
Gainesville, Florida 32610-0215
352-273-7500 (dean's office); 352-273-8309 (fax)
Web site: www.med.ufl.edu

The college of medicine accepted its first class in September 1956. It is an integral part of the University of Florida and is located on the university campus. The medical school is part of the J. Hillis Miller Health Center.

Type: public
2011 total enrollment: 536
Clinical facilities: Shands at the University of Florida, Malcom Randall Veterans Affairs Medical Center, Shands Jacksonville.

University Officials

President	J. Bernard Machen, D.D.S., Ph.D.
Provost	Joseph Glover, Ph.D.
Senior Vice President for Health Affairs	David S. Guzick, M.D., Ph.D.

Medical School Administrative Staff

Dean	Michael L. Good, M.D.
Senior Associate Dean for Clinical Affairs	Timothy C. Flynn, M.D.
Senior Associate Dean for Educational Affairs	Joseph C. Fantone III, M.D.
Senior Associate Dean for Faculty Affairs	Marian C. Limacher, M.D.
Senior Associate Dean for Faculty Group Practice	Marvin A. Dewar, M.D.
Senior Associate Dean for Financial Services	W. Wayne Tharp
Senior Associate Dean for Administration	M. Peter Pevonka, R.Ph.
Senior Associate Dean for Research Affairs	Stephen P. Sugrue, Ph.D.
Dean, Regional Campus in Jacksonville	Robert C. Nuss, M.D.
Associate Dean for Administrative Affairs	P. Jan Eller
Associate Dean for Student and Alumni Affairs	W. Patrick Duff, M.D.
Associate Dean for Continuing Medical Education	Marvin A. Dewar, M.D.
Associate Dean for Clinical Research and Training	David R. Nelson, M.D.
Associate Dean for Graduate Education	Paul A. Gulig, Ph.D.
Associate Dean for Information Technology	Richard J. Rathe, M.D.
Associate Dean for Education	Maureen A. Novak, M.D.
Associate Dean for Graduate Medical Education	Michael E. Mahla, M.D.
Associate Dean for VA Medical Center Relations	Bradley S. Bender, M.D.
Assistant Deans for Minority Relations	Donna M. Parker, M.D., and Michelle Jacobs, M.D.
Chair, Medical Selection Committee	James W. Lynch, M.D.
Vivarium Director	August H. Battles, D.V.M., Ph.D.
Librarian	Cecilia Botero
Deputy Registrar	Amy Martinsen

Department and Division or Section Chairs

Basic Sciences

Anatomy and Cell Biology	William A. Dunn, Jr., Ph.D. (Interim)
Biochemistry and Molecular Biology	James B. Flanegan, Ph.D.
Health Policy and Epidemiology	Elizabeth Shenkman, Ph.D.
Molecular Genetics and Microbiology	Henry V. Baker II, Ph.D.
Neuroscience	Lucia Notterpek, Ph.D.
Pharmacology and Therapeutics	Stephen P. Baker, Ph.D.
Physiology and Functional Genomics	Charles E. Wood, Ph.D.

Clinical Sciences

Aging and Geriatric Research. . . . . Marco Pahor, M.D.
Anesthesiology. . . . . F. Kayser Enneking, M.D.
Community Health and Family Medicine . . . . R. Whit Curry, Jr., M.D.
Emergency Medicine . . . . Joseph Adrian Tyndall, M.D.
Medicine. . . . . Robert A. Hromas, M.D.
  Cardiology. . . . . Jamie B. Conti, M.D.
  Computer Science . . . . Mario Ariet, Ph.D.
  Dermatology . . . . Franklin P. Flowers, M.D.
  Endocrinology and Metabolism. . . . . Suzanne Quinn, M.D. (Interim)
  Gastroenterology, Hepatology, and Nutrition. . . . . Christopher E. Forsmark, M.D.
  Hematology and Oncology . . . . Carmen J. Allegra, M.D.
  Hospital Medicine . . . . Robert R. Leverence, M.D.
  Infectious Diseases . . . . Reuben Ramphal, M.D. (Interim)
  Internal Medicine. . . . . Eric Rosenberg, M.D.
  Nephrology . . . . Mark Segal, M.D.
  Pulmonary Diseases . . . . Mark Brantly, M.D.
  Rheumatology and Clinical Immunology. Westley H. Reeves, M.D.
  SE National TB Center. . . . . Michael Lauzardo, M.D.
Neurological Surgery. . . . . William A. Friedman, M.D.
Neurology . . . . Tetsuo Ashizawa, M.D.
Obstetrics and Gynecology. . . . . R. Stan Williams, M.D.
Ophthalmology . . . . William T. Driebe, M.D.
Orthopaedic Surgery . . . . Mark Scarborough, M.D. (Interim)
Otolaryngology . . . . Patrick J. Antonelli, M.D.
Pathology, Immunology, and Laboratory Medicine . . . . Michael J. Clare-Salzler, M.D.
  Clinical Pathology . . . . Kenneth M. Rand, M.D.
Pediatrics . . . . Richard L. Bucciarelli, M.D.
  Cardiology. . . . . Frederick J. Fricker, M.D.
  Cellular and Molecular Therapy . . . . Arun Srivastava, Ph.D.
  Critical Care. . . . . Tara Smith, M.D. (Interim)
  Endocrinology . . . . Janet H. Silverstein, M.D.
  Gastroenterology . . . . Christopher D. Jolley, M.D.
  General Pediatrics . . . . Sanjeev Tuli, M.D.
  Genetics. . . . . Roberto T. Zori, M.D.
  Hematology and Oncology . . . . William B. Slayton, M.D. (Interim)
  Hospitalist Medicine. . . . . Shelley Collins, M.D.
  Immunology, Rheumatology, and Infectious Diseases. . . . . Melissa E. Elder, M.D.
  Neonatology. . . . . David J. Burchfield, M.D.
  Nephrology . . . . Vikas R. Dharnidharka, M.D.
  Neurology . . . . Paul R. Carney, M.D.
  Pulmonary Diseases and Cystic Fibrosis . . . . Mutasim Abu-Hasan, M.D.
Psychiatry . . . . Mark S. Gold, M.D.
  Child and Adolescent Psychiatry . . . . Ayesha Lall, M.D.
Radiation Oncology. . . . . Paul Okunieff, M.D.
Radiology . . . . Anthony A. Mancuso, M.D.
Surgery . . . . Kevin Behrns, M.D.
  Acute Care. . . . . Frederick Moore, M.D.
  General . . . . Steven J. Hughes, M.D.
  Pediatric . . . . David Kays, M.D.
  Plastic and Reconstructive. . . . . Bruce A. Mast, M.D.
  Surgical Oncology . . . . Steven Hochwald, M.D.
  Thoracic and Cardiovascular. . . . . Kevin Behrns, M.D. (Interim)
  Transplantation . . . . Kevin Behrns, M.D. (Interim)
  Vascular. . . . . Thomas S. Huber, M.D., Ph.D.
Urology. . . . . Johannes Vieweg, M.D.

University of Miami Miller School of Medicine
1600 N.W. 10th Avenue
P.O. Box 016099 (R699)
Miami, Florida 33101
305-243-6545 (dean's office); 305-243-4888 (fax)
E-mail: pgoldschmidt@med.miami.edu
Web site: www.med.miami.edu

The University of Miami School of Medicine was founded in 1952 and is located in the University of Miami-Jackson Memorial Hospital Medical Center. The Rosenstiel Medical Science Building serves as the center of the school's educational activities.

Type: private
2011 total enrollment: 761
Clinical facilities: Anne Bates Leach Eye Hospital/Bascom Palmer Eye Institute, Jackson Memorial Hospital, University of Miami Hospital and Clinics/Sylvester Comprehensive Cancer Center, University of Miami Hospital, Miami VA Medical Center.

University Officials

President. . . . . Donna E. Shalala, Ph.D.
Executive Vice President and Provost . . . . Thomas J. LeBlanc, Ph.D.
Senior Vice President for Medical Affairs and Dean . . . . Pascal J. Goldschmidt, M.D.
Senior Vice President for Business and Finance and Chief Financial Officer . . . . Joe Natoli
Senior Vice President for Univ. Advancement & External Affairs . . . . Sergio M. Gonzalez
Vice President for Medical Administration and
   Chief Operating and Strategy Officer . . . . William J. Donelan
Vice President for Government Affairs . . . . Rudy Fernandez
Vice President of Finance and Treasurer . . . . John R. Shipley
Vice President, General Counsel, and Secretary of the University. . . . . Aileen M. Ugalde, J.D.
Vice President for Student Affairs. . . . . Patricia A. Whitely, Ph.D.
Associate Vice President and Controller . . . . Theresa L. Ashman
Assistant Vice President for Business Services . . . . Humberto M. Speziani

Medical School Administrative Staff

Associate Vice President and Chief Operating
   Officer Hospital Division, Uhealth . . . . Michele Chulick
Associate Vice President and Medical Chief
   Human Resource Officer . . . . Sheri A. Keitz, M.D., Ph.D.
Chief Innovation Officer . . . . Jonathan T. Lord, M.D.
Chief Executive Officer, UHealth Physician
   Practice and Associate Vice President,
   UHealth Practice Administration . . . . David A. Lubarsky, M.D
Associate Vice President for Medical Communications . . . . Christine Morris
Chief Medical Officer, University of Miami Health System. . . . . William W. O'Neill, M.D.
Associate Vice President for Medical
   Development and Alumni Relations . . . . Mary Ann Sprinkle
Chief Financial Officer and Associate Vice
   President for Medical Financial Affairs . . . . Walter Ted Shaw
Chief Planning and Marketing Officer and
   Associate VP for Planning and Marketing . . . . Elaine Van der Put, Ph.D.
Assistant Vice President for Facilities and Services. . . . . Ronald Bogue
Executive Dean for Education and Policy . . . . Laurence B. Gardner, M.D.
Executive Dean for Research and Research Training. . . . . . . William W. O'Neill, M.D. (Interim)
Deputy Executive Dean for Research and Research Training. . . . . Jennifer McCafferty, Ph.D.
Associate Executive Dean for Practice Development . . . . Steven F. Falcone, M.D.
Associate Executive Dean for Child Health . . . . Steven E. Lipshultz, M.D.
Senior Associate Dean for Quality, Safety, and Risk Prevention . . . . David J. Birnbach, M.D.
Senior Associate Dean for Discovery Science. . . . . W. Dalton Dietrich, Ph.D.
Senior Associate Dean for Faculty Affairs . . . . Sheri A. Keitz, M.D., Ph.D.
Senior Associate Dean for Translational Science . . . . Norma Sue Kenyon, Ph.D.
Senior Associate Dean for Graduate Medical Education . . . . Michael C. Lewis, M.D.

University of Miami Miller School of Medicine: FLORIDA

Regional Dean for Medical Education - Regional Campus . . . . Daniel M. Lichtstein, M.D.
Senior Associate Dean for Undergraduate Medical Education . . . . Alex J. Mechaber, M.D.
Senior Associate Dean for Clinical Research . . . . John W. Newcomer, M.D.
Senior Associate Dean for Educational Development. . . . . Mark T. O'Connell, M.D.
Senior Associate Dean for Administration. . . . . Elaine Van der Put, Ph.D.
Associate Dean for TeleHealth and Clinical Outreach . . . . Anne E. Burdick, M.D., M.P.H.
Associate Dean for Student Affairs . . . . Ana E. Campo, M.D.
Associate Dean for International Medicine . . . . Eduardo de Marchena, M.D.
Associate Dean for Community Health Affairs. . . . . Arthur M. Fournier, M.D.
Associate Dean for Research in Medical Education . . . . Michael S. Gordon, M.D.
Associate Dean for Women's Health. . . . . Thomas M. Hooton, M.D.
Associate Dean for Student Services . . . . Hilit F. Mechaber, M.D.
Associate Dean for Graduate Medical Education . . . . Richard K. Parrish II, M.D.
Associate Dean for Human Genomics Programs . . . . Margaret A. Pericak-Vance, Ph.D.
Associate Dean for Preclinical Curriculum . . . . Richard L. Riley, Ph.D.
Faculty Ombudsperson. . . . . Richard J. Thurer, M.D.
Associate Dean for Therapeutic Innovations . . . . Claes Wahlestedt, M.D., Ph.D.
Associate Dean for Medical Admissions. . . . . Richard S. Weisman, Pharm.D.
Associate Dean for Regulatory Support and
Quality Improvement . . . . Jonelle E. Wright, Ph.D.

Department and Division or Section Chairs

Basic Sciences

Biochemistry and Molecular Biology. Sylvia Daunert, Ph.D., Pharm.D.
Cell Biology. . . . . Glen N. Barber, Ph.D.
Epidemiology and Public Health . . . . José Szapocznik, Ph.D.
Microbiology and Immunology. . . . . Eckhard R. Podack, M.D., Ph.D.
Molecular and Cellular Pharmacology . . . . Charles W. Luetje, Ph.D.
Physiology and Biophysics . . . . Karl L. Magleby, Ph.D.

Clinical Sciences

Anesthesiology. . . . . David A. Lubarsky, M.D.
Dermatology and Cutaneous Surgery . . . . Lawrence A. Schachner, M.D.
Family Medicine and Community Health . . . . E. Robert Schwartz, M.D.
Human Genetics . . . . Jeffery Vance, M.D., Ph.D.
Medicine. . . . . Marc E. Lippman, M.D.
Neurological Surgery. . . . . Barth A. Green, M.D.
Neurology. . . . . Ralph L. Sacco, M.D.
Obstetrics and Gynecology. . . . . Ira S. Karmin, M.D. (Interim)
Ophthalmology . . . . Eduardo C. Alfonso, M.D.
Orthopaedics. . . . . Frank J. Eismont, M.D.
Otolaryngology . . . . Fred F. Telischi, M.D.
Pathology . . . . Richard J. Cote, M.D.
Pediatrics . . . . Steven E. Lipshultz, M.D.
Physical Therapy . . . . Sherrill H. Hayes, Ph.D.
Psychiatry and Behavioral Sciences . . . . Charles B. Nemeroff, M.D., Ph.D.
Radiation Oncology. . . . . Alan Pollack, M.D., Ph.D.
Radiology . . . . Robert M. Quencer, M.D.
Rehabilitation Medicine. . . . . Diana D. Cardenas, M.D.
Surgery . . . . Alan S. Livingstone, M.D.
Urology. . . . . Bruce R. Kava, M.D. (Interim)

University of South Florida Health Morsani College of Medicine

12901 Bruce B. Downs Boulevard
MDC 2
Tampa, Florida 33612-4742
813-974-2196 (USF Health/Dean's office); 813-974-3886 (fax)
Web site: http://health.usf.edu/medicine/home.html

The college of medicine was open for the instruction of students in 1971. It is an integral part of the University of South Florida (USF) and is located on the campus. The medical school is part of USF Health.

Type: public
2011 total enrollment: 498
Clinical facilities: USF Health South Tampa Center for Advanced Health Care, Carol and Frank Morsani Center for Advanced Health Care, USF Medical Clinic, Harbourside Medical Tower, USF Eye Institute, USF ENT Center, USF Health at Wesley Chapel, USF Health Orthopedic Surgery and Sports Medicine, USF Children's Medical Services, USF Health Physical Therapy Center, Suncoast Alzheimer's and Gerontology Center, Johnnie B. Byrd Sr. Alzheimer's Center and Research Institute, Tampa General Hospital, James A. Haley Veterans Affairs Hospital, All Children's Hospital, Shriners Hospital for Children, USF Health Psychiatry Center, H. Lee Moffitt Cancer Center and Research Institute, Bay Pines Veterans Affairs Medical Center, Florida Hospital Tampa.

University Officials

President. . . . . Judy Lynn Genshaft, Ph.D.
Senior Vice President, USF Health . . . . Stephen K. Klasko, M.D.
Chief Administrative Liaison . . . . John C. Ekarius
Associate Vice President for Research . . . . Phillip J. Marty, Ph.D.
Associate Vice President for Administration, Finance, and Technology. . . . . . . Joann M. Strobbe
Associate Vice President, Cancer Services . . . . Mitchel Hoffman, M.D.
Associate Vice President, Children's Health . . . . Robert J. Nelson, Jr., M.D.
Associate Vice President for Clinical Quality Improvement . . . . Michael T. Parsons, M.D.
Associate Vice President for Communications and Marketing . . . . Michael J. Hoad
Associate Vice President for Continuing
   Professional Development . . . . Deborah Sutherland, Ph.D.
Associate Vice President of Development/USF Health. . . . . Steve Blair
Associate Vice President for Faculty and Academic Affairs . . . . John S. Curran, M.D.
Associate Vice President for Health Care Leadership. . . . . Robert G. Brooks, M.D.
Associate Vice President for Health Law, Policy, and Safety . . . . Jay Wolfson, Dr.P.H.
Associate Vice President for International Programs . . . . Ann DeBaldo, Ph.D.
Associate Vice President, Women's Health and Development . . . . Catherine Lynch, M.D.
Assistant Vice President for Academic Program
   Administration and Institutional Effectiveness . . . . Gretchen Koehler, Ph.D.
Assistant Vice President, Information Technology, and Chief Information Officer . . . . . . Vacant

Medical School Administrative Staff

Dean. . . . . Stephen K. Klasko, M.D.
Vice Dean, Administration, Finance, and Technology . . . . Joann M. Strobbe
Vice Dean, Clinical Affairs . . . . Robert J. Belsole, M.D.
Vice Dean, Educational Affairs . . . . Alicia D. H. Monroe, M.D.
Vice Dean, Research . . . . Phillip J. Marty, Ph.D.
Senior Executive Associate Dean for Faculty and Academic Affairs. . . . . John S. Curran, M.D.
Executive Associate Dean for Clinical and Extramural Affairs . . . . Charles N. Paidas, M.D.
Associate Dean for Cancer Services. . . . . Mitchel Hoffman, M.D.
Associate Dean for Clinical Research . . . . Vacant
Associate Dean for Continuing Professional Development . . . . Deborah Sutherland, Ph.D.
Associate Dean for Diversity Initiatives . . . . Marvin T. Williams, Ph.D.
Associate Dean for Educational Affairs - LVHN Campus . . . . J. Alan Otsuki, M.D.
Associate Dean for Graduate Medical Education . . . . Charles N. Paidas, M.D.
Associate Dean for International Affairs . . . . John Sinnott, M.D.
Associate Dean for Postdoctoral and Graduate Affairs . . . . Michael J. Barber, D.Phil.
Associate Dean for Research. . . . . Vacant
Associate Dean for Strategic Planning and Policy . . . . Vacant
Associate Dean for Veteran's Administration Affairs . . . . Charles W. Brock, M.D.

University of South Florida Health Morsani College of Medicine: FLORIDA

Associate Dean for School of Physical Therapy
and Rehabilitation Sciences .... W. Sandy Quillen, Ph.D.
Associate Dean for Student Affairs and Admissions .... Steven C. Specter, Ph.D.
Associate Dean for Undergraduate Medical Education .... Frazier Stevenson, M.D.
Assistant Dean for Clinical Finance............................ Karen M. Burdash
Assistant Dean for Finance.................................... Jean G. Nixon
Director of Area Health Education Center .... Anne M. Maynard
Director of Compliance....................................... Patricia J. Bickel
Director of Professional Relations.............................. Mathis L. Becker, M.D.
Director of Faculty Relations .... Olga J. Joanow, J.D.
Director of Faculty Recruitment and Pay........................ Diane Laya
Chief Executive Director of University of South
Florida Physicians Group .... Jeffrey D. Lowenkron, M.D.

Department and Division or Section Chairs

Basic Sciences

Molecular Medicine.. Robert J. Deschenes, Ph.D.
Molecular Pharmacology and Physiology..................... Sarah Y. Yuan, M.D., Ph.D.
Pathology and Cell Biology .... Santo V. Nicosia, M.D.

Clinical Sciences

Cardiovascular Sciences .... Leslie W. Miller, M.D.
Dermatology .... Neil A. Fenske, M.D.
Family Medicine .... Kira Zwygart, M.D. (Interim)
Internal Medicine .... Allan L. Goldman, M.D.
  Allergy and Immunology .... Richard F. Lockey, M.D.
  Digestive Diseases and Nutrition....................... Joel E. Richter, M.D.
  Emergency Medicine .... David J. Orban, M.D.
  Endocrinology and Metabolism......................... Anthony D. Morrison, M.D.
  Endocrinology and Metabolism (Research) .... Robert Farese, M.D.
  General Internal Medicine/Ambulatory................... Elizabeth P. Warner, M.D.
  General Internal Medicine/Inpatient .... Charles M. Edwards, M.D.
  Geriatric Medicine .... Howard Tuch, M.D.
  Infectious Disease and International Medicine............ John T. Sinnott, M.D.
  Ethics, Humanities, and Palliative Medicine.............. Robert M. Walker, M.D.
  Nephrology and Hypertension .... Jacques A. Durr, M.D.
  Prevention and Occupational Medicine.................. Stuart M. Brooks, M.D.
  Pulmonary, Critical Care, and Sleep Medicine........... David A. Solomon, M.D.
  Rheumatology .... John D. Carter, M.D.
Neurology.. Clifton L. Gooch, M.D.
  Neuromuscular .... Tuan H. Vu, M.D.
  Vascular and Critical Care .... Scott Burgin, M.D.
Neurosurgery... Harry R. van Loveren, M.D.
Obstetrics-Gynecology .... Jerome Yankowitz, M.D.
Oncologic Sciences .... Lynn C. Moscinski, M.D.
Ophthalmology .... Peter R. Pavan, M.D.
Orthopedics .... David Leffers, M.D.
  SMART Program .... Jeff G. Konin, Ph.D.
Otolaryngology .... Thomas V. McCaffrey, M.D., Ph.D.
Pathology and Cell Biology .... Santo V. Nicosia, M.D.
Pediatrics .... Patricia J. Emmanuel, M.D.
Physical Therapy, School of .... W. Sandy Quillen, Ph.D.
Psychiatry and Behavioral Medicine .... Francisco Fernandez, M.D.
Radiology .... Todd R. Hazelton, M.D.
Surgery .... David J. Smith, Jr., M.D.
  General Surgery..................................... Vic Velanovich, M.D.
  Pediatric Surgery .... Charles N. Paidas, M.D.
  Plastic Surgery .... David J. Smith, Jr., M.D.
  Trauma .... David J. Ciesla, M.D.
  USF HCA Trauma Network .... James Hurst, M.D.
  Vascular.. Karl Illig, M.D.
Urology.. Jorge L. Lockhart, M.D.

Emory University School of Medicine

1648 Pierce Drive
Atlanta, Georgia 30322
404-727-5640 (general information); 404-727-5631 (dean's office); 404-727-0473 (fax);
404-727-5655 (medical educ. & stud. aff.); 404-727-0045 (fax)
Web site: http://med.emory.edu

The history of the school began with the chartering of Atlanta Medical College in 1854. This was the first of a series of institutions that eventually consolidated in 1913 and became the school of medicine of Emory University in 1915. Since 1917, the school has operated and developed both in the downtown area and on the main university campus in Druid Hills. The medical school is part of the Robert W. Woodruff Health Sciences Center.

Type: private
2011 total enrollment: 531
Clinical facilities: Grady Memorial Hospital, Emory University Hospital, Atlanta Veterans Affairs Medical Center, Wesley Woods Center of Emory University, Emory Adventist Hospital, The Emory Clinic, Children's Healthcare of Atlanta, Emory University Hospital Midtown, Emory Johns Creek Hospital, Emory University Orthopaedics and Spine Hospital, Emory Children's Center.

University Officials

President. . . . . James W. Wagner, Ph.D.
Executive Vice President for Health Affairs and
   Chief Executive Officer, Woodruff Health
   Sciences Center . . . . S. Wright Caughman, M.D.

Medical School Administrative Staff

Dean. . . . . Thomas J. Lawley, M.D.
Executive Associate Dean/Administration and Faculty Affairs . . . . Vacant
Executive Associate Dean for Medical Education and Student Affairs. . . . . . J. William Eley, M.D.
Executive Associate Dean for Research . . . . Raymond J. Dingledine, Ph.D.
Executive Associate Dean for Clinical Affairs at Grady Hospital . . . . William J. Casarella, M.D.
Executive Associate Dean for Fiscal Affairs and CFO . . . . Barbara V. Schroeder
Executive Associate Dean for Clinical Services, The Emory Clinic . . . . Douglas Morris, M.D.
Associate Dean for Clinical Services, Grady Hospital . . . . William R. Sexson, M.D.
Associate Dean for Admissions . . . . Ira K. Schwartz, M.D.
Associate Dean for Graduate Medical Education . . . . James R. Zaidan, M.D.
Associate Dean for Clinical Education . . . . Joel M. Felner, M.D.
Associate Dean for Multicultural Medical Student Affairs. . . . . Robert Lee, Ph.D.
Associate Dean for Medical Education and Student Affairs . . . . Erica Brownfield, M.D.
Associate Dean for Faculty Development. . . . . Sharon W. Weiss, M.D.
Associate Dean for Business and Finance . . . . Sharen B. Olson
Associate Dean for Research. . . . . Carolyn C. Meltzer, M.D.
Associate Dean for Clinical and Translational Research. . . . . Jeffrey L. Lennox, M.D.
Associate Dean for Administration . . . . Joshua A. Barwick, J.D.
Assistant Dean for Research . . . . Patricia Haugaard
Assistant Dean for Graduate Medical Education . . . . Marilane Bond, Ed.D.
Assistant Dean for Medical Education and Student Affairs. . . . . Sheryl L. Heron, M.D.
Assistant Dean for Postdoctoral Education . . . . Mary J. Delong, Ph.D.
Assistant Dean for Business and Finance. . . . . Constance B. Nagle
Assistant Dean for Research Administration . . . . Patricia W. Davis
Assistant Dean for Staff Development. . . . . Rachelle Lehner, Ph.D.
Assistant Dean for Medical Education. . . . . Douglas S. Ander, M.D.
Senior Associate Vice President for Development . . . . Kathryn (Kat) Carrico

Department and Division or Section Chairs

Basic Sciences

Biochemistry . . . . Richard D. Cummings, Ph.D.
Biomedical Engineering. . . . . Larry McIntire, Ph.D.
Biomedical Informatics . . . . Joel Saltz, Ph.D.
Cell Biology. . . . . Winfield Sale, Ph.D. (Interim)
Human Genetics . . . . Stephen T. Warren, Ph.D.
Microbiology and Immunology. . . . . Jeremy R. Boss, Ph.D.
Pharmacology . . . . Raymond J. Dingledine, Ph.D.
Physiology . . . . Douglas Eaton, Ph.D.

Clinical Sciences

Anesthesiology. . . . . Lureen Hill, M.D.

Dermatology . . . . Robert A. Swerlick, M.D.
Emergency Medicine . . . . Katherine L. Heilpern, M.D.
Family and Preventive Medicine . . . . Katherine L. Heilpern, M.D. (Interim)
Gynecology and Obstetrics . . . . Ira Horowitz, M.D. (Interim)
Hematology and Medical Oncology . . . . Fadlo R. Khuri, M.D.
Medicine . . . . R. Wayne Alexander, M.D., Ph.D.
   Cardiology . . . . W. Robert Taylor, M.D., Ph.D.
   Digestive Diseases . . . . Frank Anania, M.D. (Interim)
   Endocrinology, Metabolism, and Lipids . . . . Roberto Pacifici, M.D.
   General Medicine . . . . William T. Branch, Jr., M.D.
   Geriatric Medicine and Gerontology . . . . Theodore Johnson II, M.D.
   Hospital Medicine . . . . Alan Wang, M.D.
   Infectious Diseases . . . . David S. Stephens, M.D.
   Pulmonary, Allergy, and Critical Care Medicine . . . . David M. Guidot, M.D.
   Renal . . . . Jeff M. Sands, M.D.
   Rheumatology and Human Immunology . . . . Doyt Conn, M.D. (Interim)
Neurology . . . . Allan J. Levey, M.D., Ph.D.
Neurosurgery . . . . Daniel L. Barrow, M.D.
Ophthalmology . . . . Timothy Olsen, M.D.
Orthopaedics . . . . James R. Roberson, M.D.
   Spine Center . . . . Scott Boden, M.D.
Otolaryngology-Head and Neck Surgery . . . . Douglas E. Mattox, M.D.
Pathology and Laboratory Medicine . . . . Tristram G. Parslow, M.D., Ph.D.
Pediatrics . . . . Barbara J. Stoll, M.D.
   Cardiology . . . . Robert Campbell, M.D.
   Critical Care Medicine . . . . Jana Stockwell, M.D.
   Neonatology and Perinatology . . . . David Carlton, M.D.
   Emergency Medicine . . . . Naghma Khan, M.D.
   Endocrinology . . . . Andrew Muir, M.D.
   Gastroenterology . . . . Saul Karpen, M.D.
   General Pediatrics at Hughes Spalding . . . . Robert Geller, M.D.
   Hematology, Oncology, and BMT . . . . William Woods, M.D.
   Hospitalists . . . . Corinne Taylor, M.D.
   Infectious Diseases and Immunology . . . . Paul Spearman, M.D.
   Marcus Autism Center . . . . Ami Klin, M.D.
   Nephrology . . . . Larry Greenbaum, M.D.
   Neurology . . . . Antonius DeGrauw, M.D.
   Pulmonology, Allergy, Cystic Fibrosis, and Sleep . . . . Arlene Stecenko, M.D.
   Rheumatology . . . . Larry B. Vogler, M.D.
Psychiatry and Behavioral Sciences . . . . Mark Rapaport, M.D.
   Child/Adolescent Psychiatry and Forensic Psychiatry . . . . Peter Ash, M.D.
   Geriatric Psychiatry . . . . William M. McDonald, M.D.
Radiation Oncology . . . . Walter Curran, M.D.
Radiology . . . . Carolyn C. Meltzer, M.D.
   Abdominal Imaging . . . . William Small, M.D., Ph.D.
   Breast Imaging . . . . Michael A. Cohen, M.D.
   Cardiothoracic Imaging . . . . Arthur E. Stillman, M.D., Ph.D.
   Community Radiology . . . . Leonel Vasquez, M.D.
   Emergency Radiology . . . . Jamlik-Omari Johnson, M.D.
   Interventional Radiology . . . . Kevin Kim, M.D.
   Musculoskeletal Imaging . . . . Michael Terk, M.D.
   Neuro-Interventional Radiology . . . . Jacques Dion, M.D.
   Neuroradiology . . . . A. Jackson Fountain, M.D.
   Nuclear Medicine . . . . David Schuster, M.D.
   Pediatric Imaging . . . . Stephen Simoneaux, M.D.
Rehabilitation Medicine . . . . David T. Burke, M.D.
Surgery . . . . Christian P. Larsen, M.D., D.Phil
   CardioThoracic . . . . Robert A. Guyton, M.D.
   General . . . . John F. Sweeney, M.D.
   Oral and Maxillofacial . . . . Steven M. Roser, D.M.D., M.D.
   Pediatric . . . . , M.D. Vacant
   Plastic and Reconstructive . . . . Grant W. Carlson, M.D.
   Surgical Oncology . . . . Charles Staley, M.D.
   Transplantation . . . . Stuart J. Knechtle, M.D.
   Trauma/Surgical Critical Care . . . . David Feliciano, M.D.
   Vascular . . . . Thomas Dodson, M.D.
Urology . . . . Chad Ritenour, M.B. (Interim)

Medical College of Georgia at Georgia Health Sciences University

1120 Fifteenth Street, AA 1002
Augusta, Georgia 30912-4750
706-721-0211 (general information); 706-721-2231 (dean's office); 706-721-7035 (fax)
Web site: www.mcg.edu/som

The Medical College of Georgia (MCG) School of Medicine was originally chartered in 1828 as the Medical Academy of Georgia; the school of medicine was the founding school of what has evolved to become Georgia's health sciences university: the Medical of Georgia. Now in its 182nd year, the MCG School of Medicine is Georgia's only public medical school. Among the health sciences schools of MCG are allied health sciences, dentistry, medicine, nursing, and graduate studies. The university's mission, to improve health and reduce the burden of illness on society, is central to every facet of MCG's educational, research, and clinical initiatives.

Type: public
2011 total enrollment: 808
Clinical facilities: Medical College of Georgia Hospital and Clinics, Augusta, Georgia; Atlanta Medical Center, Atlanta, Georgia; Charlie Norwood Veterans Administration Medical Center, Augusta, Georgia; Dwight David Eisenhower Army Medical Center, Augusta, Georgia; St. Joseph's Candler, Savannah, Georgia; Memorial Health University Medical Center, Savannah, Georgia; Phoebe Putney Memorial Hospital, Albany, Georgia.

GHSU Officials

President. . . . . Ricardo Azziz, M.D., M.P.H., M.B.A.
Executive Vice President for Academic Affairs and Provost . . . . Gretchen Caughman, Ph.D.
Interim Senior Vice President for Finance . . . . Dennis R. Roemer
Interim Vice President for Research . . . . Mark W. Hamrick, Ph.D.
Vice President for Student Services and Development. . . . . Kevin B. Frazier, D.D.S.
Vice President for Instruction and Enrollment Management . . . . Roman M. Cibirka, D.D.S.
Interim Vice President for Administration . . . . William R. Bowes
Associate Senior Vice President for Finance and
    Administration/CIO/Associate Provost . . . . Beth P. Brigdon
Associate Senior Vice President for Executive Communications . . . . Deborah L. Barshafsky
General Councel . . . . Andrew R. H. Newton
Senior Vice President for Advancement and Community relations. . . . . Susan L. Barcus
Chief of Staff. . . . . TBA

Medical College Administrative Staff

Dean. . . . . Peter F. Buckley, M.D.
Vice Dean for Academic Affairs . . . . Ruth-Marie E. Fincher, M.D.
Campus Dean, Athens . . . . Barbara L. Schuster, M.D.
Interim Associate Dean for Admissions. . . . . Kathryn Martin, Ph.D.
Associate Dean for Student Affairs . . . . Kathleen M. McKie, M.D.
Associate Dean for Curriculum. . . . . T. Andrew Albritton, M.D.
Associate Dean for Evaluation . . . . Andria Thomas, Ph.D.
Associate Dean for Diversity Affairs. . . . . Kimberly Halbur, M.D.
Associate Dean for Regional Campus Coordination. . . . . Linda Boyd, D.O.
Interim Campus Dean, Southwest Georgia Clinical Campus. . . . . George Chastain, M.D.
Campus Dean, Southeast Georgia Clinical Campus . . . . Kathryn R. Martin, Ph.D.
Campus Dean for Curriculum, Northwest Campus . . . . Leonard D. Reeves, M.D.
Senior Associate Dean for Graduate Medical
    Education and Veterans Administration Affairs . . . . Walter J. Moore, M.D.
Senior Associate Dean for Basic Research . . . . John D. Catravas, Ph.D.
Senior Associate Dean for Clinical Research . . . . Anthony L. Mulloy, Ph.D., D.O.
Senior Associate Dean for Clinical Affairs. . . . . William Kanto, M.D.
Senior Associate Dean for Primary Care and Community Affairs . . . . Joseph Hobbs, M.D.
Associate Dean for Faculty Development. . . . . Christopher B. White, M.D.
Executive Associate Dean for Administration. . . . . Vacant
Chief Operations Officer . . . . Joel J. Covar
Chief of Staff. . . . . Jeanette Balotin

Medical College of Georgia at Georgia Health Sciences University: GEORGIA

Department and Division or Section Chairs

Basic Sciences

Biochemistry and Molecular Biology. . . . . Vadivel Ganapathy, Ph.D.
Cellular Biology and Anatomy . . . . Sally S. Atherton, Ph.D.
Pharmacology and Toxicology . . . . R. William Caldwell, Ph.D.
Physiology. . . . . R. Clinton Webb, Ph.D.

Clinical Sciences

Anesthesiology and Perioperative Medicine. . . . . C. Alvin Head, M.D.
Emergency Medicine . . . . Richard B. Schwartz, M.D.
Family Medicine . . . . Joseph Hobbs, M.D.
Medicine. . . . . Michael P. Madaio, M.D.
   Allergy and Immunology . . . . Dennis R. Ownby, M.D.
   Cardiology. . . . . Robert A. Sorrentino, M.D. (Interim)
   Dermatology . . . . Jack L. Lesher, Jr., M.D.
   Endocrinology, Diabetes, and Metabolism . . . . Anthony L. Mulloy, Ph.D., D.O.
   Gastroenterology and Hepatology. . . . . Robert R. Schade, M.D.
   General Internal Medicine . . . . Lee Ann Merchan, M.D.
   Hematology and Oncology. . . . . Anand Jillella, M.D.
   Infectious Disease. . . . . J. Peter Rissing, M.D.
   Nephrology, Hypertension, and Transplantation Medicine. . . . . Laura L. Mulloy, D.O.
   Pulmonary. . . . . William B. Davis, M.D.
   Rheumatology . . . . Walter J. Moore, M.D.
Neurology. . . . . David C. Hess, M.D.
   Child Neurology. . . . . James E. Carroll, M.D.
Obstetrics and Gynecology. . . . . Ana A. Murphy, M.D.
   General Gynecology and Obstetrics. . . . . John Lue, M.D.
   Gynecologic Oncology . . . . Sharade Ghamande, M.D.
   Maternal-Fetal Medicine . . . . Andrew W. Helfgott, M.D.
   Reproductive Endocrinology, Infertility, and Genetics . . . . Lawrence C. Layman, M.D.
   Urogynecology and Pelvic Surgery. . . . . Vacant
Ophthalmology . . . . Julian J. Nussbaum, M.D.
Orthopaedics. . . . . Norman B. Chutkan, M.D.
Otolaryngology . . . . David J. Terris, M.D.
Pathology . . . . Amyn Rojiani, M.D.
   Anatomic Pathology. . . . . Paul Biddinger, M.D.
   Clinical Pathology . . . . John C. H. Steele, Jr., M.D.
Pediatrics . . . . Bernard Maria, M.D.
   Allergy and Immunology . . . . Dennis R. Ownby, M.D.
   Cardiology. . . . . Henry B. Wiles, M.D.
   Critical Care Medicine . . . . Anthony L. Pearson-Shaver, M.D.
   Endocrinology, Diabetes, and Metabolism . . . . Christopher Houk, M.D.
   Gastroenterology . . . . Sudipta Misra, M.B.B.S.
   General Pediatrics and Adolescent Medicine . . . . Reda Bassali, M.D.
   Genetics. . . . . David Flamery, M.D.
   Hematology and Oncology. . . . . Roger A. Vega, M.D.
   Infectious Diseases . . . . Dennis L. Murray, M.D.
   Neonatology. . . . . Jatinder J. S. Bhatia, M.D.
   Georgia Prevention Institute. . . . . Gregory Harshfield, Ph.D.
   Nephrology, Hypertension, and Transplantation Medicine. . . . . Luiz A. Ortiz, M.D.
   Pulmonology . . . . Valera Hudson
   Rheumatology . . . . Rita S. Jerath, M.D.
Psychiatry and Health Behavior . . . . Stewart Shevitz, M.D. (Interim)
   Child, Adolescent, and Family Psychiatry. . . . . Sandra B. Sexson, M.D.
Radiology . . . . James V. Rawson, M.D.
   Radiation Oncology . . . . James V. Rawson, M.D.
Surgery. . . . . Charles G. Howell, Jr., M.D. (Interim)
   General Surgery. . . . . Vacant
   Oral and Maxillofacial Surgery . . . . Allen L. Sisk, D.D.S.
   Pediatric Surgery . . . . Charles G. Howell, Jr., M.D.
   Plastic Surgery . . . . Jack Yu, M.D.
   Urology. . . . . Ronald W. Lewis, M.D.

Mercer University School of Medicine
1550 College Street
Macon, Georgia 31207
478-301-2600; 478-301-5570 (dean's office); 478-301-2547 (fax)
Web site: www.medicine.mercer.edu

The Mercer University School of Medicine was founded in June 1982 and graduated its charter class in June 1986. Its school of medicine is located on the main campus of Mercer University. A second campus in Savannah opened for new first-year students in August 2008.

Type: private
2011 total enrollment: 351
Clinical facilities: Medical Center of Central Georgia, Memorial Health-University Medical Center, Floyd Medical Center, Atlanta Medical Center, Columbus Medical Center, Phoebe Putney Memorial Hospital.

University Officials

President. . . . . William D. Underwood, J.D.
Senior Vice President for Marketing
    Communications and Chief of Staff . . . . Larry D. Brumley
Provost . . . . D. Scott Davis, Ph.D.
Executive Vice President for Administration and Finance . . . . James S. Netherton, Ph.D.
Senior Vice President and General Counsel . . . . William Solomon, J.D.
Senior Vice President for Enrollment Management. . . . . Penny L. Elkins, Ph.D.
Senior Vice President for University Advancement . . . . John A. Patterson
Vice President for Health Sciences. . . . . Hewitt W. Matthews, Ph.D.
Vice President for Audit and Compliance. . . . . James S. Calhoun
Associate Vice President for Regulatory Compliance . . . . David L. Innes, Ph.D.
Chancellor . . . . R. Kirby Godsey, Ph.D.

Medical School Administrative Staff

Dean. . . . . William F. Bina III, M.D.
Vice Dean/Dean, Savannah campus . . . . T. Philip Malan, M.D.
Associate Dean for Admissions and Student Affairs . . . . Alice A. House, M.D.
Associate Dean for Academic Affairs, Macon campus. . . . . Robert S. Donner, M.D.
Associate Dean for Faculty Development. . . . . TBA
Associate Dean for Academic Affairs, Savannah campus. . . . . Tina L. Thompson, Ph.D.
Associate Dean for Student Affairs, Savannah Campus. . . . . Robert J. Shelley, M.D.
Senior Associate Dean for Medical Center of
    Central Georgia Programs . . . . James Cunningham, M.D.
Associate Dean for Graduate/Continuing
    Medical Education Medical Center of Central
    Georgia Programs . . . . Marcia B. Hutchinson, M.D.
Senior Associate Dean for Clinical Affairs, Savannah campus. . . . . Ramon V. Meguiar, M.D.
Associate Dean for Graduate Medical Education,
    Savannah campus . . . . Edward E. Abrams, D.Ed.
Associate Dean for Research. . . . . Wayne Glasgow, Ph.D.
Assistant Dean for Admissions, Savannah campus . . . . Samuel D. Murray, M.D.
Assistant Dean for Faculty Development . . . . Marie Dent, Ph.D.
Assistant Dean for Research, Macon campus. . . . . Joseph M. Van De Water, M.D.
Director of Finance . . . . Christa Ward
Director, Medical Library. . . . . Jan Labeause
Registrar and Director, Financial Aid and Office
    of Practice Opportunities . . . . Youvette Hudson
Director of Information Technology and Media Services. . . . . Shane Milam

Mercer University School of Medicine: GEORGIA

Department and Division or Section Chairs

Basic Sciences

Basic Sciences, Macon campus . . . . Roy Russ, Ph.D.
Biomedical Sciences, Savannah campus . . . . Wayne Glasgow, Ph.D.

Clinical Sciences

Anesthesiology. . . . . Ken McDonald, M.D.
Community Medicine. . . . . David Parish, M.D.
Emergency Medicine, Macon campus . . . . Del Doyle, M.D.
Emergency Medicine, Savannah campus . . . . Jay Goldstein, M.D.
Family Medicine, Macon campus . . . . Fred Girton, M.D.
Family Medicine, Savannah campus . . . . Robert M. Pallay, M.D.
Internal Medicine, Macon campus . . . . Ed W. Grimsley, M.D. (Interim)
Internal Medicine, Savannah campus . . . . Steven Carpenter, M.D.
Obstetrics and Gynecology, Macon campus. . . . . William Butler, M.D.
Obstetrics and Gynecology, Savannah campus. . . . . David B. Byck, M.D. (Interim)
Pathology . . . . Robert S. Donner, M.D.
Pediatrics, Macon campus . . . . Frank P. Bowyer, M.D.
Pediatrics, Savannah campus . . . . Eric Pearlman, M.D.
Psychiatry and Behavioral Science, Macon campus . . . . Melton Strozier, Ph.D.
Psychiatry and Behavioral Science, Savannah campus . . . . William Ellien, M.D.
Radiology, Macon campus . . . . TBA
Radiology, Savannah campus . . . . Deborah Conway, M.D.
Surgery, Macon campus . . . . Don Nakayama, M.D.
Surgery, Savannah campus . . . . M. Gage Ochsner, M.D.

Morehouse School of Medicine
720 Westview Drive, S.W.
Atlanta, Georgia 30310
404-752-1500; 404-752-1720 (dean's office); 404-752-1594 (fax)
Web site: www.msm.edu

The Morehouse School of Medicine is a historically black institution established to recruit and train minority and other students as physicians, biomedical scientists, and public health professionals committed to the primary health care needs of the underserved. Founded in 1975 as the school of medicine at Morehouse College, the Morehouse School of Medicine became independent from Morehouse College in 1981 and became a member of the Atlanta University Center in 1983. An active biomedical research program tied together by an emphasis on disease processes that disproportionately affect minority communities supports Ph.D., M.D., M.P.H., and M.S.C.R. programs.

Type: private
2011 total enrollment: 330
Clinical facilities: Grady Memorial Hospital, South Fulton Medical Center, Georgia Regional Hospital, Atlanta, Tuskegee Veterans Administration Medical Center.

Medical School Administrative Staff

President. . . . . John E. Maupin, Jr., D.D.S.
Dean and Senior Vice President for Academic
  Affairs . . . . Sandra A. Harris-Hooker, Ph.D. (Interim)
Vice President for Finance and Administration . . . . Donetta Butler
Vice President for Institutional Advancement
  and Marketing and Communications . . . . Sally M. Davis
Vice President and Senior Associate Dean for
  Sponsored Research Administration . . . . Sandra A. Harris-Hooker, Ph.D.
Associate Vice President, Community Relations
  and Development . . . . Willie H. Clemons, Ph.D.
Associate Vice President of Human Resources. . . . . Denise Britt
Associate Vice President, Marketing and Communications. . . . . Frances W. Thompkins
Chief Information Officer . . . . Cigdem Delano
Senior Associate Dean, Education and Faculty Affairs . . . . Martha L. Elks, M.D., Ph.D.
Associate Dean for Administration . . . . Sandra E. Watson
Associate Dean for Clinical Affairs . . . . Lawrence L. Sanders, Jr., M.D.
Associate Dean for Clinical Research . . . . Elizabeth Ofili, M.D., M.P.H.
Associate Dean for Community Health . . . . Daniel S. Blumenthal, M.D.
Assistant Dean for Admissions and Student Affairs . . . . Ngozi Anachebe, M.D., Pharm.D.
Associate Dean for Graduate Studies . . . . Douglas F. Paulsen, Ph.D.
Director, Admissions . . . . Sterling Roaf, M.D.
Director, Campus Operations and Capital Resources. Tony Collier
Manager, Library. . . . . Joe Swanson, Jr.
Director, Graduate Medical Education Administration. . . . . William E. Booth
Director, Planning and Institutional Research. Andrea D. Fox, M.B.A.
Director, Student Information Systems, and Registrar . . . . Adrienne Wyatt (Interim)
Controller. . . . . David H. Byrd
General Counsel . . . . Harold Jordon
Senior Advisor to the President for Government
  Relations and International Programs . . . . Ginger Floyd

Department Chairs

Basic Sciences

Anatomy and Neurobiology . . . . Peter R. MacLeish, Ph.D.
Microbiology, Biochemistry, and Immunology . . . . Myrtle J. Thierry-Palmer, Ph.D. (Interim)
Pharmacology and Toxicology . . . . Gianluca Tosini, Ph.D.
Physiology . . . . Gary Gibbons, M.D.

Clinical Sciences

Community Health and Preventive Medicine . . . . Beverly Taylor, M.D., M.P.H.
Family Medicine . . . . Harry S. Strothers III, M.D.
Internal Medicine . . . . Myra E. Rose, M.D.
Medical Education . . . . Martha L. Elks, M.D., Ph.D.
Obstetrics and Gynecology . . . . Roland Matthews, M.D.
Pathology . . . . Marjorie M. Smith, M.D.
Pediatrics . . . . Frances J. Dunston, M.D., M.P.H.
Psychiatry and Behavioral Science . . . . Gail A. Mattox, M.D.
Surgery . . . . Harvey Bumpers, M.D.

University of Hawaii at Mānoa John A. Burns School of Medicine

651 Ilalo Street, Medical Education Building
Honolulu, Hawaii 96813-5534
808-692-0899 (general information); 808-692-0881 (dean's office); 808-692-1247 (fax)
Web site: http://jabsom.hawaii.edu

The school of medicine was established in 1965 and functioned as a two-year school until 1973. At that time, expansion to a full M.D. degree-granting program was approved. The first class graduated in 1975. Since 1989, Problem Based Learning (PBL) has been utilized extensively throughout the curriculum.

Type: public
2011 total enrollment: 260
Clinical facilities: Hawaii State Hospital, Hilo Medical Center, Kaiser Foundation Hospital, Kapiolani Medical Center for Women and Children, Kuakini Medical Center, Leahi Hospital, The Physician Center at Mililani, Queen Emma Clinics, The Queen's Medical Center, Rehabilitation Hospital of the Pacific, Shriner's Hospital for Children, Straub Clinic and Hospital, Straub Hospital for Children, Tripler Army Medical Center, Castle Medical Center, Department of Veterans Affairs Pacific Island Health Care System, Wahiawa General Hospital.

University Officials

President. . . . . M. R. C. Greenwood, Ph.D.
Chancellor . . . . Virginia S. Hinshaw, Ph.D.

Medical School Administrative Staff

Dean. . . . . Jerris R. Hedges, M.D.
Vice Dean and Director of Admissions . . . . Satoru Izutsu, Ph.D.
Associate Dean for Clinical Affairs . . . . A. Roy Magnusson, M.D.
Associate Dean for Medical Education . . . . Richard T. Kasuya, M.D.
Chief Financial Officer. . . . . Nancy Foster, C.P.A.
Director of Office of Medical Education . . . . Damon Sakai, M.D.
Director of Office of Medical Student Affairs . . . . Richard Smerz, D.O.
Director of Faculty Development . . . . Rosanne C. Harrigan, Ed.D.
Director of Postgraduate Medical Education . . . . Kalami Brady, M.D.
Director of Research . . . . Eric Holmes, Ph.D.
Director of Development, UH Foundation . . . . Jeffrie Jones
Director of Fiscal and Administrative Affairs . . . . Corinne Seymour
Director of Communications . . . . Tina Shelton
Contracts Officer, Hospital and External Business Affairs . . . . Lauren Kwak, J.D.
Director of Facilities Management and Planning. . . . . Francis Blanco

University of Hawaii at Mānoa John A. Burns School of Medicine: HAWAII

Department Chairs

Basic Sciences

Anatomy, Biochemistry, Physiology, and Reproductive Biology. . . . . Scott Lozanoff, Ph.D.
Cell and Molecular Biology . . . . Marla J. Berry, Ph.D.
Communication Sciences and Disorders . . . . Henry Lew, M.D.
  Medical Technology . . . . Dick Y. Teshima, M.P.H.
Pathology . . . . Jeff Killeen, M.D.
Public Health Sciences and Epidemiology. . . . . Jason E. Maddock, Ph.D.
Tropical Medicine, Medical Microbiology, and Pharmacology . . . . Vivek Nerurkar, Ph.D.

Clinical Sciences

Complementary and Alternative Medicine . . . . Rosanne C. Harrigan, Ed.D.
Family Medicine and Community Health . . . . Vacant
Geriatric Medicine. . . . . Kamal Masaki, M.D.
Medicine. . . . . Elizabeth K. Tam, M.D.
Native Hawaiian Health . . . . Keawelaimoku Kaholokula, Ph.D.
Obstetrics, Gynecology, and Women's Health . . . . Lynnae Millar Sauvage, M.D.
Pediatrics . . . . Kenneth Nakamura, M.D.
Psychiatry . . . . Naleen N. Andrade, M.D.
Surgery . . . . Danny M. Takanishi, M.D.

University of Chicago
Division of the Biological Sciences
Pritzker School of Medicine
5841 South Maryland Avenue
Chicago, Illinois 60637
773-702-1939; 773-702-9000 (dean's office); 773-702-1897 (fax)
Web site: www.uchicago.edu

The school of medicine of the University of Chicago was established in 1927. In 1968, it was renamed the Pritzker School of Medicine.

Type: private
2011 total enrollment: 428
Clinical facilities: University of Chicago Medical Center, LaRabida Children's Hospital and Research Center, Louis A. Weiss Memorial Hospital, Mercy Hospital and Medical Center, Northshore University Health System.

University Officials

President . . . . Robert J. Zimmer, Ph.D.
Provost . . . . Thomas Rosenbaum, Ph.D.

Medical School Administrative Staff

Dean and Executive Vice President for Medical Affairs . . . . Kenneth S. Polonosky, M.D.
Dean for Clinical Practice . . . . Richard Baron, M.D.
Dean for Medical Education . . . . Holly J. Humphrey, M.D.
Dean for Research and Graduate Education . . . . Conrad Gilliam, Ph.D.
Associate Dean for Academic Strategy . . . . Neil H. Shubin, Ph.D.
Associate Dean for Administration and Finance . . . . Christopher P. Kops
Associate Dean for Admissions . . . . Anthony Montag, M.D.
Associate Dean for Clinical Quality . . . . Bruce D. Minsky, M.D.
Associate Dean for Clinical Research . . . . Walter M. Stadler, M.D.
Associate Dean for Community-Based Research . . . . Eric E. Whitaker, M.D.
Associate Dean for Diversity . . . . Melissa Gilliam, M.D., M.P.H.
Associate Dean for Global Health . . . . Olufunmilayo I. Olopade, M.D.
Associate Dean for Graduate Affairs . . . . Victoria Prince, Ph.D.
Associate Dean for Graduate Medical Education . . . . Michael A. Simon, M.D.
Associate Dean and Master of The Biological
  Sciences Collegiate Division . . . . Jose Quintans, M.D.
Associate Dean for Medical School Education . . . . Halina Brukner, M.D.
Associate Dean for Multicultural Affairs . . . . Monica Vela, M.D.
Associate Dean for Postdoctoral Affairs . . . . Nancy Schwartz, Ph.D.
Associate Dean for Student Programs and Professional Development . . . . Shalini Reddy, M.D.
Associate Dean for Translational Medicine . . . . Julian Solway, M.D.
Associate Dean for Medical Center Development . . . . Laila M. Rashid
Faculty Dean for Academic Affairs . . . . Martin E. Feder, Ph.D.

Department and Division or Section Chairs

Basic Sciences

Ben May Department for Cancer Research . . . . Marsha R. Rosner, Ph.D.
Biochemistry and Molecular Biology . . . . Tobin R. Sosnick, Ph.D.
Ecology and Evolution . . . . Joy Bergelson, Ph.D.
Human Genetics . . . . Carole Ober, Ph.D. (Interim)
Microbiology . . . . Olaf Schneewind, M.D., Ph.D.
Molecular Genetics and Cell Biology . . . . Richard Fehon, Ph.D.
Neurobiology . . . . S. Murray Sherman, Ph.D.
Organismal Biology and Anatomy . . . . Robert K. Ho, Ph.D.

Clinical Sciences

Anesthesia and Critical Care . . . . Jeffrey L. Apfelbaum, M.D.
Family Medicine . . . . Bernard G. Ewigman, M.D.
Health Studies . . . . Ronald A. Thisted, Ph.D.

Medicine. . . . . Everett E. Vokes, M.D.
   Cardiology* . . . . Martin Burke, D.O. (Interim)
   Dermatology*. . . . . Christopher Shea, M.D.
   Emergency Medicine* . . . . Linda Druelinger, M.D. (Interim)
   Endocrinology, Diabetes, and Metabolism* . . . . Roy E. Weiss, M.D., Ph.D.
   Gastroenterology* . . . . Stephen Hanauer, M.D.
   Genetic Medicine. . . . . Nancy Cox, Ph.D.
   General Internal Medicine* . . . . Deborah Burnet, M.D.
   Geriatrics and Palliative Care*. . . . . William Dale, M.D., Ph.D.
   Hematology and Oncology* . . . . Richard Schilsky, M.D.
   Hospital Medicine . . . . David Meltzer, M.D., Ph.D.
   Infectious Diseases and Global Health* . . . . David Pitrak, M.D.
   Nephrology* . . . . F. Gary Toback, M.D.
   Pulmonary and Critical Care* . . . . Jesse Hall, M.D.
   Rheumatology* . . . . Marcus Clark, M.D.
Neurology. . . . . Christopher Gomez, M.D., Ph.D.
Obstetrics and Gynecology. . . . . Arthur Haney, M.D.
Pathology . . . . Vinay Kumar, M.D.
Pediatrics . . . . David Gozal, M.D.
   Academic Pediatrics* . . . . Daniel Johnson, M.D.
   Allergy and Immunology*. . . . . Raoul L. Wolf, M.D.
   Cardiology* . . . . Matthias Peuster, M.D., Ph.D.
   Chronic Diseases* . . . . Izhar Qamar, M.D.
   Critical Care. . . . . Mark Abe, M.D. (Interim)
   Developmental and Behavioral Pediatrics*. . . . . Michael Msall, M.D.
   Emergency Medicine* . . . . Michael Schreiber, M.D. (Interim)
   Endocrinology* . . . . Roy E. Weiss, M.D., Ph.D.
   Gastroenterology, Hepatology, and Nutrition* . . . . Stefano Guandalini, M.D.
   Advanced Pediatric Services . . . . Daniel Johnson, M.D.
   Hematology and Oncology* . . . . John M. Cunningham, M.D.
   Infectious Diseases* . . . . Kenneth Alexander, M.D., Ph.D.
   Neonatology. . . . . Kwang-sun Lee, M.D.
   Nephrology* . . . . Christopher Clardy, M.D.
   Neurology* . . . . Michael Schreiber, M.D. (Interim)
   Pediatric Surgery* . . . . Donald C. Liu, M.D., Ph.D.
   Pulmonology* . . . . Lucille A. Lester, M.D.
   Rheumatology* . . . . Linda Wagner-Weiner, M.D.
   Sleep Medicine. . . . . Hari Bandla, M.D.
Psychiatry and Behavioral Neuroscience . . . . Emil Coccaro, M.D.
Radiation and Cellular Oncology . . . . Ralph R. Weichselbaum, M.D.
Radiology . . . . David Paushter, M.D. (Interim)
Surgery . . . . Jeffrey B. Matthews, M.D.
   Cardiac and Thoracic Surgery*. . . . . Valluvan Jeevanandam, M.D.
   General Surgery* . . . . Mitchell C. Posner, M.D.
   Neurosurgery* . . . . David M. Frim, M.D., Ph.D.
   Ophthalmology and Visual Science . . . . Mark Greenwald, M.D. (Interim)
   Orthopaedic Surgery*. . . . . Terrance D. Peabody, M.D.
   Otolaryngology/Head and Neck Surgery* . . . . Robert M. Naclerio, M.D.
   Pediatric Surgery* . . . . Donald C. Liu, M.D., Ph.D.
   Plastic and Reconstructive*. . . . . David H. Song, M.D.
   Transplantation Surgery* . . . . J. Michael Millis, M.D.
   Urology* . . . . Arieh L. Shalhav, M.D.
   Vascular Surgery and Endovascular Therapy* . . . . Christopher Skelly, M.D.

*Specialty without organizational autonomy.

Chicago Medical School
At Rosalind Franklin University of Medicine and Science
3333 Green Bay Road
North Chicago, Illinois 60064
847-578-3000; 847-578-3301 (dean's office); 847-578-3343 (fax)
Web site: www.rosalindfranklin.edu

The Chicago Medical School was founded in 1912 as the Chicago Hospital College of Medicine. In 1919, the name of the institution was changed to the Chicago Medical School. In 1930, the school moved to the West Side Medical Center and remained there until it completed a move to North Chicago in 1980. In 1967, with the establishment of the University of Health Sciences, the academic programs were broadened to include the school of graduate and postdoctoral studies and the school of related health sciences in addition to the Chicago Medical School. In 1993, the university was renamed Finch University of Health Sciences. In 2004, the university was renamed in honor of Rosalind Franklin. In 2002, the Dr. William M. Scholl College of Podiatric Medicine became a college of the university.

Type: private
2011 total enrollment: 763
Clinical facilities: North Chicago Veterans Affairs Medical Center, Stroger Hospital of Cook County, Mount Sinai Hospital Medical Center, Lutheran General Hospital, Norwalk Hospital (CT), Illinois Masonic Hospital, Christ Hospital.

University Officials

President and Chief Executive Officer . . . . K. Michael Welch, M.B.Ch.B., F.R.C.P.
Executive Vice President and Chief Operating Officer. . . . . Margot Surridge
Chief Financial Officer. . . . . Roberta Lane
Vice President for Academic Affairs . . . . Wendy Rheault, P.T., Ph.D.
Vice President for Faculty Affairs . . . . Timothy R. Hansen, Ph.D.
Vice President for Medical Affairs
Vice President for Research . . . . Ronald Kaplan, Ph.D.
Vice President for Institutional Advancement . . . . Tina M. Erickson

University Deans and Administrative Staff

Dean, Chicago Medical School. . . . . Russell Robertson, M.D
Dean, School of Graduate and Postdoctoral Studies . . . . Joseph DiMario, Ph.D.
Dean, College of Health Professions. . . . . Wendy L. Rheault, Ph.D.
Dean, Dr. William M. Scholl College of Podiatric Medicine. . . . . Nancy L. Parsley, D.P.M.
Dean, College of Pharmacy . . . . Gloria E. Meredith, Ph.D.
Associate Vice President, Student Affairs and Enrollment Management . . . . Rebecca Durkin
Associate Vice President, Institutional Research,
    Director of Student Financial Services . . . . Maryann DeCaire
Coordinator, Student Housing . . . . Jennifer Smith

Medical School Administrative Staff

Vice Dean, Research. . . . . Ronald Kaplan, Ph.D.
Associate Dean for Clinical Affairs
Associate Dean for Student Affairs and Medical Eduation . . . . Doug Reifler, M.D.
    Associate Dean, Medical Affairs. . . . . John Tomkowiak, M.D
    Associate Dean, Undergraduate Studies. . . . . Marjorie Ariano, Ph.D.
    Associate Dean, Graduate Medical Education . . . . Vacant
    Associate Dean, Continuing Medical Education . . . . Michael Zolon, M.D.
Associate Dean for Veterans Affairs . . . . Tariq Hassan, M.D.
Associate Dean for Mount Sinai Hospital Medical Center . . . . Jack Garon, M.D.
Associate Dean for Research. . . . . Kenneth Neet, Ph.D.
Senior Associate Dean for Advocate Health Care . . . . Lee Sacks, M.D.
Associate Dean for Advocate Health Care. . . . . Ann Errichetti, M.D.
Assistant Dean for Advocate Health Care . . . . Mary Ann Clemens
    Assistant Dean, Basic Science Education . . . . Gordon Pullen, M.D.
    Assistant Dean, Evaluation and Assessment . . . . James Carlson, MS,PAC
    Assistant Dean, Clinical Science Education . . . . Lecia Apantaku, M.D.
    Assistant Dean, Planning. . . . . Terrianne Reynolds, MPH
    Assistant Dean, FHCC. . . . . Frank Maldonado, M.D.

Chicago Medical School
At Rosalind Franklin University of Medicine and Science: ILLINOIS

Department and Division or Section Chairs

Basic Sciences

Biochemistry and Molecular Biology............................ Marc Glucksman, Ph.D.
Cell Biology and Anatomy .... William N. Frost, Ph.D.
Cellular and Molecular Pharmacology .... Heinz Steiner, Ph.D.
Microbiology and Immunology.................................. Bala Chandran, Ph.D.
Neuroscience... Marina E. Wolf, Ph.D.
Pathology .... Arthur S. Schneider, M.D.
Physiology and Biophysics .... Robert Bridges, Ph.D.

Clinical Sciences

Anesthesiology... MaryKay Bissing, D.O.
Emergency Medicine .... Leslie Zun, M.D.
Family and Preventive Medicine .... Judith Gravdal, M.D.
Medicine... William Rhodes, D.O
   Cardiology.. Rohit Arora, M.D.
   Critical Care Medicine .... Raul Gazmuri, M.D.
   Endocrinology... Janice Gilden, M.D.
   Gastroenterology .... Axel Feller, M.D.
   Geriatric Medicine .... William Rhoades, D.O.
   Hematology and Oncology .... Rami Haddad, M.D.
   Infectious Diseases .... Walid Khayr, M.D.
   Nephrology .... Earl Smith, M.D.
   Pulmonary Diseases .... Ashok Fulambarker, M.D.
   Rheumatology .... Vacant
Neurology.. Nutan Vaidya, M.D. (Interim)
Obstetrics and Gynecology.................................... James Keller, M.D.
   Gynecologic Oncology .... Josef Blankstein, M.D.
   Gynecology .... Richard Trester, M.D.
   Maternal Fetal Medicine................................... E. C. Lampley, M.D.
   Reproductive Endocrinology............................... Josef Blankstein, M.D.
Ophthalmology... Alan J. Axelrod, M.D.
Pediatrics .... David Sheftel, M.D.
   Ambulatory Pediatrics..................................... Jay Mayefsky, M.D.
   Child Protective Services.................................. Michelle Lorand, M.D.
   Pediatric Allergy/Immunology .... James Moy, M.D.
   Pediatric Cardiology...................................... Zahra Naheed, M.D. (Acting)
   Pediatric Emergency Service............................... J. Thomas Senko, D.O.
   Pediatric Endocrinology .... Kanika Ghai, M.D.
   Pediatric Hematology and Oncology........................ Lilly Mathew, M.D.
   Pediatric Neonatology..................................... Suma Pyati, M.D.
Psychiatry and Behavioral Sciences .... Daniel Arizia, M.D.
   Addiction Psychiatry...................................... Vamsi Garlapati, M.D.
   Child Psychiatry .... Balasubramania P. S. Sarma, M.D.
   Community Psychiatry .... David Baron, M.D.
   Consultation Liaison Psychiatry............................ Viktoria Erhardt, M.D.
   Forensic Psychiatry....................................... Amin Daghestani, M.D.
   Gertiatric Psychiatry...................................... Zafeer Berki, M.D.
   Hospital Psychiatry....................................... Chandra Vedak, M.D.
   Neuropsychiatry .... Lori Moss, M.D.
   Psychotherapy .... Ruth Rosenthal, M.D., and Amanda Weiss, M.D.
Radiology .... John Anastos, M.D.
Surgery.. John White, M.D.
   Critical Care.. Michelle Holevar, M.D.
   General Surgery... Allan Fredland, M.D.
   Neurosurgery... Hernando Torres, M.D.
   Orthopedic Surgery .... Prahlad Pyati, M.D.
   Otolaryngology .... Nedra Joyner, M.D.
   Surgical Nutrition.. Stephen R. Wise, M.D.
   Urology .... Sangtae Park, M.D.

University of Illinois at Chicago College of Medicine

1853 West Polk Street (M/C 784)
Chicago, Illinois 60612
312-996-3500; 996-9006 (fax)
Web site: http://www.medicine.uic.edu/

Founded in 1881 as the College of Physicians and Surgeons of Chicago, the school affiliated with the University of Illinois in 1897 and became known as the University of Illinois College of Medicine in 1900. The dean's office is located on the campus of the University of Illinois at Chicago, 135 miles from the Urbana-Champaign campus of the university. In 1970, the college was regionalized to include programs of medical education on four campuses: Chicago, Peoria, Rockford, and Urbana-Champaign. The dean's office is located on the campus of the University of Illinois at Chicago.

Type: public
2011 total enrollment: 1,386
Clinical facilities: Chicago area—University of Illinois at Chicago Hospital and Health Sciences System, John H. Stroger Hospital of Cook County, Advocate Christ Medical Center, Advocated Lutheran General Medical Center, Advocate Illinois Masonic Medical Center, St. Francis Hospital, Mercy Hospital, Mt. Sinai Hospital, Jesse Brown Veterans Administration Medical Center, Northwest Community Hospital, Linden Oaks Hospital, John J. Madden Health Center.; Peoria—OSF St Francis Medical Cetner, Methodist Medical Center, and Pekin Hospital; Rockford area—Rockford Memorial Hospital, Rosecrance, Swedish American Hospital, and OSF St. Anthony; Urbana—Carle Foundation Hopsital, Provena Covenant Medical Center, Veterans Administration Health Care System, Danville, Provena United Samaritans Medical Center in Danville, OSF St. Joseph Medical Center (Bloomington), Advocate BroMenn Medical Center (Normal), Kirby Medical Center (Monticello), and Gibson Areas Hospital (Gibson City).

University Official

President. . . . . Michael J. Hogan, Ph.D.

University of Illinois at Chicago Officials

Vice President and Chancellor . . . . Paula Allen-Meares, Ph.D.
Provost and Vice Chancellor for Academic Affairs. . . . . Lon Kaufman, Ph.D.
Vice Chancellor for Student Affairs . . . . Barbara Henley, Ph.D.
Vice Chancellor for Research. . . . . Vacant
Associate Vice Chancellor for Health Affairs. . . . . John J. DeNardo
Exec. Assistant Vice President for Business & Finance . . . . Heather J. Haberaecker, Ph.D.
University Librarian. . . . . Mary M. Case

Medical School Administrative Staff

Dean. . . . . Dimitri Azar, M.D., M.B.A.
Vice Dean for Administration. . . . . Arnim Dontes, M.B.A.
Senior Associate Dean for Educational Affairs. Saul J. Weiner, M.D.
Senior Associate Dean for Research . . . . Lawrence Tobacman, M.D., Ph.D.
Senior Associate Dean for Student Affairs. . . . . Kathleen Kashima, Ph.D.
Senior Associate Dean for Faculty Affairs . . . . Karen Colley, Ph.D.
Senior Associate Dean for Development . . . . L. Keith Todd
Associate Dean for Administration . . . . Todd Van Neck
Associate Dean for Clinical Affairs (Inpatient) . . . . David Schwartz, M.D.
Associate Dean for Clinical Affairs (Outpatient) . . . . Patrick Tranmer, M.D.
Associate Dean and Director, Admissions . . . . Jorge A. Girotti, Ph.D.
Associate Dean for Educational Planning . . . . Loreen Troy, MHPE
Associate Dean for Graduate Medical Education . . . . Henry Dove, M.D.
Associate Dean for International Affairs . . . . Ara Tekian, Ph.D., MHPE
Chief Information Officer . . . . Andre Pavkovic
Director for Faculty Affairs. . . . . Gillian Coombs
Director, Medical Service Plan . . . . Brian Rasmus (Interim)
Director, Records and Registration. . . . . Susan Huhndorf
Director, Financial Aid. . . . . Peter Aiello

Programs of Undergraduate Medical Education

Assistant Dean for Curriculum . . . . Abbas Hyderi, M.D.
Assistant Dean for Student Affairs. . . . . Jean Lantz

Basic Sciences

Anatomy and Cell Biology . . . . Scott Brady, Ph.D.
Biochemisty and Molecular Genetics. . . . . Jack H. Kaplan, Ph.D.
Bioengineering . . . . Thomas J. Royston, Ph.D.
Medical Education. . . . . Ilene Harris, Ph.D.
Microbiology and Immunology. . . . . Bellur S. Prabhakar, Ph.D.
Pharmacology . . . . Asrar B. Malik, Ph.D.
Physiology and Biophysics . . . . R. John Solaro, Ph.D.

Clinical Sciences

Anesthesiology. . . . . David E. Schwarts, M.D.
Dermatology . . . . Lawrence Chan, M.D.
Emergency Medicine . . . . Terry Vanden Hoek, M.D.
Family Medicine . . . . Patrick A. Tranmer, M.D.
Medicine. . . . . Patricia Finn, M.D.
Neurological Surgery. . . . . Fady Charbel, M.D.
Obstetrics and Gynecology. . . . . Isabelle Wilkins, M.D. (Interim)
Opthalmology and Visual Sciences . . . . Joel Sugar, M.D.
Orthopaedic Surgery . . . . Mark A. Gonzalez, M.D.
Otolaryngology-Head and Neck Surgery . . . . J. Regan Thomas, M.D.
Pathology . . . . Frederick Behm, M.D.
Pediatrics . . . . Usha Raj, M.D.
Psychiatry . . . . Anand Kumar, M.D.
Radiology . . . . Masoud Hemmati, M.D.
Radiation Oncology* . . . . Jeffrey Feinstein, M.D.
Surgery . . . . Enrico Benedetti, M.D.
Urology. . . . . Craig Niederberger, M.D.
* Specialty without organizational autonomy

College of Medicine at Chicago
1853 West Polk Street (M/C 784)
Chicago, Illinois 60612
312-996-3500; 312-996-9006 (fax)

Associate Dean for Curriculum. . . . . David Mayer, M.D.
Assistant Dean for Curriculum . . . . Gary Loy, M.D., M.P.H.
Assistant Dean for Student Affairs. . . . . Jean Lantz
Associate Dean and Director, Special Curricular
    Programs; Dir., Medical College Admissions . . . . Jorge A. Girotti, Ph.D.

Basic Sciences

Anatomy and Cell Biology . . . . Scott Brady, Ph.D.
Biochemistry and Molecular Genetics. . . . . Jack H. Kaplan, Ph.D.
Medical Education. . . . . Ilene Harris, Ph.D. (Interim)
Microbiology and Immunology. . . . . Bellur S. Prabhakar, Ph.D.
Pharmacology . . . . Asrar B. Malik, Ph.D.
Physiology and Biophysics . . . . R. John Solaro, Ph.D.

Clinical Sciences

Anesthesiology. . . . . David E. Schwartz, M.D.
Dermatology. . . . . Lawrence Chan, M.D.
Emergency Medicine . . . . Timothy Erikson, M.D. (Interim)
Family Medicine . . . . Patrick A. Tranmer, M.D.
Medicine. . . . . Thomas J. Layden, M.D.

University of Illinois at Chicago College of Medicine: ILLINOIS

Allergy and Immunology*.. John Christman, M.D.
Cardiology* .... Samuel Dudley, M.D., Ph.D.
Digestive Disease and Nutrition*.. Gail A. Hecht, M.D.
Endocrinology* .... Theodore Mazzone, M.D.
General Internal Medicine* .... John Tulley, M.D.
Geriatric Medicine* .... Donald Jurivich, D.O.
Hematology* .... Howard Ozer, M.D., Ph.D.
Hepatology*... Scott Cotler, M.D.
Infectious Diseases* .... James L. Cook, M.D.
Nephrology* .... Jose A. L. Arruda, M.D.
Oncology*... Howard Ozer, M.D., Ph.D.
Respiratory and Critical Care* .... John Christman, M.D.
Rheumatology* .... William Swedler, M.D.
Neurology and Rehabilitation Medicine .... Philip B. Gorelick, M.D.
Neurological Surgery.. Fady Charbel, M.D.
Obstetrics and Gynecology.. Sara Kilpatrick, M.D., Ph.D.
Ophthalmology and Visual Sciences .... Dimitri T. Azar, M.D.
Orthopaedic Surgery.. Mark A. Gonzalez, M.D.
Otolaryngology-Head and Neck Surgery .... J. Regan Thomas, M.D.
Pathology .... Frederick Behm, M.D.
Pediatrics .... Usha Raj, M.D.
Psychiatry .... Anand Kumar, M.D.
Radiation Oncology... Jeffrey Feinstein, M.D.
Radiology .... Masoud Hemmati, M.D.
Surgery.. Enrico Benedetti, M.D.
Cardio-Thoracic Surgery*.. Malek G. Massad, M.D.
Colorectal Surgery* .... Jose Cintron, M.D.
General Surgery*.. Pier Cristoforo Giulianotti, M.D.
Pediatric Surgery* .... Mark Holterman, M.D.
Plastic Surgery* .... Mimis N. Cohen, M.D.
Transplantation Surgery* .... Jose Obherholzer, M.D.
Vascular Surgery*... Martin Borhani, M.D.
Urology.. Craig Niederberger, M.D.

*Specialty without organizational autonomy.

College of Medicine at Peoria
One Illini Drive
P.O. Box 1649
Peoria, Illinois 61656
309-671-8402 (regional dean's office); 309-671-8438 (fax)

Regional Dean... Sara L. Rusch, M.D.
Regional Vice Dean .... Vacant
Senior Associate Dean for Research .... Jasti Rao, Ph.D.
Associate Dean for Academic Affairs...................................... Vacant
Associate Dean for Community Health .... John G. Halvorsen, M.D.
Associate Dean for Graduate Medical Education .... Thomas Santoro, M.D.
Assistant Dean for Student Services .... Linda Rowe, Ed.D.
Assistant Dean for Clinical Curriculum and Evaluation .... Vacant
Assistant Dean for Education/MMCI .... Richard Anderson, M.D.
Assistant Dean for Pre-Clinical Curriculum and Evaluation .... Glenn Miller, M.D.
Assistant Dean for Education/SFMC................................. Tim Miller, M.D.
Assistant Dean for Medical Education and Evaluation .... Vacant
Director of Fiscal Services/CFO .... A. Nicholas Straub
Cancer Biology and Pharmacology.................................... Jasti Rao, Ph.D.
Dermatology .... Allan Campbell, M.D.
Family and Community Medicine................................ John G. Halvorsen, M.D.
Internal Medicine .... James Graumlich, M.D.
Neurology... Jorge C. Kattah, M.D.
Neurosurgery.. Daniel Fassett (Interim)
Obstetrics and Gynecology...................................... Salvatore LoCoco, M.D.
Pathology .... Roger Geiss, M.D.
Pediatrics .... Pedro de Alarcon, M.D.
Psychiatry and Behavioral Medicine .... Ryan Finkinbine, M.D.
Radiology .... Thomas J. Cusack, M.D.

Rehabilitation Medicine................................. Sara Rusch, M.D. (Interim)
Surgery .... Norman C. Estes, M.D.

College of Medicine at Rockford
1601 Parkview Avenue
Rockford, Illinois 61107
815-395-5600 (regional dean's office); 815-395-5887 (fax)

Regional Dean.. Martin S. Lipsky, M.D.
Associate Dean for Academic Affairs....................... Mitchell King, M.D.
Associate Dean for Fiscal Affairs and Administration...................... Rick Hampton
Assistant Dean for Medical Education and Evaluation .... Margaret Maynard, M.D.
Assistant Dean for Health Systems Research .... Joel B. Cowen
Biomedical Sciences...................................... K. Ramaswamy, Ph.D.
Family and Community Medicine..................... Vivek S. Kantayya, M.D. (Interim)
Medicine... Glenn Netto, M.D.
Obstetrics and Gynecology........................... Timothy J. Durkee, M.D., Ph.D.
Pathology .... Gary L. Anderson, M.D. (Interim)
Pediatrics .... David E. Deutsch, M.D.
Psychiatry .... Steven Kouris, D.O., M.P.H. (Interim)
Surgery .... Samuel Appavu, M.D.

College of Medicine at Urbana-Champaign
190 Medical Sciences Building
506 South Mathews
Urbana, Illinois 61801
217-333-5465 (regional dean's office); 217-333-8868 (fax)

Regional Dean....................................... Bradford S. Schwartz, M.D.
Director of Business and Financial Systems................. Dedra Mooday Williams, Ed.M.
Associate Dean for Academic Affairs....................... Richard I. Gumport, Ph.D.
Associate Dean for Student Affairs and Medical Scholars Program........ James W. Hall, Ed.D.
Associate Dean for Academic Curriculum Management................. Susan Kies, Ed.D.
Associate Dean for Clinical Affairs .... Robert W. Kirby, M.D.
Executive Assistant Dean for Student Affairs and
  Medical Scholars Program .... Nora J. Few, Ph.D.
Asociate Dean for Administration....................... Dedra Mooday Williams, Ed.M.
Director of Medical Scholars Program .... James Slauch, Ph.D.
Director of Advancement...................................... Madeleine Jaehne
Director of Computer and Information Science .... Tod A. Jebe
Medical Humanities and Social Sciences Program................. Evan M. Melhado, Ph.D.
Biochemistry.. Colin A. Wraight, Ph.D.
Cell and Structural Biology .... Martha L. U. Gillette, Ph.D.
Family Medicine .... Christian Wagner, M.D.
Internal Medicine .... Janet Jokela, M.D.
Medical Information Science .... Bruce R. Schatz, Ph.D. (Interim)
Microbiology....................................... John E. Cronan, Ph.D.
Molecular and Integrative Physiology .... Byron W. Kemper, Ph.D.
Obstetrics and Gynecology.............................. Ralph J. Kehl, M.D.
Pathology .... Gregory G. Freund, M.D.
Pediatrics .... M. Kathleen Buetow, M.D., Dr.P.H.
Pharmacology .... Byron W. Kemper, Ph.D.
Psychiatry .... Sari Gilman Aronson, M.D.
Surgery .... Uretz J. Oliphant, M.D.

Loyola University Chicago Stritch School of Medicine
2160 South First Avenue
Maywood, Illinois 60153
708-216-9000; 708-216-3326 (dean's office); 708-216-4305 (fax)
Web site: www.stritch.luc.edu

Stritch School of Medicine is one of ten professional schools of Loyola University Chicago, an urban Catholic university composed of a culturally and religiously diverse faculty, student body, and administration. Established in 1909, Stritch specifically calls upon its Jesuit tradition of education, which emphasizes the full development of its students, rigorous concern for the quality of its academic programs, and promotion of a broad educational curriculum that encourages leadership in the service of others and advances social justice. The school is located at Loyola's medical center campus in Maywood, Illinois, a suburb 12 miles west of Chicago's lake front. The 200,000 square-foot medical education building includes a variety of contemporary teaching spaces, student life/lounge/study areas, computer facilities, a clinical skills and simulation center, and administrative offices. A 62,000 square-foot health and fitness center is adjacent to the school. Stritch's curriculum relies on small-group sessions and problem-based learning as well as on traditional lectures and labs. Medical students are required to develop particular competencies to the level expected of new physicians entering graduate medical education programs. Students are broadly trained and prepared to undertake advanced training and choose careers in academic medicine, community medicine, and/or research. Faculty members are committed as teachers, mentors, and role models to support the development of these student competencies.

Type: private
2011 total enrollment: 588
Clinical facilities: Loyola University Hospital, Edward Hines Veterans Administration Medical Center, Madden Mental Health Center, Provident Hospital of Cook County, Alexian Brothers Health System, Resurrection Medical Center, MacNeal Hospital, West Suburban Medical Center, Gottlieb Memorial Hospital, St. Joseph Hospital.

University Officials

President. . . . . Michael J. Garanzini, S.J., Ph.D.
Senior Vice President and Provost for Health Sciences . . . . . . Richard L. Gamelli, M.D., F.A.C.S.

Medical School Administrative Staff

Dean, Stritch School of Medicine. . . . . Linda Brubaker, M.D.
Senior Associate Dean, Education Program. . . . . Gregory Gruener, M.D.
Senior Associate Dean, Research . . . . Richard Kennedy, Ph.D.
Associate Dean, Educational Affairs . . . . Paul Hering, M.D.
Associate Dean, Computers in Education . . . . Arcot J. Chandrasekhar, M.D.
Senior Associate Dean, Clinical and Translational Research. . . . . Linda Brubaker, M.D.
Associate Dean, Faculty Administration. . . . . Donna Halinski
Associate Dean, Fiscal Affairs . . . . Cindy Gonya
Associate Dean, Graduate Medical Education . . . . William Cannon, M.D.
Associate Dean, Health Sciences Library. . . . . Jeanne Sadlik, M.L.S. (Acting)
Associate Dean, Information Systems . . . . Ron Price, Jr.
Associate Dean, Student Affairs . . . . Teresa Wronski
Associate Dean, Veterans Affairs. . . . . Jack M. Bulmash, M.D. (Acting)
Assistant Dean, Admissions and Recruitment . . . . Adrian Jones, J.D.
Assistant Dean, Basic Science Research and Postdoctoral Studies. . . . . Ruben Mestril, Ph.D.
Assistant Dean, Biomedical and Translational Science. . . . . Allen Frankfater, Ph.D.
Assistant Dean, Clinical Performance . . . . Keith Muccino, S.J., M.D.
Assistant Dean, Comparative Studies. . . . . Lee Cera, D.V.M., Ph.D.
Assistant Dean, Development . . . . Shawn Vogen
Assistant Dean, Medical Education . . . . Patricia McNally, Ed.D.
Assistant Dean, Student Affairs. . . . . Michael Lambesis
Assistant Dean, Student Affairs. . . . . James Mendez
Director, Education Program Administration . . . . Linda Massari
Director, Financial Aid. . . . . Donna Sobie
Director, Registration and Records. . . . . Mary Van Houten
Director, Research Services . . . . Jamie Caldwell
Director, Teaching and Learning Center . . . . Beth Sonntag

Loyola University Chicago Stritch School of Medicine: ILLINOIS

Department and Division or Section Chairs

Basic Sciences

Microbiology and Immunology. . . . . Katherine Knight, Ph.D.
Molecular Pharmacology and Therapeutics. . . . . Tarun Patel, Ph.D.
Cell and Molecular Physiology . . . . Pieter deTumbe, Ph.D.

Clinical Sciences

Anesthesiology. . . . . W. Scott Jellish, M.D., Ph.D.
Family Medicine . . . . Eva Bading, M.D.
Medicine. . . . . David Hecht, M.D.
   Allergy, Immunology, and Rheumatology . . . . John A. Robinson, M.D. (Interim)
   Bioethics and Health Policy . . . . Mark Kuczewski, Ph.D.
   Cardiology. . . . . David Wilber, M.D.
   Dermatology . . . . Rebecca Tung, M.D.
   Endocrinology . . . . Nicholas Emanuele, M.D.
   Gastroenterology . . . . Claus Fimmel, M.D.
   General Internal Medicine . . . . Edward Gurza, M.D.
   Health Services Research . . . . Frances Weaver, Ph.D.
   Hematology and Oncology. . . . . Patrick Stiff, M.D.
Hospital Medicine . . . . Elizabeth Schulwolf, M.D. (Interim)
   Infectious Disease. . . . . J. Paul O'Keefe, M.D. (Interim)
   Nephrology . . . . Anil Bidani, M.D.
   Pulmonary Disease . . . . Charles Alex, M.D.
Neurological Surgery. . . . . Vikram Prabhu, M.D. (Interim)
Neurology. . . . . Jose Biller, M.D.
Obstetrics and Gynecology. . . . . Ronald K. Potkul, M.D.
Ophthalmology . . . . Charles Bouchard, M.D.
Orthopedic Surgery and Rehabilitation. . . . . Terry Light, M.D.
Otolaryngology . . . . James Stankiewicz, M.D.
Pathology . . . . Eva Wojcik, M.D.
Pediatrics . . . . Jerold Stirling, M.D.
Preventive Medicine and Epidemiology. . . . . Richard Cooper, M.D.
Psychiatry and Behavioral Neurosciences . . . . Muralidhara S. Rao, M.D.
Radiation Oncology. . . . . Bahman Emami, M.D.
Radiology . . . . Scott Mirowitz, M.D.
Surgery . . . . Paul Kuo, M.D.
   Emergency Medical Services . . . . Mark Cichon, D.O.
   General Surgery. . . . . Steven DeJong, M.D.
   Oral and Maxillofacial Surgery and Dental Medicine . . . . Victor Cimino, D.D.S., M.D.
   Peripheral Vascular Surgery . . . . Ross Milner, M.D.
   Plastic and Reconstructive Surgery . . . . Juan Angelats, M.D.
   Surgical Oncology . . . . Margo Shoup, M.D.
   Surgical Research. . . . . Elizabeth Kovacs, Ph.D.
   Trauma, Surgical Critical Care, and Burns. . . . . Thomas Esposito, M.D.
Thoracic and Cardiovascular Surgery . . . . Mamdouh Bakhos, M.D.
Urology. . . . . Robert Flanigan, M.D.

Interdisciplinary Research Institutes and Directors

Burn and Shock Trauma Institute . . . . Richard Gamelli, M.D.
Infectious Disease and Immunology Institute . . David Hecht, M.D., and Katherine Knight, Ph.D.
Leischner Institute for Medical Education . . . . Gregory Gruener, M.D.
Oncology Institute. . . . . Paul Kuo, M.D.
Cardiovascular Institute . . . . Pieter de Tombe, Ph.D.
Neiswanger Institute for Bioethics and Health Policy. . . . . Mark Kuczewski, Ph.D.
Neuroscience Institute. . . . . Wendy Kartje, Ph.D.
Institute of Signal Transduction . . . . Tarun Patel, Ph.D.

Northwestern University
The Feinberg School of Medicine

420 East Superior Avenue
Chicago, Illinois 60611-3008
312-503-8649 (campus operator); 312-503-0340 (dean's office);
312-503-7757 (dean's office fax)
Web site: www.feinberg.northwestern.edu

Northwestern University Feinberg School of Medicine was organized in 1859 as the Medical Department of Lind University. In 1863, it continued under the name of Chicago Medical College. In 1879, the college was affiliated with Northwestern University. Together with the schools of law and continuing education division, the school has been located on the Chicago campus of the university since 1926.

Type: private
2011 total enrollment: 695
Clinical facilities: Children's Memorial Hospital, Evanston Northwestern Healthcare, Northwestern Memorial Hospital, Rehabilitation Institute of Chicago, VA Chicago Health Care System.

University Officials

President. . . . . Morton O. Schapiro, Ph.D.
Provost . . . . Daniel H. Linzer, Ph.D.
Vice President for Medical Affairs. . . . . Eric G. Neilson, M.D.

Medical School Administrative Staff

Dean. . . . . Eric G. Neilson, M.D.
Vice Dean, Regulatory Affairs, Chief Compliance Officer. . . . . Robert M. Rosa, M.D.
Dean, Medical Development . . . . Katherine Kurtz
Executive Director Alumni Relations . . . . Virginia Darakjian
Vice Dean, Education . . . . Raymond H. Curry, M.D.
Associate Dean, Admissions . . . . Warren H. Wallace, M.D.
Director, Continuing Medical Education. . . . . Genevieve Napier
Vice President for Graduate Medical Education . . . . Joshua Goldstein, M.D. (Interim)
Senior Associate Dean for Medical Education
  and Competency Achievement . . . . John X. Thomas, Jr., Ph.D.
Associate Dean for Medical Education . . . . Marianne M. Green, M.D.
Associate Dean for Diversity. . . . . John E. Franklin, M.D.
Associate Dean for Student Programs and
  Career Development . . . . Sandra M. Sanguino, M.D., M.P.H.
Vice Dean, Scientific Affairs and Graduate Education . . . . Rex L. Chisholm, Ph.D.
Executive Director for Research . . . . Eric W. Boberg, Ph.D.
Senior Associate Dean for Clinical and Translational Research . . . . Philip Greenland, M.D.
Associate Dean for Research Operations. . . . . David Johnson, Ph.D.
Assistant Dean for Clinical Affairs. . . . . Michael Ruchim, M.D.
Associate Dean for Academic Affairs at Jesse
  Brown VA Medical Center . . . . Wendy Weinstock Brown, M.D.
Associate Dean for Academic Affairs, RIC. . . . . Todd A. Kuiken, M.D., Ph.D.
Associate Dean for Academic Affairs, CMH. . . . . Edward S. Ogata, M.D.
Vice Dean, Academic Affairs . . . . William L. Lowe, Jr., M.D.
Associate Dean for Faculty Recruitment and
  Professional Development . . . . Richard McGee, Ph.D.
Associate Dean for Faculty Development. . . . . Linda Van Horn, Ph.D., R.D.
Assistant Dean for Faculty Affairs . . . . Marcie Weiss
Chief Operating Officer. . . . . David Browdy
Senior Executive Director for Communications. . . . . Thomas Garritano
Executive Director for Finance and Budget, Chief Financial Officer . . . . Craig Johnson
Director, Galter Health Sciences Library. . . . . James Shedlock
Assistant Dean for Management Information Systems . . . . Jonathan C. Lewis

Department and Division or Section Chairs

Basic Sciences

Cell and Molecular Biology . . . . Robert D. Goldman, Ph.D.
Microbiology and Immunology. . . . . Laimonis Laimins, Ph.D.

Molecular Pharmacology and Biological Chemistry . . . . Eugene M. Silinsky, Ph.D.
Physiology . . . . D. James Surmeier, Jr., Ph.D.

Clinical Sciences

Anesthesiology . . . . M. Christine Stock, M.D.
Dermatology . . . . Amy Paller, M.D.
Emergency Medicine . . . . James Adams, M.D.
Family and Community Medicine . . . . Michael Fleming, M.D. (Interim)
Medical Social Sciences . . . . David Cella, Ph.D.
Medicine . . . . Douglas Vaughan, M.D.
Ken and Ruth Davee Department of Neurology . . . . John A. Kessler, M.D.
Neurological Surgery . . . . H. Hunt Batjer, M.D.
Obstetrics and Gynecology . . . . Sharon Dooley, M.D. (Interim)
Ophthalmology . . . . Nicholas Volpe, M.D.
Orthopaedic Surgery . . . . Terrance Peabody, M.D.
Orthopaedic Surgery . . . . Terrance Peabody, M.D.
Otolaryngology and Head and Neck Surgery . . . . Robert Kern, M.D.
Pathology . . . . William A. Muller, M.D., Ph.D.
Pediatrics . . . . Thomas Green, M.D.
Physical Medicine and Rehabilitation . . . . Elliot J. Roth, M.D.
Physical Therapy and Human Movement Science . . . . Julius Dewald, Ph.D.
Preventive Medicine . . . . Donald Lloyd-Jones, M.D.
Psychiatry and Behavioral Sciences . . . . John G. Csernansky, M.D.
Radiation Oncology . . . . Bharat B. Mittal, M.D.
Radiology . . . . Eric J. Russell, M.D.
Surgery . . . . Nathaniel J. Soper, M.D.
Urology . . . . Anthony J. Schaeffer, M.D.

Centers, Institutes, and Special Programs

Buehler Center on Aging, Health, and Society . . . . Linda Emanuel, M.D., Ph.D.
Northwestern Comprehensive Center for AIDS Research . . . . Steven M. Wolinsky, M.D.
Center for Bioethics, Science, and Society . . . . Laurie Zoloth, Ph.D.
Institute for BioNanotechnology in Medicine . . . . Sam Stupp, Ph.D.
Robert H. Lurie Comprehensive Cancer Center . . . . Steven T. Rosen, M.D.
Frances Evelyn Feinberg Cardiovascular
  Research Institute . . . . Douglas Vaughan, M.D. (Interim)
Northwestern University Clinical and
  Translational Sciences Institute . . . . Philip Greenland, M.D.
Cognitive Neurology and Alzheimer's Disease Center . . . . M. Marsel Mesulam, M.D.
Center for Genetic Medicine . . . . Peter Kopp, M.D. (Interim)
Global Health Center . . . . Robert Murphy, M.D.
Institute for Healthcare Studies . . . . Jane Holl, M.D., M.P.H.
Interdepartmental Immunobiology Center . . . . Stephen D. Miller, Ph.D.
Feinberg Clinical Neurosciences Research Institute . . . . John A. Kessler, M.D.
Northwestern Comprehensive Center for the
  Study of Obesity and Weight Management . . . . Lewis Landsberg, M.D.
Simulation Technology and Immersive Learning Center . . . . John A. Vozenilek, M.D.
Northwestern Comprehensive Transplant Center . . . . Michael Abecassis, M.D.
Institute for Women's Health Research . . . . Teresa K. Woodruff, Ph.D.
Medical Humanities and Bioethics . . . . Kathryn K. Montgomery, Ph.D.
Medical Humanities and Bioethics . . . . Tod S. Chambers, Ph.D.

Rush Medical College of Rush University Medical Center

600 South Paulina
Chicago, Illinois 60612
312-942-5000 (general information); 312-942-6909 (dean's office); 312-942-2828 (fax)
E-mail: medcol@rush.edu
Web site: www.rush.edu

Rush Medical College was chartered in 1837. The early Rush faculty was involved with other developing institutions in Chicago: St. Luke's Hospital, established in 1864; Presbyterian Hospital, opened at the urging of Rush faculty in 1884; and the University of Chicago, with which Rush Medical College was affiliated and later united from 1898 to 1942. In the early 1940s, Rush discontinued undergraduate education; its faculty continued to teach at the University of Illinois School of Medicine. In 1969, Rush Medical College reactivated its charter and merged with Presbyterian-St. Luke's Hospital, which itself had been formed through merger in 1956, to form Rush-Presbyterian-St. Luke's Medical Center. Rush University, which now includes colleges of medicine, nursing, health sciences, and basic science, was established in 1972. In 2003, the medical center changed its name to Rush University Medical Center.

Type: private
2011 total enrollment: 1,729
Clinical facilities: Rush University Medical Center, including 613-bed hospital serving adults and children and 61-bed rehabilitation and senior care facility; system affiliate Rush Oak Park Hospital with 176 beds. **Other system affiliates:** Rush-Copley Medical Center in Aurora, Rush North Shore Medical Center in Skokie, and Riverside HealthCare in Kankakee. Rush Medical College is the primary medical college for John H. Stroger Jr. Hospital of Cook County.

University Officials

President. . . . . Larry J. Goodman, M.D.
Provost . . . . Thomas A. Deutsch, M.D.
Vice Provost and Vice President of University Affairs. . . . . Lois A. Halstead, R.N., Ph.D.
Associate Provost, Academic Affairs . . . . Susan Chubinskaya, Ph.D.
Associate Provost, Research and Vice President, Research Affairs. . . . . . James L. Mulshine, M.D.
Associate Provost, Student Affairs. . . . . Gayle Ward, J.D.
Assistant Provost for Community Research . . . . Martha Clare Morris, Sc.D.
Dean, Rush Medical College, and Senior Vice
    President, Medical Affairs . . . . Thomas A. Deutsch, M.D.
Dean, College of Nursing. . . . . Melanie C. Dreher, R.N., Ph.D.
Dean, College of Health Sciences. . . . . David C. Shelledy, Ph.D., R.R.T.
Dean, Graduate College. . . . . Paul M. Carvey, Ph.D.
Executive Vice President and Chief Operating Officer. . . . . Peter W. Butler
Senior Vice President for Hospital Affiars,
    Executive Director, Rush University Hospital . . . . J. Robert Clapp, Jr.
Senior Vice President, Corporate and External Affairs. . . . . Avery Miller
Senior Vice President of Finance, Chief Financial Officer . . . . John Mordach
Senior Vice President, Information Services, and Chief Information Officer. . . . . . Lac Van Tran
Vice President of Medical Affairs, Clinical
    Practice, and Executive Director, Rush
    University Medical Group . . . . Brian T. Smith
Principal Business Officer . . . . Richard K. Davis
Associate Vice President, University Relations . . . . Mary Katherine Krause

Medical School Administrative Staff

Dean. . . . . Thomas A. Deutsch, M.D.
Senior Associate Dean, Clinical Affairs . . . . David A. Ansell, M.D.
Associate Dean, Medical Sciences and Services . . . . Robert E. Kimura, M.D.
Associate Dean, Surgical Sciences and Services . . . . Keith W. Millikan, M.D.
Associate Dean, Basic Sciences. . . . . Paul M. Carvey, Ph.D.
Senior Associate Dean, Education. . . . . Keith Boyd, M.D.
Associate Dean, Medical Student Programs. . . . . Susan K. Jacob, Ph.D.
Associate Dean, Postgraduate Education. . . . . Harold A. Kessler, M.D.
Associate Dean, Graduate Medical Education . . . . Susan Vanderberg-Dent, M.D.

Rush Medical College of Rush University Medical Center: ILLINOIS

Associate Dean, Academic Affiliations....................... David M. Rothenberg, M.D.
Associate Dean, Cancer Program .... Howard L. Kaufman, M.D.
Vice President, Medical Affairs.................................... Richard K. Davis
Director of Admissions... Jill M. Volk, M.S.Ed.
Assistant Dean for Student Development .... Mary C. Anderson, M.D.
Assistant Dean, Preclinical Programs.......................... Robert M. Leven, Ph.D.
Assistant Dean for Academic Affairs .... Sandra Frellsen, M.D.
Assistant Dean for Accreditation and Continuous
    Program Improvement .... Madhu Soni, M.D.
Assistant Dean, Post-Graduate Medical Education .... Claudia G. Gidea, M.D.

Department Chairs

Basic Sciences

Anatomy and Cell Biology .... R. Dale Sumner, Ph.D.
Behavioral Sciences .... Stevan E. Hobfoll, Ph.D.
Biochemistry .... Di Chen, M.D., Ph.D.
Immunology and Microbiology.................................. Alan L. Landay, Ph.D.
Molecular Biophysics and Physiology .... Robert S. Eisenberg, Ph.D.
Pharmacology .... Chunxiang ""Kevin"" Zhang, M.D., Ph.D.
Preventive Medicine.. Lynda H. Powell, Ph.D.

Medical Sciences

Dermatology .... Michael D. Tharp, M.D.
Emergency Medicine .... Dino Rumoro, D.O.
Family Medicine .... William A. Schwer, M.D.
Internal Medicine .... Stuart Levin, M.D.
Neurological Sciences .... Jacob H. Fox, M.D.
Pediatrics .... Kenneth M. Boyer, M.D.
Physical Medicine and Rehabilitation .... James A. Young, M.D.
Psychiatry .... Mark Pollack, M.D.

Surgical Sciences

Anesthesiology.. Kenneth J. Tuman, M.D.
Cardiovascular-Thoracic Surgery...................... Walter J. McCarthy, M.D. (Acting)
Diagnostic Radiology and Nuclear Medicine....................... Sharon E. Byrd, M.D.
General Surgery.. Daniel J. Deziel, M.D.
Neurosurgery... Richard W. Byrne, M.D.
Obstetrics and Gynecology................................. Howard T. Strassner, M.D.
Ophthalmology .... Kirk H. Packo, M.D.
Orthopedic Surgery... Joshua J. Jacobs, M.D.
Otolaryngology and Bronchoesophagology .... David D. Caldarelli, M.D.
Pathology .... Robert P. De Cresce, M.D.
Plastic and Reconstructive Surgery .... John W. Polley, M.D.
Radiation Oncology.. Ross A. Abrams, M.D.
Urology... Charles F. McKiel, Jr., M.D.

Southern Illinois University School of Medicine

801 North Rutledge
P.O. Box 19620
Springfield, Illinois 62794-9620
1-800-342-5748; 217-545-3625 (dean's office); 217-545-0786 (fax)
Web site: www.siumed.edu

Southern Illinois University School of Medicine was established in 1969. Teaching facilities are located on the campus of Southern Illinois University at Carbondale and Springfield.

Type: public
2011 total enrollment: 288
Clinical facilities: Memorial Medical Center and St. John's Hospital (Springfield), Veterans Affairs Medical Center (Marion).

University Official

Chancellor . . . . Rita Cheng, Ph.D.

Medical School Administrative Staff

Dean and Provost . . . . J. Kevin Dorsey, M.D., Ph.D.
Associate Dean for Clinical Affairs; and Chief
  Executive Officer, SIU Healthcare . . . . Hyung Kim, M.D.
Associate Dean for Education and Curriculum . . . . Debra Klamen, M.D., M.H.P.E.
Associate Dean for Graduate Medical Education . . . . Karen Broquet, M.D.
Associate Dean for Information Resources; and Director of Medical Library . . . . . Connie Poole
Associate Dean for Research and Faculty Affairs . . . . Linda A. Toth, Ph.D., D.V.M
Associate Dean for Student Affairs . . . . Erik Constance, M.D.
Associate Provost for External and Health Affairs . . . . Phillip Davis, Ph.D.
Associate Provost for Finance and Administration . . . . Pamela Speer
Assistant Provost for Financial Affairs . . . . Connie Hess
Assistant Provost for Institutional Planning and
  Management Information . . . . Gary Giacomelli
Assistant Provost for Project and Management Consulting . . . . M. Beth Collier
Assistant Dean for Student Affairs . . . . Linda Herrold
Assistant Dean for Minority Affairs . . . . Harold R. Bardo, Ph.D.
Chief Compliance Officer . . . . Peter Cadwell
Associate Provost for Finance and Administration . . . . Pamela J. Speer
Chief Financial Officer, SIU HealthCare . . . . Wendy Cox-Largent
Chief Medical Officer, SIU HealthCare . . . . Jeffrey Lobas, M.D.
Chief Operating Officer, SIU HealthCare . . . . Kathryn Mahaffey
Comptroller . . . . Sandra Lewis
Director of Alumni Affairs . . . . Julie Robbs
Director of Communications and Publica Relations . . . . Karen Carlson
Assistant Provost, Financial Affairs . . . . Connie Hess
Director of Continuing Education . . . . Laura Worrall
Director of Development . . . . Deborah Case
Director of Laboratory Animal Medicine . . . . Teresa Liberati, Ph.D., D.V.M.

Department and Division or Section Chairs

Director of MEDPREP . . . . Harold Bardo, Ph.D.

Basic Sciences

Anatomy . . . . Richard Clough, Ph.D.
  Biochemistry and Molecular Biology . . . . Ramesh Gupta, Ph.D.
Information and Communication Sciences . . . . Connie Poole
Executive Assistant to Dean for Diversity,
  Multicultural and Minority Affairs . . . . Wesley McNeese, M.D.
Medical Education . . . . Debra L. Klamen, M.D., M.H.P.E.
Executive Director, Capital Planning and Service Operations . . . . Gary Pezall
Executive Director of Human Resources . . . . Penny McCarty
Medical Humanities . . . . Ross D. Silverman, J.D., M.P.H.
Medical Microbiology, Immunology, and Cell Biology . . . . Morris D. Cooper, Ph.D.
Senior Associate General Counsel . . . . Virginia Cooper, J.D.
Associate General Counsel . . . . Carl L. Faingold, Ph.D., and Luke Crater, J.D.

Southern Illinois University School of Medicine: ILLINOIS

Clinical Sciences

Anesthesiology.. Reginald Bulkley, M.D.
Physiology... Dale Buchanan Hales, Ph.D.
Family and Community Medicine................................... Jerry Kruse, M.D.
  Endocrinology.. Michael Jakoby, M.D.
  Gastroenterology.................................... Russell D. Yang, M.D., Ph.D.
  General Internal Medicine................................... Alan Deckard, M.D.
  Hematology Oncology....................................... John Godwin, M.D.
  Infectious Diseases... Janak Koirala, M.D.
  Medicine and Psychiatry..................................... David Resch, M.D.
  Nephrology... Lawrence Smith, M.D.
  Pulmonary Medicine...................................... Joseph Henkle, M.D.
  Rheumatology .... Vacant
Neurology... Rodger Eible, M.D., Ph.D.
Obstetrics and Gynecology......................... J. Ricardo Loret de Mola, M.D.
  Uro/Gynecology... Sohail Siddique, M.D.
  Maternal Fetal Medicine.................................. Robert Abrams, M.D.
Patholy............................ Sanjai Nagendra, M.D., and Brian Moore, M.D.
Pediatrics.. Mark Puczynski, M.D.
Psychiatry .... Stephen Soltys, M.D.
  Child Psychiatry... Mary Dobbins, M.D.
  Psycho-Oncology... Chad Noggle, Ph.D.
Radiology... Andrew Sherrick, M.D.
Surgery... Gary Dunnington, M.D.
  Cardiothoracic Surgery.................................. Stephen Hazelrigg, M.D.
  Emergency Medicine .... David Griffen, M.D.
  General Surgery... John Mellinger, M.D.
  Neurosurgery.. Jeffrey Cozzens, M.D.
  Orthopedics.. Khaled Saleh, M.D.
  Otolaryngology... Gayle Woodson, M.D.
  Pediatric Surgery....................................... Andreas Meier, M.D.
  Plastic Surgery....................................... Michael Neumeister, M.D.
  Urology... Patrick McKenna, M.D.
  Vascular... Kim Hodgson, M.D.

Centers and Institutes

Center for Alzheimer Disease and Related Disorders............. Thomas Ala, M.D. (Interim)
Simmons Cancer Institute at SIU .... K. Thomas Robbins, M.D.
Internal Medicine .... David Steward, M.D.
  Cardiology... Frank Aquirre, M.D.
  Dermatology .... Lucinda Buescher, M.D.

Indiana University School of Medicine

340 West 10th Street
Indianapolis, Indiana 46202-3082
317-274-5000 (general information); 317-278-3048 (dean's office); 317-274-8439 (fax)
Web site: www.medicine.iu.edu

The Indiana University School of Medicine was organized in Bloomington in 1903 through a series of mergers of various medical schools. In 1958, the school was consolidated and located at Indianapolis with the exception of a basic medical science program, which remains on the Bloomington campus. In 1971, the school's programs were expanded by the addition of basic medical science programs at Evansville, Fort Wayne, Gary, Lafayette, Muncie, South Bend, and Terre Haute.

Type: public
2011 total enrollment: 1,298
Clinical facilities: Indiana University Health, Wishard Health Services, Indianapolis Veterans Affairs Hospital, Larue Carter Memorial Hospital

University Officials

President. . . . . Michael A. McRobbie, Ph.D.
Vice President and Chancellor (Indianapolis). Charles R. Bantz, Ph.D.

Medical School Administrative Staff

Dean. . . . . D. Craig Brater, M.D.
Executive Associate Dean for Administration,
   Operations, and Finance . . . . Timothy P. Brown (Interim)
Executive Associate Dean for Clinical Affairs. . . . . John F. Fitzgerald, M.D.
Executive Associate Dean for Educational Affairs . . . . Maryellen E. Gusic, M.D.
Executive Associate Dean for Faculty Affairs and
   Professional Development . . . . Stephen P. Bogdewic, Ph.D.
Executive Associate Dean for Research Affairs. David S. Wilkes, M.D.
Associate Dean for Admissions and Medical Student Affairs. . . . . James J. Brokaw, Ph.D.
Associate Dean for Bioethics . . . . Eric M. Meslin, Ph.D.
Associate Dean for Cancer Research. . . . . Patrick J. Loehrer, M.D.
Associate Dean for Clinical Effectiveness Research . . . . William M. Tierney, M.D.
Associate Dean for Clinical Research . . . . Rafat Abonour, M.D.
Associate Dean for Continuing Medical Education . . . . Alexander M. Djuricich, M.D.
Associate Dean for Development . . . . Elizabeth A. Elkas
Associate Dean for Diversity Affairs. . . . . George H. Rausch, Ed.D.
Associate Dean for Global Health. . . . . Robert M. Einterz, M.D.
Associate Dean for Graduate Medical Education . . . . Peter M. Nalin, M.D.
Associate Dean for Graduate Studies . . . . Patricia J. Gallagher, Ph.D.
Associate Dean for Indiana University Health Affairs. . . . . Eric S. Williams, M.D.
Associate Dean for Information Technology. . . . . Vincent J. Sheehan
Associate Dean for Primary Care . . . . John F. Fitzgerald, M.D.
Associate Dean for Research in Medical Education . . . . Debra K. Litzelman, M.D.
Associate Dean for Translational Research . . . . Anantha Shekhar, M.B.B.S., Ph.D.
Associate Dean of Undergraduate Medical Education . . . . Paula S. Wales, Ed.D. (Interim)
Associate Dean for VA Affairs. . . . . Vacant
Associate Dean for Wishard Affairs. . . . . Lisa E. Harris, M.D.
Assistant Deans for Diversity Affairs . . . . . Sheryl E. Allen, M.D., and Javier F. Sevilla-Martir, M.D.
Assistant Dean for Entreprenurial Research . . . . Mervin C. Yoder, Jr., M.D.
Assistant Deans for Faculty Affairs and Professional Development . . . . . Mary E. Dankoski, Ph.D.,
                            Randy R. Brutkiewicz, Ph.D., Megan M. Palmer, Ph.D.,
                            and Emily C. Walvoord, M.D.
Assistant Dean and Director, Medical Sciences
   Program (Bloomington) . . . . John B. Watkins III, Ph.D.
Assistant Dean and Director, IUSM-Evansville . . . . Steven G. Becker, M.D. (Interim)
Assistant Dean and Director, IUSM-Fort Wayne. . . . . Fen-Lei F. Chang, M.D., Ph.D.
Assistant Dean and Director, IUSM-Lafayette . . . . Gordon L. Coppoc, Ph.D., D.V.M.
Assistant Dean and Director, IUSM-Muncie. . . . . T. Stuart Walker, Ph.D.
Assistant Dean and Director, IUSM-Northwest. . . . . Patrick W. Bankston, Ph.D.
Assistant Dean and Director, IUSM-South Bend . . . . Rudolph M. Navari, M.D., Ph.D.
Assistant Dean and Director, IUSM-Terre Haute. . . . . Taihung Duong, Ph.D.
Director of Admissions. . . . . Karen A. Smartt
Director of Graduate Medical Education. . . . . Linda A. Bratcher

Department and Division or Section Chairs

Basic Sciences

Anatomy and Cell Biology .... Kathryn J. Jones, Ph.D.
Biochemistry and Molecular Biology.......................... Zhong-Yin Zhang, Ph.D.
Biostatistics .... Barry P. Katz, Ph.D.
Cellular and Integrative Physiology......................... Michael S. Sturek, Ph.D.
Medical and Molecular Genetics............................. Kenneth G. Cornetta, M.D.
Microbiology and Immunology............................... Stanley M. Spinola, M.D.
Pharmacology and Toxicology .... Michael R. Vasko, Ph.D.

Clinical Sciences

Anesthesia.. Robert G. Presson, Jr., M.D.
Dermatology .... Elliot J. Androphy, M.D.
Emergency Medicine .... Cherri D. Hobgood, M.D.
Family Medicine .... Kevin B. Gebke, M.D.
Medicine... David W. Crabb, M.D.
   Cardiology... Peng-Sheng Chen, M.D.
   Clinical Pharmacology .... David A. Flockhart, M.D., Ph.D.
   Endocrinology and Metabolism............................ Michael J. Econs, M.D.
   Gastroenterology and Hepatology...................... Naga P. Chalasani, M.B.B.S.
   General Internal Medicine and Geriatrics .... Greg A. Sachs, M.D.
   Hematology and Oncology...................... G. David Roodman, M.D., Ph.D.
   Infectious Diseases .... Byron E. Batteiger, M.D. (Interim)
   Nephrology .... Sharon M. Moe, M.D.
   Pulmonary and Critical Care Medicine .... Homer L. Twigg III, M.D.
   Rheumatology .... Steven T. Hugenberg, M.D. (Interim)
Neurological Surgery.................................... Nicholas M. Barbaro, M.D.
Neurology.. Robert M. Pascuzzi, M.D.
Obstetrics and Gynecology............................. Lee A. Learman, M.D., Ph.D.
Ophthalmology .... Louis B. Cantor, M.D.
Orthopaedic Surgery .... Randall T. Loder, M.D.
Otolaryngology-Head and Neck Surgery .... Richard T. Miyamoto, M.D.
Pathology and Laboratory Medicine .... John N. Eble, M.D.
Pediatrics .... D. Wade Clapp, M.D.
   Adolescent Health .... Vaughn I. Rickert, Psy.D.
   Cardiology... Randall L. Caldwell, M.D.
   Child Development .... John D. Rau, M.D.
   Developmental Pediatrics .... Abigail F. Klemsz, M.D. (Interim)
   Endocrinology and Diabetes............................ Erica A. Eugster, M.D.
   Gastroenterology .... Jean P. Molleston, M.D.
   General and Community Pediatrics...................... Stephen M. Downs, M.D.
   Health Services Research .... Stephen M. Downs, M.D.
   Hematology and Oncology...................... Robert J. Fallon, M.D., Ph.D.
   Infectious Diseases .... John C. Christenson, M.D.
   Neonatal and Perinatal Medicine .... David A. Ingram, Jr., M.D.
   Nephrology .... Sharon P. Andreoli, M.D.
   Pulmonary Disease .... Stephanie D. Davis, M.D.
   Rheumatology .... Suzanne L. Bowyer, M.D.
Physical Medicine and Rehabilitation .... Flora Hammond, M.D.
Psychiatry .... Alan D. Schmetzer, M.D. (Interim)
Public Health .... Eric R. Wright, Ph.D. (Interim)
Radiation Oncology..................................... Peter A. S. Johnstone, M.D.
Radiology and Imaging Sciences.......................... Valerie P. Jackson, M.D.
Surgery.. Robert J. Havlik, M.D. (Interim)
   Cardiothoracic Surgery..................... Mark W. Turrentine, M.D. (Interim)
   General Surgery............................ Don J. Selzer, M.D. (Interim)
   Pediatric Surgery .... Frederick J. Rescorla, M.D.
   Plastic Surgery .... John J. Coleman III, M.D.
   Transplant Surgery........................... A. Joseph Tector, M.D., Ph.D.
   Vascular Surgery................................... Michael C. Dalsing, M.D.
Urology... Michael O. Koch, M.D.

University of Iowa Roy J. and Lucille A. Carver College of Medicine
200 Medicine Administration Building
Iowa City, Iowa 52242-1101
319-335-8053 (admissions/student aff.); 319-384-4547 (dean's office);
319-335-8049 (fax-admissions/student aff.); 319-353-5617 (fax-dean's office)
Web site: www.medicine.uiowa.edu

The University of Iowa Roy J. and Lucille A. Carver College of Medicine originated as the Medical Department of the University of Iowa in 1850. In 1870, the medical department was moved from Keokuk to the campus at Iowa City and became known as the University of Iowa College of Medicine. In 2002, the Carver name was adopted in honor of a landmark gift to the college.

Type: public
2011 total enrollment: 586
Clinical facilities: University of Iowa Hospitals and Clinics, Veterans Affairs Medical Center (Iowa City); St. Luke's Hospital, Mercy Medical Center (Cedar Rapids); Genesis Medical Center (Davenport); Broadlawns Medical Center, Iowa Lutheran Hospital, Iowa Methodist Medical Center, Veterans Affairs Medical Center (Des Moines); Mercy Medical Center-North Iowa (Mason City); Mercy Medical Center-Sioux City; St. Luke's Regional Medical Center (Sioux City); Allen Memorial Hospital, Covenant Medical Center (Waterloo).

University Officials

President. . . . . Sally K. Mason
Executive Vice President and Provost . . . . P. Barry Butler
Senior Vice President and University Treasurer. . . . . Douglas K. True
Vice President for Research . . . . Jordan L. Cohen, Ph.D.
Vice President for Medical Affairs. . . . . Jean E. Robillard, M.D.

Medical School Administrative Staff

Dean. . . . . Paul B. Rothman, M.D.
Interim Executive Associate Dean. . . . . Donna L. Hammond, Ph.D.
Senior Associate Dean for Scientific Affairs. Michael A. Apicella, M.D.
Associate Dean, Student Affairs and Curriculum . . . . Christopher S. Cooper, M.D.
Associate Dean, Faculty Affairs and Development . . . . Lois J. Geist, M.D.
Associate Dean for Information Technology. . . . . Boyd M. Knosp
Associate Dean for Clinical & Translational Science . . . . Patricia L. Winokur, M.D.
Associate Dean, Cultural Affairs and Diversity . . . . Denise Martinez Adams, M.D. (Interim)
Assistant Dean, Student Affairs and Curriculum . . . . David P. Asprey, Ph.D.
Assistant Dean, Student Affairs and Curriculum . . . . Nancy S. Rosenthal, M.D.
Assistant Dean for Facilities Planning and Management . . . . James D. Henderson
Assistant Dean and Director, Office of Statewide
  Clinical Education Programs . . . . Roger D. Tracy
Associate Dean for Clinical Affairs and Executive
  Director, UI Physicians . . . . Craig H. Syrop, M.D.
Assistant Dean for Clinical Affairs and Associate
  Director, UI Physicians . . . . Daniel S. Fick, M.D.
Assistant Vice President for Health Policy. . . . . Stacey T. Cyphert, Ph.D.
Assistant Vice President of Finance and Assistant CFO, UI Health Care . . . . Mark J. Hingtgen

Department and Division or Section Chairs

Basic Sciences

Anatomy and Cell Biology . . . . John F. Engelhardt, Ph.D.
Biochemistry. . . . . Charles M. Brenner, Ph.D.
Microbiology. . . . . Patrick M. Schlievert, Ph.D.
Molecular Physiology and Biophysics . . . . Kevin P. Campbell, Ph.D.
Pharmacology . . . . Curt D. Sigmund, Ph.D.

Clinical Sciences

Anesthesia. . . . . Michael M. Todd, M.D.
Cardiothoracic Surgery . . . . Mark D. Iannettoni, M.D.
Dermatology. . . . . Janet A. Fairley, M.D.
Emergency Medicine . . . . Andrew Nugent, M.D. (Interim)
Family Medicine . . . . Paul A. James, M.D.
Internal Medicine . . . . Mark E. Anderson, M.D., Ph.D.

University of Iowa Roy J. and Lucille A. Carver College of Medicine: IOWA

Allergy and Immunology .... Zuhair K. Ballas, M.D.
Cardiovascular Diseases........................... Richard E. Kerber, M.D. (Interim)
Clinical Pharmacology .... William G. Haynes, M.B.Ch.B., M.D.
Endocrinology and Metabolism............................. William I. Sivitz, M.D.
Gastroenterology and Hepatology............................... David Elliott, M.D.
General Medicine, Clinical Epidemiology, and
    Health Services Research .... Peter Cram, M.D.
Hematology and Oncology...................... Steven R. Lentz, M.D., Ph.D.
Infectious Diseases...................................... Daniel Diekma, M.D.
Nephrology .... John B. Stokes III, M.D.
Pulmonary Diseases .... Joseph Zabner, M.D.
Neurology....................................... George Richerson, M.D., Ph.D.
Neurosurgery....................................... Matthew A. Howard III, M.D.
Obstetrics and Gynecology................................ Kimberly Leslie, M.D.
Ophthalmology and Visual Sciences........................... Keith Carter, M.D.
Orthopaedics and Rehabilitation .... Joseph A. Buckwalter, M.D.
Otolaryngology-Head and Neck Surgery...................... Bruce J. Gantz, M.D.
Pathology .... Michael B. Cohen, M.D.
Pediatrics .... Thomas D. Scholz, M.D. (Interim)
    Allergy and Pulmonary...................................... Paul B. McCray, M.D.
    Cardiology... Thomas Scholz, M.D.
    Child Psychology .... Lynn C. Richman, Ph.D.
    Critical Care.. Fred S. Lamb, M.D., Ph.D.
    Developmental and Behavioral Medicine .... Katherine Mathews, M.D.
    Endocrinology and Diabetes................................... Eva Tsalikian, M.D.
    Gastroenterology .... Warren P. Bishop, M.D.
    General Pediatrics and Adolescent Medicine .... Jerold C. Woodhead, M.D.
    Genetics.. Val C. Sheffield, M.D., Ph.D.
    Hematology, Oncology, and Rheumatology.................. Raymond Tannous, M.D.
    Infectious Diseases....................................... Charles Grose, M.D.
    Neonatology... Jeffrey Segar, M.D.
    Nephrology and Hypertension .... Patrick Brophy, M.D., Ph.D.
    Neurology .... Katherine D. Mathews, M.D.
    Nutrition/Metabolism....................... Thomas D. Scholz, M.D. (Interim)
    Specialized Child Health Services .... Debra Waldron, M.D.
Psychiatry .... James B. Fotash, M.D., M.P.H.
Radiation Oncology... John Buatti, M.D.
Radiology .... Laurie L. Fajardo, M.D.
    Nuclear Medicine...................... Michael M. Graham, M.D., Ph.D. (Div. Dir.)
Surgery.. Ronald J. Weigel, M.D., Ph.D.
    Gastrointestinal, Minimally Invasive and Bariatric.................... John Cromwell, M.D.
    Pediatric Surgery .... Joel Shilyansky, M.D.
    Plastic and Reconstructive Surgery .... W. Thomas Lawrence, M.D.
    Surgical Oncology and Endocrine Surgery..................... James R. Howe, V, M.D.
    Transplant Surgery.. Alan Reed, M.D.
    Trauma, Critical Care, and Burn Surgery .... Kent Choi, M.D.
    Vascular Surgery....................................... W. John Sharp, M.D.
Urology... Karl Kreder, M.D.

University of Kansas School of Medicine

3901 Rainbow Boulevard
Kansas City, Kansas 66160-7300
913-588-5200 (general information); 913-588-5287 (executive dean); 913-588-1412 (fax)
Web site: www.kumc.edu/som

The University of Kansas established a "preparatory medical course" in 1880, and began to offer a four-year medical curriculum in 1906. The school of medicine is part of the University of Kansas Medical Center, which began to develop its current site in Kansas City, Kansas, in 1924. In 1971, the school of medicine established a campus in Wichita, where a portion of each class receives its clinical training in the last two years. In 2011, the school of medicine established a 4-year campus in Salina.

Type: public
2011 total enrollment: 1,973
Clinical facilities: University of Kansas Hospital, Research Medical Center, Geary Community Hospital, St. Joseph Hospital, Wesley Hospital, Via Christi Hospital, Veteran Administration Centers (Kansas City, Missouri; Leavenworth; Topeka; Wichita).

University Officials

Chancellor . . . . Bernadette Gray-Little, Ph.D.
Executive Vice Chancellor . . . . Barbara F. Atkinson, M.D.
Chief of Staff. . . . . Shelley Gebar
Senior Vice Chancellor for Academic and Student Affairs . . . . Karen Miller, Ph.D.
Vice Chancellor for Academic Affairs . . . . Allen B. Rawitch, Ph.D.
Vice Chancellor for Administration . . . . Steffani Webb
Vice Chancellor for Research . . . . Paul Terranova, Ph.D.

Medical School Administrative Staff

Executive Dean . . . . Barbara F. Atkinson, M.D.
Vice Dean . . . . Vacant
Senior Associate Dean for Clinical Affairs . . . . Douglas A. Girod, M.D.
Senior Associate Dean for Finance . . . . Kimberly A. Meyer, Ph.D.
Senior Associate Dean for Medical Education . . . . Heidi S. Chumley, M.D.
Senior Associate Dean for Operations and Administration. . . . . Shelley Gebar
Senior Associate Dean for Research and Graduate Studies. . . . . Paul Terranova, Ph.D.
Associate Dean for Graduate Medical Education . . . . Terry Tsue, M.D.
Associate Dean for Student Affairs . . . . Mark Meyer, M.D.
Associate Dean for Cultural Enhancement and Diversity . . . . Josh Freeman, M.D. (Interim)
Associate Dean for Medical Graduate Studies . . . . Vacant
Associate Dean for Admissions . . . . Sandra J. McCurdy
Associate Dean for Continuing Medical Education . . . . Susan Pingleton, M.D.
Associate Dean for Medical Education . . . . Giulia A. Bonaminio, Ph.D.
Associate Dean for Academic Affairs. . . . . Robert Klein, Ph.D.

Department and Division or Section Chairs

Basic Sciences

Anatomy and Cell Biology . . . . Dale R. Abrahamson, Ph.D.
Biochemistry and Molecular Biology. . . . . Gerald M. Carlson, Ph.D.
Cancer Institute. . . . . Roy A. Jensen, M.D.
Health Policy and Management . . . . Glendon C. Cox, M.D.
History of Medicine. . . . . Christopher Crenner, M.D.
Microbiology, Molecular Genetics, and Immunology. . . . . Michael J. Parmely, Ph.D. (Interim)
Molecular and Integrative Physiology . . . . Paul D. Cheney, Ph.D.
Pathology and Laboratory Medicine . . . . Lowell Tilzer, M.D., Ph.D.
Pharmacology, Toxicology, and Therapeutics . . . . Gerald Carlson, Ph.D. (Interim)
Preventive Medicine. . . . . Edward F. Ellerbeck, M.D.

Clinical Sciences

Anesthesiology . . . . James D. Kindscher, M.D.
Family Medicine . . . . Joshua Freeman, M.D.
Medicine . . . . Steven Stites, M.D.
Neurology . . . . Richard Barohn, M.D.
Obstetrics and Gynecology . . . . Carl Weiner, M.D.
Ophthalmology . . . . John Sutphin, M.D.
Otolaryngology . . . . Douglas Girod, M.D.
Pediatrics . . . . Chet Johnson, M.D.
Physical Medicine and Rehabilitation . . . . Raj Mitra, M.D.
Psychiatry and Behavioral Sciences . . . . William Gabrielli, M.D., Ph.D.
Radiation Oncology . . . . Parvesh Kumar, M.D.
Radiology . . . . Stanton J. Rosenthal, M.D.
Surgery . . . . James Thomas, M.D.
   Neurological . . . . Paul Camarata, M.D.
   Orthopedic . . . . Bruce Toby, M.D.
   Plastic . . . . Richard A. Korentager, M.D.
   Urological . . . . Brantley Thrasher, M.D.

University of Kansas School of Medicine
Wichita Campus
1010 North Kansas
Wichita, Kansas 67214
316-261-2600 (dean's office)

Dean . . . . H. David Wilson, M.D.
Associate Dean, Academic and Student Affairs . . . . Garold Minns, M.D.
Associate Dean for Administration . . . . Christopher McCracken
Associate Dean for Graduate Medical Education . . . . Brad Poss, M.D.
Associate Dean for Faculty Development . . . . Anne Walling, M.D.
Associate Dean for Research . . . . Michele Mariscalco, M.D.
Associate Dean for Veterans Affairs . . . . Vacant

Department Chairs

Anesthesiology . . . . Robert McKay, M.D.
Family and Community Medicine . . . . Rick Kellerman, M.D.
Internal Medicine . . . . Jon P. Schrage, M.D.
Obstetrics and Gynecology . . . . Douglas Horbelt, M.D.
Pathology . . . . Thomas Kluzak, M.D.
Preventive Medicine and Public Health . . . . Ruth Wetta-Hall, Ph.D. (Interim)
Pediatrics . . . . Barry Bloom, M.D.
Psychiatry . . . . Russell Scheffer, M.D.
Radiology . . . . Charles McGuire, M.D.
Surgery . . . . Alex Ammar, M.D.

University of Kentucky College of Medicine

138 Leader Avenue
Lexington, Kentucky 40506-9983
859-323-5000; 859-323-6582 (dean's office); 859-323-2039 (fax)
Web site: www.mc.uky.edu/medicine

The College of Medicine opened in September, 1960. It is one of the units of the University of Kentucky A.B. Chandler Medical Center, which also includes the colleges of Dentistry, Health Sciences, Public Health, Nursing, and Pharmacy; the UK Chandler Hospital; Kentucky Clinic, with its off-site facilities; the Medical Center Library; and the University Student Health Service.

Type: public
2011 total enrollment: 445
Clinical facilities: Primary: UK Chandler Hospital, UK Good Samaritan Hospital, the Kentucky Clinic and its off-site facilities, The five Centers for Rural Health, The Markey Cancer Center, The Gill Heart Institute, and the Veterans Affairs Medical Center. **Additionally:** Appalachian Regional Medical Center, Central Baptist Hospital, Cardinal Hill Rehabilitiation Hospital, Eastern State Hospital, Samaritan Hospital, Shriner's Hospital, St. Claire Regional Medical Center, and Rockcastle Hospital and Respiratory Care Center, Georgetown Community Hospital and Harrison Memorial Hospital.

University Officials

President. . . . . Eli I. Capilouto, D.M.D.
Provost . . . . Kumble Subbaswamy, Ph.D.
Vice President for Research . . . . James W. Tracy, Ph.D.

Medical Center Campus Officials

Executive Vice President for Health Affairs. . . . . Michael Karpf, M.D.
Senior Vice President for Health Affairs and Chief Financial Officer . . . . Sergio Melgar
Vice President for Clinical Academic Affairs . . . . Frederick C. de Beer, M.D.
Vice President for Health Care Operations and
   Chief Clinical Officer . . . . Richard P. Lofgren, M.D.
Chief Medical Officer . . . . Paul DePriest, M.D.
Associate Vice President for Clinical Network Development. . . . . Joseph O. Claypool
Associate Vice President for Information Technology . . . . Tim Tarnowski
Associate Vice President for Medical Center Operations . . . . Murray Clark
Director of Strategic Marketing . . . . Bill Gombeski
Chief External Affairs Officer. . . . . Mark D. Birdwhistell
Chief Development Officer . . . . Vicky Myers
Associate Dean and Director, Medical Center Library . . . . Janet Stith

Medical School Administrative Staff

Dean. . . . . Frederick C. de Beer, M.D.
Executive Vice Dean . . . . Robert T. Means, M.D.
Senior Associate Dean for Basic Science Affairs. . . . . Vacant
Senior Associate Dean for Medical Education . . . . C. Darrell Jennings, Jr., M.D.
Senior Associate Dean for Research . . . . Alan Daugherty, Ph.D.
Senior Associate Dean for AHEC and Community Outreach . . . . Paul DePriest, M.D.
Associate Dean for AHEC and Community Outreach . . . . James C. Norton, Ph.D.
Associate Dean for Administration and Finance . . . . Vacant
Associate Dean for Admissions and Institutional Advancement . . . . Carol L. Elam, Ed.D.
Associate Dean for Clinical Affairs . . . . Paul DePriest, M.D.
Associate Dean for Faculty Advancement . . . . Mary Vore, Ph.D.
Associate Dean for Student Affairs . . . . Charles H. Griffith, M.D.
Associate Dean for Veterans Affairs . . . . Robert T. Means, M.D.
Assistant Dean for Student Affairs. . . . . Todd Cheever, M.D.
Senior Assistant Dean of Curriculum . . . . Rosemarie Conigliaro, M.D.
Assistant Dean for Student Assessment and Program Evaluation . . . . Terry D. Stratton, Ph.D.
Assistant Dean for Graduate Medical Education . . . . Susan M. McDowell, M.D.
Assistant Dean for Administration. . . . . Sandra Jaros
Assistant Dean for Morehead Regional Site. . . . . Anthony D. Weaver, M.D.
Assistant Dean for Purchase Regional Site. . . . . Richard Crouch, M.D.
Assistant Dean for Finance. . . . . Patricia Polly (Acting)
Assistant Dean for Organizational Management . . . . Christy Anderson (Acting)
Director for Clinical Contracting . . . . Jennifer Collins
Director of Finance . . . . Patricia Polly
Director of Development . . . . Vacant
Director of Communications . . . . Seth Flynn

Institute/Center Directors

Lucille P. Markey Cancer Center .... B. Mark Evers, M.D.
MRI and Spectroscopy Center .... Charles Smith, M.D.
Linda and Jack Gill Heart Institute........................... David J. Moliterno, M.D.
Center for the Advancement of Women's Health .... Leslie Crofford, M.D.
Multidisciplinary Research Center for Drug and Alcohol Abuse......... Sharon Walsh, Ph.D.
Sanders-Brown Center on Aging............................... Linda Van Eldik, Ph.D.
Spinal Cord and Brain Injury Research Center .... Edward D. Hall, Ph.D.
University of Kentucky Center for Rural Health, Hazard .... Frances Feltner
University of Kentucky Center for Rural Health, Madisonville .... Natalie Begley
University of Kentucky Center for Rural Health, Morehead......... Gregory Bausch, Pharm.D.
University of Kentucky Center for Rural Health, Murray.............. Richard Crouch, M.D.
University of Kentucky Center for Rural Health, Danville .... Rachael Fitz Gerald, Ph.D.
Dr. Sibu and Becky Saha Cardiovascular Research Center .... Alan Daugherty, Ph.D.

Department and Division or Section Chairs
Basic Sciences

Anatomy and Neurobiology..................................... Don M. Gash, Ph.D.
Behavioral Science.. Carl G. Leukefeld, D.S.W.
Graduate Center for Nutritional Sciences............................ Lisa Cassis, Ph.D.
Graduate Center for Toxicology................................. Mary Vore, Ph.D.
Molecular and Cellular Biochemistry .... Sidney Whiteheart, Ph.D. (Interim)
Microbiology, Immunology, and Molecular Genetics................. Alan M. Kaplan, Ph.D.
Molecular and Biomedical Pharmacology .... Philip S. Landfield, Ph.D.
Physiology.. Michael B. Reid, Ph.D.

Clinical Sciences

Anesthesiology... Edwin A. Bowe, M.D.
Emergency Medicine...................................... Roger L. Humphries, M.D.
Family and Community Medicine....................... Kevin Pearce, M.D. (Interim)
Internal Medicine .... Frederick C. deBeer, M.D.
   Allergy and Immunology .... Beth Miller, M.D.
   Cardiovascular Medicine.................................. David Moliterno, M.D.
   Digestive Diseases and Nutrition .... Willem de Villiers, M.D.
   Endocrinology and Molecular Medicine .... Lisa Tannock, M.D.
   General Medicine and Geriatrics............................. T. Shawn Caudill, M.D.
   Hematology, and Blood and Marrow Transplantation .... Kevin McDonagh, M.D.
   Infectious Diseases .... Ardis Hoven, M.D. (Interim)
   Medical Oncology .... John Rineheart, M.D.
   Nephrology, Bone and Mineral Metabolism.............. Hartmut H. Malluche, M.D.
   Pulmonary Critical Care and Sleep Medicine.................... James McCormick, M.D.
   Rheumatology and Women's Health.......................... Leslie Crofford, M.D.
Neurology... Joseph R. Berger, M.D.
Neurosurgery... Phillip A. Tibbs, M.D.
Obstetrics and Gynecology................................. Wendy Hansen, M.D.
Ophthalmology and Visual Science........................... Andrew Pearson, M.D.
Orthopaedic Surgery .... Darren L. Johnson, M.D.
Otolaryngology-Head and Neck Surgery...................... Raleigh O. Jones, M.D.
Pathology and Laboratory Medicine.............................. Paul Bachner, M.D.
Pediatrics .... Carmel Wallace, M.D. (Interim)
Physical Medicine and Rehabilitation .... Gerald V. Klim, D.O.
Psychiatry... Lon R. Hays, M.D.
Radiation Medicine .... Marcus E. Randall, M.D.
Radiology.. M. Elizabeth Oates, M.D.
Surgery... Joseph B. Zwischenberger, M.D.
   Cardiothoracic Surgery...................................... Mark Plunkett, M.D.
   Community .... Joseph B. Zwischenberger, M.D.
   Dermatology .... Joseph B. Zwischenberger, M.D.
   General and Vascular Surgery................................ Patrick McGrath, M.D.
   Otolaryngology-Head and Neck Surgery .... Raleigh O. Jones, M.D.
   Pediatric Surgery .... Joseph Iocono, M.D.
   Plastic and Reconstructive Surgery .... Henry C. Vasconez, M.D.
   Transplantation .... Roberto Gedaly, M.D.
   Urology.. Stephen E. Strup, M.D.

University of Louisville School of Medicine

Health Sciences Center
Abell Administration Center, 323 East Chestnut Street
Louisville, Kentucky 40202
502-852-1499 (dean's office); 502-852-1484 (fax); 502-852-5555 (general information)
Web site: www.louisville.edu/medschool

Medical education in Louisville began on February 2, 1833, with the granting of a charter for the Louisville Medical Institute. The medical school is part of the health sciences center.

Type: public
2011 total enrollment: 644
Clinical facilities: University of Louisville Hospital, Kosair Children's Hospital, VA Medical Center, James Graham Brown Cancer Center. **Other affiliates:** The Bingham Child Guidance Clinic Inc., Central State Hospital, Norton Audubon Hospital, Frazier Rehabilitation Center, Jewish Hospital, Norton Hospital, Portland Family Health Center, Trover Campus (Madisonville).

University Officials

President. . . . . James R. Ramsey, Ph.D.
Executive Vice President for Health Affairs. . . . . David L. Dunn, M.D., Ph.D.

Medical School Administrative Staff

Dean. . . . . Edward C. Halperin, M.D.
Vice Dean for Academic Affairs and Associate Vice President . . . . David L. Wiegman, Ph.D.
Vice Dean for Clinical Affairs. . . . . Richard E. Goldstein, M.D.
Vice Dean for Research . . . . Russell A. Prough, Ph.D.
Senior Associate Dean for Student and Academic Affairs. . . . . Toni M. Ganzel, M.D.
Associate Dean for Academic Affairs. . . . . V. Faye Jones, M.D.
Associate Dean for Admissions. . . . . Stephen Wheeler, M.D.
Associate Dean for Faculty Affairs. . . . . Tracy D. Eells, Ph.D.
Associate Dean for Graduate Medical Education . . . . John L. Roberts, M.D.
Associate Dean for Medical Education . . . . Ruth Greenberg, Ph.D.
Associate Dean, Postdoctoral Affairs . . . . Thomas E. Geoghegan, Ph.D.
Associate Dean for Research. . . . . Peter Rowell, Ph.D.
Associate Dean for Trover Campus. . . . . William J. Crump, M.D.

Institute/Center Directors

Center for Autism . . . . Joseph Hersh, M.D., and Allan Josephson, M.D.
Center for Health Hazard Preparedness . . . Ronald M. Atlas, Ph.D., and Richard D. Clover, M.D.
Center for Environmental Genomics and Integrative Biology. . . . . Kenneth S. Ramos, Ph.D.
Center for Genetics and Molecular Medicine . . . . Ronald Gregg, Ph.D.
Depression Center. . . . . Jesse Wright, M.D.
Diabetes and Obesity Center . . . . Aruni Bhatnagar, Ph.D.
Gheens Center on Aging . . . . Eugenia Wang, Ph.D.
Institute for Cellular Therapeutics . . . . Suzanne T. Ildstad, M.D.
Institute for Molecular Cardiology . . . . Roberto Bolli, M.D.
James Graham Brown Cancer Center . . . . Donald M. Miller, M.D., Ph.D.
Kentucky Spinal Cord Injury Research Center. . . . . Scott R. Whittemore, Ph.D.
Price Institute for Surgical Research. . . . . Susan Galandiuk, M.D.
University of Louisville Birth Defects Center. . . . . Robert M. Greene, Ph.D.
Cardiovascular Innovation Institute. . . . . Stuart Williams, Ph.D.

Department and Division or Section Chairs
Basic Sciences

Anatomical Sciences and Neurobiology. . . . . Fred J. Roisen, Ph.D.
Biochemistry and Molecular Biology. . . . . Ronald G. Gregg, Ph.D.
Microbiology and Immunology. . . . . Robert D. Stout, Ph.D.
Pathology and Laboratory Medicine . . . . Ronald J. Elin, M.D., Ph.D.
Pharmacology and Toxicology . . . . David W. Hein, Ph.D.
Physiology and Biophysics . . . . Irving G. Joshua, Ph.D.

Clinical Sciences

Anesthesiology and Perioperative Medicine. Mark Boswell, M.D.
Emergency Medicine . . . . Daniel F. Danzl, M.D.
Family and Geriatric Medicine . . . . James G. O'Brien, M.D.
Medicine. . . . . Jesse Roman, M.D.
  Cardiovascular Medicine. . . . . Roberto Bolli, M.D.
  Dermatology . . . . Jeffrey P. Callen, M.D.

Endocrinology and Metabolism. . . . . Stephen J. Winters, M.D.
Gastroenterology, Hepatology, and Nutrition. . . . . Kristine Krueger, M.D.
General Internal Medicine, Palliative Medicine, and Medical Education. . . . . Ann Shaw, M.D.
Infectious Diseases . . . . Julio A. Ramirez, M.D.
Medical Oncology and Hematology. . . . . Donald M. Miller, M.D., Ph.D.
Nephrology . . . . Eleanor Lederer, M.D.
Pulmonary, Critical Care, and Sleep Disorders. . . . . Rodney Folz, M.D., Ph.D.
Rheumatology . . . . Michael J. Edwards, M.D. (Acting)
Neurological Surgery. . . . . Jonathan Hodes, M.D.
Neurology. . . . . Robert P. Friedland, M.D.
Obstetrics, Gynecology, and Women's Health . . . . Sharmila Makhija, M.D.
Endocrinology. . . . . Steven T. Nakajima, M.D.
General Gynecology. . . . . James Shwayder, M.D.
General Obstetrics and Gynecology. Margarita Terrassa, M.D.
Family Planning and Outpatient Clinic Director . . . . Elaine Stauble, M.D.
Maternal and Fetal Medicine . . . . Jeffrey King, M.D.
Pediatric and Adolescent Gynecology . . . . Paige Hertweck, M.D.
Oncology. . . . . Lynn Parker, M.D.
Urogynecology. . . . . Susan B. Tate, M.D.
Ophthalmology and Visual Sciences . . . . Henry J. Kaplan, M.D.
Orthopedic Surgery. . . . . Craig Roberts, M.D.
Pediatrics . . . . Gerard P. Rabalais, M.D.
Adolescent and Rheumatology . . . . Kenneth N. Schikler, M.D.
Allergy and Immunology . . . . James L. Sublett, M.D.
Cardiology. . . . . Christopher L. Johnsrude, M.D. (Acting)
Child Behavior and Evaluation and Genetics. . . . . Joseph H. Hersh, M.D.
Critical Care. . . . . Vicki L. Montgomery, M.D.
Emergency Pediatrics . . . . Ronald I. Paul, M.D.
Endocrinology . . . . Michael Foster, M.D. (Acting)
Forensic Medicine . . . . Melissa L. Currie, M.D.
Gastroenterology . . . . Thomas C. Stephen, M.D.
General Inpatient Medicine . . . . Jeffrey Grill, M.D.
General Pediatrics . . . . Salvatore J. Bertolone, M.D.
Hematology and Oncology . . . . Salvatore J. Bertolone, M.D.
Infectious Diseases . . . . Gary Marshall, M.D.
International Pediatrics. . . . . George Rodgers, M.D., Ph.D.
Neonatology. . . . . David H. Adamkin, M.D.
Nephrology . . . . Salvatore J. Bertolone, M.D. (Acting)
Pathology. . . . . Robert F. Debski, M.D.
Pulmonary and Cystic Fibrosis. . . . . Nemr S. Eid, M.D.
Sleep Medicine. . . . . Vincent McCarthy, M.D.
Psychiatry and Behavioral Sciences . . . . Allan Tasman, M.D.
Addictions Psychiatry . . . . Bill Barcley, M.D.
Adult Psychiatry . . . . David A. Casey, M.D.
Children, Adolescent & Family Psychiatry . . . . Allan M. Josephson, M.D.
Consultation/Liaison (Psychosomatic) Psychiatry. . . . . Robert Frierson, M.D.
Emergency Psychiatry. . . . . Christina Terrell, M.D.
Geriatric Psychiatry. . . . . David Casey, M.D.
Memory Disorders . . . . Ben Schoenbachler, M.D.
Mood Disorders . . . . Jesse Wright, M.D., Ph.D.
Women's Mental Health. . . . . Joyce Spurgeon, M.D.
Radiation Oncology. . . . . Shiao Woo, M.D.
Radiology . . . . Gregory C. Postel, M.D.
Surgery . . . . Kelly M. McMasters, M.D., Ph.D.
Colon-Rectal Surgery . . . . Susan Galandiuk, M.D.
Communicative Disorders. . . . . David Cunningham, Ph.D.
Endoscopy . . . . Gary C. Vitale, M.D.
General . . . . J. David Richardson, M.D.
Oncology. . . . . Robert C. Martin, M.D.
Otolaryngology. . . . . Jeffrey M. Bumpous, M.D.
Pediatric . . . . Mary E. Fallat, M.D.
Plastic and Reconstructive. . . . . Bradon Wilhelmi, M.D.
Thoracic and Cardiovascular. . . . . Mark Slaughter, M.D.
Transplant . . . . Michael Marvin, M.D.
Vascular . . . . Charles Ross, M.D.
Urology. . . . . Murali Ankem, M.D.

Louisiana State University Health Sciences Center
School of Medicine in New Orleans
2020 Gravier Street
New Orleans, Louisiana 70112-2822
504-568-4007 (dean's office); 504-568-4008 (fax)
Web site: www.medschool.lsuhsc.edu

The Louisiana State University School of Medicine in New Orleans was established on October 1, 1931. The main campus of the parent university, Louisiana State University, is located in Baton Rouge. The school of medicine is one of six professional schools in the Louisiana State University Health Sciences Center.

Type: public
2011 total enrollment: 766
Clinical facilities: Clinical facilities: LSU Hospitals: LSU Interim Public Hospital; Earl K. Long Hospital (Baton Rouge); University Medical Center (Lafeyette); LSU-Bogalusa; LSU-Lake Charles; LSU-Chabert; Children's Hospital; Touro Infirmary; Oschner Foundation Hospital; Oschner-Kenner; Oschner-Baptist; East Jefferson General Hospital; West Jefferson Medical Center; Our Lady of the Lake Hospital; Baton Rouge General Hospital; Women's Hospital (Baton Rouge); Lake Charles Memorial Hospital

University Officials

President of University System and Board Secretary. . . . . John V. Lombardi, Ph.D.
Chancellor of LSU Health Science Center . . . . Larry H. Hollier, M.D.
Vice Chancellor for Academic Affairs . . . . Joseph M. Moerschbaecher III, Ph.D.
Vice Chancellor for Administration and Finance. Ronnie E. Smith
Director, Office for Research . . . . Kenneth E. Kratz, Ph.D.
Director of Information Services. . . . . Leslie L. Capo
Vice Chancellor for Clinical Affairs. . . . . Frank Opelka, M.D.
Associate Vice Chancellor for Academic and
  Multicultural Affairs . . . . Derek J. Rovaris, Sr., Ph.D.
Associate Vice Chancellor for Property and Facilities Management . . . . John Ball
Assistant Vice Chancellor for Administration and Finance . . . . Terry Ullrich
Assistant Vice Chancellor for Information Technology . . . . Bettina Owens
Vice Chancellor for Administrative and Community Affairs . . . . Ronald Gardner
Vivarium Director . . . . Reynaldo R. Gonzalez, D.V.M.

Medical School Administrative Staff

Dean. . . . . Steve Nelson, M.D.
Associate Dean for Academic Affairs. . . . . Charles Hilton, M.D.
Associate Dean for Alumni Affairs and Development. . . . . Cathi Fontenot, M.D.
Associate Dean for Community and Minority Health Education. . . . . Edward G. Helm, M.D.
Associate Dean for Faculty and Institutional Affairs . . . . Janis G. Letourneau, M.D.
Associate Dean for Finance . . . . Keith G. Schroth
Associate Dean for Health Quality and Patient Safety . . . . Dwayne Thomas, M.D.
Associate Dean for Student Affairs and Records . . . . Joseph Delcarpio, Ph.D.
Associate Dean for Clinical Affairs . . . . Vacant
Associate Dean for Admissions . . . . Samuel G. McClugage, Ph.D.
Associate Dean for Research. . . . . Wayne Backes, Ph.D.
Assistant Dean for Student Affairs. . . . . Fred Lopez, M.D.
Assistant Dean for Undergraduate Education . . . . Richard DiCarlo, M.D.
Director of Basic Science Curriculum . . . . Michael G. Levitzky, Ph.D.
Director of Clinical Science Curriculum . . . . Robin English, M.D.
Director of Research . . . . Jean Jacob, Ph.D.
Director of Faculty Development . . . . Paula Gregory, Ph.D.
Director of Rural Education. . . . . Kim E. LeBlanc, M.D., Ph.D.
Director of Community Health Clinics . . . . Mary T. Coleman, M.D., Ph.D.

Department and Division or Section Chairs

Basic Sciences

Biochemistry and Molecular Biology. . . . . Arthur Haas, Ph.D.
Genetics . . . . Vacant
Cell Biology and Anatomy . . . . Samuel G. McClugage, Ph.D.
Microbiology, Immunology, and Parasitology . . . . Alistair Ramsay, Ph.D.

Pharmacology and Experimental Therapeutics .... Kurt Varner, Ph.D.
Physiology .... Patricia E. Molina, M.D., Ph.D.

Clinical Sciences

Anesthesiology.. Alan D. Kaye, M.D., Ph.D.
Dermatology .... Lee T. Nesbitt, Jr., M.D.
Family Medicine .... Kim E. LeBlanc, M.D., Ph.D.
Medicine.. Charles V. Sanders, M.D.
  Allergy and Clinical Immunology .... Prem Kumar, M.D.
  Cardiology.. Frank Smart, M.D.
  Comprehensive Medicine..................................... David Borne, M.D.
  Emergency Medicine .... Keith W. Van Meter, M.D.
  Endocrinology and Metabolism............................... William T. Cefalu, M.D.
  Gastroenterology .... Daniel Raines, M.D. (Interim)
  Geriatric Medicine .... Charles A. Cefalu, M.D.
  Hematology and Oncology................................... John Cole, M.D.
  Hospital Medicine .... John R. Amoss, M.D.
  Infectious Diseases .... David H. Martin, M.D.
  Nephrology .... Efrain Reisin, M.D.
  Physical Medicine and Rehabilitation .... Gary Glynn, M.D.
  Pulmonary and Critical Care Medicine .... Judd E. Shellito, M.D.
  Rheumatology .... Luis R. Espinoza, M.D.
Neurology... John D. England, M.D.
Neurosurgery.. Frank Culicchia, M.D.
Obstetrics and Gynecology................................... Amy Young, M.D.
  General Obstetrics and Gynecology......................... Martha Brewer, M.D.
  Gynecologic Oncology.................................... Danny Barnhill, M.D.
  Maternal and Fetal Medicine .... Joseph M. Miller, M.D.
  Reproductive Endocrinology............................... Richard Dickey, M.D.
  Urogynecology.. Ralph Chesson, M.D.
Ophthalmology... Jayne Weiss, M.D.
Orthopaedics.. Andrew King, M.D.
Otolaryngology-Head and Neck Surgery .... Daniel Nuss, M.D.
  Kresge Hearing Research Laboratory........................... Vacant
Pathology .... Richard Vander Heide, M.D., Ph.D.
Pediatrics .... Ricardo U. Sorensen, M.D.
  Allergy and Immunology .... Ken Paris, M.D., M.P.H. (Interim)
  Ambulatory Pediatrics.................................. Suzanne LeFevre, M.D.
  Cardiology.. Robert J. Ascuitto, M.D.
  Clinical Genetics .... Yves Lacassie, M.D.
  Critical Care.. Bonnie C. Desselle, M.D.
  Developmental and Behavioral Pediatrics .... Joy D. Osofsky, Ph.D.
  Emergency Medicine .... Raghubir Mangat, M.D.
  Endocrinology, Diabetes, and Metabolic Disorders............... Stuart Chalew, M.D.
  Forensics .... Jamie Jackson, M.D.
  Gastroenterology and Nutrition .... Paul E. Hyman, M.D.
  Hematology and Oncology.................................. Lolie C. Yu, M.D.
  Hospitalists.. George Hescock, M.D.
  Infectious Diseases .... Rodolfo Begue, M.D.
  Neonatology and Perinatology .... Brian Barkemeyer, M.D.
  Nephrology .... Matti Vehaskari, M.D., Ph.D.
  Public Health.. Susan Berry, M.D.
  Rheumatology .... Abraham Gedalia, M.D.
Psychiatry .... Howard J. Osofsky, M.D., Ph.D.
  Adult Psychology .... Mark H. Townsend, M.D.
  Child Psychiatry .... Martin J. Drell, M.D.
  Psychology.. Phillip T. Griffin, Ph.D.
  Social Work .... Michelle M. Many, M.S.W., L.C.S.W.
Radiology .... Leonard R. Bok, M.D., M.B.A., J.D.
Surgery .... Robert C. Batson, M.D.
  Peripheral Vascular Surgery .... Robert C. Batson, M.D.
  Plastic Surgery .... Charles Dupin, M.D.
  Surgical Oncology .... Eugene A. Woltering, M.D.
  Thoracic Surgery .... William Risher, M.D.
  Trauma/Critical Care................................... John Hunt, M.D.
Urology.. J. Chris Winters, M.D.

Louisiana State University School of Medicine at Shreveport
P.O. Box 33932
Shreveport, Louisiana 71130-3932
318-675-5000; 318-675-5241 (dean's office); 318-675-5244 (fax)
Web site: www.lsuhscshreveport.edu

Established in 1965 by acts of the Louisiana legislature, the school of medicine in Shreveport graduated its first class of students in 1973. In 1975, the school of medicine complex was completed, and a class enrollment of 100 students per year was approved. The medical school is part of the Louisiana State University Health Sciences Center at Shreveport.

Type: public
2011 total enrollment: 439
Clinical facilities: (Shreveport) - Louisiana State University Hospital-Shreveport, E.A. Conway Medical Center (Monroe), Veterans Administration Medical Center, Schumpert Medical Center, Shriners Hospitals for Children-Shreveport, Willis-Knighton Health System, Northwest Development Center (Bossier City), Huey P. Long Medical Center (Pineville).

University Officials

President of the University System and Board Secretary. . . . . John V. Lombardi, Ph.D.
Chancellor . . . . Robert A. Barish, M.D.
Chief Financial Officer. . . . . Sheila Faour
Vice Chancellor for Clinical Affairs. . . . . Hugh E. Mighty, M.D.
Assistant Vice Chancellor for Information Technology . . . . Lee Bairnsfather, Ph.D.
Assistant Vice Chancellor for Graduate Medical Education . . . . Donnie F. Aultman, M.D.
Vice Chancellor for Business Administration. . . . . John Dailey, J.D.

Medical School Administrative Staff

Dean. . . . . Andrew L. Chesson, Jr., M.D.
Senior Associate Dean and Chief Medical Officer . . . . Kevin Sittig, M.D.
Associate Dean for Academic Affairs. . . . . Jane M. Eggerstedt, M.D.
Assistant Dean for Student Admissions . . . . F. Scott Kennedy, Ph.D.
Assistant Dean for Student Affairs. . . . . Mark Platt, Ph.D.
Assistant Dean for VA Medical Center . . . . Vacant
Hospital Administrator. . . . . Joseph M. Miciotto
Executive Director of Communications and Public Affairs. . . . . Sally Croom
Director of Public and Government Relations. . . . . Mimi Hedgcock
In-house Counsel. . . . . Susan Armstrong
Coordinator of Legal Affairs. . . . . Carol Peterson
Director, Arthritis Center of Excellence . . . . Seth M. Berney, M.D.
Acting Director, Cancer Center of Excellence. . . . . Glenn Mills, M.D.
Assistant Dean for Educational Program Development . . . . Vacant

Department and Division or Section Chairs

Basic Sciences

Biochemistry and Molecular Biology. . . . . Robert E. Rhoads, Ph.D.
Bioinformatics and Computational Biology. . . . . Lee Bairnsfather, Ph.D.
Cellular Biology and Anatomy . . . . Wm. G. Mayhan, Ph.D.
Medical Library Science. . . . . Marianne L. Comegys
Microbiology and Immunology. . . . . Dennis J. O'Callaghan, Ph.D.
Molecular and Cellular Physiology . . . . D. Neil Granger, Ph.D.
Pharmacology, Toxicology, and Neuroscience. . . . . Nicholas E. Goeders, Ph.D.

Clinical Sciences

Anesthesiology. . . . . Ashok Rao, M.D.
Emergency Medicine . . . . Thomas C. Arnold, M.D.
  Toxicology. . . . . Thomas C. Arnold, M.D.
Family Medicine and Comprehensive Care . . . . Michael Harper, M.D. (Acting)

Medicine . . . . Steven Levine, M.D. (Acting)
  Cardiology . . . . Pratap C. Reddy, M.D.
  Dermatology . . . . Vacant
  Endocrinology and Metabolic Disease . . . . David Scarborough, M.D.
  Gastroenterology . . . . Paul Jordan, M.D.
  General Medicine . . . . Gunjan Kahlon, M.D. (Acting)
  Hematology . . . . Glen Mills, M.D.
  Infectious Diseases . . . . John King, M.D.
  Nephrology . . . . Kenneth D. Abreo, M.D.
  Pulmonary and Critical Care . . . . D. Keith Payne, M.D.
  Rheumatology . . . . Seth M. Berney, M.D.
Neurology . . . . Robert Schwendimann, M.D. (Acting)
Neurosurgery . . . . Anil Nanda, M.D.
Obstetrics and Gynecology . . . . Lynn Groome, M.D.
Ophthalmology . . . . Donald E. Texada, M.D. (Acting)
Orthopaedic Surgery . . . . John Marymont, M.D.
Oral and Maxillofacial Surgery . . . . G. E. Ghali, M.D., D.D.S.
Otolaryngology and Head and Neck Surgery . . . . Cherie-Ann Nathan, M.D.
Pathology . . . . Stephen M. Bonsib, M.D.
Pediatrics . . . . Joseph A. Bocchini, M.D.
  Allergy and Immunology . . . . Sami L. Bahna, M.D.
  Cardiology . . . . Ernest Kiel, M.D.
  Clinical Pharmacology . . . . John T. Wilson, M.D.
  Endocrinology . . . . Robert McVie, M.D.
  Gastroenterology . . . . John Herbst, M.D.
  General Pediatrics . . . . Steven Bienvenu, M.D.
  Hematology and Oncology . . . . Majed A. Jeroudi, M.D.
  Infectious Diseases . . . . Joseph A. Bocchini, M.D.
  Neonatology . . . . Winston Koo, M.D.
  Nephrology . . . . Kenneth D. Abreo, M.D.
  Neurology . . . . Arun Kalra, M.D.
  Pulmonary . . . . Kimberly L. Jones, M.D.
Psychiatry . . . . Rita Horton, M.D. (Acting)
Radiology . . . . Horacio R. D'Agostino, M.D.
Surgery . . . . Benjamin Li, M.D.
  Burn* . . . . Kevin M. Sittig, M.D.
  Cardiothoracic* . . . . Mary Mancini, M.D., Ph.D.
  Oncology* . . . . Quyen Chu, M.D.
  Pediatric* . . . . Kevin Boykin, M.D. (Acting)
  Plastic* . . . . Mary Kim, M.D.
  Transplantation* . . . . Gazi B. Zibari, M.D.
  Trauma* . . . . Asser Youssef, M.D.
Urology . . . . Dennis D. Venable, M.D.

*Specialty without organizational autonomy.

Tulane University School of Medicine

1430 Tulane Avenue
New Orleans, Louisiana 70112
504-988-5462 (dean's office); 504-988-2945 (fax)
Web site: www.som.tulane.edu

Founded in 1834 as the Medical College of Louisiana, the school of medicine was incorporated into the University of Louisiana at its establishment in 1847. It has been called Tulane University since 1884. The medical school is part of the Tulane Health Sciences Center.

Type: private
2011 total enrollment: 709
Clinical facilities: Tulane University Hospital and Clinic; Tulane Lakeside Hospital; Baton Rouge General Hospital; Children's Hospital; Dermatopathology Association; East Jefferson General Hospital; East Louisiana Mental Health System; Huey P. Long Regional Medical Center Hospital; Jefferson Parish Health Service Authority; Kindred Hospital; Louisiana Heart Hospital; Lady of the Lake Hospital; Lakeview Regional Medical Center; Medical Center of Louisiana at New Orleans; MD Anderson; Ochsner Hospital; OSHA; Southeast Louisiana; Texas Heart; Touro Infirmary; University of North Carolina; Veterans Administration at Alexandria, Biloxi, Baton Rouge; West Jefferson Medical Center.

University Officials

President. . . . . Scott S. Cowen, D.B.A.
Senior Vice President. . . . . Benjamin P. Sachs, M.B., B.S., D.P.H.
Director of Continuing Education for Health Sciences . . . . Melinda A. Epperson, M.Ed.
Librarian for Health Sciences. . . . . Neville Prendergast

Medical School Administrative Staff

Dean. . . . . Benjamin P. Sachs, M.B., B.S., D.P.H.
Vice President for Health Services Systems and Vice Dean. . . . . Mary W. Brown, M.B.A.
Executive Vice Dean . . . . L. Lee Hamm, M.D.
Vice Dean for Academic Affairs . . . . N. Kevin Krane, M.D.
Vice Dean for Community Affairs and Health
    Care Policy . . . . Karen B. DeSalvo, M.D., M.P.H., M.Sc.
Senior Associate Dean for Admissions and Student Affairs. . . . . Marc J. Kahn, M.D.
Associate Dean for Admissions . . . . Barbara S. Beckman, Ph.D.
Associate Dean for Clinical Research . . . . Roy Weiner, M.D.
Associate Dean for Graduate Medical Education. Jeffrey Wiese, M.D.
Assistant Dean for Graduate Studies in Biomedical Sciences . . . . Robert F. Garry, Jr., Ph.D.
Assistant Dean for Lakeside Affairs. . . . . Gabriella Pridjian, M.D.
Assistant Dean, M.D./M.P.H. Combined Degree Program . . . . Marie A. Krousel-Wood, M.D.
Assistant Dean for Program Review and Strategic Analysis . . . . Susan K. Pollack, M.S.
Assistant Dean for Student Affairs. . . . . Ernest Sneed, M.D.

Tulane University School of Medicine: LOUISIANA

Department and Division or Section Chairs

Basic Sciences

Biochemistry . . . . Jim D. Karam, Ph.D.
Microbiology and Immunology. . . . . John D. Clements, Ph.D.
Pharmacology . . . . David Busija, Ph.D.
Physiology. . . . . Luis Gabriel Navar, Ph.D.
Structural and Cellular Biology. . . . . Steven M. Hill, Ph.D.

Clinical Sciences

Anesthesiology. . . . . Frank Rosinia, M.D.
Dermatology . . . . Erin Boh, M.D., Ph.D.
Family and Community Medicine . . . . Edwin Dennard, M.D. (Interim)
Medicine. . . . . L. Lee Hamm, M.D.
   Clinical Immunology, Allergy, and Rheumatology . . . . Laurianne G. Wild, M.D.
   Endocrinology . . . . Vivian A. Fonseca, M.D.
   Gastroenterology and Hepatology . . . . Luis Balart, M.D.
   General Internal Medicine and Geriatrics . . . . Karen B. DeSalvo, M.D.
   Hematology and Medical Oncology. . . . . Cindy A. Leissinger, M.D.
   Infectious Diseases . . . . David M. Mushatt, M.D.
   Nephrology . . . . Eric Simon, M.D.
   Pulmonary Diseases, Critical Care, and Environmental Medicine . . . . . . Joseph A. Lasky, M.D.
Heart and Vascular Institute. . . . . Karen B. DeSalvo, M.D.
Neurosurgery. . . . . Roger Smith, M.D.
Obstetrics and Gynecology. . . . . Gabriella Pridjian, M.D.
Ophthalmology . . . . Delmar R. Caldwell, M.D.
Orthopedics . . . . Raoul P. Rodriguez, M.D.
Otolaryngology . . . . Paul Friedlander, M.D.
Pathology . . . . Tong Wu, M.D.
Pediatrics . . . . Samir El-Dahr, M.D.
   Adolescent Medicine . . . . Sue Ellen Abdalian, M.D.
   Pediatric Allergy, Immunology, and Rheumatology . . . . Jane El-Dahr, M.D.
   Pediatric Cardiology. . . . . Mitch Recto, M.D.
   Pediatric Critical Care . . . . Edwin Frieberg, M.D.
   Pediatric Emergency Medicine . . . . Carla Alcid, M.D.
   Pediatric Endocrinology . . . . Vacant
   Pediatric Gastroenterology . . . . Ilana Fortgang, M.D.
   General Academic Pediatrics . . . . Hosea Doucet, M.D., M.P.H.
   Pediatric Hematology and Oncology . . . . Tammuella Singleton, M.D.
   Pediatric Infectious Diseases . . . . Russell Van Dyke, M.D.
   Neonatology. . . . . Phillip Goroon, M.D.
   Pediatric Nephrology . . . . Samir El-Dahr, M.D.
   Pediatric Pulmonary. . . . . Robert Hopkins, M.D.
   Pediatric Hospitalist . . . . Todd Washko, M.D.
   Pediatric Neurology . . . . Allison H. Conravey, M.D.
   Community Pediatrics and Global Health . . . . Alina Olteanu, M.D., Ph.D.
Psychiatry . . . . Daniel Winstead, M.D. Vacant
Radiology . . . . Harold R. Neitzschman, M.D.
Surgery. . . . . Douglas P. Slakey, M.D.
Urology. . . . . Raju Thomas, M.D.
Neurology. . . . . Roger Kelly, M.D.

Johns Hopkins University School of Medicine

733 North Broadway
Baltimore, Maryland 21205
410-955-5000; 410-955-3180 (dean's office); 410-955-0889 (fax)
Web site: www.hopkinsmedicine.org

The school of medicine was opened for the instruction of students in October 1893, four years after the opening of the Johns Hopkins Hospital.

Type: private
2011 total enrollment: 480
Clinical facilities: Johns Hopkins Hospital, Johns Hopkins Bayview Medical Center, Kennedy Kreiger Institute, Good Samaritan Hospital, Sinai Hospital of Baltimore, Greater Baltimore Medical Center, Howard County General Hospital, Suburban Hospital.

University Officials

Chair, University Board of Trustees . . . . Pamela Flaherty
Chair, Medicine Board of Trustees . . . . Frank Burcks
President . . . . Ronald Daniels
Provost and Vice President for Academic Affairs . . . . Lloyd Minor, M.D.
Senior Vice President for Administration . . . . Daniel Ennis
Secretary . . . . Gerome Schnydman
Vice President for Development and Alumni . . . . Michael C. Eicher

Medical School Administrative Staff

Dean of the Medical Faculty and Chief Executive
  Officer, Johns Hopkins Medicine . . . . Edward D. Miller, M.D.
Vice Dean for Faculty Affairs . . . . Janice E. Clements, Ph.D.
Vice Dean for Education . . . . David G. Nichols, M.D.
CEO of Johns Hopkins Medicine . . . . Steven J. Thompson
Chief Financial Officer, Johns Hopkins Medicine . . . . Richard A. Grossi
Vice Dean for Clinical Affairs . . . . William A. Baumgartner, M.D.
Vice Dean for Clinical Investigation . . . . Daniel E. Ford, M.D.
Vice Dean for Research . . . . Chi Van Dang, M.D., Ph.D.
Vice Dean for Bayview . . . . David B. Hellmann, M.D.
Associate Dean for Admissions . . . . James Weiss, M.D.
Associate Dean for Student Affairs . . . . Thomas W. Koenig, M.D.
Associate Dean for Diversity and Cultural Competency . . . . Brian K. Gibbs, Ph.D.
Associate Dean for Graduate Students . . . . Peter C. Maloney, Ph.D.
Associate Dean for Postdoctoral Affairs . . . . Levi Watkins, Jr., M.D.
Associate Dean for Graduate Medical Education . . . . Julia McMillan, M.D.
Associate Dean for Curriculum . . . . Patricia Thomas, M.D.
Associate Dean and Registrar . . . . Mary E. Foy
Associate Dean for Research Administration . . . . Michael B. Amey
Associate Dean for Continuing Medical Education . . . . Todd Dorman, M.D.
Associate Dean for Emerging Technologies . . . . Peter S. Greene, M.D.
Associate Dean, Executive Director, Clinical Practice Association . . . . Vacant
Associate Dean for Women in Science . . . . Barbara Fivush, M.D.
Assistant Dean for Admissions and Financial Aid . . . . Vacant
Assistant Dean for Bayview . . . . Melissa Helicke
Assistant Dean for Medicine . . . . Christine H. White
Assistant Dean and Director, Office of Academic Computing . . . . Harry Goldberg, Ph.D.
Assistant Dean for Part-Time Faculty . . . . Maura McGuire, M.D.
Associate Dean for Policy Coordination . . . . Julie Gottlieb
Assistant Dean for Student Diversity . . . . Daniel Teraguchi, Ed.D.
Assistant Dean for Student Affairs . . . . Sarah Clever, M.D.
Assistant Dean for Faculty, Development, and Equity . . . . Vacant
Assistant Dean for Student Affairs . . . . Michael Barone, M.D.
Assistant Dean for Human Subject Research Compliance . . . . Barbara Starklauf
Assistant Dean and Compliance Officer for
  Graduate Medical Education . . . . John Rybock, M.D.

Department and Division or Section Chairs

Basic Sciences

Biological Chemistry . . . . Gerald W. Hart, Ph.D.

Johns Hopkins University School of Medicine: MARYLAND

Biomedical Engineering. . . . . Elliot R. McVeigh, Ph.D.
Biophysics . . . . L. Mario Amzel, Ph.D.
Cell Biology. . . . . Peter M. Devreotes, Ph.D.
Comparative Medicine. . . . . M. Christine Zink, Ph.D., D.V.M.
Health Sciences Informatics* . . . . Nancy K. Roderer
History of Medicine . . . . Randall Packard, Ph.D.
Institute for Basic Biomedical Sciences . . . . Stephen Desiderio, M.D., Ph.D.
Molecular Biology and Genetics . . . . Carol Greider, Ph.D.
Neuroscience. . . . . Richard L. Huganir, Ph.D.
Pharmacology and Molecular Sciences . . . . Philip A. Cole, M.D., Ph.D.
Physiology . . . . William B. Guggino, Ph.D.

Clinical Sciences

Anesthesiology and Critical Care Medicine . . . . John Ulatowski, M.D.
Dermatology . . . . Sewon Kang, M.D.
Emergency Medicine . . . . Gabor D. Kelen, M.D.
Medicine. . . . . Myron L. Weisfeldt, M.D.
   Allergy and Clinical Immunology* . . . . Bruce Bochner, M.D.
   Cardiology* . . . . Gordon Tomaselli, M.D.
   Clinical Pharmacology* . . . . Theresa B. Shapiro, M.D., Ph.D.
   Endocrine and Metabolic* . . . . Paul W. Ladenson, M.D.
   Gastroenterology* . . . . Anthony Kalloo, M.D.
   Geriatric Medicine and Gerontology* . . . . Samuel C. Durso, M.D.
   Hematology* . . . . Robert Brodsky, M.D.
   Infectious Diseases* . . . . David Thomas, M.D.
   Internal Medicine* . . . . Frederick Brancati, M.D.
   Molecular Medicine* . . . . Andrew Feinberg, M.D.
   Nephrology* . . . . Paul Scheel, M.D.
   Pulmonary and Critical Care Medicine* . . . . Landon King, M.D.
   Rheumatology* . . . . Antony Rosen, M.D.
Neurological Surgery . . . . Henry Brem, M.D.
Neurology . . . . Justin McArthur, M.B.B.S.
Neuroscience. . . . . Richard L. Huganir, Ph.D.
Obstetrics-Gynecology . . . . Harold Fox, M.D.
Oncology. . . . . William Nelson, M.D.
Ophthalmology . . . . Peter McDonnell, M.D.
Orthopedic Surgery . . . . Frank J. Frassica, M.D.
Otolaryngology-Head and Neck Surgery . . . . John Niparko, M.D. (Interim)
   Oral* . . . . William Henderson, D.D.S. (Interim)
Pathology . . . . J. Brooks Jackson, M.D.
Pediatrics . . . . George Dover, M.D.
Plastic Surgery. . . . . W.P. Andrew Lee, M.D.
Psychiatry and Behavioral Science . . . . Raymond DePaulo, M.D.
   Child Psychiatry . . . . Margaret Bruas, Ph.D. (Interim)
Radiation Oncology. . . . . Theodore L. DeWeese, M.D.
Radiology . . . . Jonathan Lewin, M.D.
   Nuclear Medicine* . . . . Richard Wahl, M.D.
Physical Medicine and Rehabilitation . . . . Jeffrey Palmer, M.D.
Surgery . . . . Julie Freischlag, M.D.
   Acute Care Surgery-Trauma, Critical Care,
     Emergency, and General Surgery . . . . David Efron, M.D.
   Cardiac Surgery . . . . Duke Cameron, M.D.
   Gastrointestinal Surgery . . . . Jonathan Efron, M.D.
   Pediatric Surgery* . . . . Paul M. Colombani, M.D.
   Surgical Oncology . . . . Richard Schulick, M.D.
   Thoracic Surgery . . . . Stephen C. Yang, M.D.
   Transplantation . . . . Robert Montgomery, M.D.
   Vascular Surgery and Endovascular Therapy . . . . Bruce Perler, M.D.
Urology. . . . . Alan W. Partin, M.D., Ph.D.

*Specialty without organizational autonomy.

University of Maryland School of Medicine

655 West Baltimore Street
Baltimore, Maryland 21201
410-706-3100 (campus); 410-706-7410 (dean's office); 410-706-0235 (fax)
E-mail: deanmed@som.umaryland.edu
Web site: http://medschool.umaryland.edu

The University of Maryland School of Medicine was founded in 1807 as the College of Medicine of Maryland. Davidge Hall, its first building, was constructed in 1812 and is the oldest building in North America used continuously for medical education. The school of medicine is one of six professional schools that comprise the university's campus in downtown Baltimore.

Type: public
2011 total enrollment: 625
Clinical facilities: University of Maryland Medical Center (UM Marlene and Stewart Greenebaum Cancer Center and the R Adams Cowley Shock Trauma Center); Mercy Medical Center; VA Maryland Health Care System, Baltimore; Eastern Shore and Western Maryland AHEC.

University Officials

Chancellor, University System of Maryland . . . . William E. Kirwan, Ph.D.
President, University of Maryland Baltimore . . . . Jay Perman, M.D.
Vice President for Academic Affairs and Dean of
  the Graduate School . . . . Roger Ward, Ed.D., J.D.
Vice President for Medical Affairs. . . . . E. Albert Reece, M.D., Ph.D.

Medical School Administrative Staff

Dean. . . . . E. Albert Reece, M.D., Ph.D.
Executive Vice Dean . . . . Bruce E. Jarrell, M.D.
Vice Dean for Clinical Affairs. . . . . Frank M. Calia, M.D., M.A.C.P.
Associate Dean, Business Affairs, and Senior Advisor to the Dean . . . . Jerry D. Carr, J.D.
Associate Dean for Academic Administration
  and Resource Management . . . . Gregory Robinson, D.Min.
Associate Dean for Admissions . . . . Milford M. Foxwell, Jr., M.D.
Associate Dean for Faculty Affairs. . . . . Nancy Ryan Lowitt, M.D.
Associate Dean for Finance and Business Affairs . . . . Louisa A. Peartree
Associate Dean for Development . . . . Dennis J. Narango
Associate Dean for Graduate Studies . . . . Margaret M. McCarthy, Ph.D.
Associate Dean for Hospital Networks. . . . . John W. Ashworth III
Associate Dean for Medical Education . . . . David B. Mallott, M.D.
Associate Dean for Information Services. . . . . James E. McNamee, Ph.D.
Associate Dean for Interdisciplinary Research . . . . Stephen B. Liggett, M.D.
Associate Dean for Policy and Planning . . . . Claudia R. Baquet, M.D.
Associate Dean for Research. . . . . Curt I. Civin, M.D.
Associate Dean and Director, Program in Personalized Medicine. . . . . Alan R. Shuldiner, M.D.
Associate Dean for Student Affairs . . . . Donna Parker, M.D.
Associate Dean for Veterans Affairs . . . . Dorothy A. Snow, M.D.

Department and Division or Section Chairs

Basic Sciences and Allied Health Chairs

Anatomy and Neurobiology . . . . Michael T. Shipley, Ph.D.
Biochemistry and Molecular Biology. . . . . Richard L. Eckert, Ph.D.
Epidemiology and Preventive Medicine. . . . . Jay S. Magaziner, Ph.D.
Medical and Research Technology . . . . Sanford A. Stass, M.D.
Microbiology and Immunology. . . . . James B. Kaper, Ph.D.
Pharmacology and Experimental Therapeutics . . . . Margaret McCarthy, Ph.D. (Interim)
Physical Therapy and Rehabilitation Science. Mary M. Rodgers, Ph.D.
Physiology . . . . Scott M. Thompson, Ph.D. (Interim)

Clinical Sciences Chairs and Program Directors

Anesthesiology. . . . . Peter Rock, M.D.
Dermatology . . . . Anthony A. Gaspari, M.D.
Diagnostic Radiology and Nuclear Medicine . . . . William F. Regine, M.D.
Emergency Medicine . . . . Brian J. Browne, M.D.
Family and Community Medicine. . . . . David L. Stewart, M.D.
Medicine. . . . . Stephen N. Davis, M.B.B.S.
  Cardiology . . . . Mandeep Mehra, M.D.
  Endocrinology, Diabetes, and Nutrition. . . . . Alan R. Shuldiner, M.D.

Gastroenterology and Hepatology . . . . Jean-Pierre Raufman, M.D.
General Internal Medicine . . . . Louis J. Domenici, M.D.
Geographic Medicine . . . . Myron M. Levine, M.D., D.T.P.H.
Gerontology and Geriatric Medicine . . . . Andrew P. Goldberg, M.D.
Hematology and Oncology . . . . Edward A. Sausville, M.D., Ph.D. (Interim)
Infectious Diseases . . . . Robert R. Redfield, M.D.
Nephrology . . . . Matthew R. Weir, M.D.
Pulmonary and Critical Care Medicine . . . . Jeffrey D. Hasday, M.D.
Rheumatology and Clinical Immunology . . . . Marc C. Hochberg, M.D.
Neurology . . . . William J. Weiner, M.D.
Neurosurgery . . . . Howard M. Eisenberg, M.D.
Obstetrics, Gynecology, and Reproductive Sciences . . . . Christopher Harman, M.D. (Interim)
General Obstetrics and Gynecology . . . . May Blanchard, M.D.
Gynecologic Oncology . . . . Vacant
Maternal-Fetal Medicine . . . . Christopher R. Harman, M.D.
Reproductive Endocrinology . . . . Howard D. McClamrock, M.D.
Urogynecology and Pelvic Reconstruction . . . . Harry W. Johnson, M.D.
Oncology Program, UM Cancer Center . . . . Kevin J. Cullen, M.D.
Ophthalmology and Visual Sciences . . . . Robert A. Liss, M.D. (Interim)
Orthopaedics . . . . Vincent D. Pellegrini, M.D.
Otorhinolaryngology-Head and Neck Surgery . . . . Scott E. Strome, M.D.
Pathology . . . . Sanford A. Stass, M.D.
Pediatrics . . . . Steven J. Czinn, M.D.
Adolescent Medicine . . . . Ligia Peralta, M.D.
Cardiology . . . . Geoffrey Rosenthal, M.D.
Critical Care . . . . Geoffrey Rosenthal, M.D.
Emergency Medicine . . . . Vacant
Gastroenterology and Nutrition . . . . Samra Blanchard, M.D.
General Pediatrics . . . . Jack Gladstein, M.D. (Interim)
Infectious Diseases and Tropical Pediatrics . . . . Karen L. Kotloff, M.D.
Neonatology . . . . Cynthia Bearer, M.D., Ph.D.
Nephrology . . . . Susan Mendley, M.D.
Pulmonary and Allergy . . . . Sumra S. Blanchard (Interim)
Genetics . . . . Miriam Blitzer, Ph.D.
Psychiatry . . . . Anthony F. Lehman, M.D.
Adult Psychiatry . . . . Vacant
Alcohol and Drug Abuse . . . . Eric Weintraub, M.D.
Child and Adolescent Psychiatry . . . . David B. Pruitt, M.D.
Community Psychiatry . . . . Jill RachBeisel, M.D.
Consultation/Liaison Psychiatry . . . . Mark Ehrenreich, M.D.
Division of Services Research . . . . Lisa B. Dixon, M.D.
Geriatric Psychiatry . . . . William T. Regenold, M.D.
Maryland Psychiatric Research Center . . . . William T. Carpenter, Jr., M.D.
Psychology . . . . Alan S. Bellack, Ph.D.
Radiation Oncology . . . . William F. Regine, M.D.
Surgery . . . . Stephen T. Bartlett, M.D.
Cardiac Surgery . . . . Bartley P. Griffith, M.D.
General Surgery . . . . H. Richard Alexander, Jr., M.D. (Acting)
Pediatric Surgery . . . . Roger Voigt, M.B.B.S., F.R.C.S. (Acting)
Plastic and Reconstructive Surgery . . . . Sheri Slezak, M.D. (Acting)
Surgical Critical Care . . . . Steven Johnson, M.D.
Thoracic Surgery . . . . Richard J. Battafarano, M.D., Ph.D.
Transplant Surgery . . . . Jonathan S. Bromberg, M.D., Ph.D.
Urology . . . . Michael J. Naslund, M.D.
Vascular Surgery . . . . Rajobrata Sarkar, M.D.
Trauma Program-Shock Trauma Center . . . . Thomas M. Scalea, M.D.

Institute and Center Directors

Institute of Human Virology . . . . Robert C. Gallo, M.D.
University of Maryland Institute for Genome Sciences . . . . Claire M. Fraser-Liggett, Ph.D.
Integrative Medicine . . . . Brian M. Berman, M.D.
Mucosal Biology . . . . Alessio Fasano, M.D.
Vascular and Inflammatory Diseases . . . . Dudley K. Strickland, Ph.D.
Research on Aging . . . . Andrew P. Goldberg, M.D., and Jay S. Magaziner, Ph.D.
Shock, Trauma, and Anesthesiology Research . . . . Alan I. Faden, M.D.
Stem Cell Biology and Regenerative Medicine . . . . Curt I. Livin, M.D.
Vaccine Development . . . . Myron M. Levine, M.D., D.T.P.H.

Uniformed Services University of the Health Sciences
F. Edward Hébert School of Medicine
4301 Jones Bridge Road
Bethesda, Maryland 20814-4799
301-295-3016 (dean's office); 301-295-3542 (fax)
Web site: www.usuhs.mil

Upon enactment in 1972 of the Uniformed Services Health Professions Revitalization Act (PL 92-426), Congress authorized establishment of the Uniformed Services University of the Health Sciences. The governing board of regents planned and developed the school of medicine as the initial academic component within the university. The first class of 32 medical officer candidates enrolled on October 12, 1976; the present first-year enrollment is 171.

Type: public
2011 total enrollment: 670
Clinical facilities: Naval Hospital (Bethesda), Walter Reed Army Medical Center, Malcolm Grow U.S. Air Force Medical Center, Wilford Hall U.S. Air Force Medical Center.

University Officials

Chair, Board of Regents. . . . . Ronald R. Blanck, D.O.
Executive Secretary, Board of Regents . . . . William T. Bester
President. . . . . Charles L. Rice, M.D.
Senior Vice President. . . . . Dale C. Smith, Ph.D.
Vice President for Research . . . . Steven Kaminsky, Ph.D.
Vice President, External Affairs . . . . William T. Bester
Vice President, Finance and Administration . . . . Stephen C. Rice
Chief of Staff. . . . . Robert J. Thompson
General Counsel . . . . John E. Baker, J.D.
Senior Executive Director, Continuing
   Education for Health Professionals . . . . Karen Biggs, (CAPT, NC, USN)
Brigade Commander . . . . Tanis Batsel-Stewart, (CAPT, MC, USN)

Medical School Administrative Staff

Dean, School of Medicine . . . . Larry W. Laughlin, M.D., Ph.D.
Vice Dean, School of Medicine. . . . . John E. McManigle, M.D.
Commandant . . . . Lisa Pearse, M.D., (CDR, MC, USN) (Interim)
Associate Dean, Clinical Research. . . . . Kente Kester, M.D. (CCL, MC, USA)
Associate Dean, Faculty . . . . Brian V. Reamy, M.D.
Associate Dean, Graduate Education. . . . . Eleanor S. Metcalf, Ph.D.
Associate Dean, Graduate Medical Education . . . . Jerri Curtis, M.D. (CAPT, MC, USN) (Interim)
Associate Dean, Medical Education. . . . . Donna M. Waechter, Ph.D.
Associate Dean, Recruitment and Admissions . . . . . . Margaret Calloway, M.D. (CAPT, MC, USN)
Associate Dean, Simulation Education . . . . Joseph O. Lopreiato, M.D.
Associate Dean, Student Affairs . . . . Richard M. MacDonald, M.D.
Assistant Dean, Clinical Sciences. Lisa Moores, M.D. (COL, MC, USA)

Uniformed Services University of the Health Sciences
F. Edward Hébert School of Medicine: MARYLAND

Department Chairs

Basic Sciences

Anatomy, Physiology, and Genetics . . . . Harvey B. Pollard, M.D., Ph.D.
Biochemistry . . . . Teresa Dunn, Ph.D.
Biomedical Informatics . . . . Ronald Gimbel, Ph.D. (Interim)
Medical and Clinical Psychology . . . . David S. Krantz, Ph.D.
Medical History . . . . Trueman W. Sharp, M.D. (CAPT, MC, USN) (Interim)
Microbiology and Immunology . . . . Alison D. O'Brien, Ph.D.
Military and Emergency Medicine . . . . Trueman W. Sharp, M.D. (CAPT, MC, USN)
Pathology . . . . Robert M. Friedman, M.D.
Pharmacology . . . . Jeffrey M. Harmon, Ph.D.
Preventive Medicine and Biometrics . . . . Gerald V. Quinnan, Jr., M.D.
Radiation Biology . . . . Vacant

Clinical Sciences

Anesthesiology . . . . Dale F. Szpisjak, M.D. (CAPT, MC, USN) (Interim)
Dermatology . . . . Leonard B. Sperling, M.D.
Family Medicine . . . . Mark B. Stephens, M.D. (CAPT, MC, USN)
Medicine . . . . Louis Pangaro, M.D.
Neurology . . . . Geoffrey S.F. Ling, M.D. (COL, MC, USA) (Interim)
Obstetrics and Gynecology . . . . Christopher M. Zahn, M.D. (COL, USAF, MC)
Pediatrics . . . . Ildy M. Katona, M.D.
Psychiatry . . . . Robert J. Ursano, M.D.
Radiology and Nuclear Medicine . . . . Vincent B. Ho, M.D. (Interim)
Surgery . . . . Patricia L. McKay, M.D. (CDR, MC, USN) (Interim)

Boston University School of Medicine

72 East Concord Street
Boston, Massachusetts 02118
617-638-5300 (dean's office); 617-638-5258 (fax)
E-mail: busmdean@bu.edu
Web site: www.bumc.bu.edu

In 1873, Boston University established its school of medicine by merging with the New England Female Medical College, which had been founded in 1848 as the first medical college for women in the world. In 1962, the school of medicine became a constituent member of Boston University Medical Center. It is located approximately two miles from the Charles River campus of Boston University, the parent university.

Type: private
2011 total enrollment: 709
Clinical facilities: Bay Ridge Hospital, Baystate Medical Center, Beverly Hospital, Boston Medical Center, Bournewood Medical Center, Cape Cod Hospital, Carney Hospital, Solomon Carter Fuller Mental Health Center, Franciscan Children's Hospital, Human Resources Institute, Jewish Memorial Hospital, Lahey Clinic Medical Center, Columbia MetroWest Medical Center Framingham Union Campus, North Shore Childrens Hospital, Norwood Hospital, Shriners Hospital for Crippled Children, Veterans Administration hospitals (Boston, Bedford), Waltham Deaconess Hospital, Westwood Lodge Hospital, Roger Williams Hospital (Providence, Rhode Island), Central Maine Medical Center (Lewiston, Maine), Quincy Medical Center.

University Officials

President. . . . . Robert A. Brown, Ph.D.
Provost, Medical Campus . . . . Karen H. Antman, M.D.
Associate Provost . . . . Thomas J. Moore, M.D.
Associate Provost, Research . . . . Ronald B. Corley, Ph.D.
Associate Provost for Graduate Medical Sciences. . . . . Linda E. Hyman, Ph.D.
Assistant Provost for Translational Research . . . . David M. Center, M.D.
Assistant Provost for Compliance . . . . Susan Frey, J.D.
Assistant Provost . . . . Deborah Fournier, Ph.D.

Medical School Administrative Staff

Dean. . . . . Karen H. Antman, M.D.
Associate Dean for Academic Affairs. . . . . Douglas Hughes, M.D.
Associate Dean for Admissions . . . . Robert A. Witzburg, M.D.
Associate Dean for Student Affairs . . . . Phyllis L. Carr, M.D.
Associate Dean for Clinical Affairs . . . . Ravin Davidoff, M.D.
Associate Dean for Continuing Medical Education . . . . Barry M. Manuel, M.D.
Associate Dean for Graduate Medical Sciences . . . . Linda E. Hyman, Ph.D.
Associate Dean for Diversity and Multicultural Affairs . . . . Rafael Ortega, M.D.
Assistant Dean for Admissions . . . . Gary J. Balady, M.D., Shoumita Dasgupta, Ph.D.,
Philip Stone, Ph.D., and Deborah Vaughan, Ph.D.
Assistant Dean for Academic Affairs . . . . John Wiecha, M.D.
Assistant Dean for Enrichment Programs . . . . Suzanne Sarfaty, M.D.
Assistant Dean for VA Affairs . . . . Michael Charness, M.D.
Assistant Dean for RWMC Affairs . . . . Vincent Falanga, M.D.
Assistant Dean for Continuing Medical Education. Dan Alford, M.D.
Assistant Dean for Alumni Affairs. . . . . Jean Ramsey, M.D.
Assistant Dean for Student Affairs. . . . . Joel Alpert, M.D., Kenneth M. Grundfast, M.D.,
Karen Symes, Ph.D., Paul O'Bryan, Ph.D., Daniel Chen, M.D.,
and John Polk, M.D.
Assistant Dean for Diversity and Multicultural Affairs. . . . . Douglas Hughes, M.D.,
Alexander Norbash, M.D., Daniel Chen, M.D., and Samantha Kaplan, M.D.
Assistant Dean for Graduate Medical Sciences. . . . . Hee-Young Park, Ph.D.
Assistant Dean for Research . . . . Terence Keane, Ph.D.
Registrar and Coordinator for Advanced Standing Admissions. . . . . Ellen J. DiFiore
Librarian. . . . . Mary Blanchard

Boston University School of Medicine: MASSACHUSETTS

Department and Division or Section Chairs

Basic Sciences

Anatomy and Neurobiology . . . . Mark B. Moss, Ph.D.
Biochemistry . . . . David A. Harris, M.D., Ph.D.
Microbiology . . . . Ronald B. Corley, Ph.D.
Pathology and Laboratory Medicine . . . . Daniel G. Remick, M.D.
Pharmacology and Experimental Therapeutics . . . . David H. Farb, Ph.D.
Physiology and Biophysics . . . . David Atkinson, Ph.D.
Socio-Medical Sciences and Community Medicine. . . . . Robert F. Meenan, M.D.

Clinical Sciences

Anesthesiology. . . . . Keith Lewis, M.D.
Dermatology . . . . Rhoda Alani, M.D.
Emergency Medicine . . . . Jonathan S. Olshaker, M.D.
Family Medicine . . . . Charles Williams, M.D. (Interim)
Medicine . . . . David L. Coleman, M.D.
Neurology . . . . Carlos Kase, M.D.
Obstetrics and Gynecology . . . . Linda J. Heffner, M.D., Ph.D.
Ophthalmology . . . . Stephen P. Christiansen, M.D.
Pediatrics . . . . Barry S. Zuckerman, M.D.
Psychiatry . . . . Domenic A. Ciraulo, M.D.
Radiology . . . . Alexander M. Norbash, M.D.
Rehabilitation Medicine. . . . . Steve R. Williams, M.D.
Surgery . . . . Gerard M. Doherty, M.D.
    Cardiothoracic Surgery* . . . . Benedict D. T. Daly, M.D.
    Neurosurgery* . . . . James Holsapple, M.D.
    Orthopedic Surgery* . . . . Thomas A. Einhorn, M.D.
    Otolaryngology*. . . . . Kenneth M. Grundfast, M.D.
    Urology* . . . . Richard K. Babayan, M.D.

*Specialty without organizational autonomy.

Harvard Medical School

25 Shattuck Street
Boston, Massachusetts 02115
617-432-1000; 617-432-1501 (Dean's office); 617-432-3907 (fax)
Web site: www.hms.harvard.edu

On September 19, 1782, the President and Fellows of Harvard College officially adopted a plan for instituting medical instruction. The school's present buildings opened in 1906 and are located in Boston across the Charles River from the university in Cambridge.

Type: private
2011 total enrollment: 735
Clinical facilities: Beth Israel Deaconess Medical Center, Brigham and Women's Hospital, VA Boston Healthcare System, Cambridge Health Alliance, Immune Disease Institute, Children's Hospital Boston, Dana Farber Cancer Institute, Harvard Pilgrim Health Care, Joslin Diabetes Center, Judge Baker Children's Center, McLean Hospital, Massachusetts Eye and Ear Infirmary, Massachusetts General Hospital, Mount Auburn Hospital, Schepens Eye Research Institute, Spaulding Rehabilitation Hospital, Hebrew Senimite Forsyth Institute.

University Official

President. . . . . Drew G. Faust, Ph.D.

Medical School Administrative Staff

Dean. . . . . Jeffrey S. Flier, M.D.
Executive Dean for Research . . . . William W. Chin, M.D.
Executive Dean for Administration and Finance . . . . Richard G. Mills, J.D.
Dean for Academic and Clinical Affairs . . . . Nancy Tarbell, M.D.
Dean for Clinical and Translational Research . . . . Lee Nadler, M.D.
Dean for Diversity and Community Partnership . . . . Joan Reede, M.D.
Dean for Faculty Affairs . . . . Maureen Connelly, M.D.
Dean for Faculty and Research Integrity . . . . Gretchen Brodnicki, J.D.
Dean for Graduate Education and Special
  Advisor to the Dean for Global Programs . . . . David E. Golan, M.D., Ph.D.
Dean for Medical Education. . . . . Jules L. Dienstag, M.D.
Dean for Resource Development . . . . Susan Rapple
Dean for Students . . . . Nancy E. Oriol, M.D.
Associate Dean for Basic Graduate Studies . . . . David L. Cardozo, Ph.D.
Associate Dean for Basic and Interdisciplinary Research . . . . Judith Glaven, Ph.D.
Associate Dean for Communications and External Relations . . . . Gina Vild
Associate Dean for Finance and Chief Financial Officer . . . . Wesley Benbow
Chief Human Resources Officer. . . . . Julie Stanley
Assistant Dean for Faculty Affairs . . . . Mary Walsh, Ph.D.
Assistant Dean for Faculty Affairs . . . . Carol Bates, M.D
Associate Dean for Clinical and Translational Research. . . . . Elliott Antman, M.D.,
  and Anne Klibanski, M.D.
Associate Dean for Medical Education Planning and Administration . . . . Jane Neill
Associate Dean for Physical Planning and Facilities . . . . Richard M. Shea
Associate Dean for Institutional Planning and Policy. . . . . Lisa Muto, Ph.D.
Faculty Assistant Dean for Student Affairs . . . . Fidencio Saldana, M.D.
Faculty Dean for Continuing Medical Education. . . . . Sanjiv Chopra, M.D.
Faculty Associate Dean for Admissions . . . . Robert Mayer, M.D.
Faculty Associate Dean for Student Affairs . . . . Alvin F. Poussaint, M.D.
Faculty Assistant Dean for Admissions. . . . . Darrell Smith, M.D.
Chief Information Officer . . . . John D. Halamka, M.D.
Director of the Academy Center for Teaching and Learning . . . . Charles Hatem, M.D.
Director of the Countway Library. . . . . Issac S. Kohane, M.D., Ph.D.
Registrar . . . . Terese Galuszka

Department and Division or Section Chairs

Basic Sciences

Biological Chemistry and Molecular Pharmacology . . . . Stephen C. Harrison, Ph.D. (Acting)
Cell Biology. . . . . Joan S. Brugge, Ph.D.
Genetics . . . . Cliff Tabin, Ph.D.
Global Health and Social Medicine . . . . Paul Farmer, M.D., Ph.D.
Health Care Policy. . . . . Barbara J. McNeil, M.D., Ph.D.
Microbiology and Immunobiology . . . . John J. Mekalanos, Ph.D.
Neurobiology. . . . . Michael E. Greenberg, Ph.D.

Stem Cell and Regenerative Biology . . . . Douglas A. Melton, M.D., and David Scadden, M.D.
Systems Biology . . . . Marc Kirschner, Ph.D.

Clinical Science Departments

Anaesthesia . . . . Jeanine P. Weiner-Kronish, M.D. (Chair, Exec. Committee)
   Beth Israel Deaconess Medical Center. . . . . Brett Simon, M.D., Ph.D.
   Brigham and Women's Hospital . . . . Charles A. Vacanti, M.D.
   Children's Hospital . . . . Paul R. Hickey, M.D.
   Massachusetts General Hospital. . . . . Jeanine P. Weiner-Kronish, M.D.
Dermatology . . . . Robert S. Stern, M.D. (Chair, Ex Committee)
   Massachussetts General Hospital . . . . David Fisher, M.D., Ph.D.
   Beth Israel Deaconess Medical Center. . . . . Robert S. Stern, M.D.
   Brigham and Women's Hospital . . . . Thomas S. Kupper, M.D.
Medicine . . . . Joseph Loscalzo, M.D., Ph.D. (Chair, (Exec. Comm) ittee)
   Beth Israel Deaconess Medical Center. . . . . Mark L. Zeidel, M.D.
   Brigham and Women's Hospital . . . . Joseph Loscalzo, M.D., Ph.D.
   Massachusetts General Hospital. . . . . Dennis A. Ausiello, M.D.
Neurology . . . . Martin A. Samuels, M.D. (Chair, Exec. Committee)
   Beth Israel Deaconess Medical Center. . . . . Clifford B. Saper, M.D., Ph.D.
   Brigham and Women's Hospital . . . . Martin A. Samuels, M.D.
   Children's Hospital . . . . Scott L. Pomeroy, M.D., Ph.D.
   Massachusetts General Hospital. . . . . Anne B. Young, M.D., Ph.D.
Obstetrics, Gynecology, and Reproductive
   Biology . . . . Robert L. Barbieri, M.D. (Chair, Exec. Committee)
   Beth Israel Deaconess Medical Center. . . . . Hope Riciatti, M.D. (Acting)
   Brigham and Women's Hospital . . . . Robert L. Barbieri, M.D.
   Massachusetts General Hospital. . . . . Isaac Schiff, M.D.
Ophthalmology . . . . Joan Miller, M.D.
Orthopedic Surgery . . . . Harry E. Rubash, M.D. (Chair, Exec. Committee)
   Beth Israel Deaconess Medical Center. . . . . Mark Gebhardt, M.D.
   Brigham and Women's Hospital . . . . Thomas S. Thornhill, M.D.
   Children's Hospital . . . . James R. Kasser, M.D.
   Massachusetts General Hospital. . . . . Harry E. Rubash, M.D.
Otology and Laryngology. . . . . Joseph B. Nadol, Jr., M.D.
Pathology . . . . Jeffrey Saffitz, M.D., Ph.D. (Chair, Ex Commit)
   Beth Israel Deaconess Medical Center. . . . . Jeffrey Saffitz, M.D., Ph.D.
   Brigham and Women's Hospital . . . . Michael A. Gimbrone, Jr., M.D.
   Children's Hospital . . . . Mark Fleming, M.D., D.Phil.
   Massachusetts General Hospital. . . . . David N. Louis, M.D.
Pediatrics . . . . Frederick H. Lovejoy, M.D. (Chair, Exec. Committee)
   Children's Hospital . . . . Gary Fleisher, M.D.
   Massachusetts General Hospital. . . . . Ronald E. Kleinman, M.D.
Physical Medicine and Rehabilitation . . . . Ross D. Zafonte, D.O.
Population Medicine . . . . Richard Platt, M.D.
Psychiatry . . . . David R. Demaso, M.D. (Chair, Exec. Committee)
   Beth Israel Deaconess Medical Center. . . . . David Jimerson, M.D. (Acting)
   Brigham and Women's Hospital . . . . David A. Silbersweig, M.D.
   VA Boston Healthcare System . . . . Robert W. McCarley, Jr., M.D.
   Cambridge Health Alliance. . . . . Jack D. Burke, M.D.
   Children's Hospital . . . . David R. Demaso, M.D.
   McLean Hospital . . . . Scott L. Rauch, M.D.
   Massachusetts General Hospital. . . . . Jerrold F. Rosenbaum, M.D.
Radiation Oncology . . . . Jay R. Harris, M.D. (Chair, Exec. Committee)
   Brigham and Women's Hospital/Children's
   Hospital/Dana Farber Cancer Institute . . . . Jay R. Harris, M.D.
   Beth Israel Deaconess Medical Center. . . . . Mary Ann Stevenson, M.D., Ph.D.
   Massachusetts General Hospital. . . . . Jay S. Loeffler, M.D.
Radiology . . . . Jonathan Kruskal, M.D., Ph.D. (Chair, Ex Commit)
   Beth Israel Deaconess Medical Center. . . . . Jonathan Kruskal, M.D., Ph.D.
   Brigham and Women's Hospital . . . . Steven E. Seltzer, M.D.
   Children's Hospital . . . . Richard Robertson, Jr., M.D.
   Massachusetts General Hospital. . . . . James H. Thrall, M.D.
Surgery . . . . Michael J. Zinner, M.D. (Chair, Exec. Committee)
   Beth Israel Deaconess Medical Center. . . . . Elliot L. Chaikoff, M.D., Ph.D.
   Brigham and Women's Hospital . . . . Michael J. Zinner, M.D.
   Children's Hospital . . . . Robert C. Shamberger, M.D.
   Massachusetts General Hospital. . . . . Keith D. Lillemae, M.D.

University of Massachusetts Medical School

55 Lake Avenue North
Worcester, Massachusetts 01655
508-856-8000 (dean's office); 508-856-8181 (fax); 508-856-8989 (general)
E-mail: terry.flotte@umassmed.edu
Web site: www.umassmed.edu

The University of Massachusetts Medical School (UMMS) is the centerpiece of a comprehensive academic medical center committed to achievements in health sciences education, research, public service, and clinical care. The Commonwealth of Massachusetts' first and only public medical school, UMMS, was founded in 1962 to provide affordable, high-quality medical education to state residents and to increase the supply of primary care physicians.

Type: public
2011 total enrollment: 469
Clinical facilities: UMass Memorial-University and Memorial Campuses, Berkshire Medical Center, St. Vincent Hospital, St. Elizabeth's Medical Center, Milford Regional Medical Center.

University Officials

President. . . . . Robert Caret, Ph.D.
Senior Vice President for Health Sciences and Chancellor . . . . Michael F. Collins, M.D.
Chief of Staff to the Chancellor . . . . Brendan H. Chisholm
Provost and Executive Deputy Chancellor. . . . . Terence R. Flotte, M.D.
Deputy Chancellor for Commonwealth Medicine . . . . Joyce A. Murphy
Vice Chancellor for Communications. . . . . Edward J. Keohane
Vice Chancellor for Administration and Finance. . . . . Robert Jenal
Vice Chancellor for Development. . . . . Charles Pagnam
Vice Chancellor for Human Resources, Diversity & Inclusion . . . . Deborah Plummer, Ph.D.
Associate Vice Chancellor for University Relations. . . . . Mark L. Shelton
Vice Provost for School Services. . . . . Deborah Harmon Hines, Ph.D.
Vice Provost for Research. . . . . John Sullivan, M.D.
Vice Provost for Faculty Affairs. . . . . Luanne Thorndyke, M.D.
Associate Provost for Global Health . . . . Katherine Luzuriaga, M.D.
Associate Vice Provost for Research . . . . Thoru Pederson, Ph.D.
Associate Vice Provost for Research . . . . Gary Schneider, Ph.D.
Associate Vice Provost for Professional Development. . . . . Robert J. Milner, Ph.D.
Associate Vice Provost for Faculty Affairs. . . . . Judith Ockene, Ph.D.
Associate Vice Provost for Health Disparities Research . . . . Jeroan Allison, M.D., M.S.

School of Medicine Administrative Staff

Dean. . . . . Terence R. Flotte, M.D.
Assistant Dean for Administration, Chief of Staff. . . . . Lisa B. Beittel
Senior Associate Dean for Educational Affairs. . . . . Michele P. Pugnaire, M.D.
Senior Associate Dean for Clinical Affairs and
 Associate Dean for Graduate Medical
 Education . . . . Deborah M. DeMarco, M.D.
Associate Dean for Admissions. . . . . John Paraskos, M.D.
Associate Dean for Student Affairs . . . . Mai-Lan Rogoff, M.D.
Senior Associate Dean for UMass Medical Group . . . . Eric Dickson, M.D.
Associate Dean for Continuing Education
 (Interim), Associate Dean for Allied Health
 and Interprofessional Education . . . . Michael Kneeland, M.D.
Associate Dean, Berkshire Medical Center . . . . Martin Broder, M.D.
Associate Dean, Saint Vincent Hospital. . . . . Octavio Diaz, M.D.
Associate Dean, Milford Regional Medical Center. . . . . William Muller, M.D.
Associate Dean, Veterans Affairs. . . . . Neil J. Nusbaum, M.D.
Assistant Dean for Graduate Medical Education . . . . Anne Larkin, M.D.
Assistant Dean, Academic Achievement. . . . . Mark E. Quirk, M.D.
Assistant Dean, Student Advising . . . . Michael C. Ennis, M.D.
Director of Animal Medicine . . . . Jerald Silverman, D.V.M.

University of Massachusetts Medical School: MASSACHUSETTS

Department Chairs and Directors

Basic Sciences

Biochemistry and Molecular Pharmacology. . . . . C. Robert Matthews, Ph.D.
Cancer Biology . . . . Arthur Mercurio, Ph.D. (Interim)
Cell Biology. . . . . Gary S. Stein, Ph.D.
Microbiology and Physiological Systems . . . . Allan S. Jacobson, Ph.D.
Molecular Medicine. . . . . Michael P. Czech, Ph.D.
Neurobiology. . . . . Steven M. Reppert, M.D.
Program in Gene Function and Expression. . . . . Michael Green, M.D., Ph.D.
Gene Therapy Center . . . . Guangping Gao, Ph.D.
Program in Bioinformatics and Integrative Biology . . . . Zhiping Weng, Ph.D.
RNA Therapeutics Institute . . . . Victor Ambros, Ph.D., Craig Mello, Ph.D., Melissa Moore, Ph.D., and Phillip Zamore, Ph.D.
Program in Systems Biology . . . . Job Dekkar, Ph.D., and Marian Walhout, Ph.D.

Clinical Sciences

Quantitative Health Sciences . . . . Catarina I. Kiefe, M.D., Ph.D.
Anesthesiology. . . . . Stephen O. Heard, M.D.
Emergency Medicine . . . . Greg Volturo, M.D.
Family Medicine and Community Health . . . . Daniel H. Lasser, M.D., M.P.H.
Medicine. . . . . Robert W. Finberg, M.D.
Neurology. . . . . Robert Brown, M.D., D.Phil.
Obstetrics and Gynecology. . . . . Julia Johnson, M.D.
Ophthalmology . . . . George Asdourian, M.D. (Interim)
Orthopedics and Physical Rehabilitation. . . . . David Ayers, M.D.
Otolaryngology . . . . Daniel Kim, M.D. (Interim)
Pathology . . . . Kenneth L. Rock, M.D.
Pediatrics . . . . Marianne E. Felice, M.D.
Psychiatry . . . . Douglas M. Ziedonis, M.D., M.P.H.
Radiation Oncology. . . . . Thomas FitzGerald, M.D.
Radiology . . . . Joseph Ferrucci, M.D. (Interim)
Surgery . . . . Demetrius Litwin, M.D., M.B.A.

Graduate School of Biomedical Sciences Administrative Staff

Dean, Graduate School of Biomedical Sciences. . . . . Anthony Carruthers, Ph.D.
Associate Dean for Basic Biomedical Sciences . . . . Kendall Knight, Ph.D.
Associate Dean for Student Diversity. . . . . Brian Lewis, Ph.D.
Associate Dean for Clinical and Translational Research. . . . . Gyongyi Szabo, M.D., Ph.D.
Associate Dean, Graduate School of Biomedical Sciences (GSBS) . . . . Carole Upshur, Ed.D.
Associate Dean, Office for Postdoctoral Studies. . . . . Anthony Imbalzano, Ph.D.
Assistant Dean for GSBS Curriculum . . . . Mary Ellen Lane, Ph.D.

Tufts University School of Medicine
136 Harrison Avenue
Boston, Massachusetts 02111
617-636-7000; 617-636-6565 (dean's office); 617-636-0375 (fax)
Web site: www.tufts.edu/med

Tufts University School of Medicine is located in downtown Boston, two blocks south and east of the historic Boston Common. Established in 1893 as one of the component schools of Tufts College, its name was changed from Tufts College Medical School to its present title in 1955 when the original Tufts College, founded in 1852, changed to its university status. The medical and dental schools, the USDA Human Nutrition Research Center on Aging, the Gerald J. and Dorothy R. Friedman School of Nutrition Science and Policy, and the Sackler School of Graduate Biomedical Sciences are located in Boston. The Cummings School of Veterinary Medicine at Tufts University is located in Grafton, just west of Boston. The university's undergraduate campus is in Medford, just north of Boston.

Type: private
2011 total enrollment: 775
Clinical facilities: Tufts Medical Center and the Floating Hospital for Children, Baystate Medical Center, Lahey Clinic, Maine Medical Center, Newton-Wellesley Hospital, St. Elizabeth's Hospital

University Officials

President. . . . . Anthony P. Monaco, M.D., Ph.D.
Senior Vice President and Provost . . . . Margaret S. Newell, J.D. (Interim)
Vice Provost. . . . . Margaret S. Newell, J.D.
Executive Vice President . . . . Patricia L. Campbell
Associate Provost . . . . Mary Y. Lee, M.D.
Associate Provost . . . . Dawn Geronimo Terkla

Medical School Administrative Staff

Dean. . . . . Harris A. Berman, M.D.
Vice Dean for Research . . . . Naomi Rosenberg, Ph.D.
Dean for Clinical Affairs. . . . . Henry Klapholz, M.D.
Dean for Educational Affairs . . . . Scott Epstein, M.D.
Dean for Information Technology . . . . David A. Damassa, Ph.D.
Dean for Student Affairs . . . . Amy Kuhlik, M.D.
Dean for Baystate Medical Center. . . . . Kevin T. Hinchey, M.D. (Interim)
Dean for Admissions . . . . David A. Neumeyer, M.D.
Dean for Public Health and Professional Degree Programs . . . . Aviva Must, Ph.D.
Dean for International Affairs . . . . Adel Abu-moustafa, Ph.D.
Dean for Multicultural Affairs and Global Health . . . . Joyce A. Sackey, M.D.
Associate Dean for Educational Affairs . . . . Carolyn C. McVoy
Associate Dean for Students. . . . . Janet Kerle
Associate Dean for Admissions and Enrollment Services . . . . John A. Matias
Assistant Dean for Administration and Finance. Kenneth Goldsmith
Assistant Dean for Conflict of Interest Administration . . . . Marcia M. Boumil, J.D.
Assistant Dean for Faculty Affairs . . . . Kathleen Lowney
Assistant Dean for Faculty Development . . . . Maria Blanco, Ed.D.
Assistant Dean for Public Health and Professional Degree Programs . . . . Robin Glover
Executive Administrative Dean. . . . . Marsha Semuels
Senior Director of Development and Alumni Relations-Medicine. . . . . Jo Wellins (Interim)
Director of Admissions. . . . . Thomas Slavin
Director of Continuing Medical Education . . . . Rosalie Phillips
Director of Evaluation and Assessment . . . . Yung-Chi Sung, Ph.D.
Director of Financial Aid . . . . Tara Olsen
Director of the Hirsh Health Sciences Library. Eric D. Albright
Director for Multicultural Affairs and Student Programs . . . . Colleen Romain
Registrar . . . . Carol A. Duffey
Manager of Finance and Administration. . . . . Patrice Ambrosia
Academic Dean at Lahey Clinic . . . . David J. Schoetz, M.D.
Academic Dean at Maine Medical Center. Peter W. Bates, M.D.
Academic Dean at St. Elizabeth's Medical Center . . . . Nicolaos E. Madias, M.D.

Tufts University School of Medicine: MASSACHUSETTS

Department and Division or Section Chairs

Basic Sciences

Anatomy and Cellular Biology . . . . James E. Schwob, M.D., Ph.D.
Biochemistry . . . . Brian S. Schaffhausen, Ph.D.
Molecular Biology and Microbiology. . . . . John Leong, M.D., Ph.D.
Neuroscience. . . . . Philip G. Haydon, Ph.D.
Pathology . . . . Henry H. Wortis, M.D.
Molecular Physiology and Pharmacology. . . . . Eric Frank, M.D.

Clinical Sciences

Anesthesiology. . . . . B. Scott Segal, M.D.
Dermatology . . . . Alice B. Gottlieb, M.D., Ph.D.
Emergency Medicine . . . . Niels K. Rathlev, M.D.
Family Medicine . . . . Randy F. Wertheimer, M.D.
Medicine. . . . . Deeb N. Salem, M.D.
Neurology. . . . . Anish Bhardwaj, M.D.
Neurosurgery. . . . . Carl Heilman, M.D.
Obstetrics and Gynecology. . . . . Errol R. Norwitz, M.D.
Ophthalmology . . . . Jay S. Duker, M.D.
Orthopaedic Surgery . . . . Charles Cassidy, M.D.
Otolaryngology-Head and Neck Surgery . . . . Elie Rebeiz, M.D.
Pediatrics . . . . John Schreiber, M.D., Ph.D.
Physical Medicine and Rehabilitation . . . . Harry C. Webster, M.D. (Acting)
Psychiatry . . . . Paul Summergard, M.D.
Public Health and Community Medicine . . . . Aviva Must, Ph.D.
Radiation Oncology. . . . . David E. Wazer, M.D.
Radiology . . . . E. Kent Yucel, M.D.
Surgery . . . . William C. Mackey, M.D.
Urology. . . . . Gennaro A. Carpinito, M.D.

Michigan State University College of Human Medicine
A-110 East Fee Hall
East Lansing, Michigan 48824
517-353-1730 (East Lansing dean's office); 517-353-9969 (fax);
616-233-1678 (Grand Rapids dean's office); 616-458-4680 (fax)
Web site: www.humanmedicine.msu.edu

In 1960, there was a societal demand for more physicians, nationally and within the state. The College of Human Medicine thus began in 1964 with expectations that the college would make the maximum use of community health care facilities for clinical training and would place strong emphasis on training primary care and specialist physicians needed for the workforce of the state and nation. Issues of minority admissions, affirmative action, educational supports for disadvantaged students, and medical care for the poor are preeminent in the fabric of the college.

Type: public
2011 total enrollment: 690
Clinical facilities: Michigan State University Clinical Center; Flint Area Medical Education (Hurley Medical Center, McLaren Regional Medical Center, Genesys Regional Medical Center); Grand Rapids Campus (Spectrum Hospital, Saint Mary's Health Care, Gerber Memorial Hospital, Holland Community Hospital, Spectrum Health-United Memorial, Zeeland Community Hospital); Kalamazoo Center for Medical Studies (Bronson Health Care Group, Borgess Health); Lansing Campus (Sparrow Health System, Ingham Regional Medical Center); Midland Regional Campus (Gratiot Medical Center, MidMichigan Health-Midland, MidMichigan Health-Claire, MidMichigan Health-Gladwin); Traverse City Campus (Alpena Regional Medical Center, Charlevoix Area Hospital, Kalkaska Memorial Health Center, Mercy Hospital Cadilla, Munson Medical Center, Northern Michigan Regional Hospital, West Shore Medical Center); Upper Peninsula Regional Campus (Marquette General Health System, Michigan Bell Memorial Hospital, Michigan OSF St. Francis Hospital, Michigan Aspirus Keweenaw Hospital, Michigan Portage Health System, Michigan Iron County Community Hospital, Michigan Grandview Health System, Michigan Dickinson County Healthcare System, Michigan Baraga County Memorial Hospital, Michigan Helen Newberry Joy Hospital, Michigan War Memorial Hospital, Michigan Jacobetti Home for Veterans).

University Officials

President. . . . . Lou Anna Kimsey Simon, Ph.D.
Provost . . . . Kim A. Wilcox, Ph.D.

Medical School Administrative Staff

Dean. . . . . Marsha D. Rappley, M.D.
Senior Associate Dean for Academic Affairs . . . . Aron Sousa, M.D.
Associate Dean for Graduate Medical Education . . . . Peter Coggan, M.D.
Associate Dean for Prevention and Public Health . . . . Dean Sienko, M.D.
Associate Dean for College Wide Assessment . . . . Dianne Wagner, M.D.
Associate Dean for Research and Community Outreach . . . . Jeffrey Dwyer, Ph.D.
Associate Dean for Faculty Affairs and Development . . . . William Wadland, M.D.
Associate Dean for Student Affairs, Diversity, and Outreach. . . . . Wanda D. Lipscomb, Ph.D.
Assistant Dean for Capital and Strategic Planning . . . . Elizabeth Lawrence
Assistant Dean for Flint . . . . John B. Molidor, Ph.D.
Associate Dean for Grand Rapids . . . . Margaret Thompson, M.D.
Assistant Dean for Kalamazoo. . . . . Kevin Kavanaugh, M.D.
Assistant Dean for Lansing. . . . . Renuka Gera, M.D.
Assistant Dean for Midland Regional . . . . Paula Klose, M.D.
Assistant Dean for Traverse City . . . . Daniel M. Webster, M.D.
Assistant Dean for Upper Peninsula Region . . . . William Short, M.D.
Assistant Dean for Admissions . . . . Joel Maurer, M.D.
Assistant Dean for Preclinical Curriculum. . . . . Janet Osuch, M.D.
Senior Director for Advancement. . . . . Susan W. Lane
Assistant Dean for External Relations . . . . Jerry Kooiman
Assistant Dean for Graduate Medical Education . . . . Randy Pearson, M.D.

Michigan State University College of Human Medicine: MICHIGAN

Department and Division or Section Chairs

Basic Sciences

Anatomy . . . . Thomas Cooper
Biochemistry and Molecular Biology. . . . . Thomas D. Sharkey, Ph.D.
Epidemiology and Biostatistics . . . . Mathew Reeves, Ph.D.
Microbiology and Molecular Genetics. . . . . Walter Esselman, Ph.D.
Pharmacology and Toxicology . . . . William Jackson, Ph.D.
Physiology. . . . . David Kreulen, Ph.D.
Translational Science and Molecular Medicine . . . . Jack Lipton, Ph.D.

Clinical Sciences

Anesthesiology. . . . . Rodney D. Pease, D.O.
Cardiovascular Medicine . . . . M. Ashraf Mansour, M.D.
Clinical Neurosciences. . . . . Brian Smith, M.D.
Dermatology and Cutaneous Sciences. . . . . Brian Nickoloff, M.D.
Emergency Medicine . . . . Michael Brown, M.D.
Family Medicine . . . . William Wadland, M.D.
Human Pathology . . . . David Kruelen, Ph.D.
Medicine. . . . . Mary D. Nettleman, M.D.
Neurology and Ophthalmology . . . . David Kaufman, D.O.
Obstetrics, Gynecology, and Reproductive Biology. . . . . Richard E. Leach, M.D.
Pediatrics and Human Development. . . . . H. Dele Davies, M.D., M.Sc.
Psychiatry . . . . Jed Magen, D.O.
Psychiatry and Behavioral Science . . . . Eric Achtyes, M.D.
Radiology . . . . Thomas Cooper
Radiology and Biomedical Imaging . . . . Mark C. DeLano, M.D.
Surgery East . . . . Marc Basson, M.D.
Surgery West. . . . . M. Ashraf Mansour, M.D.

Institutes, Centers, and Programs

Ethics and Humanities in the Life Sciences. . . . . Tom Tomlinson, Ph.D.
Institute for HealthCare Studies. . . . . Vacant
Medical Education Research and Development. . . . . Brian Mavis, Ph.D.
Learning and Assessment Center . . . . Mary Kay Smith, M.S.N.

University of Michigan Medical School
1301 Catherine Street
4101 Medical Science Building I
Ann Arbor, Michigan 48109-5624
734-763-9600; 734-764-8175 (dean's office); 734-763-4936 (fax)
Web site: www.med.umich.edu/medschool

The University of Michigan Medical School admitted its first class of 91 entering students in 1850. Women were admitted as early as 1870. In 1880, the course was lengthened to three years, and in 1890 to four years.

Type: public
2011 total enrollment: 712
Clinical facilities: The University of Michigan Hospitals and Health Centers, including C. S. Mott Children's Hospital, University Hospital, W. K. Kellogg Eye Center, Cancer Center, Geriatrics Center, Cardiovascular Center, Depression Center, Van Voigtlander Women's Hospital and affiliated facilities; Catherine McAuley Health Center (St. Joseph Mercy Hospital); Veterans Administration Medical Center (Ann Arbor); Chelsea Hospital.

University Officials

President. . . . . Mary Sue Coleman, Ph.D.
Chancellor, University of Michigan-Dearborn . . . . Daniel E. Little, Ph.D.
Chancellor, University of Michigan-Flint. . . . . Ruth J. Person, Ph.D.
Executive Vice President for Academic Affairs and Provost . . . . Philip J. Hanlon, Ph.D.
Executive Vice President and Chief Financial Officer . . . . Timothy P. Slottow
Executive Vice President for Medical Affairs. . . . . Ora Hirsch Pescovitz, M.D.
Vice President for Development. . . . . Jerry A. May
Vice President for Research . . . . Stephen R. Forrest, Ph.D.
Vice President for Government Relations . . . . Cynthia H. Wilbanks
Vice President & General Counsel . . . . Suellyn Scarnecchia, J.D.
Vice President for Student Affairs. . . . . E. Royster Harper
Vice President and Secretary of the University . . . . Sally J. Churchhill
Vice President for Global Communications and Strategic Intiatives . . . . Lisa M. Rudgers

Medical School Administrative Staff

Dean. . . . . James O. Woolliscroft, M.D.
Senior Associate Dean for Clinical Affairs. David A. Spahlinger, M.D.
Senior Associate Dean for Research . . . . Steven L. Kunkel, Ph.D.
Senior Associate Dean for Education and Global Initiatives. . . . . Joseph C. Kolars, M.D.
Senior Associate Dean for Faculty and Faculty Development . . . . Margaret R. Gyetko, M.D.
Associate Dean for Medical Student Education . . . . Rajesh S. Mangrulkar, M.D., Ph.D.
Associate Dean for Graduate Medical Education . . . . Lisa M. Colletti, M.D.
Associate Dean for Graduate and Postdoctoral Studies . . . . Victor J. DiRita, Ph.D.
Associate Dean for Diversity and Career Development. . . . . Monica L. Lypson, M.D. (Interim)
Associate Dean for Regulatory Affairs. . . . . Raymond J. Hutchinson, M.D.
Associate Dean for Clinical and Translational Research. . . . . Thomas P. Shanley, M.D.
Assistant Dean for Admissions . . . . Steven E. Gay, M.D.
Assistant Dean for Graduate Medical Education . . . . Monica L. Lypson, M.D.
Assistant Dean for Clinical Faculty . . . . Elisabeth H. Quint, M.D.
Assistant Dean for Instructional Faculty . . . . Kevin C. Chung, M.D.
Assistant Dean for Research Faculty . . . . Nicholas W. Lukacs, Ph.D.
Assistant Dean for Clinical Affairs. . . . . Caroline S. Blaum, M.D.
Assistant Dean for Recruitment and Pre-
   Candidate Graduate Education . . . . Lori L. Isom, Ph.D.
Assistant Dean for Research . . . . Samuel M. Silver, M.D., Ph.D.
Assistant Dean for Student Programs . . . . James F. Peggs, M.D.
Assistant Dean for Longitudinal Learning &
   Educational Assessment . . . . Jennifer G. Christner, M.D.
Assistant Dean, VA Medical Center. . . . . Eric W. Young, M.D.
Assistant Dean for Educational Research and
   Quality Improvement . . . . Sally A. Santen, M.D., Ph.D.

University of Michigan Medical School: MICHIGAN

Department and Division or Section Chairs

Basic Sciences

Cell and Developmental Biology. . . . . J. Douglas Engel, Ph.D.
Biological Chemistry . . . . William L. Smith, Ph.D.
Human Genetics . . . . Sally A. Camper, Ph.D.
Medical Education. . . . . Larry D. Gruppen, Ph.D.
Microbiology and Immunology. . . . . Harry L. T. Mobley, Ph.D.
Molecular and Integrative Physiology . . . . M. Bishr Omary, M.D., Ph.D.
Pharmacology . . . . Paul F. Hollenberg, Ph.D.

Clinical Sciences

Anesthesiology. . . . . Kevin K. Tremper, M.D., Ph.D.
Dermatology . . . . John J. Voorhees, M.D.
Emergency Medicine . . . . William G. Barsan, M.D.
Family Medicine . . . . Philip Zazove, M.D. (Interim)
Internal Medicine . . . . John M. Carethers, M.D.
Neurology . . . . David J. Fink, M.D.
Neurosurgery. . . . . Karin M. Muraszko, M.D.
Obstetrics and Gynecology. . . . . Timothy R. B. Johnson, M.D.
Ophthalmology and Visual Sciences . . . . Paul R. Lichter, M.D.
Orthopaedic Surgery . . . . James E. Carpenter, M.D.
Otolaryngology . . . . Carol R. Bradford, M.D.
Pathology . . . . Jay L. Hess, M.D., Ph.D.
Pediatrics and Communicable Diseases. . . . . Valerie P. Castle, M.D.
Physical Medicine and Rehabilitation . . . . Edward A. Hurvitz, M.D.
Psychiatry . . . . Gregory W. Dalack, M.D.
Radiation Oncology. . . . . Theodore S. Lawrence, M.D., Ph.D.
Radiology . . . . N. Reed Dunnick, M.D.
Surgery . . . . Michael W. Mulholland, M.D., Ph.D.
Urology. . . . . David A. Bloom, M.D.

Institutes, Centers, and Program Directors

A. Alfred Taubman Medical Research Institute . . . . Eva L. Feldman, M.D., Ph.D.
Cardiovascular Center . . . . . Kim A. Eagle, M.D., Richard L. Prager, M.D., David J. Pinsky, M.D.,
and James C. Stanley, M.D. (co-dir.)
Center for Arrythmia Research. . . . . Jose Jalife, M.D.
Center for Computational Medicine and Bioinformatics . . . . Brian D. Athey, Ph.D.
Center for Organogenesis . . . . Gary D. Hammer, M.D., Ph.D.
Comprehensive Cancer Center. . . . . Max S. Wicha, M.D.
Depression Center. . . . . John F. Greden, M.D.
Geriatrics Center . . . . Jeffrey B. Halter, M.D.
Institute for Healthcare Policy and Innovation . . . . Rodney A. Hayward, M.D. (Interim)
Kresge Hearing Research Institute . . . . Jochen H. Schacht, Ph.D.
Medical Scientist Training Program . . . . Ronald J. Koenig, M.D., Ph.D.
Michigan Center for Translational Pathology . . . . Arul M. Chinnaiyan, M.D.
Michigan Comprehensive Diabetes Center . . . . Peter R. Arvan, M.D., Ph.D.
Michigan Institute for Clinical and Health Research . . . . Thomas P. Shanley, M.D.
Michigan Metabolomics and Obesity Center . . . . Charles Burant, M.D., Ph.D.
Michigan Nanotechnology Institute for Medicine
and Biological Sciences . . . . James R. Baker, Jr., M.D.
Molecular and Behavioral Neuroscience Institute . . . . Stanley J. Watson, M.D., Ph.D.,
and Huda Akil, Ph.D. (co-dir.)

Wayne State University School of Medicine

540 East Canfield
Detroit, Michigan 48201
313-577-1335 (dean's office); 313-577-8777 (fax)
Web site: www.med.wayne.edu

The school of medicine was founded in 1868 as the Detroit Medical College. It was the first established school of what was to become, in 1956, Wayne State University. It is one of the largest single-campus medical schools in the country.

Type: public
2011 total enrollment: 1,065
Clinical facilities: Barbara Ann Karmanos Cancer Institute, Detroit Receiving Hospital and University Health Center, Children's Hospital of Michigan, Harper University Hospital, Hutzel Womens Hospital, Sinai-Grace Hospital, Veterans Administration Medical Center, Rehabilitation Institute of Michigan, Kresge Eye Institute, Michigan Orthopaedic Specialty Hospital, William Beaumont Hospital, Huron Valley Sinai Hospital, Providence Hospital, North Oakland Medical Center, St. John Hospital and Medical Center, Oakwood Healthcare System, Bon Secours Hospital, St. Joseph Hospital (Pontiac), St. Joseph Hospital (Ann Arbor), Henry Ford Health System.

University Officials

President. . . . . Allen D. Gilmour (Interim)
Provost and Senior Vice President for Academic Affairs. . . . . Ronald T. Brown, Ph.D.
Vice President for Research . . . . Hilary Ratner, Ph.D.

Medical School Administrative Staff

Dean. . . . . Valerie M. Parisi, M.D., M.P.H., M.B.A.
Vice Dean of Business Affairs . . . . Kenneth Lee
Associate Dean of Admissions, Diversity and Inclusion. . . . . Silas Norman, M.D.
Assistant Dean for Student Affairs. . . . . Lisa MacLean, M.D.
Assistant Dean for Basic Science Education. Matthew Jackson, Ph.D.
Associate Dean for Undergraduate Medical Education . . . . Patrick Bridge, Ph.D.
Associate Dean for Graduate Medical Education . . . . Tsveti Markova, M.D., F.A.A.F.P.
Assistant Dean for Continuing Medical Education. . . . . David Pieper, Ph.D.
Vice Associate Dean for Research . . . . Bonita Stanton, M.D.
Assistant Dean for Clinical and Translational Research . . . . Michael Diamond, M.D.
Assistant Dean for Affiliate Research Programs . . . . Margot LaPointe, Ph.D.
Associate Dean for Graduate Programs. . . . . Robert Pauley, Ph.D.
Vice Dean of Clinical Affairs and Chief Medical Office . . . . Robert A. Frank, M.D.
Assistant Dean for Community Outreach and Urban Health . . . . Herbert Smitherman, M.D.
Executive Director and Chief Development Officer. . . . . Douglas Czajkowski
Manager of Public Affairs. . . . . Philip Van Hulle
Assistant Director of Financial Aid . . . . Deidre Moore
Registrar . . . . Mark Speece, M.D.
Vice Dean of Education . . . . Maryjean Schank, M.D.

Department Chairs and Division Heads

Basic Sciences

Anatomy and Cell Biology . . . . Linda Hazlett, Ph.D.
Biochemistry and Molecular Biology. Bharti Mitra, Ph.D. (Interim)
Immunology and Microbiology. . . . . Paul C. Montgomery, Ph.D.
Center for Molecular Medicine and Genetics . . . . Larry Grossman, Ph.D.
Pathology . . . . Wael Sakr, M.D.
Pharmacology . . . . Bonnie Sloane, Ph.D.
Physiology. . . . . J.P. Jin, Ph.D.

Wayne State University School of Medicine: MICHIGAN

Department and Division or Section Chairs

Clinical Sciences

Anesthesiology. . . . . Douglas Bacon, R.M.D.
Cancer Institute. . . . . Gerold Bepler, M.D., Ph.D.
Dermatology . . . . Darius Mehregan, M.D.
Emergency Medicine . . . . Suzanne White, M.D.
Family Medicine and Public Health Science . . . . John Boltri, M.D., F.A.A.F.P.
 Behavioral Science and Mental Health . . . . John Porcerelli, Ph.D.
 Occupational and Environmental Medicine. . . . . Bengt Arnetz, M.D., Ph.D.
Internal Medicine . . . . John M. Flack, M.D., M.P.H.
 Cardiology. . . . . Antonio Corillo, M.D.
 Critical Care and Pulmonary. . . . . Safwan Badr, M.D.
 Endocrinology . . . . Abdul B. Abou-Samra, M.D., Ph.D.
 Gastroenterology . . . . Milton Mutchnick, M.D.
 General Medicine. . . . . Donald Levine, M.D.
 Geriatrics. . . . . Lavoisier Cardoza, M.D.
 Hematology and Oncology . . . . Joseph P. Uberti, M.D., Ph.D.
 Infectious Diseases . . . . Jack D. Sobel, M.D.
 Nephrology . . . . Stephen Migdal, M.D.
 Rheumatology . . . . Frank Vascy, M.D.
Neurology. . . . . Robert P. Lisak, M.D.
Neurosurgery. . . . . Murali Guthikonda, M.D.
Obstetrics and Gynecology. . . . . Elizabeth Puscheck, M.D., M.S.
Ophthalmology . . . . Mark Juzych, M.D.
Orthopedic Surgery. . . . . Lawrence Morawa, M.D.
Otolaryngology . . . . Robert H. Mathog, M.D.
Pediatrics . . . . Bonita F. Stanton, M.D.
 Allergy, Immunology . . . . Elizabeth Second, M.D.
 Critical Care Medicine . . . . Mary Lieh-Lai, M.D., and Ashok Sarnaik, M.D.
 Emergency Medicine . . . . Prashant Mahajan, M.D., and Srinikasan Suresh, M.D.
 Gastroenterology . . . . Mohammed El-Baba, M.D., and Howard Fischer, M.D.
 General Pediatrics . . . . Yvonne Friday, M.D.
 Genetics and Metabolism . . . . David Stockfon, M.D.
 Hematology and Oncology . . . . . . Jeanne Lusher, M.D., and Yaddanapudi Ravindranath, M.D.
 Hospitalist . . . . Allison Ball, M.D.
 Infectious Diseases . . . . Basim Asmar, M.D.
 Neonatology. . . . . Seetha Shankaran, M.D.
 Nephrology . . . . Tej Mattoo, M.D., and Harry Chugani, M.D.
 Neurology . . . . Coyula Acsadi, M.D.
 Pediatric Education . . . . Deepak Kamat, M.D.
 Pharmacology and Toxicology . . . . Diane Chugani, M.D.
 PM&R . . . . Edward Dabrowski, M.D.
 Research Prevention. . . . . Xiaoming Li, Ph.D.
 Pulmonary Diseases . . . . Ibrahim A. Abdulhamid, M.D.
 Children's Research Center of Michigan . . . . William Lyman, Ph.D.
Physical Medicine and Rehabilitation . . . . Jay Meythaler, M.D., J.D.
Psychiatry and Behavioral Neurosciences . . . . David Rosenberg, M.D.
Radiation Oncology. . . . . Andre Konski, M.D., M.B.A.
Radiology . . . . Wilbur Smith, M.D.
Surgery . . . . Donald Weaver, M.D.
 Breast . . . . David Bouwman, M.D.
 Cardiothoracic. . . . . Larry Stephenson, M.D.
 General Surgery. . . . . Donald Weaver, M.D.
 Pediatric Surgery . . . . Michael Klein, M.D.
 Plastic and Reconstructive. . . . . Eti Gursel, M.D.
 Transplantation . . . . Scott Gruber, M.D.
 Trauma . . . . James Tyburski, M.D.
 Vascular. . . . . O.W. Brown, M.D., Ph.D.
 Veteran Affairs. . . . . Walter Salwen, M.D.
Urology. . . . . Michael Cher, M.D.

Mayo Medical School

200 First Street, S.W.
Rochester, Minnesota 55905
507-538-4897; 507-266-5299 (dean's office); 507-284-2634 (fax)
Web site: www.mayo.edu

Mayo Medical School, founded in 1972, is part of the Mayo Clinic. Other schools at the Mayo Clinic are the Mayo School of Graduate Medical Education, founded in 1915; the Mayo Graduate School, formalized in 1989; the Mayo School of Health Sciences, formalized in 1972; and the Mayo School of Continuous Professional Development, established in 1996.

Type: private
2011 total enrollment: 168
Clinical facilities: Mayo Clinic, Saint Mary's Hospital, Methodist Hospital (Rochester, Minnesota); Mayo Clinic Florida; Mayo Clinic Arizona, Mayo Clinic Hospitals in Phoenix and Jacksonville, and regional affiliates.

Mayo Clinic Officials

Chair, Board of Trustees . . . . Marilyn C. Nelson
President and Chief Executive Officer . . . . John H. Noseworthy, M.D.
Vice President and Chief Administrative Officer . . . . Shirley A. Weis
Vice President . . . . Nina M. Schwenk, M.D.
Vice President, Mayo Clinic, Florida . . . . William C. Rupp, M.D.
Vice President, Mayo Clinic, Arizona . . . . Wyatt W. Decker, M.D.
Executive Dean for Education . . . . Terrence Cascino, M.D.
Director for Research, Florida . . . . Thomas G. Brott, M.D.
Executive Dean for Research, Rochester . . . . Robert A. Rizza, M.D.
Director for Research, Arizona . . . . Laurence J. Miller, M.D.
Chair, Clinical Practice Committee, Florida . . . . Stephen M. Lange, M.D.
Chair, Clinical Practice Committee, Rochester . . . . C. Michael Harper, M.D.
Chair, Clinical Practice Committee, Arizona . . . . Richard Helmers, M.D.

Department of Education Services Officials

Chair, Department of Education Administration . . . . Paula N. Menkosky
Dean, Mayo Medical School . . . . Keith D. Lindor, M.D.
Associate Dean for Academic Affairs, Mayo Medical School . . . . Joseph Grande, M.D., Ph.D.
Associate Dean for Faculty Affairs, Mayo Medical School . . . . Thomas R. Viggiano, M.D.
Associate Dean for Student Affairs, Mayo Medical School . . . . Alexandra P. Wolanskyj, M.D.
Associate Dean for Undergraduate Education, Florida . . . . Gerardo Colon-Otero, M.D.
Associate Dean for Undergraduate Education, Arizona . . . . M. Edwyn Harrison, M.D.
Division Chair, Florida . . . . Nell Robinson
Division Chair, Arizona . . . . Tamara K. Kary
Dean, Mayo School of Graduate Medical Education . . . . Mark Warner, M.D.
Vice Dean, Mayo School of Graduate Medical Education . . . . Steve Rose, M.D.
Associate Dean, Internal Medicine and Medical Subspecialties . . . . Darrell S. Pardi, M.D.
Associate Dean, Medical and Laboratory Specialties . . . . Paula Schomberg, M.D.
Associate Dean, Surgery and Surgical Specialties . . . . Melanie Richards, M.D.
Associate Dean, Mayo School of Graduate Education, Florida . . . . Steven Petrou, M.D.
Associate Dean, Mayo School of Graduate
 Medical Education, Arizona . . . . Richard S. Zimmerman, M.D.
Dean, Mayo Graduate School . . . . L. James Maher III, Ph.D.
Associate Dean for Academic Affairs, Mayo Graduate School . . . . (TBD)
Associate Dean for Student Affairs, Mayo Graduate School . . . . Bruce F. Horazdovsky, Ph.D.
Dean, Mayo School of Health Sciences . . . . Claire E. Bender, M.D.
Associate Dean for Student Affairs, Mayo School of Health Sciences . . . . David Agerter, M.D.
Associate Dean for Academic Affairs, Mayo
 School of Health Sciences . . . . Michael Silber, M.D.
Associate Dean, Mayo School of Health Sciences, Florida . . . . Galen Perdikis, M.D.
Associate Dean, Mayo School of Health Sciences, Arizona . . . . Catherine Roberts, M.D.
Dean, Mayo School of Continuous Professional Development . . . . Richard A. Berger, M.D.
Associate Dean, Mayo School of Continuous
 Professional Development, Rochester . . . . Darryl S. Chutka, M.D.

Associate Dean, Mayo School of Continuous
  Professional Development, Florida . . . . Thomas C. Gerber, M.D., Ph.D.
Associate Dean, Mayo School of Continuous
  Professional Development, Arizona . . . . Russell I. Heigh, M.D.
Library Director, Mayo Foundation. . . . . J. Michael Homan
Chief Public Affairs Officer . . . . John La Forgia

Department and Division or Section Chairs

Basic Sciences

Anatomy. . . . . Wojciech Pawlina, M.D.
Biochemistry and Molecular Biology. . . . . Mark A. McNiven, Ph.D.
Health Sciences Research. . . . . Veronique Roger, M.D.
Immunology . . . . Larry R. Pease, Ph.D.
Laboratory Medicine and Pathology . . . . Franklin R. Cockerill, M.D.
Pharmacology . . . . Matthew M. Ames, Ph.D.
Physiology and Biomedical Engineering . . . . Gary C. Sieck, Ph.D.

Clinical Sciences

Anesthesiology. . . . . Bradley Narr, M.D.
Dentistry . . . . Sreenivas Koka, D.D.S.
Dermatology . . . . Clark C. Otley, M.D.
Diagnostic Radiology . . . . Bernard King, M.D.
Emergency Medical Services. . . . . Annie T. Sadosty, M.D.
Family Medicine . . . . Matthew E. Bernard, M.D.
Internal Medicine . . . . Morie A. Gertz, M.D.
  Allergic Diseases. . . . . James T. C. Li, M.D.
  Cardiovascular Diseases. . . . . Charanjit S. Rihal, M.D.
  Community Internal Medicine . . . . Robert J. Stroebel, M.D.
  Endocrinology and Metabolism. . . . . John C. Morris, M.D.
  Gastroenterology . . . . Gregory J. Gores, M.D.
  General Internal Medicine . . . . Paul S. Mueller, M.D.
  Hematology . . . . Dennis Gastineau, M.D.
  Infectious Diseases . . . . Larry M. Baddour, M.D.
  Nephrology and Hypertension . . . . James T. McCarthy, M.D.
  Preventive Medicine . . . . Donald Hensrud, M.D.
  Pulmonary and Critical Care Medicine . . . . Andrew H. Limper, M.D.
  Rheumatology . . . . Eric Matteson, M.D.
Medical Genetics . . . . Dusica Babovic-Vuksanovic, M.D.
Neurologic Surgery . . . . Fredric B. Meyer, M.D.
Neurology . . . . Robert Brown, M.D.
Obstetrics and Gynecology. . . . . Bobbie S. Gostout, M.D.
Oncology. . . . . Charles Erlichman, M.D.
  Divison of Oncology Research. . . . . Scott H. Kaufmann, M.D., Ph.D.
  Medical Oncology . . . . Jan C. Buckner, M.D.
  Radiation Oncology . . . . Robert Foote, M.D.
Ophthalmology . . . . Jay C. Erie, M.D.
Orthopedics . . . . Daniel J. Berry, M.D.
Otorhinolaryngology . . . . Charles W. Beatty, M.D.
Pediatrics . . . . Ann M. Reed, M.D.
Physical Medicine and Rehabilitation . . . . Carmen M. Terzic, M.D., Ph.D.
Psychiatry and Psychology . . . . Mark A. Frye, M.D.
Surgery . . . . Claude Deschamps, M.D.
  Cardiovascular . . . . Hartzell V. Schaff, M.D.
  Colon and Rectal . . . . Bruce Wolff, M.D.
  Gastroenterologic. . . . . Michael B. Farnell, M.D.
  Plastic and Reconstructive. . . . . Steve Moran, M.D.
  Pediatric Surgery . . . . Michael Ishitani, M.D.
  Thoracic and Cardiovascular. . . . . Francis C. Nichols III, M.D.
  Transplantation . . . . Charles Rosen, M.D.
  Vascular. . . . . Thomas C. Bower, M.D.
Urology. . . . . Paul E. Andrews, M.D.

University of Minnesota Medical School

Mayo Mail Code 293
420 Delaware Street, S.E.
Minneapolis, Minnesota 55455
612-625-7977 (Admissions); 612-624-8101 (Student Affairs);
612-625-3622 (curriculum affairs); 612-626-4949 (dean's office)
Web site: www.med.umn.edu

The medical school, founded in 1888, is a major unit of the academic health center of the University of Minnesota. The buildings of the medical school, the University of Minnesota Medical Center, and the other units of the academic health center are located on the east bank portion of the Twin Cities campus of the University of Minnesota in Minneapolis and on the Duluth campus. The mission of the Duluth campus is educating future rural family physicians.

Type: public
2011 total enrollment: 998
Clinical facilities: University of Minnesota Medical Center, Fairview; Hennepin County Medical Center; Regions Hospital; Veterans Affairs Medical Center (Minneapolis); Children's Health Care; and several other community hospitals. Duluth Family Practice Center, Miller-Dwan Hospital and Medical Center, St. Luke's Hospital, St. Mary's Medical Center.

University Officials

President. . . . . Eric W. Kaler, Ph.D.
Vice President, Health Sciences . . . . Aaron L. Friedman, M.D.

Medical School Administrative Staff

Dean of the Medical School. . . . . Aaron L. Friedman, M.D.
Vice Dean, Clinical Affairs . . . . Barbara S. Daniels, M.D.
Vice Dean, Education . . . . Vacant
Vice Dean, Research . . . . W. Tucker LeBien, Ph.D.
Dean, Regional Campus in Duluth. . . . . Gary L. Davis, Ph.D.
Senior Associate Dean, Planning and Evaluation. . . . . Mark S. Paller, M.D.
Associate Dean, Strategic Projects. . . . . Patricia A. Mulcahy
Assistant Dean, Assessment, Curriculum and Evaluation . . . . Majka B. Woods, Ph.D.
Associate Dean, Faculty Affairs . . . . Vacant
Chief Financial Officer. . . . . Peter J. Mitsch
Chief Administrative Officer. . . . . Ann L. Schwind
Associate Dean, Graduate Medical Education . . . . Louis J. Ling, M.D.
Senior Associate Dean, Undergraduate Medical Education . . . . Kathleen V. Watson, M.D.
Associate Dean, Admissions . . . . Paul T. White, J.D.
Director, International Medical Education and Research. . . . . Phillip K. Peterson, M.D.

University of Minnesota Medical School: MINNESOTA

Department and Division or Section Chairs

Basic Sciences

Biochemistry, Molecular Biology, and Biophysics . . . . David A. Bernlohr, Ph.D.
Genetics, Cell Biology, and Development . . . . Michael B. O'Connor, Ph.D.
Integrative Biology and Physiology . . . . Joseph M. Metzger, M.D.
Laboratory Medicine and Pathology . . . . Leo T. Furcht, M.D.
Microbiology . . . . Ashley T. Haase, M.D.
Neuroscience . . . . Timothy J. Ebner, M.D., Ph.D.
Pharmacology . . . . Horace H. Loh, Ph.D.

Clinical Sciences

Anesthesiology . . . . Richard C. Prielipp, M.D.
Dermatology . . . . Maria D. Hordinsky, M.D.
Emergency Medicine . . . . Joseph E. Clinton, M.D.
Family Medicine and Community Health . . . . Macaran A. Baird, M.D.
Medicine . . . . Wesley J. Miller, M.D.
Neurology . . . . Jerrold L. Vitek, M.D., Ph.D.
Neurosurgery . . . . Stephen J. Haines, M.D., Ph.D.
Obstetrics, Gynecology, and Women's Health . . . . Linda F. Carson, M.D.
Ophthalmology . . . . Jay H. Krachmer, M.D.
Orthopaedic Surgery . . . . Denis R. Clohisy, M.D.
Otolaryngology . . . . Bevan Yueh, M.D.
Pediatrics . . . . Joseph P. Neglia, M.D.
Physical Medicine and Rehabilitation . . . . Dennis D. Dykstra, M.D., Ph.D.
Psychiatry . . . . S. Charles Schulz, M.D.
Radiology . . . . Charles A. Dietz, M.D.
Surgery . . . . Selwyn M. Vickers, M.D.
Therapeutic Radiology and Radiation Oncology . . . . Kathryn E. Dusenbery, M.D.
Urologic Surgery . . . . Badrinath R. Konety, M.D.

Other Programs

Brain Sciences Center . . . . Apostolos P. Georgopoulos, M.D., Ph.D.
Center for Developmental Biology . . . . David A. Zarkower, Ph.D.
Deborah E. Powell Center for Women's Health . . . . Nancy C. Raymond, M.D.
Diabetes Research, Center for . . . . Elizabeth Seaquist, M.D.
Engineering in Medicine, Institute for . . . . Vacant
Genome Engineering, Center for . . . . Daniel F. Voytas, Ph.D.
History of Medicine . . . . Jennifer Gunn, Ph.D.
Immunology Center . . . . Matthew F. Mescher, Ph.D.
Infectious Disease & Microbiology Translational
   Research, Center for . . . . Paul R. Bohjanen, M.D., Ph.D.
Institute for Human Genetics . . . . Brian C. VanNess, Ph.D., and David A. Largaespada, Ph.D.
Lillehei Heart Institute . . . . Daniel J. Garry, M.D.
Lung Science and Health, Center for . . . . Marshall I. Hertz, M.D.
M.D.-Ph.D. Program . . . . Yoji Shimizu, Ph.D.
Magnetic Resonance Research, Center for . . . . Kamil Ugurbil, Ph.D.
Masonic Cancer Center . . . . Douglas Yee, M.D.
Rural Physician Associate Program . . . . Kathleen D. Brooks, M.D.
Schulze Diabetes Institute . . . . Bernard J. Hering, Ph.D.
Stem Cell Institute . . . . Jonathan M. W. Slack, M.D.

University of Mississippi School of Medicine

2500 North State Street
Jackson, Mississippi 39216-4505
601-984-1000; 601-984-1010 (dean's office); 601-984-1011 (fax)
Web site: www.umc.edu

The University of Mississippi School of Medicine was established at Oxford in 1903 as a two-year school. In 1955, it was moved to the University of Mississippi Medical Center in Jackson and expanded to a four-year program. The first degrees were awarded in 1957.

Type: public
2011 total enrollment: 485
Clinical facilities: University Hospital, Blair E. Batson Hospital for Children, Winfred L. Wiser Hospital for Women and Infants, Wallace Conerly Hospital for Critical Care, University Rehabilitation Center, Mississippi Children's Cancer Clinic, G.V. "Sonny" Montgomery Department of Veterans Affairs Medical Center (Jackson), University Hospital and Clinics-Holmes County.

University Officials

Chancellor . . . . Daniel W. Jones, M.D.
Vice Chancellor for Health Affairs and Dean, School of Medicine . . . . James E. Keeton, M.D.
Associate Vice Chancellor for Health Affairs . . . . LouAnn Woodward, M.D.
Associate Vice Chancellor for Academic Affairs . . . . Helen R. Turner, M.D., Ph.D.
Chief Financial Officer. . . . . James Wentz
Chief Executive Officer, University Hospitals and Clinics. . . . . David G. Putt, F.A.C.H.E.
Chief Administrative Officer. . . . . David L. Powe, Ed.D.
Director, Office of Strategic Research Alliances, Medical Center . . . . David Dzielak, Ph.D.
Associate Vice Chancellor for Research. . . . . John Hall, Ph.D.
Associate Vice Chancellor, Multicultural Affairs. Jasmine Taylor, M.D.
Dean, School of Graduate Studies in the Health Sciences . . . . Joey Granger, Ph.D.
Director, Student Records and Registrar. . . . . Barbara Westerfield
Chief Public Affairs and Communications Officer . . . . Thomas H. Fortner
Director, Continuing Health Professional
  Education, Medical Center . . . . Shirley Schlessinger, M.D.
Director, Rowland Medical Library. . . . . Susan B. Clark, M.L.S.

Medical School Administrative Staff

Vice Dean . . . . LouAnn Woodward, M.D.
Associate Dean, Student Affairs . . . . Jerry F. Clark, Ph.D.
Associate Dean, Admissions . . . . Steven T. Case, Ph.D.
Associate Dean, Graduate Medical Education . . . . Shirley Schlessinger, M.D.
Associate Dean for Education for VA Affairs . . . . Sharon P. Douglas, M.D.
Associate Dean, Academic Affairs . . . . Loretta Jackson-Williams, M.D., Ph.D.
Associate Dean for Faculty Affairs. . . . . Patrick Smith, Ph.D.
Associate Dean for Multicultural Affairs . . . . Jasmine P. Taylor, M.D.
Director, Laboratory Animal Facilities. . . . . Andrew W. Grady, D.V.M.

University of Mississippi School of Medicine: MISSISSIPPI

Department and Division or Section Chairs

Basic Sciences

Neurobiology and Anatomical Sciences. . . . . James C. Lynch, Ph.D. (Interim)
Biochemistry . . . . Donald B. Sittman, Jr., Ph.D.
Microbiology . . . . Richard J. O'Callaghan, Ph.D.
Pathology . . . . Steven A. Bigler, M.D.
Pharmacology and Toxicology . . . . Richard J. Roman, Ph.D.
Physiology and Biophysics . . . . John E. Hall, Ph.D.

Clinical Sciences

Anesthesiology. . . . . Thomas Allingham, M.D. (Interim)
Emergency Medicine . . . . Richard Summers, M.D.
Family Medicine . . . . Diane K. Beebe, M.D.
Medicine. . . . . Shirley Schlessinger, M.D. (Interim)
Neurology . . . . Alexander Auchus, M.D.
Neurosurgery. . . . . H. Louis Harkey, M.D.
Obstetrics and Gynecology. . . . . Michelle Owens, M.D. (Interim)
Ophthalmology . . . . Ching J. Chen, M.D.
Orthopedic Surgery. . . . . Robert A. McGuire, Jr., M.D.
Otolaryngology and Communicative Sciences . . . . Scott P. Stringer, M.D.
Pediatrics . . . . Frederick Barr, M.D.
Psychiatry . . . . Grayson Norquist, M.D.
Radiation Oncology. . . . . Srinivasan Vijayakumar, M.B.B.S.
Radiology . . . . Timothy McCowan, M.D.
Surgery . . . . Marc E. Mitchell, M.D.

University of Missouri—Columbia School of Medicine

MA202 Medical Sciences Building, DC018.00
One Hospital Drive
Columbia, Missouri 65212
573-882-2923 (medical education); 573-882-1566 (dean's office); 573-884-4808 (fax)
Web site: http://som.missouri.edu

Founded in 1841, the University of Missouri School of Medicine offered only a two-year basic sciences program for much of its early existence. The present four-year program dates from 1956 when the University Hospital opened. Partnering with the University of Missouri Health Care, the school of medicine is located on the Columbia campus.

Type: public
2011 total enrollment: 393
Clinical facilities: University Hospital; Children's Hospital; Women's and Children's Hospital; Ellis Fischel Cancer Center; Harry S Truman Veterans Affairs Hospital; Howard A. Rusk Rehabilitation Center; Missouri Psychiatric Center; Missouri Rehabilitation Center at Mt. Vernon, Missouri; Capital Region Medical Center, Jefferson City, Missouri; and Cooper County Memorial Hospital, Boonville, Missouri.

University Officials

President . . . . Timothy M. Wolfe (Interim)
Senior Associate Vice President for Academic Affairs . . . . Steven Graham, Ph.D.
Vice President for Finance and Administration . . . . Nikki Krawitz, Ph.D.
Chancellor, Columbia campus . . . . Brady Deaton, Ph.D.
Vice Chancellor for Health System . . . . Harold A. Williamson, Jr., M.D.
Provost, Columbia campus . . . . Brian L. Foster, Ph.D.

Medical School Administrative Staff

Dean . . . . Robert Churchill, M.D.
Senior Associate Dean for Administration and Finance . . . . Kenneth Hammann
Senior Associate Dean for Clinical Affairs . . . . Les W. Hall, M.D.
Senior Associate Dean for Clinical Outcomes . . . . Kevin Dellsperger, M.D., Ph.D.
Senior Associate Dean for Diversity and Inclusion . . . . Ellis Ingram, M.D.
Senior Associate Dean for Education . . . . Linda Headrick, M.D.
Senior Associate Dean for Research . . . . Jamal A. Ibdah, M.D., Ph.D.
Associate Dean for Alumni Affairs . . . . Ted D. Groshong, M.D.
Associate Dean for Curricular Improvement . . . . John W. Gay, M.D.
Senior Associate Dean for Faculty Affairs . . . . Michael L. Misfeldt, Ph.D.
Associate Dean for Graduate Medical Education . . . . Debra Koivunen, M.D.
Associate Dean for Learning Strategies . . . . Kimberly Hoffman, Ph.D.
Associate Dean for Research . . . . Jerry Parker, Ph.D.
Associate Dean for Rural Health . . . . Weldon Webb
Associate Dean for Student Programs and
    Professional Development . . . . Rachel Brown, M.B.B.S.
Director, Center for Health Care Quality . . . . Douglas Wakefield, Ph.D.
Director, Health Sciences Library . . . . Deborah H. Ward
Director, Interdisciplinary Center on Aging . . . . Steven Zweig, M.D.
Director, Diabetes and Cardiovascular Health . . . . James R. Sowers, M.D.
Director, Ellis Fischel Cancer Center . . . . Charles W. Caldwell, M.D., Ph.D.
Director, National Center for Gender Physiology . . . . Virginia Huxley, Ph.D.
Director, Radiopharmaceutical Sciences Institute . . . . Wynn A. Volkert, Ph.D.

Department and Division or Section Chairs

Basic Sciences

Biochemistry . . . . Gerald L. Hazelbauer, Ph.D.
Molecular Microbiology and Immunology . . . . Mark McIntosh, Ph.D.
Medical Pharmacology and Physiology . . . . Ronald Korthuis, Ph.D.

Clinical Sciences

Anesthesiology and Perioperative Medicine. . . . . Joseph L. Reeves-Viets, M.D.
Child Health . . . . Timothy Fete, M.D.
   Adolescent Medicine . . . . Melissa Lawson, M.D.
   Cardiology . . . . David E. Draper, M.D.
   Critical Care. . . . . Patricia Wankum, M.D.
   Developmental Pediatrics . . . . Tracy Stroud, D.O.
   Diabetes and Endocrinology. . . . . Bert Bachrach, M.D.
   Gastroenterology . . . . Alejandro Ramirez, M.D.
   General Pediatrics . . . . Thomas Selva, M.D.
   Genetics. . . . . Jerome Gorski, M.D.
   Hematology and Oncology . . . . Thomas Loew, M.D.
Hospitalist Medicine . . . . Kyle Moylan, M.D.
   Hospitalist . . . . Catalina Kersten, M.D.
   Infectious Disease, Immunology, and Rheumatology . . . . Michael Cooperstock, M.D.
   Neonatology. . . . . John A. Pardalos, M.D.
   Nephrology . . . . Ted D. Groshong, M.D.
   Neurology . . . . Nitin Patel, M.D.
   Pulmonary Medicine and Allergy . . . . James D. Acton, M.D.
Dermatology . . . . Karen Edison, M.D.
Emergency Medicine . . . . John Montgomery, M.D. (Interim)
Family and Community Medicine. . . . . Steven C. Zweig, M.D.
Internal Medicine . . . . David Fleming, M.D.
   Cardiovascular Medicine. . . . . William Fay, M.D., Ph.D.
   Endocrinology, Diabetes, and Metabolism . . . . James R. Sowers, M.D.
   Gastroenterology and Hepatology . . . . Jamal A. Ibdah, M.D., Ph.D.
   General Internal Medicine . . . . Robert Lancey, M.D.
   Hematology and Medical Oncology. Carl Freter, M.D., Ph.D.
   Immunology and Rheumatology . . . . Darcy Folzenlogen, M.D.
   Infectious Disease. . . . . William Salzer, M.D.
   Nephrology . . . . Ramesh Khanna, M.D.
   Pulmonary, Critical Care, and Environmental Medicine . . . . . . Stevan P. Whitt, M.D. (Interim)
Neurology . . . . Pradeep Sahota, M.D.
Obstetrics, Gynecology, and Women's Health . . . . Hung Winn, M.D., J.D.
   Gynecologic Oncology . . . . Mark I. Hunter, M.D.
   Maternal Fetal Medicine. . . . . Randall C. Floyd, M.D.
   Obstetrics and Gynecology Generalist . . . . Jonathan Thomas, M.D.
   Reproductive Endocrinology and Infertility . . . . Danny J. Schust, M.D.
   Urogynecology. . . . . Raymond Foster, M.D.
Ophthalmology. . . . . John W. Cowden, M.D.
Orthopaedic Surgery . . . . James Stannard, M.D.
Otolaryngology-Head and Neck Surgery . . . . Robert Zitsch, M.D.
Pathology and Anatomical Sciences . . . . Douglas Anthony, M.D., Ph.D.
Physical Medicine and Rehabilitation . . . . Greg Worsowicz, M.D.
Psychiatry . . . . John Lauriello, M.D.
   Adult and Outpatient Clinical. . . . . John Lauriello, M.D.
   Child and Adolescent. . . . . Laine Young-Walker, M.D.
Radiology . . . . Kenneth Rall, M.D.
   Diagnostic Radiology . . . . Kenneth Rall, M.D.
   Mammography. . . . . Michael Richards, M.D.
   Nuclear . . . . Amolak Singh, M.D.
   Radiation Oncology . . . . Stephen Westgate, M.D.
Surgery . . . . Jerry Rogers, M.D.
   Acute Care. . . . . Stephen Barnes, M.D.
   Cardiothoracic . . . . Ajit Tharakan, M.D.
   General Surgery. . . . . Roger de la Torre, M.D.
   Neurosurgery. . . . . N. Scott Litofsky, M.D.
   Plastic and Reconstructive Surgery . . . . Charles L. Puckett, M.D.
   Surgical Oncology . . . . Paul S. Dale, M.D.
   Urology . . . . Mark Wakefield, M.D. (Interim)
   Vascular Surgery. . . . . W. Kirt Nichols, M.D.

Other

Health Management and Informatics . . . . Lanis L. Hicks, Ph.D. (Interim)
Nutrition and Exercise Physiology . . . . Christopher D. Hardin, Ph.D.

University of Missouri—Kansas City School of Medicine

2411 Holmes Street
Kansas City, Missouri 64108-2792
816-235-1808 (dean's office); 816-235-5277 (fax)
Web site: www.med.umkc.edu

The school of medicine is part of a four-campus university system in Missouri that includes Kansas City, Columbia, St. Louis, and Rolla. It is one of four health science schools in Kansas City. The medical school offers a six-year combined B.A.-M.D. program. The first class enrolled in fall 1971.

Type: public
2011 total enrollment: 617
Clinical facilities: Children's Mercy Hospital, Truman Medical Center Hospital Hill, Truman Medical Center-Lakewood, the Center for Behavioral Health, St. Luke's Hospital of Kansas City, Kansas City Veterans Affairs Medical Center.

University Officials

President. . . . . Stephen J. Owens (Interim)
Chancellor . . . . Leo E. Morton
Provost and Vice Chancellor for Academic Affairs. Gail Hackett, Ph.D.

Medical School Administrative Staff

Dean. . . . . Betty M. Drees, M.D.
Senior Associate Dean . . . . Paul G. Cuddy, Pharm.D.
Senior Associate Dean for Women's Health . . . . Dev Maulik, M.D., Ph.D.
Chief Financial Officer. . . . . Mark Mikkelsen
Associate Dean for Student Affairs . . . . Brenda Rogers, M.D.
Associate Dean and Chair, Graduate Medical Education . . . . Jill Moormeier, M.D.
Associate Dean for Medical Education and Research. . . . . Louise M. Arnold, Ph.D.
Associate Dean for Curriculum. . . . . Stefanie Ellison, M.D.
Associate Dean, Office of Diversity and Community Partnership . . . . Susan Wilson, Ph.D.
Associate Dean for The Children's Mercy Hospital Programs. . . . . Jane F. Knapp, M.D.
Associate Dean for Truman Medical Center Programs. . . . . Mark T. Steele, M.D.
Associate Dean for St. Luke's Programs . . . . Diana Dark, M.D.
Associate Dean for the Center for Behavioral Medicine Programs . . . . J. Stuart Munro, M.D.
Associate Dean for Research. . . . . Travis B. Solomon, M.D., Ph.D.
Assistant Dean Admissions and Recruitment. . . . . Alice Arredondo
Assistant Dean of Graduate Studies. . . . . Julie Banderas, Pharm.D.
Assistant Dean for Years 1 and 2. . . . . George Harris, M.D.
Assistant Dean for Truman Medical Center, Lakewood Programs. . . . . Rose J. Zwerenz, M.D.
Assistant Dean for Career Advising. . . . . Felix Okah, M.D.
Assistant Dean for Faculty Development . . . . John Foxworth, Pharm.D.
Assistant Dean for Research . . . . Mark Hecker, Pharm.D.
Chair, Council on Continuing Education . . . . John Foxworth, Pharm.D.
Chair, Council of Docents . . . . George R. Reisz, M.D.
Chair, Faculty Council . . . . David Hermanns, M.D.
Chair, Council on Evaluation . . . . Sara E. Gardner, M.D.
Chair, Council on Selection . . . . R. Stephen Griffith, M.D.
Director, Health Sciences Library. . . . . Margaret P. Mullaly-Quijas
Assistant to the Dean. . . . . Melvin Davis

Department and Division or Section Chairs

Basic Medical Sciences

Chair of Basic Medical Sciences . . . . Christopher J. Papasian, Ph.D.
Chair of Biomedical and Health Informatics. . . . . Karen Williams, Ph.D.

Clinical Sciences

Anesthesia. . . . . Eugene E. Fibuch, M.D.
Community and Family Medicine. . . . . Michael O'Dell, M.D.
Emergency Health Services . . . . Matthew Gratton, M.D.
Medicine. . . . . George R. Reisz, M.D.
   Cardiology. . . . . Douglas Bogart, M.D.
   Dermatology and Rheumatology. . . . . Amr Edrees, M.D.

Endocrinology . . . . Lamont Weide, M.D., Ph.D.
Gastroenterology . . . . Wendell K. Clarkston, M.D.
General Internal Medicine . . . . Eyad Al-Hihi, M.D.
Hematology and Oncology . . . . Jill Moormeier, M.D.
Infectious Disease . . . . David Bamberger, M.D.
Neurology . . . . Vernita Hairston-Mitchell, M.D. (Interim)
Pharmacology and Therapeutics . . . . Paul G. Cuddy, Pharm.D.
Respiratory Diseases and Critical Care . . . . Gary A. Salzman, M.D.
Obstetrics and Gynecology . . . . Dev Maulik, M.D., Ph.D.
Adolescent Gynecology . . . . Julie Strickland, M.D.
Gynecologic Oncology . . . . Darryl L. Wallace, M.D.
Gynecology . . . . Gerard Malnar, M.D.
Obstetrics . . . . D. Mark Schnee, D.O.
Perinatology (Maternal and Fetal Medicine) . . . . David C. Mundy, M.D.
Reproductive Endocrinology . . . . Gregory Starks, M.D.
Urogynecology . . . . Richard F. Hill, M.D.
Ophthalmology . . . . Nelson R. Sabates, M.D.
Cornea/Ureitis . . . . Vacant
Glaucoma . . . . Rohit Krishna, M.D.
Neuro-Ophthalmology . . . . Billi S. Wallace, M.D.
Ocular Oncology . . . . Komal B. Desai, M.D.
Ophthalmologic Plastic Surgery . . . . David B. Lyon, M.D.
Refractive . . . . Jean Hausheer, M.D.
Retina . . . . Michael Cassell, M.D.
Orthopaedic Surgery . . . . Richard Evans, M.D.
Pathology . . . . Kamani Lankachandra, M.D. (Interim)
Pediatrics . . . . Michael Artman, M.D.
Adolescent Medicine . . . . Daryl Lynch, M.D.
Allergy and Immunology . . . . Jay M. Portnoy, M.D.
Anesthesiology . . . . Eric Weissend, M.D.
Cardiology . . . . R. Gowdamarajan, M.D.
Child Abuse and Neglect . . . . James Anderst, M.D.
Cystic Fibrosis . . . . Philip G. Black, M.D.
Dermatology . . . . Amy J. Nopper, M.D.
Development and Behavioral Sciences . . . . Michele G. Kilo, M.D.
Developmental Pharmacology and
    Experimental Therapeutics . . . . J. Steven Leeder, Pharm.D., Ph.D.
Emergency Medicine . . . . Gregory Conners, M.D.
Endocrinology and Genetics . . . . Wayne V. Moore, M.D.
Gastroenterology . . . . Craig A. Friesen, M.D.
General Pediatrics . . . . Kenneth L. Wible, M.D.
Hematology and Oncology . . . . Gerald M. Woods, M.D.
Hospital Medicine . . . . Brian M. Pate, M.D.
Infectious Disease . . . . Mary Anne Jackson, M.D.
Neonatology . . . . Howard W. Kilbride, M.D.
Nephrology . . . . Bradley A. Warady, M.D.
Neurology . . . . Robert Kruse, M.D.
Oncology . . . . Alan S. Gamis, M.D.
Ophthalmology . . . . Scott Olitsky, M.D.
Pathology and Laboratory Medicine . . . . David Zwick, M.D.
Pulmonology . . . . Robert Beckerman, M.D.
Radiology . . . . James C. Brown, M.D.
Rehabilitation Medicine . . . . Ann C. Modricin, M.D.
Rheumatology . . . . Andrew Lasky, M.D.
Surgery . . . . George Holcomb III, M.D.
Urgent Care Medicine North . . . . Thomas Tryon, M.D.
Urgent Care Medicine South . . . . Milton Fowler, M.D.
Psychiatry . . . . J. Stuart Munro, M.D.
Radiology . . . . Lisa Lowe, M.D.
Surgery . . . . Mark L. Friedell, M.D.
Critical Care . . . . Gerald Early, M.D.
Laparoscopy Surgery . . . . Vacant
Thoracic . . . . Charles Van Way III, M.D.
Neurosurgery . . . . John Gianino, M.D.
Otolaryngology . . . . Keith Sale, M.D.
Trauma . . . . Doug Geehan, M.D.
Urology . . . . Narendra K. Khare, M.D.
Vascular . . . . Scott Kujath, M.D.

Saint Louis University School of Medicine
1402 South Grand Boulevard
Saint Louis, Missouri 63104
314-577-8000 (medical center); 314-977-9801 (dean's office); 314-977-9899 (fax)
Web site: http://medschool.slu.edu

The first faculty in medicine of the university was appointed in 1836. The present school of medicine dates from 1903 when the Marion Sims-Beaumont College of Medicine came under the direction of the university. The medical school is part of the Saint Louis University Medical Center, which is located one mile from the university proper.

Type: private
2011 total enrollment: 625
Clinical facilities: Saint Louis University Hospital, Cardinal Glennon Children's Medical Center, St. Mary's Health Center, the Anheuser Busch Institute, St. John's Mercy Medical Center, Saint Louis Veterans Affairs Medical Center (John Cochran and Jefferson Barracks Divisions), St. Elizabeth's Hospital.

University Officials

President. . . . . Lawrence Biondi, Ph.D., S.J.
Vice President, Academic Affairs . . . . Manoj S. Patankar, Ph.D.
Vice President for Business and Finance. . . . . David F. Hermburger (Interim)

Medical School Administrative Staff

Vice President, Medical Affairs. . . . . Philip O. Alderson, M.D.
Dean. . . . . Philip O. Alderson, M.D.
Senior Associate Dean for Graduate Medical Education . . . . Robert M. Heaney, M.D.
Associate Dean for Admissions and Student Affairs . . . . L. James Willmore, M.D.
Associate Dean for Clinical Affairs . . . . Berton R. Moed, M.D.
Associate Dean for Curricular Affairs . . . . Stuart J. Slavin, M.D.
Associate Dean for Faculty Development. Angela M. Sharkey, M.D.
Associate Dean for Finance and Administration . . . . Michael J. Meyer
Associate Dean for Multicultural Affairs . . . . Michael T. Railey, M.D.
Associate Dean for Research. . . . . Joel C. Eissenberg, Ph.D.
Assistant Dean for Curricular Affairs. . . . . William C. Mootz, M.D.
Assistant Dean for Graduate Medical Education . . . . .Julie K. Gammack, M.D.
Assistant Dean for Student Affairs. . . . . James E. Swierkosz, Ph.D.
Assistant Dean for Educational Development . . . . Gregory S. Smith, Ph.D.
Assistant Dean for Clinical Translational Research . . . . Paul J. Hauptman, M.D.
Chief Executive Officer, University Medical Group . . . . Philip O. Anderson, M.D. (Interim)

Department and Division or Section Chairs

Basic Sciences

Biochemistry and Molecular Biology. . . . . Enrico DiCera, M.D.
Comparative Medicine. . . . . John P. Long, D.V.M.
Institute for Molecular Virology . . . . Maurice Green, Ph.D.
Molecular Microbiology and Immunology. William S. M. Wold, Ph.D.
Pathology . . . . Carole A. Vogler, M.D.
Pharmacological and Physiological Science. . . . . Thomas C. Westfall, Ph.D.

Clinical Sciences

Anesthesiology. . . . . Gary R. Haynes, M.D.
Dermatology . . . . Scott W. Fosko, M.D.
Family and Community Medicine. . . . . F. David Schneider, M.D.
Internal Medicine . . . . Adrian M. Di Bisceglie, M.D.
  Cardiology. . . . . Michael J. Lim, M.D.
  Endocrinology and Metabolism. John E. Morley, M.D. (Interim)
  Gastroenterology and Hepatology. . . . . Brent A. Tetri, M.D.

General Internal Medicine . . . . Thomas J. Olsen, M.D.
Geriatric Medicine . . . . John E. Morley, M.D.
Hematology/Oncology . . . . Friedrich G. Schuening, M.D.
Infectious Diseases, Allergy and Immunology. . . . . Daniel F. Hoft, M.D., Ph.D.
Nephrology . . . . Kevin J. Martin, M.D.
Pulmonary, Critical Care, and Sleep Medicine . . . . Ravi P. Nayak, M.D. (Interim)
Rheumatology . . . . Terry L. Moore, M.D.
Neurology and Psychiatry. . . . . Salvador Cruz-Flores, M.D. (Interim)
Geriatric Psychiatry. . . . . George T. Grossberg, M.D.
Neurosurgery (Department) . . . . Saleem I. Abdulrauf, M.D.
Obstetrics, Gynecology, and Women's Health . . . . Raul Artal, M.D.
Ophthalmology . . . . Oscar A. Cruz, M.D.
Orthopaedic Surgery . . . . Berton R. Moed, M.D.
Otolaryngology-Head and Neck Surgery . . . . Mark A. Varvares, M.D.
Pediatrics . . . . Robert W. Wilmott, M.D.
Adolescent Medicine . . . . Dianne S. Elfenbein, M.D.
Allergy and Immunology . . . . Raymond G. Slavin, M.D., and Alan P. Knutsen, M.D.
Cardiology . . . . Kenneth Schowengerdt, M.D.
Child Protection. . . . . Timothy J. Kutz, M.D.
Critical Care. . . . . Lia Lowrie, M.D.
Dermatology . . . . Elaine C. Siegfried, M.D.
Developmental Pediatrics . . . . Rolanda Maxim, M.D. (Interim)
Emergency Medicine . . . . Robert G. Flood, M.D.
Endocrinology . . . . Sherida E. Tollefsen, M.D.
Gastroenterology . . . . Jeffrey H. Teckman, M.D.
General Academic Pediatrics. . . . . M. Susan Heaney, M.D.
Hematology and Oncology . . . . William S. Ferguson, M.D.
Infectious Diseases . . . . Stephen J. Barenkamp, M.D.
Medical Genetics . . . . Stephen Braddock, M.D.
Neonatology. . . . . Farouk H. Sadiq, M.D.
Nephrology . . . . Ellen G. Wood, M.D.
Pulmonology . . . . Blakeslee E. Noyes, M.D.
Rheumatology . . . . Terry L. Moore, M.D.
Toxicology. . . . . Anthony J. Scalzo, M.D.
Radiation Oncology. . . . . Bruce J. Walz, M.D.
Radiology . . . . Jeffrey J. Brown, M.D.
Nuclear Medicine. . . . . Medhat M. Osman, M.D.
Surgery . . . . Gary J. Peterson, M.D. (Interim)
Cardiothoracic Surgery. . . . . Keith S. Naunheim, M.D.
Emergency Medicine . . . . Laurie E. Byrne, M.D.
General Surgery. . . . . Eddy C. Hsueh, M.D.
Abdominal. . . . . Janet Tuttle-Newhall, M.D.
Pediatric Surgery . . . . Dennis W. Vane, M.D.
Plastic Surgery . . . . Bruce A. Kraemer, M.D.
Trauma Service . . . . Charles H. Andrus, M.D.
Urology . . . . Michael J. Chehval, M.D.
Vascular Surgery. . . . . Gary J. Peterson, M.D.

Washington University in St. Louis School of Medicine

660 South Euclid Avenue, Box 8106
Saint Louis, Missouri 63110
314-362-5000; 314-362-6827 (dean's office); 314-367-6666 (fax)
Web site: http://medinfo.wustl.edu

Medical education began at Washington University in 1891 by affiliation between the university and the Saint Louis Medical College. Today, the medical school is part of the Washington University Medical Center.

Type: private
2011 total enrollment: 591
Clinical facilities: Washington University Medical Center: Alvin J. Siteman Cancer Center, Barnard Free Skin and Cancer Hospital, Barnes-Jewish Hospital, Central Institute for the Deaf, Saint Louis Children's Hospital. **Other facilities:** Metropolitan Psychiatric Center, Saint Louis Shriner's Hospital for Crippled Children, Saint Louis Veterans Administration (John Cochran) Hospital.

University Officials

Chancellor . . . . Mark S. Wrighton, Ph.D.
Executive Vice Chancellor for Medical Affairs. . . . . Larry J. Shapiro, M.D.

Medical School Administrative Staff

Dean. . . . . Larry J. Shapiro, M.D.
Associate Dean and Associate Vice Chancellor,
   Administration and Finance . . . . Richard J. Stanton
Associate Vice Chancellor, Clinical Affairs. . . . . James P. Crane, M.D.
Associate Dean and Associate Vice Chancellor,
   Animal Affairs . . . . Evan D. Kharasch, M.D., Ph.D.
Associate Vice Chancellor, Medical Public Affairs . . . . Donald E. Clayton
Associate Vice Chancellor, Medical Alumni and Development Programs . . . . Pamela Buell
Senior Associate Dean for Education . . . . Alison J. Whelan, M.D.
Associate Dean & Assoc. Vice Chancellor,
   Admissions & Continuing Medical Education . . . . W. Edwin Dodson, M.D.
Associate Dean, Student Affairs . . . . Lisa M. Moscoso, M.D.
Associate Dean, Graduate Medical Education . . . . Rebecca P. McAlister, M.D.
Associate Dean, Medical Student Education . . . . David W. Windus, M.D.
Associate Dean and Director, Medical Library. . . . . Paul Schoening
Associate Dean, Human Studies. . . . . Jonathan M. Green, M.D.
Associate Dean and Director, Diversity Programs. . . . . Will R. Ross, M.D.
Associate Dean, Clinical and Translational Research . . . . Brad Evanoff, M.D., M.P.H.
Assistant Dean, Admissions and Student Affairs. . . . . Koong-Nah Chung, Ph.D.
Assistant Dean, Career Counseling . . . . Kathryn Diemer, M.D.
Assistant Dean and Chief Information Officer. . . . . Michael P. Caputo
Assistant Dean and Director, Center for Clinical Studies . . . . Yi Zhang, J.D.
Assistant Vice Chancellor and Assistant Dean,
   Facilities and Chief Facilities Officer . . . . Walter W. Davis, Jr.
Assistant Vice Chancellor and Assistant Dean, Finance . . . . George E. Andersson
Assistant Dean and Director, Program in Medicine . . . . Stephen S. Lefrak, M.D.
Assistant Dean, Academic Affairs and Registrar. Deborah A. Monolo
Assistant Dean and Assistant Vice Chancellor, Special Programs . . . . Glenda Wiman
Assistant Dean, Student Affairs, and Director, Student Financial Aid . . . . Bridget O'Neal
Assistant Vice Chancellor, Veterinary Affairs. . . . . Steven L. Leary, D.V.M.
Associate Vice Chancellor and Chief Counsel . . . . John E. Powers II
Director of the Student and Employee Health
   Services, Medical Campus . . . . Karen Winters, M.D.

Department and Division or Section Chairs
Basic Sciences

Division of Biology and Biomedical Sciences. . . . . John Russell, Ph.D.
Anatomy and Neurobiology. . . . . David C. Van Essen, Ph.D.
Biochemistry and Molecular Biophysics. . . . . John A. Cooper, M.D., Ph.D. (Interim)
Cell Biology and Physiology. . . . . Helen Piwnica-Worms, Ph.D.
Genetics . . . . Jeffrey D. Milbrandt, M.D., Ph.D.
Developmental Biology . . . . Lilianna Solnica-Krezel, Ph.D.
Molecular Microbiology. . . . . Stephen M. Beverley, Ph.D.
Pathology and Immunology. . . . . Herbert W. Virgin IV, M.D., Ph.D.
Division of Biostatistics. . . . . D. C. Rao, Ph.D.
Medical Scientist Training Program . . . . Wayne Yokoyama, M.D., and Brian Sullivan

Washington University in St. Louis School of Medicine: MISSOURI

Clinical Sciences

Anesthesiology. . . . . Alex S. Evers, M.D.
Internal Medicine . . . . Victoria J. Frasier, M.D.
   Allergy and Immunology . . . . H. James Wedner, M.D.
   Bone and Mineral Diseases. . . . . Roberto Civitelli, M.D.
   Bioorganic Chemistry and Molecular Pharmacology. . . . . Richard W. Gross, M.D., Ph.D.
   Cardiology and Cardiovascular Diseases. . . . . Douglas L. Mann, M.D.
   Dermatology . . . . Lynn A. Cornelius, M.D.
   Emergency Medicine . . . . Brent E. Ruoff, M.D.
   Endocrinology, Metabolism, and Lipid Research . . . . Clay F. Semenkovich, M.D.
   Gastroenterology . . . . Nicholas O. Davidson, M.D.
   General Medical Sciences. . . . . Bradley A. Evanoff, M.D.
   Geriatrics and Nutritional Science. . . . . Samuel Klein, M.D.
   Health Behavior Research. . . . . Mario Schootman, Ph.D.
   Hematology . . . . J. Evan Sadler, M.D., Ph.D.
   Infectious Diseases . . . . Victoria Fraser, M.D., and Daniel Goldberg, M.D., Ph.D.
   Medical Education . . . . Melvin S. Blanchard, M.D.
   Oncology. . . . . John F. DiPersio, M.D., Ph.D.
   Pulmonary and Critical Care Medicine . . . . Michael J. Holtzman, M.D.
   Renal Diseases . . . . Marc R. Hammerman, M.D.
   Rheumatology . . . . John P. Atkinson, M.D.
   VA Medical Service. . . . . Scot G. Hickman, M.D.
Neurology. . . . . David M. Holtzman, M.D.
Neurological Surgery. . . . . Ralph G. Dacey, Jr., M.D.
Obstetrics and Gynecology. . . . . George A. Macones, M.D.
   Basic Science Research. . . . . Kelle H. Moley, M.D.
   Gynecology . . . . Jeffrey Peipert, M.D.
   Gynecologic Oncology . . . . David G. Mutch, M.D.
   Maternal-Fetal Medicine . . . . David Stamilio, M.D.
   Reproductive Endocrinology. . . . . Randall R. Odem, M.D.
   Research . . . . D. Michael Nelson, M.D., Ph.D.
   Urogynecology. . . . . L. Lewis Wall, M.D.
Ophthalmology and Visual Sciences . . . . Michael Kass, M.D.
Orthopaedic Surgery. . . . . Richard H. Gelberman, M.D.
Otolaryngology . . . . Richard A. Chole, M.D., Ph.D.
Pediatrics . . . . Alan L. Schwartz, M.D., Ph.D.
   Allergy and Pulmonary. . . . . Thomas W. Ferkol, M.D.
   Cardiology. . . . . George Van Hare, M.D.
   Critical Care Medicine . . . . Allan Doctor, M.D.
   Diagnostic Medicine. . . . . Katie Plax, M.D.
   Emergency Medicine . . . . David M. Jaffe, M.D.
   Endocrinology and Diabetes. . . . . Abby Hollander, M.D.
   Gastroenterology . . . . Phillip I. Tarr, M.D.
   Genetics. . . . . Dorothy Grange, M.D.
   Hematology and Oncology. . . . . Robert Hayashi, M.D.
   Immunology and Rheumatology. . . . . Andrew J. White, M.D.
   Infectious Diseases . . . . Gregory A. Storch, M.D.
   Laboratory Medicine . . . . Gregory A. Storch, M.D.
   Nephrology . . . . Keith A. Hruska, M.D.
   Newborn Medicine. . . . . F. Sessions Cole, M.D.
Psychiatry . . . . Charles F. Zorumski, M.D.
Radiology . . . . R. Gilbert Jost, M.D.
   Diagnostic Radiology . . . . Daniel D. Picus, M.D.
   Nuclear Medicine. . . . . Barry A. Siegel, M.D.
   Radiological Sciences . . . . Robert J. Gropler, M.D.
Radiation Oncology. . . . . Dennis E. Hallahan, M.D.
   Clinical . . . . Jeff M. Michalski, M.D.
   Medical Physics . . . . Eric Klien, Ph.D., and Sasa Mutic, Ph.D.
   Radiation and Cancer Biology. . . . . David Curiel, M.D., Ph.D.
   Bioinformatics and Outcomes Research. . . . . Joseph O. Deasy, Ph.D.
Surgery. . . . . Timothy J. Eberlein, M.D.
   Cardiothoracic Surgery. . . . . G. Alexander Patterson, M.D.
   Chief of Surgery at the VA . . . . Michael Crittenden, M.D.
   General Surgery. . . . . William C. Chapman, M.D.
   Pediatric Surgery . . . . Brad W. Warner, M.D.
   Reconstructive Plastic Surgery. . . . . Susan E. Mackinnon, M.D.
   Urologic Surgery . . . . Gerald L. Andriole, M.D.

Creighton University School of Medicine

2500 California Plaza
Omaha, Nebraska 68178
402-280-2900; 402-280-2600 (dean's office); 402-280-1410 (fax)
Web site: http://medicine.creighton.edu

Creighton University was founded on September 2, 1878, in accordance with the wishes of Edward and Mary Creighton, under the name of Creighton College. On August 14, 1879, the trust created was surrendered to a new corporation, the Creighton University. The Creighton University School of Medicine was opened on October 1, 1892, and became the first professional school of the university. The Creighton University Medical Center includes the schools of medicine, dentistry, nursing, pharmacy, and allied health professions. Creighton University Medical Center and the Boys Town National Research Hospital are located on a single campus with the remainder of the university community.

Type: private
2011 total enrollment: 524
Clinical facilities: Creighton University Medical Center, Boys Town National Research Hospital, Archbishop Bergan Mercy Hospital, Children's Hospital, Veterans Administration Hospital (Omaha), Immanuel Medical Center, St. Joseph's Hospital and Medical Center (Phoenix), St. Mary's Medical Center (San Francisco).

University Officials

President	Father Timothy R. Lannon, S.J.
Senior Vice President for Operations	Daniel E. Burkey
Vice President, Health Sciences	Donald R. Frey, M.D.
Associate Vice President, Health Sciences	Sade Kosoko-Lasaki, M.D.
Associate Vice President, Research	Thomas F. Murray, Ph.D.
Assistant Vice President, Health Sciences, and Director, Health Sciences Library	James Bothmer
Coordinator, Health Sciences, Public Relations	N. Kathryn Clark
Vice President, University Ministry	Father Andy Alexander, S.J.
Vice President for Academic Affairs	Patrick Borchers, J.D.
Vice President for Student Services	John C. Cernech, Ph.D.
Vice President for University Relations	Vacant
Vice President, Information Systems	Brian A. Young
Vice President for Finance, Treasurer	Jan D. Madsen
Registrar	John Krecek
Director, Media Services	Charles Lenosky
Assistant Vice President for Marketing and Public Relations	Kim Manning
Associate Vice President for Research and Compliance	Kathleen Taggart
Director, Grants Administration	Beth Herr

Medical School Administrative Staff

Dean	Rowen K. Zetterman, M.D.
Senior Associate Dean, Academic and Clinical Affairs	Stephen J. Lanspa, M.D.
Senior Associate Dean, Administration and Finance	Dale Davenport
Chief Executive Officer, Creighton Medical Associates	Todd Carlon
Chief Financial Officer	Ray Stoupa
Associate Dean, Hospital Affairs	Gary Honts
Associate Dean for Research	Thomas F. Murray, Ph.D.
Associate Dean, Graduate Medical Education	Cecile M. Zielinski, M.D.
Associate Dean, Student Affairs	Michael J. Kavan, Ph.D.
Associate Dean, Veterans Affairs	Thomas G. Lynch, M.D.
Associate Dean, Phoenix Campus	James Balducci, M.D.
Assistant Dean for Admissions	Thomas Quinn, Ph.D.
Assistant Dean, Clinical Affairs	Robert W. Dunlay, M.D.
Assistant Dean, Faculty Affairs	Archana Chatterjee, M.D.
Assistant Dean, Medical Education	Kathryn D. Haggett, Ph.D.
Assistant Dean Medical Education, Phoenix Campus	Randy Richardson, M.D.
Assistant Dean, Graduate Medical Education	Robin E. Graham, M.D.

Assistant Dean Student Affairs, Phoenix Campus. . . . . Robert Garcia, M.D.

Department and Division or Section Chairs

Basic Sciences

Biomedical Sciences. . . . . John Yee, Ph.D.
Health Policy and Ethics . . . . Amy Haddad, Ph.D.
Medical Microbiology and Immunology . . . . Richard V. Goering, Ph.D.
Pathology . . . . Robert Allen, M.D.
Pharmacology . . . . Thomas F. Murray, Ph.D.

Clinical Sciences

Anesthesiology. . . . . James L. Manion, M.D.
Emergency Medicine . . . . Wesley S. Grigsby, M.D.
Family Medicine . . . . Laeth S. Nasir, MBBS
Medicine. . . . . Syed M. Mohiuddin, M.D.
    Allergy. . . . . Thomas B. Casale, M.D.
    Cardiology. . . . . Dennis J. Esterbrooks, M.D.
    Dermatology . . . . Christopher J. Huerter, M.D.
    Endocrinology . . . . Robert R. Recker, M.D.
    Gastroenterology . . . . Bennie Upchurch, M.D.
    General Medicine. . . . . Henry Sakowski, M.D.
    Hematology and Oncology . . . . Peter Silberstein, M.D.
    Infectious Diseases . . . . Gary L. Gorby, M.D.
    Nephrology . . . . Richard Lund, M.D.
    Pulmonary Medicine. . . . . Dan Schuller, M.D.
    Rheumatology . . . . John A. Hurley, M.D., and Jay G. Kenik, M.D.
Neurology. . . . . Sanjay P. Singh, M.D.
Obstetrics and Gynecology. . . . . James F. Smith, M.D.
Pediatrics . . . . Terence L. Zach, M.D.
    Allergy and Immunology . . . . Russell J. Hopp, D.O.
    Developmental Pediatrics . . . . Andrea J. Steenson, M.D.
    General Ambulatory. . . . . Michael Moore, M.D.
    Infectious Disease. . . . . Archana Chatterjee, M.D.
    Newborn Medicine. . . . . Harold Kaftan, M.D.
    Pediatric Cardiology. . . . . John Kugler, M.D.
    Pediatric Intensive Care . . . . Mohan Mysore, M.D.
Preventive Medicine and Public Health . . . . Henry T. Lynch, M.D.
Psychiatry . . . . Daniel R. Wilson, M.D., Ph.D.
Radiology . . . . Thomas Dworak, M.D.
Surgery. . . . . Jeffrey T. Sugimoto, M.D.
    Cardiothoracic Surgery. . . . . Jeffrey T. Sugimoto, M.D.
    General Surgery. . . . . Robert J. Fitzgibbons, Jr., M.D.
    Neurosurgery. . . . . Charles Taylon, M.D.
    Ophthalmology . . . . Omofolasade K. Lasaki, M.D.
    Orthopedic Surgery . . . . Jaffrey T. Sugimoto, M.D. (Interim)
    Plastic and Reconstructive Surgery . . . . Amardip Bhuller, M.D.
    Urology . . . . Stephen Leslie, M.D.
    Vascular Surgery. . . . . Vacant

University of Nebraska College of Medicine

985520 Nebraska Medical Center
Omaha, Nebraska 68198-5520
402-559-4000 (general information); 402-559-4204 (dean's office);
402-559-4148 (dean's office fax)
Web site: www.unmc.edu

The Omaha Medical College was incorporated in 1881. When it became part of the University of Nebraska in 1902, the basic sciences years were taught in Lincoln and the clinical years were taught in Omaha. In 1913, a new campus was established in Omaha for all medical education. The medical school is part of the University of Nebraska Medical Center.

Type: public
2011 total enrollment: 491
Clinical facilities: The Nebraska Medical Center (composed of the University of Nebraska Hospital and Bishop Clarkson Memorial Hospital), Methodist Hospital, Children's Hospital, Immanuel Medical Center, Bergan Mercy Hospital, Omaha VA Hospital, Creighton University Medical Center, Boys Town National Research Hospital, Bryan LGH, St. Elizabeth's Hospital, Jennie Edmundson Hospital, Mercy Hospital, Mary Lanning Hospital, Good Samaritan Hospital, West Nebraska General Hospital, Columbus Community Hospital, Faith Regional Health Center, Fremont Area Medical Center, Great Plains Regional Medical Center, Regional West Medical Center, St. Francis Medical Center.

University Officials

President	James B. Milliken, J.D.
Chancellor and Vice President	Harold M. Maurer, M.D.
Vice Chancellor for Academic Affairs	David A. Crouse, M.D. (Interim)
Vice Chancellor for Business and Finance	Donald S. Leuenberger
Vice Chancellor for External Affairs	Robert D. Bartee
Vice Chancellor for Research	Jennifer L. Larsen, M.D.
Director, Library of Medicine	Nancy N. Woelfl, Ph.D.
Director, Public Relations	William R. O'Neill, J.D.

Medical School Administrative Staff

Dean	Bradley E. Britiban, M.D.
Senior Associate Dean for Academic Affairs	Gerald F. Moore, M.D.
Senior Associate Dean for Administration	Michael R. McGlade
Senior Associate Dean for Clinical Affairs	Carl V. Smith, M.D.
Senior Associate Dean for the Health System	Glenn A. Fosdick
Senior Associate Dean for Research Development	Howard S. Fox, M.D., Ph.D.
Associate Dean for Admissions and Student Affairs	Jeffrey W. Hill, M.D.
Associate Dean for Graduate Medical Education	Robert S. Wigton, M.D.
Associate Dean for Hospital Services	Stephen B. Smith, M.D.
Associate Dean, School of Allied Health Professions	Kyle P. Meyer, Ph.D.
Associate Dean for Veterans Affairs	Thomas G. Lynch, M.D.
Associate Dean for Pediatric Affairs	John W. Sparks, M.D.
Assistant Dean for Medical Education	Hugh A. Stoddard, Ph.D.
Assistant Dean for Admissions and Student Affairs	Jeffrey D. Harrison, M.D.
Assistant Dean for Clinical Skills and Quality	Paul M. Paulman, M.D.
Assistant Dean for Graduate Medical Education	James H. Stageman, M.D.
Assistant Dean for Government Affairs	James W. Gigantelli, M.D.
Assistant Dean for Graduate Students/International Affairs	Jialin C. Zheng, M.D.
Assistant Dean for Continuing Education	Dennis P. McNeilly, Psy.D.
Director, Dean's Business Office	Galen L. Kathol
Director, Comparative Medicine	Robert S. Dixon, D.V.M.

Department and Division or Section Chairs

Basic Sciences

Biochemistry and Molecular Biology	Surinder K. Batra, Ph.D.
Cellular and Integrative Physiology	Irving H. Zucker, Ph.D.

Genetics, Cell Biology, and Anatomy .... Vimia Band, Ph.D.
Pathology and Microbiology................................. Steven H. Hinrichs, M.D.
Pharmacology and Experimental Neuroscience................ Howard E. Gendelman, M.D.

Clinical Sciences

Anesthesiology...................................... Kenneth A. Follett, M.D. (Interim)
Emergency Medicine..................................... Robert L. Muelleman, M.D.
Family Medicine .... Michael A. Sitorius, M.D.
Internal Medicine .... Lynell W. Klassen, M.D.
    Cardiology... John R. Windle, M.D.
    Dermatology .... Vacant
    Diabetes, Endocrinology, and Metabolism .... Cyrus V. Desouza, M.D.
    Gastroenterology and Hepatology......................... Mark E. Mailliard, M.D.
    General Internal Medicine .... Thomas G. Tape, M.D.
    Geriatrics and Gerontology.................................. Jane F. Potter, M.D.
    Infectious Diseases .... Mark E. Rupp, M.D.
    Nephrology .... Troy J. Plumb, M.D. (Interim)
    Oncology-Hematology .... Julie M. Vose, M.D.
    Pulmonary, Critical Care, Sleep, and Allergy .... Joseph H. Sisson, M.D.
    Rheumatology .... James R. O'Dell, M.D.
Neurological Sciences .... Daniel L. Murman, M.D. (Interim)
Obstetrics and Gynecology................................... Carl V. Smith, M.D.
Ophthalmology and Visual Sciences......................... Thomas W. Hejkal, M.D.
Orthopedic Surgery and Rehabilitation...................... Kevin L. Garvin, M.D.
Otolaryngology-Head and Neck Surgery .... Daniel Lydiatt, D.D.S., M.D. (Interim)
Pediatrics .... John W. Sparks, M.D.
    Cardiology....................................... Christopher C. Erickson, M.D.
    Child Health Policy and City MatCH......................... John W. Sparks, M.D.
    Critical Care...................................... Mohan R. Mysore, M.D.
    Cytogenetics...................................... Warren G. Sanger, Ph.D.
    Developmental Medicine .... Cynthia R. Ellis, M.D.
    Emergency Med....................................... David M. Tolo, M.D.
    Endocrinology and Diabetes.............................. Kevin P. Corley, M.D.
    Gastroenterology and Nutrition .... Ruben Quiros, M.D.
    General Pediatrics .... John N. Walburn, M.D.
    Genetics.. Warren G. Sanger, Ph.D.
    Hematology and Oncology .... Bruce G. Gordon, M.D.
    Hospitalist .... Joseph T. Snow, M.D.
    Infectious Disease..................................... Kari A. Simonsen, M.D.
    Inherited Metabolic Diseases.......................... William B. Rizzo, M.D.
    Molecular Genetics.................................. Shelley D. Smith, Ph.D.
    Nephrology .... Helen B. Lovell, M.D.
    Neurology .... Paul D. Larsen, M.D.
    Newborn Medicine...................................... Terrence L. Zach, M.D.
    Psychology... Joseph H. Evans, Ph.D.
    Pulmonary Medicine and Cystic Fibrosis .... John L. Colombo, M.D.
    Rehabilitation Medicine .... J. Michael Leibowitz, M.D.
    Rheumatology .... Adam L. Reinhardt, M.D.
Psychiatry .... Steven P. Wengel, M.D.
Radiation Oncology....................................... Charles A. Enke, M.D.
Radiology .... Craig W. Walker, M.D.
Surgery.. David W. Mercer, M.D.
    Cardiothoracic Surgery.................................. Kim F. Duncan, M.D.
    General Surgery....................................... Jon S. Thompson, M.D.
    Neurosurgery... Kenneth A. Follett, M.D.
    Oral and Maxillofacial Surgery .... Leon F. Davis, D.D.S., M.D.
    Pediatric Surgery...................................... Stephen C. Raynor, M.D.
    Plastic and Reconstructive Surgery .... Ronald R. Hollins, M.D., D.M.D.
    Surgical Oncology .... James A. Edney, M.D.
    Transplantation Surgery .... Alan N. Langnas, D.O.
    Urologic Surgery .... George P. Hemstreet III, M.D., Ph.D.

University of Nevada School of Medicine

Pennington Medical Education Building/332
Reno, Nevada 89557-0071
775-784-6001 (general information); 775-784-8251 (fax)
Web site: www.unr.edu/med

The School of Medicine was originally approved in 1969 as a two-year school of basic sciences. In 1977, the Board of Regents and the Nevada state legislature approved the school's conversion to a four-year degree granting school and the first Doctor of Medicine degree was awarded in 1980. The School of Medicine is research-intensive and community-based, is the only public medical school in the state, and is committed to health care in Nevada. It enjoys state-of-the-art research and medical education facilities, with basic science research and integrated pre-clinical teaching located on the University of Nevada, Reno campus. Clinical teaching and residency and fellowship training are based at clinical campuses in both Reno and Las Vegas. The current enrollment is 62 students per class, with a commitment to increase to 100 students per year over the next 6 years.

Type: public
2011 total enrollment: 253
Clinical facilities: Reno: VA Medical Center, Renown Regional Medical Center, St. Mary's Regional Medical Center. Las Vegas: University Medical Center of Southern Nevada, Sunrise Hospital and Medical Center, VA Southern Nevada Healthcare System, St. Rose Dominican Hospitals, NVCI-Nevada Cancer Institute.

University Officials

Chancellor, Nevada Systems of Higher Education . . . . Daniel Klaich, J.D.
President, University of Nevada, Reno . . . . Marc Johnson, Ph.D.

Medical School Administrative Staff

Dean. . . . . Thomas L. Schwenk, M.D.
Chief of Staff. . . . . Jessica Younger
General Counsel . . . . Thomas Ray, Esq.
Director of Development . . . . Stefanie Scoppettone, Ph.D.
Chief Financial Officer. . . . . Jean Regan
Human Resources Director . . . . Feride McAlpine
Senior Associate Dean for Basic Science and Research . . . . David M. Lupan, Ph.D.
Associate Dean for Clinical Affairs . . . . Nevin Wilson, M.D.
Senior Associate Dean of Academic Affairs . . . . Melissa Piasecki, M.D.
 Associate Dean of Academic Affairs, Las Vegas . . . . Deborah Kuhls, M.D.
Associate Dean for Admissions and Student Affairs . . . . Peggy Dupey, Ph.D.
 Assistant Dean for Admissions. . . . . Beverly Neyland, M.D.
Associate Dean for Medical Education . . . . Tim Baker, M.D.
 Assistant Dean for Evaluation and Assessment . . . . Gwen Shonkwiler, Ph.D.
Associate Dean for Faculty Affairs and Development . . . . Jennifer Hagen, M.D.
Associate Dean for Graduate Medical Education . . . . Miriam Bar-on, M.D.
Associate Dean for Medical Education . . . . Gwen S. Shonkwiler, Ph.D. (Interim)
Chief Financial Officer. . . . . Jean Regan
Personnel Officer . . . . Feride McAlpine
Medical Library Director . . . . Terry Henner

University of Nevada School of Medicine: NEVADA

Department and Division or Section Chairs

Basic Sciences

Biochemistry . . . . Gary Blomquist, Ph.D.
Microbiology . . . . Gregory Pari, Ph.D.
Pharmacology . . . . Joseph Hume, Ph.D.
Physiology and Cell Biology . . . . Kenton H. Sanders, Ph.D.

Clinical Sciences

Emergency Medicine . . . . Dale Carrison, D.O
Family and Community Medicine, Las Vegas . . . . Elissa Palmer, M.D.
Family and Community Medicine, Reno . . . . Daniel Spogen, M.D.
Internal Medicine, Las Vegas . . . . John Varras, M.D.
Internal Medicine, Reno . . . . Daniel S. Shapiro, M.D.
Obstetrics and Gynecology . . . . Vani Dandolu, M.D.
Pathology and Laboratory Medicine . . . . Sanford H. Barsky, M.D.
Pediatrics, Las Vegas . . . . David Gremse, M.D.
Pediatrics, Reno . . . . Nevin Wilson, M.D.
Psychiatry and Behavioral Sciences . . . . Ole Thienhaus, M.D.
Speech Pathology and Audiology . . . . Tom Watterson, Ph.D.
Surgery . . . . William Zamboni, M.D.
Student Health Services . . . . Cheryl Hug-English, M.D.
Director of Continuing Medical Education . . . . Melissa O'Brien, M.S.

Dartmouth Medical School

Hanover, New Hampshire 03755-1404
877-367-1797 (general information); 603-650-1200 (dean's office);
603-650-5000 (medical center); 603-650-1202 (dean's fax)
Web site: http://dms.dartmouth.edu/

Dartmouth Medical School, founded as the medical department of Dartmouth College, opened with its first lecture on November 22, 1797. The medical school is a component of the Dartmouth-Hitchcock Medical Center and has facilities on the campus of Dartmouth College and at the medical center in Lebanon, New Hampshire.

Type: private
2011 total enrollment: 347
Clinical facilities: Dartmouth Hitchcock Medical Center (Lebanon, NH), Veterans Administration Medical Center (White River Juntion, VT; Manchester, NH), Dartmouth-Hitchcock Clinic (multiple locations in New Hampshire), Hartford Hospital (Hartford, CT), New Hampshire State Hospital (Concord, NH), Concord Hospital (Concord, NH), West Central Services (Lebanon, NH), Maine Medical Center (Portland, ME), Cheshire Hospital (Keene, NH), Indian Health Service Hospital (Tuba City, AZ), Yukon-Kushokwim Delta Regional Hospital (Bethel, AK) Maine-Dartmouth Family Practice (Augusta, ME), California-Pacific Medical Center (San Francisco, CA), Community-based clinics in southern New Hampshire, northern Vermont, and Maine.

Dartmouth College Officials

President . . . . Jim Yong Kim, M.D., Ph.D.
Provost . . . . Carol L. Folt, Ph.D.

Medical School Administrative Staff

Dean . . . . Wiley W. Souba, M.D., Sc.D.
Senior Associate Dean for Faculty Affairs . . . . Leslie P. Henderson, Ph.D.
Senior Associate Dean for Clinical Affairs . . . . John F. Modlin, M.D.
Senior Associate Dean for Medical Education . . . . David M. Nierenberg, M.D.
Senior Associate Dean for Research . . . . Duane A. Compton, Ph.D.
Associate Dean and Chief Operating Officer . . . . Charles R. Mannix, J.D.
Associate Dean, VA Hospital Affairs . . . . Robert M. Walton, M.P.A.
Associate Dean for Advancement . . . . Mark A. Notestine, Ph.D.
Chief Diversity Officer . . . . Susan Pepin, M.D.
Associate Dean for Student Affairs and Student Services . . . . Ann Davis, M.D.
Assistant Dean for Clinical Affairs . . . . Jocelyn D. Chertoff, M.D.
Associate Dean for Continuing Medical Education . . . . Richard I. Rothstein, M.D.
Associate Dean for Graduate Medical Education . . . . Marc L. Bertrand, M.D.
Assistant Dean for Clinical Education . . . . Eric A. Shirley, M.D.
Assistant Dean for Community-Based Education . . . . Catherine F. Pipas, M.D.
Assistant Dean for Medical Education (ORIME) . . . . Greg Ogrinc, M.D.
Assistant Dean for Medical Education (Residency Affairs) . . . . Susan N. Harper, M.D.
Senior Advising Dean and Director of Community Programs . . . . Joseph F. O'Donnell, M.D.
Director of Finance . . . . Paul F. Greeley
Medical Student Registrar . . . . Michelle W. Jaeger
Director of Admissions . . . . Andrew G. Welch
Chief, Comparative and Translational Animal Research . . . . P. Jack Hoopes, Ph.D., D.V.M.
Director, Biomedical Libraries . . . . Vacant
Director of Communications and Marketing . . . . Derik Hertel Vacant
Director of Computing and Information Technologies . . . . Stephen B. McAllister
Director of Financial Aid . . . . Gordon D. Koff

Department and Division or Section Chairs

Basic Sciences

Anatomy . . . . Rand S. Swenson, M.D.
Biochemistry . . . . Charles K. Barlowe, Ph.D.
Genetics . . . . Jay C. Dunlap, Ph.D.
Microbiology and Immunology . . . . William R. Green, Ph.D.

Pharmacology and Toxicology . . . . Ethan Dmitrovsky, M.D.
Physiology and Neurology . . . . Hermes H. Yeh, Ph.D.

Clinical Sciences

Anesthesiology. . . . . Thomas M. Dodds, M.D.
Community and Family Medicine . . . . Michael Zubkoff, Ph.D.
Medicine . . . . Richard Rothstein, M.D. (Acting)
    Cardiology . . . . Edward Catherwood, M.D. (Acting)
    Clinical Pharmacology . . . . David W. Nierenberg, M.D.
    Dermatology . . . . James G. H. Dinulos, M.D.
    Emergency Medicine . . . . Norman N. Yanofsky, M.D.
    Endocrinology . . . . Richard Comi, M.D.
    Gastroenterology and Hepatology . . . . Richard Rothstein, M.D.
    General Internal Medicine . . . . W. Blair Brooks, M.D.
    Hematology and Oncology . . . . Bradley A. Arrick, M.D., Ph.D.
    Hospital Medicine . . . . Edward J. Merrens, M.D.
    Infectious Diseases and International Health . . . . Bryan J. Marsh, M.D. (Acting)
    Nephrology and Hypertension . . . . Brian D. Remillard, M.D.
    Occupational and Environmental Medicine . . . . Robert K. McLellan, M.D.
    Pulmonary . . . . Richard I. Enelow, M.D.
    Radiation Oncology . . . . Alan C. Hartford, M.D. (Acting)
    Rheumatology . . . . Daniel A. Albert, M.D.
    VA Medicine . . . . James A. Geiling, M.D.
Neurology . . . . Gregory L. Holmes, M.D.
Obstetrics and Gynecology . . . . Richard H. Reindollar, M.D.
Orthopaedics . . . . Sohail Mirza, M.D.
Pathology . . . . Wendy A. Wells, M.D.
Pediatrics . . . . John F. Modlin, M.D.
    Allergy/Clinical Immunology . . . . Donald P. Woodmansee, M.D.
    Cardiology . . . . Michael F. Flanagan, M.D.
    Child Development . . . . Richard P. Morse, M.D.
    Critical Care . . . . James J. Filiano, M.D.
    Endocrinology . . . . Samuel J. Casella, M.D.
    General Pediatrics . . . . Henry H. Bernstein, D.O.
    Genetics . . . . John Moeschler, M.D.
    Hematology and Oncology . . . . Jack van Hoff, M.D.
    Neonatology . . . . William H. Edwards, M.D.
Psychiatry . . . . Alan I. Green, M.D.
Radiology . . . . Clifford Belden, M.D. (Acting)
Surgery . . . . Richard Freeman, M.D.
    Cardiothoracic . . . . William C. Nugent, M.D.
    General Surgery . . . . Richard J. Barth, Jr., M.D.
    Maxillofacial . . . . Rocco R. Addante, M.D.
    Neurosurgery . . . . David W. Roberts, M.D.
    Ophthalmology . . . . William J. Rosen, M.D.
    Otolaryngology and Audiology . . . . Daniel H. D. Morrison, M.D.
    Pediatric . . . . Laurie A. Latchaw, M.D.
    Plastic . . . . E. Dale L. Vidal, M.D.
    Transplantation . . . . David A. Axelrod, M.D.
    Urology . . . . William Bihrle III, M.D.
    Vascular Surgery . . . . Richard J. Powell, M.D.

Centers

Center for Health and Aging . . . . Stephen J. Bartels, M.D.
Dartmouth Lung Biology Center . . . . Bruce A. Stanton, Ph.D.
Dartmouth Psychiatric Research Center . . . . Robert E. Drake, M.D.
Heart and Vascular Research Center . . . . Nicholas Shworak, M.D., Ph.D.
Hood Center for Children and Families . . . . Madeline A. Dalton, Ph.D.
Norris Cotton Cancer Center . . . . Mark A. Israel, M.D.
The Dartmouth Institute for Health Policy and Clinical Practice . . . . Vacant

UMDNJ—New Jersey Medical School

185 South Orange Avenue
Newark, New Jersey 07103-2714
973-972-4300; 973-972-4538/4539 (dean's office); 973-972-7104 (fax)
Web site: http://njms.umdnj.edu

The UMDNJ-New Jersey Medical School was incorporated on August 6, 1954, as the Seton Hall College of Medicine and Dentistry, and in November 1954, was granted a charter by the New Jersey Department of Education. In 1965, Seton Hall College of Medicine and Dentistry became the New Jersey College of Medicine and Dentistry, a state-supported institution. The New Jersey Medical School is one of eight schools that comprise the statewide UMDNJ (University of Medicine and Dentistry of New Jersey), established in July 1970 under a single board of trustees.

Type: public
2011 total enrollment: 680
Clinical facilities: UMDNJ-University Hospital, Hackensack University Medical Center, Kessler Institute for Rehabilitation, Veterans Affairs Medical Center (East Orange).

University Official

President . . . . William F. Owen, Jr., M.D.

Medical School Administrative Staff

Dean . . . . Robert L. Johnson, M.D.
Vice Dean . . . . Maria L. Soto-Greene, M.D.
Associate Dean and Chief Financial Officer . . . . David L. Roe
Executive Director for Administration . . . . Walter L. Douglas
Senior Associate Dean, Research . . . . William C. Gause, Ph.D.
Senior Associate Dean, Clinical Affairs . . . . Kendell R. Sprott, M.D., J.D.
Senior Associate Dean, Graduate School of
    Biomedical Sciences at New Jersey Medical
    School . . . . Andrew P. Thomas, Ph.D.
Associate Dean, Graduate Medical Education . . . . Stephen R. Baker, M.D.
Associate Dean, Student Affairs . . . . James M. Hill, Ph.D.
Associate Dean, Admissions . . . . George F. Heinrich, M.D.
Executive Assistant to the Dean . . . . Michael J. Petti

Department and Division or Section Chairs

Basic Sciences

Biochemistry and Molecular Biology . . . . Michael B. Mathews, Ph.D.
Cell Biology and Molecular Medicine . . . . Junichi Sadoshima, M.D., Ph.D.
Microbiology and Molecular Genetics . . . . Carol S. Newlon, Ph.D.
Pathology and Laboratory Medicine . . . . Stanley Cohen, M.D.
Pharmacology and Physiology . . . . Andrew P. Thomas, Ph.D.

Clinical Sciences

Anesthesiology . . . . Melissa Davidson, M.D. (Interim)
Emergency Medicine . . . . Maria Soto-Greene, M.D. (Interim)
Family Medicine . . . . Rubin S. Schroeder, M.D. (Interim)
Medicine . . . . Bunyad Haider, M.D. (Interim)
    Academic Medicine, Geriatrics, and Community Programs . . . . Mary Ann Haggerty, M.D.
    Allergy, Immunology, and Rheumatology . . . . Mary Ann Haggerty, M.D. (Interim)
    Cardiology . . . . Marc Klapholz, M.D.
    Dermatology . . . . Robert A. Schwartz, M.D.
    Endocrinology and Metabolism . . . . David Bleich, M.D.
    Gastroenterology and Hepatology . . . . Arun Samanta, M.D. (Interim)
    Hematology and Oncology . . . . Lillian Pliner, M.D. (Interim)
    Infectious Diseases . . . . David Alland, M.D.
    Nephrology . . . . Alluru Reddi, M.D.
    Pulmonary Diseases and Critical Care . . . . Andrew Berman, M.D.
Neurological Surgery . . . . Peter W. Carmel, M.D.
Neurology and Neurosciences . . . . Barry Levin, M.D. (Interim)
    Cerebrovascular . . . . Andrea Hidalgo, M.D.

Neurophysiology . . . . Nizar Souayah, M.D.
   Pediatric Neurology . . . . Caroline Hayes-Rosen, M.D.
Obstetrics, Gynecology, and Women's Health . . . . Gerson Weiss, M.D.
   General Obstetrics and Gynecology . . . . Natalie E. Roche, M.D.
   Gynecologic Oncology . . . . Bernadette Cracchiolo, M.D.
   Maternal and Fetal Medicine . . . . Joseph Apuzzio, M.D.
   Reproductive Endocrinology and Infertility . . . . Peter McGovern, M.D.
   Research . . . . Laura T. Goldsmith, Ph.D.
Ophthalmology and Visual Science . . . . Marco A. Zarbin, M.D., Ph.D.
   Comprehensive Ophthalmology . . . . Suqin Guo, M.D.
   Cornea, External Diseases, and Refractive Surgery . . . . Peter S. Hersh, M.D.
   Glaucoma . . . . Robert Fechtner, M.D.
   Neuro-Ophthalmology . . . . Larry Frohman, M.D.
   Oculoplastics and Orbital Reconstructive Surgery . . . . Paul Langer, M.D.
   Ophthalmic Pathology . . . . Nina Mirani, M.D.
   Pediatric Ophthalmology and Strabismus . . . . Rudolph Wagner, M.D.
   Retina and Vitreous Surgery . . . . Neelakshi Bhagat, M.D.
   Uvietis and Infectious Disease . . . . Ronald Rescigno, M.D.
Orthopaedics . . . . Joseph Benevenia, M.D.
   Adult Reconstruction . . . . Edward Adler, M.D.
   Foot and Ankle . . . . Wayne Berberian, M.D.
   Hand Injuries and Disorders . . . . John Capo, M.D.
   Musculoskeletal Oncology . . . . Francis Patterson, M.D.
   Orthopaedic Trauma . . . . Mark Reilly, M.D.
   Pediatric Orthopaedics . . . . Sanjeev Sabharwal, M.D.
   Spine Disorders and Surgery . . . . Michael J. Vives, M.D.
   Sports Medicine and Arthroscopic Surgery . . . . Robin Gehrmann, M.D.
   Otolarngology/Head and Neck Surgery . . . . Soly Baredes, M.D. (Interim)
Pediatrics . . . . Kendell Sprott, M.D., J.D. (Acting)
   Adolescent Medicine and Young Adult . . . . Robert L. Johnson, M.D.
   Cardiology . . . . Jose R. Antillon, M.D.
   Child Development . . . . Tyrone Bentley, M.D. (Acting)
   Emergency Medicine . . . . Robert Barricella, D.O.
   Gastroenterology . . . . Iona Monteiro, M.D.
   General Pediatrics and Pediatric Education . . . . Susan Mautone, M.D.
   Genetics . . . . Franklin Desposito, M.D.
   Hematology and Oncology . . . . Franklin Desposito, M.D.
   Center for Human Development and Aging . . . . Abraham Aviv, M.D.
   Infectious Diseases, Allergy, and Immunology . . . . James Oleske, M.D.
   Nephrology . . . . Constancia Uy, M.D.
   Pulmonology . . . . Helen Aguila, M.D.
Physical Medicine and Rehabilitation . . . . Joel A. DeLisa, M.D.
   Noninvasive Ventilation and Pulmonary Rehabilitation . . . . John R. Bach, M.D.
   Occupational/Musculoskeletal Medicine . . . . Todd P. Stitik, M.D.
Preventive Medicine and Community Health . . . . William E. Halperin, M.D., Dr.P.H.
   Biostatistics and Epidemiology . . . . Bart K. Holland, Ph.D.
   Public Health . . . . Marian R. Passannante, Ph.D.
   Preventive Medicine . . . . Pauline Thomas, M.D.
Psychiatry . . . . Giovanni Caracci, M.D. (Interim)
   Child and Adolescent Psychiatry . . . . Tolga Taneli, M.D.
Radiation Oncology . . . . Bruce G. Haffty, M.D.
Radiology . . . . Stephen R. Baker, M.D.
   Diagnostic Radiology . . . . Stephen R. Baker, M.D.
   Radiation Research . . . . Roger Howell, Ph.D.
Surgery . . . . Anne Mosenthal, M.D. (Interim)
   Cardiothoracic . . . . Justin Sambol, M.D.
   Critical Care . . . . Anne Mosenthal, M.D.
   Palliative Care . . . . Anne Mosenthal, M.D.
   General and Minimally Invasive . . . . Asha Bale, M.D.
   Plastic . . . . Mark Granick, M.D.
   Transplantation . . . . Baburao Koneru, M.D.
   Trauma . . . . David H. Livingston, M.D.
   Urology . . . . Mark Jordan, M.D.
   Vascular . . . . Michael Curi, M.D.

University of Medicine and Dentistry of New Jersey
Robert Wood Johnson Medical School

125 Paterson Street, Suite 1400
New Brunswick, New Jersey 08901
732-235-5600; 732-235-6300 (dean's office); 732-235-6315 (fax)
Web site: http://rwjms.umdnj.edu

UMDNJ-Robert Wood Johnson Medical School has campuses in Piscataway, New Brunswick, and Camden, New Jersey. Established as Rutgers Medical School, its name changed to Robert Wood Johnson Medical School in 1986.

Type: public
2011 total enrollment: 667
Clinical facilities: Principal hospitals are Robert Wood Johnson University Hospital and Cooper University Hospital. University hospitals are Jersey Shore University Medical Center and the University Medical Center at Princeton. Major clinical affiliates are Somerset Medical Center and Raritan Bay Medical Center. In addition, there are 27 clinical affiliates.

University Officials

President. . . . . William F. Owen, Jr., M.D.
Executive Vice President, Academic and Clinical Affairs . . . . Denise V. Rodgers, M.D.

Medical School Administrative Staff

Dean and Chief Executive Officer, The Robert
    Wood Johnson Medical Group . . . . Peter S. Amenta, M.D., Ph.D.
Senior Associate Dean for Community Health. . . . . Eric G. Jahn, M.D.
Senior Associate Dean for Education . . . . Carol A. Terrigino (Interim)
Senior Associate Dean for Research . . . . Terri Goss-Kinzy, Ph.D. (Interim)
Senior Associate Dean for Clinical Affairs. . . . . Anthony T. Scardella, M.D.
Senior Associate Dean for the Camden campus. . . . . Carol A. Terregino, M.D. (Acting)
Senior Associate Dean for Graduate School of
    Biomedical Sciences . . . . Terri Goss-Kinzy, Ph.D.
Associate Dean for Clinical Translational Research . . . . Peter M. Scholz, M.D.
Associate Dean for Research. . . . . Celine Gelinas, Ph.D.
Associate Dean for Oncology Programs. . . . . Robert S. DiPaola, M.D.
Associate Dean for Admissions . . . . Carol A. Terregino, M.D.
Associate Dean for Postgraduate Education. . . . . Vacant
Associate Dean for Global Health. . . . . Javier Escobar, M.D.
Associate Dean for Research at Camden . . . . Peter Melera, Ph.D.
Associate Dean for Jersey Shore Univ. Med. Ctr. . . . . David Kountz, M.D.
Associate Dean for Veterans Affairs . . . . Vacant
Associate Dean for Women's Health. . . . . Gloria A. Bachmann, M.D.
Associate Dean for Graduate Medical Education . . . . Marie C. Trontell, M.D.
Associate Dean for Education and CME . . . . David Swee, M.D.
Associate Dean for Student Affairs . . . . Vacant
Assistant Dean for Student Affairs. . . . . Sonia Garcia-Laumbach, M.D.
Assistant Dean for Educational Programs . . . . Norma Saks, Ed.D.
Assistant Dean for Student Affairs. . . . . Daniel Mehan, Ph.D.
Assistant Dean for Education . . . . Archana Pradhan, M.D.
Assistant Dean for Student Affairs at Camden . . . . Robert J. Risimini, M.D.
Chief Operating and Financial Officer . . . . Alice Lustig

University of Medicine and Dentistry of New Jersey
Robert Wood Johnson Medical School: NEW JERSEY

Department Chairs

Basic Sciences

Biochemistry . . . . Michael Hampsey, Ph.D. (Acting)
Molecular Genetics, Microbiology, and Immunology . . . . Gary Brewer, Ph.D. (Interim)
Neuroscience and Cell Biology . . . . Cheryl Dreyfus, Ph.D. (Acting)
Pathology and Laboratory Medicine . . . . Evan Cadoff, M.D. (Acting)
Pharmacology . . . . Leroy F. Liu, Ph.D.
Physiology and Biophysics . . . . Jianjie Ma, Ph.D. (Acting)

Clinical Sciences

Anesthesia . . . . Christine Hunter, M.D.
Dermatology . . . . Babar Rao, M.D. (Acting)
Environmental and Occupational Medicine . . . . Howard Kipen, M.D. (Acting)
Emergency Medicine . . . . Michael E. Chansky, M.D.
Family Medicine . . . . Alfred F. Tallia, M.D.
Medicine . . . . John B. Kostis, M.D.
Neurology . . . . Suhayl Dhib-Jalbut, M.D.
Obstetrics, Gynecology, and Reproductive Sciences . . . . Gloria A. Bachmann, M.D. (Acting)
Ophthalmology . . . . Stuart N. Green, M.D.
Orthopaedic Surgery . . . . Charles J. Gatt, M.D.
Pediatrics . . . . Patricia N. Whitley-Williams, M.D. (Acting)
Physical Medicine and Rehabilitation . . . . Thomas E. Strax, M.D.
Psychiatry . . . . Matthew Menza, M.D.
Radiation Oncology . . . . Bruce G. Haffty, M.D.
Radiology . . . . John Nosher, M.D.
Surgery . . . . Alan Graham, M.D. (Interim)

UMDNJ-Robert Wood Johnson Medical School, Camden Campus
856-757-7905, (assoc. dean, acad. stud. aff.

Department Heads

Anesthesiology . . . . Michael Goldberg, M.D.
Emergency Medicine . . . . Michael E. Chansky, M.D.
Family Medicine . . . . Dyanne P. Westerberg, D.O.
Medicine . . . . Joseph E. Parrillo, M.D.
Obstetrics and Gynecology . . . . Robin L. Perry, M.D.
Orthopaedic Surgery . . . . Lawrence Miller, M.D.
Pathology . . . . Roland Schwarting, M.D.
Pediatrics . . . . Michael Goodman, M.D.
Physical Medicine and Rehabilitation Therapy . . . . Elliot Bodofsky, M.D.
Psychiatry . . . . Andres Pumariego, M.D.
Radiation Oncology and Nuclear Medicine . . . . Tamara A. LaCouture, M.D.
Radiology . . . . Raymond Baraldi, M.D.
Surgery . . . . Jeffrey P. Carpenter, M.D.

University of New Mexico School of Medicine
MSC 08 4720
Albuquerque, New Mexico 87131
505-272-2321 (dean's office); 505-272-6581 (fax)
Web site: http://hsc.unm.edu/som

The establishment of the school of medicine at the University of New Mexico was authorized by the board of regents in 1961. The first entering class enrolled in fall 1964. The school of medicine is situated on the university campus and is a part of the University of New Mexico Health Sciences Center.

Type: public
2011 total enrollment: 280
Clinical facilities: University of New Mexico Hospitals, Veterans Administration Medical Center, Bernalillo County Mental Health/Mental Retardation Center, University of New Mexico Children's Psychiatric Hospital, University of New Mexico Cancer Center, Ambulatory Care Center, Center for Non-invasive Diagnosis, Carrie Tingley Hospital.

University Officials

President. . . . . David Schmidly, Ph.D.
Provost and Executive Vice President for Academic Affairs . . . . Vacant
Executive Vice President for Administration . . . . David W. Harris
Chancellor, Health Sciences Center . . . . Paul B. Roth, M.D., M.S.
Vice President for Student Affairs. . . . . Eliseo Torres, Ph.D.
Vice President for Advancement. . . . . Henry Nemcik
Vice Provost for Research. . . . . Julia Fulghum, Ph.D.

Medical School Administrative Staff

Dean. . . . . Paul B. Roth, M.D., M.S.
Executive Vice Dean . . . . Jeffrey K. Griffith, Ph.D.
Associate Dean for Student Affairs. . . . . Eve Espey, M.D.
Assistant Dean for Admissions . . . . David Bear, Ph.D.
Associate Dean, Office of Diversity . . . . Valerie Romero-Leggott, M.D.
Associate Dean for Undergraduate Medical Education . . . . Craig Timm, M.D.
Associate Dean for Graduate Medical Education. . . . . David Sklar, M.D.
Senior Associate Dean for Medical Education . . . . Ellen M. Cosgrove, M.D.
Senior Associate Dean for Academic Affairs . . . . Leslie Morrison, M.D.
Senior Associate Dean for Clinical Affairs. . . . . Carolyn Voss, M.D.
Senior Associate Dean for Research . . . . Richard Larson, M.D.
Executive Director, Health Sciences Center
    Library and Informatics Center . . . . Holly Buchanan, Ph.D.

Department and Division or Section Chairs

Basic Sciences

Biochemistry and Molecular Biology. . . . . William Anderson, Ph.D.
Cell Biology and Physiology . . . . Paul McGuire, Ph.D.
Molecular Genetics and Microbiology. . . . . Vojo Deretic, Ph.D.
Neurosciences . . . . David D. Savage II, Ph.D.
Pathology . . . . Thomas Williams, M.D.

Clinical Sciences

Anesthesiology. . . . . John Wills, M.D.
Dermatology . . . . R. Steven Padilla, M.D.
Emergency Medicine . . . . Michael Richards, M.D.
    Pediatric Emergency Care. . . . . Robert Sapien, M.D.
Family and Community Medicine. . . . . Martha McGrew, M.D.
    Family Practice. . . . . Vacant
    Geriatrics. . . . . Robert L. Rhyne, Jr., M.D.
Medicine. . . . . Pope Moseley, M.D.

Cardiology . . . . Warren Laskey, M.D.
Dental Medicine. . . . . Gary Cuttrell, D.D.S.
Endocrinology . . . . David Schade, M.D.
Epidemiology and Preventive Medicine . . . . Marianne Berwick
Gastroenterology . . . . Thomas Ma, M.D.
General Medicine. . . . . Carolyn M. Voss, M.D.
Gerontology. . . . . Carla Herman, M.D.
Hematology and Oncology . . . . Vacant
Infectious Diseases . . . . Gregory Mertz, M.D.
Nephrology and Renal . . . . Philip G. Zager, M.D.
Pulmonary . . . . Richard Crowell, M.D.
Rheumatology . . . . Arthur D. Bankhurst, M.D.
Neurology . . . . Gary A. Rosenberg, M.D.
Pediatric Neurology . . . . Leslie Morrison, M.D.
Neurosurgery. . . . . Howard Yonas, M.D.
Obstetrics and Gynecology . . . . William F. Rayburn, M.D.
Breast Disease Program . . . . Kathleen Kennedy, M.D.
Certified Nurse Midwifery Service . . . . Laura Migliaccio, C.N.M.
Gynecologic Oncology . . . . Carolyn Mullen, M.D.
Gynecology . . . . Tony Ogburn, M.D.
Maternal Fetal Medicine. . . . . Lisa Moore, M.D.
Maternity and Infant Care . . . . Sharon Phelan, M.D.
Urogynecology . . . . Rebecca Rogers, M.D.
Reproductive Endocrinology and Infertility . . . . Francis W. Byrn, M.D.
Orthopaedics. . . . . Robert Schenk, M.D.
Adult Reconstruction . . . . Christopher Hanosh, M.D.
Foot and Ankle Reconstruction. . . . . Richard A. Miller, M.D.
General Orthopaedic Surgery . . . . Paul Echols, M.D.
Hand Surgery. . . . . Tahseen Cheema, M.D.
Occupational Therapy . . . . Terry K. Crowe, Ph.D.
Pediatrics . . . . Dale Hoekstra, M.D.
Physical Therapy . . . . Susan Queen, P.T., Ph.D.
Spine. . . . . Andrew Paterson, M.D.
Sports Medicine . . . . Daniel C. Wascher, M.D.
Trauma . . . . Thomas A. DeCoster, M.D.
Pediatrics . . . . Loretta Cordova de Ortega, M.D.
Adolescent Medicine . . . . Victor S. Strasberger, M.D.
Ambulatory . . . . Andrew Hsi, M.D.
Cardiology. . . . . M. Beth Goens, M.D.
Critical Care. . . . . Mark Crowley, M.D.
Pulmonary . . . . Lea Davies, M.D.
Developmental Disabilities . . . . Catherine McClain, M.D.
Dysmorphology . . . . Randall Heidenreich, M.D.
Endocrinology . . . . Nancy Gregor, M.D.
Hematology and Oncology . . . . Stuart Winter, M.D.
Infectious Disease. . . . . Sheila Hickey, M.D.
Neonatology. . . . . Kristi Watterberg
Pediatrics Rehabilitation Medicine . . . . Denise Taylor, M.D.
Psychiatry . . . . George Nurenberg, M.D.
Child and Adolescent Psychiatry . . . . Robert A. Bailey, M.D.
Radiation Oncology. . . . . Vacant
Radiology . . . . Philip Wiest, M.D.
Surgery . . . . John Russell, M.D.
Cardiothoracic Surgery. . . . . Jorge A. Wernly, M.D.
General Surgery. . . . . Thomas Howdieshell, M.D.
Ophthalmology . . . . Arup Das, M.D.
Pediatric Surgery . . . . David Lemon, M.D.
Plastic Surgery, Head, Neck, and Reconstructive Surgery . . . . Bret Baack, M.D.
Urology . . . . Anthony Smith, M.D.
Vascular Surgery. . . . . Mark Langsfeld, M.D.

Albany Medical College

47 New Scotland Avenue
Albany, New York 12208
518-262-6008 (dean's office); 518-262-6515 (fax)
Web site: www.amc.edu

The Albany Medical College, chartered by the legislature of New York, opened on January 2, 1839. The medical college is part of the Albany Medical Center.

Type: private
2011 total enrollment: 513
Clinical facilities: Albany Medical Center Hospital, Samuel Stratton DVA Medical Center, St. Peter's Hospital (Albany), Ellis Hospital (Schenectady), Capital District Psychiatric Center (Albany), Mary Imogene Bassett Hospital, AMC South Clinical Campus.

Albany Medical Center Officials

President and Chief Executive Officer . . . . James J. Barba
Executive Vice President for Health Affairs. . . . . Vincent P. Verdile, M.D.
Executive Vice President and Chief Operating Officer. Gary J. Kochem
Executive Vice President for Integrated Delivery
  Systems and Hospital Systems General
  Director . . . . Steven M. Frisch, M.D.
Executive Vice President and Chief Financial Officer . . . . William C. Hasselbarth
Senior Vice President for Development . . . . Terri Cerveny
Senior Vice President and General Counsel . . . . Lee R. Hessberg
Senior Vice President for Policy Planning and Communications . . . . Kim Fine

Medical School Administrative Staff

Dean. . . . . Vincent P. Verdile, M.D.
Vice Dean for Academic Administration . . . . Henry S. Pohl, M.D.
Vice Dean for Clinical Affairs. . . . . Ferdinand Venditti, M.D.
Senior Associate Dean for Clinical Research . . . . Paul J. Davis, M.D.
Associate Dean for Academic Affairs and Student Services. . . . . Elizabeth Higgins, M.D.
Associate Dean for Graduate Medical Education . . . . Joel Bartfield, M.D.
Assistant Dean for Graduate Studies Program . . . . Thomas Anderson, Ph.D.
Associate Dean for Medical Education . . . . Jonathan M. Rosen, M.D.
Associate Dean for Community Outreach and Medical Education . . . . Ingrid Allard, M.D.
Executive Associate Dean and Chief Operating Officer . . . . John DePaola
Assistant Dean for Undergraduate Medical
  Education, Years 1 and 2 . . . . Rebecca Keller, Ph.D.
Assistant Dean for Undergraduate Medical Education, Years 3 and 4 . . . . . . Kimberly Kilby, M.D.
Director, Admissions and Student Records . . . . Joanne Nanos
Director, Alumni Office . . . . Maura Mack-Hisgen
Director of Continuing Medical Education . . . . Jennifer Price
Director of Public Relations. . . . . Vacant
Associate Dean for Information Resources and Technology. . . . . Enid Geyer

Department and Division or Section Chairs

Interdisciplinary Research Centers

Cardiovascular Science. . . . . Harold A. Singer, Ph.D.
Cell Biology and Cancer Research . . Paula J. McKeown-Longo, Ph.D., and Paul J. Higgins, Ph.D.
Immunology and Microbial Disease . . . . Dennis W. Metzger, Ph.D.
Neuropharmacology and Neuroscience. Stanley D. Glick, M.D., Ph.D.

Clinical Sciences

Anesthesiology. . . . . Kevin W. Roberts, M.D.
Emergency Medicine . . . . Christopher King, M.D.
Family Practice . . . . Neil Mitnick, D.O.
Medicine. . . . . Richard Blinkhorn, M.D.
   Allergy. . . . . Jocelyn Celestin, M.D.
   Cardiology. . . . . Edward Philbin, M.D.
   Endocrinology . . . . Matthew C. Leinung, M.D.
   Gastroenterology . . . . Catherine Bartholomew, M.D.
   General Internal Medicine . . . . Alwin F. Steinmann, M.D.
   Geriatric Medicine . . . . Vacant
   Hematology and Medical Oncology. . . . . Vacant
   HIV Medicine . . . . Douglas G. Fish, M.D.
   Hospital Medicine . . . . John Tietjen, D.O.
   Medicine/Pediatrics . . . . Kathleen Zabinski-Kramer
   Pulmonary Diseases . . . . Thomas Smith, M.D.
   Renal Diseases . . . . George Eisele, M.D.
   Rheumatology . . . . Ludovico Cavaliere, M.D.
Neurology. . . . . Michael Gruenthal, M.D., Ph.D.
Neurosciences Institute . . . . Michael Gruenthal, M.D., Ph.D.
Obstetrics, Gynecology, and Reproductive Sciences. . . . . Kevin C. Kiley, M.D.
   General Gynecology and Obstetrics. Norman F. Angell, M.D., Ph.D.
   Gynecologic Oncology . . . . Vacant
   Maternal and Fetal Medicine . . . . Camille Kanaan, M.D.
   Urogynecology and Reproductive Pelvic Surgery . . . . Vacant
Ophthalmology. . . . . John Simon, M.D.
Pathology and Laboratory Medicine . . . . Jeffrey S. Ross, M.D.
Pediatrics . . . . David A. Clark, M.D.
Physical Medicine and Rehabilitation . . . . George P. Forrest, M.D.
Psychiatry . . . . Victoria I. Balkoski, M.D.
   Child Psychiatry . . . . Victoria I. Balkoski, M.D.
Radiology . . . . Gary Siskin, M.D.
   Vascular and Interventional Radiology. . . . . Gary Siskin, M.D.
Surgery . . . . Steven Stain, M.D.
   Cardiothoracic Surgery. . . . . Edward Bennett, M.D.
   General Surgery. . . . . Edward Lee, M.D.
   Neurosurgery. . . . . Alan Boulos, M.D.
   Orthopaedic Surgery . . . . Richard Uhl, M.D.
   Otolaryngology. . . . . Jason Mouzakes, M.D.
   Pediatric Surgery . . . . Mary Christine Whyte, M.D.
   Plastic Surgery . . . . Malcolm Roth, M.D.
   Urological Surgery . . . . Barry A. Kogan, M.D.
   Vascular Surgery. . . . . R. Clement Darling, M.D.
Vascular Institute. . . . . Dhiraj M. Shah, M.D.

Albert Einstein College of Medicine of Yeshiva University

1300 Morris Park Avenue
Bronx, New York 10461
718-430-2000; 718-430-2801 (dean's Office); 718-430-8822 (fax)
Web site: www:einstein.yu.edu

The Albert Einstein College of Medicine admitted its first class in fall 1955. The college of medicine is approximately seven miles from the main campus of the university.

Type: private
2011 total enrollment: 776
Clinical facilities: Beth Abraham Hospital, Beth Israel Medical Center, Bronx-Lebanon Hospital Center, Bronx Psychiatric Center and Bronx Psychiatric Children's Hospital, Four Winds Hospital, Jack D. Weiler Hospital of Albert Einstein College of Medicine (division of Montefiore Medical Center), North Shore-Long Island Jewish Health System, Montefiore Medical Center, North Bronx Care Network (Jacobi Medical Center and North Central Bronx Hospital).

University Officials

President. . . . . Richard M. Joel, J.D.
Chancellor . . . . Norman Lamm, Ph.D.
Vice President for Medical Affairs. . . . . Allen M. Spiegel, M.D.

Medical School Administrative Staff

Dean. . . . . Allen M. Spiegel, M.D.
Executive Dean . . . . Edward R. Burns, M.D.
Senior Associate Dean for Students . . . . Stephen G. Baum, M.D.
Senior Associate Dean, Medical Education . . . . Martha S. Grayson, M.D.
Senior Associate Dean, Student Academic Affairs . . . . Nadine T. Katz, M.D.
Associate Dean, Graduate Medical Education . . . . Brian L. Cohen, M.B.Ch.B.
Associate Dean, Public Affairs and Communication. . . . . Gordon W. Earle
Associate Dean, Diversity Mentoring. . . . . Genevieve S. Neal-Perry, M.D., Ph.D.
Associate Dean, Office of Diversity Enhancement . . . . Yvette Calderon, M.D.
Associate Dean, Continuing Medical Education
and Research Administration . . . . Victor B. Hatcher, Ph.D.
Associate Dean, Admissions . . . . Noreen Kerrigan
Associate Dean, Graduate Programs in Biomedical Sciences . . . . . . Victoria H. Freedman, Ph.D.
Associate Dean, Clinical Research Education. . . . . Paul R. Marantz, M.D.
Associate Dean, Institutional Advancement. . . . . Glenn Miller
Associate Dean, Clinical and Translational Research . . . . Harry Shamoon, M.D.
Associate Dean, Finance and Administration. . . . . Jed M. Shivers
Assistant Dean, Montefiore Medical Center. . . . . Brian Currie, M.D.
Assistant Dean, North Bronx Healthcare Network. . . . . Stephan L. Kamholz, M.D.
Assistant Dean, Beth Israel Medical Center. . . . . Alfred P. Burger, M.D.
Assistant Dean, Bronx-Lebanon Hospital Center . . . . Jeffrey Mark Levine, M.D.
Assistant Dean, North Shore-Long Island Jewish Health System . . . . Lawrence P. Davis, M.D.
Assistant Dean, St. Barnabas Hospital . . . . David H. Rubin, M.D.
Assistant Dean, Educational Informatics . . . . Gary Hamill, Ed.D.
Assistant Dean, Scientific Resources . . . . Harris Goldstein, M.D.
Assistant Dean, Educational Resources . . . . Penny Steiner-Grossman, Ed.D.
Assistant Dean, Faculty Development . . . . Christina M. Coyle, M.D.
Assistant Dean, Scientific Operations . . . . John L. Harb
Assistant Dean, Academic Affairs . . . . Barbara A. Levy
Assistant Dean, Academic Administration . . . . Shelly Motzkin
Assistant Dean, Office of Diversity . . . . Nilda Soto
Assistant Dean, Biomedical Science Education . . . . Howard M. Steinman, Ph.D.
Assistant Dean, Community Engagement . . . . Alvin H. Strelnick, M.D.
Director, Medical Scientist Training Program . . . . Myles Akabas, M.D., Ph.D.
Director, Belfer Institute for Advanced Biomedical Studies . . . . Jonathan M. Backer, M.D.
Director, D. Samuel Gottesman Library . . . . Racheline Habousha
Director, Clinical Research Training Program. . . . . Ellie E. Schoenbaum, M.D.

Albert Einstein College of Medicine of Yeshiva University: NEW YORK

Department and Division or Section Chairs

Basic Sciences

Anatomy and Structural Biology. . . . . John S. Condeelis, Ph.D., and Robert H. Singer, Ph.D.
Biochemistry . . . . Vern L. Schramm, Ph.D.
Cell Biology. . . . . Arthur I. Skoultchi, Ph.D.
Developmental and Molecular Biology . . . . Liang Zhu, M.D., Ph.D. (Interim)
Genetics . . . . Jan Vijg, Ph.D.
Molecular Pharmacology . . . . Charles S. Rubin, Ph.D., and Susan B. Horwitz, Ph.D.
Microbiology and Immunology. . . . . Arturo Casadevall, M.D., Ph.D.
Neuroscience. . . . . Donald S. Faber, Ph.D.
Pathology . . . . Michael B. Prystowsky, M.D.
Physiology and Biophysics . . . . Denis L. Rousseau, Ph.D.
Systems and Computational Biology . . . . Aviv Bergman, Ph.D.

Clinical Sciences

Anesthesiology. . . . . Ellise S. Delphin, M.D., M.P.H.
Cardiothoracic Surgery . . . . Robert E. Michler, M.D.
Dentistry . . . . Richard A. Kraut, D.D.S.
Emergency Medicine . . . . E. John Gallagher, M.D.
Epidemiology and Population Health . . . . Thomas E. Rohan, M.D., Ph.D.
Family and Social Medicine . . . . Peter A. Selwyn, M.D.
Medicine. . . . . Victor L. Schuster, M.D.
Neurological Surgery . . . . Eugene S. Flamm, M.D.
Neurology. . . . . Mark F. Mehler, M.D.
Nuclear Medicine . . . . M. Donald Blaufox, M.D., Ph.D.
Obstetrics and Gynecology and Women's Health . . . . Irwin R. Merkatz, M.D.
Ophthalmology and Visual Sciences . . . . Roy Chuck, M.D., Ph.D.
Otorhinolaryngology . . . . Marvin P. Fried, M.D.
Pediatrics . . . . Phillip Ozuah, M.D.
Physical Medicine Rehabilitation . . . . Mark A. Thomas, M.D. (Interim)
Psychiatry and Behavioral Sciences . . . . T. Byram Karasu, M.D.
Radiation Oncology. . . . . Shalom Kalnicki, M.D.
Radiology . . . . E. Stephen Amis, Jr., M.D.
Surgery . . . . Robert E. Michler, M.D.
  Orthopedic Surgery . . . . Neil J. Cobelli, M.D.
Urology. . . . . Reza Ghavamian, M.D. (Interim)

Columbia University College of Physicians and Surgeons

630 West 168th Street
New York, New York 10032
212-305-3592 (dean's office); 212-304-4201
Web site: www.cumc.columbia.edu

Columbia University began as King's College, which was founded in 1754 by royal grant of George II, King of England. In 1814, the medical faculty of Columbia College was merged with the college of physicians and surgeons. In 1860, the college of physicians and surgeons became the medical department of Columbia College. In 1891, the college was incorporated as an integral part of the university. The medical school is part of the Columbia-Presbyterian Medical Center.

Type: private
2011 total enrollment: 659
Clinical facilities: Presbyterian Hospital (Sloane Hospital for Women, Babies and Children's Hospital, Vanderbilt Clinic, Neurological Institute, Eye Institute, New York Orthopedic Hospital, Squier Urological Clinic); New York State Psychiatric Institute; Mary Imogene Bassett Hospital (Cooperstown); Harlem Hospital Center; Helen Hayes Hospital (Haverstraw); Overlook Hospital (Summit, New Jersey); St. Luke's-Roosevelt Hospital Center; Valley Hospital (Ridgewood, New Jersey); Horton Memorial Hospital (Middletown); Lawrence Hospital (Bronxville); White Plains Hospital Center; New Milford Hospital (Connecticut); Stamford Hospital (Connecticut); Nyack Hospital (New York); St. Luke's (Newburgh, New York); St. Mary's Hospital for Children (New York); St. Vincent's Hospital (Connecticut); Cornwall Hospital (New York); Holy Name Hospital (Teaneck, New Jersey).

University Officials

President. . . . . Lee C. Bollinger, J.D.
Provost . . . . Claude Steele, Ph.D.
Executive Vice President for Health and Biomedical Sciences . . . . Lee Goldman, M.D.
Executive Vice President for Research . . . . Michael Purdy, Ph.D.
Chief Operating Officer. . . . . Mark McDougle
Chief Financial Officer. . . . . Joanne M. Quan
Chief Human Resources Officer. . . . . Diane Tucker
Chief Information Officer . . . . Robert V. Sideli, M.D.
Associate General Counsel . . . . Patricia Sachs Catapano, J.D.
Vice President for Development. . . . . Amelia Alverson
Deputy Vice President for Government and Community Affairs. . . . . Ross A. Frommer, J.D.
Controller. . . . . Francine Caracappa
General Council . . . . Jane Booth, J.D.
Vice President for Public Safety . . . . James F. McShane
Vice President for Facilities Management . . . . Amador Centeno
Associate Vice President for Budget and Planning. . . . . William P. McKoy
Associate Vice President and Chief Billing Compliance Officer . . . . Diane Lloyd Yaeger, J.D.
Associate Vice President, Environmental Health and Safety. . . . . Kathleen Crowley
Associate Vice President for HIPAA Compliance/Privacy Officer . . . . Karen Pagliaro-Meyer
Assistant Vice President, Campus Operations . . . . Herman Matte

Medical School Administrative Staff

Dean of the Faculties of Health Sciences and Medicine. . . . . Lee Goldman, M.D.
Senior Vice Dean. . . . . Steven Shea, M.D.
Vice Dean for Research . . . . Robert Kass, Ph.D.
Vice Dean for Administration. . . . . Martha Hooven
Vice Dean for Academic Affairs . . . . Anne Taylor, M.D.
Vice Dean for Education . . . . Ronald E. Drusin, M.D.
Chief Financial Officer. . . . . Alan D. Johns
Senior Associate Dean for Student Affairs. . . . . Lisa A. Mellman, M.D.
Senior Associate Dean for St. Luke's-Roosevelt Hospital Center. . . . . . . Richard Rosenthal, M.D.
Senior Associate Dean for Bassett Healthcare . . . . Walter A. Franck, M.D.
Senior Associate Dean at Stamford Health System. . . . . Noel I. Robin, M.D.
Associate Dean for Admissions . . . . Stephen W. Nicholas, M.D.
Associate Dean for Graduate Affairs . . . . Richard B. Robinson, Ph.D.
Associate Dean for Diversity and Minority Affairs . . . . Hilda Hutcherson, M.D.

Columbia University College of Physicians and Surgeons: NEW YORK

Executive Director of the Office of Clinical Trials . . . . Rudina Odeh-Ramada, Ph.D.
Director of Science and Technology Ventures. . . . . Ofra Weinberger, Ph.D.
Director of Institutional Review Board . . . . George Gasparis
President, Faculty Practice Organization . . . . Louis Bigliani, M.D.

Department and Division or Section Chairs

Basic Sciences

Biochemistry and Molecular Biophysics. . . . . Thomas Maniatis, Ph.D.
Genetics and Development. . . . . Gerard Karsenty, M.D., Ph.D.
Microbiology. . . . . Sankar Ghosh, Ph.D.
Pathology and Cell Biology . . . . Michael L. Shelanski, M.D., Ph.D.
Pharmacology . . . . Robert S. Kass, Ph.D.
Physiology and Cellular Biophysics . . . . Andrew Marks, M.D.

Clinical Sciences

Anesthesiology. . . . . Margaret Wood, M.D.
Biomedical Informatics . . . . George M. Hripcsak, M.D.
Dermatology . . . . David R. Bickers, M.D.
Medicine. . . . . Donald W. Landry, M.D., Ph.D.
Neurological Surgery. . . . . Robert A. Solomon, M.D.
Neurology . . . . Richard Mayeux, M.D.
Neuroscience. . . . . Steven Siegelbaum, Ph.D.
Obstetrics and Gynecology. . . . . Mary E. D'Alton, M.D.
Ophthalmology . . . . Stanley Chang, M.D.
Orthopedic Surgery. . . . . Louis U. Bigliani, M.D.
Otolaryngology-Head and Neck Surgery . . . . Lanny Garth Close, M.D.
Pediatrics . . . . Lawrence R. Stanberry, M.D., Ph.D.
Psychiatry . . . . Jeffrey Lieberman, M.D.
Radiation Oncology. . . . . K. S. Clifford Chao, M.D.
Radiology . . . . Lawrence Schwartz, Ph.D.
Rehabilitation Medicine. . . . . Joel Stein, M.D.
Surgery . . . . Craig R. Smith, M.D.
Urology. . . . . Mitchell Benson, M.D.

Weill Cornell Medical College of Cornell University

New York, New York 10021
212-746-5454; 212-746-6005 (dean's office); 212-746-8424 (fax)
E-mail: dean@med.cornell.edu
Web site: www.med.cornell.edu

Cornell University Medical College was established in New York City in 1898, and its graduate school of medical sciences in 1952 by the trustees of Cornell University in order to take advantage of New York City's extensive opportunities for clinical instruction. The medical college moved to its present location in 1932 as the research and educational component of the New York Hospital-Cornell Medical Center. In 1998, the medical college and graduate school were renamed the Joan and Sanford I. Weill Medical College and Graduate School of Medical Sciences of Cornell University, and the college is now known as the Weill Cornell Medical College of Cornell University.

Type: private
2011 total enrollment: 417
Clinical facilities: Amsterdam Nursing Home, Brooklyn Hospital Center, Burke Rehabilitation Hospital, Cayuga Medical Center at Ithaca, Community Health Network, New York Community Hospital, Hospital for Special Surgery, Lincoln Medical and Mental Health Center, Memorial Sloan-Kettering Cancer Center, New York Presbyterian Hospital, New York Downtown Hospital, New York Hospital Medical Center of Queens, New York Methodist Hospital, the Rogosin Institute, The Methodist Hospital (Houston, Texas), Westchester Square Medical Center, Wyckoff Heights Medical Center.

University Officials

President . . . . David J. Skorton, M.D.
Provost for Medical Affairs . . . . Laurie H. Glimcher, M.D.

Medical School Administrative Staff

Dean . . . . Laurie H. Glimcher, M.D.
Dean, Graduate School of Medical Sciences,
   Executive Vice Provost and Senior Executive
   Vice Dean . . . . David P. Hajjar, Ph.D.
Dean, Weill Cornell Medical College (Qatar) . . . . Javaid I. Sheikh, M.D., M.B.A.
Executive Vice Provost . . . . Stephen M. Cohen
Vice Provost (Development) . . . . Larry Schafer
Vice Provost (Public Affairs) . . . . Myrna Manners
Senior Associate Dean (Clinical Affairs) . . . . Michael G. Stewart, M.D., M.P.H.
Senior Associate Dean (Education) . . . . Carol Storey-Johnson, M.D.
Associate Dean (Academic Affairs) . . . . Shari R. Midoneck, M.D.
Associate Dean (Admissions) . . . . Charles L. Bardes, M.D.
Associate Dean (Affiliations) . . . . Oliver T. Fein, M.D.
Associate Dean (Billing Compliance) . . . . Stephen J. Thomas, M.D.
Associate Dean (Burke Rehabilitation Hospital) . . . . Mary Beth Walsh, M.D.
Associate Dean (Clinical Research) . . . . Ralph L. Nachman, M.D.
Associate Dean (Continuing Medical Education) . . . . Scott J. Goldsmith, M.D.
Associate Dean (Curricular Affairs) . . . . Peter M. Marzuk, M.D.
Associate Dean (Graduate School of Medical Sciences) . . . . Randi B. Silver, Ph.D.
Associate Dean (Healthcare System) . . . . Eliot J. Lazar, M.D.
Associate Dean (Intercampus Affairs) . . . . Caren A. Heller, M.D.
Associate Dean (MSK Cancer Center) . . . . Thomas J. Fahey, Jr., M.D.
Associate Dean (Pre-Medical Education-Qatar) . . . . Michael D. Johnson, Ph.D.
Associate Dean (Research Strategy-Qatar) . . . . Eelco A. Slagter, M.B.A.
Associate Dean (Student Affairs and Equal Opportunity Programs) . . . . Carlyle Miller, M.D.
Associate Dean (Translational Research) . . . . Julianne Imperato-McGinley, M.D.
Assistant Provost (Research Administration) . . . . Harry M. Lander, Ph.D.
Librarian of Medicine . . . . Colleen Cuddy
Assistant Dean (Admissions) . . . . Lori Nicolaysen
Assistant Dean (Departmental Associates) . . . . Marcus M. Reidenberg, M.D.
Assistant Dean (Faculty Affairs) . . . . Mark A. Albano, Ph.D.
Assistant Dean (Education Administration) . . . . Jason Korenkiewicz, M.A.
Assistant Dean (Graduate School) . . . . Francoise Freyre, M.A.

Weill Cornell Medical College of Cornell University: NEW YORK

Assistant Dean (Research Development/Outreach) . . . . Brian D. Lamon, Ph.D.
Assistant Dean (Student Affairs) . . . . Elizabeth Wilson Anstey
Deputy University Counsel and Sec. of the Medical College. . . . . James R. Kahn, J.D.
Chief Medical Officer, Physician Organization . . . . Daniel M. Knowles, M.D.
Chief Administrative Officer, Physician Organization. . . . . <PB> Nancy L. Farrell

Department Chairs and Basic Sciences

Biochemistry . . . . Frederick R. Maxfield, Ph.D.
Cell and Developmental Biology. . . . . Katherine A. Hajjar, M.D.
Genetic Medicine . . . . Ronald G. Crystal, M.D.
Microbiology and Immunology. . . . . Carl F. Nathan, M.D.
Pathology and Laboratory Medicine . . . . Daniel M. Knowles, M.D.
Pharmacology . . . . Lorraine J. Gudas, Ph.D.
Physiology and Biophysics . . . . Harel Weinstein, D.Sc.

Clinical Sciences

Anesthesiology. . . . . John J. Savarese, M.D.
Cardiothoracic Surgery . . . . O. Wayne Isom, M.D.
Dermatology . . . . Richard D. Granstein, M.D.
Medicine. . . . . Andrew I. Schafer, M.D.
Neurology and Neuroscience . . . . Matthew E. Fink, M.D. (Interim)
Neurological Surgery . . . . Philip E. Stieg, M.D., Ph.D.
Obstetrics and Gynecology. . . . . Frank A. Chervenak, M.D., Ph.D.
Ophthalmology . . . . Donald J. D'Amico, M.D.
Orthopaedic Surgery . . . . Thomas P. Sculco, M.D.
Otorhinolaryngology . . . . Michael G. Stewart, M.D., M.P.H.
Pediatrics . . . . Gerald M. Loughlin, M.D.
Psychiatry . . . . Jack D. Barchas, M.D.
Public Health . . . . Alvin I. Mushlin, M.D., Sc.M.
Radiology . . . . Robert J. Min, M.D.
Rehabilitation Medicine. . . . . Joel Stein, M.D.
Surgery . . . . Fabrizio Michelassi, M.D.
Urology. . . . . Peter N. Schlegel, M.D.

Centers and Institutes

Ansary Stem Cell Institute . . . . Shahin Rafii, M.D.
Center for Aging Research and Clinical Care . . . . Ronald D. Adelman, M.D.,
and Mark S. Lachs, M.D.
Center for Complementary and Integrative Medicine . . . . Mary E. Charlson, M.D., M.P.H.
Center for Global Health . . . . Warren D. Johnson, Jr., M.D.
Center for the Study of Hepatitis C, Medical Director. . . . . Ira M. Jacobson, M.D. **
Center for Vascular Biology . . . . Timothy Hla, Ph.D.
Institute for Computational Biomedicine . . . . Harel Weinstein, D.Sc.
Institute for Reproductive Medicine
　　Women's Service Center. . . . . Zev Rosenwaks, M.D.
　　Men's Service Center . . . . Marc Goldstein, M.D.
Sackler Institute for Developmental Psychobiology . . . . B. J. Casey, Ph.D.
Iris Cantor Women's Health Center . . . . Orli R. Etingin, M.D.
The Arthur and Rochelle Belfer Institute of
　　Hematology and Medical Oncology . . . . Barbara L. Hempstead, M.D., Ph.D.,
and David M. Nanus, M.D.
Neuberger Berman Lung Cancer Research Center . . . . Nasser Altorki, M.D.

**Medical Director

141

Mount Sinai School of Medicine

One Gustave L. Levy Place
New York, New York 10029-6574
212-241-6500; 212-241-8884 (dean's office); 212-824-2302 (fax)
Web site: www.mssm.edu

The school of medicine was granted a provisional charter by the board of regents of the State University of New York in 1963 and an absolute charter on May 24, 1968, to establish a medical school on the campus of the Mount Sinai Hospital. The school matriculated its first students in September 1968.

Type: private
2011 total enrollment: 1187
Clinical facilities: The Mount Sinai Hospital, Bronx Veterans Affairs Medical Center, Elmhurst Hospital Center, Englewood Hospital and Medical Center, Good Samaritan Hospital Medical Center, Jersey City Medical Center, Jewish Home and Hospital, Morristown Memorial Hospital, Mount Sinai Hospital of Queens, North General Hospital, Overlook Hospital, Phelps Memorial Hospital Center, Pilgrim Psychiatric Center, Queens Hospital Center, St. Joseph's Regional Medical Center.
University Official President, The Mount Sinai Medical Center . . . . Kenneth L. Davis, M.D.

Medical School Administrative Staff

Dean, Mount Sinai School of Medicine and
  Executive Vice President for Academic Affairs,
  The Mount Sinai Medical Center . . . . Dennis S. Charney, M.D.
Dean for Basic Science and the Graduate School
  of Biological Sciences . . . . John Morrison, Ph.D.
Dean for Genetics and Genomic Sciences. . . . . Robert J. Desnick, Ph.D., M.D.
Dean for Translational Biomedical Research. . . . . Hugh Sampson, M.D.
Dean for Medical Education. . . . . David Muller, M.D.
Dean for Clinical Affairs. . . . . Douglas Jabs, M.D.
Dean for Operations . . . . Jeffrey Silberstein
Dean for Queens/Elmhurst Programs. . . . . Jasmin Moshirpur, M.D.
Dean for Global Health . . . . Philip J. Landrigan, M.D., M.Sc.
Dean for Clinical and Population-Based Research . . . . Barbara Murphy, M.D.
Dean for International Clinical Affiliations . . . . Samin Sharma, M.D.
Senior Vice President for Finance. . . . . Stephen T. Harvey
Senior Vice President for Development . . . . Mark Kostegan
Associate Dean for Graduate Medical Education . . . . Scott Barnett, M.D.
Associate Dean for Education and Translational Research Operations . . . . Phyllis Schnepf
Associate Dean for Research. . . . . Jeffrey Silverstein, M.D.
Associate Dean for Research Resources. . . . . Reginald Miller, D.V.M.
Associate Dean for Diversity Programs and Policy . . . . Gary C. Butts, M.D.
Associate Dean for Faculty Affairs and Administration. . . . . Leslie Schneier
Associate Dean for Planning and Resource Management. . . . . Rama Iyengar
Associate Dean for Research. . . . . Glenn Martin, M.D.
Associate Dean for Sponsored Programs. . . . . Jessica Moise
Associate Dean for Clinical Research . . . . Mary Sano, Ph.D.
Associate Dean for Medical Student Research . . . . Karen Zier, Ph.D.
Associate Dean for Education Assessment and Scholarship . . . . Erica Friedman, M.D.
Associate Dean for Graduate Medical Education . . . . Kevin M. Troy, M.D.
Associate Dean for Admissions. . . . . Valerie Parkas, M.D.
Associate Dean for Information Resources and Systems. . . . . Lynn Kasner Morgan
Associate Dean for Academic Development and Mentoring. . . . . Lakshmi Devi, Ph.D.
Associate Dean for Alliance Development. . . . . Robert Southwick
Associate Dean for Atlantic Health System . . . . Susan Kaye, M.D.
Associate Dean for Bronx Veterans Administration Affairs. . . . . Eric Langhoff, M.D., Ph.D.
Associate Dean for Cancer Program Operations . . . . Sharon Mias
Associate Dean for Curricular Affairs and
  Undergraduate Medical Education . . . . Reena Karani, M.D.
Associate Dean of the Graduate School of Biological Sciences. . . . . Ross Cagan, Ph.D.
Associate Dean Queens/Elmhurst Programs . . . . Kenneth Feifer
Associate Dean for Clinical Excellence . . . . Mark Callahan, M.D.

Associate Dean for Undergraduate Medical
    Education and Student Affairs .... Peter Gliatto, M.D.
Associate Dean for Scientific Computing .... Patricia Kovatch
Associate Dean for Global Health................................. Jagat Narula, M.D.

Department Chairs

Basic Sciences

Center for Comparative Medicine and Surgery .... Reginald W. Miller, D.V.M.
Genetics and Genomic Sciences.................................. Eric E. Schadt, Ph.D.
Microbiology.. Peter Palese, Ph.D.
Developmental and Regenerative Biology .... Marek Mlodzik, Ph.D.
Neuroscience... Eric J. Nestler, M.D., Ph.D.
Oncological Sciences.. Stuart Aaronson, M.D.
Pharmacology and Systems Therapeutics .... Ravi Iyengar, Ph.D.
Structural and Chemical Biology .... Ming-Ming Zhou, Ph.D.

Clinical Sciences

Anesthesiology.. David Reich, M.D.
Cardiothoracic Surgery .... David Adams, M.D.
Cardiovascular Institute .... Valentin Fuster, M.D.
Preventive Medicine.. Philip J. Landrigan, M.D.
Dentistry.. John Pfail, D.D.S.
Dermatology.. Mark G. Lebwohl, M.D.
Emergency Medicine .... Andy S. Jagoda, M.D.
Geriatrics and Palliative Medicine............................. Albert Siu, M.D.
Health Evidence and Policy .... Eric A. Rose, M.D.
Medical Education.. David Muller, M.D.
Medicine... Mark W. Babyatsky, M.D., F.A.C.P.
    Cardiology.. Valentin Fuster, M.D., Ph.D.
    Clinical Immunology .... Lloyd Mayer, M.D.
    Endocrinology.. Yaron Tomer, M.D.
    Gastroenterology .... Bruce Sands, M.D.
    General Medicine....................................... Alex Federman, M.D.
    Hematology and Medical Oncology......................... William Oh, M.D.
    Infectious Diseases .... Michael Mullen, M.D. (Interim)
    Liver Diseases... Scott Friedman, M.D.
    Nephrology .... Barbara Murphy, M.D.
    Pulmonary and Critical Care............................ Charles A. Powell, M.D.
    Rheumatology .... Yousef Ali, M.D.
Neurology.. Stuart Sealfon, M.D.
Neurosurgery.. Joshua Bederson, M.D.
Obstetrics, Gynecology, and Reproductive Science .... Michael Brodman, M.D.
Ophthalmology... Douglas Jabs, M.D.
Orthopaedics.. Evan Flatow, M.D.
Otolaryngology .... Eric Genden, M.D.
Pathology .... Carlos Cordon-Cardo, M.D., Ph.D.
Pediatrics .... Lisa Satlin, M.D.
Psychiatry .... Wayne Goodman, M.D.
Radiation Oncology.. Kenneth Rosenzweig, M.D.
Radiology .... Burton P. Drayer, M.D.
Rehabilitation Medicine...................................... Kristjan T. Ragnarsson, M.D.
Surgery... Michael Marin, M.D.
Transplant Institute .... Sander Florman, M.D.
Urology... Simon Hall, M.D.

New York Medical College
Administration Building
Valhalla, New York 10595
914-594-4900 (provost and dean's office); 914-594-4145 (fax)
Web site: www.nymc.edu

New York Medical College was founded by William Cullen Bryant and received its charter from the legislature of New York state in April 1860. New York Medical College is a health sciences university and a member of the Tauro college and university system, that includes two graduate schools: the graduate school of basic medical sciences and the school of health sciences and practice. For over 100 years, the college was located in New York City. During the late 1970s, the college moved to its present location in Westchester County.

Type: private
2011 total enrollment: 669
Clinical facilities: Academic Medical Center - Westchester Medical Center. **University hospital** - Metropolitan Hospital Center. **Affiliated hospitals** - Benedictine Hospital; Calvary Hospital; Good Samaritan Hospital, Suffern; Greenwich Hospital; Kingston Hospital; Montefiore Medical Center, North Division; Mount Vernon Hospital; Northern Westchester Hospital Center; Norwalk Hospital; Phelps Memorial Hospital Center; Richmond University Medical Center; Saint Joseph's Medical Center, Yonkers; Saint Vincent's Medical Center, Bridgeport; Sound Shore Medical Center of Westchester; Terence Cardinal Cooke Health Care Center; VA Hudson Valley Health Care System. **Specialty Hospitals** - The New York Eye and Ear Infirmary; St. Vincent's Hospital Westchester. **Ambulatory Care Programs** - Center for Comprehensive Health Practice; Westchester Institute for Human Development.

University Officials

President. . . . . Alan H. Kadish, M.D.
Chief Executive Officer . . . . Karl P. Adler, M.D.
Provost and Dean, School of Medicine . . . . Ralph A. O'Connell, M.D.
Senior Vice President, Chief Financial Officer, and Vice Provost . . . . Stephen Piccolo, Jr.
Vice Provost and Senior Associate Dean for
    Academic Administration . . . . William A. Steadman II
Vice President and General Counsel. . . . . Waldemar A. Comas, J.D.
Vice President for University Development and University Planning. . . . . Julie A. Kubaska
Dean, Graduate School of Basic Medical Sciences. . . . . Francis L. Belloni, Ph.D.
Dean, School ofHealth Sciences and Practice . . . . Robert W. Amler, M.D.

Medical College Administration

Vice Dean for Graduate Medical Education and Affiliations. . . . . Richard G. McCarrick, M.D.
Vice Dean for Westchester Medical Center . . . . Renee Garrick, M.D.
Vice Dean for Medical Education . . . . Paul M. Wallach, M.D.
Senior Associate Dean for Metropolitan Hospital Center. . . . . Richard K. Stone, M.D.
Senior Associate Dean for Montefiore Medical
    Center, North Division . . . . T. S. Dharmarajan, M.D.
Senior Associate Dean for Graduate Medical Education . . . . Frederick Z. Bierman, M.D.
Senior Associate Dean for Student Affairs. . . . . Gladys M. Ayala, M.D.
Senior Associate Dean for Pre-Internship Program . . . . Saverio S. Bentivegna, M.D.
Senior Associate Dean for Admissions. . . . . Fern Juster, M.D.
Associate Dean for Continuing Medical Education . . . . Joseph F. Dursi, M.D.
Associate Dean for Student Affairs . . . . Elliott N. Perla, M.D.
Associate Dean for Student Financial Planning . . . . Anthony M. Sozzo
Associate Dean for Richmond University Medical Center. . . . . Edward L. Arsura, M.D.
Associate Dean for Sound Shore Medical Center. . . . . Stephen Jesmajian, M.D.
Associate Dean for Medical Education . . . . Jennifer Koestler, M.D.
Associate Dean for Research Administration . . . . Catharine Crea
Associate Dean and Director of Medical Sciences Library . . . . Diana J. Cunningham
University Registrar and Associate Provost. . . . . Judith A. Ehren
Associate Vice President for Communications . . . . Donna Moriarty
Director of Comparative Medicine . . . . Sulli J. Popilakis, D.V.M.
Executive Assistant to the Provost and Dean . . . . Vilma E. Bordonaro

Department and Division or Section Chairs

Basic Sciences

Biochemistry and Molecular Biology............................ Ernest Y. C. Lee, Ph.D.
Cell Biology and Anatomy .... Joseph D. Etlinger, Ph.D.
Microbiology and Immunology................................. Ira Schwartz, Ph.D.
Pharmacology .... Michal L. Schwartzman, M.D. (Acting)
Physiology .... Thomas H. Hintze, Ph.D.

Clinical Sciences

Anesthesiology... Kathryn E. McGoldrick, M.D.
Dental Medicine .... Joseph F. Morales, D.D.S.
Dermatology .... Bijan Safai, M.D., D.Sc.
Emergency Medicine .... Gregory L. Almond, M.D.
Family and Community Medicine......................... Montgomery Douglas, M.D.
Medicine... William H. Frishman, M.D.
   Vice Chair for Administration........................... Stephen J. Peterson, M.D.
   Vice Chair for Education .... Robert G. Lerner, M.D.
   Vice Chair for Research and Scientific Affairs .... Gary P. Wormser, M.D.
Neurology... Brij Singh Ahluwalia, M.D.
Neurosurgery.. Raj Murali, M.D.
Obstetrics and Gynecology............................. Howard Blanchette, M.D.
   Vice Chair, Montefiore Medical Center, North Division .... Kevin D. Reilly, M.D.
   Vice Chair, Richmond University Medical Center................. Michael Moretti, M.D.
Ophthalmology .... Joseph B. Walsh, M.D.
Orthopedic Surgery.................................... David E. Asprinio, M.D.
Otolaryngology .... Edward J. Shin, M.D. (Acting)
Pathology .... John T. Fallon III, M.D.
Pediatrics .... Leonard J. Newman, M.D.
   Vice Chair, Westchester Medical Center .... Michael H. Gewitz, M.D.
Psychiatry and Behavioral Sciences........................ Joseph T. English, M.D.
   Vice Chair, Westchester Medical Center .... Neil Zolkind, M.D.
Radiation Medicine .... Chitti R. Moorthy, M.D.
Radiology .... Zvi Lefkovitz, M.D.
Rehabilitation Medicine................................ Maria P. de Araujo, M.D.
Surgery .... John A. Savino, M.D.
   Vice Chair, Westchester Medical Center .... Patricia A. Sheiner, M.D.
Urology.. Muhammad S. Choudhury, M.D.

New York University School of Medicine

550 First Avenue
New York, New York 10016
212-263-7300; 212-263-3269 (dean's office); 212-263-1828 (fax)
Web site: www.med.nyu.edu/education

The New York University School of Medicine admitted its first class in 1841. The parent university is a private institution, receiving no tax support and having no geographic restrictions on its student body. The medical school is part of the NYU Langone Medical Center.

Type: private
2011 total enrollment: 736
Clinical facilities: Bellevue Hospital Center, Veterans Affairs Medical Center, Tisch Hospital, Howard A. Rusk Institute of Rehabilitation Medicine, Hospital for Joint Diseases Orthopaedic Institute, Gouverneur Hospital, Woodhull Hospital Medical Center.

Medical School Administrative Staff

President . . . . John Sexton
Dean and Chief Executive Officer . . . . Robert I. Grossman, M.D.
Vice Dean, Chief of Staff . . . . Anthony Shorris
Vice Dean, Chief of Hospital Operations . . . . Bernard A. Birnbaum, M.D.
Vice Dean, Chief Information Officer . . . . Nader Mherabi
Vice Dean, Corporate Chief Financial Officer . . . . Michael Burke
Vice Dean for Clinical Affairs and Strategy . . . . Andrew Brotman, M.D.
Vice Dean and General Counsel . . . . Annette B. Johnson, Esq.
Vice Dean for Education, Faculty, and Academic Affairs . . . . Steven B. Abramson, M.D.
Vice Dean for Science . . . . Dafna Bar-Sagi, Ph.D.
Vice Dean for Human Resources . . . . Nancy Sanchez
Senior Associate Dean for Biomedical Sciences . . . . Joel D. Oppenheim, Ph.D.
Senior Associate Dean for Community Health Affairs . . . . Mariano J. Rey, M.D.
Associate Dean for Graduate Medical Education . . . . Michael Ambrosino, M.D.
Associate Dean for Student Affairs . . . . Lynn Buckvar-Keltz, M.D.
Associate Dean for Postgraduate Programs . . . . Norman Sussman, M.D.
Associate Dean for Diversity and Academic Affairs . . . . Fritz Francois, M.D.
Vice Dean for Real Estate Development and Facilities . . . . Vicki Match Suna
Senior Director of Sponsored Programs Administrations . . . . Anthony Carna
Associate Dean for Medical Education and Technology . . . . Thomas Riles, M.D.
Associate Dean for Admissions and Financial Aid . . . . Rafael Rivera, M.D.
Associate Dean for Collaborative Science . . . . David Levy, D.ch., Ph.D.
Associate Dean for Medical Education . . . . Melvin Rosenfeld, Ph.D.
Asssociate Dean for Basic Science . . . . Linda Miller, Ph.D.
Associate Dean for Collaborative Science . . . . David Levy, Ph.D.
Associate Dean for Education Informatics . . . . Marc Triola, Ph.D.
Vice President for Medical Center Government Affairs . . . . Gilda Ventresca Ecroyd
Director, Office of Registration and Student Records . . . . Maureen A. Doran
Vice President for Development and Alumni Affairs . . . . Lisa Silverman
Assistant Dean (VA Medical Center) . . . . Michael S. Simberkoff, M.D.
Assistant Dean for Advanced Applications . . . . Jonathan H. Weider
Assistant Dean for Admissions and Financial Aid . . . . Joanne McGrath
Assistant Dean for Diversity and Community Affairs . . . . Mekbib Gemeda
Associate Dean for Alumni Relations and Academic Events . . . . Anthony Grieco, M.D.
Assistant Dean for Curriculum . . . . Vicky Harnick, Ph.D.

Department and Division or Section Chairs

Basic Sciences

Biochemistry . . . . Hannah Klein, Ph.D. (Interim)
Cell Biology . . . . Daniel Rifkin, Ph.D. (Interim)
Environmental Medicine . . . . Max Costa, Ph.D.
Forensic Medicine . . . . Charles S. Hirsch, M.D.
Microbiology . . . . Claudio Basilico, M.D.

Pathology . . . . Joan Cangiarella, M.D. (Interim)
Pharmacology . . . . Herbert H. Samuels, M.D.
Physiology and Neuroscience . . . . Richard Tsien, Dphil

Clinical Sciences

Anesthesiology. . . . . Thomas Blanck, M.D., Ph.D.
Cardiothoracic Surgery. . . . . Aubrey Galloway, M.D.
Child and Adolescent Psychiatry. . . . . Glenn Saxe, M.D.
Dermatology . . . . Seth Orlow, M.D., Ph.D.
Emergency Medicine . . . . Lewis R. Goldfrank, M.D.
Medicine. . . . . Martin Blaser, M.D.
   Cardiology* . . . . Glenn Fishman, M.D.
   Translational Medicine* . . . . Bruce Cronstein, M.D.
   Endocrinology* . . . . Ann Danoff, M.D.
   Gastroenterology* . . . . Robert Raicht, M.D.
   Hematology and Medical Oncology* . . . . Abraham Chachoua, M.D. (Interim),
      and Lawrence Gardner, M.D. (Interim)
   Nephrology* . . . . Edward Skolnik, M.D.
   Infectious Diseases and Immunology* . . . . Judith Aberg, M.D.
   Medical Humanities . . . . Robert Anderson, M.D.
   Pulmonary Critical Care Medicine and Sleep Medicine* . . . . William N. Rom, M.D.
   General Internal Medicine . . . . Marc Gourevitch, M.D.
   Rheumatology* . . . . Steven B. Abramson, M.D.
Neurology. . . . . David Levine, M.D. (Interim)
Neurosurgery. . . . . John Golfinos, M.D.
Obstetrics and Gynecology. . . . . David Keefe, M.D.
Ophthalmology . . . . Jack Dodick, M.D.
Orthopedic Surgery. . . . . Joseph D. Zuckerman, M.D.
Otolaryngology . . . . Thomas Roland, M.D.
Pediatrics . . . . Catherine Manno, M.D.
Plastic Surgery. . . . . Joseph G. McCarthy, M.D.
Psychiatry . . . . Charles Marmar, M.D.
Radiation Oncology. . . . . Silvia Formenti, M.D.
Radiology . . . . Michael Recht, M.D.
Rehabilitation Medicine. . . . . Steven Flanagan, M.D.
Surgery . . . . H. Leon Pachter, M.D.
   Bariatric Surgery. . . . . Christine Ren, M.D.
   Endocrine Surgery* . . . . Keith Heller, M.D.
   General* . . . . Kenneth Eng, M.D.
   Pediatric Surgery . . . . Howard Ginsburg, M.D.
   Surgical Oncology*. . . . . Daniel Roses, M.D.
   Transplant* . . . . Lewis Teperman, M.D.
   Trauma/Critical Care* . . . . Ronald Simon, M.D.
   Vascular*. . . . . Mark Adelman, M.D.
   Wound Healing and Regenerative Medicine* . . . . Vacant
Urology. . . . . Herbert Lepor, M.D.

*Specialty without organizational autonomy.

University of Rochester School of Medicine and Dentistry

601 Elmwood Avenue, Box 706
Rochester, New York 14642
585-275-0017 (Dean's office); 585-256-1131 (fax)
Web site: www.rochester.edu

The school of medicine and dentistry was founded in 1920 and accepted its first class in 1925. The medical center adjoins the university's River campus with its programs in arts and science and major intellectual disciplines.

Type: private
2011 total enrollment: 436
Clinical facilities: The Strong Memorial Hospital, Highland Hospital, Rochester Health System, Monroe Community Hospital, Unity Health System, Eastman Dental Center.

University Officials

President and Chief Executive Officer . . . . Joel Seligman
Provost and Executive Vice President . . . . Ralph W. Kuncl, M.D., Ph.D.
Senior University Vice President for Health
Sciences and Chief Executive Officer,
University of Rochester Medical Center. . . . . Bradford C. Berk, M.D., Ph.D.
Senior Vice President for Administration and
Finance and Chief Financial Officer . . . . Ronald J. Paprocki
Vice Provost and University Dean for Graduate Studies. . . . . Margaret H. Kearney, Ph.D.
Deputy to the President and Vice Provost for
Faculty Development and Diversity . . . . Vivian Lewis, M.D.
Senior Vice President for Institutional Resources . . . . Douglas Phillips
Senior Vice President and General Counsel . . . . Sue S. Stewart
General Secretary and Chief of Staff. . . . . Lamar R. Murphy

Medical School Administrative Staff

Senior University Vice President for Health
Sciences and Chief Executive Officer,
University of Rochester Medical Center. . . . . Bradford C. Berk, M.D., Ph.D.
Dean and University Vice President for Health Sciences . . . . Mark B. Taubman, M.D.
President and Chief Executive Officer, Strong
Memorial Hospital and Highland Hospital . . . . Steven I. Goldstein
Medical Center Vice President and Chief Operating Officer . . . . Peter G. Robinson
Medical Center Vice President and Chief Financial Officer . . . . Michael C. Goonan
Vice President and Chief Medical Officer. . . . . Raymond J. Mayewski, M.D.
Vice President for Clinical Services. . . . . Richard I. Fisher, M.D.
Senior Associate Dean for Graduate and Postdoctoral Education. . . . . Edith M. Lord, Ph.D.
Senior Associate Dean for Academic Affairs . . . . Richard I. Burton, M.D.
Senior Associate Dean for Clinical Research . . . . Thomas A. Pearson, M.D., Ph.D.
Senior Associate Dean for Basic Research. . . . . J. Edward Puzas, Ph.D.
Senior Associate Dean for Clinical Affairs. Raymond J. Mayawski, M.D.
Senior Associate Dean for Medical Education . . . . David R. Lambert, M.D.
Senior Associate Dean for Graduate Medical Education . . . . Diane M. Hartmann, M.D.
Associate Dean for Admissions . . . . John T. Hansen, Ph.D.
Associate Dean for Clinical Affairs . . . . Regis J. O'Keefe, M.D., Ph.D.
Associate Dean for Diversity. . . . . Linda Chaudron, M.D.
Associate Dean for Educational Evaluation and Research . . . . Ronald M. Epstein, M.D.
Associate Dean for Faculty Development. . . . . Janine Shapiro, M.D.
Senior Associate Dean for Finance and Administration . . . . William P. Passalacqua
Assistant Dean for Medical Education and Student Affairs. . . . . Brenda D. Lee
Assistant Dean for Medical Simulation . . . . Linda L. Spillane, M.D.
Director of Continuing Medical Education . . . . Jeffrey M. Lyness, M.D.
Director of Admissions. . . . . Pat Samuelson
Director, Edward G. Miner Library. . . . . Julia F. Sollenberger

University of Rochester School of Medicine and Dentistry: NEW YORK

Department, Center, and Division or Section Chairs

Basic Sciences

Biochemistry and Biophysics. . . . . Robert A. Bambara, Ph.D.
Biomedical Engineering. . . . . Richard E. Waugh, Ph.D.
Biomedical Genetics . . . . Hartmut Land, Ph.D.
Biostatistics and Computational Biology . . . . David Oakes, Ph.D. (Interim)
Aab Cardiovascular Research Institute . . . . Charles J. Lowenstein, M.D.
Center for Community Health . . . . Nancy M. Bennett, M.D.
Center for Human Experimental Therapeutics . . . . Karl D. Kieburtz, M.D., M.P.H.
Center for Neural Development and Disease. . . . . Harris Gelbard, M.D., Ph.D.
Center for Musculoskeletal Research . . . . Edward M. Schwarz, Ph.D.
Center for Oral Biology. . . . . Robert G. Quivey, Jr., Ph.D.
Center for RNA Biology. . . . . Lynne Maquat, Ph.D.
Center for Translational Neuromedicine . . . . Steven A. Goldman, M.D., Ph.D.,
and Maiken Nedergaard, M.D., D.M.Sc.
Center for Vaccine Biology and Immunology . . . . Tim R. Mosmann, Ph.D.
Community and Preventive Medicine . . . . Susan Fisher, Ph.D.
Environmental Medicine . . . . Thomas A. Gasiewicz, Ph.D.
Laboratory Animal Medicine* . . . . Jeffrey D. Wyatt, D.V.M.
Microbiology and Immunology. . . . . Stephen Dewhurst, Ph.D.
Neurobiology and Anatomy . . . . Gary D. Paige, M.D., Ph.D.
Pharmacology and Physiology. . . . . A. William Tank, Ph.D.

Clinical Sciences

Anesthesiology. . . . . Michael P. Eaton, M.D. (Interim)
Cancer Center. . . . . Richard I. Fisher, M.D.
Dentistry . . . . Cyril Meyerowitz, D.D.S.
Dermatology . . . . Alice P. Pentland, M.D.
Emergency Medicine . . . . Michael F. Kamali, M.D.
Family Medicine . . . . Thomas L. Cambell, M.D.
Imaging Sciences. . . . . David L. Waldman, M.D., Ph.D.
Medicine. . . . . Paul C. Levy, M.D.
Neurology. . . . . Steven A. Goldman, M.D., Ph.D.
Neurosurgery. . . . . Webster H. Pilcher, M.D., Ph.D.
Obstetrics and Gynecology. . . . . James R. Woods, M.D.
Ophthalmology . . . . Steven E. Feldon, M.D.
Orthopaedics and Rehabilitation . . . . Regis J. O'Keefe, M.D., Ph.D.
Otolaryngology-Head and Neck Surgery . . . . Shawn D. Newlands, M.D., Ph.D., M.B.A.
Pathology and Laboratory Medicine . . . . Daniel H. Ryan, M.D.
Pediatrics . . . . Nina F. Schor, M.D., Ph.D.
Physical Medicine and Rehabilitation . . . . K. Rao Poduri, M.D.
Psychiatry . . . . Eric D. Caine, M.D.
Radiation Oncology. . . . . Yuhchyau Chen, M.D. (Interim)
Surgery . . . . Jeffrey H. Peters, M.D.
Urology. . . . . Edward M. Messing, M.D.

State University of New York, Downstate Medical Center
College of Medicine
450 Clarkson Avenue, Box 97
Brooklyn, New York 11203-2098
718-270-1000; 718-270-3776 (dean's office); 718-270-4074 (fax)
Web site: www.downstate.edu

The college of medicine was founded in 1860 as the teaching division of the Long Island College Hospital in Brooklyn. In 1930, it was incorporated as the Long Island College of Medicine, and in 1950, it was merged with the State University of New York to become the first unit of the Downstate Medical Center.

Type: public
2011 total enrollment: 775
Clinical facilities: Clinical facilities: Major affiliates - Brookdale Hospital Medical Center, Kings County Hospital Center, Maimonides Medical Center, Staten Island University Hospital, University Hospital of Brooklyn, VA, New York Harbor Healthcare System, Lenox Hospital, Lutheran Medical Center, Coney Island Hospital **Limited affiliates** - Brooklyn Hospital Center, Kingsboro Psychiatric Center, Kingsbrook Jewish Center, New York Method Hospital, Jamaica Hospital, Long Island Jewish Medical Center, North Shore University Hospital, Richmond University Medical Center, Woodhull Medical and Mental Health Center, St. John's Episcopal Hospital—South Shore, Interfaith Medical Center. **Graduate affiliates** — Beth Israel Hospital, Memorial Sloan-Kettering Cancer Center, NYS Institute for Basic Research in Developmental Disabilities, NY Hospital-Queens, Calvary Hospital, Elmhurst Hospital, Rutland Nursing Home, Wyckoff Heights Medical Center.

University Official
Chancellor . . . . Nancy L. Zimpher

Health Science Center Administrative Staff
President. . . . . John C. LaRosa, M.D.
Executive Vice President and Chief Operating Officer. . . . . Ivan M. Lisnitzer
Senior Vice President for Institutional
    Advancement and Philanthropy and Vice
    President for Academic Affairs . . . . Jo Ann Bradley, Ed.D.
Assistant Vice President for Institutional Advancement . . . . Ellen Watson
Assistant Vice President for Planning . . . . Dorothy R. Fyfe
Chief Financial Officer. . . . . Paul Davis (Interim)
Chief Executive Officer, University Hospital of Brooklyn . . . . Debra D. Carey
Vice President, Office of Compliance and Audit Services. . . . . Renee Poncet

College of Medicine
Dean, College of Medicine. . . . . Ian L. Taylor, M.D., Ph.D.
Vice Dean . . . . Roger Q. Cracco, M.D.
Vice Dean for Graduate Medical Education . . . . Frank E. Lucente, M.D.
Vice President for Student Affairs and Dean of Students . . . . Lorraine Terracina, Ph.D.
Senior Associate Dean for Education . . . . Stanley Friedman, M.D.
Senior Associate Dean for Academic Affairs . . . . Pamela Sass, M.D.
Associate Dean for Student Affairs . . . . Sophie R. Christoforou
Associate Dean for Administration . . . . Ross Clinchy, Ph.D.
Associate Dean of Admissions. . . . . Marcia Gerber, M.D.
Associate Dean of Minority Affairs . . . . Constance Hill, M.D.
Associate Dean for Graduate Medical Education . . . . Stephen Wadowski, M.D.
Assistant Dean for Clinical Education . . . . Sheldon Landesman, M.D.
Assistant Dean for Program and Faculty Development. . . . . Fredric Volkert, Ph.D.
Assistant Dean for Student Affairs. . . . . Jeffrey Putman
Registrar . . . . Anne Shonbrun
Director, Academic Fiscal Affairs . . . . Richard D. Katz
Director of Admissions. . . . . Shushawna DeOliveira, D.H.A.
Director, Continuing Medical Education. . . . . Edeline Mitton, M.Ed.
Director, Graduate Medical Education . . . . Monica Dweck, M.D.
Director, Institutional Research and Educational Evaluation . . . . Vacant
Director, Financial Aid. . . . . James Newell
Director, Alumni Affairs. . . . . Jill Ditchik

Department and Division or Section Chairs
Basic Sciences
Cell Biology. . . . . M. A. Q. Siddiqui, Ph.D.
Pathology . . . . Suzanne S. Mirra, M.D.
Physiology and Pharmacology. . . . . Robert K. Wong, Ph.D.

State University of New York, Downstate Medical Center
College of Medicine: NEW YORK

Clinical Sciences

Anesthesiology . . . . James E. Cottrell, M.D.
  Ambulatory Surgery . . . . Rebecca Twersky, M.D.
  Cardiac . . . . Ketan Shevde, M.D.
  Critical Care . . . . Jean Charchaflieh, M.D.
  Neuroanesthesia . . . . Audree A. Bendo, M.D.
  Obstetrical . . . . David Wlody, M.D., and Alexandru Apostol, M.D.
  Pain Management . . . . Neolle Best, N.P.
  Pediatrics . . . . Khosrow Mojdehi, M.D.
  Transplant . . . . Lijin Liang, M.D.
Dermatology . . . . Alan R. Shalita, M.D.
Emergency Medicine . . . . Michael Lucchesi, M.D.
Family Practice . . . . Miriam T. Vincent, M.D., Ph.D.
Medicine . . . . Jeffrey Borer, M.D.
  Allergy and Immunology . . . . Rauno Joks, M.D. (Interim)
  Cardiology . . . . Jeffrey Borer, M.D.
  Digestive Diseases and Hepatology . . . . Frank Gress, M.D.
  Endocrinology, Hypertension, and Diabetes . . . . Maryann Bauer
  Geriatrics . . . . Everton Prospere, M.D.
  Hematology and Oncology . . . . Albert Braverman, M.D.
  Infectious Diseases . . . . Michael Augenberg
  Internal Medicine . . . . Jeffrey Borer, M.D. (Acting)
  Palliative Care . . . . Eduard Porosnicu, M.D.
  Pulmonary Medicine and Critical Care . . . . Spiro Demetis, M.D. (Interim)
  Renal Diseases . . . . Moro O. Salifu, M.D., M.P.H.
  Rheumatology . . . . Ellen Ginzler, M.D.
  Student Health . . . . Sigrid Ulrich, M.D.
Neurology . . . . Daniel Rosenbaum, M.D.
Obstetrics and Gynecology . . . . Ovadia Abulafia, M.D.
  Gynecologic Oncology . . . . Yi-Chun Lee, M.D.
  Maternal Fetal Medicine . . . . David Sherer, M.D.
  Reproductive Endocrinology . . . . Ozgul Muneyyirici-Delale, M.D.
Ophthalmology . . . . Douglas Lazzaro, M.D.
Orthopedic Surgery and Rehabilitation Medicine . . . . William P. Urban, Jr., M.D.
Otolaryngology . . . . Richard Rosenfeld, M.D., M.P.H.
Pediatrics . . . . Stanley E. Fisher, M.D.
  Adolescent Medicine . . . . Amy Suss, M.D.
  AIDS Program . . . . Hermann Mendez, M.D.
  Allergy and Immunology . . . . Hamid Moallem, M.D.
  Ambulatory Care . . . . Eugene Dinkevich, M.D.
  Asthma Center . . . . Haesoon Lee, M.D.
  Cardiology . . . . Sarita Dhuper, M.D.
  Child Development . . . . Harris Huberman, M.D.
  Critical Care . . . . Stephen Piecuch, M.D.
  Endocrinology . . . . Svetlana Ten, M.D.
  Gastroenterology . . . . Steven Schwartz, M.D.
  Genetics . . . . Vacant
  Hematology and Oncology . . . . S. P. Rao, M.D.
  Infectious Diseases . . . . Margaret Hammerschlag, M.D.
  Neonatology . . . . Jacob Aranda, M.D.
  Nephrology . . . . Morris Schoeneman, M.D.
  Neurology . . . . Joan Cracco, M.D.
  Pulmonology . . . . Haesoon Lee, M.D.
Psychiatry . . . . Stephen Goldfinger, M.D.
Radiation Oncology . . . . Marvin Rotman, M.D.
Radiology . . . . Marvin Rotman, M.D. (Interim)
Surgery . . . . Antonio Alfonso, M.D.
  Cardiothoracic Surgery . . . . Vinay Tak, M.D.
  Dental and Oral Medicine . . . . Susan Pugliese, D.D.S.
  General Surgery and Surgical Oncology . . . . Alexander Schwartzman, M.D.
  Pediatric Surgery . . . . Nicholas Shorter, M.D.
  Transplantation Surgery . . . . Devon John, M.D.
  Trauma and Surgical Critical Care . . . . Patricia O'Neill, M.D., and Robert Kurtz, M.D.
  Vascular Surgery . . . . Mark Songe, M.D.
Urology . . . . Jeffrey Weiss, M.D.

University at Buffalo, School of Medicine and Biomedical Sciences
State University of New York
3435 Main Street
Buffalo, New York 14214
716-829-3955 (dean's office); 716-829-2179 (fax)
Web site: www.medicine.buffalo.edu

The University of Buffalo School of Medicine was founded in 1846, and in 1898, the school of medicine absorbed the medical department of Niagara University. In September 1962, the University at Buffalo was merged with and became a unit of the State University of New York.

Type: public
2011 total enrollment: 581
Clinical facilities: Erie County Medical Center, KALEIDA Health Buffalo General Division, KALEIDA Health Women's and Children's Hospital of Buffalo, KALEIDA Health Millard Fillmore Health System, Veterans Administration Medical Center, Roswell Park Cancer Institute, Sisters of Charity Hospital, Mercy Hospital.

University Officials

President. . . . . Satish Tripathi, Ph.D.
Provost . . . . Harvey G. Stenger, Sc.D. (Interim)
Vice President for Health Sciences . . . . Michael E. Cain, M.D.

Medical School Administrative Staff

Dean, School of Medicine and Biomedical Sciences . . . . Michael E. Cain, M.D.
Senior Staff Assistant . . . . Deborah L. Kelsch
Senior Associate Dean for Faculty Affairs and Facilities . . . . Suzanne Laychock, Ph.D.
Senior Associate Dean for Clinical and Translational Research . . . . Timothy Murphy, M.D.
Senior Associate Dean for Graduate Medical Education . . . . Roseanne C. Berger, M.D.
Senior Associate Dean for Health Policy. . . . . Nancy H. Nielsen, M.D., Ph.D.
Senior Associate Dean for Communications . . . . Kathleen A. Wiater
Senior Associate Dean for Medical Curriculum. . . . . Avery Ellis, M.D.
Senior Associate Dean for Resource Management. . . . . Sandra Drabek
Senior Associate Dean for Development. . . . . Eric C. Alcott
Senior Associate Dean for Student and Academic Affairs. . . . . David Milling, M.D.
Senior Associate Dean for Research and
    Biomedical Education . . . . Kenneth Blumenthal, Ph.D.
Associate Dean for Biomedical Research and Education . . . . Mulchand Patel, Ph.D.
Associate Dean for Support Services. . . . . Ray Dannenhoffer, Ph.D.
Associate Dean for Medical Education and Admissions . . . . Charles Severin, Ph.D., M.D.
Associate Dean for Student Affairs . . . . Andrea Manyon, M.D.
Assistant Dean and Director of Continuing Medical Education . . . . Lori McMann
Assistant Dean for Biomedical Undergraduate Education . . . . David Schubert
Assistant Dean for Evaluation: Research . . . . Frank Schimpfhauser, Ph.D.
Assistant Dean for Student Services . . . . Debra Stamm
Registrar. . . . . James Rosso

Department and Division or Section Chairs

Basic Sciences

Biochemistry. . . . . Kenneth Blumenthal, Ph.D.
Biotechnical and Clinical Sciences . . . . Paul Kostyniak, Ph.D.
Microbiology. . . . . John Hay, Ph.D.
Pathology and Anatomical Sciences . . . . John Tomaszewski, M.D.
Pharmacology and Toxicology . . . . Margarita Dubocovich, Ph.D.
Physiology and Biophysics . . . . Perry Hogan, Ph.D. (Interim)
Structural Biology . . . . Robert Blessing, Ph.D. (Interim)

University at Buffalo, School of Medicine and Biomedical Sciences
State University of New York: NEW YORK

Clinical Sciences

Anesthesiology. . . . . Mark Lema, M.D., Ph.D.
Dermatology . . . . Animesh A. Sinha, M.D., Ph.D.
Emergency Medicine . . . . G. Richard Braen, M.D.
Family Medicine . . . . Thomas Rosenthal, M.D.
Gynecology and Obstetrics. . . . . Armando Arroyo, M.D. (Interim)
Medicine. . . . . Anne B. Curtis, M.D.
Neurology . . . . Gil I. Wolfe, M.D.
Neurosurgery. . . . . L. Nelson Hopkins III, M.D.
Nuclear Medicine . . . . Robert Miletich, M.D. (Interim)
Ophthalmology . . . . James Reynolds, M.D.
Orthopaedics. . . . . Lawrence Bone, M.D.
Otolaryngology . . . . David Sherris, M.D.
Pediatrics . . . . Teresa Quattrin, M.D.
Psychiatry . . . . Steven Dubovsky, M.D.
Radiation Oncology. . . . . Michael Kuettel, M.D., Ph.D.
Radiology . . . . Angelo M. DelBalso, M.D., D.D.S.
Surgery . . . . Merril Dayton, M.D.
Urology. . . . . Gerald Sufrin, M.D.

Stony Brook University Medical Center

Health Sciences Center
HSC Level 4-225
Stony Brook, New York 11794-8430
631-444-8234 (dean's office); 631-444-6266 (fax); 631-444-2113 (admissions)
Web site: www.stonybrookmedicalcenter.org

The medical center at Stony Brook University, a union of the school of medicine and University Hospital, is located on the university campus. The first medical students were accepted for the 1971-72 year. Instruction occurs in the academic tower, University Hospital, and affiliated institutions.

Type: public
2011 total enrollment: 513
Clinical facilities: Stony Brook University Hospital and affiliated teaching hospitals including Nassau University Medical Center, Winthrop-University Hospital, Brookhaven National Lab, Peconic Bay Medical Center, flushing Hospital, and VA Medical Center (Northport) provide both clinical and academic facilities. Special teaching programs are provided in associated community hospitals.

University Official

President. . . . . Samuel L. Stanley, Jr., M.D.

Medical Center Administrative Staff

Dean. . . . . Kenneth Kausbansky, M.D.
Dean, Nassau University Medical Center. . . . . Robert M. Yost, M.S.
Vice Dean for Faculty Affairs . . . . Sharon Nachman, M.D.
Vice Dean for Clinical Affairs. . . . . Thomas M. Biancaniello, M.D.
Vice Dean for Graduate Medical Education . . . . Frederick Schiavone, M.D.
Vice Dean for Scientific Affairs. . . . . Wadie Bahou, M.D.
Vice Dean for Undergraduate Medical
  Education and Curriculum Evaluation . . . . Latha Chandran, M.D., M.P.H.
Chief Executive Officer of Stony Brook University Hospital. . . . . Steven Strongwater, M.D.
Associate Dean for Admissions . . . . Jack Fuhrer, M.D.
Associate Dean for Continuing Medical Education . . . . Dorothy S. Lane, M.D.
Associate Dean for Student and Minority Affairs. . . . . Aldustus E. Jordan, Ed.D.
Associate Dean for Finance, Personnel, and Administration. . . . . John H. Riley
Associate Dean for Clinical Trials. . . . . Sharon Nachman, M.D.
Associate Dean for Clinical Affairs . . . . William Greene, M.D.
Associate Dean for VA Medical Center, Northport . . . . Edward J.C. Mack, M.D.
Associate Dean, Winthrop-University Hospital. . . . . John F. Aloia, M.D.
Associate Dean for Faculty Development. . . . . Elza Mylona, Ph.D.
Associate Dean, International Students. . . . . John Shanley, M.D., M.P.H.
Assistant Dean for Admissions . . . . Grace Agnetti
Assistant Dean for Faculty Personnel . . . . Karen M. Wilk
Assistant Dean for Medical Education. . . . . Andrew Wackett, M.D.
Assistant Dean for Student Affairs. . . . . Mary Jean Allen
Assistant Dean of Operations for Scientific Affairs. . . . . Glen Itzkowitz
Associate Lab Director for Life Sciences &
  Environment, Brookhaven National Lab . . . . Reinhold Mann, Ph.D.
Director, Health Sciences Library. . . . . Andrew White, Ph.D.
Director, Laboratory Animal Resources. . . . . Thomas Zimmerman
Director of Budget and Finance. . . . . Glenn Schmidt

Department and Division or Section Chairs
Basic Sciences

Anatomical Sciences . . . . William Jungers, Ph.D.
Biochemistry and Cell Biology . . . . Robert Haltiwanger, Ph.D.
Biomedical Engineering. . . . . Clinton Rubin, Ph.D.
Molecular Genetics and Microbiology. . . . . Jorge Benach, Ph.D.
Neurobiology and Behavior . . . . Lorna Role, Ph.D.
Pathology . . . . Kenneth R. Shroyer, M.D., Ph.D.
Pharmacological Sciences. . . . . Michael Frohman, M.D., Ph.D.
Physiology and Biophysics . . . . Peter R. Brink, Ph.D.

Clinical Sciences

Anesthesiology. . . . . Peter Glass, M.D.
Dermatology . . . . Evan Jones, M.D.
Emergency Medicine . . . . Mark C. Henry, M.D.
Family Medicine . . . . Jeffery S. Trilling, M.D.

Medicine. . . . . Margaret Parker, M.D. (Acting)
   Cardiology. . . . . Luis Gruberg, M.D. (Interim)
   General Medicine/Geriatrics. . . . . Suzanne Fields, M.D.
   Hematology and Medical Oncology. . . . . Theodore Gabig, M.D.
   Infectious Diseases . . . . Jack Fuhrer, M.D. (Acting)
   Gastroenterology . . . . Basil Rigas, M.D.
   Nephrology . . . . Edward Nord, M.D.
   Pulmonary and Critical Care. . . . . Gerald Smaldone, M.D.
   Rheumatology . . . . Heidi Roppelt, M.D.
   VA Medical Center (Northport) . . . . Hussein Fode, M.D. (Acting)
   Winthrop-University Hospital . . . . Michael S. Niederman, M.D.
Neurological Surgery. . . . . Raphael Davis, M.D.
Neurology. . . . . Patricia Coyle, M.D. (Acting)
Obstetrics, Gynecology, and Reproductive Medicine . . . . J. Gerald Quirk, M.D., Ph.D.
   Gynecologic Oncology . . . . Michael L. Pearl, M.D.
   Gynecology and General Obstetrics. . . . . James N. Droesch, M.D.
   Maternal / Fetal Medicine . . . . Paul L. Ogburn, Jr., M.D.
   Midwifery. . . . . Christina Kocis
   Reproductive Endocrinology and Infertility . . . . Richard A. Bronson, M.D.
Ophthalmology. . . . . Patrick A. Sibony, M.D.
Orthopaedics. . . . . Lawrence Hurst, M.D.
Pediatrics . . . . Margaret M. McGovern, M.D., Ph.D.
   Adolescent Medicine . . . . Joseph Puccio, M.D.
   Allergy and Immunology . . . . Kalpana Patel, M.D.
   Cardiology. . . . . Thomas M. Biancaniello, M.D.
   Critical Care. . . . . Margaret M. Parker, M.D.
   Developmental Disabilities/Cody Center . . . . John Pomeroy, M.D.
   Developmental and Behavioral Pediatrics . . . . Janet E. Fischel, Ph.D.
   Endocrinology . . . . Thomas A. Wilson, M.D.
   Gastroenterology . . . . Anupama Chawla, M.D.
   Genetics. . . . . Patricia A. Galvin-Parton, M.D.
   Hematology and Oncology . . . . Robert I. Parker, M.D.
   Infectious Diseases . . . . Sharon A. Nachman, M.D.
   Neonatology. . . . . Shanthy Sridhar, M.D.
   Nephrology . . . . Dilys Whyte, M.D.
   Pediatric Emergency Medicine . . . . Sergey Kunkou, M.D.
   Primary Care Medicine. . . . . Susmita Patel, M.D.
   Pediatric Rheumatology . . . . Julie Cherian, M.D.
   Pulmonology . . . . Catherine E. Kier, M.D.
Preventive Medicine. . . . . Iris Granek, M.D.
Psychiatry and Behavioral Sciences . . . . Mark J. Sedler, M.D., M.P.H.
   Adult Psychiatry (Director) . . . . Mark J. Sedler, M.D., M.P.H.
   Adult Consultation/Liaison. . . . . Mark J. Sedler, M.D., M.P.H.
   Adult Inpatient. . . . . Andrew Francis, Ph.D.
   Adult Outpatient . . . . Eric Fink, M.D.
   Child and Adolescent Psychiatry (Director) . . . . Gabrielle Carlson, M.D.
   Child Consultation/Liaison. . . . . Darla Broberg, Ph.D.
   Child Inpatient. . . . . David Margulies, M.D.
   Child Outpatient . . . . Deborah Weisbrot, M.D.
Radiation Oncology. . . . . Allen G. Meek, M.D.
Radiology. . . . . John Ferretti, M.D. (Acting)
   Nuclear Medicine. . . . . Dinko Franceschi, M.D.
Surgery. . . . . Todd Rosengart, M.D.
   Cardiothoracic. . . . . Todd Rosengart, M.D.
   Otolaryngology. . . . . David Schessel, M.D.
   Pediatric Surgery . . . . Thomas Lee, M.D.
   Trauma . . . . Marc Shapiro, M.D.
   Surgical Oncology . . . . Brian O'Hea, M.D.
   Upper Gland General Oncology . . . . Kevin Watkins, M.D.
   Vascular Surgery. . . . . Apostolos Tassiopoulos, M.D.
   Plastic . . . . Alexander Dagum, M.D.
   Nassau University Medical Center . . . . Gerald Shaftan, M.D.
   VA Medical Center, Northport . . . . Eugene Mohan, M.D.
   Winthrop-University Hospital . . . . William P. Reed, Jr., M.D.
Urology. . . . . Wayne C. Waltzer, M.D.
   Transplantation Surgery . . . . Wayne C. Waltzer, M.D.

State University of New York
Upstate Medical University
College of Medicine
750 East Adams Street
Syracuse, New York 13210-2399
315-464-9720; 315-464-9721 (fax)
Web site: www.upstate.edu

The college of medicine traces its history back to 1834, when it was organized as the medical department of Geneva College. The college remained in Geneva until 1872, when it moved to Syracuse as the college of medicine of Syracuse University. It became part of the State University of New York (SUNY) in 1950, and was renamed the Upstate Medical Center. In 1999, it was renamed the SUNY Upstate Medical University. The main campus is located in Syracuse, and a satellite clinical campus is in Binghamton. The main office of the State University of New York is located in Albany.

Type: public
2011 total enrollment: 614
Clinical facilities: University Hospital, Crouse Hospital, Veterans Administration Medical Center, St. Joseph's Hospital Health Center, Community-General Hospital, Hutchings Psychiatric Center, United Health Services, Inc., Our Lady of Lourdes Memorial Hospital, Guthrie Medical Center/Robert Packer Memorial Hospital.

University Officials

Chancellor, State University of New York . . . . Nancy L. Zimpher, Ph.D.
President, SUNY Upstate Medical University . . . . David R. Smith, M.D.
Interim Dean, College of Medicine. . . . . David B. Duggan, M.D.
Senior Vice President for Administration and Finance. . . . . Steven C. Brady, M.B.A.
Chief Executive Officer, University Hospital, and
    Senior Vice President for Hospital Affairs . . . . John McCabe, M.D.
Associate Senior Vice President for Operations . . . . Wanda M. Thompson, Ph.D.
Vice President for Research . . . . Steven Goodman, Ph.D.
Vice President for Academic Affairs . . . . Lynn M. Cleary, M.D.
Vice President and Associate Dean for Clinical Affairs. . . . . David B. Duggan, M.D.
Assistant Vice President for Academic Affairs . . . . Paul L. Grover, Ph.D.
Chief Administrative Officer, Upstate University
    Hospital, Community General . . . . Meredith Price, C.P.A.
Assistant Vice President for Diversity and Inclusion . . . . Maxine S. Thompson, MSW,LCSW-R

Medical School Administrative Staff

Dean, College of Medicine. . . . . David Duggan, M.D. (Interim)
Dean for Student Affairs . . . . Julie White, Ph.D.
Associate Dean Student Affairs. . . . . Sharon Huard
Dean for Binghamton Campus. . . . . Rajesh J. Davé, M.D.
Dean, Graduate Studies . . . . Steven Goodman, M.D.
Chief of Staff. . . . . MaryGrace VanNortwick
Senior Associate Dean for Education . . . . Lynn M. Cleary, M.D.
Senior Associate Dean for Faculty Affairs and Faculty Development . . . . Paula Trief, Ph.D.
Senior Associate Dean for Finance . . . . Richard Gardner
Associate Dean for Graduate Medical Education . . . . William Grant, M.D. (Interim)
Associate Dean for Clinical Affairs . . . . David B. Duggan, M.D.
Associate Dean, VA Medical Center . . . . William Marx, D.O.
Assistant Dean for Student Affairs. . . . . Margaret M. Maimone, Ph.D.
Associate Dean for Curriculum. . . . . Vacant
Associate Dean for Continuing Medical Education . . . . Paul L. Grover, Ph.D.
Assistant Vice President, Governmental and Community Relations. . . . . Daniel N. Hurley
Director, Vivarium . . . . Robert H. Quinn, D.V.M.
Director, Health Science Library . . . . Cristina A. Pope

Department and Division or Section Chairs

Basic Sciences

Cell and Developmental Biology. . . . . Joseph W. Sanger, Ph.D.
Biochemistry and Molecular Biology. . . . . Patricia M. Kane, Ph.D.
Microbiology and Immunology. . . . . Rosemary Rochford, Ph.D.
Pharmacology . . . . Ziwei Huang, Ph.D.
Neuroscience and Physiology. . . . . Barry Knox, Ph.D.

Clinical Sciences

Anesthesiology. . . . . Colleen O'Leary, M.D. (Interim)
Emergency Medicine . . . . Gary Johnson, M.D.
Family Medicine . . . . John Epling, M.D.
Medicine. . . . . Michael Iannuzzi, M.D.
Neurology. . . . . Jeremy M. Shefner, M.D.
Neurosurgery. . . . . Lawrence Chin, M.D.
Obstetrics and Gynecology. . . . . Robert Silverman, M.D.
Ophthalmology . . . . John A. Hoepner, M.D.
Orthopedic Surgery. . . . . Stephen A. Albanese, M.D.
Otolaryngology and Communication Sciences. . . . . Robert M. Kellman, M.D.
Pathology . . . . Gregory A. Threatte, M.D.
Pediatrics . . . . Thomas R. Welch, M.D.
Physical Medicine and Rehabilitation . . . . Robert J. Weber, M.D.
Psychiatry and Behavioral Science . . . . Robert Gregory, M.D.
Radiation Oncology. . . . . Jeffrey A. Bogart, M.D.
Radiology . . . . David Feiglin, M.D.
Surgery. . . . . Robert Cooney, M.D.
Urology. . . . . Gennady Bratslavsky, M.D.

Other

Bioethics and Humanities . . . . Kathy Faber-Langendoen, M.D.
Public Health and Preventive Medicine . . . . Donna Bacchi, M.D., M.P.H.

Duke University School of Medicine

P.O. Box 2927
Durham, North Carolina 27710
919-684-2455 (dean's office); 919-684-0208 (dean's office fax)
Web site: http://medschool.duke.edu

Duke University School of Medicine, which is a part of the Duke University Medical Center, is located on the campus of Duke in Durham. The hospital opened in 1930, and its first medical students were admitted in October 1930.

Type: private
2011 total enrollment: 421
Clinical facilities: Duke University Hospital, Durham Regional Hospital, Duke Raleigh Hospital.

University Officials

President . . . . Richard Brodhead, Ph.D.
Chancellor for Health Affairs . . . . Victor J. Dzau, M.D.
Vice Chancellor for Academic Affairs . . . . Nancy C. Andrews, M.D., Ph.D.
Vice Chancellor for Corporate and Venture Development . . . . Robert L. Taber, Ph.D.
Vice Chancellor for Clinical Research . . . . Robert M. Califf, M.D.
Vice Chancellor for Duke-National University of
   Singapore Affairs . . . . Michael H. Merson, M.D.

Medical School Administrative Staff

Dean, School of Medicine . . . . Nancy C. Andrews, M.D., Ph.D.
Vice Dean for Education . . . . Edward G. Buckley, M.D.
Executive Vice Dean for Administration . . . . J. Scott Gibson
Vice Dean for Basic Sciences . . . . Sally Kornbluth, Ph.D. TBA
Vice Dean for Clinical Research . . . . Mark A. Stacy, M.D. TBA
Vice Dean, Finance and Resource Planning . . . . Billy R. Newton, Jr.
Vice Dean, Medical Affairs . . . . Theodore N. Pappas, M.D.
Associate Vice Dean for Faculty Development . . . . Ann J. Brown, M.D.
Associate Dean and Director for Student Affairs . . . . Caroline P. Haynes, M.D., Ph.D.
Associate Dean and Director, Graduate Medical Education . . . . John L. Weinerth, M.D.
Associate Dean for Biomedical Graduate
   Education and Leadership Services . . . . Dona M. Chikaraishi, Ph.D.
Associate Dean for Medical Education . . . . Robert P. Drucker, M.D.
Associate Dean for Medical Education . . . . Phillip C. Goodman, M.D.
Associate Dean for Medical Education . . . . Delbert R. Wigfall, M.D.
Associate Dean, Admissions . . . . Brenda E. Armstrong, M.D.
Associate Dean, Curriculum Development . . . . Colleen O. Grochowski, Ph.D.
Associate Dean, Continuing Medical Education. . . . . Katherine P. Grichnik, M.D.
Assistant Dean, Undergraduate Primary Care Education . . . . Barbara L. Sheline, M.D.
Assistant Dean for Education Technology . . . . Jeff M. Taekman, M.D.

Department and Division or Section Chairs

Basic Sciences

Biochemistry . . . . Richard Brennan, Ph.D.
Biostatistics and Bioinformatics. . . . . Elizabeth R. DeLong, Ph.D.
Cell Biology. . . . . Brigid L. Hogan, Ph.D.
Immunology . . . . Michael S. Krangel, Ph.D.
Molecular Genetics and Microbiology. . . . . Joseph B. Heitman, M.D., Ph.D.
Neurobiology. . . . . Stephen G. Lisberger, Ph.D.
Pharmacology and Cancer Biology . . . . Donald P. McDonnell, Ph.D.

Clinical Sciences

Anesthesiology. . . . . Mark F. Newman, M.D.
Community and Family Medicine. . . . . J. Lloyd Michener, M.D.
Dermatology . . . . Russell P. Hall III, M.D.
Medicine. . . . . Mary E. Klotman, M.D.
Obstetrics and Gynecology. . . . . Haywood L. Brown, M.D.
Orthopaedic Surgery . . . . James A. Nunley II, M.D. (Interim)
Ophthalmology . . . . David L. Epstein, M.D.
Pathology . . . . Salvatore V. Pizzo, M.D., Ph.D.
Pediatrics . . . . Joseph W. St. Geme, M.D.
Psychiatry . . . . Sarah H. 'Holly' Lisanby, M.D.
Radiation Oncology. . . . . Christopher G. Willett, M.D.
Radiology . . . . Geoff D. Rubin, M.D.
Surgery . . . . Danny O. Jacobs, M.D.

The Brody School of Medicine at East Carolina University

600 Moye Boulevard, AD-52
Greenville, North Carolina 27834-4354
252-744-1020 (general information); 252-744-2201 (dean's office); 252-744-9003 (fax)
Web site: www.ecu.edu/med

In 1972, East Carolina University enrolled students in a one-year program in medical education. The present four-year school was established in 1975.

Type: public
2011 total enrollment: 309
Clinical facilities: Vidant Medican Center, Pitt County Mental Health Center, Walter B. Jones Alcoholic Rehabilitation Center, Childrens Developmental Services Agency.

University Official
Chancellor . . . . Stephen C. Ballard, Ph.D.

Medical School Administrative Staff
Vice Chancellor. . . . . Phyllis N. Horns, R.N., D.S.N.
Dean. . . . . Paul R. G. Cunningham, M.D., F.A.C.S.
Vice Dean . . . . Nicholas H. Benson, M.D.
Senior Associate Dean for Academic Affairs . . . . Kathleen Previll, M.D. (Interim)
Associate Dean for Admissions . . . . James G. Peden, Jr., M.D.
Associate Dean for Medical Education and Student Development . . . . . . David W. Musick, Ph.D.
Chief Financial Officer. . . . . Gary Vanderpool (Interim)
Associate Dean for Continuing Medical Education . . . . Stephen E. Willis, M.D.
Associate Dean for Graduate Medical Education . . . . Lorraine Basnight, M.D.
Associate Dean for Research and Graduate Studies . . . . Robert M. Lust, Ph.D. (Interim)
Associate Dean for Faculty Development. . . . . Carl E. Haisch, M.D.

Department and Division or Section Chairs
Basic Sciences
Anatomy and Cell Biology . . . . Cheryl B. Knudson, Ph.D.
Biochemistry and Molecular Biology. Phillip H. Pekala, Ph.D. (Interim)
Comparative Medicine. . . . . Dorcas P. O'Rourke, D.V.M.
Bioethics and Interdisciplinary Studies . . . . Maria C. Clay, Ph.D.
Microbiology and Immunology. . . . . C. Jeffrey Smith, Ph.D.
Pharmacology and Toxicology . . . . David A. Taylor, Ph.D.
Physiology. . . . . Robert M. Lust, Ph.D.
Public Health . . . . Lloyd F. Novick, M.D.

Clinical Sciences
East Carolina Heart Institute, Director . . . . W. Randolph Chitwood, Jr., M.D.
Cardiovascular Sciences . . . . J. Mark Williams, M.D. (Interim)
  Cardiology. . . . . Harry DeAntonio, D.O.
  Cardiovascular Sciences, Vascular Surgery . . . . Michael C. Stoner, M.D.
Emergency Medicine . . . . Theodore R. Delbridge, M.D.
  EastCare Air Medical Services . . . . Jeffrey D. Ferguson, M.D.
  Eastern Carolina Injury Prevention Program . . . . Herbert G. Garrison, M.D.
  Clinical Simulation Lab . . . . Walter C. Robey, M.D.
  EM Residency Program. . . . . Leigh A. Patterson, M.D.
  EM/IM Residency Program. . . . . Reuben D. Johnson, M.D.
  Toxicology. . . . . William J. Meggs, M.D.
Family Medicine . . . . Kenneth K. Steinweg, M.D.
  Clinical Services . . . . Robert J. Newman, M.D.
  Educational Development. . . . . Lars C. Larsen, M.D.
  Firetower Clinic . . . . Tommy Ellis, M.D.
  Geriatric Division . . . . Kenneth K. Steinwig, M.D. (Interim)
  Geriatric Fellowship . . . . Tae Joon Lee, M.D.
  Research . . . . Doyle M. Cummings, Pharm.D.
  Residency Program. . . . . Gary Levine, M.D.
  Medical Student Education. . . . . Susan Schmidt, M.D.
  Sports Medicine Residency . . . . Joseph Armen, D.O.
  Women's Health . . . . Vacant
Internal Medicine . . . . Paul Bolin, Jr., M.D.
  Dermatology . . . . Charles Phillips, M.D.
  Endocrinology . . . . Almond J. Drake III, M.D.
  Gastorenterology . . . . Hossam Kandil, M.D.
  General Medicine. . . . . James R. Powell, M.D.
  Hematology and Oncology . . . . Adam Asch, M.D.

The Brody School of Medicine at East Carolina University: NORTH CAROLINA

Infectious Disease. . . . . Paul Cook, M.D.
Nephrology . . . . Cynthia Christiano, M.D.
Pulmonary, Critical Care and Sleep Medicine . . . . Mark Mazer, M.D.
Residency Program. . . . . M. Suzanne Kraemer, M.D.
Obstetrics and Gynecology. . . . . Cliford C. Hayslip, M.D. (Interim)
General Obstetrics and Gynecology. . . . . Thomas Kraemer, M.D.
Gynecologic Oncology . . . . Diane Semer, M.D.
Maternal-Fetal Medicine . . . . Jeffrey Livingston, M.D.
Reproductive Endocrinology and Infertility . . . . Clifford C. Hayslip, Jr., M.D.
Reproductive Physiology Lab. . . . . Charles A. Hodson, Ph.D.
Residency Program. . . . . Clifford C. Hayslip, Jr., M.D.
Oncology. . . . . Peter J. Kragel, M.D.
Pathology and Laboratory Medicine . . . . Peter J. Kragel, M.D.
Autopsy and Forensic Pathology . . . . William Oliver, M.D.
Clinical Chemistry . . . . Vacant
Cytology-Thin Needle Biopsy . . . . Les Burke, M.D.
Electron Microscopy. . . . . Paul H. Strausbauch, M.D., Ph.D.
Hematology, Coagulation, and Urinalysis. . . . . Gregory A. Gagnon, M.D.
HLA-Tissue Transplantation . . . . Lorita Rebellato-deVente, Ph.D.
Immunochemistry and Allergy . . . . Donald R. Hoffman, Ph.D.
Immunohistochemistry. . . . . Ming Yin, M.D.
Medical Informatics . . . . Vacant
Microbiology and Serology . . . . John D. Christie, M.D., Ph.D.
Molecular Pathology. . . . . Larry J. Dobbs, Jr., M.D., Ph.D.
Regional Pathology. . . . . Gregory A. Gagnon, M.D.
Residency Program. . . . . Peter J. Kragel, M.D.
Surgical Pathology . . . . Jamie Shutter, M.D.
Transfusion Service . . . . Emmanuel Fadeyi, M.D.
Pediatrics . . . . Ronald M. Perkin, M.D.
Adolescent. . . . . Sharon Mangan, M.D.
Behavior and Development. . . . . Michael Reichel, M.D.
Cardiology. . . . . David W. Hannon, M.D.
Critical Care. . . . . Irma Fiordalisi, M.D.
Endocrinology . . . . Jennifer Sutter, M.D.
Gastroenterology . . . . Vacant
General and Ambulatory. . . . . Dale Newton, M.D.
Genetics and Child Development . . . . John Wiley, Ph.D.
Hematology and Oncology . . . . Charles Daeschner, M.D.
Infectious Disease. . . . . Debra Tristram, M.D.
Neonatology. . . . . James Cummings, M.D.
Nephrology . . . . Guillermo Hidalgo, M.D.
Pulmonary. . . . . Gerald Strope, M.D.
Residency Program. . . . . Karin Hillenbrand, M.D.
Physical Medicine and Rehabilitation . . . . Daniel Moore, M.D.
Pain Medicine . . . . Thurman B. Whitted, M.D.
Residency Program. . . . . Raymundo D. Millan, M.D.
Wound Care and Hyperbaric Medicine . . . . Daniel Moore, M.D.
Psychiatric Medicine . . . . Sy Saeed, M.D.
Adult Psychiatry . . . . Stanley Oakley, M.D.
Adult Residency Program . . . . Diana S. Antonacci, M.D.
Child and Adolescent Psychiatry . . . . John Diamond, M.D.
Child and Adult Residency Program . . . . Kaye McGinty, M.D.
Radiation Oncology. . . . . Emmanuel E. Zervos, M.D. (Interim)
Surgery. . . . . Michael F. Rotondond, M.D.
Bariatric and Minimally Invasive Surgery . . . . William H. H. Chapman III, M.D.
Chowan General Surgery . . . . Alden Davis, M.D.
Clinical Effectiveness . . . . Claudia E. Goettler, M.D.
General Surgery, Advanced Laparoscopic,
   Gastrointestinal, and Endocrine Surgery . . . . Walter E. Pofahl, M.D.
Pediatric Surgery . . . . David A. Rodeberg, M.D.
Plastic Surgery and Reconstructive Surgery . . . . Richard Zeri, M.D.
Residency Program. . . . . Paul J. Schenarts, M.D.
Surgical Education . . . . Carl E. Haisch, M.D.
Surgical Immunology and Transplantation . . . . Robert C. Harland, M.D.
Surgical Oncology . . . . Emmanuel E. Zervos, M.D.
Trauma and Surgical Critical Care . . . . Scott G. Sagraves, M.D.
Neurosurgery . . . . Stuart Lee, M.D.

University of North Carolina at Chapel Hill School of Medicine

Bondurant Hall, 301 Columbia Street, Campus Box 7000
Chapel Hill, North Carolina 27599
919-966-4161 (dean's office); 919-966-8623 (fax)
Web site: www.med.unc.edu

The school of medicine of the University of North Carolina was established in 1879. It is located on the campus of the University of North Carolina at Chapel Hill.

Type: public
2011 total enrollment: 650
Clinical facilities: UNC Hospitals, Wake Medical Center, Moses H. Cone Memorial Hospital, Carolinas Medical Center, New Hanover Regional Medical Center, Nash Health Care Systems, Mission Memorial Hospital, Heritage Hospital.

University Officials

President of University System . . . . Thomas W. Ross
Chancellor, UNC at Chapel Hill. . . . . H. Holden Thorp, Ph.D.
Executive Vice Chancellor and Provost . . . . Bruce Carney, Ph.D.
Vice Chancellor for Human Resources . . . . Brenda R. Malone

Medical School Administrative Staff

Dean, School of Medicine; Vice Chancellor of
Medical Affairs, CEO of UNC Health Care
System . . . . William L. Roper, M.D., M.P.H.
Associate Vice Chancellor for Strategic Alliances. . . . . Margaret B. Dardess, Ph.D., J.D.
Associate Vice Chancellor for Global Health . . . . Myron S. Cohen, M.D.
Executive Dean . . . . Marschall S. Runge, M.D., Ph.D.
Executive Associate Dean for Academic Programs . . . . Amelia Drake, M.D.
President, UNC Hospitals. . . . . Gary L. Park
Executive Vice President and Chief Operating Officer . . . . Brian P. Goldstein, M.D.
Chief Financial Officer, UNC Health Care System. . . . . John P. Lewis
Vice Dean for Finance and Administration . . . . Cam Enarson, M.D.
Assistant Dean for Planning . . . . Gene Bober, and Patricia Oliver
Assistant Dean for Human Resources . . . . Harvey L. Lineberry II, Ph.D.
Vice Dean for Medical Education . . . . Warren P. Newton, M.D., M.P.H.
Assistant Dean for Medical Education Operations . . . . Karen Stone
Associate Dean for Admissions . . . . Robert A. Bashford, M.D.
Associate Dean for Student Affairs . . . . Georgette A. Dent, M.D.
Assistant Dean for Admissions and Director of Special Programs . . . . Cedric Bright, M.D.
Executive Associate Dean for Faculty Affairs . . . . Paul Godley, M.D.
Executive Associate Dean for Clinical Affairs and Chief of Staff. . . . . B. Tony Lindsey, M.D.
Executive Associate Dean for Graduate Medical Education . . . . Clark Denniston, M.D.
Vice Dean for Research . . . . Terry Magnuson, Ph.D.
Assistant Dean for Core Facilities . . . . Michael D. Topal, Ph.D.
Assistant Dean for Graduate Education . . . . Virginia Miller, Ph.D.
Executive Associate Dean for Clinical Research . . . . John B. Buse, M.D., Ph.D.
Executive Associate Dean for Population Research . . . . Timothy S. Carey, M.D.
Executive Associate Dean for Translational Research. . . . . Richard C. Boucher, M.D.
Executive Associate Dean and Director, NC AHEC . . . . Thomas Bacon, Dr.P.H.
Associate Dean for Allied Health Sciences . . . . Lee K. McLean, Ph.D.
Associate Dean for Medical Alumni Affairs . . . . James R. Harper, M.D.
Associate Dean for Advancement . . . . David B. Anderson
Asst. Dean for Institutional Advancement . . . . Greg Duyck, and Deborah C. Dibbert
Director, Office of Public Affairs and Marketing . . . . Karen McCall
Director, Division of Laboratory Animal
Medicine . . . . Dwight Bellinger, Ph.D., D.V.M. (Interim)
Librarian. . . . . Carol G. Jenkins

Department and Division or Section Chairs
Basic Sciences

Biochemistry and Biophysics. . . . . Leslie Parise, Ph.D.
Biomedical Engineering. . . . . Nancy Allbritton, M.D., Ph.D.
Cell and Developmental Biology. Patrick Brenwald, Ph.D. (Interim)
Cell and Molecular Physiology . . . . Carol Otey, Ph.D. (Interim)
Genetics . . . . Terry Magnuson, Ph.D.
Microbiology and Immunology. . . . . William Goldman, Ph.D.
Nutrition. . . . . June Stevens, Ph.D.
Pathology and Laboratory Medicine . . . . J. Charles Jennette, M.D.
Pharmacology . . . . Gary L. Johnson, Ph.D.

University of North Carolina at Chapel Hill School of Medicine: NORTH CAROLINA

Clinical Sciences

Allied Health Sciences . . . . Lee K. McLean, Ph.D.
Anesthesiology . . . . David A. Zvara, M.D.
Dermatology . . . . Luis A. Diaz, M.D.
Emergency Medicine . . . . Charles B. Cairns, M.D.
Family Medicine . . . . Warren P. Newton, M.D.
Medicine . . . . Marschall S. Runge, M.D., Ph.D.
   Cardiology . . . . W. Cam Patterson, M.D.
   Endocrinology and Metabolism . . . . John B. Buse, M.D., Ph.D.
   Gastroenterology and Hepatology . . . . Robert S. Sandler, M.D., M.P.H.
   General Medicine and Clinical Epidemiology . . . . Michael Pignone, M.D., M.P.H.
   Geriatric Medicine . . . . Jan Busby-Whitehead, M.D.
   Hematology and Oncology . . . . Thomas Shea, M.D. (Interim)
   Infectious Diseases . . . . Myron S. Cohen, M.D.
   Nephrology and Hypertension . . . . Ronald J. Falk, M.D.
   Pulmonary and Critical Care Medicine . . . . Shannon Carson, M.D.
   Rheumatology, Allergy, and Immunology . . . . Joanne Jordan, M.D., M.P.H.
Neurology . . . . William Powers, M.D.
Neurosurgery . . . . Matthew G. Ewend, M.D.
Obstetrics and Gynecology . . . . Daniel L. Clarke-Pearson, M.D.
   Advanced Laparascopy and Pelvic Pain . . . . John F. Steege, M.D.
   Gynecologic Oncology . . . . Paola Gehrig, M.D.
   Maternal and Fetal Medicine . . . . M. Kathryn Menard, M.D.
   Midwifery . . . . Kathy Higgins, C.N.M.
   Reproductive Endocrinology and Infertility . . . . Marc A. Fritz, M.D.
   Urogynecology and Reconstructive Pelvic Surgery . . . . Catherine Matthews, M.D.
   Women's Primary Health Care . . . . John M. Thorp, M.D.
Ophthalmology . . . . Donald Budenz, M.D.
Orthopaedics . . . . Douglas R. Dirschl, M.D.
Otolaryngology-Head and Neck Surgery . . . . Harold C. Pillsbury III, M.D.
Pediatrics . . . . A. Wesley Burks, M.D.
   Developmental Disorders . . . . James Bodfish, Ph.D.
   General Pediatrics and Adolescent Medicine . . . . Michael Steiner, M.D.
   Neonatal-Perinatal Medicine . . . . Wayne A. Price, M.D.
   Allergy, Immunology, Rheumatology, and Infectious Diseases . . . . David Peden, M.D.
   Pediatric Cardiology . . . . Elman G. Frantz, M.D.
   Pediatric Critical Care Medicine . . . . Tina Schade-Willis, M.D.
   Pediatric Endocrinology and Diabetes . . . . Ali Calikoglu, M.D.
   Pediatric Gastroenterology . . . . Steven N. Lichtman, M.D.
   Pediatric Genetics and Metabolism . . . . Cynthia M. Powell, M.D.
   Pediatric Hematology and Oncology . . . . Stuart Gold, M.D.
   Pediatric Nephrology and Hypertension . . . . Bill Primack, M.D.
   Pediatric Pulmonary Medicine . . . . Stephanie Davis, M.D.
Physical Medicine and Rehabilitation . . . . George Retsch-Bogart, M.D.
Psychiatry . . . . David R. Rubinow, M.D.
   Adult Psychiatry . . . . A. Jack Naftel, M.D.
   Child Psychiatry . . . . A. Jack Naftel, M.D.
   TEACCH . . . . Laura Klinger, Ph.D. Vacant
Radiation Oncology . . . . Lawrence Marks, M.D.
Radiology . . . . Matthew A. Mauro, M.D.
Social Medicine . . . . Gail E. Henderson, Ph.D.
Surgery . . . . Anthony A. Meyer, M.D., Ph.D.
   Abdominal Transplant . . . . David A. Gerber, M.D.
   Burn Center . . . . Bruce A. Cairns, M.D.
   G. I. Surgery . . . . Michael Mill, M.D., and Mark J. Koruda, M.D.
   G. I. Surgery . . . . Timothy Farrell, M.D.
   Pediatric Surgery . . . . William T. Adamson, M.D.
   Plastic Surgery . . . . C. Scott Hultman, M.D.
   Surgical Oncology . . . . Benjamin F. Calvo, M.D.
   Trauma and Critical Care . . . . Preston B. Rich, M.D.
   Urology . . . . Raj Pruthi, M.D.
   Vascular Surgery . . . . William A. Marston, M.D.

Wake Forest School of Medicine of Wake Forest Baptist Medical Center

Medical Center Boulevard
Winston-Salem, North Carolina 27157
336-716-2011; 336-716-4424 (dean's office); 336-716-3368 (fax)
Web site: wwwwakehealth.edu

The school of medicine, established at Wake Forest, North Carolina, in 1902, operated as a two-year medical school until 1941, when it was moved to Winston-Salem and expanded to a four-year medical college. At that time, it was renamed the Bowman Gray School of Medicine of Wake Forest College. The name of the parent institution was officially changed to Wake Forest University in 1967. The medical school and the North Carolina Baptist Hospitals, Inc., were formally organized as the Medical Center of Bowman Gray School of Medicine and North Carolina Baptist Hospital in 1974. The medical center organization became a corporation in 1976. The name of the school was changed to the Wake Forest University School of Medicine in 1997 and to Wake Forest School of Medicine in 2011.

Type: private
2011 total enrollment: 452
Clinical facilities: Forsyth Memorial Hospital, North Carolina Baptist Hospitals, Inc., Reynolds Family Health Center, Veterans Administration Medical Center—Salisbury.

University Officials

President, Wake Forest University . . . . Nathan O. Hatch, Ph.D.
President and COO, Wake Forest Baptist Health . . . . Thomas E. Sibert, M.D., M.B.A.

Medical School Administrative Staff

Dean . . . . Edward Abraham, M.D.
Executive Vice President and Chief Operations Officer . . . . Douglas L. Edgeton
Senior Associate Dean . . . . Steven M. Block, M.B.B.Ch.
Senior Associate Dean for Research . . . . Janice Wagner, D.V.M., Ph.D.
Associate Dean for Academic Computing and
  Information Services . . . . Johannes M. Boehme II
Associate Dean for Medical Student Admissions . . . . Gretchen L. Wells, M.D.
Associate Dean for Graduate Medical Education . . . . Patricia H. Petrozza, M.D.
Associate Dean for Education . . . . K. Patrick Ober, M.D.
Associate Dean for Student Services . . . . Mark P. Knudson, M.D.
Assistant Dean for Education . . . . M. Ann Lambros, Ph.D.
Assistant Dean for Research . . . . Paula Means
Assistant Dean for Resource Management . . . . Laurie Molloy
Assistant Dean for Student Services and Director
  of Diversity and Development Initiatives . . . . Brenda A. Latham-Sadler, M.D.
Vice President for Development and Alumni Affairs . . . . Norman D. Potter, Jr.
Vice President for Facilities Planning and Construction . . . . Karen Huey
Vice President and Chief Information Officer, Information Services . . . . Sheila Sanders
Vice President for Financial Planning and Chief Financial Officer . . . . Terry L. Hales, Jr.
Vice President for Human Resources . . . . Cheryl Locke
Vice President for Government Relations . . . . Joanne C. Ruhland
Dean, Graduate School . . . . Lorna C. Moore, Ph.D.
Director, AHEC . . . . Michael P. Lischke, Ed.D.
Director, Emeritus Affairs . . . . M. Robert Cooper, M.D.
Director, Libraries . . . . E. Parks Welch

Department and Division or Section Chairs
Basic Sciences

Biochemistry . . . . Douglas Lyles, Ph.D.
Cancer Biology . . . . Frank M. Torti, M.D.
Microbiology and Immunology . . . . Griffith Parks, Ph.D.
Neurobiology and Anatomy . . . . Barry E. Stein, Ph.D.
Pathology . . . . A. Julian Garvin, M.D., Ph.D.
  Comparative Medicine . . . . Jay R. Kaplan, Ph.D.
  Lipid Sciences . . . . Lawrence L. Rudel, Ph.D.
  Tumor Biology . . . . Mark C. Willingham, M.D.
Physiology and Pharmacology . . . . Linda Porrino, Ph.D.
Public Health Sciences . . . . Gregory L. Burke, M.D.
  Biostatistical Sciences . . . . Mark A. Espeland, Ph.D.
    Biostatistics . . . . Gregory W. Evans
    Statistical Genetics and Bioinformatics . . . . Carl D. Langefeld, Ph.D.
  Epidemiology . . . . David C. Goff, Jr., M.D., Ph.D.

Wake Forest School of Medicine of Wake Forest Baptist Medical Center: NORTH CAROLINA

Social Sciences and Health Policy . . . . Doug Easterling, Ph.D.
    Health Care Systems and Policy. . . . . Ann M. Geiger, Ph.D.
    Social and Behavioral Sciences . . . . Michelle J. Naughton, Ph.D.
    Society and Health . . . . Mark Wolfson, Ph.D.
Regenerative Medicine (Tissue Engineering) . . . . Anthony Atala, M.D.

Clinical Sciences

Anesthesiology. . . . . Joseph R. Tobin, M.D.
    Section on Ambulatory and Outpatient. . . . . Vacant
    Cardiothoracic Anesthesia. . . . . Thomas Slaughter, M.D.
    Section on Chronic Pain. . . . . Vacant
    Critical Care. . . . . David L. Bowton, M.D.
    Section on Inpatient Anesthesia . . . . Scott A. Miller, M.D.
    Neuroanesthesia. . . . . John E. Reynolds, M.D.
    Obstetric Anesthesia. . . . . Robert D'Angelo, M.D.
    Pediatric Anesthesia and Pediatric Critical Care. . . . . TBA
    Section on Regional Anes and Acute Pain. . . . . J. C. Gerancher, M.D.
Dentistry. . . . . Raymond S. Garrison, D.D.S.
Dermatology. . . . . Alan B. Fleischer, Jr., M.D.
Emergency Medicine . . . . James W. Hoekstra, M.D.
Family and Community Medicine. . . . . Michael L. Coates, M.D.
Internal Medicine . . . . Thomas D. DuBose, Jr., M.D.
    Cardiology. . . . . William C. Little, M.D.
    Endocrinology and Metabolism. . . . . TBA
    Gastroenterology . . . . Kenneth L. Koch, M.D.
    General Internal Medicine . . . . Catherine M. Jones, M.D.
    Gerontology and Geriatric Medicine. . . . . Jeff D. Williamson, M.D.
    Hematology and Oncology . . . . Bayard Powell, M.D.
    Infectious Diseases . . . . Kevin High, M.D.
    Molecular Medicine . . . . Richard F. Loeser, Jr., M.D.
    Nephrology . . . . Barry I. Freeman, M.D.
    Pulmonary and Critical Care Medicine . . . . Vacant
    Rheumatology . . . . Kevin High, M.D.
Neurology. . . . . Allison Brashear, M.D.
    Neuromuscular Diseases. . . . . James Caress, M.D.
    Neuropsychology . . . . Cecile Naylor, M.D.
    Pediatric Neurology . . . . Annette Grefe, M.D.
Obstetrics and Gynecology. . . . . Sarah Bergg, M.D.
    General Obstetrics and Gynecology. . . . . Andrea Fernandez, M.D.
    General Gynecology . . . . Karen Gerancher, M.D.
    Gynecologic Oncology . . . . Samuel S. Lentz, M.D.
    Maternal and Fetal Medicine . . . . Heather Mertz, M.D.
Pediatrics . . . . Jon S. Abramson, M.D.
Physician Assistant Studies . . . . Reamer L. Busharett, Pharm.D., PA-C
Psychiatry and Behavioral Medicine . . . . W. Vaughn McCall, M.D.
    Child and Adolescent Psychiatry . . . . Guy K. Palmes, M.D.
    Geriatric Psychiatry. . . . . W. Vaughn McCall, M.D.
Radiation Oncology. . . . . A. William Blackstock, M.D.
    Clinical Radiation. . . . . Allan deGuzman, Ph.D.
    Radiation Physics Research/Education . . . . Michael Munley, Ph.D.
    Radiation Biology. . . . . Michael E. C. Robbins, Ph.D.
Radiologic Sciences . . . . Ronald J. Zagoria (Interim)
    Medical Engineering . . . . Craig Hamilton, Ph.D. (Interim)
    Radiology, Diagnostic. . . . . Ronald J. Zagoria (Interim)
Surgical Sciences . . . . J. Wayne Meredith, M.D.
    Cardiothoracic. . . . . Neal D. Kon, M.D.
    General . . . . J. Wayne Meredith, M.D.
    Neurosurgery. . . . . Charles L. Branch, M.D.
        Section on Brain Tumor Biology . . . . Waldemar Debinski, M.D., Ph.D.
    Ophthalmology . . . . Craig Greven, M.D.
    Orthopedic . . . . L. Andrew Koman, M.D.
    Otolaryngology. . . . . J. Dale Browne, M.D.
    Plastic and Reconstructive. . . . . Malcolm Marks, M.D.
    Urology . . . . Anthony Atala, M.D.

University of North Dakota School of Medicine and Health Sciences

501 North Columbia Road, Stop 9037
Grand Forks, North Dakota 58202-9037
701-777-2515 (general information); 701-777-2514 (dean's office); 701-777-3527 (fax)
Web site: www.med.und.edu

The University of North Dakota School of Medicine was founded in 1905 as a two-year school of basic science. Its expansion to an M.D. degree-granting program was approved in 1973, and its first class graduated in 1976. The first two years of medical education are provided in Grand Forks, while the third and fourth years are provided in Bismarck, Fargo, Grand Forks, Minot, and other communities across the state. The school's name was changed in 1996 to the University of North Dakota School of Medicine and Health Sciences to reflect the diversity of educational and research activities that occur at the school.

Type: public
2011 total enrollment: 241
Clinical facilities: Veterans Administration Center Hospital, Altru Health System, Sanford Health System, Essentia Health, St. Alexius Medical Center, Medcenter One, Trinity Medical Center, Minot Air Force Base Hospital, and community hospitals throughout North Dakota.

University Officials

President. . . . . Robert O. Kelley, Ph.D.
Vice President for Academic Affairs and Provost. . . . . Paul LeBel, J.D.
Vice President for Student Affairs and Outreach Services . . . . Lori Reesor, Ph.D.
Vice President for Operations and Finance. . . . . Alice Brekke
Vice President for Health Affairs . . . . Joshua Wynne, M.D., M.B.A., M.P.H.
Vice President for Research and Economic Development . . . . Phyllis E. Johnson, Ph.D.

Medical School Administrative Staff

Dean. . . . . Joshua Wynne, M.D., M.B.A., M.P.H.
Associate Dean, Student Affairs and Admissions . . . . Steffen Christensen, M.D.
Associate Dean, Southeast Campus. . . . . Julie A. Blehm, M.D.
Associate Dean, Southwest Campus. . . . . Nicholas H. Neumann, M.D.
Associate Dean, Administration and Finance. . . . . Randy S. Eken
Senior Associate Dean, Academic and Faculty Affairs. . . . . Gwen W. Halaas, M.D., M.B.A.
Associate Dean, Clinical Education . . . . Charles E. Christianson, M.D.
Assistant Dean, Faculty Development . . . . Patrick A. Carr, Ph.D.
Assistant Dean, Preclinical Medical Education. Thomas M. Hill, Ph.D.
Assistant Dean, Undergraduate and Graduate Education. . . . . Kenneth G. Ruit, Ph.D.
Assistant Dean, Graduate Medical Education. . . . . David J. Theige, M.D.
Assistant Dean, Veterans Affairs . . . . William P. Newman, M.D.
Assistant Dean, Northeast Campus . . . . Jon W. Allen, M.D.
Assistant Dean, Northwest Campus. . . . . Martin L. Rothberg, M.D.
Assistant Dean for Students, Southeast Campus. . . . . Steffen P. Christensen, M.D.
Director, Medical Education. . . . . Thomas M. Hill, Ph.D.
Director, Center for Rural Health. . . . . L. Gary Hart, Ph.D.
Director, Alumni and Community Relations . . . . Jessica Sobolik
Director, Continuing Medical Education. . . . . Gwen W. Halaas, M.D., M.B.A.
Director, Development. . . . . Dave Miedema
Director, Harley French Library of the Health Sciences. . . . . Lila Pedersen
Director, Indians Into Medicine (INMED) . . . . Eugene L. Delorme, J.D.
Chief Information Officer . . . . Nasser Hammami
Chief of Staff. . . . . Judy Solberg

University of North Dakota School of Medicine and Health Sciences:
NORTH DAKOTA
Department and Division or Section Chairs

Basic Sciences

Anatomy and Cell Biology . . . . Jonathan D. Geiger, Ph.D. (Interim)
Biochemistry and Molecular Biology. . . . . Katherine A. Sukalski, Ph.D. (Interim)
Microbiology and Immunology. . . . . David S. Bradley, Ph.D.
Pathology . . . . Mary Ann Sens, M.D., Ph.D.
   Clinical Laboratory Science Program. . . . . Ruth A. Paur, Ph.D.
   Cythotechnology Program. . . . . Katherine Hoffman
Pharmacology, Physiology, and Therapeutics. . . . . Jonathan D. Geiger, Ph.D.

Clinical Sciences

Family and Community Medicine. . . . . Robert W. Beattie, M.D.
   Athletic Training Program . . . . Steven Westereng
   Physician Assistant Program . . . . Jeanie McHugo, Ph.D.
Internal Medicine . . . . William P. Newman, M.D.
   Ambulatory . . . . Julie A. Blehm, M.D.
   Cardiology. . . . . Jonathan L. Dickson, M.D.
   Critical Care Medicine . . . . Hasrat Khan, M.D.
   Endocrinology Metabolism . . . . William P. Newman, M.D.
   Epidemiology. . . . . Abe E. Sahmoun, M.D.
   Gastroenterology . . . . Sajid Jalil, M.D.
   General Medicine. . . . . Julie A. Blehm, M.D.
   Geriatrics . . . . Darin W. Lang, M.D.
   Hematology and Oncology . . . . Amit Panwalkar, M.D.
   Hospitalist . . . . Mohammed Sanaullah, M.D.
   Nephrology . . . . Adit S. Mahale, M.D.
   Infectious Disease. . . . . David R. McNamera, M.D.
   Pulmonary . . . . Naeem R. Adhami, M.D.
   Rheumatology . . . . Umbreen Hasan, M.D.
Clinical Neuroscience . . . . James E. Mitchell, M.D.
   Neurology . . . . Vacant
   Psychiatry. . . . . James E. Mitchell, M.D.
Obstetrics and Gynecology. . . . . Dennis J. Lutz, M.D.
Pediatrics . . . . Stephen J. Tinguely, M.D.
Radiology . . . . Edward F. Fogarty III, M.D.
Surgery . . . . Robert P. Sticca, M.D.
   Orthopedic Surgery . . . . J. Donald Opgrande, M.D.

Allied Health Sciences

Occupational Therapy . . . . Janet S. Jedlicka, Ph.D.
Physical Therapy . . . . Thomas M. Mohr, Ph.D.

Case Western Reserve University School of Medicine

10900 Euclid Avenue
Cleveland, Ohio 44106-4915
216-368-2000; 216-368-2825 (dean's office); 216-368-2820 (dean's office fax)
Web site: http://mediswww.cwru.edu

The school was organized in 1843 as the Cleveland Medical College in cooperation with Western Reserve College, then located at Hudson, Ohio. The school of medicine is now legal successor to all of the regular medical schools that have existed from time to time in Cleveland and is located on the Case Western Reserve University campus. In 2004, the Cleveland Clinic Lerner College of Medicine of Case Western Reserve University, a distinct five-year M.D. program within the School of Medicine and based at the nearby Cleveland Clinic, accepted its first annual class of 32 students. The CCLCM offers a unique program designed to prepare its graduates as careers as physician investigators.

Type: private
2011 total enrollment: 854
Clinical facilities: University Hospitals Case Medical Center, Cleveland Clinic, Louis Stokes Cleveland Veterans Affairs Medical Center, MetroHealth Medical Center.

University Officials

President. . . . . Barbara R. Snyder, J.D.
Provost and Executive Vice President . . . . William A. Baeslack III, Ph.D.
Vice President for Medical Affairs. . . . . Pamela B. Davis, M.D., Ph.D.

Medical School Administrative Staff

Dean, School of Medicine . . . . Pamela B. Davis, M.D., Ph.D.
Vice Dean for Clinical Affairs, Case Medical Center . . . . Achilles Demetriou, M.D.
Vice Dean for Community Health . . . . George E. Kikano, M.D.
Interim Vice Dean for Education and Academic Affairs. . . . . Clint W. Snyder, Ph.D.
Vice Dean for External Affairs and Vice
  President for Medical Development . . . . Carol L. Moss, M.S.
Vice Dean for Finance and Administration . . . . Christopher D. Masotti, C.P.A., M.B.A.
Vice Dean for Research . . . . Mark Chance, Ph.D.
Executive Dean, CCLCM . . . . James Young, M.D.
Senior Associate Dean and Chief of Staff . . . . Lisa M. Mencini, C.P.A., M.B.A.
Senior Associate Dean for Louis Stokes Veterans
  Affairs Medical Center . . . . Murray D. Altose, M.D.
Senior Associate Dean for Students . . . . C. Kent Smith, M.D.
Senior Associate Dean for MetroHealth System. . . . . Alfred F. Connors, Jr., M.D.
Associate Dean and Director of Graduate Medical Education . . . . Jerry M. Shuck, M.D.
Associate Dean for Admissions . . . . Lina Mehta, M.D.
Associate Dean for Admissions and Student Affairs, CCLCM . . . . Kathleen Franco, M.D.
Associate Dean for Curricular Affairs . . . . Terry W. Wolpaw, M.D.
Associate Dean for Curricular Affairs, CCLCM . . . . Alan L. Hull, M.D., Ph.D.
Associate Dean for Development . . . . Robert B. Daroff, M.D.
Associate Dean for Faculty Affairs, CCLCM. Gene H. Barnett, M.D.
Associate Dean for Graduate Education . . . . Alison Hall, Ph.D.
Associate Dean for Space and Facilities Planning . . . . Jill Stanley
Associate Dean for Student Affairs . . . . Robert Haynie, M.D., Ph.D.
Registrar . . . . Siu Yan Scott

Department and Division or Section Chairs

Basic Sciences

Anatomy . . . . Daniel B. Ornt, M.D. (Interim)
Biochemistry . . . . Michael A. Weiss, M.D., Ph.D.
Bioethics. . . . . Stuart Youngner, M.D.
Biomedical Engineering. . . . . Jeffrey Duerk, Ph.D.
Environmental Health Sciences . . . . Dorr Dearborn, M.D., Ph.D.
Epidemiology and Biostatistics . . . . Robert Elston, Ph.D.
General Medical Sciences. . . . . Pamela B. Davis, M.D., Ph.D.
  Cancer Center . . . . Stanton Gerson, M.D.
  Center of the Study of Kidney Biology and Disease . . . . John Sedor, M.D.
  Center for Clinical Investigation . . . . Pamela B. Davis, M.D., Ph.D.

Case Western Reserve University School of Medicine: OHIO

Center for Global Health and Diseases .... James W. Kazura, M.D.
Center for Medical Education........................ Terry W. Wolpaw, M.D. (Interim)
Center for Proteomics and Bioinformatics...................... Mark R. Chance, Ph.D.
Center for Regenerative Medicine............................ Stanton Gerson, M.D.
Center for Science, Health and Society....................... Nathan A. Berger, M.D.
Center for RNA Molecular Biology .... Timothy W. Nilsen, Ph.D.
Genetics .... Mark R. Chance, Ph.D. (Interim)
Molecular Biology and Microbiology............................ Jonathan Karn, Ph.D.
Molecular Medicine, Cleveland Clinic Lerner
  College of Medicine .... Paul E. DiCorleto, Ph.D.
Neurosciences.. Lynn Landmesser, Ph.D.
Nutrition.. Henri Brunengraber, M.D., Ph.D.
Pathology .... Clifford V. Harding, M.D., Ph.D.
Pharmacology .... Krzysztof Palczewski, Ph.D.
Physiology and Biophysics .... Walter Boron, M.D., Ph.D.

Clinical Sciences

Anesthesiology and Perioperative Medicine-
  University Hospitals of Case Medical Center .... Howard S. Nearman, M.D.
Anesthesiology-Cleveland Clinic Foundation .... David L. Brown, M.D.
Anesthesiology-MetroHealth Medical Center........................ Tejbir S. Sidhu, M.D.
Dermatology-University Hospitals of Case Medical Center .... Kevin D. Cooper, M.D.
Dermatology-MetroHealth Medical Center .... Stephen C. Somach, M.D. (Interim)
Emergency Medicine-University Hospitals of
  Case Medical Center .... Edward Michelson, M.D.
Emergency Medicine-MetroHealth Medical Center .... Charles L. Emerman, M.D.
Family Medicine-University Hospitals of Case Medical Center .... George E. Kikano, M.D.
Family Medicine, Cleveland Clinic .... John M. Hickner, M.D.
Family Medicine-MetroHealth Medical Center .... James W. Campbell, M.D.
Medicine-University Hospitals of Case Medical Center............. Richard A. Walsh, M.D.
Medicine-Cleveland Clinic Foundation .... Brian Mandell, M.D., Ph.D.
Medicine-MetroHealth Medical Center........................ M. Michael Wolfe, M.D.
Neurological Surgery-University Hospitals of
  Case Medical Center .... Warren R. Selman, M.D.
Neurology-University Hospitals of Case Medical Center.............. Anthony J. Furlan, M.D.
Neurology-MetroHealth Medical Center .... Joseph P. Hanna, M.D.
Ophthalmology and Visual Sciences-University
  Hospitals of Case Medical Center .... Jonathan H. Lass, M.D.
Ophthalmology-Cleveland Clinic Foundation .... Vacant
Orthopaedics-University Hospitals of Case Medical Center............. Randall Marcus, M.D.
Orthopaedics-MetroHealth Medical Center.................... Brendan M. Patterson, M.D.
Otolaryngology-Head and Neck Surgery-
  University Hospitals of Case Medical Center .... James E. Arnold, M.D.
Otolaryngology-Head and Neck Surgery-MetroHealth Medical Center ...... Joseph Carter, M.D.
Pathology-University Hospitals of Case Medical Center .... Clifford V. Harding, M.D., Ph.D.
Pathology-Cleveland Clinic Foundation.............. Kandice Kottke-Marchant, M.D., Ph.D.
Pathology-MetroHealth Medical Center .... Joseph Tomashefski, M.D.
Pediatrics-University Hospitals of Case Medical Center .... Michael W. Konstan, M.D.
Pediatrics-Cleveland Clinic Foundation............................ Robert Wyllie, M.D.
Pediatrics-MetroHealth Medical Center.................... Nazha Abughali, M.D. (Interim)
Physical Medicine and Rehabilitation-MetroHealth Medical Center .... Gary S. Clark, M.D.
Plastic Surgery-University Hospitals of Case Medical Center........... Bahman Guyuron, M.D.
Psychiatry-University Hospitals of Case Medical Center .... Robert Ronis, M.D.
Psychiatry-MetroHealth Medical Center .... Ewald Horwath, M.D.
Radiation Oncology-University Hospitals of Case Medical Center....... Mitchell Machtay, M.D.
Radiology-University Hospitals of Case Medical Center .... Pablo Ros, M.D., Ph.D.
Radiology-Cleveland Clinic Foundation........................ Gregory Borkowski, M.D.
Radiology-MetroHealth Medical Center .... Robert Ferguson, M.D.
Reproductive Biology-University Hospitals of Case Medical Center............ James Liu, M.D.
Reproductive Biology-MetroHealth Medical Center.......... William J. Todia, M.D. (Interim)
Surgery-University Hospitals of Case Medical Center.................. Jeffrey Ponsky, M.D.
Surgery-Cleveland Clinic Foundation .... John Fung, M.D.
Surgery-MetroHealth Medical Center .... Christopher Brandt, M.D.
Urology-University Hospitals of Case Medical Center............... Firouz Daneshgari, M.D.

Northeast Ohio Medical University formerly known as Northeastern Ohio Universities College of Medicine
4209 State Route 44
P.O. Box 95
Rootstown, Ohio 44272-0095
330-325-2511; 330-325-6255 (President's office); 330-325-5919 (President's office fax)
Web site: www.neomed.edu

Northeast Ohio Medical University (NEOMED) is a community-based state medical school established in November 1973. NEOMED awards the M.D. degree and through consortial relationships with the University of Akron, Kent State University, and Youngstown State University, offers a combined B.S./M.D. degree program. The administration, basic sciences, and community health sciences are located on the Rootstown campus, and the clinical sciences are community-based in hospitals in Akron, Canton, Youngstown, and a newly formed relationship with Cleveland State University that will begin a cohort of students. The charter class graduated in May 1981. NEOMED also offers the Pharm.D. degree and is a cosponsor of the Consortium of Eastern Ohio Master of Public Health Program.

Type: public
2011 total enrollment: 503
Clinical facilities: Major Teaching Hospitals (Associated): Akron City Hospital, Akron Children's Hospital, Aultman Hospital, Valley Care Health, Mercy Medical Center, St. Elizabeth Health Center, Summa Barberton Hospital, Summa Health System. Affiliated hospitals (associated): Alliance Community Hospital, Ashtabula County Medical Center, Edwin Shaw (on hold), Heartland Behavioral Health Center, Hillside Rehabilitation Hospital, Med Central Health System (Mansfield), Medina Community Hospital, Riverside Methodist (Columbus), Robinson Memorial Hospital, Salem Community Hospital, Southwest General Health Center, St. Thomas Hospital, St. Vincent Charity Hospital, Trumbull Memorial Hospital (Valley Center), Union Hospital (Dover), Wadsworth/Rittman. Health Departments (associated): Akron Health Department, Canton City Health Department, Mahoning County District Board of Health, Portage County Combined Health District, Stark County Health Department, Summit County Health Department

College Officials

President	Jay A. Gershaw, D.D.S., Ph.D.
Vice President for Administration and Finance	John Wray
Vice President for External Afffairs	Kathleen C. Ruff, M.B.A.
General Counsel	Maria R. Schimer, J.D.

Medical School Administration

Dean of Medicine	Jeffrey L. Susman, M.D.
Associate Dean for Academic Affairs COM	Elisabeth H. Young, M.D.
Associate Dean for Community Partnerships	Anthony J. Costa, M.D.
Dean of Pharmacy	Richard J. Kasmer, PharmD., J.D. (Interim)
Associate Dean for Academic Affairs COP	Richard J. Kasmer, PharmD., J.D.
Vice President for Research	Walter E. Horton, Ph.D.
Associate Dean for Clinical Education (Akron)	Joseph Zarconi, M.D.
Associate Dean for Clinical Education (Akron)	Eugene Moward, M.D.
Associate Dean for Clinical Education (Akron)	Paul Lecat, M.D.
Associate Dean for Clinical Education (Barberton)	Nancy Flicking, M.D.
Associate Dean for Clinical Education (Canton)	Martha W. Magoon, M.D.
Associate Dean for Clinical Education (Canton)	J. Richard Ziegler, Jr., M.D.
Associate Dean for Clinical Education (Youngstown)	Rebecca S. Bailey, M.D.
Associate Dean for Clinical Education (Youngstown)	Rudolph Krafft, M.D.
Director, Admissions	Michelle L. Cassetty
Director for Institutional Research	Margarita D. Kokinova, Ph.D.
Director, Area Health Education Center	Patricia Thornborough
Director, Center for Studies of Clinical Performance	Holly A. Gerzina
Director, Chief Medical Librarian	Beth Layton
Director, Comparative Medicine	Walter I. Horne, D.V.M.
Director, Continuing Professional Education	Vacant
Senior Development Officer	Tiffany Edwards
Senior Development Officer	Lindsey Loftus
Senior Development Officer	Michael Wolff
Director, Governmental Relations	Richard W. Lewis
Director, Graduate Programs	Walter E. Horton, Ph.D.

Northeast Ohio Medical University formerly known as Northeastern Ohio Universities College of Medicine: OHIO

Director, Human Resources . . . . Vacant
Director, Public Relations and Marketing . . . . Cristine D. Boyd
Registrar . . . . Michelle L. Cassetty
Director, Professional Development . . . . Anita R. Pokorny
Chief Student Affairs Officer . . . . Sandra Emerick, M, Ed.

Basic Medical and Community Health Sciences

Anatomy and Neurobiology . . . . Jeffrey J. Wenstrup, Ph.D.
Integrative Medical Sciences. . . . . William M. Chilian, Ph.D.

Clinical Sciences

Emergency Medicine . . . . Nicholas Jouriles, M.D.
  Pediatric Emergency Medicine* . . . . Jeffrey A. Kempf, D.O.
Family Medicine . . . . Anthony J. Costa, M.D.
Internal Medicine . . . . George I. Litman, M.D.
  Allergy-Immunology* . . . . Joseph F. Alexander, Jr., M.D.
  Cardiology* . . . . J. Ronald Mikolich, M.D.
  Dermatology*. . . . . Eliot N. Mostow, M.D., M.P.H.
  Endocrinology* . . . . James K. Salem, M.D.
  Gastroenterology* . . . . Edward Esbcr, M.D.
  General Medicine*. . . . . Kathleen Seyza, M.D.
  Geriatric Medicine* . . . . Mary Jo Cleveland, M.D.
  Hematology-Oncology*. . . . . John J. Petrus, M.D.
  Infectious Disease*. . . . . Thomas M. File, Jr., M.D.
  Nephrology* . . . . John F. Jacobs, Jr., M.D.
  Neurology* . . . . Christopher A. Sheppard, M.D.
  Pulmonary and Critical Care*. . . . . Rebecca S. Bailey, M.D.
  Rehabilitation Medicine* . . . . Michael J. Delahanty, D.O.
  Rheumatology* . . . . Andrew C. Raynor, M.D.
Obstetrics and Gynecology. . . . . Michael P. Hopkins, M.D.
Orthopaedic Surgery . . . . Thomas S. Boniface, M.D.
Pathology . . . . Robert W. Novak, M.D.
Pediatrics . . . . Norman C. Christopher, M.D.
  Neonatology. . . . . Anand D. Kantak, M.D.
Psychiatry . . . . Mark R. Munetz, M.D.
  Community Psychiatry . . . . Mark R. Munetz, M.D.
  Psychology* . . . . Sharon Irwin, Ph.D.
Radiology . . . . William Demas, M.D.
  Medical Radiation Biophysics* . . . . Dale E. Starchman, Ph.D.
  Nuclear Medicine*. . . . . John M. Lahorra, M.D.
  Pediatric Radiology*. . . . . Godfrey Gaisie, M.D.
  Radiation Oncology* . . . . Michael J. Seider, M.D., Ph.D.
  Sectional Imaging*. . . . . Laura A. Cawthon, M.D., M.P.H.
Surgery . . . . Daniel P. Guyton, M.D.
  Anesthesiology* . . . . vacant
  Neurosurgery*. . . . . Ghassan F. Khayyat, M.D.
  Ophthalmology*. . . . . Deepak Edward, M.D.
  Otolaryngology*. . . . . vacant
  Plastic Surgery* . . . . James A. Lehman, Jr., M.D.
  Thoracic and Cardiovascular*. . . . . Robert W. Kamienski, M.D.
Urology. . . . . Raymond Bologna, M.D.

*Specialty without organizational autonomy.

Ohio State University College of Medicine

254 Meiling Hall
370 West Ninth Avenue
Columbus, Ohio 43210
614-292-2220; 614-292-2600 (dean's office); 614-292-4254 (fax)
Web site: www.medicine.osu.edu

The college of medicine of Ohio State University was established in 1914 by an act of the Ohio legislature.

Type: public
2011 total enrollment: 863
Clinical facilities: Ohio State University Hospitals; Ohio State University Hospital East; Ohio State University Harding Hospital; Arthur G. James Cancer Hospital and Richard J. Solove Research Institute; Richard M. Ross Heart Hospital; Mount Carmel Medical Center; Grant Medical Center; Riverside Methodist Hospitals; Nationwide Children's Hospital; St. Ann's Hospital; Veterans Affairs Medical Center (Dayton); Bethesda Hospital Center of Zanesville (Ohio); Veterans Hospital (Chillicothe, Ohio); Veterans Outpatient Clinic; Medical Center Hospital (Chillicothe, Ohio).

University Officials

President. . . . . E. Gordon Gee
Senior Vice President and Executive Dean for Health Sciences . . . . Steven G. Gabbe, M.D.

Medical School Administrative Staff

Dean. . . . . Catherine R. Lucey, M.D. (Interim)
Vice Dean for Clinical Affairs. . . . . E. Christopher Ellison, M.D.
  Associate Dean for Ancillary Services. . . . . Douglas A. Rund, M.D.
  Associate Dean for Medical Services . . . . Michael Grever, M.D.
  Associate Dean for Primary Care. . . . . Mary Jo Welker, M.D.
  Associate Dean for Surgical Services . . . . E. Christopher Ellison, M.D.
Vice Dean for Education . . . . Robert Ruberg, M.D. (Interim)
  Associate Dean for Admissions . . . . Quinn Capers, M.D.
  Associate Dean for Graduate Medical Education . . . . Bryan Martin, M.D.
    Associate Dean for Student Life. . . . . Joanne Lynn, M.D.
  Associate Dean for Medical Education. . . . . Daniel Clinchot, M.D.
  Assistant Dean, Clinical Skills and Medical Education . . . . Carol Hasbrouck
    Assistant Dean for Medical Education,
      Nationwide Children's Hospital . . . . Mary McIlroy, M.D.
  Assistant Dean for Medical Education, Mount Carmel Hospital. . . . . Patrick Ecklar, M.D.
  Assistant Dean for Medical Education, Grant Hospital . . . . Bruce T. Vanderhoff, M.D.
  Assistant Dean for Medical Education, Ohio Health, Inc. . . . . Douglas Knutson, M.D.
  Assistant Dean for Rural Medical Education. . . . . Randall Longenecker, M.D.
Vice Dean for Research . . . . Clay B. Marsh, M.D.
  Associate Dean for Translational and Applied Research . . . . Chandan Sen, Ph.D.
  Associate Dean for Basic Research. . . . . Joanna Groden, Ph.D.
  Associate Dean for Clinical Research. . . . . Rebecca Jackson, M.D.
  Associate Dean for Graduate Studies. . . . . James King, Ph.D.
  Associate Dean for Outcomes Research. . . . . Michael F. Para, M.D.
  Associate Dean for Research Education. . . . . Ginny Bumgardner, M.D., Ph.D.
  Assistant Dean for Research . . . . James King, Ph.D.
Vice Dean for Academic Affairs and Secretary of the College . . . . Robert A. Bornstein, Ph.D.
Associate Dean for Faculty Affairs. . . . . Philip Binkley, M.D.
Assistant Dean for Diversity and Cultural Affairs . . . . Leon McDougle, M.D.
Associate Dean and Director, School of Allied Medical Professions . . . . . Deborah Larsen, Ph.D.
Senior Fiscal Officer and Principal Admin Exec. . . . . John Lahey
Director, Center for Continuing Medical Education . . . . Barbara Berry

Ohio State University College of Medicine: OHIO

Department and Division or Section Chairs

Basic Sciences

Biomedical Informatics . . . . Philip Payne, Ph.D.
Molecular and Cellular Biochemistry . . . . Michael Ostrowski, Ph.D.
Molecular Virology, Immunology, and Medical Genetics . . . . Carlo Croce, M.D.
Neuroscience. . . . . Randy J. Nelson, Ph.D.
Pharmacology . . . . Wolfgang Sadee, Dr.rer.nat
Physiology and Cell Biology . . . . Muthu Periasamy, Ph.D.

Clinical Sciences

Anesthesiology. . . . . Ronald Harter, M.D.
Emergency Medicine . . . . Mark Angelos, M.D. (Interim)
Family Medicine . . . . Mary Jo Welker, M.D.
Internal Medicine . . . . Michael Grever, M.D.
   Cardiovascular Medicine. . . . . William T. Abraham, M.D.
   Dermatology . . . . Mark Bechtel, M.D.
   Gastroenterology Hepatology and Nutrition . . . . Nicholas Verne, M.D.
   Endocrinology, Diabetes, and Metabolism . . . . Kwame Osei, M.D.
   General Internal Medicine . . . . Linda Strout, M.D.
   Hematology. . . . . John Byrd, M.D.
   Hospital Medicine . . . . Nathan O'Dorisio, M.D.
   Human Genetics . . . . Albert de la Chapelle, M.D. (Interim)
   Immunology and Rheumatology. . . . . Wael Jarjour, M.D.
   Infectious Diseases . . . . Larry S. Schlesinger, M.D.
Medical Oncology . . . . Miguel Villalona, M.D.
   Nephrology . . . . Brad Rovin, M.D.
   Pulmonary, Allergy, Critical Care, and Sleep Medicine. . . . . Stephen Hoffman, M.D. (Interim)
Neurological Surgery. . . . . E. Antonio Chiocca, M.D., Ph.D.
Neurology. . . . . Michael Racke, M.D.
Obstetrics and Gynecology. . . . . Mark Landon, M.D.
Ophthalmology. . . . . Thomas Mauger, M.D.
Orthopaedics. . . . . Jason Calhoun, M.D.
Otolaryngology . . . . D. Bradley Welling, M.D., Ph.D.
Pathology . . . . Daniel Sedmak, M.D.
Pediatrics . . . . Michael Brady, M.D.
Physical Medicine and Rehabilitation . . . . W. Jerry Mysiw, M.D. (Interim)
Psychiatry . . . . John Campo, M.D. (Interim)
Radiation Medicine . . . . Arnab Chakravarti, M.D.
Radiology . . . . Richard White, M.D.
   Abdominal Imaging . . . . William Bennett, M.D.
   Interventional Radiology. . . . . Gregory Guy, M.D., and Hooman Khabiri, M.D.
   Breast Imaging. . . . . Adele Lipari, D.O.
   Musculoskeletal Radiology . . . . Alan Rogers, M.D.
   Neuroradiology . . . . Andrew Kalnin, M.D.
   Nuclear Medicine. . . . . Nathan Hall, M.D., Ph.D.
   Radiobiology . . . . Altaf Wani, Ph.D.
   Thoracic Imaging. . . . . Mark King, M.D.
   Ultrasound. . . . . Vacant
Surgery . . . . E. Christopher Ellison, M.D.
   Cardiothoracic Surgery. . . . . Patrick Ross, M.D., Ph.D. (Interim)
   Critical Care, Trauma, and Burns . . . . Steven M. Steinberg, M.D.
   General and Gastrointestinal Surgery . . . . W. Scott Melvin, M.D.
   Pediatric Surgery . . . . Donna A. Caniano, M.D.
Plastic Surgery . . . . Michael Miller, M.D. (Interim)
   Surgical Oncology . . . . William B. Farrar, M.D.
   Transplantation Surgery. . . . . Robert Higgins, M.D.
   Vascular Diseases and Surgery. . . . . Patrick Vaccaro, M.D.
Urology. . . . . Robert R. Bahnson, M.D.

University of Cincinnati College of Medicine

P.O. Box 670555
Cincinnati, Ohio 45267-0555
513-558-7391 (dean's office); 513-558-1165 (fax)
Web site: www.med.uc.edu

The college of medicine is a descendant of the Medical College of Ohio, which was chartered in 1819. In 1896, this college became the medical department of the University of Cincinnati by incorporation into that institution. The medical college is part of the University of Cincinnati Academic Health Center.

Type: public
2011 total enrollment: 641
Clinical facilities: Cincinnati Children's Hospital Medical Center, Christ Hospital, Drake Center, Inc., Good Samaritan Hospital, Jewish Hospital, Shriners Burns Hospital, Veterans Affairs Medical Center, University of Cincinnati Health-University Hospital, University of Cincinnati Health, Inc., Franciscan Hospital.

University Officials

President. . . . . Gregory H. Williams, J.D., Ph.D.
Vice President for Health Affairs . . . . Thomas F. Boat, M.D.

Medical School Administrative Staff

Dean. . . . . Thomas F. Boat, M.D.
Senior Associate Dean for Clinical Affairs. . . . . Myles Pensak, M.D.
Senior Associate Dean for Academic Affairs . . . . Andrew T. Filak, M.D.
Senior Associate Dean for Operations and Finance, CFO . . . . Lori Mackey Vacant
Senior Associate Dean for Research . . . . Stephen M. Strakowski, M.D.
Associate Dean for Student Affairs and Admissions . . . . Aurora J. Bennett, M.D.
Associate Dean for Faculty and Legal Affairs. . . . . M. Kathleen Robbins, J.D.
Associate Dean for Diversity and Community Affairs . . . . Charles Collins, M.D.
Associate Dean for Clinical Research . . . . James Heubi, M.D.
Associate Dean for Clinical Research . . . . Joel Tsevat, M.D.
Associate Dean for Graduate Education . . . . Robert Highsmith, Ph.D.
Associate Dean for Medical Education . . . . Anne Gunderson, Ed.D.
Assistant Dean for Admissions . . . . R. Stephen Manual, Ph.D.
Assistant Dean for Continuing Medical Education. . . . . John R. Kues, Ph.D.
Assistant Dean for Medical Education. . . . . Kenneth Davis, M.D., and Michael Sostok, M.D.
Assistant Dean for Graduate Education. . . . . Laura Hildreth
Assistant Dean for Student Affairs and Registrar . . . . Iva Dean Lair-Adolph
Assistant Dean for Student Affairs. . . . . Denise D. Gibson, Ph.D.
Assistant Dean, Medical School Financial Aid . . . . Daniel Burr, Ph.D.
Associate Dean for Finance . . . . Jan Hawk

Department and Division or Section Chairs

Basic Sciences

Cancer and Cell Biology . . . . Jerry Lingrel, Ph.D. (Interim)
Environmental Health . . . . Shuk-Mei Ho, Ph.D.
  Biostatistics and Epidemiology*. . . . . Kim N. Dietrich, Ph.D.
  Industrial Hygiene, Occupational Safety, and Ergonomics* . . . . Carol Rice, Ph.D.
  Molecular Toxicology* . . . . Howard Shertzer, Ph.D.
  Occupational Environmental Medicine* . . . . James Lockey, M.D.
Molecular and Cellular Physiology . . . . Marshall Montrose, Ph.D.
Molecular Genetics, Biochemistry, and Microbiology. . . . . Malak Kotb, Ph.D.
Pathology . . . . David Witte, M.D.
  Anatomic Pathology* . . . . Mohammed Nazek, M.D.
  Autopsy* . . . . Fred Lucas, M.D.
  Nephropathology. . . . . Lois Arend, M.D.
  Neuro-Pathology*. . . . . Ady Kendler, M.D.

174

University of Cincinnati College of Medicine: OHIO

Surgical Pathology* .... Fred Lucas, M.D.
Pharmacology and Cell Biophysics .... John J. Hutton, M.D. (Interim)

Clinical Sciences

Anesthesiology... William E. Hurford, M.D.
University of Cincinnati Cancer Institute .... George Atweh, M.D.
Dermatology... Diya F. Mutasim, M.D.
Emergency Medicine..................................... Arthur Pancioli, M.D.
Family Medicine .... Philip M. Dniza, M.D.
Internal Medicine .... Gregory Rouan, M.D. (Interim)
   Cardiology* .... Neal Weintraub, M.D.
   Digestive Diseases*.............................. Kenneth Sherman, M.D.
   General Medicine*.................................. Mark Eckman, M.D.
   Hematology and Oncology* .... George Atweh, M.D.
   Infectious Diseases* .... George Deepe, M.D.
   Medical Immunology, Rheumatic Disease, and Allergy*............ William Ridgeway, M.D.
   Metabolism and Endocrinology*......................... David D'Alessio, M.D.
   Nephrology and Hypertension* .... Manoocher Soleimani, M.D.
   Pulmonary Diseases*................................ Francis X. McCormack, M.D.
Neurology... Joseph P. Broderick, M.D.
Neurosurgery.. Mario Zuccarello, M.D.
Obstetrics and Gynecology............................... Arthur T. Evans, M.D.
Ophthalmology....................................... James J. Augsburger, M.D.
Orthopedic Surgery.................................... Peter Stern, M.D.
Otolaryngology and Head and Neck Surgery...................... Myles Pensak, M.D.
Pediatrics .... Arnold Strauss, M.D.
Physical Medicine and Rehabilitation .... Mark Goddard, M.D.
Psychiatry .... Stephen Strakowski, M.D.
Public Health Sciences............................... Ronnie Horner, Ph.D.
Radiation Oncology................................... William Barrett, M.D.
Radiology .... Jannette Collins, M.D.
   Abdominal Imaging .... Jonathan Moulton, M.D.
   Breast Imaging.................................... Mary Mahoney, M.D.
   Cardiothoracic Imaging .... Ralph Shipley, M.D.
   Interventional Imaging............................. Ross Ristagno, M.D.
   Musculoskeletal Radiology .... Robert Wissman, M.D.
   Neuroradiology .... Thomas Tomsick, M.D.
   Nuclear Medicine.............................. Mariano Fernandez-Ulla, M.D.
   Pediatric Radiology................................ Lane Donnelly, M.D.
Surgery .... Michael Edwards, M.D.
   Burn .... Richard Kagan, M.D.
   Cardiac* .... J. Michael Smith, M.D.
   Colorectal .... Janice Rafferty, M.D.
   General Surgery* .... David Fischer, M.D.
   Oral Surgery*...................................... Robert Marciani, M.D.
   Pediatric Surgery* .... Richard G. Azizkhan, M.D.
   Plastic Surgery* .... W. John Kitzmiller, M.D.
   Surgical Oncology*................................. Jeffrey Sussman, M.D.
   Thoracic*.. Sandra Starnes, M.D.
   Transplantation and Surgical Immunology*..................... E. Steve Woodle, M.D.
   Trauma and Critical Care* .... Jay Johannigman, M.D.
   Urology* .... James Donovan, M.D.
   Vascular Surgery*.................................. George Meier, M.D.

*Specialty without organizational autonomy.

The University of Toledo, College of Medicine

3000 Arlington Avenue
Toledo, Ohio 43614
419-383-4000; 419-383-4243 (dean's office); 419-383-6100 (fax)
Web site: http://hsc.utoledo.edu/

The University of Toledo College of Medicine came into existence July 1, 2006, as a result of the merger of the former Medical University of Ohio, a free-standing, state-supported academic health center, and the University of Toledo, one of 14 state-supported universities in Ohio. The Medical University of Ohio was formerly the Medical College of Ohio. The University of Toledo College of Medicine falls under the policy-making authority of the Ohio Board of Regents. The first class of medical students was admitted in 1969.

Type: public
2011 total enrollment: 586
Clinical facilities: University Medical Center at The University of Toledo, St. Vincent Mercy Medical Center, the Toledo Hospital, Northwest Psychiatric Hospital.

University of Toledo Administrative Staff

President. . . . . Lloyd A. Jacobs, M.D.
Chancellor and Executive Vice President for
  Biosciences and Health Affairs, Dean of the
  College of Medicine . . . . Jeffrey P. Gold, M.D.
Interim UTMC Executive Director and Senior
  Vice President for Finance and Administration . . . . Scott Scarborough, Ph.D.
Vice President for Institutional Advancement . . . . Vernon Snyder
Administrator and Chief Information Officer . . . . Godfrey Ovwhigo
Senior Director for Research Administration. . . . . James P. Trempe, Ph.D.
Associate Dean for Graduate Programs, College of Medicine. . . . . Dorothea L. Sawicki, Ph.D.
Vice Chancellor and Associate Dean for Student
  Affairs, College of Medicine . . . . Patricia J. Metting, Ph.D.
Associate Dean for Clinical Undergraduate
  Medical Education, Professionalism, and
  Diversity . . . . Imran Ali, M.D.
Associate Dean for Admissions . . . . James Kleshinski, M.D.
  Assistant Dean for Admissions. . . . . Richard Lane, Ph.D.
Associate Dean for Clinical Affairs . . . . Ronald McGinnis, M.D.
Associate Dean for Faculty Development and
  Curriculum Evaluation . . . . Constance J. Shriner, Ph.D.
Associate Dean for Graduate Medical Education . . . . Mary R. Smith, M.D.
Associate Dean for Preclinical Medical Education . . . . Carol Bennett-Clarke, Ph.D.
Associate Dean for Continuing Medical Education . . . . William Davis, D.D.S.
Associate Dean for Research and Center for Clinical Research . . . . Debra Gmerek, Ph.D.
Director, Alumni Affairs and Development . . . . Daniel Saevig
Director, Division of Laboratory Animal Medicine. . . . . Phillip Robinson, D.V.M.
Director, Health Science Campus Library . . . . Jolene M. Miller, M.L.S., A.H.I.P.
Director of Communications . . . . Tobin Klinger
Director, Financial Aid. . . . . Carolyn Baumgartner
Registrar . . . . Sherri Armstrong

The University of Toledo, College of Medicine: OHIO

Department and Division or Section Chairs

Basic Sciences

Biochemistry and Cancer Biology . . . . William Maltese, Ph.D.
Medical Microbiology and Immunology . . . . Akira Takashima, Ph.D.
Neurosciences . . . . Brian Yamamoto, Ph.D.
Physiology, Pharmacology, Metabolism, and
    Cardiovascular Science . . . . Nader G. Abraham, Ph.D.

Clinical Science

Anesthesiology. . . . . Alan Marco, M.D.
Family Medicine . . . . Linda French, M.D.
Medicine. . . . . Joseph Shapiro, M.D.
    Cardiology. . . . . Christopher Cooper, M.D.
    Dermatology . . . . Lori Gottwald, M.D.
    General Internal. . . . . Basil Akpunonu, M.D.
    Hematology and Oncology . . . . Iman Mohamed, M.D.
    Hepatology . . . . Thomas Sodeman, M.D.
    Infectious Disease. . . . . Julia Westerink, M.D.
    Nephrology . . . . Deepak Malhotra, M.D.
    Pulmonary. . . . . Jeffrey Hammersley, M.D.
    Rheumatology . . . . M. Bashar Kahaleh, M.D.
Neurology. . . . . Gretchen Tietjen, M.D.
Obstetrics and Gynecology. . . . . Kelly Manahan, M.D. (Interim)
Orthopaedic Surgery . . . . Nabil Ebraheim, M.D.
Pathology . . . . Robert Mrak, M.D.
Pediatrics . . . . Jeffrey Blumer, M.D.
Psychiatry . . . . Marijo Tamburrino, M.D.
Radiation Oncology. . . . . John J. Feldmeier, D.O.
Radiology . . . . Lee Woldenberg, M.D.
Surgery . . . . Gerald Zelenock, M.D.
Urology. . . . . Stephen Selman, M.D.

Wright State University Boonshoft School of Medicine

3640 Col. Glenn Highway
Dayton, Ohio 45435-0001
937-775-2933 (dean's office); 937-775-2211 (fax)
E-mail: SOM_dean@wright.edu
Web site: www.med.wright.edu

Wright State University was first established in 1964 as a campus of the Ohio University System operated conjointly by the Ohio State University and Miami University of Ohio; in 1967, independent status as one of 12 state-assisted universities was conferred. The school of medicine was authorized in 1973 by the state of Ohio. The administration and the basic sciences departments are located on the parent university campus in Fairborn, a suburb of Dayton. The clinical sciences departments are community-based in six affiliated hospitals in the Dayton area. The charter class matriculated in September 1976.

Type: public
2011 total enrollment: 431
Clinical facilities: Atrium Medical Center, Children's Medical Center, Dayton Health Centers, Good Samaritan Hospital and Health Center, Greene Memorial Hospital, Kettering Medical Center, Mercy Memorial Hospital, Miami Valley Hospital, Mount Carmel Hospital, Springfield Regional Medical Center, Upper Valley Medical Center, Department of Veterans Affairs Medical Center (Dayton), Wayne Hospital, Wilson Memorial Hospital, Wright-Patterson Medical Center.

University Officials

President	David R. Hopkins, Ph.D.
Director, Biomedical Sciences Ph.D. Program	Gerald M. Alter, Ph.D.
Provost	Steven R. Angle, Ph.D.

Medical School Administrative Staff

Dean	Howard M. Part, M.D.
Executive Associate Dean	Margaret M. Dunn, M.D.
Associate Dean for Academic Affairs	Dean X. Parmelee, M.D.
Associate Dean for Air Force Affairs	Colonel Stephen Higgins, M.D.
Associate Dean for Premier Health Partners	Molly J. Hall, M.D.
Associate Dean for Research Affairs	Robert E. W. Fyffe, Ph.D.
Associate Dean for Fiscal Affairs	John L. Bale
Associate Dean for Student Affairs and Admissions	Gary LeRoy, M.D.
Associate Dean for Veterans Affairs	William Germann, M.D.
Assistant Dean for Admissions	Stephen E. Peterson, Ph.D.
Assistant Dean for Diversity and Inclusion	Kevin J. Watt, M.D.
Assistant Dean for Faculty Affairs	Albert F. Painter, Psy.D.
Assistant Dean for Quality and Primary Care Research	Richard W. Pretorius, M.D.
Assistant to the Dean	Betty Kangas
Assistant Vice President for Advancement	Robert S. Copeland
Clinical Medicine Librarian	Bette S. Sydelko
Director, Interdisciplinary Teaching Laboratory	Debra M. Hendershot
Director, Laboratory Animal Resources	Gregory Boivin, D.V.M.
Director of Marketing and Communications	Cindy Young

Department and Division or Section Chairs

Basic Sciences

Biochemistry and Molecular Biology	Steven J. Berberich, Ph.D.
Neuroscience, Cell Biology and Physiology	Timothy Cope, Ph.D.
Cellular and Molecular Microscopy Facility	Robert E.W. Fyffe, Ph.D.
Pharmacology and Toxicology	Mariana Morris, Ph.D.

Clinical Sciences

Community Health	Arthur Pickoff, M.D.
Aerospace Medicine	Robin Dodge, M.D.
Medical Humanities	Mary T. White, Ph.D.
Dermatology	Julian J. Trevino, M.D.
Emergency Medicine	James E. Brown, M.D.
Family Medicine	Cynthia G. Olsen, M.D.
Geriatric Medicine	Larry Lawhorne, M.D.

Wright State University Boonshoft School of Medicine: OHIO

Medicine . . . . Glen D. Solomon, M.D.
  Cardiology . . . . Mukul Chandra, M.D.
  Endocrinology . . . . Thomas Koroscil, M.D., Ph.D.
  Gastroenterology . . . . Gregory J. Beck, M.D.
  General Internal Medicine . . . . Dean Bricker, M.D.
  Hematology and Oncology . . . . Michael Baumann, M.D.
  Infectious Disease . . . . John S. Czachor, M.D.
  Nephrology . . . . Mohammed Saklayen, M.D.
  Neurology . . . . Bradley Jacobs, M.D.
  Nuclear Medicine . . . . Joseph C. Mantil, M.D., Ph.D.
  Pulmonary . . . . Amaresh Nath, M.D.
  Rheumatology . . . . William E. Venanzi, M.D.
Obstetrics and Gynecology . . . . Gary Ventolini, M.D.
  Gynecologic Oncology . . . . John W. Moroney, M.D.
  Maternal and Fetal Medicine . . . . Christopher Croom, M.D.
  Obstetrics and Gynecology . . . . Janice M. Duke, M.D.
  Reproductive Endocrinology . . . . Lawrence Amesse, M.D., Ph.D.
  Research . . . . Vacant
  Urogynecology . . . . Geoffrey D. Towers, M.D.
Orthopaedic Surgery, Sports Medicine, and Rehabilitation . . . . Richard T. Laughlin, M.D.
Pathology . . . . Paul Koles, M.D.
Pediatrics . . . . Arthur Pickoff, M.D.
  Cardiology . . . . Joseph Ross, M.D.
  Child Advocacy . . . . Lori Vavul-Rodeiger, M.D.
  Critical Care . . . . Vipul V. Patel, M.B.B.S.
  Endocrinology and Metabolism . . . . Paul R. Breyer, M.D.
  Gastroenterology and Nutritional Support . . . . Farhat N. Ashai-Khan, M.D.
  General and Community Pediatrics . . . . John Pascoe, M.D.
  Hematology and Oncology . . . . Emmett Broxson, M.D.
  Infectious Disease . . . . Sherman J. Alter, M.D.
  Medical Genetics . . . . Marvin Miller, M.D.
  Nephrology . . . . Leonardo M. Canessa, M.D.
  Neurology . . . . Daniel J. Lacey, M.D., Ph.D.
  Pulmonary Medicine and Cystic Fibrosis . . . . Robert Fink, M.D.
  Sleep Medicine . . . . Samuel Dzodzomenyo, M.D.
Psychiatry . . . . Jerald Kay, M.D.
Surgery . . . . Mary C. McCarthy, M.D.
  Anesthesiology . . . . Erin D. Underwood, D.O
  Burn Surgery . . . . Travis L. Perry, M.D.
  Cardiothoracic . . . . Mark P. Anstadt, M.D.
  General Surgery . . . . Linda M. Barney, M.D.
  Neurosurgery . . . . Cynthia Z. Africk, M.D.
  Ophthalmology . . . . Richard L. Liston, M.D.
  Otolaryngology . . . . Peter G. Michaelson, M.D.
  Pediatric Surgery . . . . David P. Meagher, M.D.
  Surgical Oncology . . . . James R. Ouellette, D.O.
  Transplantation Surgery . . . . Rick B. Stevens, M.D.
  Trauma/Emergency Surgery/Critical Care . . . . Akpofure P. Ekeh, M.D.
  Urology . . . . Lawrence J. Litscher, M.D.
  Vascular . . . . Kian Mostafavi, M.D.

Centers

Center for Genomics Research . . . . Michael Markey, Ph.D.
Center for Global Health . . . . James R. Ebert, Ph.D.
Center for Interventions, Treatment, and Addictions Research . . . . Robert G. Carlson, Ph.D.
Neuroscience Institute . . . . Timothy C. Cope, Ph.D.
Lifespan Health Research Center . . . . Richard Sherwood, Ph.D.
National Center for Medical Readiness . . . . Glenn C. Hamilton, M.D.

University of Oklahoma College of Medicine

P.O. Box 26901, BMSB 357
Oklahoma City, Oklahoma 73126
405-271-2265 (dean's office); 405-271-3032 (fax)
Web site: www.medicine.ouhsc.edu

The college of medicine is one of seven health professions colleges that make up the University of Oklahoma Health Sciences Center, located 20 miles from the university's main campus in Norman. The college of medicine was established in 1900.

Type: public
2011 total enrollment: 659
Clinical facilities: OU Medical Center, Children's Hospital, Veterans Affairs Medical Center, Integris Baptist Medical Center, Saint Anthony Hospital, Bone and Joint Hospital.

University Officials

President. . . . . David L. Boren
Senior Vice President and Provost . . . . M. Dewayne Andrews, M.D.
Vice President for Administrative Affairs. . . . . Kenneth Rowe
Vice President for Research . . . . John J. Iandolo, Ph.D.

Medical School Administrative Staff

Executive Dean . . . . M. Dewayne Andrews, M.D.
Senior Associate Dean . . . . Robert H. Roswell, M.D.
Associate Dean for Academic Affairs. . . . . Christopher S. Candler, M.D., Ed.D
Associate Dean for Student Affairs . . . . Herman Jones, Ph.D.
Associate Dean for Graduate Medical Education . . . . John P. Zubialde, M.D.
Associate Dean for Research. . . . . Darrin Akins, Ph.D.
Associate Dean for Administration and Finance . . . . Anne Barnes
Associate Dean for Executive Affairs. . . . . Jon S. Brightbill
Associate Dean for Clinical Affairs . . . . Lynn V. Mitchell, M.D.
Associate Dean for Clinical Practice . . . . Brian L. Maddy
Associate Dean for Admissions . . . . Sherri Baker, M.D.
Associate Dean for Continuing Professional Development . . . . C.A. Sivaram, M.D.

Department and Division or Section Chairs

Basic Sciences

Biochemistry and Molecular Biology. . . . . Paul H. Weigel, Ph.D.
Cell Biology. . . . . Lawrence I. Rothblum, Ph.D.
Microbiology and Immunology. . . . . Jimmy Ballard, Ph.D.
Pathology . . . . Michael L. Talbert, M.D.
Physiology. . . . . Jay Ma, M.D., Ph.D.

Clinical Sciences

Anesthesiology. . . . . Jane C. K. Fitch, M.D.
Dermatology . . . . Pam Allen, M.D. (Interim)
Family Medicine . . . . Steven Crawford, M.D.
Geriatric Medicine. . . . . Laurence Z. Rubenstein, M.D.
Medicine. . . . . Michael Bronze, M.D.
   Cardiology. . . . . Dwight Reynolds, M.D.
   Digestive Disease and Nutrition. . . . . Courtney W. Houchen, M.D.
   Endocrinology and Diabetes . . . . Timothy Lyons, M.D.
   General Internal Medicine . . . . Michael Bronze, M.D.
   Hematology-Oncology . . . . George Selby, M.D. (Interim)
   Rheumatology, Immunology, and Allergy . . . . Ira Targoff, M.D. (Interim)
   Infectious Diseases . . . . Douglas Drevets, M.D.
   Nephrology . . . . Benjamin Cowley, Jr., M.D.
   Pulmonary Disease . . . . Gary T. Kinasewitz, M.D.
Neurology. . . . . David Lee Gordon, M.D.
Neurosurgery. . . . . Timothy Mapstone, M.D.
Obstetrics and Gynecology. . . . . Robert S. Mannel, M.D.
   Gynecologic Oncology . . . . D. Scott McMeekin, M.D.

Maternal and Fetal Medicine . . . . Eric Knudtson, M.D.
Reproductive Endocrinology and Infertility . . . . Karl Hansen, M.D.
Ophthalmology . . . . Gregory L. Skuta, M.D.
Orthopaedic Surgery and Rehabilitation . . . . David C. Teague, M.D.
Otorhinolaryngology . . . . Greg A. Krempl, M.D.
Pediatrics . . . . Terrence L. Stull, M.D.
  Adolescent Medicine . . . . Philip W. Rettig, M.D.
  Cardiology . . . . Ed Overholt, M.D.
  Critical Care . . . . Morris R. Gessouroun, M.D.
  Developmental and Behavioral Pediatrics . . . . Mark Wolraich, M.D.
  Diabetes and Endocrinology . . . . Kenneth Copeland, M.D.
  Gastroenterology . . . . John E. Grunow, M.D.
  General and Community Pediatrics . . . . Paul M. Darden, M.D.
  Genetics . . . . John Mulvihill, M.D.
  Hematology and Oncology . . . . William Meyer, M.D.
  Infectious Disease . . . . Robert Welliver, M.D.
  Neonatology . . . . Marilyn Escobedo, M.D.
  Nephrology . . . . Martin Turman, M.D.
  Pulmonology and Cystic Fibrosis . . . . James Royall, M.D.
  Rheumatology . . . . Vacant
Psychiatry and Behavioral Sciences . . . . Betty Pfefferbaum, M.D., J.D.
Radiation Oncology . . . . Terence S. Herman, M.D.
Radiological Sciences . . . . Susan M. Edwards, M.D.
Surgery . . . . Russell Postier, M.D.
  Pediatric Surgery . . . . David Tuggle, M.D.
  Plastic Surgery . . . . Kamal Sawan, M.D.
  Thoracic Surgery . . . . Marvin Peyton, M.D.
  Transplant . . . . Anthony Sebastian, M.D.
Urology . . . . Bradley Kropp, M.D. (Interim)

University of Oklahoma College of Medicine-Tulsa
School of Community Medicine
4502 East 41st Street
Tulsa, Oklahoma 74135-2553
918-660-3000; 918-660-3095 (dean's office); 918-660-3090 (fax)

The school of community medicine was established in 1974 as a community-based branch campus for third- and fourth-year students where to up to 25 percent of the class may complete their education.
Clinical facilities: Hillcrest Medical Center, Saint Francis Hospital, St. John Medical Center, Laureate Psychiatric Clinic and Hospital, and OU Clinics.

Administrative Staff

Dean . . . . F. Daniel Duffy, M.D.
Senior Associate Dean for Clinical Affairs . . . . Charles J. Foulks, M.D.
Associate Dean for Academic Services . . . . Meredith A. Davison, Ph.D.
Associate Dean for Academic Programs . . . . Ronald B. Saizow, M.D.
Associate Dean for Community Medicine and
  Research Development . . . . Mark D. Fox, M.D., Ph.D.
Associate Dean for Finance and Administration . . . . Jonathan E. Joiner

Department Chairs

Emergency Medicine . . . . Stephen H. Thomas, M.D.
Family Medicine . . . . John W. Tipton, M.D.
Medicine . . . . Charles J. Foulks, M.D.
Obstetrics and Gynecology . . . . Michael O. Gardner, M.D.
Pediatrics . . . . Michael Gomez, M.D.
Psychiatry . . . . Ondria C. Gleason, M.D.
Surgery . . . . John Blebea, M.D.

Oregon Health & Science University School of Medicine

3181 S.W. Sam Jackson Park Road, Mailcode L102
Portland, Oregon 97239-3098
503-494-7677; 503-494-8220 (dean's office); 503-494-3400 (fax)
Web site: www.ohsu.edu/som

The University of Oregon School of Medicine in Portland, Oregon, was established in 1887. In 1913, it was merged with the medical department of Willamette University in Salem, and all students were transferred to Portland. In 1974, the schools of medicine, dentistry, and nursing were combined into the University of Oregon Health Sciences Center. The center was renamed Oregon Health & Science University in 2001.

Type: public
2011 total enrollment: 507
Clinical facilities: University Hospital, Doernbecher Memorial Hospital for Children, Child Development Rehabilitation Center, Outpatient Clinics, Veterans Administration Medical Center, Emanuel Hospital and Health Center, Good Samaritan Hospital and Medical Center, Kaiser Foundation Hospitals - Northwest Region, Portland Adventist Medical Center, Providence Medical Center, Shriners Hospital for Children, St. Charles Medical Center of Bend, St. Vincent Hospital and Medical Center, Cascades East Family Practice Center at Klamath Falls, Merle West Medical Center at Klamath Falls, Family Health Centers at Gabriel Park, Richmond, Sellwood-Moreland, Beaverton, Scappoose, Hillsboro, Oregon City, University Fertility Consultants.

University Officials

President. . . . . Joseph E. Robertson, M.D.
Chief Financial Officer. . . . . Lawrence J. Furnstahl
Vice President for Academic Affairs and Provost . . . . Jeannette Mladenovic, M.D.
Vice President and Executive Director, OHSU Healthcare. . . . . Peter F. Rapp
Vice President and General Counsel. . . . . Amy Wayson, J.D.
Vice President Medical Affairs . . . . Mark A. Richardson, M.D.
Vice President for Research . . . . Daniel Dorsa, Ph.D.
President, OHSU Foundation. . . . . Allan Price
Registrar and Director of Financial Aid. . . . . A. Cherie Honnell

Medical School Administrative Staff

Dean. . . . . Mark A. Richardson, M.D.
Dean-Emeritus. . . . . . . John A. Benson, M.D., Joseph D. Bloom, M.D., and John W. Kendall, M.D.
Senior Associate Dean, Finance & Administration . . . . Irene M. Barhyte, C.P.A.
Senior Associate Dean, Clinical Practice . . . . Tom Heckler
Senior Associate Dean, Research . . . . Daniel M. Dorsa, Ph.D
Associate Dean, Clinical and Veterans Affairs . . . . Jeffrey R. Kirsch, M.D.
Associate Dean, Clinical Science. . . . . Eric S. Orwoll, M.D.
Associate Dean, CME & GME. . . . . Donald E. Girard, M.D.
Associate Dean, Faculty Development . . . . M. Patrice Eiff, M.D. (Interim)
Associate Dean, Graduate Studies. . . . . Allison D. Fryer, Ph.D.
Associate Dean, Student Affairs . . . . Molly L. Osborne, M.D., Ph.D.
Assistant Dean, Admissions. . . . . Cynthia D. Morris, Ph.D.
Assistant Dean, Faculty Affairs and Administration . . . . Nicole Lockart, M.B.A.
Assistant Dean, Faculty Development . . . . M. Patrice Eiff, M.D.
Assistant Dean, Medical Education . . . . Vicki Fields, B.S.
Assistant Dean, Student Development. . . . . Anita D. Taylor, M.A.Ed.

Department and Division or Section Chairs
Basic Sciences

Behavioral Neuroscience . . . . Robert J. Hitzemann, Ph.D.
Biochemistry and Molecular Biology. . . . . Peter S. Rotwein, M.D.
Biomedical Engineering. . . . . Joe Gray, Ph.D.
Cell and Developmental Biology. . . . . Lisa Coussens, Ph.D.
Division of Management . . . . James Huntzicker, Ph.D.
Heart Research Center. . . . . Kent L. Thornburg, Ph.D.
Molecular and Medical Genetics. . . . . Susan Hayflick, M.D.
Molecular Microbiology and Immunology. . . . . Mary Stenzel-Poore, Ph.D.
Physiology and Pharmacology. . . . . David C. Dawson, Ph.D.
Clinical Sciences

Anesthesiology and Perioperative Medicine. . . . . Jeffrey R. Kirsch, M.D.
Center for Women's Health . . . . Aaron B. Caughey, M.D., Ph.D.
Dermatology . . . . Alfons Krol, M.D.
Diagnostic Radiology . . . . Steven L. Primack, M.D. (Interim)
    Nuclear Medicine. . . . . Jeffrey S. Stevens, M.D.
Dotter Interventional Institute . . . . Frederick S. Keller, M.D.
Emergency Medicine . . . . O. John Ma, M.D.
Family Medicine . . . . John W. Saultz, M.D.

Medical Informatics and Clinical Epidemiology. . . . . William R. Hersh, M.D.
Medicine. . . . . D. Lynn Loriaux, M.D., Ph.D.
   Allergy and Clinical Immunology . . . . Anthony Montanaro, M.D. (Interim)
   Arthritis and Rheumatic Diseases . . . . James T. Rosenbaum, M.D.
   Cardiovascular Medicine. . . . . Sanjiv Kaul, M.D.
   Endocrinology, Diabetes, and Clinical Nutrition . . . . James R. Lundblad, M.D. (Interim)
   Gastroenterology and Hepatology. . . . . David A. Lieberman, M.D.
   General Internal Medicine and Geriatrics . . . . Katherine Bensching, M.D. (Interim)
   Health Promotion and Sports Medicine . . . . Linn Goldberg, M.D.
   Hematology and Medical Oncology. . . . . Alan Sandler, M.D.
   Hospital Medicine . . . . Alan J. Hunter, M.D.
   Infectious Diseases . . . . Brian Wong, M.D.
   Nephrology and Hypertension . . . . David H. Ellison, M.D.
   Pulmonary and Critical Care Medicine . . . . David B. Jacoby, M.D.
Neurological Surgery. . . . . Kim J. Burchiel, M.D.
Neurology. . . . . Dennis N. Bourdette, M.D.
Obstetrics and Gynecology. . . . . Aaron B. Caughey, M.D., Ph.D.
OHSU Institute on Development & Disability . . . . Brian Rogers, M.D.
OHSU Knight Cancer Institute. . . . . Brian J. Druker, M.D.
Ophthalmology . . . . David Wilson, M.D.
Orthopaedics and Rehabilitation . . . . Jung Yoo, M.D.
Otolaryngology, Head, and Neck Surgery . . . . Paul W. Flint, M.D.
   Audiology/Vestibular Services/Cochlear Implants . . . . TBD
   Facial Plastic and Reconstructive Surgery. . . . . Tom Wang, M.D.
   Head and Neck Surgery. . . . . Peter Andersen, M.D.
   NW Clinic for Voice and Swallowing . . . . Joshua Schindler, M.D.
   Oral and Maxillofacial Surgery . . . . Thomas Albert, M.D.
   Oregon Hearing Research Center. . . . . Alred Nuttall, Ph.D.
   Otology/Neurotology/Skull Base Surgery . . . . Sean McMenomey, M.D.
   Pediatric Otolaryngology. . . . . Henry Milczuk, M.D.
   Rhinology and Sinus Surgery . . . . Timothy Smith, M.D.
Pathology . . . . Douglas Weeks, M.D.
   Anatomic Pathology. . . . . Ken Gatter, M.D.
   Laboratory Medicine . . . . Richard Scanlan, M.D.
Pediatrics . . . . H. Stacy Nicholson, M.D.
   Adolescent Medicine . . . . C. Wayne Sells, M.D.
   Cardiology. . . . . Mark Reller, M.D.
   Critical Care. . . . . Dana Braner, M.D.
   Developmental Pediatrics. . . . . Brian Rogers, M.D.
   Endocrinology . . . . Bruce A. Boston, M.D.
   Gastroenterology . . . . William Byrne, M.D.
   General Pediatrics . . . . Cindy Ferrell, M.D. (Interim)
   Hematology/Oncology. . . . . Linda Stork, M.D.
   Infectious Disease. . . . . Deborah Lewinsohn, M.D.
   Metabolics . . . . David M. Koeller, M.D.
   Neonatology. . . . . Robert Schelonka, M.D.
   Neurology . . . . Thomas Koch, M.D.
   Pediatric Kidney Services and Hypertension . . . . David Rozansky, M.D.
   Pulmonary. . . . . Mike Powers, M.D.
   Rheumatology and Immunology. . . . . Michael Borzy, M.D.
Physician Assistant Education Division . . . . Ted Ruback
Psychiatry . . . . George A. Keepers, M.D.
   Child and Adolescent Psychiatry. . . . . Ajit Jetmalani, M.D.
   Clinical Psychiatry . . . . George A. Keepers, M.D.
Public Health and Preventive Medicine . . . . Thomas M. Becker, M.D.
Radiation Medicine . . . . Charles R. Thomas, M.D.
Surgery. . . . . John G. Hunter, M.D.
   Abdominal Organ Transplantation . . . . Susan L. Orloff, M.D.
   Cardiothoracic Surgery. . . . . Steven Guyton, M.D. (Acting)
   Gastrointestinal and General Surgery . . . . Robert G. Martindale, M.D.
   Pediatric Surgery . . . . Mark L. Silen, M.D.
   Plastic and Reconstructive Surgery . . . . Juliana E. Hansen, M.D.
   Surgical Oncology . . . . Kevin G. Billingsley, M.D.
   Trauma Critical Care and Acute Care Surgery. . . . . Martin A. Schrieber, M.D.
   Urology. . . . . Christopher L. Amling, M.D.
   Vascular Surgery. . . . . Gregory L. Moneta, M.D.

Drexel University College of Medicine (Formerly MCP Hahnemann School of Medicine)

245 North 15th Street, MS400
Philadelphia, Pennsylvania 19102
215-991-8560; 215-762-3500 (dean's office); 215-991-8561 (education & acad. affairs)
Web site: www.drexelmed.edu

Drexel University College of Medicine represents the union of the Women's Medical College of Pennsylvania and Hahnemann Medical College, whose roots go back 157 years. In 2002, the combined medical schools, then MCP-Hahnemann, merged with Drexel University, a 100-year-old institution recognized for its focus on technology across the curriculum. Fostering interdisciplinary research between the college of medicine and its other schools and colleges is a university priority.

Type: private
2011 total enrollment: 1,080
Clinical facilities: Abington Memorial Hospital, Allegheny General Hospital, Bayhealth Medical Center, Bryn Mawr Hospital, Capital Health System, Chambersburg Hospital, Coatsville VA Medical Center, Crozer-Chester Medical Center, Eagleville Hospital, Easton Hospital, Friends Hospital, Hahnemann University Hospital, Holy Redeemer Hospital and Medical Center, Lancaster General Hospital, Lehigh Valley Hospital, Mercy Catholic Medical Center, Monmouth Medical Center, Pinnacle Hospitals, Reading Hospital and Medical Center, St. Christopher's Hospital for Children, St. Peter's University Hospital, York Hospital.

University Officials

President. . . . . John A. Fry
Vice President. . . . . Mary M. Moran, M.D.
Provost . . . . Mark L. Greenberg, Ph.D.
Senior Vice President for Finance and Treasurer . . . . Helen Y. Boarman
Dean, College of Medicine. . . . . Daniel V. Schidlow, M.D. (Interim)
Dean, College of Nursing and Health Professions . . . . Gloria Donnelly, Ph.D.
Dean, School of Public Health. . . . . Marla Gold, M.D.

Medical School Administrative Staff

Vice President for Health Affairs . . . . Mary M. Moran, M.D.
Dean. . . . . Daniel V. Schidlow, M.D. (Interim)
Associate Dean for Administration and Chief of Staff . . . . Claire A. Tillman
Executive Assistant to the Dean . . . . Tina Callaghan
Vice Dean, Educational and Academic Affairs. . . . . Barbara A. Schindler, M.D.
  Associate Dean, Admissions. . . . . Cheryl Hanau, M.D.
  Associate Dean, Assessment and Evaluation . . . . Burton J. Landau, Ph.D.
  Associate Dean, Clincal Skills, Education, and Assessment . . . . Dennis H. Novack, M.D.
  Associate Dean, Community Outreach Programs . . . . Vincent Zarro, M.D.
  Assistant Dean, Continuing Medical Education . . . . Cynthia Johnson
  Associate Dean, Information Technology. . . . . Arnold Smolen, Ph.D.
  Assistant Dean, Interdisciplinary Foundations of Medicine . . . . Donna Russo, Ph.D.
  Associate Dean, Student Affairs and Diversity. . . . . Anthony Rodriguez, M.D.
  Associate Dean, Program for Integrated Learning . . . . Donna Russo, M.D.
  Senior Associate Dean for Student Affairs and Admissions . . . . Samuel K. Parrish, M.D.
    Associate Dean, Student Affairs . . . . Amy C. Fuchs, M.D.
  Vice Dean, Faculty Affairs and Professional Development. . . . . Mary M. Moran, M.D.
  Senior Associate Dean, Student Affairs and
    Medical Education (AGH) . . . . James Wilberger, M.D.
  Vice Dean for Research . . . . Kenny J. Simansky, Ph.D.
  Vice Dean for Biomedical Graduate Studies. . . . . Barry Waterhouse, Ph.D.
Vice Dean for Professional Studies in the Health Sciences. . . . . Gerald Soslau, Ph.D.
Director of Graduate Medical Education and
  Designated Institutional Official . . . . Jay Yanoff, Ed.D.
    Associate Dean, Graduate Medical Education. . . . . Mark Woodland, M.D.

Drexel University College of Medicine (Formerly MCP Hahnemann School of Medicine): PENNSYLVANIA

Department Chairs

Basic Sciences

Biochemistry . . . . Jane Clifford, Ph.D.
Microbiology and Immunology. . . . . Brian Wigdahl, Ph.D.
Neurobiology and Anatomy . . . . Itzhak Fischer, Ph.D.
Pharmacology and Physiology. . . . . James E. Barrett, Ph.D.

Clinical Sciences

Anesthesiology. . . . . George Mychaskiw, M.D.
Cardiovascular Medicine and Surgery. . . . . Glenn Laub, M.D.
Dermatology . . . . Herbert Allen, M.D.
Emergency Medicine . . . . Richard Hamilton, M.D.
Family, Community, and Preventive Medicine . . . . Eugene Hong, M.D.
Medicine. . . . . James C. Reynolds, M.D.
Neurology . . . . Robert J. Schwartzman, M.D.
Neurosurgery. . . . . James Wilburger, M.D.
Obstetrics and Gynecology. . . . . Owen Montgomery, M.D.
Ophthalmology . . . . Myron Yanoff, M.D.
Orthopedic Surgery. . . . . Norman Johanson, M.D.
Otolaryngology-Head and Neck Surgery . . . . Robert Sataloff, M.D.
Pathology and Laboratory Medicine . . . . Cheryl A. Hanau, Ph.D.
Pediatrics . . . . Robert S. McGregor, M.D. (Interim)
Psychiatry . . . . Susan McLeer, M.D.
Radiation Oncology. . . . . Lydia Komarnicky, M.D.
Radiologic Sciences . . . . Michael Hallowell, M.D.
Surgery . . . . D. Scott Lind, M.D.

Centers and Institute

Director, Institute for Women's Health. . . . . Lynne Yeakel

Jefferson Medical College of Thomas Jefferson University

1025 Walnut Street
Philadelphia, Pennsylvania 19107-5083
215-955-6000; 215-955-6980 (dean's office); 215-503-2654 (fax)
E-mail: dean.jmc@mail.tju.edu
Web site: www.tju.edu

Jefferson Medical College was established in 1824; classes have been graduated annually since 1826. It is a private, nondenominational, coeducational medical school. On July 1, 1969, Thomas Jefferson University was established with the Jefferson Medical College as one of its colleges.

Type: private
2011 total enrollment: 1,035
Clinical facilities: Thomas Jefferson University Hospital, Thomas Jefferson University Hospital—Methodist Division, Jefferson Hospital for the Neurosciences. **Affiliated hostpials:** Abington Memorial Hospital, Albert Einstein Medical Center, Bryn Mawr Hospital, Bryn Mawr Rehab, Christina Care Health Services, Crozer-Keystone Health System, A.I. duPont Hospital for Children, Lankenau Hospital, Latrobe Hospital, Magee Rehabilitation Hospital, Paoli Hospital, Reading Hospital and Medical Center, Underwood Memorial Hospital, Veterans Affairs Medical Center, Virtua Health, Wills Eye Institute, York Hospital.

University Officials

President. . . . . Robert L. Barchi, M.D., Ph.D.
Senior Vice President and Dean, Jefferson Medical College. . . . . Mark L. Tykocinski, M.D.

Medical School Administrative Staff

Dean. . . . . Anthony F. DePalma, and Gertrude M. DePalma
Chief Operating Officer. . . . . John Ogunkeye
Senior Associate Dean, Clinical Affairs . . . . William M. Keane, M.D.
Associate Dean, Cancer-related Services . . . . Richard G. Pestell, M.D., Ph.D.
Vice Dean for Research . . . . Leonard Freedman, Ph.D.
Associate Dean for Research. . . . . Theodore Taraschi, Ph.D.
The Lillian H. Brent Dean of Students and Admissions. . . . . Clara A. Callahan, M.D.
    Senior Associate Dean, Student Affairs and Career Counseling. . . . . Charles A. Pohl, M.D.
        Associate Dean, Student Affairs and Career Counseling . . . . Kristin L. DeSimone, M.D.
        Associate Dean, Student Affairs and Career Counseling . . . . Bernard L. Lopez, M.D.
Assistant Dean, Student Affairs and Career Counseling . . . . Kathryn Trayes, M.D.
Senior Associate Dean, Continuing Medical Education . . . . Joseph L. Seltzer, M.D.
    Associate Dean, Alumni Relations, Executive
        Director of Alumni Association . . . . Phillip J. Marone, M.D.
    Vice Dean, Faculty Affairs and Professional Development. . . . . Karen D. Novielli, M.D.
Vice Dean, Graduate Medical Education and Affiliations. . . . . David L. Paskin, M.D.
    Associate Dean, Graduate Medical Education and Affiliations. . . . . John Caruso, M.D.
    Associate Dean, Graduate Medical Education and Affliliations . . . . John Kairys, M.D.
Vice Dean, Academic Affairs/Undergraduate Medical Education. . . . . Susan L. Rattner, M.D.
    Associate Dean, Academic Affairs/
        Undergraduate Medical Education . . . . Karen M. Glaser, Ph.D.
    Assistant Dean, Academic Affairs/
        Undergraduate Medical Education . . . . Steven K. Herrine, M.D.
The Roger B. Daniels Associate Dean of
    Professionalism in Medicine . . . . John M. Spandurfer, M.D.
    Assistant Dean, Diversity and Minority Affairs . . . . Luz Ortiz
Assistant Dean, Medical Education, Albert Einstein Medical Center . . . . . . Douglas McGee, D.O.
Assistant Dean, Medical Education, Christiana Care . . . . Brian W. Little, M.D.
Assistant Dean, Medical Education, Main Line Health. . . . . James F. Burke, M.D.
Chief Executive of the Practice, Nemours
    Children's Clinic–Wilmington/A.I. duPont
    Hospital for Children . . . . Bernard J. Clark, M.D.
Director, Center for Research in Medical
    Education and Health Care . . . . Joseph S. Gonnella, M.D.

Jefferson Medical College of Thomas Jefferson University: PENNSYLVANIA

Department and Division or Section Chairs

Basic Sciences

Biochemistry and Molecular Biology......................... Jeffrey Benovic, Ph.D.
Cancer Biology .... Richard G. Pestell, M.D., Ph.D.
Microbiology and Immunology.............................. Timothy Manser, Ph.D.
Molecular Physiology and Biophysics .... Marion J. Siegman, Ph.D.
Neuroscience... Irwin Levitan, Ph.D.
Pharmacology and Experimental Therapeutrics .... Scott Waldman, M.D., Ph.D.
Stem Cell Biology and Regenerative Medicine............... Michael P. Lisanti, M.D., Ph.D.

Clinical Sciences

Anesthesiology.. Zvi Grunwald, M.D.
Dermatology and Cutaneous Biology .... Jouni J. Uitto, M.D., Ph.D.
Emergency Medicine .... Theodore A. Christopher, M.D.
Family and Community Medicine............................ Richard C. Wender, M.D.
Medical Oncology .... Neal Flomenberg, M.D.
Medicine... Arthur M. Feldman, M.D., Ph.D.
Neurology.. Abdolmohamad Rostami, M.D., Ph.D.
Neurological Surgery.................................... Robert H. Rosenwasser, M.D.
Obstetrics and Gynecology............................... Joseph Montella, M.D. (Acting)
Ophthalmology.. Julia A. Haller, M.D.
Orthopaedic Surgery.................................... Todd J. Albert, M.D.
Otolaryngology-Head and Neck Surgery .... William M. Keane, M.D.
Pathology, Anatomy, and Cell Biology .... Stephen Peiper, M.D.
Pediatrics .... Jay S. Greenspan, M.D.
Psychiatry and Human Behavior........................... Michael J. Vergare, M.D.
Radiation Oncology...................................... Adam P. Dicker, M.D., Ph.D.
Radiology .... Vijay M. Rao, M.D.
Rehabilitation Medicine................................. John L. Melvin, M.D.
Surgery .... Charles J. Yeo, M.D.
Urology.. Leonard G. Gomella, M.D.

Institute Directors

Farber Institute for Neurosciences .... Irwin B. Levitan, Ph.D.
Kimmel Cancer Institute .... Richard G. Pestell, M.D., Ph.D.

Pennsylvania State University College of Medicine
500 University Drive
P.O. Box 850
Hershey, Pennsylvania 17033
717-531-8521; 717-531-8323 (dean's office); 717-531-5351 (fax)
E-mail: hpaz@psu.edu
Web site: www.pennstatehershey.org

Penn State Milton S. Hershey Medical Center of the Pennsylvania State University was established in August 1963 and admitted its first class of medical students in 1967. Located on a 549-acre campus on the western edge of Hershey, the medical center is 12 miles from the state capital, Harrisburg, and approximately 105 miles from the university's main campus at University Park.

Type: private
2011 total enrollment: 581
Clinical facilities: A 484-bed university and children's hospital is located on the campus as part of a single, continuous structure housing both the hospital and the Medical Sciences Building. The Health System includes a rehabilitation and a psychiatric hospital. Core clinical clerkships and elective clerkships are given at the medical center hospital and at affiliated hospitals.

University Official
President . . . . Rodney A. Erickson, Ph.D.

Medical School Administrative Staff
Senior Vice President for Health Affairs and Dean . . . . Harold L. Paz, M.D.
Associate Vice President for Finance and Business and Controller . . . . Wayne W. Zolko
Vice Dean for Clinical Affairs . . . . A. Craig Hillemeier, M.D.
Vice Dean for Educational Affairs . . . . Richard J. Simons, M.D.
Vice Dean for Research and Graduate Studies . . . . Daniel A. Notterman, M.D.
Senior Associate Dean, Regional Campus (State College) . . . . E. Eugene Marsh, M.D.
Associate Dean for Primary Care . . . . James M. Herman, M.D.
Associate Dean for Admissions and Student Affairs . . . . Dwight Davis, M.D.
Associate Dean for Administration . . . . Donald E. Martin, M.D.
Associate Dean for Diversity . . . . Harjit Singh, M.D.
Associate Dean for Faculty Affairs . . . . Carol S. Weisman, Ph.D.
Associate Dean for Graduate Studies . . . . Michael Verderame, Ph.D.
Associate Dean for Graduate Medical Education . . . . Ronald Domen, M.D.
Associate Dean for Clinical Education . . . . Eileen Moser, M.D.
Associate Dean for Research . . . . Sheila L. Vrana, Ph.D.
Associate Dean for Faculty and Professional Development . . . . Ann Ouyang, M.D.
Associate Dean for Continuing Medical Education . . . . William L. Hennrikus, M.D.
Associate Dean for Preclinical Curriculum . . . . Carol Whitfield, Ph.D.
Associate Dean for Medical Education (York Hospital) . . . . Richard Sloan, M.D.
Associate Dean for Medical Education (Pinnacle Health) . . . . Nirmal Joshi, M.D.
Associate Dean for Clinical Science Research . . . . Thomas Terndrup, M.D.
Associate Dean for Clinical Simulation . . . . Elizabeth Sinz, M.D.
Associate Vice President for Development . . . . Kristen B. Rozansky

Department and Division or Section Chairs
Basic Sciences
Biochemistry and Molecular Biology . . . . Judith S. Bond, Ph.D.
Cellular and Molecular Physiology . . . . Leonard S. Jefferson, Ph.D.
Comparative Medicine . . . . Ronald P. Wilson, V.M.D.
Humanities . . . . Daniel Shapiro, Ph.D.
Microbiology and Immunology . . . . Richard J. Courtney, Ph.D.
Neural and Behavioral Sciences . . . . Colin J. Barnstable, D.Phil.
Pharmacology . . . . Kent Vrana, Ph.D.
Public Health Sciences . . . . Vernon M. Chinchilli, Ph.D.

Clinical Sciences
Anesthesiology . . . . Berend Mets, M.B.,Ch.B., Ph.D.
  Cardiac Anesthesia . . . . Kane High, M.D.
  Critical Care Medicine . . . . John K. Stene, Jr., M.D., Ph.D., and Kane High, M.D.
  Pain Medicine . . . . Vitaly Gordin, M.D.
  Pediatric Anesthesia . . . . Patrick McQuillan, M.D.
  Regional Anesthesia . . . . Patrick McQuillan, M.D.
Dermatology . . . . James Marks, M.D.
Emergency Medicine . . . . Thomas Terndrup, M.D.

Pennsylvania State University College of Medicine: PENNSYLVANIA

Family and Community Medicine . . . . James M. Herman, M.D.
Medicine . . . . Robert C. Aber, M.D.
   Cardiology . . . . Gerald V. Naccarelli, M.D.
   Endocrinology . . . . Andrea Manni, M.D.
   Gastroenterology . . . . Thomas J. McGarrity, M.D.
   Hematology and Oncology . . . . Wafik El-Deiry, M.D., Ph.D.
   Infectious Diseases . . . . Leslie J. Parent, M.D.
   Internal Medicine . . . . Christopher N. Sciamanna, M.D.
   Pulmonary . . . . Kevin Gleeson, M.D.
   Renal Medicine . . . . William Reeves, M.D.
   Rheumatology . . . . Nancy J. Olsen, M.D.
Neurology . . . . David C. Good, M.D.
Neurosurgery . . . . Robert E. Harbaugh, M.D.
Obstetrics, Gynecology, and Women's Health . . . . John T. Repke, M.D.
   Gynecologic Oncology . . . . James Fanning, D.O.
   Maternal and Fetal Medicine . . . . Serdar H. Ural, M.D.
   Reproductive Endocrinology and Infertility . . . . William C. Dodson, M.D.
   Women's Health . . . . Holly Thomas, M.D.
Ophthalmology . . . . David Quillen, M.D.
Orthopaedics and Rehabilitation . . . . Kevin Black, M.D.
Pathology . . . . Dani S. Zander, M.D.
   Anatomic Pathology . . . . Catherine S. Abendroth, M.D.
   Clinical Laboratories . . . . Michael Creer, M.D.
Pediatrics . . . . A. Craig Hillemeier, M.D.
   Adolescent Medicine . . . . Richard Levine, M.D.
   Cardiology . . . . Howard Weber, M.D. (Interim)
   Critical Care . . . . Steven E. Lucking, M.D.
   Endocrinology . . . . Ying Chang, M.D.
   Gastroenterology and Nutrition . . . . Douglas Field, M.D.
   General Pediatrics . . . . Mark Widome, M.D.
   Genetics . . . . Roger Ladda, M.D.
   Hematology and Oncology . . . . Barbara Miller, M.D.
   Infectious Diseases . . . . George McSherry, M.D.
   Nephrology . . . . Steven J. Wassner, M.D.
   Neurology . . . . William Trescher, M.D.
   Newborn Medicine . . . . Charles Palmer, M.D.
   Pulmonology . . . . Gavin Graff, M.D.
   Rheumatology . . . . Brandt P. Groh, M.D.
Physical Medicine and Rehabilitation . . . . Brenda Mallory, M.D. (Interim)
Psychiatry . . . . Alan J. Gelenberg, M.D.
   Autism Services . . . . Michael Murray, M.D.
   Consult Psychiatry . . . . Mark Rapp, M.D.
   Education and Training Programs . . . . Aftab Khan, M.D.
   Molecular Neuropharmacology Research . . . . John Ellis, Ph.D.
   Child and Adolescent Psychiatry . . . . J. Lynn Taylor, M.D.
Radiology . . . . Kathleen Dunne Eggli, M.D.
   Abdominal Imaging . . . . Thomas Dykes, M.D.
   Breast Imaging . . . . Susann Schetter, D.O.
   CVI . . . . Peter N. Waybill, M.D.
   Diagnostic Radiology . . . . Rickhesvar P. M. Mahraj, M.D.
   Musculoskeletal . . . . Timothy J. Mosher, M.D.
   Neuroradiology . . . . Dan Nguyen, M.D.
   Nuclear Medicine . . . . Thomas W. Allen, M.D.
   Pediatric Radiology . . . . Danielle K. Boal, M.D.
   Radiation Oncology . . . . Henry Wagner, M.D.
   Thoracic Imaging . . . . Rickhesvar P. M. Mahraj, M.D.
Surgery . . . . Peter W. Dillon, M.D.
   Cardiothoracic Surgery . . . . Walter E. Pae, Jr., M.D.
   Colon and Rectal Surgery . . . . Walter Koltun, M.D.
   General Surgery . . . . David Soybel, M.D.
   Otolaryngology-Head and Neck Surgery . . . . Fred Fedok, M.D.
   Pediatric Surgery . . . . Robert E. Cilley, M.D.
   Plastic and Reconstructive Surgery . . . . Donald Mackay, M.D.
   Surgical Oncology . . . . David I. Soybel, M.D.
   Transplantation . . . . Zakiyah Kadry, M.D.
   Trauma and Critical Care . . . . Dan Galvan, M.D.
   Urology . . . . Ross M. Decter, M.D.
   Vascular Surgery . . . . Amy B. Reed, M.D.

Temple University School of Medicine
3500 North Broad Street
Philadelphia, Pennsylvania 19140-5104
215-707-7000; 215-707-8773 (dean's office); 215-707-8431 (fax)
E-mail: tusmdean@temple.edu
Web site: www.temple.edu/medicine

The school of medicine was opened as a department of Temple University in 1901.

Type: private
2011 total enrollment: 778
Clinical facilities: Abington Memorial Hospital (Abington), Crozer-Chester Medical Center (Upland), Western Pennsylvania Allegheny Health System (Pittsburgh), Conemaugh Valley Memorial Hospital (Johnstown), Forbes Regional Hospital (Monroeville), Fox Chase Cancer Center, Geisinger Medical Center (Danville), Jeanes Hospital, Lancaster General Hospital (Lancaster), Lehigh Valley Medical Center (Allentown), Mercy Hospital (Scranton), Montgomery Hospital (Norristown), Reading Hospital and Medical Center (Reading), St. Christopher's Hospital for Children, St. Luke's Hospital and Health Network (Bethlehem), Sacred Heart Hospital (Allentown), Shriner's Hospital for Children, Temple University Hospital, Virtua West Jersey Hospitals (Voorhees, NJ).

University Officials

President. . . . . Ann Weaver Hart, Ph.D.
Senior Vice President and Provost . . . . Richard M. Englert, Ed.D. (Interim)
Senior Executive Vice President of Health
   Sciences and Chief Executive Officer, Temple
   University Health System . . . . Larry R. Kaiser, M.D.

Medical School Administrative Staff

Executive Dean and Chief Academic Officer,
   Temple University Health System . . . . Arthur Feldman, M.D., Ph.D.
Dean. . . . . Larry R. Kaiser, M.D.
Executive Associate Dean. . . . . Richard J. Kozera, M.D.
Assistant Dean for Graduate Medical Education . . . . Darilyn Moyer, M.D.
Assistant Dean and Director of the Recruitment,
   Retention, and Admissions Program . . . . Raul A. De La Cadena, M.D.
Assistant Dean for Continuing Medical Education. . . . . Melinda M. Somasekhar, Ph.D.
Assistant Dean for Finance. . . . . Ann Untalan
Senior Associate Dean for Medical Education . . . . Gerald H. Sterling, Ph.D.
Associate Dean for Admissions . . . . Audrey Uknis, M.D.
Associate Dean for Student Affairs . . . . Kathleen Reeves, M.D.
Associate Dean for the Graduate and M.D./Ph.D. Programs . . . . Dianne Soprano, Ph.D.
Associate Dean for Graduate Studies . . . . Scott Shore, Ph.D.
Associate Dean for Academic Affiliations . . . . Stephen R. Permut, M.D., J.D.
Assistant Dean for Academic Affiliations. . . . . William F. Schulze
Assistant Dean for Clinical Education . . . . Larry Kaplan, M.D.
Senior Associate Dean for Research . . . . Steven Houser, Ph.D. (Interim)
Associate Dean for Faculty Affairs and Faculty Development . . . . Helen E. Pearson, Ph.D.
Assistant Dean for Institutional Affiliate Faculty Development . . . . Beth Moughan, M.D.
Vice Dean for Finance and Administration and
   Executive Director, Temple University
   Physicians . . . . Thomas Kupp
Vice Dean for Information Technology, School
   of Medicine, and Chief Information Officer,
   Temple University Physicians . . . . Frank Erdlen
Associate Dean at Abington Memorial Hospital. . . . . David Gary Smith, M.D.
Associate Dean at Crozer Chester Medical Center. . . . . Guy Hewlett, M.D.
Associate Dean at Geisinger Medical Center . . . . Linda Famiglio, M.D.
Senior Associate Dean at St. Luke's Regional Campus. . . . . Joel C. Rosenfeld, M.D.
Senior Associate Dean at West Penn-Allegheny Campus . . . . Elliot Goldberg, M.D.
Assistant Dean for International Affiliations . . . . Christopher Loftus, M.D.
Assistant Dean for Institutional Advancement . . . . Eric Abel

Temple University School of Medicine: PENNSYLVANIA

Assistant Dean for Minority Affairs . . . . Donald Parks, M.D.
Director of Bioresources . . . . David Schabdach, D.V.M.
Director, Health Sciences Library . . . . Barbara Kuchan (Interim)

Department Chairs and Section Chiefs

Basic Science Departments and Research Centers

Anatomy and Cell Biology . . . . Steven N. Popoff, Ph.D.
Biochemistry . . . . Donald Gill, Ph.D.
Cardiovascular Research Center . . . . Steven Houser, Ph.D.
Center for Neural Repair and Rehabilitation . . . . Michael E. Selzer, M.D., Ph.D.
Center for Obesity Research and Education . . . . Gary D. Foster, Ph.D.
Center for Substance Abuse . . . . Ellen Unterwald, Ph.D.
Fels Institute for Cancer Research and Molecular Biology . . . . Jean-Pierre Issa, M.D.
Microbiology and Immunology . . . . Doina Ganea, Ph.D.
Neuroscience . . . . Kamel Khalili, Ph.D.
Pathology and Laboratory Medicine . . . . Yuri Persidsky, M.D.
Pharmacology . . . . Nae Dun, Ph.D.
Physiology . . . . Steven Houser, Ph.D.
Sol Sherry Thrombosis Research Center . . . . Satya P. Kunapuli, Ph.D.

Clinical Science Departments

Anesthesiology . . . . Rodger Barnette, M.D.
Emergency Medicine . . . . Robert McNamara, M.D.
Family Practice and Community Health . . . . Stephen R. Permut, M.D., J.D.
Internal Medicine . . . . José C. Missri, M.D. (Interim)
   Cardiology . . . . José C. Missri, M.D.
   Endocrinology and Metabolism . . . . Kevin J. Williams, M.D.
   Gastroenterology . . . . Oleh Haluszka, M.D.
   General Internal Medicine . . . . Anuradha Paranjape, M.D.
   Hematology . . . . A. Koneti Rao, M.D.
   Infectious Diseases . . . . Thomas Fekete, M.D.
   Nephrology . . . . Crystal A. Gadegbeku, M.D.
   Oncology . . . . Michael Bromberg, M.D.
   Pulmonary Diseases . . . . Gerard J. Criner, M.D.
   Rheumatology . . . . Philip Cohen, M.D.
Neurology . . . . S. Ausim Azizi, M.D.
Neurosurgery . . . . Christopher Loftus, M.D.
Obstetrics, Gynecology, and Reproductive Science . . . . Enrique Hernandez, M.D.
Ophthalmology . . . . Jeffrey Henderer, M.D.
Orthopedic Surgery . . . . Joseph Thoder, M.D.
Otorhinolaryngology-Head and Neck Surgery . . . . John Krouse, M.D.
Pediatrics . . . . Stephen Aronoff, M.D.
   Ambulatory Pediatrics . . . . Beth Moughan, M.D.
   Hospital-based Pediatrics . . . . Michael Del Vecchio, M.D.
Physical Medicine and Rehabilitation . . . . Ian Maitin, M.D.
Psychiatry and Behavioral Science . . . . William Dubin, M.D.
Radiation Oncology . . . . Curtis Miyamoto, M.D.
Radiology . . . . Charles Jungreis, M.D.
Surgery . . . . John M. Daly, M.D. (Interim)
   Bariatric . . . . John Meilahn, M.D.
   Cardiothoracic . . . . T. Sloane Guy, M.D.
   General . . . . Sean Harbison, M.D.
   Trauma . . . . Amy Goldberg, M.D.
   Vascular . . . . Eric Choi, M.D.
Urology . . . . Jack Mydlo, M.D.

University of Pennsylvania Perelman School of Medicine

3620 Hamilton Walk
Philadelphia, Pennsylvania 19104-6055
215-898-8034 (academic programs); 215-898-6796 (dean's office); 215-573-2030 (fax)
Web site: www.med.upenn.edu

Founded in 1765, the school of medicine of the University of Pennsylvania has the distinction of being the oldest medical school in the United States. It is located on the campus of the university in west Philadelphia.

Type: private
2011 total enrollment: 770
Clinical facilities: Hospital of the University of Pennsylvania, Children's Hospital of Philadelphia, Veterans Administration Medical Center, Penn Presbyterian Medical Center (including Scheie Eye Institute), Children's Seashore House, Chestnut Hill Hospital, Englewood Hospital, York Hospital, Pennsylvania Hospital, Chester County Hospital, St. Luke's Hospital-Bethlehem, Virtua-Burlington Hospital, Underwood Memorial Hospital, Reading Hospital.

University Officials

President. . . . . Amy Gutmann, Ph.D.
Provost . . . . Vincent E. Price, Ph.D.
Executive Vice President of the University for
  the Health System and Dean, Perelman
  School of Medicine . . . . J. Larry Jameson, M.D., Ph.D.
Chief Executive Officer, Health System. . . . . Ralph W. Muller

Medical School Administrative Staff

Executive Vice President and Dean. . . . . J. Larry Jameson, M.D., Ph.D.
  Associate Dean and Chief of Staff . . . . Thomas R. Hecker, Ph.D.
  Senior Vice President for Public Affairs and
  Senior Advisor to Executive Vice President/
  Dean . . . . Susan E. Phillips
  Associate Dean, Health Promotion and Disease Prevention . . . . . . Shiriki K. Kumanyika, Ph.D.
Vice Dean, Institutional Affairs. . . . . Brian L. Strom, M.D., M.P.H.
Vice Dean for Education . . . . Gail Morrison, M.D.
  Associate Dean for Curriculum . . . . Stanley Goldfarb, M.D.
  Assistant Dean, Diversity for Undergraduate Medical Education . . . . Karen E. Hamilton, Ph.D.
  Associate Dean, Student Affairs. . . . . Jon B. Morris, M.D.
  Associate Dean, Continuing Medical Education . . . . Zalman S. Agus, M.D.
  Associate Dean, Medical Education Research
  and Director, Evaluation and Assessment . . . . Judy A. Shea, Ph.D.
  Associate Dean, Professionalism and Humanism . . . . Paul N. Lanken, M.D.
  Chief Administrative Officer and Director, Curriculum Office . . . . Anna T. Delaney
  Director of Admissions and Financial Aid . . . . Gaye W. Sheffler
Vice Dean, Faculty and Resident Affairs . . . . Lisa M. Bellini, M.D.
Associate Dean, Graduate Medical Education . . . . Jeffrey S. Berns, M.D.
Executive Vice Dean and Chief Scientific Officer . . . . Glen N. Gaulton, Ph.D.
  Associate Dean, Research . . . . Arnold Levinson, M.D.
  Associate Dean, Combined Degree and Physician Scholars. . . . . . Lawrence F. Brass, M.D., Ph.D.
  Associate Dean for Research Program Development . . . . Jonas H. Ellenberg, Ph.D.
  Associate Dean for Clinical Research. . . . . Susan S. Ellenberg, Ph.D.
  Associate Dean for Graduate Education and
  Director, Biomedical Graduate Studies . . . . Susan R. Ross, Ph.D.
  Associate Dean, Biomedical Postdoctoral Programs . . . . Susan R. Weiss, Ph.D.
  Associate Dean, Global Health Programs. Neal Nathanson, M.D.
  Associate Dean, Core Facilities . . . . Morris J. Birnbaum, M.D., Ph.D.
  Associate Dean, Master's Programs . . . . Donna George, Ph.D.
  Managing Director, Office of Corporate Alliances . . . . Terry J. Fadem
  Senior Executive Director, Research and Research Training. . . . . Susan R. Passante
Vice Dean, Professional Services and Senior Vice President. . . . . . Peter D. Quinn, D.M.D., M.D.
  Executive Director, Clinical Practices of the
  University of Pennsylvania . . . . Elizabeth B. Johnston

University of Pennsylvania Perelman School of Medicine: PENNSYLVANIA

Vice Dean, Integrative Services. . . . . Kevin B. Mahoney
Vice Dean, Administration and Finance . . . . Rebecca Cooke
  Executive Director, Administration . . . . Robert J. Dugan
  Executive Director, Finance . . . . Kathleen F. Bramwell
  Executive Director, Office of Research Compliance and Integrity. . . . . Debbi Gilad, J.D.
  Executive Director, Information Services. . . . . Janet Lind
  Executive Director, Space Planning and Operations. . . . . Eric M. Weckel
  Executive Director, Research Support Services. . . . . Marianne Achenbach
  Executive Director, Faculty Affairs and Professional Development . . . . Victoria A. Mulhern
  Executive Director, Strategic Planning. . . . . James R. Cunningham
  Director, Decision Support and Analysis . . . . Lynn K. Meaney
  Director, Biomedical Library. . . . . Barbara Cavanaugh
Chief Advancement Officer . . . . Katharine J. Griffo
Senior Director, Alumni Development and Alumni Relations . . . . Vanessa Marinari
Associate Dean, Resource Development . . . . John Glick, M.D.

Department and Division or Section Chairs

Basic Sciences

Biochemistry and Biophysics. . . . . Mark A. Lemmon, Ph.D.
Biostatistics and Epidemiology . . . . Brian L. Strom, M.D.
Cancer Biology . . . . Lewis A. Chodosh, M.D., Ph.D.
Cell and Developmental Biology. . . . . Jonathan A. Epstein, M.D.
Genetics . . . . Stephen A. Liebhaber, M.D. (Interim)
Medical Ethics and Health Policy . . . . Ezekiel J. Emanuel, M.D., Ph.D.
Microbiology. . . . . Robert W. Doms, M.D., Ph.D.
Neuroscience. . . . . Jonathan A. Raper, Ph.D. (Interim)
Pharmacology . . . . Garret A. FitzGerald, M.D.
Physiology. . . . . H. Lee Sweeney, Ph.D.

Clinical Sciences

Anesthesiology and Critical Care . . . . Lee A. Fleisher, M.D.
Dermatology . . . . George Cotsarelis, M.D.
Emergency Medicine . . . . Jill M. Baren, M.D.
Family Medicine and Community Health . . . . Marjorie A. Bowman, M.D.
Medicine. . . . . Richard P. Shannon, M.D.
  Cardiovascular Medicine. . . . . Michael S. Parmacek, M.D.
  Endocrinology, Diabetes, and Metabolism . . . . Mitchell A. Lazar, M.D., Ph.D.
  Experimental Therapeutics. . . . . Garret A. FitzGerald, M.D.
  Gastroenterology . . . . Anil K. Rustgi, M.D.
  General Internal Medicine . . . . Katrina Armstrong, M.D.
  Geriatrics Medicine . . . . Jerry C. Johnson, M.D.
  Hematology and Oncology . . . . Lynn M. Schuchter, M.D.
  Infectious Diseases . . . . Harvey M. Friedman, M.D.
  Medical Genetics . . . . Reed E. Pyeritz, M.D., Ph.D.
  Pulmonary Allergy and Critical Care . . . . John H. Hansen-Flaschen, M.D.
  Renal Electrolyte and Hypertension . . . . Lawrence B. Holzman, M.D.
  Rheumatology . . . . Sharon L. Kolasinski, M.D. (Interim)
  Sleep Medicine. . . . . Allan I. Pack, M.D., Ph.D.
Neurology. . . . . H. Branch Coslett, M.D. (Interim)
Neurosurgery. . . . . M. Sean Grady, M.D.
Obstetrics and Gynecology. . . . . Deborah A. Driscoll, M.D.
Ophthalmology . . . . Joan M. O'Brien, M.D.
Orthopaedic Surgery. . . . . L. Scott Levin, M.D.
Otorhinolaryngology-Head and Neck Surgery . . . . Bert W. O'Malley, M.D.
Pathology and Laboratory Medicine . . . . David B. Roth, M.D, Ph.D.
Pediatrics . . . . Alan R. Cohen, M.D.
Physical Medicine and Rehabilitation . . . . Timothy R. Dillingham, M.D., M.S.
Psychiatry . . . . Dwight L. Evans, M.D.
Radiation Oncology. . . . . Stephen Hahn, M.D.
Radiology . . . . R. Nick Bryan, M.D., Ph.D.
Surgery. . . . . Jeffrey A. Drebin, M.D., Ph.D.

193

University of Pittsburgh School of Medicine
Alan Magee Scaife Hall of the Health Professions
3550 Terrace Street
Pittsburgh, Pennsylvania 15261
412-648-9891 (admissions); 412-648-9040 (student affairs);
412-648-8975 (dean's office); 412-648-1236 (fax)
Web site: www.medschool.pitt.edu

The school of medicine was originally chartered in 1886 as the Western Pennsylvania Medical College and, in 1892, became affiliated with the Western University of Pennsylvania. In 1908, its name was changed to the school of medicine of the University of Pittsburgh. The University of Pittsburgh became a state-related institution in 1966. The medical school is located on the university campus.

Type: private
2011 total enrollment: 629
Clinical facilities: University of Pittsburgh Medical Center (UPMC) includes: Children's Hospital of Pittsburgh of UPMC, Eye and Ear Institute, Magee Womens Hospital of UPMC, UPMC Presbyterian-Shadyside, Western Psychiatric Institute and Clinic as well as UPMC community hospitals, the VA Pittsburgh Health System, and international venues.

University Officials

Chancellor . . . . Mark A. Nordenberg
Provost and Senior Vice Chancellor . . . . Patricia E. Beeson, Ph.D.
Senior Vice Chancellor, Health Sciences. . . . . Arthur S. Levine, M.D.
Associate Senior Vice Chancellor for Clinical
 Policy and Planning, Health Sciences . . . . Loren H. Roth, M.D.
Associate Senior Vice Chancellor, Health Sciences Administration . . . . Jeffrey L. Masnick
Associate Senior Vice Chancellor for Science
 Strategy and Planning, Health Sciences . . . . Jeremy Berg, Ph.D.
Associate Vice Chancellor for Cancer Research. . . . . Nancy E. Davidson, M.D.
Associate Vice Chancellor for Basic Biomedical Research . . . . Michelle S. Broido, Ph.D.
Associate Vice Chancellor for Clinical Research . . . . Steven E. Reis, M.D.
Associate Vice Chancellor for Academic Affairs. . . . . Margaret C. McDonald, Ph.D.
Associate Vice Chancellor for Continuing
 Education and Industry Relations . . . . Barbara E. Barnes, M.D.
Associate Vice Chancellor for Diversity Programs, Health Sciences. . . . . Paula K. Davis
Associate Vice Chancellor for Health Policy and
 Planning, Health Sciences . . . . A. Everette James, J.D.

Medical School Administrative Staff

Dean. . . . . Arthur S. Levine, M.D.
Vice Dean . . . . Steven L. Kanter, M.D.
Associate Dean for Admissions and Financial Aid . . . . Beth M. Piraino, M.D.
Associate Dean for Faculty Affairs. . . . . Ann E. Thompson, M.D.
Associate Dean for Graduate Medical Education. . . . . Rita M. Patel, M.D.
Associate Dean for Graduate Studies . . . . John P. Horn, Ph.D.
Associate Dean for Medical Education . . . . John F. Mahoney, M.D.
Associate Dean for the Medical Scientist Training Program. . . . . . . Clayton A. Wiley, M.D., Ph.D.
Associate Dean for Medical Student Research . . . . David J. Hackman, M.D., Ph.D.
Associate Dean for Postdoctoral Affairs. . . . . Darlene F. Zellers
Associate Dean for Student Affairs . . . . Joan Harvey, M.D.
Assistant Dean for Graduate Medical Education . . . . Frank J. Kroboth, M.D.
Assistant Dean for Student Affairs and Diversity . . . . Chentis Pettigrew, Ph.D.
Assistant Dean for Veterans Administrative Affairs. . . . . Ali F. Sonel, M.D.

Department and Division or Section Chairs

Centers and Institutes

Thomas E. Starzl Transplantation Institute . . . . Fadi G. Lakkis, M.D. (Sci. Dir.)
University of Pittsburgh Cancer Institute. . . . . Nancy E. Davidson, M.D. (Director)
McGowan Institute for Regenerative Medicine . . . . William Wagner, M.D. (Interim)
Cardiovascular Institute . . . . Barry London, M.D., Ph.D. (Director)
Drug Discovery Institute. . . . . D. Lansing Taylor, Ph.D. (Director)
Systems Neuroscience Institute. . . . . Peter L. Strick, Ph.D. (Director)

University of Pittsburgh School of Medicine: PENNSYLVANIA

Basic Sciences

Biomedical Informatics . . . . Michael J. Becich, M.D., Ph.D.
Cell Biology and Physiology . . . . Alexander D. Sorkin, Ph.D.
Computational and Systems Biology . . . . Ivet Bahar, Ph.D.
Developmental Biology . . . . Cecilia Lo, Ph.D.
Immunology . . . . Olivera J. Finn, Ph.D.
Microbiology and Molecular Genetics . . . . Thomas E. Smithgall, Ph.D.
Neurobiology . . . . Susan G. Amara, Ph.D.
Pharmacology and Chemical Biology . . . . Bruce A. Freeman, Ph.D.
Structural Biology . . . . Angela M. Gronenborn, Ph.D.

Clinical Sciences

Anesthesiology . . . . John P. Williams, M.D.
Cardiothoracic Surgery . . . . James D. Luketich, M.D.
Critical Care Medicine . . . . Derek Angus, M.D.
Dermatology . . . . Louis D. Falo, M.D., Ph.D.
Emergency Medicine . . . . Donald M. Yealy, M.D.
Family Medicine . . . . Jeannette E. South-Paul, M.D.
Medicine . . . . John J. Reilly, Jr., M.D.
   Cardiology . . . . Barry London, M.D., Ph.D.
   Endocrinology and Metabolism . . . . Andrew F. Stewart, M.D.
   Gastroenterology . . . . David C. Whitcomb, M.D., Ph.D.
   General Internal Medicine . . . . Wishwa N. Kapoor, M.D., M.P.H.
   Geriatric Medicine . . . . Neil M. Resnick, M.D.
   Hematology and Oncology . . . . Edward Chu, M.D.
   Infectious Diseases . . . . John W. Mellors, M.D.
   Pulmonary and Critical Care . . . . Mark T. Gladwin, M.D.
   Renal-Electrolyte . . . . Thomas R. Kleyman, M.D.
   Rheumatology . . . . Larry W. Moreland, M.D.
Neurological Surgery . . . . Robert M. Friedlander, M.D.
Neurology . . . . Lawrence R. Wechsler, M.D.
Obstetrics, Gynecology, and Reproductive Sciences . . . . W. Allen Hogge, M.D.
Ophthalmology . . . . Joel S. Schuman, M.D.
Orthopedic Surgery . . . . Freddie H. Fu, M.D.
Otolaryngology . . . . Jonas T. Johnson, M.D.
Pathology . . . . George K. Michalopoulos, M.D., Ph.D.
   Anatomic/Surgical Pathology . . . . Samuel A. Yousem, M.D.
   Laboratory Medicine . . . . Alan Wells, M.D., D.M.S.
Pediatrics . . . . David H. Perlmutter, M.D.
   Adolescent Medicine . . . . Elizabeth Miller, M.D., Ph.D.
   Cardiology . . . . Steven Webber, M.B.Ch.B., M.R.C.P.
   Child Neurology . . . . Ira Bergman, M.D.
   Endocrinology . . . . Dorothy J. Becker, MBBCh
   Gastroenterology . . . . Mark E. Lowe, M.D., Ph.D.
   General Academic Pediatrics . . . . Alejandro Hoberman, M.D.
   Medical Genetics . . . . Gerard Vockley, M.D., Ph.D.
   Hematology and Oncology . . . . A. Kim Ritchey, M.D.
   Infectious Disease . . . . Toni Darville, M.D.
   Neonatology and Developmental Biology . . . . Gary A. Silverman, M.D., Ph.D.
   Nephrology . . . . Carlton M. Bates, M.D.
Physical Medicine and Rehabilitation . . . . Michael L. Boninger, M.D.
Psychiatry . . . . David A. Lewis, M.D.
   Adult Psychiatry . . . . Kurt Ackerman, M.D., Ph.D.
   Child and Adolescent Psychiatry, Autism, and
      Developmental Disorders . . . . Martin J. Lubetsky, M.D.
   Geriatrics . . . . Jules R. Rosen, M.D.
Radiation Oncology . . . . Joel S. Greenberger, M.D.
Radiology . . . . Kyongtae (Ty) Bae, M.D., Ph.D.
Surgery . . . . Timothy R. Billiar, M.D.
   General Surgery . . . . Andrew Peitzman, M.D.
   Pediatric Surgery . . . . George K. Gittes, M.D.
   Plastic Surgery . . . . J. Peter Rubin, M.D.
   Surgical Oncology . . . . David Bartlett, M.D.
   Transplant Surgery . . . . Abhinav Humar, M.D.
   Vascular Surgery . . . . Michel Makaroun, M.D.
Urology . . . . Joel B. Nelson, M.D.

Ponce School of Medicine and Health Sciences

P.O. Box 7004
Ponce, Puerto Rico 00732
787-840-2575 (general information); 787-844-3710 (dean's office); 787-840-9756 (fax)
E-mail: mleon@psm.edu
Web site: www.psm.edu

The Ponce School of Medicine and Health Sciences is one of the premier medical schools with Hispanic heritage in the entire Western Hemisphere. Thirty years after its unique foundation by Ponce's community action and resolve, Ponce School of Medicine and Health Sciences has gained extraordinary recognition and prestige in Puerto Rico and abroad for its educational, service, and research achievements. It now holds nationally accredited graduate programs in the disciplines of medicine, clinical psychology, and biomedical sciences, and a master's degree program in public health.

Type: private
2011 total enrollment: 597
Clinical facilities: Damas Hospital, Dr. Pila Metropolitan Hospital, Dr. Tito Mattei Metropolitan Hospital, La Concepción Hospital, San Lucas Hospital, Hospital Oncológico Andrés Grillasca, First Hospital Panamericano, San Cristobal Hospital, Med Center, San Antonio Hospital, Dr. Ramón E Betances University Hospital; VA Medical Center (San Juan), MultiMed, CSCO Aguadilla General Hospital, CSCO Mayaguez Hospital, San Lucas Guayama, Inc, Hospital, Castañer Clinic, Castañer Hospital, VA Clinic-Ponce, La Casa del Veterano.

Medical School Administrative Staff

President. . . . . Joxel García, M.D., M.B.A.
Dean of Medicine . . . . Joxel García, M.D., M.B.A.
Associate Dean for Academic Affairs. . . . . Olga Rodriguez, M.D.
Senior Vice President and Executive Dean for Administration and Finance . . . . . . Reinaldo Diaz
Associate Dean for Faculty and Clinical Affairs . . . . Raúl A. Armstrong, M.D.
Dean of Health Sciences . . . . Olga Rodriguez, M.D.
Provost . . . . Leon Ferder, M.D. (Acting)
Medical Director, Ambulatory Clinics . . . . Olga Rodriguez, M.D.
Assistant Dean for Behavioral Health Services. . . . . José E. Cangiano, Ph.D.
Assistant Dean for Administration and Finance. Bethzaida Cruz
Assistant Dean for Student Affairs. . . . . Arvin Báez, Ph.D.
Director of Admissions. . . . . Wanda Vélez, M.D.
Assistant Dean for Education . . . . Gladys Pereles, Ed.D.
Director, Office of Continued Medical Education . . . . Augusto Sepúlveda, M.D.
Director, Office of Development and Community Relations. . . . . María E. Avilés-Albors
Director, Office of Graduate Medical Education (Ponce) . . . . Luisa Alvarado, M.D.
Director, Office of Graduate Medical Education
     (Mayaguez) . . . . Norman Ramirez Lluch, M.D.
Finance Director . . . . Héctor Pérez
Registrar . . . . Clarimir Castro
Librarian. . . . . Carmen G. Malavet
Director of Student Financial Aid. . . . . Héctor Pérez
Director of Personnel . . . . Evelyn Lugo
Budget Director and Legal Counselor. . . . . Waleska Murphy

Ponce School of Medicine and Health Sciences: PUERTO RICO

Department and Division or Section Chairs

Basic Sciences

Anatomy . . . . Juan B. Fernández, Ph.D.
Cell Biology . . . . Maritza La Paix, M.D.
Biochemistry . . . . José Torres, Ph.D.
Microbiology . . . . Nilda Zapata, M.D.
Infectious Diseases . . . . Nilda Zapata, M.D.
Physiology, Pharmacology, and Toxicology . . . . León Ferder, M.D.

Clinical Sciences

Family and Community Medicine . . . . Georgina Aguirre (Acting)
Preventive Medicine . . . . Iván Iriarte, M.D.
Medicine . . . . Miguel Magraner, M.D.
Obstetrics and Gynecology . . . . Joaquin Laboy, M.D.
Pathology . . . . Adalberto Mendoza, M.D.
Pediatrics . . . . Ivonne Galarza, M.D.
Psychiatry . . . . Pedro Castaing, M.D.
Surgery . . . . Aníbal Torres, M.D.

Ph.D. Program in Biomedical Sciences

Director . . . . José Torres, Ph.D.

Public Health Program

Director . . . . E. Anne Peterson, M.D.

Psy.D. Program

Director . . . . José Pons, Ph.D.

Special Programs

Clinical Research Center . . . . Elizabeth Barranco, M.D.

*Includes all programs: M.D., Ph.D., Psy.D., and M.P.H.

Universidad Central del Caribe School of Medicine

P.O. Box 60-327
Bayamón, Puerto Rico 00960-6032
787-798-3001; 787-269-4510 (dean's office); 787-269-1352 (fax)
E-mail: jose.ginel@uccaribe.edu
Web site: www.uccaribe.edu

The school of medicine of Universidad Central del Caribe started operations in September 1976. All basic science and clinical facilities are located on the grounds of the Dr. Ramón Ruiz Arnau University Hospital at Bayamón, Puerto Rico. The new Basic Sciences Building started operation in August 1990.

Type: private
2011 total enrollment: 253
Clinical facilities: Dr. Ramón Ruiz Arnau University Hospital, San Juan City Hospital, San Pablo Hospital, First Hospital Panamericano, Family Practice Centers Northeast Health Region, San Jorge Children's Hospital, Veteran's Administration Hospital, Hospital Interamericano de Medicina Avanzada, P.R. Children's Hospital, Hospital Hermanos Melendez.

University Officials

President of the University . . . . José Ginel Rodríguez, M.D.
President of the Board of Trustees . . . . Joaquin Arbona
Dean of Academic Affairs . . . . Nereida Diaz, Ph.D.
Dean for Admissions and Student Affairs . . . . Omar Perez, Ph.D.
Dean of Administration . . . . Emilia Soto
Institutional Development Office . . . . Yvonne Corsino

Medical School Administrative Staff

Dean . . . . José Ginel Rodríguez, M.D.
Associate Dean of Medicine . . . . Zilka Ríos
Associate Dean of Clinical and Faculty Affairs . . . . Harry Mercado, M.D.
Associate Dean for Research and Graduate Studies . . . . Luis Cubano, Ph.D.
Director of CME . . . . Frances García, M.D.
Director of GME . . . . Frances García, M.D.
Admissions Officer . . . . Irma Cordero
Counselor . . . . Yari M. Marrero
Financial Aid Officer . . . . Lisandra Viera
Registrar . . . . Nilda Montanez
Librarian . . . . Mildred Rivera
Office of Assessment and Academic Research . . . . Michael Vélez
Office of Curriculum and Faculty Development . . . . Elsa Gilbes
Director of Learning and Information Resources Center . . . . Legier Rojas, Ph.D.

Universidad Central del Caribe School of Medicine: PUERTO RICO

Center for the Development of Clinical Skills . . . . José L. Oliver, D.M.D.

Department and Division or Section Chairs

Office of Elective Courses . . . . Gustavo Flores

Basic Sciences

Anatomy and Cell Biology . . . . Sofía Jiménez, Ph.D.
Biochemistry . . . . Richard M. Hann, M.D.
Microbiology and Immunology. . . . . Eddy O. Ríos-Olivares, Ph.D.
Neuroscience. . . . . Maria Bykhovskaia, Ph.D.
Pharmacology . . . . Hector Maldonado, Ph.D.
Physiology . . . . Priscila Sanabria, Ph.D.

Clinical Sciences

Family Medicine and Community Health . . . . Eric Gonzalez, M.D.
Internal Medicine . . . . Melba Colón, M.D.
   Cardiovascular* . . . . Elvin Rivera, M.D.
   Critical Care* . . . . Juan Ruiz, M.D.
   Dermatology*. . . . . Limarie Aguila, M.D.
   Endocrinology* . . . . Luis M. Reyes, M.D.
   Gastroenterology* . . . . Roberto Vendrell, M.D.
   Hematology and Oncology* . . . . Robert Hunter, M.D.
   Infectious Disease* . . . . Melba Colón, M.D.
   Nephrology* . . . . Luis Quesada, M.D.
   Neurology* . . . . Damaris Torres, M.D.
   Pneumology* . . . . Miriam Melendez-Rosa, M.D.
   Rhcumatology* . . . . Salvador Vila, M.D.
Obstetrics and Gynecology. . . . . Stanley Asensio, M.D.
Pathology and Laboratory Medicine . . . . Angelissa Franceschini, M.D.
Pediatrics . . . . Fermín Sánchez, M.D.
   Allergy* . . . . Carmen Acantilado, M.D.
   Cardiology* . . . . Rafael Villavicencio, M.D.
   Critical Care* . . . . Gilberto Puig, M.D.
   Developmental Pediatrics* . . . . Jorge Arzola-Rivera, M.D.
   Endocrinology* . . . . Fermín Sánchez, M.D.
   Gastroenterology* . . . . Jaime Rosado, M.D.
   Hematology and Oncology* . . . . Carmen L. Bartolomei, M.D.
   Infectology* . . . . Haydeé Garcia, M.D.
   Neonatology* . . . . Alvaro Santaella, M.D.
   Nephrology* . . . . Melvin Bonilla, M.D.
   Neurology* . . . . Carlos R. Laó, M.D.
   Pneumology* . . . . William de la Paz, M.D.
   Rheumatology . . . . Annette Lopez, M.D.
Psychiatry . . . . José A. Franceschini, M.D.
Radiology . . . . Zoraida Estela, M.D.
Surgery . . . . Julio Soto, M.D.
   Emergency Medicine . . . . Juan Garcia-Castro, M.D.

*Specialty without organizational autonomy.

University of Puerto Rico School of Medicine

Medical Sciences Campus
P.O. Box 365067
San Juan, Puerto Rico 00936-5067
787-758-2525; 787-765-2363 (dean's office); 787-756-8475 (dean's fax)
E-mail: pedro.santiago9@upr.edu
Web site: www.md.rcm.upr.edu/

The University of Puerto Rico School of Medicine accepted its first class in August 1950. The school of medicine developed originally from the school of tropical medicine of the university (which had been established under joint auspices with Columbia University in 1924). Since 1972, the school of medicine has been located on the medical sciences campus on the grounds of the Puerto Rico Medical Center, two miles from the main university campus at Rio Piedras.

Type: public
2011 total enrollment: 431
Clinical facilities: University Hospital, University Pediatric Hospital, Veterans Administration Medical Center, U.P.R. University Hospital, Pavia Hospital, Auxillo Mutuo Hospital, Perea Hospital, De La Concepción Hospital, San Pablo Hospital, First PanAmerican Hospital, San Antonio Hospital, San Juan Oncological Hospital, Cardiovascular Center, San Juan City Hospital and Puerto Rico Medical Center. Nineteen primary care settings located throughout the island are also in use.

University Officials

President, Board of Trustees . . . . Ygri Rivera de Martinez, J.D.
President, University of Puerto Rico . . . . Miguel A. Munoz, Ph.D.

Medical Sciences Campus Officials

Chancellor . . . . Rafael Rodriguez Mercado, M.D.
Dean of Academic Affairs. . . . . Ilka Rios, D.M.D.
Dean of Students. . . . . Maria M. Hernández, Ph.D.
Dean of Administration . . . . Eleuterio Pomales
Librarian. . . . . Irma Quinones, Ed.D.
Registrar . . . . Reynaldo Pomales

Medical School Administrative Staff

Dean. . . . . Pedro J. Santiago-Borrero, M.D. (Acting)
Associate Dean for Clinical Affairs . . . . Yolanda Gómez, M.D.
Associate Dean for Academic Affairs. . . . . Guido E. Santacana, Ph.D.
Associate Dean for Biomedical Sciences and
    Director, Graduate School . . . . Jorge D. Miranda, Ph.D.
Director, Curriculum Office. . . . . Maria Padilla, M.D.
Associate Dean for Student Affairs . . . . Gladys González, M.D.
Chair, Admissions Committee. . . . . Gladys González, M.D.
Associate Dean for Graduate Medical Education . . . . Yolanda Gómez, M.D.
Director, Evaluation and Research in
    Medical Education Office . . . . Irma Rivera
Chair, Planning and Development Committee . . . . Pedro J. Santiago-Borrero, M.D.
Associate Dean for Administrative Affairs . . . . Roberto Acevedo, M.H.S.A.

Department and Division or Section Chairs

Basic Sciences

Anatomy and Neurobiology. . . . . Maria Sosa, Ph.D.
Biochemistry and Nutrition . . . . José Rodríguez, Ph.D.
Microbiology and Medical Zoology. . . . . Guillermo Vázquez, M.D.
Pathology . . . . Maria Sante, M.D.
Pharmacology and Toxicology . . . . Walmor C. De Mello, M.D., Ph.D.
Physiology and Biophysics . . . . Nelson Escobales, Ph.D.

University of Puerto Rico School of Medicine: PUERTO RICO

Clinical Sciences

Anesthesiology . . . . Miguel Marrero, M.D.
Dermatology . . . . Néstor Sanchez, M.D.
Family Medicine . . . . Richard de Andino, M.D.
Medicine . . . . Ivonne Jiminéz, M.D. (Acting)
   Cardiology* . . . . Mario R. García-Palmieri, M.D.
   Endocrinology* . . . . Miriam Allende, M.D.
   Gastroenterology* . . . . Pablo Costas, M.D.
   General Internal Medicine* . . . . Carlos González, M.D.
   Geriatrics . . . . Juan Rosado, M.D.
   Hematology* . . . . Eileen Pacheco, M.D.
   Infectious Diseases* . . . . Carlos Sánchez, M.D.
   Nephrology* . . . . Rafael Burgos-Calderón, M.D.
   Neurology . . . . Carlos Luciano, M.D.
   Pulmonary Diseases* . . . . Angel F. Laureano, M.D.
   Rheumatology* . . . . Luis M. Vilá, M.D.
Obstetrics and Gynecology . . . . Juana Rivera, M.D.
Ophthalmology . . . . Luis Serrano, M.D.
Pediatrics . . . . Melvin Bonilla, M.D.
   Cardiology . . . . Angel F. Espinosa, M.D.
   Emergency Care* . . . . Milagros Pumarejo, M.D.
   Endocrinology* . . . . Lilliam González-Pijem, M.D.
   Gastroenterology . . . . David Fernández, M.D.
   General Pediatrics* . . . . Debora H. Silva, M.D.
   Hematology and Oncology . . . . Melvin Bonilla, M.D. (Acting)
   Infectious Diseases . . . . Inés Esquilin, M.D.
   Intensive Care . . . . Alicia Fernandez-Seins, M.D.
   Medical Genetics* . . . . Maria del Carmen González, M.D.
   Neonatology* . . . . Marta Valcárcel, M.D.
   Nephrology* . . . . Juan O. Peréz, M.D.
   Neurology . . . . Marisel Vázquez, M.D.
   Pneumology* . . . . Maria Alvarez, M.D.
Physical Medicine, Rehabilitation, and Sports Medicine . . . . William Micheo, M.D.
Psychiatry . . . . Lelis Nazario, M.D.
   Child Psychiatry* . . . . Lelis Nazario, M.D.
   General Psychiatry* . . . . Luz N. Colón, M.D.
Radiological Sciences . . . . Frieda Silva, M.D.
   Diagnostic Radiology . . . . Edgar Colón, M.D.
   Nuclear Medicine . . . . Frieda Silva, M.D.
   Radiotherapy . . . . José Santana, M.D.
Surgery . . . . Segundo Rodriguez, M.D. (Acting)
   Neurosurgery . . . . Juan Vigo, M.D. (Acting)
   Orthopedics . . . . Manuel Garcia, M.D.
   Otolaryngology . . . . Carlos González Aquino, M.D.
   Urology . . . . Antonio Puras, M.D.
Emergency Medicine . . . . Juan González, M.D.

Special Programs

Animal Resources Unit . . . . Malween Martinez, D.V.M.
Biomedical Sciences Core Laboratories . . . . Walter Silva, Ph.D.
Caribbean Primate Research Center . . . . Edmundo Kraiselburd, M.D.
Clinical Research Center . . . . Julio Benabe, M.D.
Clinical Skills Laboratory . . . . Nerian Ortiz, M.D.
Comprehensive Cancer Center . . . . Reynold López, M.D.
Center for Informatic and Technology . . . . José L. Quiñones
Neurobiology Laboratory . . . . Steven Treistman, Ph.D.
Raffucci Surgical Research Laboratory . . . . Reynold López, M.D.
Trauma Center . . . . Pablo Rodriguez, M.D.

*Specialty without organizational autonomy.

201

San Juan Bautista School of Medicine

P.O. Box 4968
Caguas, Puerto Rico 00726-4968
787-743-3038 x 231 (Dean's Office); 787-743-3038 x 225 (Student Affairs' Office);
787-746-3093 (fax)
Web site: www.sanjuanbautista.edu

The San Juan Bautista School of Medicine (SJBSM) was founded in 1978 with the mission to advance the health of the community by focusing on community medicine and the need for having more physicians serving vulnerable and medically underserved populations. Geographically located in the city of Caguas, the School has an established network of ambulatory clinics and hospitals for clerkship rotations and clinical electives that include local and national facilities. The latter care facilities by agreement and tradition are closely integrated with the SJBSM faculty. The School has expanded its academic offers to have medical, public health, and nursing education under the same organizational structure; expecting to develop an integrative educational model that facilitates the teaching of team-based care.

Type: private
2011 total enrollment: 231
Clinical facilities: Hospital teaching facilities: Mennonite Health System, including Caugas Hospital, Cayey Hospital, Aibonito Hospital, and CIMA; San Juan City Hospital; VA Caribbean Healthcare System; Metro-Pavia Hospital, Pavia Hato Rey Hospital, First PanAmerican Hospital; Psychiatric Correctional Health Services Hospital; Ryder Memorial Hospital; Santa Rosa Hospital; Professional Hospital; University of Puerto Rico clinical teaching facilities. Primary care settings: Gurabo Community Health Center; COSSMA; Mennonite Community Health Centers; SANOS, and Center for Family Health and Geriatrics - Luis Izquierdo Mora.

Medical School Administrative Staff

President, Board of Trustees . . . . Aracelis Arroyo, M.D.
President and Dean . . . . Yocasta Brugal-Mena, M.D.
Dean for Academic Affairs . . . . Miriam Marquez, M.D.
Dean for Administration and Human Resources . . . . Carlos Fco. Abreu
Chief Financial Officer . . . . Aurea Vázquez
Associate Dean for Student Affairs . . . . Nelly Rivera, Ed.D.
Associate Dean for Graduate Medical Education . . . . Myrna Morges, M.D.
Dean of Students . . . . Nelly Rivera, Ed.D.
Associate Dean for Research . . . . Irvin M. Maldonado-Rivera, Ph.D. (Interim)
Library Director . . . . Carlos A. Altamirano
Associate Dean for Biomedical Sciences . . . . Mirian Ramos, M.D. (Interim)
Office of Financial Aid . . . . Beatriz De Leon Rivera
Associate Dean for Clinical Sciences . . . . Miriam Ramos, M.D.
Registrar . . . . Lissette Torres
Admissions Officer . . . . Jaymi Sánchez
Financial Aid Officer . . . . Beatriz De Leon-Rivera

Medical Faculty

Library Director . . . . Carlos A. Altamirano

Department Chairs

Basic Sciences

Anatomy . . . . (Recruiting)
Biochemistry and Pharmacology . . . . Marielis Rivera, Ph.D.
Microbiology . . . . Shirley D. Valentin, Ph.D.
Physiology and Pathology . . . . José Santiago, Ph.D.

Clinical Sciences

Clinical Skills . . . . Manuel Pérez Pabón, M.D.
Anesthesiology . . . . José Rodriguez, M.D.

San Juan Bautista School of Medicine: PUERTO RICO

Emergency Medicine . . . . Wilfredo Cordero, M.D.
Family Medicine . . . . Edgardo Soto, M.D.
Internal Medicine . . . . Edgardo Cartagena, M.D.
Obstetrics and Gynecology . . . . Rafael Figueroa-De Los Reyes, M.D.
Pathology . . . . Yocasta Brugal, M.D.
Pediatrics . . . . Milagros Reyes, M.D.
Psychiatry . . . . (Recruiting)
Radiology . . . . Silverio Perez, M.D.
Surgery . . . . Jorge Cordero, M.D.
Family Medicine Clerkship Coordinator . . . . Rolance Chavier, M.D.
Internal Medicine Clerkship Coordinator . . . . Luz V. Alicea, M.D.
Obstetrics/Gynecology Clerkship Coordinator . . . . Ruben Guadalupe, M.D.
Pediatric Clerkship Coordinator . . . . Michelle Moringlane, M.D.
Psychiatry Clerkship Coordinator . . . . Myrta N. Sifonte, M.D.
Surgery Clerkship Coordinator . . . . Carols Roque, M.D.

Training Programs

Director, Graduate Medical Education . . . . Myrna Borges, M.D.

The Warren Alpert Medical School of Brown University

97 Waterman Street
Providence, Rhode Island 02912
401-863-3991; 401-863-3330 (dean's office); 401-863-3431 (fax)
Web site: http://bms.brown.edu

Brown University was founded in 1764. Its first M.D. program, initiated in 1811, was temporarily suspended in 1827. The master of medical science program was begun in 1963, and the M.D.-conferring program started in 1973. Its first class of physicians was graduated in June 1975. The medical school operates in conjunction with seven hospitals in the Providence metropolitan area.

Type: private
2011 total enrollment: 413
Clinical facilities: Butler Hospital, Memorial Hospital of Rhode Island, Miriam Hospital, Women and Infants Hospital, Rhode Island Hospital, Veterans Administration Medical Center, Bradley Hospital.

University Officials

President. . . . . Ruth J. Simmons, Ph.D.
Provost . . . . Mark S. Schlissel, M.D., Ph.D.
Dean of the Faculty . . . . Kevin McLaughlin, Ph.D.

Medical School Administrative Staff

Dean of Medicine and Biological Sciences . . . . Edward J. Wing, M.D.
Executive Dean for Administration. . . . . Lindsay J. Graham
Senior Associate Dean for Biomedical Advancement . . . . John A. Perry, C.F.R.E.
Associate Dean for Biology. . . . . Edward Hawrot, Ph.D.
Associate Dean of Medicine (Public Health and Public Policy) . . . . Terrie Wetle, Ph.D.
Associate Dean for Medical Education . . . . Philip A. Gruppuso, M.D.
Associate Dean for Academic Affairs. . . . . Michele G. Cyr, M.D.
Associate Dean for Graduate and Postdoctoral Studies . . . . Elizabeth Harrington, Ph.D.
Associate Dean of Medicine (Minority Affairs) . . . . Emma Simmons, M.D., M.P.H.
Associate Dean for Clinical Affairs . . . . Glenn A. Tung, M.D., F.A.C.R.
Associate Dean of Medicine (Women in
  Medicine and Graduate Medical Education) . . . . Michele G. Cyr, M.D.
Associate Dean of Medicine (Minority
  Recruitment and Retention) . . . . Mercedes Domenech, M.D., Ph.D.
Associate Dean of Medicine (Program in Liberal Medical Education) . . . . . . Julianne Y. Ip, M.D.
Associate Dean of Medicine (Continuing
  Medical Education) . . . . Glenn A. Tung, M.D., F.A.C.R.
Assistant Dean of Medicine (Advising) . . . . Anne Cushing-Brescia, M.D.
Assistant Dean of Medicine (Advising) . . . . Timothy M. Empkie, M.D.
Associate Dean for Finance and Planning. . . . . James W. Patti, M.B.A.
Director, Medical Student Affairs . . . . Alexandra Morang-Jackson
Director, Admissions . . . . Barbara Fuller
Director, Financial Aid. . . . . Linda Gillette
Associate Dean of Biological Sciences. . . . . Marjorie Thompson, Ph.D.
Associate Dean of Medicine (Admissions) . . . . Arnold-Peter C. Weiss, M.D.
Director of Biomed Advancement Communications . . . . Sarah Baldwin-Beneich

The Warren Alpert Medical School of Brown University: RHODE ISLAND

Assistant Director of Medical Student Affairs. . . . . Emily Green
Director of Medical Education Administration . . . . Kathleen Chien

Department and Division or Section Chairs

Basic Sciences

Ecology and Evolutionary Biology. . . . . Mark D. Bertness, Ph.D.
Molecular Biology, Cell Biology, and Biochemistry . . . . Kimberly Mowry, Ph.D.
Molecular Microbiology and Immunology. . . . . Laurent Brossay, Ph.D. (Interim)
Molecular Pharmacology, Physiology, and Biotechnology. . . . . Wayne Bowen, Ph.D.
Neuroscience. . . . . Barry W. Connors, Ph.D.

Clinical Sciences

Clinical Neurology. . . . . James Gilchrist, M.D. (Interim)
Clinical Neurosurgery . . . . Garth R. Cosgrove, M.D.
Community Health . . . . Garth R. Cosgrove, M.D.
Dermatology . . . . Charles J. McDonald, M.D.
Diagnostic Imaging . . . . John J. Cronan, M.D.
Emergency Medicine . . . . Brian J. Zink, M.D.
Family Medicine . . . . Jeffrey M. Borkan, M.D., Ph.D.
Medicine. . . . . Louis B. Rice, M.D.
   The Memorial Hospital of Rhode Island . . . . Louis B. Rice, M.D.
   The Miriam Hospital . . . . Louis B. Rice, M.D.
   Rhode Island Hospital . . . . Louis B. Rice, M.D.
   Veterans Administration Medical Center . . . . Louis B. Rice, M.D.
   Women and Infants Hospital . . . . Louis B. Rice, M.D.
Obstetrics and Gynecology. . . . . Maureen Phipps, M.D. (Interim)
Orthopaedics. . . . . Michael Ehrlich, M.D.
   The Miriam Hospital . . . . Michael Ehrlich, M.D.
   Rhode Island Hospital . . . . Michael Ehrlich, M.D.
   Veterans Administration Medical Center . . . . Richard M. Terek, M.D.
Pathology and Laboratory Medicine . . . . Agnes B. Kane, M.D., Ph.D.
   The Memorial Hospital of Rhode Island . . . . Noubar Kessimian, M.D.
   The Miriam Hospital . . . . Ronald A. DeLellis, M.D.
   Rhode Island Hospital . . . . Ronald A. DeLellis, M.D.
   Women and Infants Hospital . . . . W. Dwayne Lawrence, M.D.
Pediatrics . . . . Robert B. Klein, M.D.
Psychiatry and Human Behavior. Steven Rasmussen, M.D. (Interim)
   Bradley Hospital. . . . . Gregory K. Fritz, M.D.
   Butler Hospital. . . . . Steven Rasmussen, M.D.
   The Miriam Hospital . . . . Richard J. Goldberg, M.D.
   Rhode Island Hospital . . . . Richard J. Goldberg, M.D.
   Veterans Administration Medical Center . . . . Michael Goldstein, M.D.
Radiation Medicine . . . . David E. Wazer, M.D.
Surgery . . . . William G. Cioffi, M.D.
   The Miriam Hospital . . . . Vacant
   Rhode Island Hospital . . . . William G. Cioffi, M.D.
   Veterans Administration Medical Center . . . . Michael P. Vezeridis, M.D.

Medical University of South Carolina College of Medicine
171 Ashley Avenue
Charleston, South Carolina 29425
843-792-2300; 843-792-2081 (dean's office); 843-792-2967 (fax)
Web site: www.musc.edu/com

Founded in 1824, the Medical College of South Carolina graduated its first class in 1825. In 1969, its name was changed to the Medical University of South Carolina.

Type: public
2011 total enrollment: 672
Clinical facilities: Charleston Memorial Hospital, Greenville Hospital System, McLeod Regional Medical Center, Medical University Hospital, Naval Regional Medical Center, Richland Memorial Hospital, Roper Hospital, St. Francis Xavier Hospital, Veterans Administration Medical Center (Charleston), Anderson Area Medical Center, Self Memorial Hospital, Spartanburg Regional Medical Center, Allendale County Hospital, Hampton General Hospital.

University Officials

President. . . . . Raymond S. Greenberg, M.D., Ph.D.
Vice President for Academic Affairs and Provost. . . . . Mark S. Sothmann, Ph.D.
Vice President for Medical Affairs. . . . . Etta D. Pisano, M.D.
Vice President for Finance and Administration. . . . . Lisa P. Montgomery
Vice President for Clinical Operations and
  Executive Director of the Medical Center . . . . W. Stuart Smith
Vice President for Development. . . . . Jim Fisher
Director of Libraries and Learning Resource Center. . . . . Thomas G. Basler, Ph.D.
Director of Office of Diversity . . . . Willette Burnham
Executive Director, Enrollment Services. . . . . George Ohlandt
University Counsel. . . . . Joseph C. Good, Jr.

Medical School Administrative Staff

Dean. . . . . Etta D. Pisano, M.D.
Senior Associate Dean, Research . . . . Craig Crosson, Ph.D.
Executive Senior Associate Dean, Clinical Affairs. . . . . John R. Feussner, M.D.
Senior Associate Dean, Clinical Affairs . . . . Bruce M. Elliott, M.D.
Senior Associate Dean, Medical Education . . . . Deborah Deas, M.D.
Associate Dean, Admissions . . . . Paul B. Underwood, M.D.
Associate Dean, Evaluation and Integration (Basic Sciences) . . . . Debra Hazen-Martin, Ph.D.
Associate Dean, Evaluation and Integration (Clinical Sciences) . . . . Donna Kern, M.D.
Associate Dean, Students . . . . Christopher Pelic, M.D.
Associate Dean, Graduate Medical Education . . . . Harry S. Clarke, M.D., Ph.D.
Associate Dean, Resident Inclusion and Diversity Education . . . . Wanda Gonsalves, M.D.
Associate Dean, Continuing Medical Education. . . . . Robert J. Malcolm, M.D.
Associate Dean for Faculty Affairs and Faculty Development . . . . Marc Chimowitz, M.B.Ch.B.
Associate Dean for Faculty Affairs and Faculty Development . . . . Gary Gilkeson, M.D.
Associate Dean for Faculty Affairs and Faculty Development . . . . Leonie Gordon, M.B.Ch.B.
Associate Dean for Faculty Affairs and Faculty Development . . . . Paul McDermott, Ph.D.
Associate Dean for Faculty Affairs and Faculty Development . . . . Daniel Smith, Ph.D.
Associate Dean, Finance. . . . . Stephen Valerio
Associate Dean, Administration and Planning. . . . . Robert Marriott
Assistant Dean, Academic Affairs . . . . Jennifer Nall
Associate Dean, Development. . . . . Terry Stanley
Associate Dean, Corporation, Foundation, and Organization Relations . . . . Helen Snow
Associate Dean, Clinical Research. . . . . Kathleen Brady, M.D., Ph.D.
Associate Dean, Interdisciplinary Research . . . . Andrew Kraft, M.D.
Associate Dean, Statewide Clinical Effectiveness Education . . . . John Schaefer, M.D.
Associate Dean, Area Health Education Consortium . . . . David R. Garr, M.D.
Associate Dean, Veteran Affairs . . . . Florence N. Hutchinson, M.D.

Medical University of South Carolina College of Medicine: SOUTH CAROLINA

Department and Division or Section Chairs

Basic Sciences

Comparative Medicine . . . . M. Michael Swindle, D.V.M.
Biochemistry and Molecular Biology . . . . Yusuf A. Hannun, M.D.
Cell and Molecular Pharmacology and
Experimental Therapeutics . . . . Kenneth D. Tew, Ph.D., D.Sc.
Microbiology and Immunology . . . . Zihai Li, M.D., Ph.D.
Neurosciences (Research) . . . . Peter W. Kalivas, Ph.D.
Pathology and Laboratory Medicine . . . . Janice M. Lage, M.D.
Regenerative Medicine and Cell Biology . . . . Roger R. Markwald, Ph.D.

Clinical Sciences

Anesthesia and Perioperative Medicine . . . . Scott T. Reeves, M.D.
Dermatology . . . . Bruce H. Thiers, M.D.
Family Medicine . . . . William J. Hueston, M.D.
Medicine . . . . Richard M. Silver, M.D. (Interim)
    Biostatistics, Bioinformatics, and Epidemiology . . . . Yuko Palesch, Ph.D.
    Cardiovascular . . . . Michael R. Gold, M.D., Ph.D.
    Emergency Medicine . . . . Edward C. Jauch, M.D. (Interim)
    Endocrinology, Metabolism, and Nutrition . . . . Louis M. Luttrell, M.D., Ph.D.
    Gastroenterology . . . . Mark Payne, M.D.
    General Internal Medicine and Gerontology . . . . William Moran, M.D.
    Hematology and Oncology . . . . Harry Drabkin, M.D.
    Infectious Diseases . . . . Michael Kilby, M.D.
    Nephrology . . . . Michael Ullian, M.D. (Interim)
    Pulmonary and Critical Care . . . . Steven Sahn, M.D.
    Rheumatology and Immunology . . . . James C. Oates, M.D.
Neurosciences (Clinical) . . . . Sunil J. Patel, M.D.
Obstetrics and Gynecology . . . . J. Peter VanDorsten, M.D.
Ophthalmology . . . . Lucian V. DelPriore, M.D., Ph.D.
Orthopaedic Surgery . . . . Langdon Hartsock, M.D.
Otolaryngology and Communicative Sciences . . . . Paul R. Lambert, M.D.
Pediatrics . . . . Rita M. Ryan, M.D.
Psychiatry and Behavioral Sciences . . . . Thomas W. Uhde, M.D.
Radiation Oncology . . . . Joseph M. Jenrette III, M.D.
Radiology . . . . Philip Costello, M.D.
Surgery . . . . David J. Cole, M.D.
    Cardiothoracic . . . . John Ikonomidis, M.D., Ph.D.
    GI and Laparoscopic Surgery . . . . David Adams, M.D.
    General Surgery . . . . Samir Fakhry, M.D.
    Pediatric Surgery . . . . Andre Hebra, M.D.
    Plastic and Reconstructive Surgery . . . . Milton Armstrong, M.D.
    Surgical Oncology . . . . Nestor Esnaola, M.D.
    Transplant Surgery . . . . Prabhakar Baliga, M.D.
    Vascular Surgery . . . . Bruce Elliott, M.D.
Urology . . . . Thomas E. Keane, M.B.B.Ch.

University of South Carolina School of Medicine
Columbia, South Carolina 29208
803-216-3301 (dean's office); 803-216-3331 (fax)
Web site: www.med.sc.edu

The University of South Carolina School of Medicine was authorized by the South Carolina legislature in June 1973 and is established under the Veterans Administration Medical School Assistance and Health Manpower Training Act of 1972. The new school of medicine campus, located approximately four-and-a-half miles from the main campus of the University of South Carolina, was completed in 1983 and houses basic science departments, administrative offices, and the medical library. Most clinical departments are located at affiliated hospitals in the Columbia area. The school's first class matriculated in September 1977.

Type: public
2011 total enrollment: 315
Clinical facilities: Dorn Veterans Administration Medical Center, Palmetto Health, South Carolina Department of Mental Health, Moncrief Army Hospital, Greenville Hospital System.

University Officials

President. . . . . Harris Pastides, Ph.D.
Provost . . . . Michael D. Amiridis, Ph.D.

Medical School Administrative Staff

Dean. . . . . Richard A. Hoppmann, M.D.
Associate Dean for Clinical Affairs . . . . O. Marion Burton, M.D.
Associate Dean for Medical Education and Academic Affairs . . . . . . Joshua T. Thornhill IV, M.D.
Assistant Dean for Continuing Medical Education. . . . . Morris J. Blachman, Ph.D.
Assistant Dean for Preclinical Curriculum. . . . . Lynn K. Thomas, Dr.P.H.
Assistant Dean for Clinical Curriculum and Assessment. . . . . Nancy A. Richeson, M.D.
Associate Dean (Dorn VA Medical Center) . . . . Alfred B. Boykin, Jr., M.D.
Assistant Dean (Greenville Hospital System) . . . . Paul V. Catalana, M.D.
Associate Dean (Palmetto Health Alliance). . . . . James I. Raymond, M.D.
Assistant Dean for Innovative Education and
 Faculty Support . . . . Norman W. Pedigo, Jr., Ph.D.
Assistant Dean for Minority Affairs . . . . Carol L. McMahon, M.D.
Administrator, Office of Admissions and Registrar . . . . Jeanette H. Ford, Ed.D.
Associate Dean for Administration and Finance . . . . Jeffrey L. Perkins
Director of Information Technology. . . . . D. Lindsie Cone, M.D.
Director of Legal Affairs. . . . . Hedy S. Zaragoza, J.D.
Director of Medical Library . . . . Ruth A. Riley
Director of Student and Career Services . . . . Donald J. Kenney, Ph.D.

University of South Carolina School of Medicine: SOUTH CAROLINA

Department and Division or Section Chairs

Basic Sciences

Biochemistry . . . . James M. Sodetz, Ph.D.
Cell and Developmental Biology and Anatomy . . . . Joseph S. Janicki, Ph.D.
Pathology, Microbiology, and Immunology . . . . Mitzi Nagarkatti, Ph.D.
Pharmacology, Physiology, and Neuroscience . . . . Marlene A. Wilson, Ph.D.

Clinical Sciences

Family and Preventive Medicine . . . . Elizabeth G. Baxley, M.D.
Internal Medicine . . . . Shawn A. Chillag, M.D.
   Allergy and Immunology . . . . David J. Amrol, M.D.
   Cardiology . . . . Augustine E. Agocha, M.D.
   Endocrinology . . . . Ali Rizvi, M.D.
   General Internal Medicine . . . . Allan S. Brett, M.D.
   Geriatrics . . . . Victor A. Hirth, M.D.
   Infectious Diseases . . . . Helmut Albrecht, M.D.
   Rheumatology . . . . James W. Fant, Jr., M.D.
Neurology . . . . Souvik Sen, M.D.
Neuropsychiatry and Behavioral Science . . . . Meera Narasimhan, M.D. (Interim)
   Child and Adolescent Psychiatry . . . . Craig Stuck, M.D.
   Forensic Psychiatry . . . . Richard L. Frierson, M.D.
   Psychoanalysis . . . . Clyde H. Flanagan, Jr., M.D.
   Rehabilitation Counseling . . . . Kerry R. Lachance
Neurosurgery . . . . Lenwood P. Smith, Jr., M.D.
Obstetrics and Gynecology . . . . Judith T. Burgis, M.D.
   Adolexcent Gynecology . . . . Judith T. Burgis, M.D.
   Maternal Fetal Medicine . . . . Paul C. Browne, M.D.
   OB Ultrasound . . . . Paul C. Browne, M.D.
   GYN Ultrasound . . . . Kerry M. Sims, M.D.
   Genetic Counseling . . . . Janice G. Edwards
   Benign Gynecology . . . . Judith T. Burgis, M.D.
Ophthalmology . . . . Edward W. Cheeseman, M.D.
Orthopaedic Surgery . . . . John J. Walsh IV, M.D.
Pediatrics . . . . R. Caughman Taylor, M.D.
Radiology . . . . Francis H. Neuffer, M.D.
Surgery . . . . James M. Nottingham, M.D. (Interim)
   Cardiothoracic Surgery . . . . Reid W. Tribble, M.D.
   General Surgery . . . . Richard M. Bell, M.D.
   Pediatric Surgery . . . . P. Prithvi Reddy, M.D.
   Plastic Surgery . . . . Harold I. Friedman, M.D., Ph.D.
   Trauma . . . . Raymond P. Bynoe, M.D.
   Vascular Surgery . . . . Robert R. M. Gifford, M.D.

University of South Dakota Sanford School of Medicine
1400 West 22nd Street
Sioux Falls, South Dakota 57105-1570
605-357-1300 (dean's office); 605-357-1311 (fax)
Web site: www.usd.edu/med

Medical course work began at the University of South Dakota in 1907 with the organization of the college of medicine offering the first two years of the standard four-year medical degree program. The program was expanded in 1974 to degree-granting status and graduated its first class in 1977. The school has a community-based philosophy, and clinical training (Years 3 and 4) is conducted in the community facilities affiliated with the program throughout South Dakota.

Type: public
2011 total enrollment: 213
Clinical facilities: Avera Sacred Heart Hospital, South Dakota Human Services Center, Avera McKennan Hospital and University Health Center, Sanford USD Medical Center, Sioux Falls Veterans Administration Hospital, Children's Care Hospital, Rapid City Regional Hospital, Fort Meade Veterans Administration Hospital.

University Officials

President. . . . . James Abbott
Vice President of Health Affairs . . . . Rodney Parry, M.D.

Medical School Administrative Staff

Dean. . . . . Rodney Parry, M.D.
Executive Dean . . . . Ron Lindahl, Ph.D.
Dean, Student Affairs. . . . . Paul Bunger, Ph.D.
Dean of Clinical Faculty. . . . . Tim Ridgway, M.D.
Dean, Graduate Medical Education . . . . G. Michael Tibbitts, M.D.
Dean, Health Sciences. . . . . Michael Lawler, Ph.D.
Dean, Medical Student Education . . . . Janet Lindemann, M.D.
Dean, Rapid City Campus . . . . Matthew Simmons, M.D.
Dean, Yankton Campus . . . . Lori Hansen, M.D.
Dean, Sioux Falls Campus . . . . Tim Ridgway, M.D.
Dean, Vermillion Campus . . . . Ron Lindahl, Ph.D.
Associate Director of Medical Education. . . . . Matt Bien, M.D.
Director of Continuing Professional Development. . . . . Jason Kemnitz, Ed.D.
Director of Evaluation and Assessment . . . . Edward Simanton, Ph.D.
Director of Finance . . . . Julie Kriech
Director of Graduate Medical Education. . . . . Nedd Brown, Ph.D.
Director of Human Resources . . . . Lisa Sorensen

University of South Dakota Sanford School of Medicine: SOUTH DAKOTA

Department and Division or Section Chairs
Basic Biomedical Sciences

Dean.. Ron Lindahl, Ph.D.
Associate Dean .... Steve Waller, Ph.D.
Pathology .... Michael Koch, M.D.

Clinical Sciences

Family Medicine .... H. Bruce Vogt, M.D.
   Area Health Education Center (AHEC) .... Amy Jacobson, Ed.D.
   Emergency Medicine .... Darren Manthey, M.D.
Internal Medicine .... LuAnn Eidsness, M.D.
   Allergy and Immunology .... R. Maclean Smith, M.D.
   Cardiology... Scott Pham, M.D.
   Critical Care... Ashraf Elshami, M.D.
   Dermatology .... Brian Knutson, M.D.
   Endocrinology .... Richard Barth, M.D.
   Ethics and Palliative Care .... Joann Bennett, D.O.
   Gastroenterology .... Larry Schafer, M.D.
   Geriatrics.. David Sandvik, M.D.
   Hematology and Oncology .... Michael McHale, M.D., and David Elson, M.D.
   Hospitalist Medicine.................................. Jitendra Thakkar, M.D.
   Infectious Diseases .... Veronica Soler, M.D.
   Nephrology .... Richard Jensen, M.D.
   Pulmonology .... Brian Hurley, M.D.
   Radiology.. Christopher Fischer, M.D.
   Research .... Karen Munger, Ph.D.
   Rheumatology .... Joseph Fanciullo, M.D.
Neurosciences .... Jerome Freeman, M.D.
Obstetrics and Gynecology................................. Keith Hansen, M.D.
Pediatrics .... Dennis Stevens, M.D. (Interim)
   Cardiology.. Theresa Stamato, M.D.
   Child Advocacy... Jerome Blake, M.D.
   Clinical Services .... James Wallace, M.D.
   Critical Care.. Joseph Segeleon, M.D.
   Developmental Pediatrics .... Jerome Blake, M.D.
   Education .... Lawrence Wellman, M.D.
   Endocrinology, Genetics, and Metabolic Disease .... Laura Davis-Keppen, M.D.
   Gastroenterology .... Gary Neidich, M.D.
   General Pediatrics .... Joseph Zenel, M.D.
   Hematology and Oncology............................... Kaye Lyn Wagner, M.D.
   Hospitalist .... Yamen Smadi, M.D.
   Infectious Diseases .... Maria Carrillo-Marquez, M.D.
   Neonatology... Dennis Stevens, M.D.
   Neurology .... Bonnie Bunch, M.D., Ph.D.
   Nephrology .... John Sanders, M.D.
   Pulmonology .... James Wallace, M.D.
   Research .... Amy Elliott, Ph.D.
   Surgery .... Adela Casas-Melley, M.D.
   Urology... Romano DeMarco, M.D.
Psychiatry .... Timothy Soundy, M.D.
Surgery... Gary Timmerman, M.D.
   Anesthesiology... Jack Gaspari, M.D.
   Neurosurgery.. Quentin J. Durward, M.D.
   Ophthalmology .... Gregory D. Osmundson, M.D.
   Orthopedic Surgery .... Robert Van Demark, Jr., M.D.
   Otolaryngology.. Kenneth Scott, M.D.
   Urology .... Matthew Witte, M.D.

East Tennessee State University
James H. Quillen College of Medicine
P.O. Box 70694
Johnson City, Tennessee 37614
423-439-1000; 423-439-6315 (dean's office); 423-439-2033 (admissions);
423-439-8090 (fax)
E-mail: medcom@etsu.edu
Web site: http://etsu.edu/com

The James H. Quillen College of Medicine of East Tennessee State University was authorized by the Tennessee legislature in March 1974 and is established under the Veterans Administration Medical School Assistance and Health Manpower Training Act of 1972. Consistent with its mission, the Quillen College of Medicine is noted for its emphasis on primary care and rural medicine training, placing 75 to 85 percent of its graduates in medically underserved and/or rural communities.

Type: public
2011 total enrollment: 269
Clinical facilities: ETSU Physicians and Associates, Family Medicine Centers (Kingsport, Bristol, Johnson City); Johnson City Medical Center; Indian Path Medical Center; Bristol Regional Medical Center; Holston Valley Medical Center (Kingsport); Frontier Health; Woodridge Hospital; James H. Quillen Veterans Affairs Medical Center (Mountain Home); Ambulatory Clinics (Mountain City, Rogersville).

University Officials

President . . . . Brian E. Noland, Ph.D.
Vice President for Health Affairs . . . . Wilsie S. Bishop, D.P.A.

Medical School Administrative Staff

Dean . . . . Philip C. Bagnell, M.D.
Executive Associate Dean for Academic and Faculty Affairs . . . . Kenneth E. Olive, M.D.
Associate Dean for Clinical Affairs . . . . T. Watson Jernigan, M.D.
Associate Dean for Continuing Medical Education . . . . Barbara J. Sucher
Associate Dean for Finance and Administration . . . . Gregory L. Wilgocki
Associate Dean for Graduate Studies . . . . Mitchell E. Robinson, Ph.D.
Associate Dean for Learning Resources . . . . Biddanda (Suresh) Ponnappa
Associate Dean for Student Affairs . . . . Thomas E. Kwasigroch, Ph.D.
Assistant Dean and Director of Operations . . . . M. David Linville, M.D.
Assistant Dean for Academic Affairs . . . . Penny Little Smith, Ed.D.
Assistant Dean for Admissions and Records . . . . Edwin D. Taylor
Assistant Dean for Women in Medicine . . . . Theresa F. Lura, M.D.
Assistant Dean for Graduate Medical Education . . . . Debra A. Shaw
Assistant Dean for Finance and Administration . . . . Joyce Sue Taylor
Assistant Vice President for Government Relations . . . . Robert V. Acuff, Ph.D.
Director for Government Relations . . . . Olga A. Cabello, Ph.D.
Associate Chief of Staff for Education VAMC . . . . Stephen D. Loyd, M.D.
Office Manager for Dean's Office . . . . Donna D. Gage
Media Relations Coordinator . . . . Bradley A. Lifford

Department and Division or Section Chairs

Basic Sciences

Anatomy and Cell Biology . . . . Paul J. Monaco, Ph.D. (Interim)
Cell and Tissue Biology . . . . Paul J. Monaco, Ph.D.
Gross Anatomy . . . . Thomas E. Kwasigroch, Ph.D.
Neurobiology . . . . Ronald H. Baisden, Ph.D.
Biochemistry and Molecular Biology . . . . W. Scott Champney, Ph.D. (Interim)
Microbiology . . . . Priscilla B. Wyrick, Ph.D.
Pharmacology . . . . Gregory A. Ordway, Ph.D.
Physiology . . . . William L. Joyner, Ph.D.

Clinical Sciences

Family Medicine .... John P. Franko, M.D.
  Division of Medical Student Education .... Reid Blackwelder, M.D.
  Division of Graduate Medical Education .... Raymond Feierabend, M.D.
  Division of Primary Care Research .... Fraser (Fred) G. Tudiver, M.D.
  Division of Rural Programs............................... Joseph A. Florence IV, M.D.
  Residency-Kingsport .... Beth A. Fox, M.D.
  Residency-Bristol .... Greg Clarity, M.D.
  Residency-Johnson City...................................... Diana L. Heiman, M.D.
Internal Medicine .... J. Kelly Smith, M.D. (Interim)
  Allergy.. Guha Krishnaswamy, M.D.
  Basic Sciences .... David Chi, Ph.D.
  Cardiology... Philip D. Henry, M.D.
  Dermatology .... Stuart S. Leicht, M.D.
  Endocrinology .... Charles Stuart, M.D., and Alan Peiris, M.D., Ph.D.
  Gastroenterology .... Mark Young, M.D.
  General Internal Medicine .... Rebecca J. Copeland, M.D.
  Hematology and Oncology..................... Koyamangalath Krishnan, M.D.
  Immunology... Guha Krishnaswamy, M.D.
  Infectious Disease... Jonathan P. Moorman, M.D.
  Preventive Medicine and Epidemiology............................ Jay B. Mehta, M.D.
  Pulmonary... Thomas M. Roy, M.D.
  Rheumatology .... William Wason, M.D.
Obstetrics and Gynecology.......................... T. Watson Jernigan, M.D.
  Gynecologic Oncology .... Paul R. Kramer, M.D.
  Maternal Fetal Medicine..................................... Selman Welt, M.D.
Pathology .... John B. Schweitzer, M.D.
Pediatrics .... David K. Kalwinsky, M.D.
  Adolescent Medicine .... David Chastain, M.D.
  Developmental and Behavioral .... H. Patrick Stern, M.D.
  Research .... William L. Stone, Ph.D.
  Cardiology.. Rajani Anand, M.D.
  Gastroenterology .... Ayman Abdel-Wahab, M.D.
  General Pediatrics .... Debra Quarles Mills, M.D.
  Genetics... Apostolos Psychogios, M.D.
  Hematology and Oncology........................... Kathryn Klopfenstein, M.D.
  Neonatology.. W. Michael DeVoe, M.D.
  Neurology .... Pyar Noorani, M.D.
  Nephrology .... Ahmad Wattad, M.D.
  Pulmonary and Intensive Care .... Ricky T. Mohon, M.D.
Psychiatry .... Merry N. Miller, M.D.
  VA Psychiatry Services..................................... George R. Brown, M.D.
  Child and Adolescent Psychiatry .... Steve Shulruff, M.D., Jill McCarley, M.D.,
                                         and Martha Bird, M.D.
Surgery... I. William Browder, M.D.
  Critical Care...................................... Tiffany Lasky, M.D.
  General Surgery... Carlos Floresguerra, M.D.
  Ophthalmology .... Barbara O. Kimbrough, M.D.
  Plastic Surgery .... Daniel F. Haynes, M.D.
  Research .... David Williams, Ph.D.
  Surgical Oncology .... Mary A. Hooks, M.D.
  Trauma Surgery-Johnson City .... Chris R. Kaufmann, M.D.
  Trauma Surgery-Kingsport .... Tiffany Lasky, M.D.
  Vascular Surgery.. Dan Rush, M.D.

Meharry Medical College School of Medicine
1005 Dr. D. B. Todd Jr. Boulevard
Nashville, Tennessee 37208
615-327-6204 (dean's office); 615-327-6568 (fax); 615-327-6111 (general information)
Web site: www.mmc.edu/medschool

Meharry Medical College was organized in 1876 as the medical department of Central Tennessee College. In 1900, Central Tennessee College was reorganized as Walden University, and the medical department became known as Meharry Medical College of Walden University. Later, a separate corporate existence was sought, and in 1915, a new charter was granted by the state of Tennessee. Through contributions from various sources, property was acquired in northwest Nashville, and the present school and hospital were erected in 1930-31. The school of medicine is the oldest and largest of the college's three schools.

Type: private
2011 total enrollment: 431
Clinical facilities: Alvin C. York Veterans Administration Medical Center (Murfreesboro), Meharry Medical Group Ambulatory Care Centers, Matthews Walker Comprehensive Health Center, Middle Tennessee Medical Center, Nashville General Hospital at Meharry, Vanderbilt University Medical Center, Blanchard Army Community Hospital (Fort Campbell, Kentucky).

Medical College Officials

President and Chief Executive Officer . . . . Wayne J. Riley, M.D., M.P.H., M.B.A.
Executive Vice President and Provost . . . . Vacant
Senior Vice President, General Counsel and
   Corporate Secretary . . . . Benjamin E. Rawlins, M.D.
Senior Vice President for Finance and Chief Financial Officer. . . . . . . LaMel Bandy-Neal, M.B.A.
Senior Vice President for Institutional Advancement. . . . . Robert S. Poole, B.A.
Senior Vice President for Health Affairs & Dean,
   School of Medicine . . . . Charles P. Mouton, M.D., M.S.
Dean, School of Dentistry . . . . Janet Southerland, D.D.S., Ph.D.
Dean, School of Graduate Studies and Research . . . . Maria F. Lima, Ph.D.

School of Medicine Administrative Staff

Assistant Dean, Student and Academic Affairs. Brenda Merritt, M.P.A.
Associate Dean, Administration, and Chief of Staff . . . . Cassandra S. Ward, Ed.D.
Associate Dean, Curriculum Evaluation and CME . . . . Etheleen McGinnis-Hill, Ph.D.
Associate Dean, Business and Finance. . . . . Trea McMillan, M.B.A., C.P.A.
Associate Dean, Clinical Affiliations . . . . Susanne Tropez-Sims, M.D.
Associate Dean, Clinical Affairs. . . . . Chike M. Nzerue, M.D.
Assistant Dean, Special Programs . . . . Sharon Turner-Friley, M.S.W.

Meharry Medical College School of Medicine: TENNESSEE

Department Chairs

Basic Sciences

Biochemistry and Cancer Biology............................. Samuel Adunyah, Ph.D.
Microbiology and Immunology................................ Fernando Villalta, Ph.D.
Neuroscience and Pharmacology .... Clivel Charlton, Ph.D.
Physiology....................................... Herbert Rucker, Ph.D. (Interim)
Professional and Medical Education .... George Breaux, M.D.

Clinical Sciences

Family and Community Medicine.............................. Roger Zoorob, M.D.
Internal Medicine .... Duane T. Smoot, M.D.
Internal Medicine
Obstetrics and Gynecology............................. Gloria Richard-Davis, M.D.
Pathology .... Billy R. Ballard, D.D.S., M.D.
Pediatrics .... Xylina Bean, M.D.
Psychiatry and Behavioral Sciences.......................... Rahn K. Bailey, M.D.
Radiology .... Anthony Disher, M.D.
Surgery
Surgery... Lemuel Dent, M.D. (Interim)

Center Directors

Center for AIDS Health Disparities Research .... Fernando Villalta, Ph.D. (Interim)
Center for Women's Health Research.............. Charles P. Mouton, M.D., M.S. (Interim)

*Specialty without organizational autonomy.

University of Tennessee Health Science Center, College of Medicine
910 Madison, Suite 1002
Memphis, Tennessee 38163
901-448-5529 (dean's office); 901-448-7683 (fax)
Web site: www.uthsc.edu

The University of Tennessee College of Medicine was established in 1851 as the medical department of Central Tennessee College. In 1900, Central Tennessee College was reorganized as Walden University, and the medical department became known as Meharry Medical College of Walden University. Later, a separate corporate existancey mergers and agreements, it became part of the University of Tennessee and was moved to Memphis in 1911. It is one of six colleges comprising the University of Tennessee Health Science Center, and has programs in Chattanooga, Jackson, Knoxville, and Nashville as well as in Memphis.

Type: public
2011 total enrollment: 671
Clinical facilities: Regional Medical Center at Memphis, Baptist Memorial Hospital, Le Bonheur Children's Medical Center, Memphis Mental Health Institute, Department of Veterans' Affairs Medical Center, St. Jude Children's Research Hospital, Methodist University Hospital, the University of Tennessee Medical Center (James K. Dobbs Research Institute, Doctors Office Building), Saint Francis Hospital (Memphis), Baroness Erlanger and T. C. Thompson Hospitals (Chattanooga), University of Tennessee Medical Center (Knoxville), Jackson-Madison County General Hospital (Jackson), Baptist Hospital (Nashville).

University Officials

President. . . . . Joseph D. Pietro, D.V.M.
Chancellor, Health Science Center. . . . . Steve J. Schwab, M.D.
Executive Dean, College of Medicine . . . . David M. Stern, M.D.
Dean, College of Medicine-Chattanooga. . . . . David C. Seaberg, M.D.
Dean, College of Medicine-Knoxville . . . . James J. Neutens, Ph.D.
Dean, College of Medicine-Memphis . . . . David M. Stern, M.D.

Medical School Administrative Staff

Executive Dean . . . . David M. Stern, M.D.
Associate Dean for Finance and Administration . . . . J. Timothy Mashburn, M.B.A.
Associate Dean for Graduate Medical Education
    and Continuing Medical Education . . . . Eugene Mangiante, M.D.
Associate Dean for Clinical Affairs . . . . David M. Stern, M.D.
Associate Dean, Medical Education. . . . . Robert G. Shreve, Ed.D.
Associate Dean, Faculty Affairs . . . . Polly Hofmann, Ph.D.
Associate Dean, Student Affairs . . . . Owen Phillips, M.D.
Assistant Dean, Academic Programs at St. Jude
    Children's Research Hospital . . . . P. Joan Chesney, M.D.
Assistant Dean, Admissions and Enrollment Services . . . . E. Nelson Strother, Jr.
Assistant Dean, Baptist Hospital-Nashville . . . . Paul C. McNabb, M.D.
Assistant Dean, Basic Science Curriculum . . . . James Patrick Ryan, M.D.
Assistant Dean, Clinical Curriculum . . . . Susan Brewer, M.D.

Department Chairs

Basic Sciences–Memphis Campus

Anatomy and Neurobiology . . . . Matthew Ennis, Ph.D.
Biomedical Engineering and Imaging. . . . . Steve Bares, Ph.D., M.B.A.
Molecular Sciences . . . . Gerald Byrne, Ph.D.
Pharmacology . . . . Burt M. Sharp, M.D.
Physiology. . . . . Gabor J. Tigyi, Ph.D.

Clinical Sciences–Memphis Campus

Anesthesiology. . . . . John Zanella, M.D., Ph.D.

University of Tennessee Health Science Center, College of Medicine: TENNESSEE

Comparative Medicine . . . . Timothy D. Mandrell, D.V.M.
Family Medicine . . . . David L. Maness, D.O., M.S.S.
Medicine . . . . Guy L. Reed, M.D.
Neurology . . . . William A. Pulsinelli, M.D., Ph.D.
Neurosurgery . . . . Jon H. Robertson, M.D.
Obstetrics and Gynecology . . . . Mari Giancarlo, M.D.
Ophthalmology . . . . Barrett G. Haik, M.D.
Orthopaedic Surgery . . . . S. Terry Canale, M.D.
Otolaryngology-Head and Neck Surgery . . . . Jerome W. Thompson, M.D.
Pathology . . . . Charles Handorf, M.D., Ph.D.
Pediatrics . . . . Keith English, M.D.
Preventive Medicine . . . . Karen Johnson (Interim)
Psychiatry . . . . James A. Greene, M.D., and Kenneth A. Sakauye, M.D.
Radiology . . . . Harris Cohen, M.D.
Surgery . . . . Timothy C. Fabian, M.D.
Urology . . . . Robert Wake, M.D.

Chattanooga Campus

Family Medicine . . . . J. Mack Worthington, M.D.
Medicine . . . . Mukta Panda, M.D.
Obstetrics and Gynecology . . . . Paul Stumpf, M.D.
Orthopaedic Surgery . . . . Vacant
Pediatrics . . . . Alan Kohrt, M.D.
Plastic Surgery . . . . Larry A. Sargent, M.D.
Radiology . . . . R. Kent Hutson, M.D.
Surgery . . . . R. Phillip Burns, M.D.
Emergency Medicine . . . . R. Phillip Burns, M.D.

Knoxville Campus

Anesthesiology . . . . Jerry L. Epps, M.D.
Family Medicine . . . . Gregory H. Blake, M.D.
Medicine . . . . Timothy Panella, M.D.
Obstetrics and Gynecology . . . . Bobby Howard, M.D.
Pathology . . . . Stuart Van Meter, M.D.
Radiology . . . . J. Mark McKinney, M.D.
Surgery . . . . Mitchell H. Goldman, M.D.

Vanderbilt University School of Medicine

21st Avenue South at Garland Avenue
Nashville, Tennessee 37232
615-322-5000 (general information); 615-322-2151 (dean's office); 615-343-7286 (fax)
E-mail: jeff.balser@vanderbilt.edu
Web site: www.mc.vanderbilt.edu/medschool

Vanderbilt University issued its first M.D. degrees in 1875. During a reorganization in 1925, the medical school was moved to the main campus of Vanderbilt University. The medical school is part of the Vanderbilt University Medical Center.

Type: private
2011 total enrollment: 442
Clinical facilities: Vanderbilt University Hospital, Vanderbilt Stallworth Rehabilitation Hospital, Nashville Veterans Administration Medical Center, Vanderbilt Psychiatric Hospital, Nashville Metropolitan General Hospital, Monroe Carell Jr. Children's Hospital at Vanderbilt.

University Official

Chancellor . . . . Nicholas S. Zeppos

Medical Center Officials

Vice Chancellor for Health Affairs . . . . Jeffrey R. Balser, M.D., Ph.D.
Deputy Vice Chancellor for Health Affairs; CEO,
  Vanderbilt Health System . . . . C. Wright Pinson, M.D.
Associate Vice Chancellor for Clinical and
  Translational Research . . . . Gordon R. Bernard, M.D.
Associate Vice Chancellor for Health Affairs;
  Senior Vice Pres., Vanderbilt University
  Medical Center Finance . . . . Warren Beck, M.B.A.
Associate Vice Chancellor for Health Affairs;
  CAO, Vanderbilt University Medical Center . . . . John F. Manning, Jr., Ph.D.
Associate Vice Chancellor for Health Affairs;
  Chief Compliance Officer . . . . David S. Raiford, M.D.
Associate Vice Chancellor for Health Affairs; Chief Strategy and Information Officer . . . William
W. Stead, M.D.
Associate Vice Chancellor for Basic Science Research . . . . Susan R. Wente, Ph.D.

Medical School Administrative Staff

Dean. . . . . Jeffrey R. Balser, M.D., Ph.D.
Senior Associate Dean for Biomedical Research,
  Education, and Training . . . . G. Roger Chalkley, D.Phil.
Senior Associate Dean for Biomedical Sciences. Susan R. Wente, Ph.D.
Senior Associate Dean, Clinical Affairs . . . . C. Wright Pinson, M.D.
Senior Associate Dean for Clinical Sciences . . . . Gordon R. Bernard, M.D.
Senior Associate Dean for Faculty Affairs . . . . David S. Raiford, M.D.
Senior Associate Dean for Health Sciences Education . . . . Bonnie M. Miller, M.D.
Senior Associate Dean for Population Health Sciences . . . . Robert Dittus, M.D., M.P.H.
Associate Dean of Admissions. . . . . John A. Zic, M.D.
Associate Dean for Adult Clinical Affairs. . . . . Paul Sternberg, M.D.
Associate Dean for Alumni Affairs . . . . Ann H. Price, M.D.
Associate Dean for Clinical & Translational
  Scientist Development . . . . Katherine E. Hartmann, M.D.
Associate Dean for Diversity in GME & Faculty Affairs. . . . . André L. Churchwell, M.D.
Associate Dean for Diversity in Medical Education . . . . George C. Hill, Ph.D.
Associate Dean for Faculty Affairs. . . . . Gerald B. Hickson, M.D.
Associate Dean for Graduate Medical Education . . . . Donald W. Brady, M.D.
Associate Dean for Medical Student Affairs. . . . . Scott M. Rodgers, M.D.
Associate Dean for Operations and Administration . . . . John F. Manning, Jr., Ph.D.
Associate Dean for Undergraduate Education. . . . . Kimberly D. Lomis, M.D.

Department and Division or Section Chairs

Basic Sciences

Biochemistry. . . . . F. Peter Guengerich, Ph.D. (Interim)
Biomedical Informatics . . . . Kevin B. Johnson, M.D.

Vanderbilt University School of Medicine: TENNESSEE

Biostatistics . . . . Frank E. Harrell, Jr., Ph.D.
Cancer Biology . . . . Harold L. Moses, M.D. (Interim)
Cell and Development Biology . . . . Susan R. Wente, Ph.D. (Interim)
Molecular Physiology and Biophysics . . . . Roger D. Cone, Ph.D.
Pathology, Microbiology, and Immunology . . . . Samuel A. Santoro, M.D., Ph.D.
Pharmacology . . . . Heidi E. Hamm, Ph.D.

Clinical Sciences

Anesthesiology . . . . Warren S. Sandberg, M.D., Ph.D.
Emergency Medicine . . . . Corey M. Slovis, M.D.
Hearing and Speech Sciences . . . . Anne Marie Tharpe, Ph.D.
Medicine . . . . Nancy J. Brown, M.D.
  Allergy, Pulmonary, and Critical Care . . . . Timothy S. Blackwell, M.D.
  Cardiovascular Medicine . . . . Douglas B. Sawyer, M.D., Ph.D.
  Clinical Pharmacology . . . . David G. Harrison, M.D.
  Dermatology . . . . George P. Stricklin, M.D., Ph.D.
  Epidemiology . . . . Wei Zheng, M.D.
  Endocrinology and Diabetes . . . . Alvin C. Powers, M.D.
  Gastroenterology . . . . Richard M. Peek, Jr., M.D.
  General Internal Medicine . . . . Robert S. Dittus, M.D.
  Genetic Medicine . . . . Alfred L. George, Jr., M.D.
  Hematology and Oncology . . . . Carlos L. Arteaga, M.D.
  Infectious Disease . . . . Richard T. D'Aquila, M.D.
  Nephrology . . . . Raymond C. Harris, Jr., M.D.
  Rheumatology and Clinical Immunology . . . . James Ward Thomas II, M.D.
Neurology . . . . Robert L. Macdonald, M.D., Ph.D.
Obstetrics and Gynecology . . . . Howard W. Jones III, M.D.
Ophthalmology and Visual Sciences . . . . Paul Sternberg, Jr., M.D.
Orthopaedics and Rehabilitation . . . . Herbert S. Schwartz, M.D.
Otolaryngology . . . . Roland D. Eavey, M.D.
Pediatrics . . . . Margaret G. Rush, M.D. (Acting)
  Adolescent Medicine . . . . Lynn S. Walker, Ph.D.
  Cardiology . . . . H. Scott Baldwin, M.D.
  Critical Care . . . . Fred S. Lamb, M.D., Ph.D.
  Developmental Medicine . . . . Tyler E. Reimschisel, M.D.
  Emergency Medicine . . . . Thomas J. Abramo, M.D.
  Endocrinology . . . . William E. Russell, M.D.
  Gastroenterology and Nutrition . . . . Sari A. Acra, M.D. (Interim)
  General Pediatrics . . . . Shari L. Barkin, M.D.
  Genetics . . . . John A. Phillips III, M.D.
  Hematology and Oncology . . . . Debra L. Friedman, M.D.
  Hospital Medicine . . . . Kris P. Rehm, M.D.
  Infectious Disease . . . . Terence S. Dermody, M.D.
  Neonatology . . . . Judy L. Aschner, M.D.
  Nephrology . . . . Kathy L. Jabs, M.D.
  Pulmonology, Allergy, and Immunology . . . . Paul E. Moore, M.D.
  Rheumatology . . . . T. Brent Graham, M.D.
  Toxicology . . . . Michael Aschner, Ph.D.
Preventive Medicine . . . . William Schaffner, M.D.
Psychiatry . . . . Stephan H. W. Heckers, M.D.
  Addiction Psychiatry . . . . Peter R. Martin, M.D.
  Child and Adolescent Psychiatry . . . . D. Catherine Fuchs, M.D.
Radiation Oncology . . . . Arnold W. Malcolm, M.D.
Radiology and Radiological Sciences . . . . Jeremy J. Kaye, M.D.
Section of Surgical Sciences . . . . R. Daniel Beauchamp, M.D.
  Cardiac Surgery . . . . John G. Byrne, M.D.
  General Surgery . . . . Naji N. Abumrad, M.D.
  Neurosurgery . . . . Reid Thompson, M.D.
  Oral Surgery and Dentistry . . . . Samuel J. McKenna, D.D.S., M.D.
  Pediatric Surgery . . . . Dai H. Chung, M.D.
  Plastic Surgery . . . . R. Bruce Shack, M.D.
  Thoracic Surgery . . . . Joe B. Putnam, Jr., M.D.
  Urologic Surgery . . . . Joseph A. Smith, Jr., M.D.

Baylor College of Medicine
One Baylor Plaza
Houston, Texas 77030
713-798-4951 (general information); 713-798-4800 (president's office);
713-798-6353 (fax)
Web site: www.bcm.edu

Baylor College of Medicine, founded in Dallas in 1900, is the only private medical school in the greater Southwest. The college moved to Houston in 1943 to become the educational cornerstone of the new Texas Medical Center. In 1903, the medical school began an affiliation with Baylor University that lasted until 1969, when Baylor College of Medicine became an independent institution.

Type: private
2011 total enrollment: 1489
Clinical facilities: DeBakey Veterans Affairs Medical Center, Harris County Hospital District and Community Health Program (Ben Taub General Hospital and Quentin Mease Community Hospital), Menninger Clinic, St. Luke's Episcopal Hospital, Texas Children's Hospital, The Institute for Research and Rehabilitation and The Methodist Hospital. **Other affiliated clinical institutions:** Cullen Bayou Place, DePelchin Children's Center, Houston Child Guidance Center, Jewish Family Service Cancer Center, Kelsey-Seybold Clinic, Park Plaza Hospital, Seven Acres Jewish Geriatric Center, Shriners Hospital for Children, The University of Texas M.D. Anderson Cancer Center and The Woman's Hospital of Texas.

Medical College Officials

President, Chief Executive Officer, and Executive Dean . . . . Paul Klotman, M.D.
Chancellor Emeritus . . . . William T. Butler, M.D.
Vice President, Primary Care . . . . Stephen J. Spann, M.D.
Vice President, Research . . . . Adam Kuspa, Ph.D.
Vice President and General Counsel, Corporate Secretary . . . . Robert Corrigan, J.D.
Chief Compliance Officer . . . . James R. Banfield, J.D.
Dean, Graduate School of Biomedical Sciences. . . . . Hiram Gilbert, Ph.D.
Dean, Medical Education . . . . Stephen B. Greenberg, M.D.
Dean, School of Allied Health Sciences . . . . J. David Holcomb, Ed.D.
Vice President for Development . . . . Kristi Cooper
Dean, National School of Tropical Medicine. . . . . Peter J. Hotez, M.D., Ph.D.
Vice President for Government Relations . . . . Thomas W. Kleinworth
Vice President for Communications . . . . Claire M. Bassett
Chief Human Resources Officer . . . . Dane Friend, J.D.
Vice President for Finance and Chief Financial Officer . . . . Kim David, C.P.A., M.B.A.
Chief Investment Officer . . . . William D. Walker, J.D., M.B.A.

Medical College Academic Administration

President, Chief Executive Officer, and Executive Dean . . . . Paul Klotman, M.D.
Dean of the Graduate School of Biomedical Sciences . . . . Hiram Gilbert, Ph.D.
Dean, Medical Education . . . . Stephen B. Greenberg, M.D.
Dean of the School of Allied Health Sciences . . . . J. David Holcomb, Ed.D.
Dean, National School of Tropical Medicine. . . . . Peter J. Hotez, M.D., Ph.D.
Senior Associate Dean, Graduate Medical Education . . . . Linda B. Andrews, M.D.
Associate Dean, Student Affairs . . . . Mary Brandt, M.D.
Senior Associate Dean, Continuing Medical Education . . . . C. Michael Fordis, Jr., M.D.
Assistant Dean, Admissions, Graduate School of Biomedical Sciences. . . . . . Gad Shaulsky, Ph.D.
Senior Associate Dean, Admissions . . . . Lloyd Michael, Ph.D. (Interim)
Associate Dean, Admissions . . . . Karen Johnson, M.D.
Assistant Dean, Student Affairs and Diversity. . . . . Toi Harris, M.D.
Senior Associate Dean, Undergraduate Medical Education . . . . Elizabeth A. Nelson, M.D.
Senior Associate Dean . . . . James L. Phillips, M.D.
Associate Dean, Post-Doctoral Affairs, Graduate
  School of Biomedical Sciences . . . . Richard Sifers, Ph.D.
Associate Dean for Research Assurances . . . . Stacey L. Berg, M.D.
Associate Dean, Undergraduate Medical Education. . . . . J. Clay Goodman, M.D.
Assistant Dean, Graduate Medical Education. . . . . Jacqueline E. Levesque, A.Ed.

Senior Associate Dean, Graduate Education and
Diversity, Graduate School of Biomedical
Sciences . . . . Gayle R. Slaughter, Ph.D.
Assistant Dean for Curriculum, Graduate School
of Biomedical Sciences . . . . Carolyn Smith, Ph.D.
Assistant Dean, Continuing Medical Education . . . . William A. Thomson, Ph.D.
Director, Human Genome Sequencing Center . . . . Richard A. Gibbs, Ph.D.
Director, Lester and Sue Smith Breast Center. . . . . C. Kent Osborne, M.D.
Director, Huffington Center on Aging . . . . Hui Zheng, Ph.D.
Director, Center for Medical Ethics and Health Policy . . . . Baruch A. Brody, Ph.D.
Director, Dan L. Duncan Cancer Center. . . . . C. Kent Osborne, M.D.
Director, Center for Cell and Gene Therapy. . . . . Malcolm K. Brenner, M.D., Ph.D.

Department and Division or Section Chairs

Basic Sciences

Biochemistry and Molecular Biology. . . . . Theodore G. Wensel, Ph.D. (Interim)
Molecular and Cellular Biology . . . . Bert W. O'Malley, M.D.
Molecular and Human Genetics. . . . . Arthur L. Beaudet, M.D.
Molecular Physiology and Biophysics . . . . Susan L. Hamilton, Ph.D.
Molecular Virology and Microbiology. . . . . Janet S. Butel, Ph.D.
Neuroscience. . . . . Dora Angelaki, Ph.D.
Pathology and Immunology . . . . Thomas M. Wheeler, M.D.
Pharmacology . . . . Timothy G. Palzkill, Ph.D.

Clinical Sciences

Anesthesiology. . . . . Maya S. Suresh, M.D.
Dermatology . . . . John E. Wolf, Jr., M.D.
Family and Community Medicine. . . . . Stephen Spann, M.D.
Medicine. . . . . Robert F. Todd III, M.D.
Neurology . . . . Eli M. Mizrahi, M.D.
Neurosurgery. . . . . Raymond A. Sawaya, M.D.
Obstetrics and Gynecology. . . . . Michael Belfort, M.D., Ph.D.
Ophthalmology . . . . Dan B. Jones, M.D.
Orthopedic Surgery. . . . . Charles Reitman, M.D. (Interim)
Otolaryngology-Head and Neck Surgery . . . . Donald T. Donovan, M.D. (Interim)
Pediatrics . . . . Mark W. Kline, M.D.
Physical Medicine and Rehabilitation . . . . Martin Grabois, M.D.
Psychiatry and Behavioral Sciences. . . . . Stuart C. Yudofsky, M.D.
Radiology . . . . Michel E. Mawad, M.D.
Surgery. . . . . David Wesson, M.D. (Interim)
Urology. . . . . Michael Coburn, M.D.

221

Texas A&M Health Science Center College of Medicine

Health Professions Education Bldg., 8447 Highway 47
Bryan, Texas 77807
979-436-0200 (dean's office); 979-436-0092 (fax)
Web site: http://medicine.tamhsc.edu

Texas A&M Health Science Center College of Medicine was authorized by the Texan legislature in 1971. Its first class graduated in 1981. The college is located on the main campus of the parent Health Science Center with clinical and research facilities in affiliated institutions.

Type: public
2011 total enrollment: 638
Clinical facilities: Scott & White Memorial Hospital and Clinic (Temple, College Station, Round Rock); Central Texas Veterans Health Care System (Temple, Waco, Marlin, Austin); Carl R. Darnall Army Medical Center (Ft. Hood); Brazos Family Medicine Residency (Bryan-College Station); St. Joseph Regional Health Center (Bryan-College Station); College Station Medical Center (College Station); Physician's Centre Hospital (College Station); Lone Star Circle of Care (Round Rock); Seton Medical Center Williamson (Round Rock); Dell Children's Medical Center (Austin); Austin State Hospital (Austin); St. David's Round Rock Medical Center (Round Rock); Driscoll Children's Hospital (Corpus Christi); CHRISTUS Spohn Memorial Hospital (Corpus Christi); Tarrant County Hospital District (Fort Worth); University of Texas M.D. Anderson Cancer Center (Houston); St. Joseph Medical Center (Houston); Memorial Hermann Southwest Hospital (Houston); St. Luke's Episcopal Hospital (Houston); Memorial Family Medicine Residency Program, and Physicians at Sugar Creek (Houston); Baylor University Medical Center (Dallas).

Health Science Center Officials

President and Vice Chancellor for Health Affairs . . . . Nancy W. Dickey, M.D.
Vice President for Academic Affairs . . . . Roderick E. McCallum, Ph.D.
Vice President for Clinical Affairs . . . . Thomas Samuel Shomaker, M.D., J.D.
Vice President for Finance and Administration . . . . Barry C. Nelson, Ph.D.
Vice President for Governmental Affairs . . . . Jenny E. Jones
Vice President for Institutional Advancement and Communications. . . . . . . Russ Gibbs, D.Min.
Vice President for Research and Graduate Studies . . . . David S. Carlson, Ph.D.
Associate Vice Chancellor for Health Affairs and Chief of Staff . . . . Lee Ann Ray, Ed.D.
Chief Legal Officer . . . . Cullen M. Godfrey, J.D.

Medical School Administrative Staff (Bryan/College Station)

Dean. . . . . Thomas Samuel Shomaker, M.D., J.D.
Vice Dean for Academic Affairs . . . . Paul E. Ogden, M.D.
Vice Dean for Graduate and Continuing Medical Education . . . . Edward J. Sherwood, M.D.
Vice Dean for Clinical and Translational Research . . . . David P. Huston, M.D.
Vice Dean for Finance and Administration . . . . Matthew D. Brown
Vice Dean for Research and Graduate Studies . . . . Van Wilson, Ph.D.
Senior Associate Dean for Student Affairs. . . . . Kathleen Fallon, M.D.
Associate Dean for Admissions . . . . Filomeno Maldonado
Associate Dean for Development . . . . A. Nelson Avery, M.D.
Associate Dean for Faculty Affairs and Curriculum Management . . . . Vernon L. Tesh, Ph.D.
Associate Dean for Student Affairs . . . . Gary C. McCord, M.D.
Associate Dean for Technology and Curriculum Innovation . . . . Paul C. Brandt, Ph.D.
Associate Dean for Veterans Affairs . . . . William F. Harper, M.D.
Assistant Dean for Admissions and Diversity . . . . Leila Diaz
Assistant Dean for Planning and Evaluation and Chief of Staff . . . . Karan Chavis
Assistant Dean for Veterans Affairs . . . . Kevin J. Carlin, M.D.
Assistant Dean for Institutional Effectiveness and
   Process Improvement . . . . Courtney Dodge (Interim)

Department and Division or Section Chairs
Basic Sciences

Humanities in Medicine. . . . . Charles W. Sanders, M.D.
Microbial and Molecular Pathogenesis . . . . James E. Samuel, Ph.D.
Molecular and Cellular Medicine . . . . Geoffrey Kapler, Ph.D. (Interim)
Neuroscience and Experimental Therapeutics. . . . . William H. Griffith, Ph.D.
Systems Biology and Translational Medicine . . . . Harris J. Granger, Ph.D.

Clinical Sciences

Anesthesiology. . . . . Timothy M. Bittenbinder, M.D.
Emergency Medicine . . . . C. Keith Stone, M.D.
Family and Community Medicine . . . . Michael Reis, M.D.

Internal Medicine . . . . Alejandro Arroliga, M.D.
Obstetrics and Gynecology . . . . Steven R. Allen, M.D.
Pathology . . . . John Greene, M.D. (Interim)
Pediatrics . . . . Madhava Beeram, M.D.
Psychiatry and Behavioral Science . . . . Brian Kirkpatrick, M.D.
Radiology . . . . L. Gill Naul, M.D.
Surgery . . . . W. Roy Smythe, M.D.

Texas A&M Health Science Center College of Medicine - Temple Campus
2401 South 31st Street
Temple, Texas 76508
254-724-2368 (phone); 254-724-7113 (fax)

Vice Dean . . . . Donald E. Wesson, M.D.
Associate Dean for Education . . . . Ruth L. Bush, M.D.
Assistant Dean for Continuing Medical Education . . . . John P. Erwin, M.D.
Assistant Dean for Educational Technologies . . . . Jose F. Pliego, M.D.
Assistant Dean for Quality Development and Patient Safety . . . . Russell K. McAllister, M.D.
Assistant Dean for Research . . . . Richard A. Beswick, Ph.D., M.B.A.
Assistant Dean for Student Affairs . . . . Wei-Jung Chen, Ph.D.

Texas A&M Health Science Center College of Medicine - Bryan/College Station Campus
St. Joseph Regional Health Center - First Floor
2801 Franciscan Drive
Bryan, Texas 77802
979-436-0514 (phone); 979-776-6903 (fax)

Vice Dean for Clinical Affairs and CMO of Practice Plan . . . . Christopher Cargile, M.D.
Regional Chair, Anesthesiology . . . . Patrick Ryan, M.D.
Regional Chair, Family and Community Medicine . . . . David A. McClellan, M.D. (Interim)
Regional Chair, Internal Medicine . . . . Paul E. Ogden, M.D.
Regional Chair, Obstetrics and Gynecology . . . . William L. Rayburn, M.D.
Regional Chair, Psychiatry . . . . Darlene McLaughlin, M.D. (Interim)
Regional Chair, Surgery . . . . Jonathan Friedman, M.D.
Regional Chair, Family and Community Medicine (Houston Area) . . . . . . David W. Bauer, M.D.

Texas A&M Health Science Center College of Medicine - Round Rock
Office of the Vice Dean
3950 North A.W. Grimes Boulevard, Suite N403
Round Rock, Texas 78665
512-341-4915 (phone); 512-341-4212 (fax)

Vice Dean . . . . Edward J. Sherwood, M.D.
Regional Chair, Family and Community Medicine . . . . Jim Donovan, M.D.
Regional Chair, Obstetrics and Gynecology . . . . Paul Murphree, M.D.
Regional Chair, Internal Medicine . . . . Lianne Marks, M.D.
Regional Chair, Pediatrics . . . . Laura E. Ferguson, M.D.
Regional Chair, Surgery . . . . Michael Craun, M.D.

Texas A&M Health Science Center College of Medicine - Dallas
Baylor University Medical Center, Dept of Medical Education
3500 Gaston Avenue
Dallas, Texas 75246
214-820-6727 (phone); 214-820-7272 (fax)

Vice Dean . . . . Cristie Columbus, M.D.

Texas Tech University Health Sciences Center
School of Medicine
3601 4th Street, MS 6207
Lubbock, Texas 79430
806-743-3000 (dean's office); 806-743-3021 (fax)
Web site: www.ttuhsc.edu/som

In May 1969, the Texas legislature and governor system authorized the establishment of an M.D. degree-granting school of medicine on the campus of Texas Tech University in Lubbock. The school is governed by the board of regents of Texas Tech University, which meets in separate sessions for each institution. Each is subject to the supervision and regulations of the coordinating board, Texas College and University System. The medical school, with regional academic health centers in Amarillo, and the Permian Basin, is part of the Texas Tech University Health Sciences Center.

Type: public
2011 total enrollment: 571
Clinical facilities: Texas Tech University Health Sciences Center Ambulatory Clinics, University Medical Center, Covenant Medical Center, Texas Tech Southwest, Veterans Administration Outpatient Clinitcs (in Lubbock), Northwest Texas Hospital and Psychiatric Pavillion, Baptist St. Anthony Hospital, Harrington Cancer Center, Veterans Administration Hospital (in Amarillo and Big Spring).

University Officials

President	Tedd Mitchell, M.D.
Executive Vice President for Research	Doug Stocco, Ph.D.
Senior Vice President for Academic Affairs	Rial Rolfe, Ph.D.
Executive Vice President and Provost	Steven L. Berk, M.D.
Vice President for Rural and Community Health	Billy Phillips, Ph.D.
Vice President for Information Technology and CIO	Chip Shaw, Ed.D.
Director of Libraries	Richard Wood
Director of Student Services and Registrar	David Carter

Medical School Administrative Staff (Lubbock)

Dean, School of Medicine	Steven L. Berk, M.D.
Associate Dean for Correctional Managed Health	Cynthia Jumper, M.D.
Associate Dean for GME and Resident Affairs	Surendra Varma, M.D.
Associate Dean for Clinical Affairs	Dale M. Dunn, M.D.
Associate Dean for Faculty Affairs and Development	Thomas Tenner, Ph.D.
Associate Dean for Academic Affairs	Simon Williams, Ph.D.
Associate Dean for Women in Health and Science	Marjorie Jenkins, M.D.
Associate Dean for Medical Practice Income Plan (MPIP)	Brent Magers
Associate Dean for Admissions	Kim Peck, M.D.
Assistant Dean for Student Affairs	Lauren S. Cobbs, M.D.
Assistant Dean for Administration	Bryce McGregor

Department and Division or Section Chairs
Basic Sciences

Cell Biology and Biochemistry	Harry M. Weitlauf, M.D.
Microbiology and Immunology	Matthew Grisham, Ph.D.
Pharmacology	Reid Norman, Ph.D.
Cell Physiology and Molecular Biophysics	Luis Reuss, M.D., Ph.D.

Clinical Sciences

Anesthesiology	John Wasnick, M.D.
Dermatology	Cloyce Stetson, M.D.
Family and Community Medicine	Ron Cook, D.O. (Interim)
Internal Medicine	Cynthia Jumper, M.D.
Neurology	John C. DeToledo, M.D.
Obstetrics and Gynecology	Edward Yeomans, M.D.
Ophthalmology and Visual Sciences	David McCartney, M.D.
Orthopaedic Surgery	George Brindley, M.D.
Pathology	Dale M. Dunn, M.D.
Pediatrics	Richard M. Lampe, M.D.
Psychiatry	Terry McMahon, M.D.
Surgery	John A. Griswold, M.D.
Urology	Werner deRiese, M.D.

Texas Tech University Health Sciences Center at Amarillo
1400 South Coulter
Amarillo, Texas 79106
806-354-5401

Regional Dean. . . . . Richard Jordan, M.D.
Assistant Academic Dean . . . . Kristin Stutz (Interim)
Assistant Regional Dean for Finance and Administration. . . . . Deborah Cain
Assistant Regional Dean for Research . . . . Thomas Hale, Ph.D.
Family Medicine . . . . Rodney Young, M.D.
Internal Medicine . . . . Roger Smalligan, M.D.
Obstetrics and Gynecology. . . . . Robert Kauffman, M.D.
Pediatrics . . . . Todd Bell, M.D.
Psychiatry . . . . Michael Jenkins, M.D.
Surgery. . . . . Mark Arredondo, M.D.

Texas Tech University Health Sciences Center at the Permian Basin
800 West 4th Street
Odessa, Texas 79763
432-335-5113

Regional Dean. . . . . John Jennings, M.D.
Executive Associate Regional Dean for Hospital
and Community Affairs and Vice President for
Fiscal Affairs . . . . Kandy Stewart (Interim)
Family Medicine . . . . Romona Burdine, M.D.
Internal Medicine . . . . William R. Davis, M.D.
Obstetrics and Gynecology. . . . . R. Moss Hampton, M.D.
Pediatrics . . . . Robert Bennett, Jr., M.D.
Psychiatry . . . . Shailesh Jain, M.D.
Surgery. . . . . Shelton Viney, M.D.

University of Texas Health Science Center at San Antonio
School of Medicine
7703 Floyd Curl Drive
San Antonio, Texas 78229
210-567-4420 (dean's office); 210-567-3435 (fax)
Web site: www.uthscsa.edu

The University of Texas Medical School at San Antonio was established in 1959 by the Texas legislature as a separate component unit of the University of Texas System. The medical school opened at its present site in September 1968. In October 1972, the Board of Regents of the University of Texas System directed the establishment of the University of Texas Health Science Center at San Antonio. The school of medicine is an integral part of the center.

Type: public
2011 total enrollment: 800
Clinical facilities: University Health System (University Hospital and University Health Center Downtown), Audie L. Murphy Memorial Veterans Hospital, Christus Santa Rosa Medical Center, Medical Arts and Research Center, Cancer Therapy and Research Center, St. Luke's Hospital, Wilford Hall USAF Medical Center, Brooke Army Medical Center, Community Guidance Center, San Antonio Children's Center, Baptist Memorial Hospital System.

University Officials
Chancellor (Austin)..................................... Francisco G. Cigarroa, M.D.
Executive Vice Chancellor for Health Affairs (Austin)........ Kenneth I. Shine, M.D. (Interim)

Health Science Center Administrative Staff
President.. William L. Henrich, M.D.
Senior Executive Vice President and Chief Operating Officer .... Michael E. Black

School of Medicine Administrative Staff
Dean, School of Medicine, & Vice President,
  Medical Affairs .... Francisco González-Scarano, M.D.
Vice Dean for Clinical Affairs.................................. Carlos Rosende, M.D.
Vice Dean for Undergraduate Medical Education .... Florence Eddins-Folensbee, M.D.
Vice Dean for Research .... Paula Shireman, M.D.
Senior Associate Dean for Finance .... Gabe Hernandez, C.P.A., M.B.A.
Senior Associate Dean for Admissions........................ David J. Jones, Ph.D.
Senior Associate Dean for Graduate Medical Education .... Lois L. Bready, M.D.
Regional Academic Health Center Dean........................ Leonel Vela, M.D., Ph.D.
Associate Dean for Administration .... Jan Wilson, Ed.D.
Associate Dean for Clinical Affairs .... Luci K. Leykum, M.D.
Associate Dean for Quality and Lifelong Learning .... Jan E. Patterson, M.D.
Associate Dean for Faculty and Diversity........................ Janet Williams, M.D.

Department and Division or Section Chairs
Clinical Sciences
Anesthesiology.. J. Jeffrey Andrews, M.D.
Epidemiology and Biostatistics .... Bradley Pollock, Ph.D.
Family and Community Medicine........................... Carlos R. Jaén, M.D., Ph.D.
Medicine .... L. David Hillis, M.D.
  Cardiology....................................... Steven Bailey, M.D.
  Clinical Immunology and Rheumatology................... Michael D. Fischbach, M.D.
  Clinical Pharmacology .... Alexander M. Shepherd, M.D., Ph.D.
  Dermatology .... Sandra Osswald, M.D.
  Diabetes... Ralph De Fronzo, M.D.
  Gastroenterology and Human Nutrition .... Glenn W. Gross, M.D.
  General Medicine.................................. Andrew K. Diehl, M.D.
  Geriatrics and Gerontology........................... Michael J. Lichtenstein, M.D.
  Hematology and Oncology............................ Athanassios Argins, M.D.
  Infectious Diseases .... Thomas F. Patterson, M.D.
  Nephrology .... Hanna Abboud, M.D.
  Pulmonary Diseases .... Jay I. Peters, M.D.
Neurology.. Robin L. Brey, M.D.
Neurosurgery... David F. Jimenez, M.D.
Obstetrics and Gynecology............................... Robert S. Schenken, M.D.
  Gynecology / Oncology .... Kevin Hall, M.D.
  Maternal and Fetal Medicine .... Elly M. J. Xenakis, M.D.
  Reproductive Endocrinology and Infertility................ Robert Brzyski, M.D.
  Reproductive Research.............................. Rajeshwar R. Tekmal, Ph.D.
Ophthalmology....................................... Steven Chalfin, M.D. (Interim)

Orthopaedics. . . . . Robert H. Quinn, M.D.
  Podiatry. . . . . Thomas Zgonis, D.P.M.
Otolaryngology-Head and Neck Surgery . . . . Randall A. Otto, M.D.
Pediatrics . . . . Thomas C. Mayes, M.D.
  Cardiology . . . . Steven Neish, M.D.
  Child Abuse Pediatrics . . . . Nancy Kellogg, M.D.
  Community Pediatrics. . . . . Victor F. German, M.D., Ph.D.
  Critical Care. . . . . Richard P. Taylor, M.D.
  Endocrinology and Diabetes. . . . . Daniel Hale, M.D.
  Gastroenterology . . . . Naveen K. Mittal, M.D.
  General Pediatrics . . . . Juan Parra, M.D. (Interim)
  Hematology-Oncology . . . . Gail Tomlinson, M.D., Ph.D.
  Immunology and Infectious Diseases. . . . . Anthony J. Infante, M.D., Ph.D.
  Inpatient Pediatrics . . . . Shawn Ralston, M.D.
  Neonatology. . . . . Steven Seidner, M.D.
  Nephrology . . . . Mazen Arar, M.D.
  Genetics, Developmental Pediatrics and Child Neurology. . . . . Sidney Atkinson, M.D.
  Pulmonology . . . . Donna Beth Willey-Courand, M.D.
Psychiatry . . . . Pedro L. Delgado, M.D.
  Aging and Geriatric Psychiatry . . . . Donald R. Royall, M.D.
  Alcohol and Drug Addiction. . . . . John D. Roache, Ph.D.
  Behavioral Medicine. . . . . Alan Peterson, Ph.D.
  Bewell Clinical Trials . . . . John D. Roache, Ph.D.
  Child and Adolescent Psychiatry . . . . Steven R. Pliszka, M.D.
  Data/Biostatistics . . . . Jim Mintz, Ph.D.
  Functional Genomics . . . . Consuelo Walss-Bass, Ph.D.
  Mood and Anxiety Disorders. . . . . Mauricio Tohen, M.D.
  Neurobehavioral Research . . . . Donald Dougherty, Ph.D.
  Psychopharmacology. . . . . Martin A. Javors, Ph.D.
  Schizophrenia and Related Disorders . . . . Dawn Velligan, Ph.D.
  Southwest Brain Bank . . . . Peter M. Thompson, M.D.
  Translational and Genetic Epidemiology. . . . . Douglas E. Williamson, Ph.D.
Radiology . . . . Michael J. McCarthy, M.D. (Interim)
  Diagnostic Radiology . . . . Ralph Blumhardt, M.D.
  Research Imaging Institute . . . . Peter T. Fox, M.D.
  Radiological Sciences . . . . Geoffrey D. Clarke, Ph.D.
Radiation Oncology. . . . . Chul S. Ha, M.D.
Rehabilitation Medicine. . . . . Nicolas E. Walsh, M.D.
Surgery . . . . Ronald M. Stewart, M.D.
  Emergency Medicine . . . . Justin B. Williams, M.D. (Interim)
  General Surgery. . . . . Wayne H. Schwesinger, M.D. (Interim)
  Organ Transplant. . . . . Glenn A. Halff, M.D.
  Plastic and Reconstructive Surgery . . . . Howard Wang, M.D.
  Trauma and Emergency Surgery. . . . . John G. Myers, M.D.
  Surgical Oncology . . . . Ismail Jakoi, M.D., Ph.D.
  Vascular Surgery. . . . . Boulos Toursarkissian, M.D.
Thoracic Surgery. . . . . John H. Calhoon, M.D.
Urology. . . . . Dennis S. Peppas, M.D. (Interim)
  Neuro-Urology. . . . . Stephen R. Kraus, M.D.
  Pediatric Urology. . . . . Dennis S. Peppas, M.D.
  Urology Research. . . . . Robin J. Leach, Ph.D.
  Urologic Oncology. . . . . Dipen J. Parekh, M.D.

University of Texas Southwestern Medical Center
Southwestern Medical School

5323 Harry Hines Boulevard
Dallas, Texas 75390
214-648-3111; 214-648-2509 (dean's office); 214-648-8955 (dean's office fax)
Web site: www.utsouthwestern.edu

The University of Texas Southwestern Medical Center at Dallas was founded as Southwestern Medical College in 1943, affiliated with the University of Texas System in 1949, and was given health center form in 1972. The three components of the UT Southwestern Medical Center are Southwestern Medical School, UT Southwestern Graduate School of Biomedical Sciences, and UT Southwestern School of Health Professions.

Type: public
2011 total enrollment: 932
Clinical facilities: UT Southwestern University Hospitals and Clinics, Parkland Memorial Hospital, Children's Medical Center, Dallas VA Medical Center, Baylor University Medical Center, Callier Center for Communication Disorders, John Peter Smith Hospital, Presbyterian Hospital of Dallas, Seton Family of Hospitals (Austin), Southwestern Institute of Forensic Sciences, Texas Scottish Rite Hospital for Crippled Children, Terrell State Hospital, Methodist Hospitals of Dallas, Methodist Charlton Medical Center, University of Texas Health Center at Tyler, McLennan County Family Practice Center (Waco), Wichita General Hospital (Wichita Falls).

University Officials

Chancellor (Austin) . . . . Francisco G. Cigarroa, M.D.
Executive Vice Chancellor for Health Affairs (Austin) . . . . Kenneth I. Shine, M.D.

Medical Center Administrative Staff

President . . . . Daniel K. Podolsky, M.D.
Executive Vice President for Academic Affairs and Provost . . . . J. Gregory Fitz, M.D.
Executive Vice President for Business Affairs . . . . Arnim Dantes
Executive Vice President for Health System Affairs . . . . Bruce A. Meyer, M.D.
Vice Provost and Dean of Basic Research . . . . David W. Russell, Ph.D.
Dean, Medical School . . . . J. Gregory Fitz, M.D.
Dean, Graduate School of Biomedical Sciences . . . . Michael G. Roth, Ph.D. (Interim)
Dean, UT Southwestern School of Health Professions . . . . Raul Caetano, M.D., Ph.D.
Vice President for Clinical Operations . . . . John D. Rutherford, M.D.
Vice President for Corporate and Community Relations . . . . Ruben E. Esquivel
Vice President for Development . . . . Randy Farmer
Vice President for Human Resources . . . . William Behrendt, Ph.D.
Vice President for Legal Affairs . . . . Leah A. Hurley, J.D.
Vice President for Technology Development . . . . Ray Wheatley (Interim)
Vice President for External Relations . . . . Cynthia B. Bassel
Vice President for Information Resources . . . . Kirk A. Kirksey
Vice President for Student and Alumni Affairs . . . . J. Wesley Norred
Vice President for Communications, Marketing, and Public Affairs . . . . Tim Doke

Medical School Administrative Staff

Dean . . . . J. Gregory Fitz, M.D.
Senior Associate Dean for Academic Affairs . . . . Charles M. Ginsburg, M.D.
Senior Associate Dean for Strategic Development . . . . Dwain L. Thiele, M.D.
Regional Dean, Austin Programs . . . . Susan Cox, M.D.
Associate Dean for Undergraduate Medical Education . . . . Stephen C. Cannon, M.D.
Associate Dean for Faculty Diversity and Development . . . . Bryon L. Cryer, M.D.
Associate Dean for Global Health . . . . Ohwofiemu E. Nwariaku, M.D.
Associate Dean for Student Affairs . . . . James M. Wagner, M.D.
Associate Dean for Student Affairs . . . . Angela P. Mihalic, M.D.
Associate Dean for Minority Student Affairs . . . . Shawna D. Nesbitt, M.D.
Associate Dean for Graduate Medical Education . . . . Bradley F. Marple, M.D.
Associate Dean for Oncology Programs . . . . James K.V. Willson, M.D.
Associate Dean for M.D.-Ph.D. Training Program . . . . Andrew R. Zinn, M.D., Ph.D.

Department and Division or Section Chairs

Basic Sciences

Biochemistry . . . . Steven L. McKnight, Ph.D.
Cell Biology . . . . Sandra L. Schmio, Ph.D.
Developmental Biology . . . . Luis F. Parada, Ph.D.
Immunology . . . . Edward K. Wakeland, Ph.D.
Microbiology . . . . Michael V. Norgard, M.D.
Molecular Biology . . . . Eric N. Olson, Ph.D.
Molecular Genetics . . . . Joseph L. Goldstein, M.D.
Neuroscience . . . . Joseph Takahashi, Ph.D.
Pharmacology . . . . David J. Mangelsdorf, Ph.D.
Physiology . . . . James T. Stull, Ph.D.

Clinical Sciences

Anesthesiology . . . . Charles W. Whitten, M.D.
Cardiovascular and Thoracic Surgery . . . . Michael E. Jessen, M.D.
Clinical Sciences . . . . Milton Packer, M.D.
Dermatology . . . . Kim B. Yancey, M.D.
Family and Community Medicine . . . . Alison Dobbie, M.D.
Internal Medicine . . . . David H. Johnson, M.D.
   Allergy . . . . Rebecca Gruchalla, M.D., Ph.D.
   Cardiology . . . . Joseph Hill, M.D., Ph.D.
   Clinical Genetics . . . . Helen H. Hobbs, M.D.
   Digestive and Liver Diseases . . . . Don Rockey, M.D.
   Endocrinology and Metabolism . . . . Abhimanyu Garg, M.D. (Interim)
   Epidemiology . . . . Robert W. Haley, M.D.
   General Internal Medicine . . . . Ethan Halm, M.D.
   Hematology-Oncology . . . . Joan Schiller, M.D.
   Nutrition and Metabolic Diseases . . . . Abhimanyu Garg, M.D.
   Infectious Disease . . . . Mark Swancutt, M.D. (Interim)
   Mineral Metabolism . . . . Khashayar Sakhaee, M.D.
   Nephrology . . . . Peter Igarashi, M.D.
   Pulmonary and Critical Care Medicine . . . . Lance S. Terada, M.D.
   Rheumatic Diseases . . . . David Karp, M.D., Ph.D.
   Touchstone Diabetes Center . . . . Philipp E. Scherer, M.D.
Neurological Surgery . . . . Duke S. Samson, M.D.
Neurology and Neurotherapeutics . . . . Mark P. Goldberg, M.D.
Obstetrics-Gynecology . . . . Steven L. Bloom, M.D.
Ophthalmology . . . . James P. McCulley, M.D.
Orthopaedic Surgery . . . . Joseph Borrelli, Jr., M.D.
Otolaryngology-Head and Neck Surgery . . . . Peter S. Roland, M.D.
Pathology . . . . James S. Malter, M.D.
Pediatrics . . . . Julio Perez-Fontan, M.D. (Interim)
Physical Medicine and Rehabilitation . . . . Karen J. Kowalske, M.D.
Plastic Surgery . . . . Rodney J. Rohrich, M.D.
Psychiatry . . . . Carol A. Tamminga, M.D.
   Psychology . . . . C. Munro Cullum, Ph.D.
Radiation Oncology . . . . Hak Choy, M.D.
Radiology . . . . Neil M. Rofsky, M.D.
Surgery . . . . Robert Rege, M.D.
   Burn/Trauma/Critical Care . . . . Joseph Minei, M.D.
   Emergency Medicine . . . . Paul Pepe, M.D.
   GI/Endocrine . . . . Edward Livingston, M.D.
   Oral Surgery . . . . John Zuniga, D.D.S., Ph.D.
   Pediatric Surgery . . . . Robert Foglia, M.D.
   Surgical Oncology . . . . Roderich Schwarz, M.D., Ph.D.
   Transplant Surgery . . . . Juan Arenas, M.D.
   Vascular Surgery . . . . R. James Valentine, M.D.
Urology . . . . Claus Roehrborn, M.D.

University of Texas Medical Branch
University of Texas Medical School at Galveston

301 University Boulevard
Galveston, Texas 77555-0133
409-772-1011; 409-772-2671 (dean's office); 409-772-9598 (fax)
E-mail: ganderso@utmb.edu
Web site: www.utmb.edu

The University of Texas Medical Branch at Galveston was established in 1881 as a branch of the University of Texas and accepted its first class in 1891. In addition to the medical school, the campus includes the graduate school of biomedical sciences, school of health professions, school of nursing, Institute for Translational Sciences, Institute for the Medical Humanities, and the Institute for Human Infections and Immunity.

Type: public
2011 total enrollment: 920
Clinical facilities: John Sealy Hospital, Children's Hospital, Primary Care Pavillion, Texas Department of Criminal Justice Hospital. **Other facility:** Shriners Burns Institute.

University Officials

Chancellor (Austin) . . . . Francisco G. Cigarroa, M.D.
Executive Vice Chancellor for Health Affairs (Austin) . . . . Kenneth I. Shine, M.D.

Medical Branch Administrative Staff

President. . . . . David L. Callender, M.D., F.A.C.S.
Executive Vice President and Provost . . . . Garland D. Anderson, M.D.
Executive Vice President and Chief Business and Finance Officer . . . . William R. Elger
Executive Vice President and Chief Executive
 Officer, UTMB Health System . . . . Donna K. Sollenberger
Senior Vice President for Health Policy and Legislative Affairs . . . . Ben G. Raimer, M.D.
Vice President for Education . . . . Pamela G. Watson, Sc.D.
Director, Moody Medical Library and Associate
 VP for Academic Resources and Director of
 Libraries . . . . Brett A. Kirkpatrick

Medical School Administrative Staff

Dean of Medicine . . . . Garland D. Andersen, M.D.
Vice Dean for Academic Affairs . . . . Steven A. Lieberman, M.D.
Chief Physician Executive, Faculty Group Practice. . . . . Rex McCallum, M.D.
Vice President for Finance, Academic Enterprise . . . . Cameron Slocum, M.B.A.
Senior Associate Dean for Faculty Affairs . . . . Linda G. Phillips, M.D.
Associate Dean for Educational Affairs . . . . Michael A. Ainsworth, M.D.
Associate Dean for Graduate Medical Education . . . . Thomas A. Blackwell, M.D.
Associate Dean for Research Services Administration. . . . . William New
Associate Dean for Student Affairs and Admissions . . . . Lauree Thomas, M.D.
Assistant Dean for Continuing Medical Education. . . . . Lois A. Killewich, M.D., Ph.D.
Assistant Dean for Educational Affairs . . . . Gregory K. Asimakis, Ph.D.
Assistant Dean for Educational Affairs . . . . Judith L. Rowen, M.D.
Assistant Dean for Educational Development . . . . Ann W. Frye, Ph.D.
Assistant Dean for Osler Student Societies . . . . Michael H. Malloy, M.D.
Assistant Dean for Regional Medical Education. . . . . John C. Luk, M.D.
Assistant Dean for Student Affairs and Admissions . . . . Jeffrey P. Rabek, Ph.D.

Department and Division or Section Chairs

Basic Sciences

Biochemistry and Molecular Biology. . . . . J. Regino Perez-Polo, Ph.D.
Microbiology and Immunology. . . . . David W. Niesel, Ph.D.
Neuroscience and Cell Biology. . . . . Henry F. Epstein, M.D.
Pathology . . . . David H. Walker, M.D.
Pharmacology and Toxicology . . . . Lawrence Sowers, Ph.D.
Preventive Medicine and Community Health . . . . Harvey Bunce III, Ph.D. (ad interim)

Clinical Sciences

Anesthesiology. . . . . Donald S. Prough, M.D.
Dermatology . . . . Sharon S. Ramier, M.D.
Family Medicine . . . . Barbara L. Thompson, M.D.
Internal Medicine . . . . Randall J. Urban, M.D.
  Allergy and Immunology . . . . Rana Bonds, M.D.
  Cardiology. . . . . Ken Fujise, M.D.
  Endocrinology . . . . Nicola Abate, M.D.
  Gastroenterology . . . . G. Nicholas Verne, M.D.
  General Medicine. . . . . Randall J. Urban, M.D. (ad interim)
  Geriatrics. . . . . Mukaila Raji, M.D.
  Hematology and Oncology. . . . . Avi Markowitz, M.D.
  Infectious Diseases . . . . A. Clinton White, M.D.
  Nephrology and Hypertension . . . . John Badalamenti, M.D.
  Pulmonary, Sleep, and Critical Care . . . . Gulshan Sharma, M.D., M.P.H.
  Rheumatology . . . . Emilio B. Gonzalez, M.D.
Neurology. . . . . R. Glenn Smith, M.D. (ad interim)
Obstetrics and Gynecology. . . . . Gary Hankins, M.D., D.V.
Ophthalmology and Visual Sciences . . . . Bernard F. Godley, M.D., Ph.D.
Orthopaedics and Rehabilitation . . . . Ronald W. Lindsey, M.D.
Otolaryngology . . . . Vicente A. Resto, M.D., Ph.D.
Pediatrics . . . . C. Joan Richardson, M.D.
Psychiatry and Behavioral Sciences . . . . Robert M. A. Hirschfeld, M.D.
Radiation Oncology. . . . . Martin Colman, M.D.
Radiology . . . . Val M. Runge, M.D.
Surgery . . . . Courtney M. Townsend, Jr., M.D.
  Cardiovascular and Thoracic. . . . . Vincent R. Conti, M.D.
  General Surgery. . . . . Courtney M. Townsend, Jr., M.D.
  Neurosurgery. . . . . Joel T. Patterson, M.D. (ad interim)
  Oral Surgery . . . . Elgene G. Mainous, D.D.S.
  Plastic Surgery . . . . Linda G. Phillips, M.D.
  Urology . . . . Eduardo Orihuela, M.D.

University of Texas Medical School at Houston

6431 Fannin
Houston, Texas 77030
713-500-5160 (student affairs); 713-500-5010 (dean's office); 713-500-0602 (fax)
Web site: www.med.uth.tmc.edu

The University of Texas Medical School at Houston was authorized by the Texas Legislature in May 1969 as a component of The University of Texas System. With cooperation of the other three University of Texas medical schools, the first class enrolled in September 1970 and was graduated in 1973. The medical school is a part of the University of Texas Health Science Center at Houston with schools of dentistry, public health, nursing, health information sciences, and the graduate school of biomedical sciences.

Type: public
2011 total enrollment: 942
Clinical facilities: Memorial Hermann Texas Medical Center, The University of Texas M. D. Anderson Cancer Center, Lyndon B. Johnson General Hospital/Harris County Hospital District, Memorial Hermann Hospital System, Shriners Hospital for Crippled Children, St. Joseph Hospital, UT Harris County Psychiatric Center, St. Luke's Episcopal Hospital-Texas Heart Institute.

University Officials

Chancellor (Austin)... Francisco G. Cigarroa, M.D.
Executive Vice Chancellor for Health Affairs (Austin)............... Kenneth I. Shine, M.D.

Health Science Center Administrative Staff

President.. Giuseppe N. Colasurdo, M.D. (Ad Interim)
Senior Executive Vice President, Chief
    Operating and Financial Officer .... Kevin Dillon, M.B.A., C.P.A.
Executive Vice President for Academic and Research Affairs......... George M. Stancel, Ph.D.

Medical School Administrative Staff

Dean... Giuseppe N. Colasurdo, M.D.
Executive Vice Dean for Clinical Affairs .... Brent R. King, M.D.
Vice Dean for Clinical Research and Healthcare Quality.......... Jon E. Tyson, M.D., M.P.H.
Vice Dean for Research... John F. Hancock, M.B., B.Chir., Ph.D.
Senior Associate Dean for Educational Programs .... Patricia M. Butler, M.D.
Associate Dean for Administrative Affairs .... Nancy O. McNiel, Ph.D.
Associate Dean for Admissions and Student Affairs.............. Margaret C. McNeese, M.D.
Associate Dean for Clinical Business Affairs..................... Julie T. Page, C.P.A.
Associate Dean for Faculty Affairs and Alumni Relations............ Henry W. Strobel, Ph.D.
Associate Dean for Harris County Programs .... Carmel B. Dyer, M.D. (Interim)
Associate Dean for Healthcare Quality .... Eric Thomas, M.D., M.P.H.
Associate Dean for Hospital Affairs and
    Community Partnerships .... Craig Cordola, M.B.A., M.H.A.
Associate Dean for Information Technology..................... William A. Weems, Ph.D.
Associate Dean for Research...................................... John H. Byrne, Ph.D.
Associate Dean for Research.................................. David G. Gorenstein, Ph.D.
Assistant Dean for Admissions and Student Affairs .... Wallace A. Gleason, M.D.
Assistant Dean for Admissions and Student Affairs .... Latanya J. Love, M.D.
Assistant Dean for Admissions and Student Affairs .... Sheela L. Lahoti, M.D.
Assistant Dean for Educational Programs .... R. Andrew Harper, M.D.
Assistant Dean for Educational Programs .... Philip R. Orlander, M.D.
Assistant Dean for Educational Programs .... Gary C. Rosenfeld, Ph.D.
Assistant Dean for Educational Programs .... Margaret O. Uthman, M.D.
Assistant Dean for Graduate Medical Education .... John R. Potts, M.D.
Assistant Dean for Healthcare Quality (Adult) .... Bela Patel, M.D.
Assistant Dean for Healthcare Quality (Pediatrics) .... Eric C. Eichenwald, M.D.
Assistant Dean for Healthcare Quality (Women's & Perinatal)........... Sean Blackwell, M.D.
Director, Graduate Medical Education .... David E. Kusnerik
Director, Educational Programs .... Allison R. Ownby, Ph.D., M.Ed.
Director, Biomedical Information Technology .... Stephen J. Fath, Ph.D.
Director, Center for Laboratory Animal
    Medicine and Care .... Bradford S. Goodwin, Jr., D.V.M.
Executive Director of Finance .... Angela Hintzel Smith, C.P.A.
Director, Management Services .... Claire Brunson
Executive Director, Development................................... Shernaz Boga
Director, Admissions and Student Affairs .... Patricia E. Caver

University of Texas Medical School at Houston: TEXAS

Coordinator, Faculty Affairs . . . . Faye W. Viola
Coordinator, Postdoctoral Affairs . . . . Leslie Beckman

Department Chairs and Division Directors

Basic Sciences

Biochemistry and Molecular Biology. . . . . Rodney E. Kellems, Ph.D.
Integrative Biology and Pharmacology . . . . John F. Hancock, M.B., B.Chir., Ph.D.
Microbiology and Molecular Genetics. . . . . Theresa M. Koehler, Ph.D. (Interim)
Nanomedicine and Biomedical Engineering . . . . David G. Gorenstein, Ph.D. (Interim)
Neurobiology and Anatomy . . . . John H. Byrne, Ph.D.

Clinical Sciences

Anesthesiology. . . . . Carin A. Hagberg, M.D.
Cardiothoracic and Vascular Surgery . . . . Hazim J. Safi, M.D.
Dermatology . . . . Ronald P. Rapini, M.D.
Diagnostic and Interventional Imaging. . . . . Susan D. John, M.D.
Emergency Medicine. . . . . Brent R. King, M.D.
Family and Community Medicine. . . . . Carlos A. Moreno, M.D.
Internal Medicine . . . . David D. McPherson, M.D.
    Cardiology. . . . . David D. McPherson, M.D.
    Critical Care Medicine . . . . Bela Patel, M.D., F.C.C.P.
    Endocrinology, Diabetes, and Metabolism . . . . Philip R. Orlander, M.D.
    Gastroenterology, Hepatology, and Nutrition. . . . . Michael B. Fallon, M.D.
    General Medicine. . . . . Philip C. Johnson, M.D.
    Geriatric Medicine . . . . Carmel B. Dyer, M.D.
    Hematology. . . . . Harinder S. Juneja, M.D.
    Infectious Diseases . . . . Barbara E. Murray, M.D.
    Medical Genetics . . . . Dianna M. Milewicz, M.D., Ph.D.
    Oncology. . . . . Robert J. Amato, D.O. (Acting)
    Pulmonary and Sleep Medicine. Richard J. Castriotta, M.D., Ph.D.
    Renal Diseases and Hypertension . . . . Kevin W. Finkel, M.D.
    Rheumatology and Clinical Immunogenetics . . . . John D. Reveille, M.D.
Neurology . . . . James C. Grotta, M.D.
Neurosurgery. . . . . Dong H. Kim, M.D.
Obstetrics, Gynecology, and Reproductive Sciences . . . . Sean C. Blackwell, M.D. (Interim)
Ophthalmology and Visual Science. . . . . Robert M. Feldman, M.D.
Orthopaedic Surgery . . . . Walter R. Lowe, M.D.
Otorhinolaryngology-Head and Neck Surgery . . . . Martin J. Citardi, M.D.
Pathology and Laboratory Medicine . . . . Robert L. Hunter, Jr., M.D., Ph.D.
Pediatric Surgery . . . . Kevin P. Lally, M.D.
Pediatrics . . . . Brent R. King, M.D. (Interim)
    Adolescent Medicine . . . . Mona Eissa, M.D.
    Cardiology. . . . . J. Timothy Bricker, M.D.
    Children's Learning Institute . . . . Susan H. Landry, Ph.D.
    Community and General . . . . Robert J. Yetman, M.D.
    Critical Care. . . . . Ikram Haque, M.D.
    Endocrinology . . . . Michael Yafi, M.D.
    Gastroenterology . . . . J. Marc Rhoads, M.D.
    Genetics. . . . . Hope Northrup, M.D.
    Hematology . . . . Deborah L. Brown, M.D.
    Infectious Diseases . . . . Gloria P. Heresi, M.D.
    Neonatology. . . . . Eric C. Eichenwald, M.D.
    Nephrology . . . . Rita Swinford, M.D.
    Neurology . . . . Ian J. Butler, M.D.
    Pulmonology and Allergy-Immunology Medicine . . . . James M. Stark, M.D.
Physical Medicine and Rehabilitation . . . . Gerard E. Francisco, M.D.
Psychiatry and Behavioral Sciences. . . . . Jair C. Soares, M.D.
Surgery . . . . Richard J. Andrassy, M.D.
    Acute Care. . . . . John B. Holcomb, M.D.
    Elective General Surgery. . . . . Eric B. Wilson, M.D.
    General (LBJ) . . . . Tien C. Ko, M.D.
    Immunology and Organ Transplantation. . . . . John S. Bynon, M.D., F.A.C.S.
    Oral and Maxillofacial . . . . James W. Wilson, D.D.S.
    Plastic and Reconstructive. . . . . Donald H. Parks, M.D.
    Urology . . . . Richard J. Andrassy, M.D. (Interim)

University of Utah School of Medicine
30 North 1900 East
Salt Lake City, Utah 84132-2101
801-581-7201; 801-581-6436 (dean's office); 801-585-3300 (fax)
Web site: http://medicine.utah.edu

Founded as a two-year school in 1905, the college of medicine was expanded to a four-year program in 1943. In 1965, it became completely integrated into the university with the completion of the University of Utah Medical Center on the upper campus. In 1981, the name was changed formally to the University of Utah School of Medicine.

Type: public
2011 total enrollment: 373
Clinical facilities: University Hospital and Clinics, Intermountain Healthcare, Salt Lake Regional Medical Center, St. Mark's Hospital, Shriners Hospitals for Crippled Children, Primary Children's Medical Center, McKay-Dee Hospital Center, Veterans Affairs Medical Center (Salt Lake City), University of Utah Neuropsychiatric Institute, Huntsman Cancer Hospital.

University Officials

President. . . . . A. Lorris Betz, M.D., Ph.D. (Interim)
Senior Vice President, Academic Affairs . . . . David W. Pershing, Ph.D.
Senior Vice President for Health Sciences. Vivan S. Lee, M.D., Ph.D.
Chief Executive Officer, University Hospital . . . . David Entwistle

Medical School Administrative Staff

Dean. . . . . Vivian S. Lee, M.D., Ph.D.
Senior Associate Dean . . . . Jayne M. Samuelson, M.D.
Associate Dean for Finance . . . . Cynthia Best
Associate Dean for Student Affairs . . . . Edward Junkins, M.D.
Associate Dean for Professionalism, Accountability, and Assessment. . . . . . . Barbara Cahill, M.D.
Associate Dean for Veteran's Affairs . . . . Ronald Gebhart, M.D.
Associate Dean for Admissions . . . . Wayne M. Samuelson, M.D.
Associate Dean for Curriculum. . . . . Sara Lamb, M.D.
Associate Dean for Graduate Medical Education . . . . Larry Reimer, M.D.
Associate Dean for CME; Medical Graphics/Photography . . . . Jack Dolcourt, M.D.
Assistant Dean for Inclusion and Outreach. . . . . Evelyn Gopez, M.D.
Assistant Dean for Idaho; International Medical Education . . . . DeVon C. Hale, M.D.
Assistant Dean for Dental Education. . . . . G. Lynn Powell, D.D.S.
Assistant Dean for Graduate Medical Education . . . . Alan Smith, M.D.
Director of Administration . . . . Karen Anastasopoulos
Director of Admissions. . . . . Kathy Z. Doulis
Director of Faculty Administration . . . . Jennifer Allie
Director of Medical Education . . . . Korriedu M. Lauder
Director of Student Affairs. . . . . Carol Stevens
Chief Assessment Officer . . . . Steven Baumann, Ed.D.
Chief Education Officer. . . . . Michelle Haight, Ph.D.
Financial Aid Officer . . . . Wendy Clark

Department and Division or Section Chairs
Basic Sciences

Biochemistry . . . . Chris Hill, Ph.D., and Wes Sundquist, Ph.D.
Human Genetics . . . . Lynn Jorde, Ph.D.
Human and Molecular Biology and Genetics . . . . Dean Li, Ph.D.
Biomedical Informatics . . . . Joyce Mitchell, Ph.D.
Neurobiology and Anatomy . . . . Monica Vetter, Ph.D.
Oncological Sciences . . . . Jon Ayer, Ph.D. (Interim)
Pathology . . . . Peter Jensen, M.D.
Physiology . . . . Ed Dudek, Ph.D.

Clinical Sciences

Anesthesiology. . . . . Michael K. Cahalan, M.D.
Dermatology . . . . John J. Zone, M.D.
Family and Preventive Medicine . . . . Michael K. Magill, M.D.
    Family Medicine Division . . . . Jennifer Leiser, M.D.
    Physician Assistant Program . . . . John Houchins, M.D.
    Public Health . . . . Stephen C. Alder, Ph.D.
    Occupational & Environ. Health . . . . Kurt Hegmann, M.D.

Internal Medicine . . . . John R. Hoidal, M.D.
   Cardiology . . . . John Michael, M.D. (Acting)
   Endocrinology . . . . E. Dale Abel, M.B.B.S.
   Gastroenterology . . . . Curt Hagedorn, M.D.
   General Internal Medicine . . . . Barry M. Stults, M.D.
   Geriatrics . . . . Mark A. Supiano, M.D.
   Hematology . . . . James P. Kushner, M.D.
   Infectious Disease . . . . John B. Hibbs, Jr., M.D.
   Nephrology . . . . Alred Cheung, M.D.
   Oncology . . . . John H. Ward, M.D.
   Pulmonary . . . . Robert Paine, M.D.
   Rheumatology . . . . Daniel O. Clegg, M.D.
Neurology . . . . Stefan M. Pulst, M.D.
Neurosurgery . . . . William T. Couldwell, M.D.
Obstetrics and Gynecology . . . . C. Matthew Peterson, M.D.
   General Obstetrics and Gynecology . . . . Howard T. Sharp, M.D.
   Gynecologic Oncology . . . . Andrew Soison, M.D.
   Maternal-Fetal Medicine . . . . Robert M. Silver, M.D.
   Reproductive Endocrinology and Infertility . . . . Mark Gibson, M.D.
   Urogynecology and Pelvic Reconstructive Surgery . . . . Peggy A. Norton, M.D.
Ophthalmology and Visual Sciences . . . . Randall J. Olson, M.D.
Orthopedics . . . . Charles Saltzman, M.D.
Pediatrics . . . . Edward B. Clark, M.D.
   Adolescent Medicine . . . . Michael Spigarelli, M.D.
   Clinical Pharmacology . . . . Michael Spigarelli, M.D.
   Critical Care . . . . J. Michael Dean, M.D.
   Emergency Medicine . . . . Howard Kadish, M.D.
   Endocrinology and Metabolism . . . . Mary Murray, M.D.
   General Clinical Pediatrics . . . . Karen Buchi, M.D.
   Genetics . . . . Nicola Longo, M.D., Ph.D.
   Inpatient Medicine . . . . Chris Maloney, M.D., Ph.D.
   Neonatology . . . . Robert Lane, M.D.
   Pediatric Behavioral Health . . . . D. Richard Martini, M.D.
   Pediatric Cardiology . . . . Lloyd Y. Tani, M.D.
   Pediatric Clinical Immunology and Rheumatology . . . . William Gershan, M.D.
   Pediatric Gastroenterology . . . . Linda S. Book, M.D.
   Pediatric Hematology and Oncology . . . . Richard S. Lemons, M.D., Ph.D.
   Pediatric Infectious Diseases . . . . Andrew T. Pavia, M.D.
   Pediatric Nephrology . . . . Raoul D. Nelson, M.D.
   Pediatric Neurology . . . . Francis M. Filloux, M.D.
   Pediatric Pulmonology . . . . John Bohnsack, M.D. (Interim)
   Pediatric Surgery . . . . Rebecka Meyers, M.D.
   Child Protection and Family Health . . . . David Corwin, M.D.
Physical Medicine and Rehabilitation . . . . Elie Elovic, M.D.
Psychiatry . . . . William M. McMahon, M.D.
Radiation Oncology . . . . Dennis C. Shrieve, M.D., Ph.D.
   Medical Physics . . . . Bill J. Salter, M.D.
   Radiation Therapy . . . . David K. Gaffney, M.D., Ph.D.
Radiology . . . . Edwin A. Stevens, M.D.
   Chest Radiology . . . . Howard Mann, M.D.
   General Radiology, Body Imaging . . . . Tom Winter, M.D.
   Interventional Radiology . . . . Ryan O'Hara, M.D.
   Musculoskeletal Radiology . . . . Julia R. Crim, M.D.
   Neuroradiology . . . . Karen Salzman, M.D.
   Nuclear Medicine . . . . John Hoffman, M.D.
   Utah Center for Advanced Imaging Research . . . . Dennis Parker, Ph.D.
   Vice Chair . . . . Anne Kennedy, M.D.
   Women's Imaging . . . . Matthew Stein, M.D.
Surgery . . . . Sean J. Mulvihill, M.D.
   Cardiothoracic Surgery . . . . David Bull, M.D.
   Emergency Medicine . . . . Erik Barton, M.D.
   General Surgery . . . . Edward W. Nelson, M.D.
   Otolaryngology-Head and Neck Surgery . . . . Clough Shelton, M.D.
   Pediatric Surgery . . . . Rebecka Meyers, M.D.
   Plastic and Reconstructive Surgery . . . . W. Bradford Rockwell, M.D.
   Urology . . . . Patrick C. Cartwright, M.D.
   Vascular Surgery . . . . Larry Kraiss, M.D.
   Andrology . . . . Douglas Carrell, Ph.D.

University of Vermont College of Medicine
E126 Given Building 89, Beaumont Avenue
Burlington, Vermont 05405
802-656-2156 (general information); 802-656-2156 (dean's office); 802-656-8577 (fax)
Web site: www.med.uvm.edu

Instruction in what was to become the University of Vermont College of Medicine was initiated in 1803, when Dr. John Pomeroy was appointed to the staff to teach chirurgery (surgery) and anatomy. The first full and regular course of medical lectures, however, was not offered until fall 1822. In 1836, the medical department was forced to close because of lack of students and professors. The school was reorganized and reopened in 1853. In 1899, the medical college became a coordinate department of the university under the control of its board of trustees. In 1911, the college of medicine became an intergal part of the university.

Type: public
2011 total enrollment: 445
Clinical facilities: Fletcher Allen Health Care, Inc., Danbury Hospital (CT), St. Mary's Medical Center (FL), Eastern Maine Medical Center (Bangor). Cooperating hospitals: Central Vermont Hospital, Champlain Valley Physicians Hospital, Vermont State Hospital.

University Officials

President . . . . A. John Bramley, Ph.D. (Interim)
Provost . . . . Jane Knodell, Ph.D.
Librarian, Health Sciences . . . . Marianne D. Burke
Director, Sponsored Programs . . . . Ruth A. Farrell
Associate Director, Sponsored Programs . . . . Beverly A. Blakeney

Medical School Administrative Staff

Dean . . . . Frederick C. Morin III, M.D.
Executive Assistant to the Dean . . . . Maura L. Randall
Senior Associate Dean for Finance and Administration . . . . Brian L. Cote
Senior Associate Dean for Clinical Affairs . . . . Paul Taheri, M.D.
Senior Associate Dean for Research . . . . Ira Bernstein, M.D.
Senior Associate Dean for Medical Education . . . . William Jeffries, Ph.D.
Associate Dean for Faculty and Staff
    Development and Diversity . . . . Karen Richardson-Nassif, Ph.D.
Associate Dean for Student Affairs . . . . G. Scott Waterman, M.D.
Associate Dean for Continuing Medical Education . . . . Cheung Wong, M.D.
Associate Dean for Primary Care . . . . Charles MacLean, M.D.
Associate Dean for Patient Oriented Research . . . . Richard Galbraith, M.D., Ph.D.
Associate Dean for Graduate Medical Education . . . . David Adams, M.D.
Associate Dean for Public Health . . . . Jan K. Carney, M.D.
Associate Dean for Admissions . . . . Janice M. Gallant, M.D.
Director Clinical Trials Research . . . . Kimberly Luebbers
Assistant Dean for Communications and Planning . . . . Carole L. Whitaker
Assistant Dean for Development and Alumni Affairs . . . . Vacant
Executive Secretary of Medical Alumni Association . . . . John P. Tampas, M.D.
Assistant Dean for Facilities Administration and Planning . . . . Susan W. Ligon

Department and Division or Section Chairs

Basic Sciences

Anatomy and Neurobiology . . . . Rodney L. Parsons, Ph.D.
Biochemistry . . . . Paula B. Tracy, Ph.D. (Interim)
Microbiology and Molecular Genetics . . . . Susan S. Wallace, Ph.D.
Molecular Physiology and Biophysics . . . . David M. Warshaw, Ph.D.
Pathology . . . . Edwin G. Bovill, M.D.
    Clinical Pathology* . . . . Edwin G. Bovill, M.D.
Pharmacology . . . . Mark T. Nelson, Ph.D.
    Clinical Pharmacology . . . . Richard Galbraith, M.D., Ph.D.

236

University of Vermont College of Medicine: VERMONT

Clinical Sciences

Anesthesiology. . . . . Howard M. Schapiro, M.D.
Family Practice . . . . Thomas C. Peterson, M.D.
Medicine. . . . . Polly E. Parsons, M.D.
   Cardiology* . . . . David J. Schneider, M.D.
   Dermatology*. . . . . Glenn Goldman, M.D.
   Endocrinology and Metabolism*. . . . . John L. Leahy, M.D.
   Gastroenterology* . . . . James Vecchio, M.D.
   General Internal Care*. . . . . Benjamin Littenberg, M.D.
   Gerontology*. . . . . Naomi Fukagawa, M.D. (Acting)
   Hematology-Oncology*. . . . . Claire F. Verschraegen, M.D.
   Human Medical Genetics* . . . . Vacant
   Immunobiology . . . . Ralph C. Budd, M.D.
   Infectious Diseases* . . . . Christopher J. Grace, M.D.
   Nephrology* . . . . Richard J. Solomon, M.D.
   Pulmonary and Critical Care*. . . . . Anne E. Dixon, M.D.
   Rheumatology* . . . . Edward Leib, M.D. (Interim)
   Vascular Biology. . . . . David J. Schneider, M.D.
Neurology. . . . . Robert W. Hamill, M.D.
Obstetrics and Gynecology. . . . . Mark Phillippe, M.D.
Orthopedics and Rehabilitation . . . . Claude E. Nichols, M.D.
Pediatrics . . . . Lewis R. First, M.D.
   Ambulatory Pediatrics*. . . . . Jerry G. Larrabee, M.D.
   Cardiology*. . . . . Scott B. Yeager, M.D.
   Inpatient Pediatrics and Critical Care* . . . . Barry W. Heath, M.D.
   Endocrinology . . . . Paul J. Zimakas, M.D.
   Gastrointestinal*. . . . . Michael A. D'amico, M.D.
   Genetics*. . . . . Leah W. Burke, M.D.
   Hematology-Oncology*. . . . . Alan C. Homans, M.D.
   Immunology*. . . . . Barry A. Finette, M.D., Ph.D.
   Infectious Disease*. . . . . William V. Raszka, M.D.
   Neonatal* . . . . Charles E. Mercier, M.D.
   Nephrology* . . . . Ann P. Guillot, M.D.
   Pulmonary* . . . . Thomas Lahiri, M.D.
   Rheumatology . . . . Leslie S. Abramson, M.D.
Psychiatry . . . . Robert A. Pierattini, M.D.
Radiology . . . . Steven P. Braff, M.D.
Surgery. . . . . Marion E. Couch, M.D., Ph.D. (Interim)
   Emergency Medicine* . . . . Stephen M. Leffler, M.D.
   General* . . . . James Hebert, M.D.
   Maxillofacial*. . . . . Kevin Risko, M.D.
   Neurosurgery* . . . . Michael Horgan, M.D. (Interim)
   Ophthalmology*. . . . . Marion E. Couch, M.D., Ph.D.
   Otolaryngology*. . . . . William J. Brundage, M.D.
   Pediatric*. . . . . Kennith Sartorelli, M.D.
   Plastic* . . . . Donald Laub, M.D.
   Surgical Oncology*. . . . . Seth P. Harlow, M.D.
   Thoracic and Cardiac* . . . . Frank P. Ittleman, M.D.
   Transplantation* . . . . Antonio Di Carlo, M.D.
   Trauma and Surgical Critical Care*. . . . . William Charash, M.D.
   Urology* . . . . Mark K. Plante, M.D.
   Vascular* . . . . Andrew Stanley, M.D.

*Specialty without organizational autonomy.

Eastern Virginia Medical School

P.O. Box 1980
Norfolk, Virginia 23501
757-446-5200 (president's office); 757-446-5600 (general);
757-446-5800 (dean's office); 757-446-8444 (fax)
Web site: www.evms.edu

Eastern Virginia Medical School (EVMS) is governed by the Eastern Virginia Medical School Board of Visitors and was established by the General Assembly of the Commonwealth of Virginia in 1964. In September 1976, the medical school graduated 23 physicians in its first class. With the support of the communities of Norfolk, Virginia Beach, Chesapeake, Hampton, Portsmouth, Newport News, Suffolk, and other cities and counties throughout eastern Virginia, the medical school gained recognition as an academic health center. Now, in addition to M.D. and graduate medical education programs, EVMS offers programs in biomedical sciences, clinical psychology, public health, art therapy, physician assistant, clinical embryology, ophthalmic technology, and surgical assistant. Over the years, EVMS has grown into a nationally recognized center for biomedical research, especially in the areas of reproductive medicine, diabetes, geriatrics, pediatrics, and cancer.

Type: public
2011 total enrollment: 800
Clinical facilities: Eastern Virginia Medical School Health Services, Bon Secours DePaul Medical Center, Bon Secours Maryview Medical Center, Chesapeake General Hospital, Children's Hospital of The King's Daughters, Lake Taylor Transitional Care Hospital, Naval Hospital (Portsmouth), Riverside Regional Medical Center, Sentara Bayside Hospital, Sentara Leigh Hospital, Sentara Norfolk General Hospital, Sentara Obici Hospital, Sentara Virginia Beach General Hospital, Veterans Administration Center (Hampton), Williamsburg Community Hospital, Eastern State Hospital.

Eastern Virginia Medical School

President. . . . . Harry T. Lester
Dean and Provost . . . . Richard V. Homan, M.D.
Vice President for Administration and Finance . . . . Mark R. Babashanian
Executive VP and Chief of Staff . . . . Claudia Keenan

Medical School Administrative Staff

Dean and Provost . . . . Richard V. Homan, M.D.
Assistant Dean, Student Affairs. . . . . Ann E. Campbell, Ph.D.
Director, Community Outreach . . . . Terri Babineau, M.D.
Assistant Dean, Enrollment . . . . Donald Meyers, Ph.D.
Associate Dean, Graduate Medical Education . . . . Linda R. Archer, Ph.D.
Associate Dean, Business Management . . . . David E. Huband
Director, Minority Affairs. . . . . Gail C. Williams
Associate Dean, Library and Director, Educational Technology . . . . Judith G. Robinson
Associate Dean, Research . . . . William Wasilenko, Ph.D.
Associate Dean, Human Research Subjects Protection . . . . Robert F. Williams, Ph.D.
Dean, School of Health Professions . . . . C. Donald Combs, Ph.D.
Associate Dean, Clinical Affairs. . . . . Alfred Z. Abuhamad, M.D.
Director, Faculty Affairs . . . . Alice E. Fretwell
Associate Dean, Education . . . . Ronald Flenner, M.D.

Department and Division or Section Chairs

Basic Sciences

Microbiology and Molecular Cell Biology . . . . Julie Kerry, Ph.D.
Pathology and Anatomy . . . . Nancy F. Fishback, M.D.
Physiological Sciences . . . . Gerald J. Pepe, Ph.D.

Clinical Sciences

Dermatology . . . . Antoinette F. Hood, M.D.
Emergency Medicine . . . . Francis L. Counselman, M.D.
Family and Community Medicine . . . . Christine C. Matson, M.D.
Internal Medicine . . . . Jerry L. Nadler, M.D.
Neurology . . . . Richard Zweisler, M.D.
Obstetrics and Gynecology . . . . Alfred Z. Abuhamad, M.D.
Ophthalmology . . . . Earl R. Crouch, M.D.
Otolaryngology . . . . Barry Strasnick, M.D.
Pediatrics . . . . Donald Lewis, M.D.
Physical Medicine and Rehabilitation . . . . Antonio Quidgley-Nevares, M.D.
Psychiatry and Behavioral Sciences . . . . Steven Deutsch, M.D.
Radiation Oncology and Biophysics . . . . Mark S. Sinesi, M.D., Ph.D.
Radiology . . . . Lester S. Johnson, M.D.
Surgery . . . . I.D. Britt, M.D.
Urology . . . . Kurt McCammon, M.D.

Virginia Commonwealth University
School of Medicine
P.O. Box 980565
Richmond, Virginia 23298
804-828-9000 (general); 804-828-9788 (dean's office); 804-828-9629 (admissions);
804-828-9793 (registrar); 804-828-7628 (dean's office fax)
Web site: www.medschool.vcu.edu

The Medical College of Virginia was established in 1838 as a department of Hampden-Sydney and was conducted as such until 1860 when it became a state institution. In 1913, it was consolidated with the University College of Medicine, and in 1914, all students were transferred to the Medical College of Virginia. The 1969 General Assembly of Virginia created, as of July 1, 1968, Virginia Commonwealth University through merging of Richmond Professional Instituteäwhich became the general academic divisionäand the Medical College of Virginia. The official school name is Virginia Commonwealth University School of Medicine.

Type: public
2011 total enrollment: 750
Clinical facilities: VCU Medical Center, VCU Treatment Center for Children, McGuire Veterans Administration Medical Center. **Affiliated hospitals:** Riverside Hospital, Chippenham Medical Center, INOVA Fairfax Hospital, INOVA Fair Oaks Hospital, Bon Secours St. Mary's Hospital, Children's Hospital, Eastern State Hospital, Piedmont Geriatric Hospital, Reston Hospital Center.

University Officials

President. . . . . Michael Rao, Ph.D.
Vice President for Health Sciences and Chief
    Executive Officer, VCU Health System . . . . Sheldon M. Retchin, M.D.

Medical School Administrative Staff

Executive Vice President for Medical Affairs,
    VCU Health System, and Dean . . . . Jerome F. Strauss III, M.D., Ph.D.
Senior Associate Dean, Clinical Affairs . . . . John D. Ward, M.D.
Senior Associate Dean, Faculty Affairs. . . . . PonJola Coney, M.D.
Senior Associate Dean, Medical Education and Student Affairs . . . . Isaac K. Wood, M.D.
Senior Associate Dean, Research . . . . Gordon L. Archer, M.D.
Associate Dean, Admissions . . . . Michelle Whitehurst-Cook, M.D.
Associate Dean, Clinical Activities. . . . . Ralph R. Clark, M.D.
Associate Dean, Assessment and Evaluation Studies. . . . . Paul E. Mazmanian, Ph.D.
Associate Dean, Development. . . . . Thomas E. Holland
Associate Dean, Faculty and Instructional Development. . . . . Vacant
Associate Dean, Finance and Administration. . . . . Amy S. Sebring
Associate Dean, Graduate Education. . . . . Jan F. Chlebowski, Ph.D.
Associate Dean, Graduate Medical Education . . . . Mary Alice O'Donnel, Ph.D.
Associate Dean, McGuire Vet Affairs. . . . . Julie Beales, M.D. (Interim)
Associate Dean, Medical Education-INOVA Campus . . . . Craig E. Cheifetz, M.D.
Associate Dean, Medical Informatics. . . . . Vacant
Associate Dean, Practice Plan . . . . James J. Potyraj
Associate Dean, Professional Education
    Programs and President, UHS-PEP . . . . John W. Seeds, M.D.
Associate Dean, Student Affairs . . . . Christopher M. Woleben, M.D.
Assistant Dean, Finance and Administration . . . . Kimberley G. Blowe
Assistant Dean, Medical Education . . . . Allan W. Dow III, M.D.
Assistant Dean, Medical Education and Student Affairs . . . . Douglas Franzen, M.D.
Assistant Dean, Medical Education-INOVA Campus. . . . . Vacant
Assistant Dean, Medical Education . . . . Susan R. DiGiovanni, M.D.
Assistant Dean, Sponsored Programs . . . . George F. Ford, Ph.D.
Assistant Dean, Student Affairs. . . . . Glenda U. Palmer, Ph.D.
Assistant to the Dean . . . . Joan M. Barrett

Department and Division or Section Chairs

Basic Health Sciences

Anatomy and Neurobiology . . . . John T. Povlishock, Ph.D.
Biochemistry and Molecular Biology. . . . . Sarah Spiegel, Ph.D.
Biostatistics . . . . Shumei S. Sun, Ph.D.
Epidemiology and Community Health . . . . Kate L. Lapane, Ph.D.
Human and Molecular Genetics. . . . . Paul B. Fisher, Ph.D.
Microbiology and Immunology. . . . . Dennis E. Ohman, Ph.D.
Pharmacology and Toxicology . . . . William L. Dewey, Ph.D.
Physiology and Biophysics . . . . Diomedes E. Logothetis, Ph.D.
Public Health Management and Policy . . . . Cathy J. Bradley, Ph.D.
Social and Behavioral Health . . . . Laura A. Siminoff, Ph.D.

Clinical Sciences

Anesthesiology. . . . . John F. Butterworth, M.D.
Dermatology . . . . Algin B. Garrett, M.D.
Emergency Medicine . . . . Joseph P. Ornato, M.D.
Family Practice . . . . Anton J. Kuzel, M.D.
Internal Medicine . . . . John E. Nestler, M.D.
Legal Medicine . . . . Leah L. Bush, M.D.
Massey Cancer Center . . . . Gordon D. Ginder, M.D.
Neurology. . . . . James P. Bennett, M.D.
Neurosurgery. . . . . Harold F. Young, M.D.
Obstetrics and Gynecology. . . . . David P. Chelmow, M.D.
Ophthalmology . . . . William H. Benson, M D
Orthopaedic Surgery . . . . Robert S. Adelaar, M.D.
Otolaryngology . . . . Laurence J. DiNardo, M.D.
Pathology . . . . David S. Wilkinson, M.D., Ph.D.
Pediatrics . . . . Bruce K. Rubin, M.D.
Physical Medicine and Rehabilitation . . . . David X. Cifu, M.D.
Psychiatry . . . . Joel J. Silverman, M.D.
Radiation Oncology. . . . . Mitchell S. Anscher, M.D.
Radiology . . . . Ann S. Fulcher, M.D.
Surgery . . . . James P. Neifeld, M.D.

University of Virginia School of Medicine
Health System, P.O. Box 800793
McKim Hall
Charlottesville, Virginia 22908-0793
434-924-5118 (dean's office); 434-982-0874 (fax)
Web site: www.healthsystem.virginia.edu

According to Thomas Jefferson, medical education was to become part of the curriculum and of general education at the University of Virginia. A school of anatomy and medicine was one of the original eight schools authorized by the General Assembly on January 25, 1819. The school opened on March 7, 1825, and is located on the grounds of the University of Virginia. The medical school is part of the University of Virginia Health System.

Type: public
2011 total enrollment: 555
Clinical facilities: Centra Health, Inc., Martha Jefferson Hospital, Carilion Roanoke Community Hospital, Carilion Roanoke Memorial Hospital, University of Virginia—Health South Rehabilitation Hospital, University of Virginia Kluge Children's Rehabilitation Center, University of Virginia Hospital, Veterans Affairs Medical Center (Salem), Western State Hospital, Winchester Memorial Hospital, Woodrow Wilson Rehabilitation Center, INOVA Fairfax Hospital.

University Officials

President. . . . . Teresa A. Sullivan, Ph.D.
Executive Vice President and Chief Operating Officer. . . . . Michael Strine, Ph.D.
Executive Vice President and Provost . . . . J. Milton Adams, Ph.D. (Interim)

Medical Center Administrative Staff

Vice President and Chief Executive Officer,
    University of Virginia Medical Center . . . . R. Edward Howell
Associate Vice President for Hospital and Clinics
    Operations . . . . Robert (Bo) Cofield, Dr.P.H.
Chief Nursing Officer . . . . Lorna Facteau
Chief Environmental of Care Officer . . . . Thomas A. Harkins
Chief Executive Officer, Health Services Foundation. . . . . Bradley E. Haws
Associate Vice President for Business Development . . . . Larry L. Fitzgerald
Associate Vice President for Strategic Relations and Marketing . . . . Patricia L. Cluff
Chief Information Officer . . . . Barbara S. Baldwin
Chief Technology and Health Information Officer . . . . Mark Andersen (Interim)
President, Clinical Staff . . . . Robert S. Gibson, M.D.
President, Health Services Foundation . . . . Raymond F. Morgan, M.D.
Associate Vice President for Health System Development . . . . Karen Rendleman
Special Advisor to the Vice President and Chief
    Executive Officer of the Medical Center . . . . Sally N. Barber
Chief Corporate Compliance and Privacy Officer . . . . Lori Strauss

School of Medicine Administrative Staff

Vice President and Dean . . . . Steven T. DeKosky, M.D.
Senior Associate Dean . . . . Sharon L. Hostler, M.D.
Senior Associate Dean for Clinical Affairs . . . . Jonathon D. Truwit, M.D.
Senior Associate Dean for Clinical Strategy . . . . Raymond A. Costabile, M.D.
Senior Associate Dean for Continuing Medical
    Education and External Affairs . . . . Karen S. Rheuban, M.D.
Senior Associate Dean for Education . . . . Randolph J. Canterbury, M.D.
Senior Associate Dean and CAO. . . . . Bradley E. Haws
Senior Associate Dean for Research . . . . Margaret A. Shupnik, Ph.D.
Associate Dean for Admissions . . . . Randolph J. Canterbury, M.D.
Associate Dean for Basic Research . . . . John S. Lazo, Ph.D.
Associate Dean and Director, Claude Moore Health Sciences Library. . . . . . Gretchen M. Arnold
Associate Dean for Clinical Research . . . . Ronald B. Turner, M.D.
Associate Dean for Undergraduate Medical Education . . . . Donald J. Innes, Jr., M.D.
Associate Dean for Diversity . . . . Vacant
Associate Dean for Graduate and Medical Scientist Programs . . . . Amy H. Bouton, Ph.D.
Associate Dean of Graduate Medical Education. . . . . Susan E. Kirk, M.D.

Associate Dean for International Programs . . . . Leigh Grossman, M.D.
Associate Dean for Medical Educaion, Research, and Evaluation . . . . Vacant
Associate Dean for Medical Alumni Affairs . . . . Barry J. Collins
Assistant Dean for Medical Education Support . . . . Troy S. Buer
Associate Dean for the Roanoke Program . . . . Daniel P. Harrington, M.D.
Associate Dean for Academic Affairs - Salem, Veterans Affairs . . . . Maureen McCarthy, M.D.
Associate Dean for Administrative Affairs-Salem, Veterans Affairs . . . . Vacant
Associate Dean for Student Affairs . . . . Richard D. Pearson, M.D.
Assistant Dean for Administration . . . . Polly E. King
Assistant Dean for Admissions . . . . Gabrielle Marzani-Nissen, M.D.
Assistant Dean for Admissions and Student Affairs . . . . Lesley L. Thomas, J.D.
Associate Dean for Faculty Development . . . . Susan M. Pollart, M.D.
Assistant Dean for Clinical Skills . . . . Keith Littlewood, M.D.
Associate Dean for Finance and Administration . . . . Anne C. Kromkowski
Assistant Dean for Graduate Research and Training . . . . Joel W. Hockensmith, Ph.D.
Assistant Dean for Medical Education . . . . Michael Moxley, M.D.
Assistant Dean for Medical Education . . . . Christine M. Peterson, M.D.
Assistant Dean for Research and Scientific
   Director of the Research Advisory Committee . . . . Steven S. Wasserman, Ph.D.
Assistant Dean for Research Infrastructure . . . . Jay W. Fox, Ph.D.
Assistant Dean for Records and Student Affairs . . . . Allison H. Innes, Ph.D.
Assistant Dean for Student Affairs . . . . Rasheed Balogun, M.D.
Associate Dean for Admissions and Student Affairs . . . . John J. Densmore, M.D., Ph.D.
Assistant Dean for Student Affairs . . . . Meg Keeley, M.D.
Director, Faculty and Administrator Development Programs . . . . Vacant
Chief Technology Officer . . . . Sean Jackson
Assistant Dean for Research Administration . . . . Stewart P. Craig
Director, Space Management . . . . Richard B. Allen

Department and Division or Section Chairs

Basic Sciences

Biochemistry and Molecular Genetics . . . . Joyce L. Hamlin, Ph.D.
Biomedical Engineering . . . . Frederick H. Epstein, Ph.D.
Cell Biology . . . . Barry M. Gumbiner, Ph.D.
Microbiology . . . . Kodi S. Ravichandran, Ph.D.
Molecular Physiology and Biological Physics . . . . Mark Yeager, M.D., Ph.D.
Neuroscience . . . . Kevin S. Lee, Ph.D.
Pharmacology . . . . Douglas A. Bayliss, Ph.D.

Clinical Sciences

Anesthesiology . . . . George F. Rich, M.D., Ph.D.
Dentistry . . . . Thomas E. Leinbach, D.D.S.
Dermatology . . . . Thomas G. Cropley, M.D.
Emergency Medicine . . . . Robert E. O'Connor, M.D.
Family Medicine . . . . M. Norman Oliver, M.D.
Internal Medicine . . . . Mitchell H. Rosner, M.D. (Interim)
Neurology . . . . Karen C. Johnston, M.D.
Neurosurgery . . . . Mark E. Shaffrey, M.D.
Obstetrics and Gynecology . . . . James E. Ferguson, M.D.
Ophthalmology . . . . Peter A. Netland, M.D.
Orthopaedic Surgery . . . . Mark F. Abel, M.D.
Otolaryngology-Head and Neck Surgery . . . . Paul A. Levine, M.D.
Pathology . . . . Dennis J. Templeton, M.D., Ph.D.
Pediatrics . . . . James P. Nataro, M.D., Ph.D.
Physical Medicine and Rehabilitation . . . . Robert P. Wilder, M.D.
Plastic and Maxillofacial Surgery . . . . Raymond F. Morgan, M.D.
Psychiatry and Neurobehavioral Sciences . . . . Bankole A. Johnson, D.Sc., M.D., Ph.D.
Public Health Sciences . . . . Ruth G. Bernheim, J.D.
Radiation Oncology . . . . James M. Larner, M.D.
Radiology and Medical Imaging . . . . Alan H. Matsumoto, M.D.
Surgery . . . . Irving L. Kron, M.D.
Urology . . . . William D. Steers, M.D.

University of Washington School of Medicine

Box 356340
Seattle, Washington 98195
206-543-1515 (dean's office); 206-616-3341 (fax)
E-mail: askuwsom@u.washington.edu
Web site: www.uwmedicine.org

The University of Washington School of Medicine was established in 1945 as a unit of the division of health sciences and an integral part of the total university campus. The school serves the five-state WWAMI (Washington, Wyoming, Alaska, Montana, and Idaho) region.

Type: public
2011 total enrollment: 968
Clinical facilities: (Hospitals only): Fred Hutchinson Cancer Research Center, Group Health Cooperative, Harborview Medical Center, Seattle Cancer Care Alliance, Seattle Children's Hospital, Swedish Medical Center - Ballard/Cherry Hill/First Hill/Pacific Medical, University of Washington Medical Center, VA Puget Sound Healthcare System, Virginia Mason Medical Center - Seattle/Federal Way (Seattle, WA); Naval Hospital Bremerton (Bremerton, WA); Stevens Hospital (Edmonds, WA); Northwest Hospital and Medical Center, Providence Everett Medical Center (Everett, WA); St. Francis Hospital (Federal Way, WA); Samaritan Healthcare (Moses Lake, WA); Skagit Valley Hospital (Mount Vernon, WA); Olympic Medical Center (Port Angeles, WA); Valley Medical Center (Renton, WA); Empire Health Services/Deaconess Medical Center, Sacred Heart Medical Center (Spokane, WA); Madigan Army Medical Center, Western State Hospital (Tacoma, WA); Yakima Valley Memorial Hospital (Yakima, WA); Wenatchee Valley Medical Center (Wenatchee, WA); Alaska Native Medical Center, Providence Health Services (Anchorage, AK); Banner Health/Fairbanks Memorial Hospital (Fairbanks, AK); Boise VA Medical Center, St. Alphonsus Regional Medical Center, St. Luke's Regional Medical Center Boise/Twin Falls (Boise, ID); McCall Memorial Hospital (McCall, ID); Portneuf Medical Center (Pocatello, ID); St. Patrick Hospital (Missoula, MT); Sheridan VA Medical Center (Sheridan, WY); Legacy Emanuel Hospital and Health Center (Portland, OR); Hospital for Special Surgery, Memorial Sloan Kettering Cancer Center (New York, NY). University of Washington Residency Network (WA, WY, AK, MT, ID).

University Officials

President of the University . . . . Michael K. Young
Provost . . . . Ana Mari Cauce, Ph.D.
Chief Executive Office of UW Medicine and
   Executive Vice President for Medical Affairs . . . . Paul G. Ramsey, M.D.

Medical School Administrative Staff

Dean . . . . Paul G. Ramsey, M.D.
Vice Dean, Academic Affairs . . . . Ellen M. Cosgrove, M.D.
Vice Dean, Clinical Affairs and Graduate Medical Education . . . . . . Lawrence R. Robinson, M.D.
Vice Dean, Regional Affairs . . . . Suzanne M. Allen, M.D.
Vice Dean, Research and Graduate Education . . . . John T. Slattery, Ph.D.
Vice President and Chief Business Officer . . . . Ruth M. Mahan
Associate Vice President and Financial Planning Officer . . . . Paul S. Ishizuka
Associate Vice President and Financial Operations Officer . . . . Lori Mitchell
Associate Vice President and Director of Legal and Business Matters . . . . Lori A. Oliver
Associate Vice President and Controller . . . . Liz Shirley
Senior Adviser to the Dean . . . . Harry R. Kimball, M.D., Nelson Fausto, M.D.,
                                            and Carol A. MacLaren, Ph.D.
Associate Dean, Administration and Finance . . . . Mary F. Joseph
Associate Dean for Business . . . . Mark S. Green
Associate Dean for Graduate Medical Education . . . . Byron Joyner, M.D.
Associate Dean and Chief Administrative Officer,
   Seattle Children's . . . . F. Bruder Stapleton, M.D.
Associate Dean, Curriculum . . . . Michael J. Ryan, M.D.
Associate Dean and Chief Administrative Officer, Student Affairs . . . . E. Peter Eveland, Ed.D.
Associate Dean and Director, Multicultural Affairs . . . . David A. Acosta, M.D.
Associate Dean, Admissions . . . . Carol C. Teitz, M.D.
Associate Dean for Translational Science . . . . Nora L. Disis, M.D.
Assistant Dean, Faculty Development . . . . Christina M. Surawicz, M.D.
Assistant Dean, Graduate Medical Education . . . . Amity L. Neumeister
Assistant Dean for Research, Harborview Medical Center . . . . Sheila A. Lukehart, Ph.D.
Assistant Dean for Research, Seattle Children's Hospital . . . . James Hendricks, M.D.
Associate Vice President for Compliance . . . . Sue Clausen

Associate Vice President for Medical Affairs and
Director, Health Sciences/UW Medicine News
& Community Relations . . . . Tina Mankowski
Chief of Staff and Associate Vice President . . . . Marjorie D. Wenrich
Director, Medex Program. . . . . Ruth Ballweg, P.A-C.
Associate Dean and Medical Director, University
of Washington Medical Center . . . . Thomas O. Staiger, M.D.
Associate Dean and Medical Director, Harborview Medical Center. . . . . J. Richard Goss, M.D.
Associate Dean and Medical Director, Seattle Children's Hospital . . . . David Fisher, M.D.
Associate Dean and Chief of Staff, VA Puget
Sound Health Care System (Seattle and
American Lake, Tacoma) . . . . William H. Campbell, M.D.
Vice President and Chief Health System Officer . . . . Johnese M. Spisso
Associate Vice President and Chief Advancement Officer . . . . Lynn K. Hogan, Ph.D.
Director, Medical Policy Affairs . . . . Jackie L. Der
Executive Assistant to the CEO UW Medicine /
Executive Vice President / Dean . . . . Julie A. Monteith
WWAMI Coordinators and Assistant Deans
Washington State University (Pullman) and
University of Idaho (Moscow) . . . . Andrew Turner, Ph.D.
Washington State University (Spokane) . . . . Ken Roberts, Ph.D.
University of Wyoming (Laramie) . . . . Matthew McEchron, Ph.D.
University of Alaska (Anchorage) . . . . Robert Furilla, Ph.D. (Interim)
Montana State University (Bozeman) . . . . Jane Shelby, Ph.D., and Martin Teintze, Ph.D.
Clinical Phase-Eastern and Central WA . . . Deborah J. Harper, M.D., and John McCarthy, M.D.
Clinical Phase-Wyoming . . . . J. Richard Hillman, M.D.
Clinical Phase-Alaska . . . . Tom Nighswander, M.D., and Suzanne Tryck
Clinical Phase-Boise, ID . . . . Mary Barinaga, M.D.
Clinical Phase-Whitefish, MT. . . . . Jay Erickson, M.D.

Department Chairs

Basic Sciences

Biochemistry . . . . Trisha N. Davis, Ph.D. (Acting)
Bioengineering . . . . Paul Yager, Ph.D.
Bioethics and Humanities . . . . Wylie G. Burke, M.D., Ph.D.
Biological Structure . . . . John I. Clark, Ph.D.
Comparative Medicine . . . . H. Denny Liggitt, D.V.M., Ph.D.
Immunology . . . . Joan M. Goverman, Ph.D.
Medical Education and Biomedical Informatics. . . . . Peter Tarczy-Hornoch, M.D. (Acting)
Microbiology . . . . James J. Champoux, Ph.D.
Genome Sciences. . . . . Robert H. Waterston, M.D., Ph.D.
Global Health . . . . King K. Holmes, M.D., Ph.D.
Pathology . . . . Thomas J. Montine, M.D. (Interim)
Pharmacology . . . . William A. Catterall, Ph.D.
Physiology and Biophysics . . . . Stanley C. Froehner, Ph.D.

Clinical Sciences

Anesthesiology. . . . . Debra A. Schwinn, M.D.
Family Medicine . . . . Thomas E. Norris, M.D.
Laboratory Medicine . . . . James S. Fine, M.D.
Medicine. . . . . William J. Bremner, M.D., Ph.D.
Neurological Surgery. . . . . Richard G. Ellenbogen, M.D.
Neurology. . . . . Bruce R. Ransom, M.D., Ph.D.
Obstetrics and Gynecology. . . . . David A. Eschenbach, M.D.
Ophthalmology . . . . Russell N. Van Gelder, M.D., Ph.D.
Orthopaedics and Sports Medicine. . . . . Jens R. Chapman, M.D.
Otolaryngology-Head and Neck Surgery . . . . Neal D. Futran, M.D.
Pediatrics . . . . F. Bruder Stapleton, M.D.
Psychiatry and Behavioral Sciences . . . . Richard C. Veith, M.D.
Radiation Oncology. . . . . George E. Laramore, M.D., Ph.D.
Radiology . . . . Norman J. Beauchamp, M.D.
Rehabilitation Medicine. . . . . Peter C. Esselman, M.D.
Surgery . . . . Carlos A. Pellegrini, M.D.
Urology. . . . . Hunter Wessells, M.D.

Marshall University Joan C. Edwards School of Medicine

1600 Medical Center Drive, Suite 3400
Huntington, West Virginia 25701-3655
304-691-1700 (dean's office); 304-691-1726 (fax)
Web site: http://musom.marshall.edu/

The Joan C. Edwards School of Medicine at Marshall University was developed under the Veterans Administration Medical School Assistance and Health Manpower Training Act (Public Law 92-541), enacted by Congress in 1972. The school of medicine received provisional accreditation from the Liaison Committee on Medical Education, and the first class of 24 students enrolled in January 1978. The school of medicine received full accreditation in 1981, and the charter class was graduated in May of that year. Present enrollment is 75 students per class. Marshall University is located in Huntington, which is situated on the Ohio River. The school of medicine's administrative and clinical facility is adjacent to Cabell Huntington Hospital, and the school has educational facilities at the Veterans Affairs Medical Center. Community hospitals in Huntington provide additional educational and clinical facilities.

Type: public
2011 total enrollment: 195
Clinical facilities: Cabell-Huntington Hospital, St. Mary's Medical Center, Mildred Mitchell-Bateman Hospital, Veterans Affairs Medical Center; University Physicians and Surgeons, Village Medical Center (ambulatory care centers).

University Officials

President	Stephen J. Kopp, Ph.D.
Vice President for Health Sciences Advancement	Charles H. McKown, Jr., M.D.
Vice President for Academic Affairs and Provost	Gayle Ormiston, Ph.D.
Assistant Vice President for Administration	Karen Kirtley (Interim)
Vice President for Alumni Development	Lance West
Vice President of Multicultural Affairs	Shari Clarke, Ph.D.
Dean, Student Affairs	Stephen W. Hensley
Chair	Joseph E. Evans, M.D. (Acting)

Medical School Administrative Staff

Dean	Robert C. Nerhood, M.D.
Executive Vice Dean	Vacant
Chief Medical Officer	Joseph W. Werthammer, M.D.
Senior Associate Dean for Clinical Affairs	Joseph W. Werthammer, M.D.
Senior Associate Dean for Finance and Administration	James J. Schneider
Senior Associate Dean for Graduate Medical Education	Paulette S. Wehner, M.D.
Senior Associate Dean for Medical Student Education	Aaron McGuffin, M.D.
Senior Associate Dean for Research and Graduate Education	Richard M. Niles, Ph.D.
Associate Dean for Academic Affairs	Tracy LeGrow, Psy.D.
Associate Dean for Admissions	Jennifer T. Plymale, M.D.
Associate Dean for Admissions and Development	John B. Walden, M.D.
Associate Dean for External Affairs	Karen Bledsoe
Associate Dean for Faculty Affairs and Professional Development	Darshana Shah, Ph.D.
Associate Dean for Student Affairs	Marie Veitia, Ph.D.
Assistant Dean for Clinical Research	Todd W. Gress, M.D.
Assistant Dean for Admissions	Cynthia A. Warren
Assistant Dean for Information Technology and Medical Informatics	Michael McCarthy
Assistant Dean and Director of Continuing Medical Education	David N. Bailey
Assistant Dean and Director of Center for Rural Health	Jennifer T. Plymale
Director of Animal Resources	Billy Howard, D.V.M.
Director of Development and Alumni Affairs	Linda Holmes
Director of Forensic Sciences	Terry Fenger, Ph.D.
Director of Health Science Libraries	Edward M. Dzierzak
Director of Compliance and Risk Management and COO	Beth L. Hammers

Department and Division or Section Chairs

Basic Sciences

Biochemistry and Molecular Biology	Richard M. Niles, Ph.D.
Microbiology, Immunology, and Molecular Genetics	Donald Primerano, Ph.D.
Pharmacology	Gary O. Rankin, Ph.D.
Physiology	Elsa I. Mangiarua, Ph.D.

Clinical Sciences

Cardiovascular Services	Mark A. Studeny, M.D.
Cardiovascular Medicine	Mark A. Studeny, M.D.

Marshall University Joan C. Edwards School of Medicine: WEST VIRGINIA

Interventional Cardiology . . . . Mark A. Studeny, M.D.
Family and Community Health . . . . John B. Walden, M.D.
   Community Medicine* . . . . Richard Crespo, Ph.D.
   Family Medicine* . . . . Stephen Petrany, M.D.
   Geriatrics* . . . . Charles McCormick, M.D.
   International Health . . . . John B. Walden, M.D.
   Occupational Health* . . . . Mohammed I. Ranavaya, M.D.
   Sports Medicine* . . . . Ross Patton, M.D.
Medicine . . . . Larry D. Dial, M.D. (Acting)
   Endocrinology* . . . . Henry K. Driscoll, M.D.
   Gastroenterology* . . . . Waseem Shora, M.D.
   General Internal Medicine* . . . . Shirley M. Neitch, M.D.
   Geriatrics* . . . . Shirley M. Neitch, M.D.
   Hematology-Oncology* . . . . Maria R. Tirona, M.D.
   Infectious Diseases* . . . . Thomas Rushton, M.D.
   Nephrology* . . . . M. Arif Goreja, M.D., and April Kilgore, M.D.
   Pulmonary Diseases* . . . . Imran T. Khawaja, M.D.
   Rheumatology* . . . . Ralph W. Webb, M.D.
Neuroscience . . . . Anthony M. Alberico, M.D.
Obstetrics-Gynecology . . . . David C. Jude, M.D.
   Endocrine Infertility . . . . William N. Burns, M.D.
   Gynecologic Oncology . . . . Gerard J. Oakley, M.D.
   Maternal-Fetal Medicine . . . . David B. Chafin, M.D., and Ryan Stone, M.D.
Opthamology . . . . Michael A. Krasnow, D.O.
Orthopedics . . . . Ali Oliashirazi, M.D.
Orthopedic Oncology . . . . Felix H. Cheung, M.D.
Pathology . . . . Linda G. Brown, M.D.
   Anatomical Pathology* . . . . Linda G. Brown, M.D.
   Anatomy, Cell, and Neurobiology . . . . Laura Richardson, Ph.D.
   Clinical Pathology* . . . . Linda G. Brown, M.D.
   Pathology Academic Unit* . . . . Darshana Shah, Ph.D.
Pediatrics . . . . Joseph E. Evans, M.D.
   Adolescent Medicine* . . . . Patricia Kelly, M.D.
   Allergy / Immunology . . . . Jeffrey L. Shaw, M.D.
   Behavioral Pediatrics / Mental Health . . . . James T. Binder, M.D.
   Cardiology* . . . . Mahmood Heydarian, M.D.
   Critical Care . . . . Eduardo Pino, M.D.
   Development Pediatrics . . . . James M. Lewis, M.D.
   Emergency Medicine* . . . . Brian Dunlap, M.D.
   Endocrinology* . . . . Vacant
   Forensic Pediatrics . . . . Samantha Cook, M.D.
   Gastroenterology* . . . . Yoram Elitsur, M.D.
   General Pediatrics* . . . . Joseph Evans, M.D.
   Hematology-Oncology* . . . . Andrew L. Pendleton, M.D.
   Infectious Diseases* . . . . April Kilgore, M.D., and Guada Lopez, M.D.
   Intensive Care* . . . . J. Michael Waldeck, M.D.
   Mental Health* . . . . Vacant
   Neonatology* . . . . Joseph W. Werthammer, M.D.
   Nephrology* . . . . Vacant
   Neurology . . . . Mary S. Payne, M.D.
Psychiatry and Behavioral Medicine . . . . Samuel Januszkiewcz, M.D.
Radiology . . . . Peter A. Chirico, M.D.
Surgery . . . . David A. Denning, M.D.
   Minimally Invasive Surgery . . . . Gerald McKinney, M.D.
   General Surgery* . . . . David A. Denning, M.D.
   Breast Specialists . . . . Shawn A. McKinney, M.D.
   Burn Care/Trauma . . . . Vacant
   Pediatric Surgery* . . . . Bonnie Beaver, M.D.
   Plastic Surgery* . . . . Adel P. Faltaous, M.D.
   Vascular Surgery . . . . David A. Denning, M.D.
   Oral and Maxillofacial Surgery . . . . Raj K. Khanna, D.M.D., M.D.
   Thoracic Surgery . . . . Rebecca Wolfer, M.D.
   Urology . . . . Vacant

*Specialty without organizational autonomy.

West Virginia University School of Medicine

Suite 1040, Box 9100
Robert C. Byrd Health Sciences Center South
Morgantown, West Virginia 26506-9100
304-293-6607 (dean's office); 304-293-6627 (dean's office fax);
304-293-2408 (student affairs)
E-mail: jworth@hsc.wvu.edu
Web site: www.hsc.wvu.edu

In 1902, West Virginia University (WVU) initiated a two-year medical curriculum, and in 1912, the WVU Board of Regents recognized a separate division of the university to be known as the school of medicine. In 1960, the school was expanded to a four-year program. Currently, the Robert C. Byrd Health Sciences campus is comprised of the 522-bed Ruby Memorial Hospital, Physicians Office Center, WVU Eye Institute, Mary Babb Randolph Cancer Center, WVU Children's Hospital, Betty Puskar Breast Care Center, Chestnut Ridge Psychiatric Hospital, and Mountainview Rehabilitation Center. The Charleston Division was established in October 1972, and is affiliated with Charleston Area Medical Center. The Eastern Division, located in Martinsburg, West Virginia, was established in 2001 as a two-year clinical campus. The Educational and Administrative Building (Erma Byrd Center) was completed in March 2006.

Type: public
2011 total enrollment: 440
Clinical facilities: WVU Hospitals, Monongalia General Hospital, HealthSouth Rehabilitation Hospital, Mary Babb Randolph Cancer Center, and WVU Eye Institute, all in Morgantown; Charleston Area Medical Center, WVU School of Medicine, and Thomas Memorial Hospital in Charleston; United Hospital Center and Louis A. Johnson VA Medical Center in Clarksburg; Martinsburg VA Center, City Hospital in Martinsburg, WV; and Jefferson Memorial Hospital in Ranson, WV.

University Officials

President. . . . . James P. Clements, Ph.D.
Chancellor for Health Sciences . . . . Christopher C. Colenda, M.D., M.P.H.

Medical School Administrative Staff

Dean. . . . . Arthur J. Ross III, M.D., M.B.A.
Senior Associate Dean / Chief Administrative Officer . . . . John Worth, Jr.
Senior Associate Dean for Medical Education . . . . Norman D. Ferrari III, M.D.
Associate Dean, Student Services and Professional Development . . . . Scott Cottrell, Ed.D.
Associate Dean, Research and Graduate Studies . . . . James M. O'Donnell, Ph.D.
Associate Dean, Clinical Affairs. . . . . Judie F. Charlton, M.D.
Associate Dean, Development. . . . . James M. Stevenson, M.D.
Associate Dean, Finance. . . . . Timothy Palencik
Associate Dean, Medical Education. . . . . James M. Shumway, Ph.D.
Associate Dean for Professional Programs. . . . . MaryBeth Mandich, Ph.D.
Assistant Dean, Veterans Administration Affairs. . . . . Maria Kolar, M.D.
Chairperson, Committee on Admissions . . . . Maurice Grant, M.D.

Institute Directors

Mary Babb Randolph Cancer Center . . . . Scot Remick, M.D.
Center for Health Ethics and Law . . . . Alvin H. Moss, M.D.
Center for Rural Emergency Medicine . . . . Jeffrey H. Coben, M.D.
Center of Excellence Women's Health . . . . Barbara Ducatman, M.D.
Heart Institute. . . . . Robert Beto II, M.D.

Department and Division or Section Chairs

Basic Sciences

Biochemistry . . . . Michael D. Schaller, Ph.D.
Microbiology, Immunology, and Cell Biology . . . . John B. Barnett, Ph.D.
Neurobiology and Anatomy . . . . Richard D. Dey, Ph.D.
Physiology amd Pharmacology . . . . Robert L. Goodman, Ph.D.

Clinical Sciences

Anesthesiology. . . . . Richard P. Driver, M.D.
Behavioral Medicine and Psychiatry . . . . James M. Stevenson, M.D.
Community Medicine and Public Health . . . . Alan M. Ducatman, M.D.
Emergency Medicine . . . . Todd J. Crocco, M.D.
Family Medicine . . . . James Arbogast, M.D.
Human Performance and Applied Exercise Science . . . . MaryBeth Mandich, Ph.D.
   Exercise Physiology. . . . . Stephen E. Always, Ph.D.
   Occupational Therapy . . . . Randy P. McCombie, Ph.D.

Physical Therapy .... MaryBeth Mandich, Ph.D.
Medicine.. James E. Brick, M.D.
    Cardiology... Robert Beto, M.D.
    Dermatology .... Rodney Kovach, M.D.
    Digestive Diseases... Vacant
    General Internal Medicine .... Shanthi Manivannan, M.D.
    Hematology-Oncology .... Jame Abraham, M.D.
    Infectious Diseases .... Rashida Khakoo, M.D.
    Metabolism-Endocrinology .... Tim Jackson, M.D.
    Nephrology .... Rebecca Schmidt, D.O.
    Pulmonary and Critical Care................................. John Parker, M.D.
    Rheumatology .... Joann Hornsby, M.D.
Neurosurgery.. Charles Rosen, M.D. (Interim)
Neurology.. John F. Brick, M.D.
Obstetrics and Gynecology....................................... Michael Vernon, Ph.D.
Ophthalmology .... Lee Wiley, M.D. (Interim)
Orthopedic Surgery... Sanford E. Emery, M.D.
Otolaryngology .... Stephen J. Wetmore, M.D.
Pathology .... Barbara S. Ducatman, M.D.
    Clinical Pathology .... Peter Perrotta, M.D.
    Medical Technology Program .... Martha Lake, Ed.D.
    Pathology and Cytopathology .... Melina Flanagan, M.D.
Pediatrics .... Giovanni Piedimonte, M.D.
    Adolescent Medicine .... Pamela J. Murray, M.D.
    Birth Score... Martha Mullet, M.D.
    Cardiology... Larry A. Rhodes, M.D.
    Critical Care.. Charles J. Mullet, M.D.
    Endocrinology .... Evan Jones, M.D., Ph.D.
    Gastroenterology .... Brian Ridel, M.D.
    Genetics and Metabolic .... Marybeth Hummel, M.D.
    Hematology and Oncology .... Stephen Paul, M.D.
    Infectious Diseases .... Kathryn Moffett, M.D.
    Neonatal .... Mark Polak, M.D.
    Neurology and Child Development............................. Margaret Jaynes, M.D.
    Section for Allergy, Immunology, and Pulmonary Medicine .... Kathryn Moffett, M.D.
Radiology .... Mathis Frick, M.D.
    Advanced Imaging and M.R.I.................................. Jeffrey S. Carpenter, M.D.
    Breast Imaging.. Judith S. Schreiman, M.D.
    Diagnostic .... Gary D. Marano, M.D.
Surgery... Richard Vaughan, M.D.
Urology... Stanley Zaslau, M.D.

Charleston Division
Charleston, WV 25304-1299
304-347-1298; 304-347-1209 (fax); 304-347-1206 (dean's office)

Associate Vice President for Health Sciences,
    Dean Clinical Campus .... L. Clark Hansbarger, M.D.
Chancellor for Health Sciences .... Christopher C. Colenda, M.D., M.P.H.
Associate Dean for Student Services .... James Griffith, M.D.
Behavioral Medicine and Psychiatry .... Martin Kommor, M.D.
Family Medicine .... Jeffrey V. Ashley, M.D.
Internal Medicine .... Gregory Rosencrance, M.D.
Obstetrics and Gynecology...................................... Stephen Bush, M.D.
Pediatrics .... John Udall, M.D.
Surgery.. James P. Boland, M.D.

Eastern Division
Martinsburg, WV 25402
304-264-9202 (dean's office); 304-264-9042 (fax)

Associate Vice President for Health Services,
    Dean Clinical Campus .... C. H. Mitch Jacques, M.D.
Family Medicine .... K. C. Nau, M.D.

Medical College of Wisconsin

8701 Watertown Plank Road
Milwaukee, Wisconsin 53226
414-955-8296; 414-955-8213 (dean's office); 414-955-6560 (fax)
Web site: www.mcw.edu

The Medical College of Wisconsin was founded in 1893 as the Wisconsin College of Physicians and Surgeons. In 1913, the Wisconsin College of Physicians and Surgeons and the Milwaukee Medical College merged to become the Marquette University School of Medicine. In 1967, the school of medicine seperated from Marquette and was reorganized to become a totally freestanding corporation. In 1970, the name of the college was changed to the Medical College of Wisconsin.

Type: private
2011 total enrollment: 820
Clinical facilities: Major affiliates: Froedtert Lutheran Hospital, Children's Hospital of Wisconsin, Milwaukee County Behavioral Health Division, Curative Care Network, Clement J. Zablocki Veterans Affairs Medical Center and the Blood Center of Wisconsin. **Community Affiliates:** Advanced Pain Management, AIDS Resource Center of Wisconsin, Aurora Psychiatric Hospital, Aurora Sinai Medical Center, Aurora St. Luke's Medical Center, Columbia St. Mary's Health System, Flight for Life, Marshfield Clinic, Mendota Mental Health Institute, Midwest Orthopedic Specialty Hospital, Milwaukee County Medical Examiner's Office, Orthopaedic Associates of Wisconsin, Rogers Memorial Hospital, Village at Manor Park Continuing Care Retirement Community, Vitas Innovative Hospice Care, Waukesha County Medical Examiner's Office, ProHealth Care, Inc., Waukesha Memorial Hospital, Wheaton Franciscan Healthcare-St. Joseph's Milwaukee.

Medical School Administrative Staff

President. . . . . John R. Raymond, M.D.
Dean and Executive Vice President. . . . . Joseph E. Kerschner, M.D. (Interim)
Senior Vice President and Chief Operating Officer. . . . . G. Allen Bolton
Chief Financial Officer. . . . . Marjorie M. Spencer
Vice President for Institutional Advancement . . . . James W. Heald
Senior Associate Dean for Education . . . . Karen Moredante, M.D.
Associate Dean for Student Affairs . . . . Richard L. Holloway, Ph.D.
Associate Dean for Curriculum. . . . . Philip N. Redlich, M.D., Ph.D.
Associate Dean, Student Affairs/Diversity . . . . Dawn S. Bragg, Ph.D.
Senior Associate Dean, Public and Community Health . . . . Cheryl A. Maurana, Ph.D.
Senior Associate Dean for Clinical Affairs-
  Medical College Physicians . . . . Jon L. Pryor, M.D., M.B.A.
Senior Associate Dean for Clinical Affairs-
  Children Specialty Group . . . . Marc H. Gorelick, M.D.
Senior Associate Dean for Graduate Medical Education . . . . Kenneth B. Simons, M.D.
Associate Dean for the Zablocki Veterans Affairs
  Medical Center . . . . Michael D. Erdmann, M.D., M.S.
Senior Associate Dean for Research . . . . David D. Gutterman, M.D.
Associate Dean for Research and Mentoring. David R. Harder, Ph.D.
Dean, Graduate School . . . . R Misra, Ph.D.
Director of Admissions. . . . . Jennifer Haluzak
Executive Director of Alumni Relations . . . . William A. Schultz
Director of Biomedical Resource Center. . . . . Joseph Thulin, D.V.M.
Vice President, Corporate Compliance and Risk Management. . . . . Daniel Wickeham
Director of Continuing Medical Education . . . . Linda Caples, M.D.
Associate Dean for Educational Support and Evaluation . . . . Deborah E. Simpson, Ph.D.
Director of Financial Aid . . . . Linda L. Paschal
Registrar . . . . Lesley A. Mack
Associate Vice President of Development . . . . Pamela J. Garvey
Senior Associate Dean for Faculty Affairs/Diversity . . . . Alonzo Walker, M.D.
Director of Libraries . . . . Mary B. Blackwelder
Vice President of Human Resources and Faculty Affairs . . . . Sherri DuCharme-White
Vice President, Campus Operations . . . . Tye V. Minckler
Vice President of Government Affairs/Community Relations. . . . . Kathryn A. Kuhn
Associate Vice President of Public Affairs . . . . Richard N. Katschke
Vice President and General Counsel. . . . . Sarah D. Cohn, J.D.
Assistant Dean for Clinical Research. . . . . David Clark, Ph.D.
Associate Dean for Clinical Informatics. . . . . Rick D. Gillis, M.D.
Associate Dean for Clinical Quality. . . . . John A. Weigelt, M.D., D.V.M.
Associate Dean for Clinical Research . . . . Theodore A. Kotchen, M.D.
Associate Dean for Froedert Hospital . . . . Andrew J. Norton, M.D.
Associate Dean for Research-Blood Research Institute. . . . . Gilbert White, M.D.

250

Associate Dean for Research-Children's Research Institute. . . . . Ellis D. Avner, M.D.
Associate Dean for Research-Zablocki VA Medical Center . . . . Elizabeth R. Jacobs, M.D.
Chief Medical Officer and Associate Dean for
   Medical Affairs-Medical College Physicians . . . . Lee A. Biblo, M.D.
Executive Director of Clinical Practice Services . . . . Marion Livingstone
Senior Associate Dean for Clinical and Translational Research . . . . Reza Shaker, M.D.
Vice President of Information Services . . . . Gregg Tushaus

Department Chairs and Division Chiefs

Basic Sciences

Biochemistry . . . . John Corbett, Ph.D.
Biophysics . . . . Balaraman Kalyanaraman, Ph.D.
Cell Biology, Neurobiology, and Anatomy. Joseph L. Besharse, Ph.D.
Microbiology and Molecular Genetics. . . . . Paula Traktman, Ph.D.

Clinical Sciences

Anesthesiology. . . . . David C. Warltier, M.D., Ph.D.
Dermatology . . . . Samuel Hwang, M.D., Ph.D.
Emergency Medicine . . . . Stephen W. Hargarten, M.D.
Family and Community Medicine. . . . . Alan K. David, M.D.
Medicine. . . . . Ray L. Silverstein, M.D.
   Cardiovascular Medicine. . . . . Michael P. Cinquegrani, M.D. (Interim)
   Endocrinology, Metabolism, and Clinical Nutrition . . . . Irene O'Shaughnessy, M.D.
   Gastroenterology and Hepatology. . . . . Reza Shaker, M.D.
   General Internal Medicine . . . . Ann B. Nattinger, M.D.
   Geriatrics and Gerontology. Edmund H. Duthie, Jr., M.D.
   Neoplastic Diseases and Related Disorders. . . . . Mary M. Horowitz, M.D. (Interim)
   Infectious Diseases . . . . Mark A. Bielke, M.D.
   Nephrology . . . . Sundaram Hariharan, M.D.
   Pulmonary and Critical Care. . . . . Elizabeth R. Jacobs, M.D.
   Rheumatology . . . . Lawrence M. Ryan, M.D.
Neurology . . . . Jeffery L. Binder, M.D. (Interim)
Neurosurgery. . . . . Dennis J. Maiman, M.D., Ph.D.
Obstetrics and Gynecology. . . . . Janet S. Rader, M.D.
Ophthalmology . . . . Dale K. Heuer, M.D.
Orthopaedic Surgery . . . . Jeffrey P. Schwab, M.D.
Otolaryngology and Communication Sciences. . . . . John S. Rhee, M.D.
Pathology . . . . Saul Suster, M.D.
Pediatrics . . . . Robert M. Kliegman, M.D.
Pharmacology and Toxicology . . . . William B. Campbell, Ph.D.
Physical Medicine and Rehabilitation . . . . Timothy R. Dillingham, M.D.
Physiology . . . . Allen W. Cowley, Jr., Ph.D.
Plastic and Reconstructive Surgery . . . . David Larson, M.D.
Psychiatry and Behavioral Medicine . . . . Jon Lehrmann, M.D. (Interim)
Radiation Oncology. . . . . J. Frank Wilson, M.D.
Radiology . . . . James E. Youker, M.D.
Surgery . . . . Douglas Evans, M.D. (Interim)
   Cardiothoracic. . . . . James S. Tweddell, M.D.
   Oral and Maxillofacial . . . . Steven R. Sewall, D.D.S.
   Pediatric . . . . Keith T. Oldham, M.D.
   Transplant . . . . Christopher P. Johnson, M.D.
   Trauma/Critical Care. . . . . John Weigelt, M.D.
   Vascular. . . . . Gary R. Seabrook, M.D.
Urology. . . . . William A. See, M.D.

Centers/Institutes

Center for Bioethics and Medical Humanities . . . . Arthur R. Derse, M.D., J.D.
Midwest Children's Cancer Center . . . . Bruce Camitta, M.D.
Cancer Center . . . . Ming You, Ph.D.
Cardiovascular Center. . . . . Allen W. Cowley, Jr., Ph.D.
Center for Infectious Diseases. . . . . Dara W. Frank, Ph.D.
Center for Imaging Research . . . . Shi-Jiang Li, Ph.D.
Clinical Translational Science Institute . . . . Reza Shaker, M.D.
Biotechnology and Bioengineering Center . . . . Andrew S. Greene, Ph.D.

University of Wisconsin School of Medicine and Public Health

750 Highland Avenue
Madison, Wisconsin 53705-2221
608-263-4900; 608-263-4910 (dean's office)
Web site: www.med.wisc.edu

The School of Medicine and Public Health is located on the Madison campus of the University of Wisconsin in clinical facilities, occupied since April 1, 1979, adjoining the Madison Veterans Administration Hospital. The school was established in 1907, offering a two-year program. With the construction of Wisconsin General Hospital in 1925, a four-year program was initiated. Its first four-year class graduated in 1927.

Type: public
2011 total enrollment: 683
Clinical facilities: University of Wisconsin Hospital and Clinics, American Family Children's Hospital, William S. Middleton Memorial Veterans Administration Hospital, St. Mary's Hospital, Meriter Hospital, Mendota Mental Health Institute, Central Wisconsin Center for the Developmentally Disabled, Aurora Healthcare (Milwaukee), Gundersen Lutheran (LaCrosse), Marshfield Clinic and Foundation-St. Joseph's Hospital (Marshfield).

University Officials

President, University of Wisconsin System . . . . Kevin P. Reilly, Ph.D.
Chancellor, University of Wisconsin-Madison . . . . David Ward, Ph.D. (Interim)

School of Medicine and Public Health Administrative Staff

Vice Chancellor for Medical Affairs and Dean. . . . . Robert N. Golden, M.D.
Senior Associate Dean, Academic Affairs. . . . . Elizabeth M. Petty, M.D. (Interim)
Senior Associate Dean, Basic Research,
    Biotechnology, and Graduate Studies . . . . Richard L. Moss, Ph.D.
Senior Associate Dean, Clinical Affairs . . . . Jeffrey E. Grossman, M.D.
Senior Associate Dean, Clinical and Translational Research. . . . . Marc Drezner, M.D.
Associate Dean, Medical Education. . . . . Christine S. Seibert, M.D.
Associate Dean, Hospital Affairs . . . . Vacant
Associate Dean, Public Health . . . . Patrick L. Remington, M.D., M.P.H.
Associate Dean, Rural and Community Health . . . . Byron J. Crouse, M.D.
Associate Dean, Students . . . . Patrick E. McBride, M.D., M.P.H.
Associate Dean, Marshfield Academic Campus . . . . Vacant
Associate Dean, Milwaukee Academic Campus . . . . Andy Anderson, M.D.
Assistant Dean, Clinical Affairs, Meriter Hospital. . . . . Geoffrey R. Priest, M.D.
Assistant Dean, Clinical Affairs, VA Hospital . . . . Alan J. Bridges, M.D.
Associate Dean, Clinical Affairs, Western Academic Campus . . . . David H. Chestnut, M.D.
Assistant Dean, Community Programs. . . . . Nancy Sugden
Assistant Dean, Facilities. . . . . Mark C. Wells
Associate Dean, Fiscal Affairs . . . . Kenneth J. Mount
Associate Dean, Administrative Affairs. . . . . Elizabeth T. Bolt
Associate Dean, Continuing Professional Development . . . . George C. Mejicano, M.D., M.S.
Associate Dean, Faculty Development and Faculty Affairs . . . . Patricia K. Kokotailo, M.D.
Assistant Dean, Multicultural Affairs . . . . Gloria V. Hawkins, Ph.D.
Assistant Dean, Student Affairs . . . . Patricia C. DeMarse
Assistant Dean, Technology Transfer . . . . Stephen G. Harsy, Ph.D.
Assistant Dean, Wisconsin Partnership Program . . . . Eileen Smith
Director, Medical Alumni Association and
    Assistant Dean, Alumni Relations . . . . Karen S. Peterson
Vice President, Health and Life Sciences . . . . Mark Lefebvre
Assistant Dean, Admissions. . . . . Kurt Hansen, M.D.
Director, Health Sciences Library. . . . . Julie Schneider

University of Wisconsin School of Medicine and Public Health: WISCONSIN

Department and Division or Section Chairs

Basic Sciences

Biomolecular Chemistry. . . . . Robert H. Fillingame, Ph.D.
Biostatistics and Medical Informatics . . . . Paul J. Rathouz, Ph.D.
Cell and Regenerative Biology . . . . Daniel S. Greenspan, Ph.D. (Interim)
Medical Genetics. . . . . Michael R. Culbertson, Ph.D.
Medical History and Bioethics . . . . Susan E. Lederer, Ph.D.
Medical Microbiology and Immunology . . . . Rodney A. Welch, Ph.D.
Medical Physics . . . . James A. Zagzebski, Ph.D.
Neuroscience. . . . . Tom C.T. Yin, Ph.D. (Interim)
Oncology. . . . . James D. Shull, Ph.D.
Pathology and Laboratory Medicine . . . . Andreas Friedl, M.D.
Population Health Sciences . . . . F. Javier Nieto, M.D., Ph.D.

Clinical Sciences

Anesthesiology. . . . . Robert A. Pearce, M.D., Ph.D.
Dermatology . . . . Gary S. Wood, M.D.
Family Medicine . . . . Valerie J. Gilchrist, M.D.
Human Oncology . . . . Paul Harari, M.D.
Medicine. . . . . Richard Page, M.D.
  Allergy, Pulmonary, and Critical Care . . . . Nizar N. Jarjour, M.D.
  Cardiovascular Medicine. . . . . Charles Stone, M.D.
  Emergency Medicine . . . . Azita Hamedani, M.D., M.P.H.
  Endocrinology, Diabetes, and Metabolism . . . . Marc K. Drezner, M.D.
  Gastroenterology and Hepatology. . . . . Michael R. Lucey, M.D.
  General Internal Medicine . . . . Elizabeth Trowbridge, M.D.
  Geriatrics and Gerontology. . . . . Sanjay Asthana, M.D.
  Hematology and Oncology. . . . . George Wilding, M.D.
  Hospital Medicine . . . . Ann Sheehy, M.D.
  Infectious Disease. . . . . David Andes, M.D.
  Nephrology . . . . Arjang Djamali, M.D.
  Rheumatology . . . . Kevin McKown, M.D.
Neurological Surgery. . . . . Robert J. Dempsey, M.D.
Neurology. . . . . Thomas P. Sutula, M.D., Ph.D.
Obstetrics and Gynecology. . . . . Laurel W. Rice, M.D.
Ophthalmology and Visual Sciences . . . . Paul L. Kaufman, M.D.
Orthopedics and Rehabilitation . . . . Thomas A. Zdeblick, M.D.
Pediatrics . . . . Ellen R. Wald, M.D.
Psychiatry . . . . Ned H. Kalin, M.D.
Radiology . . . . Thomas M. Grist, M.D.
  Abdominal Imaging . . . . J. Louis Hinshaw, M.D.
  Breast Imaging. . . . . Lonie Salkowski, M.D.
  Cardiothoracic Imaging . . . . Mark Schiebler, M.D.
  Magnetic Resonance Imaging . . . . Scott Reeder, M.D., Ph.D.
  Musculoskeletal Imaging. . . . . Michael Tuite, M.D.
  Neuroradiology . . . . Howard A. Rowley, M.D.
  Nuclear Medicine. . . . . Scott Perlman, M.D.
  Vascular Interventional Radiology . . . . Orhan Ozkan, M.D.
Surgery . . . . K. Craig Kent, M.D.
  Cardiothoracic. . . . . Takushi Kohmoto, M.D.
  General Surgery. . . . . Herb Chen, M.D.
  Otolaryngology-Head and Neck. . . . . Timothy M. McCulloch, M.D.
  Plastic/Reconstructive. . . . . Michael L. Bentz, M.D.
  Transplantation . . . . Dixon Kaufman, M.D.
  Vascular Surgery. . . . . Jon Matsumura, M.D.
Urology. . . . . Stephen Y. Nakada, M.D.

Provisional Medical School Members

2012

Florida Atlantic University Charles E. Schmidt College of Medicine

777 Glades Road
Boca Raton, Florida 33431
561-297-2219; 561-297-4341 (dean's office); 561-297-2462 (fax)
Web site: http://med.fau.edu/medicine

In the late 1990s, the Florida Board of Regents (BOR), then the governing body for the Florida State University System, established a regional campus of the University of Miami (UM) School of Medicine, a private institution, on the main, Boca Raton campus of Florida Atlantic University (FAU). The decision by FAU to seek LCME accreditation for an independent FAU College of Medicine is the culmination of this process that began over a decade ago. On April 7, 2010, the Florida Board of Governors authorized FAU to award the M.D. degree. Legislation authorizing the FAU College of Medicine was passed by the Florida legislature on April 22, 2010, and signed into law by the governor on May 15, 2010. On June 23, 2010, the FAU Board of Trustees renamed the Charles E. Schmidt College of Biomedical Science, in which the FAU regional medical program had been located for administrative purposes, the Charles E. Schmidt College of Medicine.

Type: public
2011 total enrollment:
Clinical facilities: Bethesda Memorial Hospital, Boca Raton Regional Hospital, Cleveland Clinic, Delray Medical Center, Memorial Healthcare System/Joe DiMaggio, St. Mary's Medical Center, West Boca Medical Center.

University Officials

President. . . . . Mary Jane Saunders, Ph.D.
Provost . . . . Diane Elias Alperin, Ph.D. (Interim)

Medical School Administrative Staff

Dean and Vice President for Medical Programs. . . . . Michael L. Friedland, M.D.
Vice Dean, Research, Graduate Programs, and Faculty Affairs . . . . Willis Paull, Ph.D.
Vice Dean, Graduate Medical Education and Student Affairs. . . . . . Lindsey Hensen, M.D., Ph.D.
Vice Dean, Graduate Medical Education and Clinical Affairs. . . . . Vacant
Senior Associate Dean, Geriatric Programs . . . . Joseph Ouslander, M.D.
Senior Associate Dean, Medical Education and Faculty Development. . . . . Barry Linger, E.D.
Senior Associate Dean, Student Affairs and Career Counseling . . . . Stuart Markowitz, M.D.
Assistant Dean, Diversity, Cultural, and Student Affairs . . . . Julie Servoss, M.D., P.M.H.
Assistant Dean, Finance . . . . Elizabeth Swerdloff
Assistant Dean, Prebaccalaureate Programs. . . . . Ira J. Gelb, M.D.
Associate Dean, Admissions and Enrollment. . . . . Robert Hinkley, Ph.D.
Assosciate Dean for Bethesda Memorial Hospital . . . . Al Biehl, M.D.
Associate Dean for Boca Raton Regional Hospital. . . . . Charles Posternack, M.D.
Associate Dean for Cleveland Clinic . . . . Steven Wexner, M.D.
Associate Dean for Delray Medical Center . . . . Anthony Dardano, M.D.
Associate Dean for Memorial Healthcare System. . . . . Stanley Marks, M.D.
Associate Dean for St. Mary's Medical Center . . . . Jeff Davis, D.O.
Associate Dean for West Boca Medical Center. . . . . Jack Harari, M.D.

Florida Atlantic University Charles E. Schmidt College of Medicine: FLORIDA

Department Chairs

Biomedical Science . . . . Keith Brew, Ph.D.
Integrated Medical Science . . . . Mort Levitt, M.D.

Florida International University Herbert Wertheim College of Medicine

11200 S.W. Eighth Street, AHC2 693
Miami, Florida 33199
305-348-0570; 305-348-0123 (fax)
Web site: http://medicine.fiu.edu

Florida International University Herbert Wertheim College of Medicine is transforming the future of public health and educational opportunity in the region. Established in 2006 amid pressing community health concerns and a projected critical shortage of physicians in the state and nationwide, the FIU College of Medicine curriculum reflects an innovative, 21st century approach to health care and medical education. In addition to the traditional basic science and clinical education, the FIU Doctor of Medicine (M.D.) program includes a formal curriculum in professional development; a required research component; and a novel service learning program that seeks to inculcate cultural competence by immersing medical students in the community as members of interdisciplinary teams with nursing and social work students. To provide medical students with diverse clinical experiences during their medical education, the college has established affiliation agreements with various private and public hospitals and clinics in the South Florida region. The M.D. degree program enrolled its first cohort of 43 students in 2009 and anticipates 480 students at full capacity.

Type: public
2011 total enrollment: 167
Clinical facilities: Baptist Health South Florida, Broward Health, Cleveland Clinic Florida, Jackson Health System (Public Health Trust), Leon Medical Centers, Memorial Healthcare System, Mercy Hospital, Miami Children's Hospital, and Mount Sinai Medical Center.

University Officials

President. . . . . Mark B. Rosenberg, Ph.D.
Provost, Executive Vice President and Chief Operating Officer . . . . Douglas Wartzok, Ph.D.
Chief Financial Officer and Senior Vice
    President of Administration . . . . Kenneth Jessell, Ph.D.
Senior Vice President for External Relations. Sandra Gonzalez-Levy
Chief Information Officer and Vice President of Information Technology . . . . Robert Grillo
Senior Vice President for University
    Advancement and President & CEO of the
    FIU Foundation . . . . Howard R. Lipman
Vice President for Government Relations . . . . Steve Sauls
Vice President for Human Resources . . . . Jaffus Hardrick, Ed.D.
Vice President of Student Affairs . . . . Rosa L. Jones, Ph.D.
Vice Provost, Academic Affairs . . . . Irma Becerra-Fernandez, Ph.D.
General Counsel . . . . M. Kristina Raattama, Esq.
Dean, University Graduate School . . . . Lakshmi N. Reddi, Ph.D.
Vice President, Office of Research . . . . Andres Gil, Ph.D.
Director of Intercollegiate Athletics . . . . Pete Garcia

Medical School Administrative Staff

Founding Dean and Senior Vice President for Medical Affairs. . . . . John A. Rock, M.D.
Founding Director of the College of Medicine Library . . . . David W. Boilard, A.M.L.S.
Executive Associate Dean for Academic Affairs . . . . Carolyn D. Runowicz, M.D.
Executive Associate Dean for Clinical Affairs. . . . . J. Patrick O'Leary, M.D.
Executive Associate Dean for Finance and Administration. . . . . Liane Martinez
Executive Associate Dean for Student Affairs. . . . . Sanford Markham, M.D.
Associate Dean for Curriculum and Medical Education. . . . . George Dambach, Ph.D.
Associate Dean for Clinical Medical Education . . . . David Graham, M.D.
Associate Dean for Graduate Medical Education . . . . Yolangel Hernandez-Suarez, M.D.
Associate Dean for International Affairs . . . . Manuel Viamonte, Jr., M.D.
Associate Dean for Academic Advising . . . . Karin Esposito, M.D., Ph.D.
Assistant Dean for Learning and Teaching . . . . Carla Lupi, M.D.
Associate Dean for Basic Research and Graduate Programs . . . . Barry P. Rosen, Ph.D.
Associate Dean for Clinical Research . . . . Maria I. New, M.D.
Associate Dean for International Affairs . . . . Manuel Viamonte, Jr., M.D.
Associate Dean for Student Affairs . . . . Robert Hernandez, Jr., M.D.

Florida International University Herbert Wertheim College of Medicine: FLORIDA

Associate Dean for Academic Affairs/Academic
  Teaching Hospital (West Kendall Baptist) .... Javier Hernandez-Lichtl
Assistant Dean for Academic Affairs .... Pedro Jose 'Joe' Greer, Jr., M.D.
Assistant Dean for Community and Clinical Affairs .... Fernando J. Valverde, M.D.
Assistant Deans for Student Affairs .... Robert Dollinger, M.D., and Barbra Roller, Ph.D.
Assistant Dean for Diversity .... Cheryl Brewster
Deputy General Counsel and Chief Legal Officer
  for Health Affairs, FIU Office of the General
  Counsel .... Jody Lehman, Esq.
Director, Accreditation... Sandra Allen
Director, Assessment .... Rodolfo Bonnin, Ph.D.
Director, Community Service Learning and NeighborhoodHELPå...... Luther Brewster, Ph.D.
Director, Counseling and Wellness........................... Heidi von Harscher, Ph.D.
Director, Educational Technology .... Leslie Bofill
Director, Finance.. Danielle Miller
Director, Financial Aid... Pemra Cetin
Director, Human Resources... Ana Poveda
Director, Operations .... Claire M. Wicker (Interim)
Director, Records.. Betty L. Monfort
Associate Director, Research...................................... Jonathan Sussman
Associate Director, Admissions .... Andria Williams-Garcia

Department and Division or Section Chairs

Cellular Biology and Pharmacology .... Georg Petroianu, M.D., Ph.D.
Human and Molecular Genetics............................. Joe Leigh Simpson, M.D.
Humanities, Health and Society............................ Pedro J. Greer, Jr., M.D.
Immunology .... Madhavan Nair, Ph.D.
Medicine.. Mark Multach, M.D.
Molecular Microbiology and Infectious Diseases .... Kalai Mathee, Ph.D.
Neurology... Jeffrey Horstmyer, M.D.
Obstetrics and Gynecology................................ Manuel A. Penalver, M.D.
Ophthalmology .... Pedro F. Lopez, M.D.
Orthopedics .... John Uribe, M.D.
Pathology .... Robert J. Poppiti, M.D.
Pediatrics .... Jefry Biehler, M.D.
Psychiatry .... Daniel Castellanos, M.D.
Radiology .... David Graham, M.D.
Surgery... Jaime Rodriguez, M.D.

Florida State University College of Medicine

1115 West Call Street
Tallahassee, Florida 32306-4300
850-644-1855 (general information); 850-644-1346 (dean's office); 850-645-1420 (fax)
E-mail: info@med.fsu.edu
Web site: www.med.fsu.edu

The first new allopathic medical school to open in the United States in more than 20 years, the Florida State University College of Medicine was established in June 2000 by the Florida Legislature for the purpose of training physicians with special emphasis on the needs of rural, underserved, minority, and elderly populations. The college's educational program uses cutting-edge information technology and focuses on producing compassionate physicians who will practice patient-centered medicine in a rapidly changing health care environment. As a community-based medical school, the college of medicine partners with existing community medical facilities and practitioners throughout the state rather than operating a teaching hospital. Students have an opportunity to learn on the front lines of the health care delivery system. The college of medicine occupies a state-of-the-art building that houses student communities, classrooms, auditoria, research labs, a clinical learning center, clinical simulation center, and administrative and faculty offices. In addition to the main campus in Tallahassee, the college has regional campuses in Daytona Beach, Fort Pierce, Orlando, Pensacola, Sarasota, and Tallahassee, along with rural clinical training sites in Marianna and Immokalee.

Type: public
2011 total enrollment: 480
Clinical facilities: Stewart-Marchman-Act Behavioral Healthcare, Daytona Beach; Apalachee Center, Inc., Tallahassee; Baptist Health Care, Pensacola; Bay Pines, VA, Bay Pines; Bayfront Medical Center, St. Petersburg; Bert Fish Medical Center, New Smyrna Beach; Big Bend Hospice, Tallahassee; Bond Community Health Center, Inc., Tallahassee; Cape Surgery Center, Sarasota; Capital Health Plan, Tallahassee; Capital Regional Medical Center, Tallahassee; Cleveland Clinic Florida, Weston; Collier Health Services, Inc., Immokalee; Community Health Centers Inc., Winter Park, DeSoto Memorial Hospital, Arcadia; Doctors Hospital of Sarasota, Sarasota; Doctors' Memorial Hospital, Perry; Doctors Same Day Surgery Center, Sarasota; Downtown Surgery Center, Orlando; Escambia County Health Department, Pensacola; Flagler County Health Department, Bunnell, Florida Community Health Center, Inc., Fort Pierce; Florida Department of Health, Children's Medical Services, Fort Pierce; Florida Health Care Plans, Inc., Holly Hill; Florida Hospital DeLand, DeLand; Florida Hospital Flagler, Flagler; Florida Hospital, Orlando; Florida State Hospital, Chattahoochee; Fort Walton Beach Medical Center, Fort Walton; Gadsden County Health Department, Quincy; Grove Place Surgery Center, Vero Beach; Intercoastal Medical Group Ambulatory Surgery Center, Sarasota; GulfCoast Surgery Center, Inc., Sarasota; H. Lee Moffitt Cancer Center, Tampa; Halifax Medical Center, Daytona Beach; Haven of Our Lady of Peace, Pensacola; HealthSouth Physicians' Surgical Care Center, Winter Park; HealthSouth Corp., Tallahassee; HealthSouth Treasure Coast Rehabilitation Hospital, Vero Beach; Indian River Medical Center, Vero Beach; Jackson Hospital, Marianna; Lakeview Center, Inc., Pensacola; Lakewood Ranch Medical Center, Bradenton; Lawnwood Regional Medical Center, Fort Pierce; M.D. Anderson Center Orlando, Orlando; Manatee Memorial Hospital, Bradenton; Martin Memorial Health Systems, Stuart; Mayo Clinic, Jacksonville; Miller School of Medicine, Miami; Morton Plant Hospital, Clearwater; Naval Hospital of Pensacola, Pensacola; Neighborhood Health Services, Tallahassee; Nemours Children's Clinic, Orlando; Nemours Children's Clinic, Pensacola; North Okaloosa Medical Center, Crestview; Orange County Medical Examiner's Office, Orlando; Orlando Health, Orlando; Orlando VA Clinic, Orlando; Pensacola VA Clinic, Pensacola; Port St. Lucie Hospital, Port St. Lucie; Raulerson Hospital, Okeechobee; Refuge House, Tallahassee; Riverchase Care Center, LLC., Quincy; Sacred Heart Health System, Pensacola; Santa Rosa Medical Center, Milton; Sarasota County Health Department, Sarasota; Sarasota Memorial Healthcare System, Sarasota; Sebastian River Medical Center, Sebastian; St. Cloud Regional Medical Center, St. Cloud; St. Lucie Medical Center, Port St. Lucie; Santa Rosa County Health Department, Milton; St. Lucie Surgery Center, Port St. Lucie; St. Vincent's, Inc., Jacksonville; Surgery Center of Fort Pierce, Fort Pierce; Surgery Center of Volusia County, Daytona Beach; Surgery Center of Okeechobee, Okeechobee; Surgical Center at Jensen Beach, Jensen Beach; Surgical Center of the Treasure Coast, Port St. Lucie; Tallahassee Memorial Healthcare, Tallahassee; Tallahassee Outpatient Surgery Center, Tallahassee; Tallahassee Plastic Surgery Clinic, Tallahassee; Tallahassee Single Day Surgery, Tallahassee; Tallahassee VA Clinic, Tallahassee; Thagard Student Health Center, Tallahassee; Twin Lakes Surgical Center, Daytona Beach; Treasure Coas

Florida State University College of Medicine: FLORIDA

University Officials

President, Florida State University . . . . Eric J. Barron, Ph.D.
Provost . . . . Garnett S. Stokes, Ph.D.
Senior Vice President for Finance and Administration. . . . . John R. Carnaghi
Vice President for Research . . . . Kirby Kemper, Ph.D.

College of Medicine Administrative Staff

Dean. . . . . John P. Fogarty, M.D.
Senior Associate Dean for Medical Education and Academic Affairs . . . . Alma Littles, M.D.
Senior Associate Dean for Research and Graduate Programs. . . . . Myra Hurt, Ph.D.
Associate Dean for Student Affairs and Admissions . . . . Christopher Leadem, Ph.D.
Executive Associate Dean for Administrative Affairs. . . . . Robert Watson, M.D.
Associate Dean of Finance and Accounting. . . . . Sharon Woodall, C.P.A.
Associate Dean for Health Affairs. . . . . Leslie Beitsch, M.D., J.D.
Associate Dean for Curriculum Development and Evaluation. . . . . Lynn Romrell, Ph.D.
Associate Dean for Medical Education . . . . Mary Johnson, Ph.D.
Associate Dean for Faculty Development. . . . . Dennis Baker, Ph.D.
Assistant Dean for Admissions . . . . Graham Patrick, Ph.D.
Assistant Dean, Daytona Beach Campus . . . . Luckey Dunn, M.D.
Assistant Dean, Fort Pierce Campus . . . . Randall Bertolette, M.D.
Assistant Dean, Orlando Campus . . . . Michael Muszynski, M.D.
Senior Associate Dean for Regional Campuses, Pensacola Campus. . . . . Paul McLeod, M.D.
Assistant Dean, Sarasota Campus . . . . Bruce Berg, M.D.
Assistant Dean, Tallahassee Campus . . . . Ronald Hartsfield, M.D.
Assistant Dean for Student Affairs. . . . . Rob Campbell, M.D.
Assistant Dean for Faculty Development . . . . Greg Turner, Ed.D.
Assistant Dean for Graduate Medical Education . . . . Christopher Mulrooney, Ph.D.
Assistant Dean for Undergraduate and Graduate Programs . . . . Helen Livingston, Ed.D.
Assistant Dean for Development. . . . . Wayne Munson, M.A.
Assistant Dean for Information Management . . . . John Van Wingen, Ph.D.
Director of Community Clinical Relations. . . . . Mollie Hill
Director of Public Affairs and Communications . . . . Doug Carlson
Associate General Counsel . . . . Robert Jurand, J.D.

Department Chairs

Biomedical Sciences. . . . . Richard Nowakowski, Ph.D.
Clinical Sciences . . . . Ricardo Gonzalez-Rothi, M.D.
Family Medicine and Rural Health. . . . . Daniel Van Durme, M.D.
Geriatrics. . . . . Kenneth Brummel-Smith, M.D.
Medical Humanities and Social Sciences. . . . . Janine Edwards, Ph.D.

University of Central Florida College of Medicine

Health Sciences Campus at Lake Nona
6850 Lake Nona Boulevard
Orlando, Florida 32827-7408
407-266-1000; 407-266-1489 (fax)
Web site: www.med.ucf.edu

The University of Central Florida College of Medicine was established in 2006 by the Florida Board of Governors, Florida legislature, and governor to increase opportunities for medical education in Florida and address the future need for physicians in the state. The college currently offers a doctor of Medicine (M.D.) degree program and undergraduate and graduate programs in biomedical sciences, biotechnology, medical laboratory sciences, and molecular biology and microbiology. The M.D. program began in fall 2009 with a charter class of 41 students and will eventually graduate 120 M.D.s per year at full enrollment. The M.D. program learning experience at the University of Central Florida is a unique and exciting blend of state-of-the-art technology, virtual patients, clinical and laboratory experiences, research, facilitator-directed small-group sessions, and interactive didactic lectures. The M.D. program integrates basic and clinical sciences across all four years. The first two years of the curriculum are structured into modules, with the first year focusing on a fundamental understanding of how the various basic science disciplines relate to the normal human body. The second year takes an organ system-based approach and applies the basic knowledge of the first year to the study of clinical disease, pathological processes, and treatment. The third and fourth years of the curriculum are devoted to clinical experience through clerkships. During each of the clerkships, the fundamental knowledge from the first two years is reinforced through lectures, simulations, journal clubs, and conferences. The four-year medical program capitalizes on the school's existing strengths in biomedical sciences, modeling and simulation, and optics and photonics.

Type: public
2011 total enrollment: 2900
Clinical facilities: Nemours Children's Hospital, Orlando VA Medical Center, Florida Hospital, Orlando Health, Sanford-Burnham Medical Research Institute, M. D. Anderson Cancer Research Institute, Orange County Health Department, Lakeside Behavioral Healthcare, Health Care Center for the Homeless, Planned Parenthood, Osceola Council on Aging.

University Officials

President. . . . . John C. Hitt, Ph.D.
Provost and Executive Vice President . . . . Tony Waldrop, Ph.D.
Vice President and General Counsel. . . . . W. Scott Cole, J.D.
Vice President for Community Relations. . . . . Helen Donegan
Vice President for Medical Affairs. . . . . Deborah C. German, M.D.
Vice President for Strategy, Marketing,
 Communications, and Admissions . . . . Alfred G. Harms, Jr.
Vice President for Alumni Relations and
 Development and CEO, UCF Foundation, Inc. Robert J. Holmes, Jr.
Vice President for University Relations . . . . Daniel C. Holsenbeck, Ph.D.
Vice President for Administration and Finance . . . . William F. Merck II
Vice President and Chief of Staff . . . . John F. Schell, Ph.D.
Director of Athletics and Executive Vice
 President, UCF Athletics Association . . . . Alfred G. Harms, Jr. (Interim)
Vice President for Student Development and Enrollment Services . . . . Maribeth Ehasz, Ph.D.
Vice President for Research and Commercialization . . . . M. J. Soileau, Ph.D.
Associate Provost and Associate General Counsel . . . . Sheryl Andrews, J.D.
Executive Vice Provost, Academic, Faculty, and
 International Affairs . . . . Diane Z. Chase, Ph.D.
Vice Provost, Regional Campuses . . . . Joyce Dorner (Interim)
Vice Provost, Information Technologies and Resources . . . . Joel L. Hartman, Ed.D.
Vice Provost and Dean, Undergraduate Studies. . . . . Elliot Vittes, Ph.D. (Interim)
Vice Provost, Space Planning, Analysis and Administration . . . . Ed Neighbor, Ph.D.
Dean, College of Arts and Humanities . . . . Jose Fernandez, Ph.D.
Dean, College of Business Administration. . . . . Foard Jones, Ph.D. (Interim)
Dean, College of Education . . . . Sandra L. Robinson, Ph.D.
Dean, College of Engineering and Computer Science . . . . Marwan Simaan, Ph.D.
Vice Provost and Dean, College of Graduate Studies . . . . Patricia J. Bishop, Ph.D.

University of Central Florida College of Medicine: FLORIDA

Dean, College of Health and Public Affairs. . . . . Michael J. Frumkin, Ph.D.
Dean, The Burnett Honors College . . . . Alvin Wang, Ph.D.
Dean, Rosen College of Hospitality Management . . . . Abraham Pizam, Ph.D.
Dean, College of Medicine. . . . . Deborah C. German, M.D.
Dean, College of Nursing. . . . . Jean D. Leuner, Ph.D.
Dean, College of Optics and Photonics. . . . . Bahaa Saleh, Ph.D.
Dean, College of Sciences . . . . Michael Johnson, Ph.D. (Interim)

Medical School Administrative Staff

Dean. . . . . Deborah C. German, M.D.
Associate Dean, Clinical Affairs and Chair, Clinical Sciences . . . . Ralph Caruana, M.D.
Associate Dean, Research. . . . . (TBA)
Associate Dean, Students . . . . Marcia Verduin, M.D.
Associate Dean, Faculty and Academic Affairs . . . . Richard Peppler, Ph.D.
Associate Dean, Planning and Knowledge Management. . . . . Julia Pet-Armacost, Ph.D.
Associate General Counsel . . . . Shainoor Ladha-Karmali, J.D.
Associate Vice President for Medical Affairs and
    Chief Legal Officer . . . . Jeanette Schreiber, J.D.
Associate Dean, Administration and Finance. . . . . Scott Sumner
Assistant Vice President, Development . . . . Charles Roberts
Director, Burnett School of Biomedical Sciences. . . . . Pappachan Kolattukudy, Ph.D.
Director, Academic Support Services . . . . Geovanna Abreu
Chair, Medical Education. . . . . David Balkwill, Ph.D.
Special Advisor to the Dean. . . . . Robert Armacost, D.Sc.
Special Assistant to the Dean . . . . Karen Smith
Assistant Dean, Diversity and Inclusion. . . . . Lisa Barkley, M.D.
Assistant Dean, Simulation and Medical
    Director, Clinical Skills and Simulation Center . . . . Juan Cendan, M.D.
Assistant Dean, Undergraduate Medical Education . . . . Lori Boardman, M.D.
Assistant Dean, Undergraduate Medical Education . . . . Jonathan Kibble, Ph.D.
Assistant Dean, Graduate Medical Education. . . . . Diane Davey, M.D.
Director, Admissions . . . . Robert Larkin
Director, Advancement/Alumni Affairs. . . . . Carlee Thomas
Director, Analysis, Accreditation and Planning . . . . Basma Selim, Ph.D.
Director, Anatomical Facilities . . . . Jennifer Parsons
Director, Assessment . . . . Basma Selim, Ph.D. (Interim)
Director, Clinical Operations . . . . Linda Smelser
Director, Faculty Development. . . . . Andrea Berry
Director, Finance and Accounting . . . . Steven Omli
Director, Health Planning . . . . Josue Rodas
Director, Health Sciences and Campus Operations . . . . Barbara O'Hara
Director, Health Sciences Library. . . . . Nadine Dexter, M.L.S.
Director, Human Resources . . . . Allen Abramson
Director, Information Technology . . . . Henry Glaspie
Director, Knowledge Management . . . . Matthew Gerber, Ph.D.
Director, Learning Systems. . . . . Dale Voorhees
Director, Marketing and Communications . . . . Wendy Sarubbi
Director, Student Financial Services . . . . Lisa Minnick (Interim)
Director, Student Affairs . . . . Soraya Smith
Director, Systems Engineering . . . . Eric Baker
Assistant Director, Database Applications . . . . Micah Marshall
Assistant Director, Development. . . . . Lorraine Scholler
Assistant Director, Health Sciences Campus Operations. . . . . Larry Langford
Assistant Director, Marketing . . . . Stephen Toth
Assistant Director, Network and Server Management. . . . . Kevin Smith
Assistant Director, Student Financial Services . . . . Lisa Minnick
Registrar . . . . Teresa Lyons-Oten

Oakland University William Beaumont School of Medicine

472 O'Dowd Hall
2200 North Squirrel Road
Rochester, Michigan 48309
248-370-3634 (dean's office); 248-370-3630 (fax)
Web site: http://www.oakland.edu/medicine

Oakland University and Beaumont Health System have partnered to form the Oakland University William Beaumont School of Medicine. Oakland, a vibrant research university, has a longstanding commitment to strong biomedical and health education programs. Beaumont's three hospital system includes campuses in Royal Oak, Troy, and Grosse Pointe. The Royal Oak campus is the major academic referral center with Level 1 trauma status. Ninety-one medical and surgical specialties are represented on the Beaumont medical staff of more than 3,100 physicians.

Type: public
2011 total enrollment: 50
Clinical facilities: Beaumont Health System

University Officials

President. . . . . Gary D. Russi, Ph.D.
Provost . . . . Virinder K. Moudgil, Ph.D.

Medical School Administrative Staff

Founding Dean . . . . Robert Folberg, M.D.
Assistant Dean for Community Integration and Outreach . . . . Nelia Afonso, M.D.
Director, Medical Library. . . . . Nancy Bulgarelli, M.S.L.S.
Associate Dean for Graduate Medical Education . . . . Jeffrey Devries, M.D., M.P.H.
Assistant Dean, Diversity and Multicultural Affairs. . . . . Vonda Douglas-Nikitin, M.D.
Associate Dean for Research. . . . . David Felten, M.D., Ph.D.
Associate Dean for Academic and Faculty Affairs. . . . . Linda Gillum, Ph.D.
Assistant Dean for Admissions . . . . Christina Grabowski, M.S.A.
Assistant Dean for Student Services . . . . Krista Malley, Ph.D.
Associate Dean for Educational Information Technology. . . . . Robert McAuley, Ph.D.
Associate Dean for Undergraduate Clinical Education. . . . . . . Lynda Misra, D.O., F.A.C.P, M.Ed.
Assoociate Dean for Medical Education . . . . Robert Noiva, Ph.D.
Associate Dean for Student Affairs . . . . Angela Nuzzarello, M.D., M,H.P.E.
Assistant Dean for Continuing Medical Education. . . . . Brooke Taylor, M.P.H., C.C.M.E.P.
Assistant Dean for Development. . . . . Tracy Utech, M.P.A.
Vice Dean for Business and Administration. Cheryl Verbruggen, M.S.A.

Oakland University William Beaumont School of Medicine: MICHIGAN

Department and Division or Section Chairs

Anesthesiology. . . . . James Grant, M.D.
Biomedical Sciences. . . . . Wanda Reygaert, Ph.D.
Cardiology. . . . . Simon Dixon, M.D.
Emergency Medicine . . . . James Ziadeh, M.D. (Interim)
Family Medicine . . . . Paul Misch, M.D.
Internal Medicine . . . . Michael Maddens, M.D.
Neurosurgery. . . . . Fernando Diaz, M.D.
Obstetrics & Gynegology . . . . Robert Starr, M.D. (Interim)
Opthalmology . . . . George Williams, M.D.
Orthopaedic Surgery . . . . Harry Herkowitz, M.D.
Pathology . . . . Mark Kolins, M.D.
Pediatrics . . . . Jeffrey Maisels, M.D.
Physical Medicine & Rehabilitation. . . . . Ronald Taylor, M.D.
Psychiatry . . . . Neil Talon, M.D.
Radiation Oncology. . . . . John Roberts, M.D. (Interim)
Radiology . . . . Duane Mezwa, M.D.
Surgery . . . . Alan Koffron, M.D. (Interim)
Urology. . . . . Kenneth Peters, M.D.

Cooper Medical School of Rowan University
400 South Broadway
Camden, New Jersey 08103
856-361-2800 (main number); 856-361-2801 (fax)
Web site: http://www.rowan.edu/coopermed

Cooper Medical School of Rowan University was formed in 2009 as a partnership between Rowan University and the Cooper Health System to create the first four-year allopathic medical school in southern New Jersey. The partnership brings together two institutions with national recognition and a historic commitment to education, patient care, and the health of the region. Our mission states the ongoing commitment to provide a humanistic education, in which inclusivity, excellence in patient care, innovative teaching, research, and service to our community are valued. Our core values include a commitment to diversity, personal mentorship, professionalism, collaboration and mutual respect, civic responsibility, patient advocacy, and life-long learning.

Type: public
2011 total enrollment: 50
Clinical facilities: The Cooper Health System.

University Officials

President, Rowan University . . . . Ali Houshmand, Ph.D. (Interim)

Medical School Administrative Staff

Founding Dean . . . . Paul Katz, M.D.
Founding Vice Dean and Senior Associate Dean
    for Faculty Affairs . . . . Annette C. Reboli, M.D.
Associate Dean for Student Affairs and Admissions . . . . John F. McGeehan, M.D.
    Director of Admissions . . . . Catherine Dayton, Ph.D.
    Chief Student Affairs Officer . . . . Marion Lombardi Munley
    Assistant Director of Financial Aid . . . . Kyhna Bryant
Associate Dean for Academic Affairs . . . . Michael E. Goldberg, M.D.
    Assistant Dean for Faculty and Student Assessment and Development . . . . . . Cindi Hasit, Ph.D.
    Assistant Dean for Curriculum - Phase I . . . . Lawrence S. Weisberg, M.D.
    Assistant Dean for Curriculum - Phase II . . . . Vijaykumar K. Rajput, M.D.
    Director of Simulation . . . . Amanda Burden, M.D.
Associate Dean for Finance, Administration, and Operations . . . . Valerie P. Weil, M.D.
Associate Dean for Multicultural and
    Community Affairs . . . . Jocelyn Mitchell-Williams, M.D., Ph.D.
Associate Dean for Program and Business Development . . . . Patricia Davis Vanston
Associate Dean for Research . . . . Harry Mazurek, Ph.D.
Associate Dean for Clinical Affairs and GME . . . . Carolyn Bekes, M.D.

Cooper Medical School of Rowan University: NEW JERSEY

Department and Division or Section Chairs

Anesthesiology . . . . Michael E. Goldberg, M.D.
Biomedical Sciences . . . . William Kocher, M.D.
Diagnostic Imaging . . . . Raymond L. Baraldi, M.D.
Emergency Medicine . . . . Michael E. Chansky, M.D.
Family Medicine . . . . Dyanne P. Westerberg, D.O.
Medicine . . . . Joseph E. Parrillo, M.D.
Neurology . . . . John Kelly, M.D.
Neurosurgery . . . . H. Warren Goldman, M.D., Ph.D.
Obstetrics and Gynecology . . . . Robin L. Perry, M.D.
Orthopaedics . . . . Lawrence S. Miller, M.D.
Pathology . . . . Roland Schwarting, M.D.
Pediatrics . . . . Michael H. Goodman, M.D.
Physical Medicine and Rehabilitation . . . . Elliot B. Bodofsky, M.D.
Psychiatry . . . . Andres J. Pumariega, M.D.
Radiation Oncology . . . . Tamara A. LaCouture, M.D.
Surgery . . . . Jeffrey P. Carpenter, M.D.

Hofstra North Shore-LIJ School of Medicine at Hofstra University
Hempstead, New York 11549-1000
516-463-7516
Web site: http://medicine.hofstra.edu

In 2006, the Association of American Medical Colleges, citing population increases, a doubling of the number of citizens over the age of 65 between 2000 and 2030, and an aging physician workforce, recommended that medical school enrollment be increased by 30 percent by 2015. Concurrently, the university and the health system each had reached a rapid-growth stage of development at which collaborating to develop a nationally renowned medical school became a highly attractive and advantageous endeavor. Aligned in their institutional visions, Hofstra University and the North Shore-LIJ Health System began to explore the advantages of collaborating to create an innovative and outstanding school of medicine. In October 2007, the two institutions announced the intent to establish the Hofstra North Shore-LIJ School of Medicine at Hofstra University. This unique partnership brought together two outstanding Long Island institutions, ensuring that the medical school would have excellent clinical training opportunities, research records and academic infrastructure from the outset. Hofstra provided its accomplished faculty and an existing admissions and student services infrastructure, as well as a beautiful campus with room for a new medical education building and residence hall. North Shore-LIJ Health System, as one of the largest integrated health systems in the nation, provided a first class group of hospitals, health care facilities and research institutions, and some of the nation's most respected physicians and researchers. On March 27, 2008, Hofstra University and North Shore-LIJ Health System entered into a formal partnership to establish the Hofstra North Shore-LIJ School of Medicine at Hofstra University, the first allopathic medical school in Nassau County and the first new medical school in the New York metropolitan area in more than 35 years. With preliminary LCME accreditation accomplished in 2010, the school matriculated its first class in 2011.

Type: private
2011 total enrollment: 40
Clinical facilities: North Shore-LIJ Health System Hospitals and ambulatory facilities.

University Officials

President. . . . . Stuart Rabinowitz
Senior Vice President for Planning and Administration. . . . . M. Patricia Adamski
Vice President for Facilities and Operations . . . . Joseph M. Barkwill
Provost and Senior Vice President for Academic Affairs. . . . . Herman A. Berliner, Ph.D.
Vice President for University Relations . . . . Melissa Kane Connolly
Vice President for Enrollment Management . . . . Jessica Eads
Vice President for Legal Affairs and General Counsel . . . . Dolores Fredrich, Esq.
Vice President for Business Development . . . . Robert V. Guardino, Jr., Esq.
Vice President for Financial Affairs and Treasurer. . . . . Catherine Hennessy
Vice President for Student Affairs. . . . . Sandra S. Johnson
Vice President for Information Technology . . . . Robert W. Juckiewicz
Vice President for Development. . . . . Alan J. Kelly

Medical School Administrative Staff

Dean. . . . . Lawrence G. Smith, M.D.
Senior Associate Dean for Education . . . . David Battinelli, M.D.
Senior Associate Dean for Academic Affairs . . . . Veronica M. Catanese, M.D.
Senior Associate Dean for Administration. . . . . June E. Scarlett
Associate Dean for Research. . . . . Kevin J. Tracey, M.D.
Associate Dean for Strategic Planning. . . . . Jeffrey A. Kraut
Associate Dean for Knowledge Management. . . . . Alan Cooper, Ph.D.
Assistant Dean for Medical Education - Faculty Development. . . . . Alice Fornari, Ed.D.
Assistant Dean for Medical Education - Case Development . . . . Samara Ginzburg, M.D.
Assistant Dean for Medical Education - Simulation . . . . Thomas Kwiatkowski, M.D.
Associate Dean for Student Affairs . . . . Jodi M. Langsfeld
Assistant Dean for Library Services . . . . Debra Rand
Assistant Dean for Admissions . . . . Rona Woldenberg, M.D.
Assistant Dean for Curricular Integration . . . . Judith Brenner, M.D.
Assistant Dean for Diversity and Inclusion. . . . . Adam Aponte, M.D.

Hofstra North Shore-LIJ School of Medicine at Hofstra University: NEW YORK

Department and Division or Section Heads

Anesthesiology. . . . . John DiCapua, M.D.
Cardiology. . . . . Stanley Katz, M.D.
Cardiovascular and Thoracic Surgery . . . . Alan Hartman, M.D.
Dental Medicine . . . . Ronald Burakoff, D.M.D.
Emergency Medicine . . . . Andrew Sama, M.D.
Family Medicine . . . . Tochi Iroke-Malize, M.D.
Medicine. . . . . Thomas McGinn, M.D.
Molecular Medicine. . . . . Bettie M. Steinberg, Ph.D.
Neurology. . . . . Ronald Kanner, M.D.
Neurosurgery. . . . . Raj K. Narayan, M.D.
Obstetrics and Gynecology. . . . . Adiel Fleischer, M.D.
Ophthalmology . . . . Ira Udell, M.D.
Orthopedic Surgery. . . . . Nicolas Sgaglione, M.D.
Otolaryngology . . . . Allan Abramson, M.D.
Pathology and Laboratory Medicine . . . . James Crawford, M.D., Ph.D.
Pediatrics . . . . Steven Shelov, M.D. (Acting)
Physical Medicine and Rehabilitation . . . . Adam Stein, M.D.
Population Health. . . . . Jacqueline Moline, M.D.
Psychiatry . . . . John Kane, M.D.
Radiation Medicine . . . . Louis Potters, M.D.
Radiology . . . . Lawrence P. Davis, M.D. (Acting)
Science Education . . . . Patrick Cannon, Ph.D.
Surgery . . . . Gene Coppa, M.D.
Urology. . . . . Louis Kavoussi, M.D.

The Commonwealth Medical College
525 Pine Street
Scranton, Pennsylvania 18509
570-504-7000 (campus); 570-504-9660 (fax)
Web site: http://thecommonwealthmedical.com

The Commonwealth Medical College (TCMC) is one of the nation's newest medical colleges located in northeast Pennsylvania. TCMC features a community-based model of education with three regional campuses- north (Scranton), south (Wilkes-Barre) and west (Williamsport). TMC offers a Medical Degree (MD) program, Master of Biomedical Sciences (MBS) degree, and Professional Science of Masters (PSM) degree. TCMC was awarded degree granting authority by the Commonwealth of Pennsylvania in 2008, received preliminary LCME (Liaison Committee on Medical Education) accreditation in 2008 and accepted its first class of medical and master's students n 2009. The College attracts students from within its 16-county region as well as across Pennsylvania and the nation who are interested in studying evidence- and community-based medicine and who have a strong desire to serve their community. In 2011, TCMC opened the 185,000 sqaure foot Medical Sciences Building that houses the academic and research programs.

Type: private
2011 total enrollment:
Clinical facilities: Allied Services/John Heinz Institute; Berwick Clinic Company, LLC; Bloomsburg Hospital; Blue Mountain Health System; Community Medical Center; Children's Service Center of Wyoming Valley; Evangelical Hospital; Geisinger Wyoming Valley Medical Center; Guthrie Healthcare System; Hazleton General Hospital; Jersey Shore Hospital; Pocono Medical Center; Moses Taylor Hospital; Muncy Hospital; Regional Hospital of Scranton; Susquehanna Health System; Schuylkill Health System; Wayne Hospital; Wyoming Valley Health Care System; and Wilkes-Barre Department of Veteran Affairs Medical Center.

University Official

President and Dean, The Commonwealth
   Medical College .... Lois Margaret Nora, M.D., J.D., M.B.A. (Interim)

Medical School Administrative Staff

Senior Associate Dean for Academic Affairs .... Maurice Clifton, M.D., M.D.Ed
Associate Dean for Student Affairs .... David Axler, Ph.D.
Associate Dean for Research and Economic Development.............. Daniel Flynn, Ph.D.
Associate Dean for Educational Development .... Raymond Smego, M.D.
Vice President and Associate Dean for Planning .... Virginia Hunt, M.U.A.
Chief Financial Officer............................... Michael Learai, M.B.A. (Interim)
Vice President, Community Engagement and Equity.................. Ida Castro, M.A., J.D.
Associate Dean for Regional Campus Development, Williamsport ...... Keith Shenberger, M.D.
Associate Dean for Regional Campus Development, Wilkes-Barre .... Richard English, M.D.
Associate Dean for Regional Campus Development, Scranton .... Gerald Tracy, M.D.

The Commonwealth Medical College: PENNSYLVANIA

Department and Division or Section Chairs

Basic Sciences

Co-Chair of Basic Sciences . . . . Daniel Flynn, Ph.D.
Co-Chair of Basic Sciences . . . . John Szarek, Ph.D.

Chairs

Family, Community and Rural Health. . . . . Janet Townsend, M.D.
Clinical Sciences . . . . Valerie Weber, M.D.
Obstetrics and Gynecology. . . . . Vacant
Pediatrics . . . . Vacant
Psychiatry . . . . Vacant
Surgery . . . . Vacant

University of South Carolina School of Medicine - Greenville

Health Sciences Administration Building
701 Grove Road
Greenville, South Carolina 29605
864-455-7992 (dean's office); 864-455-8404 (fax);
864-455-9807 (medical student affairs)
Website: http://www.greenvillemed.sc.edu

The University of South Carolina School of Medicine - Greenville (USCSOM-Greenville) is located on the Greenville Memorial Hospital campus of Greenville Hospital System (GHS). For nearly 100 years, GHS has been responding to the medical needs of the South Carolina Upstate by providing compassionate, comprehensive patient care and by training future caregivers. This invigorating environment motivated the University of South Carolina School of Medicine to create in 1990 a regional campus in Greenville for its Columbia medical school, where a portion of its medical students relocate after their second year to perform their entire clinical education at GHS. Building on that successful program and in response to the needs of society, a decision was made to expand the Greenville medical campus to offer all four years of medical education. USCSOM-Greenville received preliminary accreditation by the LCME in October of 2011.

Type:
2011 total enrollment: 50
Clinical facilities: Greenville Hospital System.

University Officials

President, University of South Carolina. . . . . Harris Pastides, Ph.D.
Provost . . . . Michael D. Amiridis, Ph.D.
Chief Executive Officer, Health System. . . . . Michael C. Riordan
Vice President of Communications. . . . . Luanne M. Lawrence

Medical School Administrative Staff

Dean. . . . . Jerry R. Youkey, M.D.
Senior Associate Dean for Academic Affairs and Diversity . . . . Spence M. Taylor, M.D.
Associate Dean for Education. . . . . Lynn M. Crespo, M.D.
Associate Dean for Faculty Affairs. . . . . Robert G. Best, Ph.D.
Associate Dean for Student Affairs . . . . James Buggy, Ph.D.
Assistant Dean for Admissions . . . . Paul V. Catalana, M.D.

University of South Carolina School of Medicine - Greenville: SOUTH CAROLINA

Department Chairs

Basic Sciences

Biomedical Sciences (Acting Chair) .... Robert G. Best, Ph.D.

Clinical Sciences

Anesthesiology... C. Wendall James III, M.D.
Emergency Medicine .... Jack Colker, M.D.
Family Medicine .... W. Patrick Marshall, M.D.
Internal Medicine .... Angelo Sinopoli, M.D.
Obstetrics and Gynecology.................................. Donald W. Wiper, M.D.
Orthopedics .... Edward W. Bray III, M.D.
Pathology .... Jesse Stafford, M.D.
Pediatrics .... William F. Schmidt III, M.D., Ph.D.
Psychiatry .... Kenneth M. Rogers, M.D.
Radiology .... C. David Williams III, M.D.
Surgery .... Eugene M. Langan III, M.D.

Texas Tech University Health Sciences Center
Paul L. Foster School of Medicine

5001 El Paso Drive
El Paso, Texas 79905
915-783-5510
Web site: www.ttuhsc.edu/fostersom

The Paul L. Foster School of Medicine at Texas Tech University Health Sciences Center in El Paso seeks to educate physicians, provide health care, and perform focused research in an environment of border and Hispanic health. Relying on its 40-year history as a teaching clinical campus, the faculty at Paul L. Foster School of Medicine have crafted a curriculum organized around clinical presentations, community and cultural sensitivity, as well as clinical and communication skills. It relies on clinical locations throughout El Paso County for student and resident rotations, while providing health care to multiple diverse populations. The school has focused its research efforts on border and Hispanic populations by creating research centers in the areas of diabetes/obesity, cancer, neurosciences, and infectious diseases.

Type: public
2011 total enrollment: 39

University Officials

President. . . . . Tedd Mitchell, M.D.
Chief of Staff. . . . . Pureza (Didit) Martinez
Special Assistant to the President . . . . Keono McWhinney
Executive Vice President and Provost . . . . Steven L. Berk, M.D.
Executive Vice President for Finance and Administration . . . . Elmo M. Cavin
Executive Vice President for Research, Dean,
    Graduate School of Biomedical Sciences . . . . Douglas M. Stocco, Ph.D.
Senior Vice President for Academic Affairs . . . . Rial Rolfe, Ph.D., M.B.A.
Vice President for Information Technology and
    Chief Information Officer . . . . Chip Shaw, Ed.D.
Vice President for Medical Affairs. . . . . Steven L. Berk, M.D.
Vice President for Rural and Community Affairs. . . . . Billy Philips, Ph.D.
Vice President for Health Affairs . . . . Jose Manuel de la Rosa, M.D.

Medical School Administrative Staff

Founding Dean. . . . . Jose Manuel de la Rosa, M.D.
Senior Associate Dean for Medical Education . . . . David J. Steele, Ph.D.
Associate Dean for Admissions and Recruitment. . . . . Manuel Schydlower, M.D.
Associate Dean for Faculty Affairs and Development . . . . Hoi Ho, M.D.
Associate Dean for Student Affairs . . . . Kathryn V. Horn, M.D.
Associate Dean for Graduate Medical Education . . . . Armando Meza, M.D.
Associate Dean for Research. . . . . Charles C. Miller III, Ph.D.
Associate Dean for Clinical Affairs . . . . Michael Romano, M.D.
Associate Dean for the Graduate School of
    Biomedical Sciences . . . . Charles C. Miller III, Ph.D.
Associate Dean for Finance and Administration . . . . Frank Stout, M.B.A.

Texas Tech University Health Sciences Center
Paul L. Foster School of Medicine: TEXAS

Department Chairs

Basic Sciences

Biomedical Sciences.................................... Charles C. Miller III, Ph.D.
Medical Education...................................... Richard Brower, M.D.

Clinical Sciences

Anesthesiology... Ahmed E. Badr, M.D.
Emergency Medicine.................................... Brian K. Nelson, M.D.
Family and Community Medicine......................... Gurjeet J. Shokar, M.D.
Internal Medicine .... Richard W. McCallum, M.D.
Neurology... David Briones, M.D. (Interim)
Obstetrics and Gynecology............................. Veronica Mallett, M.D.
Orthopaedic Surgery and Rehabilitation................. Miguel E. Pirela-Cruz, M.D.
Pathology .... Darius Boman, M.D.
Pediatrics .... Bradley Fuhrman, M.D.
Psychiatry .... Michael A. Escamilla, M.D., Ph.D.
Radiology .... Arvin E. Robinson, M.D., M.P.H.
Surgery .... Alan H. Tyroch, M.D.

Virginia Tech Carilion School of Medicine

2 Riverside Circle
Suite 102
Roanoke, Virginia 24016
540-526-2500 (general information); 540-581-0741 (fax)
E-mail: vtc@vt.edu
Web site: www.vtc.vt.edu

The Virginia Tech Carilion School of Medicine and Research Institute (VTC) is a public-private partnership formed by Virginia Tech and Carilion Clinic that leverages Virginia Tech's world-class strength in basic sciences, bioinformatics, and engineering and Carilion Clinic's highly experienced medical staff and rich history in medical education. Utilizing an innovative patient-centered curriculum, VTC addresses the increasing need for physicians who can translate research from the bench to the bedside and into the community. The curriculum provides an exemplary education in basic sciences and clinical sciences and skills, but transcends the traditional medical education model by providing a solid foundation in, and opportunities to explore, the disciplines of research and interprofessionalism. Our small class size of 42 students allows for individualized attention and participation by each student, which will in turn foster an intense and highly rich educational experience. Our rigorous admissions process will select students with the resilience to thrive in the challenging environment posed by healthcare reform. We envision that Virginia Tech Carilion School of Medicine graduates will be highly sought after by residency programs and will go on to become physician thought leaders in their chosen field of medicine, whether it be community or academic medicine, research, health policy, health care administration, or health information technology.

Type: private
2011 total enrollment: 42
Clinical facilities: Carilion Clinic.

University Officials

Associate Dean for Medical Education . . . . Richard C. Vari, Ph.D.
President and Founding Dean . . . . Cynda Ann Johnson, M.D., M.B.A.
Secretary-Treasurer and Vice Dean . . . . F. Terri Workman, J.D., M.B.A.

Medical School Administrative Staff

Senior Dean for Academic Affairs. . . . . Daniel P. Harrington, M.D.
Senior Dean for Research . . . . Michael J. Friedlande, Ph.D.
Associate Dean for Faculty Affairs . . . . Bruce E. Johnson, M.D.
Associate Dean for Student Affairs . . . . Mark H. Greenawald, M.D.
Associate Dean for Community and Culture . . . . David B. Trinkle, M.D.
Associate Dean for Admissions and Administration . . . . Stephen M. Workman, Ph.D.
Assistant Dean for Clinical Sciences (Clerkship Years)
Assistant Dean for Clinical Sciences (Pre-Clerkship Years)
Chief Financial Officer. . . . . Donna M. Littlepage, M.B.A.
Chief Development Officer . . . . Elizabeth McBride, M.B.A.

Virginia Tech Carilion School of Medicine: VIRGINIA

Department and Division or Section Chairs

Emergency Medicine . . . . John H. Burton, M.D.
Family Medicine . . . . Mark H. Greenawald, M.D.
Internal Medicine . . . . Ralph E. Whatley, M.D.
Obstetrics and Gynecology. . . . . Patrice M. Weiss, M.D.
Pediatrics . . . . Alice D. Ackerman, M.D., M.B.A.
Psychiatry . . . . Mark D. Kilgus, M.D., Ph.D.
Radiology . . . . Evelyn M. Garcia, M.D.
Surgery . . . . Christopher C. Baker, M.D.
Basic Sciences . . . . Ludeman A. Eng, Ph.D.
Interprofessionalism. . . . . Nathanial Bishop, D.Min.

Affiliate Members

2012

University of Alberta Faculty of Medicine and Dentistry

2J2 Walter Mackenzie Health Sciences Centre
8440 112th Street
Edmonton, Alberta Canada T6G 2R7
780-492-6350 (general-M.D. program); 780-492-6621 (dean's office);
780-492-7303 (fax)
Web site: www.med.ualberta.ca

The faculty of medicine at the University of Alberta was founded in 1913. The first complete M.D. degrees were granted in 1925. The faculty of dentistry merged with the faculty of medicine on April 1, 1996, to form the new faculty of medicine and dentistry.

Type: public
2011 total enrollment: 523
Clinical facilities: University of Alberta Hospitals, Royal Alexandra Hospitals, Grey Nuns Hospital, Edmonton Misericordia Hospital, Glenrose Rehabilitation Hospital, Alberta Hospital (Edmonton), Alberta Hospital (Ponoka), Cross Cancer Institute, St. Mary's Hospital (Camrose), and Red Deer General Hospital (Red Deer).

University Officials

Chancellor of the University. . . . . L. Hughes
President and Vice Chancellor . . . . I. V. Samerasekera, Ph.D.
Vice President (Academic) and Provost . . . . C. Amrhein, Ph.D.
Vice President (Finance and Administration) . . . . P. Clark
Vice President (Research) . . . . L. Babiuk, Ph.D., D.Sc.
Vice President (External Relations) . . . . D. Osburn, Ph.D.
Registrar . . . . G. Kendal

Medical School Administrative Staff

Interim Dean. . . . . V. Yiu, M.D.
Vice-Dean, Research . . . . M. Michalak, Ph.D.
Vice-Dean, Education. . . . . F. Brenneis, M.D.
Vice-Dean, Faculty Affairs. . . . . D. Kunimato, M.D. (Acting)
Chief Operating Officer. . . . . V. Wulff, C.A., C.M.C.
Associate Dean, Undergraduate Medical Education. . . . . K. Stobart, M.D.
Associate Dean, Dentistry. . . . . P. Major, D.D.S.
Associate Dean, Postgraduate Medical Education . . . . R. Kearney, M.D.
Associate Dean, Continuous Professional Learning . . . . W. Dafoe, M.D.
Assistant Dean, Research . . . . T. Krukoff, Ph.D.
Associate Dean, Clinical Research. . . . . B. Rowe, M.D.
Associate Dean, Faculty Development and Education Support. . . . . B. Fisher, M.D.
Asspcoate Dean, Clinical Faculty. . . . . T.K. Lee, M.D.
Assistant Dean, Admissions. . . . . M. Moreau, M.D.
Associate Dean, Learner Advocacy & Wellness. . . . . Mel Lewis, M.D.
Director, Clinical Education. . . . . R. Lee, M.D. (Acting)
Director, Pre-Clinical Education. . . . . R. Damant, M.D.
Program Director, Undergraduate Medical Education. . . . . M. Diduck
Director, Communications. . . . . J. Nugent
Development and Alumni Affairs . . . . Vacant
Associate Dean, Health Informatics . . . . R. Hayward, M.D.
Director, Research. . . . . M. Taylor
Associate Dean, Community Engagement . . . . J. Konkin, M.D.

Faculty Directors

Department and Division or Section Chairs

Anatomy . . . . A. Walji, M.D., Ph.D.
Biochemistry . . . . C. Holmes, Ph.D.
Biomedical Engineering. . . . . R. E. Burrell, Ph.D.
Cell Biology. . . . . R. Rachubinski, Ph.D.

University of Alberta Faculty of Medicine and Dentistry: ALBERTA

Medical Laboratory Science . . . . M. Mengal, M.D. (Acting)
Medical Microbiology and Immunology . . . . D. Evans, Ph.D.
Pharmacology . . . . A. Clanachan, Ph.D. (Acting)
Physiology . . . . K. Pearson, Ph.D. (Interim)

Clinical Sciences

Anesthesiology and Pain Medicine . . . . M. Murphy, M.D.
Critical Care Medicine . . . . N. Gibney, M.D.
Dentistry . . . . P. Major, D.D.S.
Emergency Medicine . . . . M. Bullard, M.D. (Acting)
Family Medicine . . . . G. Spooner, M.D.
Laboratory Medicine and Pathology . . . . M. Mengal, M.D. (Acting)
Medical Genetics . . . . M. A. Walter, Ph.D.
Medicine . . . . B. Ballerman, M.D.
   Cardiology . . . . B. O'Neill, M.D.
   Clinical Hematology . . . . L. Larratt, M.D.
   Dermatology and Cutaneous Sciences . . . . T. Salopek, M.D.
   Endocrinology . . . . C. Chik, M.D.
   Gastroenterology . . . . S. VanZanten, M.D.
   General Internal Medicine . . . . A. Colbourne, M.D.
   Geriatrics . . . . A. Wagg, M D
   Hematology . . . . Loree Larratt, M.D.
   Infectious Diseases . . . . G. Taylor, M.D.
   Nephrology . . . . K. Jindel, M.D. (Acting)
   Neurology . . . . T. Roberts, M.D.
   Pulmonary Medicine . . . . I. Mayers, M.D.
   Preventative Medicine . . . . Nicola Cherry, m.D.
   Rheumatology . . . . J. Homik, M.D.
Obstetrics and Gynecology . . . . M. Sagle, M.D. (Interim)
Oncology . . . . A. McEwan, M.D.
Ophthalmology . . . . I. MacDonald, M.D.
Pediatrics . . . . S. Gilmour, M.D.
Physical and Rehabilitation Medicine . . . . S. Gray, M.D.
Psychiatry . . . . K. J. Todd, Ph.D. (Interim)
Radiology and Diagnostic Imaging . . . . R. Lambert, M.B.Ch.B.
Surgery . . . . D. Hedden, M.D.
   Cardiac Surgery . . . . D.B. Ross, M.D.
   General Surgery . . . . D. Williams, M.D. (Acting)
   Neurosurgery . . . . K. Aronyk, M.D.
   Orthopaedic Surgery . . . . D. D. Otto, M.D.
   Otolaryngology Surgery . . . . H. Seikaly, M.D.
   Pediatric Surgery . . . . W. Cole, M.D.
   Plastic Surgery . . . . G. Wilkes, M.D.
   Surgical and Medical Research Group (Experimental) . . . . E. E. Tredget, M.D.
   Thoracic Surgery . . . . K. Stewart, M.D.
   Urology . . . . G. Todd, M.D.

University of Calgary Faculty of Medicine
3330 Hospital Drive N.W.
Calgary, Alberta Canada T2N 4N1
403-220-4404; 403-220-6843 (dean's office); 403-283-4740 (fax)
Web site: http://faculty.med.ucalgary.ca

The University of Calgary Faculty of Medicine was initiated in 1967. Its first class of student physicians enrolled in September 1970 and graduated in 1973. The Calgary Health Sciences Centre is located on the Foothills Hospital site, approximately two kilometers from the main campus.

Type: public
2011 total enrollment: 529
Clinical facilities: Foothills Medical Centre, Peter Lougheed Centre, Rockyview General Hospital, University of Calgary Health Sciences Centre, Alberta Children's Hospital.

University Officials

President and Vice Chancellor . . . . E. Cannon, Ph.D.
Provost and Vice President (Academic) . . . . D. Marshall, Ph.D.

Medical School Administrative Staff

Dean . . . . T. E. Feasby, M.D.
Vice Dean . . . . J. B. Meddings, M.D.
Senior Associate Dean, Clinical Affairs . . . . R. J. Bridges, M.D.
Senior Associate Dean, Education . . . . B. Hallgrimsson, Ph.D.
Senior Associate Dean, Research . . . . R. B. Hawkes, Ph.D.
Associate Dean, Basic Research . . . . J. D. Reynolds
Associate Dean, Clinical Research . . . . M. D. Hill, M.D.
Associate Dean, Continuing Medical Education . . . . J. Lockyer, Ph.D.
Associate Dean, Equity and Teacher-Learner Relations . . . . J. M. de Groot, M.D.
Associate Dean, Faculty Assessment and Development . . . . K. D. Patel, Ph.D.
Associate Dean, Graduate Sciences Education . . . . F. A. van der Hoorn, Ph.D.
Associate Dean, Global Health and International Partnerships . . . . J. M. Hatfield, Ph.D.
Associate Dean, Postgraduate Medical Education . . . . J. M. Todesco, M.D.
Associate Dean, Distributed Learning and Rural Initiatives . . . . D. L. Myhre, M.D.
Associate Dean, Undergraduate Medical Education . . . . B. J. Wright, M.D.
Associate Dean, Undergraduate Science Education . . . . A. B. Schryvers, Ph.D., M.D.
Executive Director . . . . G. Levy

University of Calgary Faculty of Medicine: ALBERTA

Department and Division or Section Chairs

Basic Sciences

Biochemistry and Molecular Biology. . . . . J. Lytton, Ph.D.
Cell Biology and Anatomy . . . . N. I. Syed, Ph.D.
Microbiology, Immunology, and Infectious Diseases . . . . G. D. Armstrong, Ph.D.
Physiology and Pharmacology. . . . . G. W. Zamponi, Ph.D.

Clinical Sciences

Anaesthesia . . . . J. N. Armstrong, M.D.
Cardiac Sciences . . . . T. J. Anderson, M.D.
Clinical Neurosciences. . . . . J. G. Cairncross, M.D.
Community Health Sciences. . . . . C. J. Doiq, M.D.
Critical Care Medicine. . . . . P. J. E. Boiteau, M.D.
Family Medicine . . . . C. A. MacLean, M.D.
Medical Genetics . . . . J. E. Cherros, Ph.D. (Interim)
Medicine. . . . . S. Ghosh, M.D.
Obstetrics and Gynecology. . . . . R. D. Wilson, M.D.
Oncology. . . . . P. S. Craighead, M.B.Ch.B.
Paediatrics. . . . . J. D. Kellner, M.D.
Pathology and Laboratory Medicine . . . . J. R. Wright, Jr., M.D., Ph.D.
Psychiatry . . . . G. M. MacQueen, M.D., Ph.D.
Radiology . . . . R. J. Sevick, M.D.
Surgery . . . . J. B. Kortbeek, M.D.

*Specialty without organizational autonomy.

University of British Columbia Faculty of Medicine
317-2194 Health Sciences Mall
Vancouver, British Columbia Canada V6T 1Z3
604-822-2421 (dean's office); 822-6061 (fax)
Web site: www.med.ubc.ca

The faculty of medicine at the University of British Columbia was established in 1950. It is distributed to three university campuses, seven clinical academic campuses, and numerous affiliated teaching hospitals.

Type: public
2011 total enrollment: 1053
Clinical facilities: Clinical Academic Campus: Royal Columbian Hospital, Surrey Memorial Hospital, University Hospital of Northern BC, BC Cancer Agency, BC Children's Hospital, BC Women's Hospital & Health Centre, St. Paul's Hospital, Vancouver General Hospital, Victoria General Hospital, Royal Jubilee Hospital (Victoria), Kelowna General Hospital. Affiliated Regional Centres: Abbotsford Regional Hospital, Campbell River & District General Hospital, Chilliwack General Hospital, Cowichan District Hospital, Dawson Creek & District Hospital, Fort St. John General Hospital, Lions Gate Hospital (North Vancouver), Mills Memorial Hospital, Nanaimo Regional General Hospital, Penticton Regional Hospital, Richmond Hospital, Royal Inland Hospital (Kamloops), St. Joseph's General Hospital (Comox), Vernon Jubilee Hospital.

University Officials

President and Vice Chancellor . . . . Stephen J. Toope, Ph.D.
Vice-President, Academic, and Provost . . . . David Farrar, Ph.D.
Vice-Provost, Health. . . . . Gavin Stuart, M.D.
Vice-President, Finance, Resources, and Operations . . . . Pierre Ouillet, M.B.A.
Vice-President, Development and Alumni Engagement . . . . Barbara Miles
Vice-President, External, Legal, and Community Relations . . . . . . Stephen Owen, L.L.B., L.L.M.
Vice-President, Research and International . . . . John Hepburn, Ph.D.
Vice-President, Students. . . . . Louise Cowan, Ph.D.
University Librarian . . . . Ingrid Parent
Associate Vice-President and Registrar . . . . James Ridge

Medical School Administrative Staff

Dean. . . . . Gavin Stuart, M.D.
Vice-Dean, Academic Affairs. . . . . Ross MacGillivray, M.D.
Executive Associate Dean, Education . . . . David Snadden, M.B., Ch.B.
Executive Associate Dean, Research . . . . George Mackie, Ph.D.
Executive Associate Dean, Clinical Affairs . . . . Dr. Robert Liston, M.D. Vacant
Associate Dean, M.D. Undergraduate Program-
  Admissions . . . . Dr. Bruce Fleming, M.D. (Acting)
Associate Dean, M.D. Undergraduate Program-Student Affairs. . . . . Sharon Salloum, M.D.
Associate Dean, M.D. Undergraduate Education-
  Curriculum and Vancouver Fraser Medical
  Program . . . . Karen Joughin, M.D. (Interim)
Associate Dean, Postgraduate Education . . . . Jill Kernahan, M.D.
Regional Associate Dean, Island Medical Program. . . . . Oscar G. Casiro, M.D.
Regional Associate Dean, Interior British Columbia . . . . Allan Jones, M.D.
Regional Associate Dean, Northern Medical Program . . . . Dr. Geoff Payne, M.D. (Acting)
Associate Dean, Equity and Professional Affairs. . . . . Gurdeep Parhar, M.D.
Associate Dean, Graduate and Postdoctoral Education . . . . Peter Leung, Ph.D.
Assistant Dean, Postgraduate Medical Education . . . . Roger Wong, M.D.
Assistant Dean, Development and Alumni Affairs . . . . Sarah Roth, M.B.A.
Assistant Dean, Continuing Professional Development. . . . . Ran Goldman, M.D.
Special Advisor to the Dean, Government Relations . . . . Cindi Valensky, M.B.A.
Associate Dean, Health Professions. . . . . Brenda Loveridge, Ph.D.
Special Advisor to the Dean on Planning . . . . David F. Hardwick, M.D.
Executive Director, Faculty Affairs . . . . Tammy Brimner
Chief Operating Officer. . . . . Mark Vernon, C.A., C.P.A.
Executive Director, Education . . . . Jane Eibner, M.B.A., C.M.A.

University of British Columbia Faculty of Medicine: BRITISH COLUMBIA

Department Heads and School Directors

Basic Sciences

Biochemistry and Molecular Biology............................. Roger Brownsey, Ph.D.
Cellular and Physiological Sciences........... John Church, M.D., and Calvin Roskelley, M.D.
Medical Genetics... Carolyn Brown, Ph.D.

Clinical Sciences

Anaesthesiology, Pharmacology, and Therapeutics .... Brian Warriner, M.D.
Dermatology and Skin Science..................................... Harvey Lui, M.D.
Emergency Medicine... Jim Christenson, M.D.
Family Practice .... Martin Dawes, M.D.
School of Population and Public Health........................... David Patrick, M.D.
Medicine.. Graydon Meneilly, M.D.
Obstetrics and Gynaecology..................................... Geoff Cundiff, M.D.
Occupational Sciences and Occupational Therapy .... William Miller, Ph.D. (Acting)
Ophthalmology and Visual Sciences .... Frederick Mikelberg, M.D.
Orthopaedics.. Bassam Masri, M.D.
Paediatrics.. Ralph Rothstein, M.D. (Acting)
Pathology and Laboratory Medicine .... Michael Allard, M.D.
Physical Therapy .... S. Jayne Garland, Ph.D.
Psychiatry .... William Honer, M.D.
Radiology .... Bruce Foster, M.D.
Surgery... Garth Warnock, M.D.
School of Audiology and Speech Sciences......................... Valter Ciocca, Ph.D.
Urologic Sciences .... Larry Goldenberg, M.D.

University of Manitoba Faculty of Medicine

260 Brodie - 727 McDermot Avenue
Winnipeg, Manitoba Canada R3E 3P5
204-789-3557 (general office); 204-789-3485 (dean's office); 204-789-3928 (fax)
Web site: www.umanitoba.ca/faculties/medicine

Manitoba Medical College was established in 1883. In 1918, it ceased to exist as a separate institution and became known as the faculty of medicine of the University of Manitoba. It is located in Winnipeg near the Health Sciences Centre, whereas the university proper is located in the suburb of Fort Garry, seven miles away.

Type: public
2011 total enrollment: 443
Clinical facilities: Winnipeg Regional Health Authority (Health Sciences Centre, St. Boniface General Hospital, Deer Lodge Centre, Grace General Hospital, Seven Oaks General Hospital, Victoria General Hospital, Concordia Hospital, Misericordia Health Centre); Brandon General Hospital; Dauphin General Hospital; Thompson General Hospital.

University Officials

President. . . . . David T. Barnard, Ph.D.
Vice President (Administration) . . . . Deborah McCallum
Vice President (Academic) and Provost . . . . Joanne Keselman, Ph.D.
Director of Enrollment Services . . . . P. Dueck

Medical School Administrative Staff

Dean. . . . . Brian Postl, M.D.
Associate Dean (Academic) . . . . T. Klassen, M.D.
Associate Dean (Research). . . . . P. Nickerson, M.D.
Associate Dean (Undergraduate Medical Education). . . . . I. Ripstein, M.D.
Associate Dean (Postgraduate Medical Education) . . . . C. Yaffe, M.D.
Assistant Dean (Students) . . . . B. Martin, M.D.
Associate Dean (Continuing Medical Education
   & Professional Development) . . . . J. Francois, M.D.
Administrator, Admissions and Enrollment. . . . . H. Christensen, B.Sc.
Associate Dean (Clinical Affairs). . . . . B. Wright, M.D.
Assistant Dean (Graduate Studies) . . . . E. Kroeger, Ph.D.
Assistant Dean (Research) . . . . K. Coombs, Ph.D.
Associate Dean (International Development) . . . . P. Choy
Associate Dean (Professionalism & Diversity) . . . . S. Barakat, M.D.
Assistant Dean (First Nations, Metis, & Inuit Health) . . . . C. Cook, M.D.
Assistant Dean. . . . . H. Dean, M.D.

Department and Division or Section Chairs

Basic Sciences

Biochemistry and Medical Genetics . . . . L. Simard, Ph.D.
Community Health Sciences. . . . . S. Macdonald
Human Anatomy and Cell Science. . . . . T. Klonisch, Ph.D.
Immunology . . . . R. Moqbel, Ph.D.
Medical Microbiology. . . . . J. Embree, M.D.
Pathology . . . . J. Gartner, M.D.
Pharmacology and Therapeutics. . . . . F. Parkinson
Physiology. . . . . J. Dodd, Ph.D.
Medical Education. . . . . J. Francois, M.D. (Acting)

University of Manitoba Faculty of Medicine: MANITOBA

Clinical Sciences

Anesthesia . . . . E. Jacobsohn, M.D.
Clinical Health Psychology . . . . R. McIlwraith, M.D.
Emergency Medicine . . . . A. Chochinov, M.D.
Family Medicine . . . . J. Boyd, M.D.
Internal Medicine . . . . D. Roberts, M.D.
   Allergy & Clinical Immunology . . . . C. Kalicinsky, M.D. TBA
   Cardiology . . . . J. Tam, M.D.
   Clinical Pharmacology . . . . F. Parkinson
   Critical Care . . . . F. Siddiqui, M.D.
   Dermatology . . . . J. E. Toole, M.D.
   Endocrinology and Metabolism . . . . C. J. Richardson, M.D.
   Gastroenterology . . . . M. Cantor, M.D.
   Geriatric Medicine . . . . C. van Ineveld, M.D.
   Haemotology . . . . C. Moltzan, M.D.
   Hepatology . . . . S. Wong, M.D.
   Immunology . . . . R. Moqbel, M.D.
   Infectious Diseases . . . . J. Embil, M.D.
   Medical Oncology . . . . D. Grenier, M.D.
   Nephrology . . . . B. Cohen, M.D.
   Neurology . . . . A. Jackson, M.D.
   Physical Medicine and Rehabilitation . . . . D. Hooper, M.D.
   Respiratory . . . . G. Eschun, M.D.
   Rheumatology . . . . D. Robinson, M.D.
Obstetrics, Gynecology, and Reproductive Sciences . . . . M. Morris, M.D.
Ophthalmology . . . . L. Bellan, Ph.D.
Otolaryngology . . . . P. Kerr, M.D.
Pediatrics and Child Health . . . . C. Rockman-Greenberg, M.D.
Psychiatry . . . . M. Enns, M.D.
Radiology . . . . S. Demeter, M.D.
Surgery . . . . R. Nason, M.D.
   Cardiac Surgery . . . . A. Menkis, M.D.
   Dental and Oral Surgery . . . . J. Curran, M.D.
   General Surgery . . . . C. Yaffe, M.D.
   Neurosurgery . . . . N. Berrington, M.D.
   Orthopaedics . . . . P. Macdonald, M.D.
   Pediatric General Surgery . . . . B.J. Hancock, M.D.
   Plastic Surgery . . . . E. Buchel, M.D.
   Thoracic Surgery . . . . H. Unruh, M.D.
   Urology . . . . K. Psooy, M.D.
   Vascular Surgery . . . . R. Guzman, M.D.

Memorial University of Newfoundland Faculty of Medicine

Health Sciences Centre
300 Prince Philip Drive
St. John's, Newfoundland Canada A1B 3V6
709-777-6602 (dean's office); 709-777-6615 (admissions);
709-777-6669 (undergraduate medical educ.);
709-777-6680 (postgraduate medical educ.); 709-777-6746 (dean's office fax)
Web site: www.med.mun.ca

The faculty of medicine was founded in 1967 as part of a combined health sciences and life sciences complex on the campus of Memorial University. The first undergraduate class was admitted in September 1969. The medical school is part of the health sciences centre.

Type: public
2011 total enrollment: 264
Clinical facilities: Eastern Regional Health Authority (St. John's); Central Regional Health Authority (Grand Falls-Windsor); Western Regional Health Authority (Corner Brook); Labrador-Grenfell Regional Health Authority (Happy Valley-Goose Bay, Labrador); Horizon Health Network (New Brunswick).

University Officials

Chancellor	General Rick Hillier
President and Vice Chancellor	Gary Kachanoski
Vice President (Academic) and Pro Vice Chancellor	David Wardlaw
Associate Vice President (Academic)	Doreen Neville
Associate Vice President	Grant Gardiner
Vice President (Administration and Finance)	Kent Decker
Vice President (Research)	Chris Loomis
Registrar	Glen W. Collins

Medical School Administrative Staff

Dean of Medicine	James Rourke, M.D.
Vice Dean	Sharon Peters, M.D.
Associate Dean, BioMedical Sciences	Karen Mearow, Ph.D.
Associate Dean, Clinical Research	Patrick Parfrey, M.D.
Associate Dean, Community Health and Humanities	Shree Mulay, Ph.D.
Associate Dean, Research and Graduate Studies	Don McKay, Ph.D. Acting
Associate Dean, Undergraduate Medical Education	Tanis Adey, M.D. Acting
Assistant Dean, Admissions	Wanda Parsons, M.D.
Assistant Dean, Postgraduate Medical Education	Asoka Samarasena, M.D.
Assistant Dean, Graduate Studies	Diana Gustafson, Ph.D. Acting
Assistant Dean, Rural Clinical School Medical Education Network	Mohamed Ravalia, M.B.B.S.
Assistant Dean, Student Affairs	Paul Dancey, M.D. Acting
Director of Animal Care	Jennifer Keyte, B.Sc., DVM
Manager of Medical Education Laboratory Support Services	Judy Foote
Associate University Librarian (Health Sciences)	Linda Barnett, MLIS Acting

Department and Division or Section Chairs

Clinical Sciences

Anesthesia* . . . . Jeremy Pridham, M.D.
Family Medicine* . . . . Marshall Godwin, M.D. (Interim)
Genetics . . . . Bridget Fernandez, M.D.
Medicine* . . . . Alan Goodridge, M.D. (Acting)
Obstetrics and Gynecology* . . . . Terry O'Grady, M.D.
Oncology . . . . David Saltman, M.D., Ph.D.
Pathology* . . . . Simon Avis, M.D.
Pediatrics* . . . . Cathy Vardy, M.D.
Psychiatry* . . . . Ted Callanan, M.D.
Radiology* . . . . Benvon Cramer, M.D.
Surgery* . . . . Darrell Boone, M.D.

Biomedical Sciences Resource People

Anatomy . . . . Shakti Chandra, Ph.D.
Biochemistry . . . . Sudesh C. Vasdev, Ph.D.
Immunology . . . . Michael Grant, Ph.D.
Neuroscience . . . . John McLean, Ph.D.
Physiology . . . . Don McKay, Ph.D.

*Specialty with partial organizational autonomy.

Dalhousie University Faculty of Medicine

Clinical Research Center
5849 University Avenue, P.O. Box 15000
Halifax, Nova Scotia Canada B3H 4R2
902-494-6592 (dean's office); 902-494-1874 (admissions office); 902-494-7119 (fax)
Web site: www.medicine.dal.ca

The faculty of medicine of Dalhousie University was organized in 1868, but the medical teaching was carried out by the independent Halifax Medical College from 1875 to 1911, when the faculty of medicine was reestablished by the university.

Type: public
2011 total enrollment: 450
Clinical facilities: Queen Elizabeth II Health Sciences Centre (Victoria General Campus and Camp Hill Campus), IWK Health Centre; Archie McCullum Hospital (Department of National Defense); Nova Scotia Hospital; Sydney Community Health Centre; Queen Elizabeth Hospital; Prince County Hospital; Region 1 Hospital Corporation, South-East (Moncton, New Brunswick); Atlantic Health Sciences Corporation (Saint John, New Brunswick); Region 3 Hospital Corporation (Fredericton, New Brunswick); Region 7 Hospital Corporation (Miramichi, New Brunswick). A Clinical Skills Learning Centre is located at 1256 Barrington Street, Halifax.

University Officials

President. . . . . T. Traves, Ph.D.
Vice President (Academic and Provost) . . . . C. Watters
Vice President (Finance and Administration) . . . . K. Burt
Vice President (Student Services). . . . . B. Neuman, Ph.D.
Vice President (External). . . . . F. Dykeman
Vice President (Research) . . . . M. Crago, Ph.D.

Medical School Administrative Staff

Dean. . . . . T. Marrie, M.D.
Associate Dean, Postgraduate Medical Education . . . . M. Gardner, M.D.
Associate Dean, Undergraduate Medical Education. . . . . D. Delva, M.D.
Associate Dean, Research. . . . . G. C. Johnston, Ph.D.
Associate Dean, Operations and Policy. . . . . D. Gorsky, M.B.A.
Associate Dean, Dalhousie Medicine New Brunswick. . . . . J. Steeves, M.D.
Assistant Dean, Admissions and Student Affairs. . . . . E. Sutton, M.D.
Assistant Dean (New Brunswick). . . . . T. Lambert, M.D.
Assistant Dean, Research (New Brunswick). . . . . T. Reiman, M.D.
Assistant Dean, Research (Clinical Departments) . . . . R. Brownstone, M.D.
Assistant Dean, Graduate and Postdoctoral Studies. . . . . C. McMaster, Ph.D.
Director, Health Law Institute . . . . (Vacant)
Director, Admissions and Student Affairs . . . . S. Graham
Director, Animal Care . . . . B. Hildebrand, D.V.M.
Acting Head, Division of Medical Education. . . . . J. Sargeant, Ph.D.
Director, Finance. . . . . C. MacNeil
Director, Human Resources . . . . L. Power
Director, Governance and Planning . . . . A. Weeden
Director of Information Technology. . . . . G. Power
Health Sciences Librarian . . . . P. Ellis
Medical Alumni Affairs Executive Director . . . . J. Webber

Department and Division or Section Chairs

Basic Sciences

Anatomy and Neurobiology. . . . . R. Leslie, Ph.D.
Biochemistry and Molecular Biology. . . . . D. Byers, Ph.D.
Microbiology and Immunology. . . . . J. S. Marshall, Ph.D.
Pharmacology . . . . J. Sawynok, Ph.D.
Physiology and Biophysics . . . . P. R. Murphy, Ph.D.

Clinical Sciences

Anaesthesia. . . . . R. Shukla, M.D.
Bioethics. . . . . C. Simpson, Ph.D.
Community Health and Epidemiology . . . . A. Levy, Ph.D.

Radiology . . . . D. Barnes, M.D.
    Nuclear Medicine. . . . . A. Ross, M.D.
Emergency Medicine . . . . D. Petrie, M.D. (Interim)
Family Medicine . . . . G. Archibald, M.D.
Medicine. . . . . D. Anderson, M.D.
    Cardiology . . . . C. Kells, M.D.
    Critical Care. . . . . W. Patrick, M.D. (Acting)
    Palliative Care . . . . P. F. McIntyre, M.D.
    Dermatology . . . . L. Finlayson, M.D.
    Endocrinology and Metabolism. . . . . S. Kaiser, M.D.
    Gastroenterology . . . . K. Peltekian, M.D.
    General Medicine. . . . . D Simpson, M.D. (Acting)
    Geriatric Medicine . . . . L. Mallery, M.D.
    Hematology . . . . S. Coubon, M.D. (Acting)
    Infectious Diseases . . . . B. L. Johston, M.D.
    Medical Oncology . . . . M. Doreen, M.D.
    Nephrology . . . . K. West, M.D. (Acting)
    Neurology . . . . C. Maxner, M.D.
    Physical Medicine and Rehabilitation . . . . C. Short, M.D.
    Respirology . . . . G. Rocker, M.D. (Acting)
    Rheumatology . . . . E. Sutton, M.D.
Obstetrics and Gynaecology . . . . B. A. Armson, M.D.
    Gynaecology. . . . . S. Farrell, M.D.
    Maternal and Fetal Medicine . . . . M. Van den Hof, M.D.
    Obstetrics. . . . . D. Ritthenberg, M.D.
    Oncology. . . . . J. Bentley, M.D.
    Reproductive Endocrinology. . . . . R. Bouzaven, M.D.
    Urolgynecology . . . . B. Amir, M.D.
Ophthalmology and Visual Sciences . . . . A. Cruess, M.D.
Pathology and Laboratory Medicine . . . . G. Heathcote, Ph.D.
    Anatomical Pathology. . . . . N. M. G. Walsh, M.D.
    Clinical Chemistry . . . . B. A. Nassar, Ph.D.
    Hematopathology. . . . . I. Sadek, M.D.
    Medical Microbiology. . . . . K. Forward, M.D.
    Molecular Pathology and Molecular Genetics . . . . D. Guernsey, Ph.D.
Pediatrics . . . . M. Bernstein, M.D.
    Atlantic Research Centre . . . . N. Ridgway, Ph.D.
    Cardiology . . . . A. Warren, M.D.
    Medical Genetics . . . . M. Ludman, M.D.
    Developmental Pediatrics . . . . S. Shea, M.D.
    Endocrinology . . . . E. Cummings, M.D.
    Gastroenterology and Nutrition . . . . A. Otley, M.D.
    General Pediatric Medicine. . . . . A. Larson, M.D.
    Hematology/Oncology. . . . . M. Bernstein, M.D.
    Immunology. . . . . T. Issekutz, M.D.
    Infectious Diseases . . . . S. Halperin, M.D.
    Neonatal Pediatric Medicine. . . . . D. MacMillan, M.D.
    Nephrology . . . . J. Crocker, M.D.
    Neurology . . . . J. Dooley, M.D.
    Palliative Care . . . . G. Frager, M.D.
    Respirology . . . . D. Hughes, M.D.
    Rheumatology . . . . B. Lang, M.D.
Psychiatry . . . . N. Delva, M.D.
Radiation Oncology. . . . . C. T. Ago, M.D.
Surgery. . . . . D. Kirkpatrick, M.D. (Interim)
    Cardiac . . . . G. Hirsch, M.D.
    General . . . . T. Topp, M.D.
    Neurosurgery. . . . . D. Clarke, M.D.
    Orthopaedics. . . . . D. Amirault, M.D.
    Otolaryngology. . . . . M. Bance, M.D. (Acting)
    Pediatric . . . . M. Giacomantonio, M.D.
    Plastic . . . . J. Paletz
    Thoracic . . . . D. Bethune, M.D.
    Vascular. . . . . G. MacKean, M.D.
Urology. . . . . D. Bell, M.D.

McMaster University Faculty of Health Sciences
1200 Main Street West
Hamilton, Ontario Canada L8N 3Z5
905-525-9140 Ext. 22141 (general info.); 905-546-0800 (fax)
Web site: www.fhs.mcmaster.ca

In 1967, the college of health sciences was formed as part of McMaster University. In 1969, in accordance with the McMaster Act of 1968-69, the structure was changed to the division of health sciences, incorporating the faculty of medicine and the school of nursing. The university structure was reorganized in 1974, at which time the division of health sciences became the faculty of health sciences. In 1989, the school of occupational therapy and physiotherapy was established. In 1993, a midwifery program was added.

Type: public
2011 total enrollment: 434
Clinical facilities: Hamilton Health Sciences (Hamilton General Hospital, McMaster Children's Hospital, and the Hamilton Regional Cancer Centre), St. Joseph's Hospital, St. Peter's Hospital and various other community partners who provide clinical experience to the students.

University Officials

Chancellor	Lynton Wilson
President and Vice Chancellor	Patrick Deane, Ph.D.
Provost and Vice President (Academic)	Ilene Busch-Vishniac, Ph.D.
Vice President (Research and International Affairs)	Mo Elbestawi, Ph.D.
Dean and Vice President (Health Sciences)	John G. Kelton, M.D.
Vice President (Administration)	Roger Couldrey
Vice President (University Advancement)	Mary Williams
Associate Vice President (Academic)	F. A. Hall, Ph.D.
Associate Vice President (International Affairs)	M. W. L. Chan, Ph.D.
Associate Vice President (Student Affairs) and Dean of Students	P. E. Wood, Ph.D.
Registrar	L. R. Ariano
University Librarian	C. Stewart (Acting)
Principal of McMaster Divinity College	S. E. Porter, Ph.D.
University Secretary and Secretary of the Board of Governors and the Senate	W. B. Frank, Ph.D.
Assistant Vice President (Administration)	L. M. Scime
Assistant Vice President (Human Resources)	M. E. Haley

Michael G. DeGroote School of Medicine Administrative Staff

Dean and Vice President, Faculty of Health Sciences	J. G. Kelton, M.D.
Associate Vice President, Academic and Associate Dean, Education	S. D. Denburg, Ph.D., M.D.
Associate Dean (Research)	S. Collins, M.D.
Associate Dean, Health Sciences (Nursing)	C. H. Tompkins, Ph.D.
Associate Dean, Health Sciences (School of Rehabilitation Science)	M. C. Law, Ph.D.
Assistant Dean, Bachelor of Health Sciences (Honours) Program	Delsworth G. Harnish, Ph.D.
Assistant Dean, Clinical Health Sciences (OT) Program	D. A. Stewart, M.D.
Assistant Dean, Clinical Health Sciences (PT) Program	L. R. Wishart, Ph.D.
Assistant Dean, Continuing Health Sciences Education Program	Gregory O. Peachey, M.D.
Assistant Dean, Midwifery Education Program	E. Hutton, Ph.D.
Postgraduate Medical Education Program	J. M. Walton, M.D.
Assistant Dean, Program for Educational Research and Development	G. R. Norman, Ph.D.
Assistant Dean, Program for Faculty Development	A. E. Walsh, M.D.
Assistant Dean, Undergraduate Medical Education Program	Rob Whyte, M.D.
Assistant Dean, Undergraduate Nursing Education Program	Janet Landeen, Ph.D.

McMaster University Faculty of Health Sciences: ONTARIO

Department and Division or Section Chairs

Basic Sciences

Biochemistry . . . . Eric D. Brown, M.D.
Clinical Epidemiology and Biostatistics . . . . Holger Schunemann, M.D.
Pathology and Molecular Medicine. . . . . Fiona Smaill, Ph.D.

Clinical Sciences

Anaesthesia . . . . Norman Buckley, M.D.
Family Medicine . . . . David Price, M.D.
Medicine. . . . . Paul O'Byrne, M.D.
Obstetrics and Gynecology. . . . . Nicholas Leyland, M.D.
Paediatrics. . . . . Lennox Huang, M.D.
Psychiatry and Behavioural Neurosciences . . . . Robert Zipursky, M.D.
Radiology . . . . David A. Koff, M.D.
Surgery . . . . William Orovan, M.D.

Northern Ontario School of Medicine

East Campus, Laurentian University
935 Ramsey Lake Road
Sudbury, Ontario Canada P3E 2C6
705-671-3874; 705-675-4883; 705-675-4858 (fax)
Web site: www.nosm.ca

The Northern Ontario School of Medicine is the first new medical school in Canada in the 21st century. It serves as the Faculty of Medicine of Lakehead University, Thunder Bay, and of Laurentian University of Sudbury. With university campuses in Thunder Bay and Sudbury, the school has multiple teaching and research sites distributed across Northern Ontario, including large and small communities.

Type: public
2011 total enrollment: 241
Clinical facilities: Health Sciences North/Horizon Santé-Nord (formerly Hospitol Regional Sudbury Regional Hospital), Thunder Bay Regional Health Sciences Centre, other hospitals and health services throughout northern Ontario.

University Officials

President (Lakehead University)................................. Brian Stevenson, Ph.D.
President (Laurentian University)............................. Dominic Giroux, M.B.A.

Medical School Administrative Staff

Dean.. Roger Strasser, M.B.B.S., M.Cl.Sc.
Associate Dean, Community Engagement............................ David Marsh, M.D.
Assistant Dean, Learner Affairs... Vacant
Associate Dean, Faculty Affairs.................... William McCready, M.B.B.Ch., M.R.C.P.
Assistant Dean, Integrated Clinical Learning............................... Sue Berry
Associate Dean, Postgraduate Medical Education .... Catherine Cervin, M.D.
Associate Dean, Undergraduate Medical Education..................... Lisa Graves, M.D.
Chief Administrative Officer.. Ken Adams
Associate Dean, Research.. Greg Ross, Ph.D.
Assistant Dean, Admissions............................... Blair Schoales, M.D., F.R.C.P.
Assistant Dean, UME Curriculum and Planning .... Rachel Ellaway, Ph.D.
Director, Undergraduate Medical Education................................ Vacant
Director, Postgraduate Education................................... Tina Vrbanic
Director, Aboriginal Affairs .... Tina Armstrong
Director, Finance... Joe Lipinski
Director, Health Sciences Library..................................... Patty Fink
Director, Human Resources...................................... Jonathan Barrett
Director, Technology and Information Management Support .... Tariq Al-idrissi
Director, Communications.. Kim Daynard

Department and Division or Section Chairs

Medical Sciences

Division Head .... Garry Ferroni, Ph.D.
Biochemistry........................ Tom Kovala, Ph.D., and Amadeo Parissenti, Ph.D.
Cell and Molecular Biology .... Rob Lafrenie, Ph.D., Leslie Sutherland, Ph.D.,
and Hoyun Lee, Ph.D.
Haematology..................... Nicole Laferriere, M.D., and Dimitrios Vergidis, M.D.
Immunology .... Marina Ulanova, M.D., Ph.D., and Stacey Ritz, Ph.D.
Molecular Genetics .... Carita Lanner, Ph.D.
Pharmacology .... Zacharias Suntres, Ph.D., and Brian Ross, Ph.D.
Physiology .. Neelam Khaper, Ph.D., David MacLean, Ph.D., Simon Lees, Ph.D., T. C. Tai, Ph.D.,
and Greg Ross, Ph.D.
Anatomy... Donna Newhouse
Medical Microbiology....................................... Garry Ferroni, Ph.D.

Northern Ontario School of Medicine: ONTARIO

Human Sciences

Acting Division Head . . . . Carry Ferroni, Ph.D.
Behavioral Medicine . . . . Patricia Smith, Ph.D.
Biostatistics . . . . Bruce Weaver, M.Sc.
History of Medicine . . . . Geoff Hudson, Ph.D.
Medical Anthropology . . . . Kristen Jacklin, Ph.D., and Marion Maar, Ph.D.
Program Evaluation . . . . Elaine Hogard, Ph.D.
Education Informatics . . . . Rachel Ellaway, Ph.D.

Section Chairs

Child Health . . . . Vacant
Emergency Medicine . . . . Gary Bota, M.D.
Family Medicine . . . . C. Rossi, M.D.
Health Sciences . . . . S. Prystanski, M.D.
Internal Medicine . . . . S. Malik, M.D.
Psychiatry . . . . R. Koka, M.D.
Surgery . . . . Vacant
Women's Health . . . . Vacant

Queen's University Faculty of Health Sciences

Kingston, Ontario Canada K7L 3N6
613-533-2542 (medicine); 613-533-2668 (nursing);
613-533-6103 (rehabilitation therapy); 613-533-2544 (general); 613-533-6884 (fax)
Web site: http://meds.queensu.ca

Established in 1854, the faculty of health sciences of Queen's University is situated on the main campus. It was reorganized in 1866 as the Royal College of Physicians and Surgeons in affiliation with the university. In 1892, the original status was resumed. Effective July 1, 1997, Queen's University established the faculty of health sciences, integrating the schools of nursing, medicine, and rehabilitation therapy into a single academic unit.

Type: public
2011 total enrollment: 1,119
Clinical facilities: Kingston General Hospital, Hotel Dieu Hospital, Providence Care (St. Mary's of the Lake Hospital and Mental Health Services sites), Cancer Centre of Southeastern Ontario, Ongwanada Hospital.

University Officials

Chancellor . . . . David Dodge, L.L.D.
Principal and Vice Chancellor . . . . Daniel Woolf, Ph.D.

Health Sciences Administrative Staff

Dean. . . . . Richard K. Reznick, M.D.
Director, School of Medicine . . . . Richard K. Reznick, M.D.
Associate Dean, Postgraduate Medical Education . . . . Ross Walker, M.D.
Vice-Dean, Academic . . . . Iain D. Young, M.D.
Vice-Dean, Medical Education . . . . Lewis L. Tomalty, Ph.D.
Director, Research. . . . . John Fisher, Ph.D.
Vice-Dean, Research . . . . Roger G. Deeley, Ph.D.
Associate Dean, Undergraduate Medical Education. . . . . Anthony J. Sanfilippo, M.D.
Associate Dean, Health Institutions and Regional Liaison . . . . Vacant
Associate Dean, Health Sciences and Director,
   School of Nursing . . . . Jennifer M. Medves, Ph.D.
Associate Dean, Health Sciences and Director,
   School of Rehabilitation Therapy . . . . Elsie G. Culham, Ph.D.
Director, Student Affairs, Undergraduate Medical Education. . . . . . . Jennifer L. Carpenter, M.D.
Associate Dean, Continuing Professional Development . . . . Karen Smith, M.D.
Associate Dean, Life Sciences and Biochemistry . . . . P. Ken Rose, Ph.D.
Secretary of the Faculty . . . . David R. Edgar
Assistant Dean, Operations and Finance . . . . David R. Edgar
Finance Manager. . . . . Joan Lee
Manager, Undergraduate Medical Education/Studies . . . . (Vacant)
Education Coordinator, Continuing Medical Education. . . . . Patricia A. Payne
Manager, Postgraduate Medical Education . . . . Jordan Sinnett
Manager, Budgets and Administration . . . . Jessie R. Griffin
Senior Staffing Officer. . . . . Gail L. Knutson

Department and Division or Section Chairs

Department of Biomedical and Molecular Sciences. . . . . Michael Adams, Ph.D.

Clinical Sciences

Anesthesiology. . . . . Joel Parlow, M.D.
Emergency Medicine . . . . Gordon R. Jones, M.D.
Family Medicine . . . . Glenn Brown, M.D.
Medicine. . . . . John L. McCans, M.D.
   Allergy and Immunology . . . . Anne Ellis, M.D.
   Cardiology. . . . . Christopher S. Simpson, M.D.
   Endocrinology . . . . Robyn Houldon, M.D.

Gastroenterology . . . . William G. Paterson, M.D.
General Internal Medicine . . . . D. Phillip Wattam, M.D., F.R.C.P.C.
Geriatric Medicine . . . . John A. H. Puxty, M.D.
Haematology and Oncology . . . . David Lee, M.D.
Infectious Diseases . . . . Dick E. Zoutman, M.D.
Nephrology . . . . Edwin B. Toffelmire, M.D.
Neurology . . . . Donald G. Brunet, M.D.
Respiratory and Critical Care Medicine . . . . Michael Fitzpatrick, M.D.
Rheumatology . . . . Tassos P. Anastassiades, M.D.
Obstetrics and Gynaecology . . . . Michael M. J. McGrath, M.D.
Oncology. . . . . Jim Bragi, M.D.
Ophthalmology . . . . Sherif El-Defrawy, M.D., Ph.D.
Otolaryngology . . . . Russell Hollins, M.D.
Paediatrics. . . . . Sarah Jones, M.D.
Critical Care. . . . . Ellen Tsai, M.D.
Hematology and Oncology . . . . Mariana Silva, M.D.
Developmental Pediatrics . . . . Garth Smith, M.D.
Neonatology. . . . . Michael P. Flavin, M.D.
Pathology and Molecular Medicine. . . . . Victor A. Tron, M.D.
Anatomical Pathology. . . . . Alexander H. Boag, M.D.
Clinical Chemistry . . . . Christine P. Collier
Genetics. . . . . Harriet E. Feilotter
Laboratory Hematopathology . . . . Dilys A. Rapson, M.B.Ch.B.
Microbiology . . . . Dick E. Zoutman, M.D.
Psychiatry . . . . Roumen V. Milev, M.D., Ph.D.
Adult Psychiatry . . . . Susan Finch, M.D.
Adult Treatment and Rehabilitation Psychiatry . . . . Simon O'Brien, M.D.
Child and Adolescent Psychiatry . . . . Nasreen Roberts, M.D.
Community Psychiatry . . . . J. Kenneth LeClair, M.D., and H. Joseph Burley, M.D.
Consultant, Liaison Psychiatry. . . . . Dijana Oliver, M.D. (Acting)
Developmental Disabilities . . . . Cherie Jones-Hiscock, M.D. (Acting)
Forensic and Correctional Psychiatry. Duncan Scott, M.D. (Acting)
Geriatric Psychiatry. . . . . D. J. Kenneth Leclair, M.D.
Diagnostic Radiology . . . . Annette McCallum, M.D.
Physical Medicine and Rehabilitation . . . . Stephen D. Bagg, M.D.
Surgery . . . . John F. Rudan, M.D.
Cardiac . . . . Andrew Hamilton, M.D.
Thoracic . . . . Kenneth R. Reid, M.D.
General Surgery. . . . . Hugh MacDonald, M.D.
Maxillofacial. . . . . Allan M. Rees, D.D.
Neurosurgery. . . . . Ronald Pokrupa, M.D.
Orthopaedics . . . . Dan Borschneck, M.D.
Plastic Surgery . . . . John S. D. Davidson, M.D.
Vascular. . . . . David T. Zelt, M.D.
Urology. . . . . James W. L. Wilson, M.D.

University of Ottawa Faculty of Medicine

451 Smyth Road
Ottawa, Ontario Canada K1H 8M5
613-562-5800 x 8117 (dean's office); 613-562-5457 (fax)
E-mail: infomed@uottawa.ca
Web site: www.medicine.uottawa.ca

The faculty of medicine was established in 1945. Between 1978 and 1988, the school of medicine was regrouped into a faculty of health sciences along with the school of nursing and school of human kinetics. The faculty of medicine was reestablished as an entity in 1989.

Type: public
2011 total enrollment: 166
Clinical facilities: The Ottawa Hospital, Royal Ottawa Health Care Group, Children's Hospital of Eastern Ontario, Montfort Hospital, Queensway Carleton Hospital, Sisters of Charity of Ottawa, Winchester District Memorial, Pembroke Regional Hospital.

University Officials

President . . . . Allan Rock
Vice President, Academic & Provost . . . . François Houle
Vice President, Resources . . . . Victor Simon
Vice President, Research . . . . Mona Nemer, Ph.D.
Vice President, Governance . . . . Diane Davidson
Vice President, External Relations . . . . Louis de Melo
Chief of Staff of the President . . . . Stéphane Émard-Chabot
Chief Negotiator . . . . Caroline Roy-Egner
Internal Audit . . . . Alain Decelles
Pension Fund . . . . Barbara Miazga
Associate V-P Institutional Research and Planning . . . . Pierre Mercier

Medical School Administrative Staff

Dean . . . . Jacques Bradwejn, M.D.
Assistant Dean, Office of Francophone Affairs . . . . Jean Roy, M.D.
Associate Dean, Postgraduate Medical Education . . . . Paul Bragg, M.D.
Director, Distributed Medical Education . . . . Charles Su, M.D.
Assistant Dean, Admissions . . . . Gary Hollingworth, M.D.
Associate Dean, Undergraduate Medical Education . . . . Melissa Forgie, M.D.
Assistant Dean, Continuing Medical Education . . . . Paul Hendry, M.D.
Director, E-curriculum . . . . Pippa Hall, M.D.
Associate Dean, Professional Affairs . . . . Rama C. Nair, Ph.D.
Assistant Dean, Academy for Innovation in
  Medical Education (AIME) . . . . Stanley Hamstra, Ph.D.
Assistant Dean, Clinical and Translational Research . . . . Marc Ruel, M.D.
Director, Faculty Development . . . . Catharine Robertson, M.D.
Director, Faculty Wellness Program . . . . Derek Puddester, M.D.
Director, Office of Equity, Diversity, and Gender Issues . . . . Catherine Tsilfidis, M.D.
Vice Dean, Research . . . . Bernard Jasmin, Ph.D.
Assistant Dean, Research and Special Projects . . . . David Park, Ph.D.
Assistant Dean, Graduate and Postdoctoral Studies . . . . Ruth Slack, Ph.D.
Associate Dean, Student Affairs . . . . Louise Laramée, M.D., D.D.S.
Assistant Dean, Health and Hospital Services . . . . Sharon Whiting, M.D.
Director of Alumni and Student Affairs - Aboriginal Studies . . . . Darlene Kitty, M.D. Vacant
Director, Global Health . . . . Anne McCarthy, M.D.
Secretary of the Faculty . . . . Vasek Mezl, Ph.D.
Director, Animal Care Service . . . . Marilyn Keaney, D.V.M.
Director, Health Sciences Library . . . . Lee-Anne Ufholz
Chief Administrative Officer . . . . Vanessa Sutton, F.C.I.S., C.M.A.
Operations Manager . . . . Linda Chenard
Human Resources Manager . . . . Heidi Baier
Director of Advancement . . . . Sharon Cardiff
Financial Services Manager . . . . Yudy Bengoa

Marketing & Communications Manager . . . . Susan Maroun

Department and Division or Section Chairs

Basic Sciences

Biochemistry, Microbiology, and Immunology. . . . . Zemin Yao, Ph.D.
Cellular and Molecular Medicine . . . . David Lohnes, Ph.D. (Acting)
Epidemiology and Community Medicine . . . . Julian Little, Ph.D.

Clinical Sciences

Anaesthesia . . . . Homer Yang, M.D.
Emergency Medicine . . . . Ian Stiell, M.D.
Family Medicine . . . . Jacques Lemelin, M.D.
 Care of the Elderly. . . . . Frank Knoefel, M.D.
Medicine. . . . . Phil Wells, M.D.
 Cardiology. . . . . Terrence Ruddy, M.D.
 Clinical Epidemiology. . . . . Jeremy Grimshaw, M.D.
 Critical Care. . . . . John Kim, M.D.
 Dermatology . . . . James Walker, M.D.
 Endocrinology . . . . Alexander Sorisky, M.D.
 Gastroenterology . . . . Linda Scully, M.D. (Acting)
 General Internal Medicine . . . . Alan Karovitch, M.D.
 Geriatrics. . . . . Barbara Power, M.D.
 Hematology . . . . Marc Rodger, M.D.
 Infectious Diseases . . . . Mark Tyndall, M.D.
 Medical Oncology . . . . Jean Maroun, M.D. (Acting)
 Nephrology . . . . Peter Magner, M.D.
 Neurology . . . . Pierre Bourque, M.D.
 Nuclear Medicine. . . . . Terrence Ruddy, M.D.
 Palliative Care . . . . José Pereira, M.D.
 Rehabilitation Medicine . . . . Scott Wiebe, M.D. (Acting)
 Respirology . . . . Shawn Aaron, M.D.
 Rheumatology . . . . Douglas Smith, M.D.
Obstetrics and Gynaecology . . . . Wylam Faught, M.D.
 Maternal Fetal Medicine (Perinatology) . . . . Lawrence Oppenheimer, M.D.
 Gynaecologie Oncology . . . . Tien Le, M.D.
 Reproductive Medicine. . . . . Delani Kotarba, M.D.
 Urogynaecology and Pelvic Reconstructive Surgery . . . . Dante Pascali, M.D.
Ophthalmology . . . . Steven Gilberg, M.D.
Otolaryngology . . . . Martin Corsten, M.D.
Paediatrics. . . . . Ciarán Duffy, M.D.
Pathology and Laboratory Medicine . . . . John Veinot, M.D.
Psychiatry . . . . Katherine Gillis, M.D.
 Addictions Psychiatry . . . . Allan Wilson, M.D., Ph.D.
 Child Psychiatry . . . . Simon Davidson, M.D.
 Forensic Psychiatry. . . . . John Bradford, M.B.Ch.B.
 Geriatric Psychiatry. . . . . Catherine Shea, M.D.
Radiology . . . . Mark E. Schweitzer, M.D.
 Radiation Oncology . . . . Gad Perry, M.D. (Acting)
Surgery. . . . . Éric Poulin, M.D.
 Cardiac Surgery . . . . Thierry Mesana, M.D.
 General Surgery. . . . . Joseph Mamazza, M.D.
 Neurosurgery. . . . . Richard Moulton, M.D.
 Orthopaedic Surgery . . . . Geoffrey Dervin, M.D.
 Plastic Surgery . . . . Mario Jarmusk, M.D.
 Thoracic Surgery . . . . Sudhir Sundaresan, M.D.
 Urology. . . . . Ron Gerridzen, M.D.
 Vascular Surgery. . . . . Andrew Hill, M.D.

University of Toronto Faculty of Medicine
1 King's College Circle
Toronto, Ontario Canada M5S 1A1
416-978-6585 (dean's office); 416-978-1774 (fax)
Web site: www.facmed.utoronto.ca

The medical school was founded in 1843 as a part of King's College, which later became the University of Toronto. The faculty of medicine was established in 1888. The former school of hygiene merged with the faculty on July 1, 1975.

Type: public
2011 total enrollment: 963
Clinical facilities: Baycrest, Holland Bloorview, Centre for Addiction and Mental Health, Hospital for Sick Children, Mount Sinai Hospital, St. Michael's, Sunnybrook Health Sciences Centre, University Health Network (includes the Toronto Western Hospital, Princess Margaret Hospital, Toronto General), Women's College Hospital. Bridgepoint Health, Credit Valley Hospital and Trillium Health Centre, George Hull Centre for Children and Families, Hincks-Dellcrest Centre, Humber River Regional, Lakeridge Health Network, Markham-Stouffville Hospital, North York General Hospital, Ontario Shores Centre for Mental Health Sciences, Providence Healthcare, The Royal Victoria Hospital, The Scarborough Hospital, Southlake Regional Health Centre, St. John's Rehabilitation Hospital, St. Joseph's Health Centre, Surry Place Centre, Toronto East General Hospital, Waypoint Centre for Mental Heath Care, West Park Healthcare Centre.

University Administration

President. . . . . C. David Naylor, M.D., D.Phil.
Vice President and Provost. . . . . C. Misak, Ph.D.
Vice Provost, Faculty and Academic Life. . . . . E. Hillan, Ph.D.
Vice Provost, Relations with Health Care Institutions. . . . . C. Whiteside, M.D., Ph.D.
Vice President, Research . . . . P. Young, Ph.D., F.R.F.C.
Vice President, Advancement . . . . D. Palmer, Ph.D.
Vice President, Business Affairs . . . . C. Riggall
Vice President, Human Resources and Equity. . . . . A. Hildyard, Ph.D.
Assistant Vice President, Government, Institutional and Community Relations . . . . M. Scully
Vice President and Principal, University of Toronto at Mississauga. . . . . D. Saini
Assistant Dean, Medical Education and Student Affairs . . . . Douglas Franzen, M.D.
Vice President and Principal, University of Toronto at Scarborough . . . . F. Vaccarino, Ph.D.
Vice Provost, Student. . . . . J. Matus

Faculty of Medicine Administrative Staff

Dean. . . . . C. Whiteside, M.D., Ph.D.
Deputy Dean. . . . . S. Verma, L.L.B, M.D.
Vice Dean, Research and International Relations . . . . A. Buchan
Vice Dean, Continuing Education and Professional Development . . . . D. Anastakis (Interim)
Vice Dean, Graduate Affairs. . . . . A. Gotlieb (Acting)
Vice Dean, Postgraduate Medical Education . . . . Sal Spadafora
Vice Dean, Undergraduate Medical Education . . . . J. Rosenfield, M.D., Ph.D.
Associate Vice Provost, Relations with Health Care Institutions . . . . L. Ferris, Ph.D., C. Psych.
Associate Dean, Health Professions Student Affairs . . . . Leslie Nickell, M.D.
Associate Dean, Research and International Relations. . . . . G. Fantus, M.D.
Associate Dean, Postgraduate Medical Education Admissions and Evaluation . . . . G. Bandiera
Associate Dean, Undergraduate Medicine
    Admissions and Student Finance . . . . Mark Hansen, M.D.
Chief Administrative Officer. . . . . Tim Neff, C.M.A., M.B.A.

Department and Division or Section Chairs

Basic Sciences

Chief Student Affairs Officer . . . . Sandra Emerick, M.Ed.
Banting and Best Department of Medical Research. . . . . B. Andrews, Ph.D.
Biochemistry. . . . . R. Reithmeier, Ph.D.

Biomaterials and Biomedical Engineering. . . . . Paul Santerre, Ph.D.
Donnelly Centre for Cellular and Biomolecular Research . . . . B. Andrews
Immunology . . . . M. Ratcliffe, Ph.D.
Medical Biophysics. . . . . P. Burns, Ph.D.
Molecular Genetics . . . . H. Lipshitz, Ph.D.
Nutritional Sciences. . . . . Mary R. L'Abbe, Ph.D.
Pharmacology and Toxicology . . . . D. Grant, Ph.D.
Physiology . . . . S. Matthews, Ph.D.

Clinical Sciences

Anesthesia. . . . . B. Kavanagh, M.D.
Laboratory Medicine and Pathobiology. . . . . Richard G. Hegele, M.D.
Medical Imaging . . . . Patrice M. Bret, M.D.
Medical Radiation Sciences Program . . . . Pamela Catton, M.D.
Medical Science, Institute of . . . . A. Kaplan, M.D.
Medicine. . . . . W. Levinson, M.D.
Obstetrics and Gynaecology . . . . A. Bocking, M.D.
Ophthalmology and Vision Sciences. . . . . J. Hurwitz, M.D.
Otolaryngology-Head and Neck Surgery . . . . P. Gullane, M.D.
Paediatrics. . . . . D. Daneman, M.D.
Psychiatry . . . . L.T. Young, M.D.
Radiation Oncology. . . . . M. Gospodarowicz, M.D.
Surgery . . . . J. Rutka, M.D.

Community Health

Family and Community Medicine. . . . . Lynn Wilson, M.D.
Health Policy, Management, and Evaluation . . . . L. Lemieux-Charles, Ph.D.
Public Health, Dalla Lana School of. . . . . L. Lemieux-Charles, Ph.D. (Acting)

Rehabilitation Sciences

Occupational Sciences and Occupational Therapy . . . . Susan Rappolt, Ph.D.
Rehabilitation Sciences Sector . . . . K. F. Berg, Ph.D.
Physical Therapy . . . . Katherine Berg, Ph.D.
Speech-Language Pathology. . . . . L. Girolametto, Ph.D.

*Specialty without organizational autonomy.

University of Western Ontario
Schulich School of Medicine & Dentistry
Clinical Skills Building Room 3700
London, Ontario Canada N6A 5C1
519-661-3744 (admissions); 519-661-3459 (dean's office); 519-661-3797 (fax)
Web site: www.schulich.uwo.ca

The University of Western Ontario's Schulich School of Medicine & Dentistry is home to a range of undergraduate, professional, graduate and postgraduate programs and has more than 1,800 faculty and 3,080 student/trainees. Its mission is "to be a global leader in optimizing life-long health through innovations in research, education, and active engagement with our communities."

Type: public
2011 total enrollment: 3,080
Clinical facilities: London Health Sciences Centre (including University Hospital, South Street Hospital, Victoria Hospital, Children's Hospital, London Regional Cancer Program), St. Joseph's Health Care, London (including St. Joseph's Hospital, Parkwood Hospital, Regional Mental Health Care/ London and St. Thomas), Windsor Regional Hospital, Hotel Dieu-Grace Hospital, Child and Parent Resource Institute, Thames Valley Children's Centre.

University Officials

The Lieutenant Governor of Ontario and
Chancellor . . . . Joseph Rotman
President and Vice Chancellor . . . . Amit Chakma, Ph.D.
Vice President (Academic) and Provost . . . . Janice Deakin
Vice President (Resources and Operations) . . . . Gitta P. Kulczycki
Vice Provost (Academic Planning, Policy, and Faculty) . . . . Alan C. Weedon, Ph.D.
Vice President, External. . . . . Kevin Goldthrop
Vice President, Research and International Relations . . . . Janice Deakin
Vice Provost (Academic Programs and Students) [Registrar] . . . . John Doerksen, Ph.D.

Medical School Administrative Staff

Dean. . . . . Mike Strong, M.D.
Vice Dean, Education . . . . Bertha Garcia, M.D.
Vice Dean, Hospital & Interfaculty Relations. Margaret Steele, M.D.
Director & Vice Dean, Dentistry. . . . . Harinder Sandhu, D.D.S.
Assistant Dean, Student Affairs. . . . . Michael Rieder, M.D.
Assistant Dean, Admissions. . . . . Robert Hammond, M.D.
Associate Dean, Basic Medical Sciences, Academic Affairs . . . . Doug Jones, Ph.D.
Associate Dean, Equity and Professionalism . . . . Terri Paul, M.D.
Associate Dean, Postgraduate Medical Education . . . . C. Watling, M.D.
Associate Dean, Research . . . . Victor Han, M.D.
Associate Dean, Windsor Program . . . . Gerry Cooper, M.D.
Associate Dean, Continuing Professional Development . . . . Jatinder Takhar, M.D.
Chief Operating Officer. . . . . Dwayne Martins
Associate Director of Finance. . . . . Cindy Servos
Associate Director, Human Resources. . . . . Connie Zrini
Associate Director, Education. . . . . John Ruicci
Manager, Admissions/Student and Equity Affairs . . . . Pam Bere
Manager, Postgraduate Medical Education . . . . M. Morris
Manager, Research . . . . M. Hymowitz
Manager, Undergraduate Medical Education . . . . Lesley DePauw
Assistant Dean, Research (Graduate and Postdoctoral Studies) . . . . Andy Watson, Ph.D.
Assistant Dean, Rural and Regional Medicine . . . . Shamin Tejrar, M.D.

Department and Division or Section Chairs

Basic Sciences

Anatomy . . . . Kem Rogers, Ph.D.
Biochemistry . . . . David Litchfield, Ph.D.

Clinical Biochemistry . . . . C. A. Rupar, Ph.D.
  Epidemiology and Biostatistics . . . . K. Campbell, Ph.D.
History of Medicine and Science . . . . TBA
Medical Biophysics. . . . . Jerry Battista, Ph.D.
Microbiology and Immunology. . . . . M. Valvano, M.D.
Pathology . . . . Subrata Chakrabarti, M.D.
Physiology and Pharmocology . . . . Jane Rylett, Ph.D.

Clinical Sciences

Anesthesia. . . . . D. Cheng, M.D.
Clinical Neurological Sciences . . . . Paul Cooper, M.D. (Acting)
Medical Imaging . . . . Andrea Lum, M.D.
  Imaging Sciences . . . . A. Fenster, Ph.D.
  Nuclear Medicine. . . . . J. Romsa, M.D.
Family Medicine . . . . S. Wetmore, M.D.
Medicine. . . . . D. J. Hollomby, M.D.
  Cardiology. . . . . S. Siu, M.D.
  Clinical Immunology and Allergy . . . . J. A. Mazza, M.D.
  Clinical Pharmacology . . . . Richard B. Kim, M.D.
  Critical Care Medicine . . . . C. Martin, M.D.
  Emergency Medicine . . . . G. I. E. Joubert
  Endocrinology and Metabolism. . . . . I. Hramiak, M.D.
  Gastroenterology . . . . P. C. Adams, M.D.
  General Internal Medicine . . . . K. Myers, M.D.
  Geriatric Medicine . . . . J. Wells, M.D.
  Hematology and Oncology . . . . I. Chin-Yee, M.D.
  Infectious Disease. . . . . E. D. Ralph, M.D.
  Nephrology . . . . P. Blake, M.D.
  Respiratory Medicine . . . . C. George, M.B., B.S.
  Rheumatology . . . . J. Pope, M.D.
Obstetrics and Gynecology. . . . . Bryan Richardson, M.D.
Oncology. . . . . Glenn Bauman, M.D.
  Experimental Oncology . . . . Gabriel E. DiMattia, Ph.D.
  Medical Oncology . . . . Scott Ernst, M.D.
  Radiation Oncology . . . . George Rodrigues, M.D.
Surgical Oncology . . . . Joseph Chin, M.D.
Ophthalmology . . . . William Hodge, M.D.
Otolaryngology, Neck and Head Surgery . . . . John Yoo, M.D.
Paediatrics. . . . . Guido Filler, M.D., Ph.D.
  Medical Genetics . . . . J. H. Jung, M.D.
Physical Medicine and Rehabilitation . . . . R. Teasell, M.D.
Psychiatry . . . . S. Fisman, M.D.
Surgery . . . . J. Denstedt, M.D.
  Cardiac Surgery . . . . B. Kaii, M.D.
  General Surgery. . . . . E. Davies, M.D.
  Orthopaedic. . . . . J. H. Roth, M.D.
  Paediatric Surgery . . . . L. Scott, M.D.
  Plastic and Reconstructive Surgery . . . . D. Ross, M.D.
  Urology Surgery. . . . . H. A. Razvi, M.D.
  Vascular Surgery. . . . . T. Forbes, M.D.
  Thoracic Surgery . . . . R. I. Inculet, M.D.
Robarts Research Institute . . . . M. Strong, M.D. (Interim)

Laval University Faculty of Medicine

Pavillon Ferdinand-Vandry
1050 Medicine Avenue, Local 4684
Quebec City, Quebec Canada G1V 0A6
418-656-2301 (dean's office); 418-656-5062 (fax)
Web site: www.fmed.ulaval.ca

The present medical school was established in fall 1852, less than a year after the founding of Laval University. Before that time, there had been a medical school incorporated by the city of Quebec. The medical school is located on the campus of Laval University on the outskirts of Quebec City.

Type: private
2011 total enrollment: 3,358
Clinical facilities: Centre hospitalier de l'Universite Laval, Hôtel-Dieu de Québec, Hôpital Laval, Hôpital du Saint-Sacrement, Hôpital de l'Enfant-Jésus, Hôpital Saint-Francois d'Assise, Hôtel-Dieu de Lévis.

University Officials

Rector . . . . Denis Brière, Ph.D.
Vice Rector (Teaching and International Development) . . . . Bernard Garnier
Vice Rector (Human Resources) . . . . Michel Beauchamp
Vice Rector (Research) . . . . Edwin Bourget
Vice Rector (Administration and Finance) . . . . Josée Germain
Secretary General . . . . Monique Richer
Executive Vice Rector (Executive Administration) . . . . Éric Bauce
Registrar . . . . Danielle Fleury

Medical School Administrative Staff

Dean . . . . Rénald Bergeron, M.D.
Associate Dean (Executive) . . . . Denis Beauchamp, Ph.D.
Associate Dean (Research) . . . . Michel J. Tremblay, Ph.D.
Associate Dean (Relations and Development) . . . . Gaëtane Routhier, M.D.
Associate Dean (Teaching) . . . . Jean-François Montreuil, M.D.
Associate Dean (Clinical Affairs) . . . . Julien Poitras, M.D.
Secretary of the Faculty . . . . Jean Talbot, M.D.
Director, Continuing Medical Education . . . . Michel Rouleau, M.D.
Assistant to the Dean (Student Affairs) . . . . Fabien Gagnon, M.D.
Administrative Assistant . . . . Patrice Lemay

Associate Dean (Rehabilitation) .... Claude Côté, Ph.D.

Department and Division or Section Chairs

Basic Sciences

Microbiology-Infectiology and Immunology .... Sylvie Trottier, M.D.
Molecular Biology, Medical Biochemistry, and Pathology.......... Pierre Leclerc, M.D., Ph.D.
   Molecular Medicine .... Serge Rivest, Ph.D.

Clinical Sciences

Anesthesiology.. Jean Beaubien, M.D.
Family Medicine and Emergency Medicine......................... Gilles Lortie, M.D.
Medicine.. Pierre Leblanc, M.D.
   Cardiology*... Can Manh Nguyên, M.D.
   Dermatology*.. Jimmy Alain, M.D.
   Endocrinology* .... Vacant
   Gastroenterology .... Claude Parent, M.D.
   Geriatrics... Michel Dugas, M.D.
   Hematology* .... Christine Demers, M.D.
   Internal Medicine*..................................... Patrick Couture, M.D.
   Medical Oncology*...................................... Danièle Marceau, M.D.
   Nephrology* .... Paul Isenring, M.D.
   Neurology* .... Steve Verreault, M.D.
   Palliative Care .... Anne Moreau, M.D.
   Physiatry*... Isabelle Côté, M.D.
   Pulmonary and Critical Care*........................... Johanne Côté, M.D.
   Radio-oncology*.. Isabelle Valli'eres, M.D.
   Rheumatology* .... Louis Bessette, M.D. (Interm)
Obstetrics and Gynecology..................................... Normand Brassard, M.D.
Ophthalmology and Otorhinolaryngology-Cervico-Facial Surgery......... Yolande Dubé, M.D.
   Ophthalmology*... Nathalie Labrecque, M.D.
Pediatrics .... Bruno Piedboeuf, M.D.
Psychiatric... Nathalie Gingras, M.D.
Radiology .... Ghislain Brousseau, M.D.
Surgery .... Yvan Douville, M.D.
   General Surgery*....................................... Simon Biron, M.D.
   Neurosurgery*.. Geneviève Milot, M.D.
   Orthopedics*... Jean Lamontagne, M.D.
   Urology*... Jean-François Audet, M.D.

Public Health Sciences

Social and Preventive Medicine .... Yv Bonnier-Viger, M.D.
Rehabilitation .... Joe L. Macoir, Ph.D.
Psychiatry .... Nathalie Gingras, M.D.
Surgery... Yvan Douville, M.D.
   Neurosurgery... Genevi'eve Milot, M.D.
   Orthopedics.. Jean Lamontagne, M.D.

*Specialty without organizational autonomy.

McGill University Faculty of Medicine
Room 600, 3655 Promenade Sir-William-Osler
Montreal, Quebec Canada H3G 1Y6
514-398-1768 (general information); 514-398-3595 (fax)
E-mail: recepmed@mcgill.ca, recept3605.med@mcgill.ca
Web site: www.med.mcgill.ca

The faculty of medicine of McGill University was established in 1829.

Type: public
2011 total enrollment: 708
Clinical facilities: McGill University Health Centre (Montreal Children's Hospital, Montreal General Hospital, Montreal Neurological Hospital, Royal Victoria Hospital) Sir Mortimer B. Davis-Jewish General Hospital; Lakeshore General Hospital; Lasalle General Hospital; Montreal Chest Hospital; St. Mary's Hospital; Shriners Hospital; Douglas Mental Health University Institute.

University Officials

Principal and Vice Chancellor . . . . Heather Munroe-Blum, Ph.D.
Provost . . . . Anthony C. Masi, Ph.D.
Vice Principal (Administration and Finance) . . . . Michael DiGrappa
Deputy Provost (Student Life and Learning). . . . . Morton J. Mendelson, Ph.D.
Vice Principal (Research and International Relations). . . . . Rosie Golstein, Ph.D.
Vice Principal (Development, Alumni, and University Relations) . . . . Marc Weinstein
Vice Principal (External Relations). . . . . Olivier Marcil
Vice Principal (Health Affairs) . . . . David Eidelman, M.D.

Medical School Administrative Staff

Dean. . . . . David Eidelman, M.D.
Executive Director, Health Affairs . . . . TBA
Assistant Dean (Admissions). . . . . Saleem Razack, M.D.
Director (Admissions) . . . . Charmaine Lyn
Associate Dean (Faculty Affairs) . . . . Mara Ludwig, M.D.
Associate Dean (Center for Continuing Health
    Professional Education) . . . . Ivan Rohan, M.D. (Interim)
Associate Dean (Faculty Development) . . . . Miriam Boillat, M.D.
Associate Vice Principal and Associate Dean (Interhospital Affairs) . . . . Sam Benaroya, M.D.
Associate Dean (Medical Education). . . . . Robert L. Primavesi, M.D.
Associate Dean (Postgraduate Medical Education
    and Professional Affairs) . . . . Sarkis Meterissian, M.D.
Assistant Dean (Resident Professional Affairs). . . . . Richard Montoro, M.D.
Associate Dean (Research). . . . . Marianna Newkirk, M.D.
Assistant Dean (Biomedical BSC and Graduate Studies) . . . . Elaine Davis, M.D.
Assistant Dean (Student Affairs) . . . . Namta Gupta, M.D.
Director, Centre for Medical Education . . . . Yvonne Steinert, Ph.D.
Director, Animal Resources Centre. . . . . Jim Gourdon
Life Sciences Area Librarian. . . . . Susan Murray

McGill University Faculty of Medicine: QUEBEC

Department and Division or Section Chairs

Basic Sciences

Anatomy and Cell Biology . . . . TBA
Biochemistry . . . . David Thomas, Ph.D.
Biomedical Engineering. . . . . Henrietta Galiana, Ph.D.
Epidemiology, Biostatistics, and Occupational Health . . . . Rebecca Fuhrer, Ph.D.
Human Genetics . . . . David Rosenblatt, M.D.
Microbiology and Immunology. . . . . Joaquin Madrenas, M.D.
Pathology . . . . David Haegert, M.D.
Pharmacology and Therapeutics. . . . . Gerhard Multhaup, M.D.
Physiology. . . . . John Orlowski, Ph.D.
Social Studies of Medicine . . . . Thomas Schlich, M.D. (Acting)

Clinical Sciences

AIDS Research Centre* . . . . Mark Wainberg, Ph.D.
Anesthesia. . . . . Steven Backman, M.D., Ph.D.
Family Medicine . . . . TBA
Rosalind and Morris Goodman Cancer Centre . . . . TBA
McGill Nutrition and Food Science Center* . . . . Errol B. Marliss, M.D.
Medicine. . . . . TBA
Neurology and Neurosurgery. . . . . Lesley Fellows, M.D. (Interim)
Obstetrics and Gynecology. . . . . Dennis Querleu, M.D.
Oncology. . . . . Eduardo Franco, M.D. (Interim)
Ophthalmology . . . . Susan Lindley, M.D. (Interim)
Otolaryngology . . . . Saul Frenkiel, M.D.
Pediatrics . . . . Michael Shevell, M.D.
Psychiatry . . . . Mimi Israel, M.D.
Radiology (Diagnostic). . . . . Robert Lisbona, M.D.
Surgery . . . . Gerald Fried, M.D.

*Specialty without organizational autonomy.

Université de Montréal, Faculty of Medicine

2900 Boulevard Edouard-Montpetit
P.O. Box 6128, Succ. Centre-ville
Montreal, Quebec Canada H3C 3J7
514-343-6267; 514-343-6351 (dean's office); 514-343-5850 (fax)
E-mail: facmed@umontreal.ca
Web site: www.med.umontreal.ca

The faculty of medicine of the Université de Montréal can be traced back to a school established in Montreal in 1843 and incorporated in 1845 under the name of "Ecole de Médecine et de Chirurgie de Montréal." In 1891, this school merged with the faculty of medicine of the Montreal branch of Laval University, which had been founded in 1877. This agreement was approved by the Quebec legislature in the same year, and henceforth, the school of medicine and surgery of Montreal became the faculty of medicine of Laval University of Montreal. In 1920, by an act of the Quebec legislature, the Montreal branch of Laval University was granted its independence, and the school of medicine became known as the Université de Montréal Faculty of Medicine.

Type: private
2011 total enrollment: 6,000
Clinical facilities: Centre Hospitalier de l'Université de Montréal, Hôpital Maisonneuve-Rosemont, Hôpital Rivière-des-Prairies, Hôpital du Sacré-Coeur de Montréal, Hôpital Louis-H. Lafontaine, Hôpital Sainte-Justine, Institut de Cardiologie de Montréal, Institut de Réadaptation de Montréal, Cité de la Santé de Laval, Institut Philippe-Pinel de Montréal, Institut Universitaire de Gériatrie de Montréal, Centre Hospitalier de Verdun, Institut de Recherches Cliniques de Montréal, Complexe Hospitalier de la Sagamie.

University Officials

Chancellor . . . . Louise Roy (Interim)
Rector . . . . Guy Breton, M.D.
Vice Rector, Academic Affairs . . . . Raymond Lalande, M.D.
Vice-Rector, Human Resources and Planning . . . . A.H. Boisvert, L.L.M.
Vice-Rector, Finance and Infrastructure . . . . Eric Filteau, M.B.A.
Vice-Rector, International Affairs and Francophonie . . . . Hél[ene David, Ph.D.
Vice-Rector, Student Affairs and Sustainable Development . . . . Louise Béliveau, Ph.D.
Vice-Rector, Major Academic Projects . . . . Joseph Hubert, Ph.D.
Vice-Rector, Research, Creation, and Innovation . . . . Genevi[eve Tanguay, Ph.D.
Secretary-General . . . . Alexandre Chabot
Financial Officer . . . . André Racette
Registrar . . . . Pierre Chénard, Ph.D.

Medical School Administrative Staff

Dean . . . . Héléne Boisjoly, M.D.
Vice-Dean, Executive and Clinical Affairs . . . . Pierre Bourgouin, M.D.
Vice-Dean, Faculty Affairs . . . . Pierre Belhumeur, Ph.D.
Vice-Dean, Research and Innovation . . . . Daniel Bourbonnais, Ph.D.
Vice-Dean, Pedagogy and Continuing Professional Development . . . . Andrée Boucher, M.D.
Vice-Dean, Basic Sciences, Health Sciences,
    Public Health, and Graduate Studies . . . . André Ferron, Ph.D.
Vice-Dean, Undergraduate Studies . . . . Christian Bourdy, M.D.
Vice-Dean, Postgraduate Medical Studies . . . . Josée Dubois, M.D.
Secretary of the Faculty . . . . Chantal Lambert, B.Pharm., Ph.D.
Associate Vice-Dean, Research . . . . Vincent Castellucci, Ph.D.
Assistant to the Dean, Communications . . . . Geneviéve Bouchard, Ph.D.
Assistant to the Dean, Human Resources . . . . Josée V[eronneau
Assistant to the Dean, Regional Training . . . . Alan Papineau, M.D.
Assistant to the Dean, Financial Resources . . . . Sylvie Monier
Assistants to the Vice-Dean, Executive
    Physical Resources, Materials and Planning . . . . Martine Jalbert
    Agreement and Special Projects . . . . Vacant
    Human Resources . . . . Josée Veronneau
    Responsible for Regional Training . . . . Alain Papineau, M.D.

Université de Montréal, Faculty of Medicine: QUEBEC

Financial Resources . . . . Sylvie Monier
Coordinator of RUIS . . . . Richard Klein
Assistant to the Vice-Dean, Postgraduate Medical Studies. . . . . Lorraine Locas
Assistants to the Vice-Dean, Undergraduate Studies
Pregraduate Clerkship . . . . Martine Jolivet-Tremblay, M.D.
Administrative Affairs . . . . Jolaine Frigault
Assistant to the Vice-Dean, Professoral Affairs
Assistant to the Vice-Dean, Human Resources . . . . Line Ginchereau
Director of M.D. Programs. . . . . Éric Drouin, M.D.
Coordinator, Student Affairs . . . . Hugues Cormier, M.D.
Coordinator, Student Affairs . . . . Ramses Wassef, M.D.
President, Curriculum Committee . . . . Serge Querin, M.D.
President, Admission Committee . . . . Vacant
Director, Medical Library. . . . . Monique St-Jean

Department and Division or Section Chairs

Basic Sciences

Biochemistry . . . . Christian Baron, Ph.D.
Microbiology and Immunology. . . . . Marc Drolet, Ph.D. (Interim)
Pathology and Cellular Biology. . . . . Pierre Drapeau, Ph.D.
Pharmacology . . . . Patrick Du Souich, M.D., Ph.D.
Physiology . . . . Michéle Brochu, Ph.D.

Clinical Sciences

Anesthesia. . . . . Pierre Drolet, M.D.
Family Medicine . . . . Jean Pelletier, M.D.
Medicine. . . . . Mario Talajic, M.D.
Obstetrics and Gynecology. . . . . Line Leduc, M.D.
Ophthalmology . . . . Jean-Daniel Arbour, M.D.
Pediatrics . . . . Marc Girard, M.D.
Psychiatry . . . . Emmanuel Stip, M.D.
Radiology, Radio-Oncology, and Nuclear Medicine . . . . Louise Samson, M.D. (Interim)
Surgery . . . . Luc Valiquette, M.D.

Health Sciences

Nutrition. . . . . Marielle LeDoux, M.D.
Rehabilitation . . . . Rhoda Weiss Lambrou, Ph.D.
Speech Therapy and Audiology . . . . Louise Getty

Public Health Sciences

Environmental Health . . . . André Dufresne, Ph.D.
Health Administration . . . . Régis Blais, Ph.D.
Social and Preventive Medicine . . . . Slim Haddad, Ph.D.

Université de Sherbrooke Faculty of Medicine and Health Sciences
3001 12th Avenue North
Sherbrooke, Quebec Canada J1H 5N4
819-564-5200; 819-564-5201 (dean's office); 819-564-5420 (fax)
Web site: www.usherbrooke.ca/medecine/

The faculty of medicine and health sciences of the Université de Sherbrooke was founded in March 1961. It is the last faculty of medicine to be organized in the province of Quebec since 1853. The first M.D. degrees were granted in 1970. The medical school is part of the Université de Sherbrooke.

Type: public
2011 total enrollment: 560
Clinical facilities: In 1995, the merger of hospitals created a new 725-bed university hospital of acute care with large ambulatory care facilities, a new 400-bed chronic and long-term care university center, and a university-affiliated community care center. Five major regional hospitals are affiliated along with a number of private clinics.

University Officials

Chancellor . . . . His Excellency, and Monsignor André Gaumond, D.D.S.
Rector. . . . . Luce Samoisette, L.L.B.
Vice-Rector, Administration . . . . Joanne Roch, Ph.D.
Vice-Rector, Campus Longueuil and Vice-Rector
of Technologies of Information . . . . Lyne Bouchard
Vice-Rector, Human Resources and Student Affairs. . . . . Martin Buteau, D.Sc.
Vice-Rector, International Relations and General Secretary . . . . Jocelyne Faucher, M.D.
Vice-Rector, Research. . . . . Jacques Beauvais, Ph.D.
Vice-Rector, Studies . . . . Lucie LaFlamme, L.L.B.
Vice-Rector, Sustainable Development and Government Relations . . . . Alain Webster, M.Sc.
Registrar . . . . France Myette

Medical School Administrative Staff

Dean. . . . . Réjean Hébert, M.D.
Vice-Dean, Executive . . . . Gilles Faust, M.D.
Vice-Dean, Research . . . . Darel Hunting, Ph.D.
Vice-Dean, Graduate Studies . . . . Claude Asselin, Ph.D.
Vice-Dean, Undergraduate Medical Education . . . . Paul Grand'Maison, M.D.
Vice-Dean, Postgraduate Medical Education . . . . François Lajoie, M.D.
Secretary and Vice-Dean, Student Affairs . . . . Sophie LaFlamme, M.D.
Vice-Dean, Nursing Sciences. . . . . Luc Mathieu, D.B.A.
Vice-Dean, Rehabilitation. . . . . Johanne Desrosiers, Ph.D.
Director, Continuing Education . . . . Gilles Voyer, M.D.
Director, Office of Medical Education . . . . Diane Clavet, M.D.
Chairperson of Admission Committee . . . . Daniel J. Côté, M.D.
Executive Director. . . . . Marc Lauzière
Administrative Director . . . . René Gagnon
Administrative Assistant for Undergraduate Medical Education . . . . Sylvie Lamarche
Medical Librarian . . . . Marthe Brideau
Director, Computer Science Office. . . . . David Serouge

Department and Division or Section Chairs

Basic Sciences

Anatomy and Cellular Biology . . . . Nathalie Rivard, Ph.D.
Biochemistry . . . . Jean-Pierre Perreault, Ph.D.
    Clinical Biochemistry . . . . Jean Dubé, Ph.D.
Microbiology and Infectiology . . . . Raymund Wellinger, Ph.D.
Nuclear Medicine and Radiobiology. . . . . Benoit Paquette, Ph.D.
Nursing School . . . . Luc Mathieu, D.B.A.
Pharmacology . . . . Emanuel Escher, Ph.D.
Physiology and Biophysics . . . . Eric Rousseau, Ph.D.

Rehabilitation School. . . . . Johanne Desrosiers, Ph.D.
Physiatry . . . . Anne Harvey, M.D.

Clinical Sciences

Anesthesia. . . . . René Martin, M.D.
Community Health Sciences. . . . . Maryse Guay, M.D.
  Drug Addiction . . . . Elise Roy, M.D.
Family Medicine . . . . Marie Giroux, M.D.
  Emergency. . . . . Colette Bellavance, M.D.
  UMF Alma. . . . . Robert Charron, M.D.
  UMF Charles-LeMoyne. . . . . Louise Champagne, M.D.
  UMF Chicoutimi . . . . Catherine Hudon, M.D.
  UMF Estrie . . . . Isabelle Germain, M.D.
  UMF du Grand-Moncton . . . . Michel Landry, M.D.
  UMF Horizon Rouyn-Noranda . . . . Marie-Josée Paquin, M.D.
  UMF Richelieu-Yamaska. . . . . Jocelyne Bonin, M.D.
Medicine. . . . . Pierre Cossette, M.D.
  Cardiology. . . . . Michel Nguyen, M.D.
  Dermatology . . . . Bruno Maynard, M.D.
  Endocrinology . . . . Patrice Perron, M.D.
  Gastroenterology . . . . Serge Langevin, M.D.
  Geriatrics. . . . . Tamas Fülöp, M.D.
  Haematology . . . . Patrice Beauregard, M.D.
  Internal Medicine. . . . . Luc Lanthier, M.D.
  Nephrology . . . . Paul Montambault, M.D.
  Neurology . . . . Jean Rivest, M.D.
  Respiratory Diseases . . . . Pierre Larivée, M.D.
  Rheumatology . . . . Artur De Brum Fernandes, M.D.
Microbiology and Infectiology (see Basic Sciences) . . . . Raymund Wellinger, Ph.D.
  Infectiology. . . . . Jacques Pépin, M.D.
Nuclear Medicine and Radiobiology (see Basic Sciences) . . . . Benoit Paquette, Ph.D.
  Nuclear Medicine. . . . . Jean Verreault, M.D.
  Radio-Oncology . . . . Rachel Bujold, M.D.
Obstetrics and Gynaecology . . . . Guy Waddell, M.D.
Pathology . . . . Edmund Rizcallah, M.D.
Pediatrics . . . . Hervé Walti, M.D.
  Pediatrics Endocrinology . . . . Nancy Gagué, M.D.
  General Pediatrics . . . . Thérése Côté-Baileau, M.D.
  Genetics. . . . . Hervé Walli, M.D.
  Immuno-Allergology. . . . . Marek Rola-Pleszczynski, M.D.
  Neonatology. . . . . Valérie Bertelle, M.D.
  Neuropediatrics . . . . Guillaume Sébire, M.D.
  Pediatrics Pneumology . . . . Jean-Paul Praud, M.D.
Psychiatry . . . . Pierre Beauséjour, M.D.
  Gerontopsychiatry . . . . Paule Hottin, M.D.
  Child Psychiatry . . . . Carmen Beauregard, M.D.
  Adult Psychiatry . . . . William Semann, M.D.
  Legal Psychiatry . . . . Pierre Gagné, M.D.
Radiology . . . . The-Bao Bui, M.D.
Surgery. . . . . Gaétan Langlois, M.D.
  Cardiovascular . . . . David Greentree, M.D.
  General Surgery. . . . . Francois Mosimann, M.D.
  Neurosurgery. . . . . David Fortin, M.D.
  Ophthalmology . . . . Anne Faucher, M.D.
  Orthopedic Surgery . . . . Nicolas Patenaude, M.D.
  Ortorhinolaryngology. . . . . Dominique Dorion, M.D.
  Urology. . . . . Michel Carmel, M.D.
  Vascular. . . . . Véronique Lapie, M.D.
  Thoracic . . . . Marco Sirois, M.D.

University of Saskatchewan College of Medicine
B103 Health Sciences Building
107 Wiggins Road
Saskatoon, Saskatchewan Canada S7N 5E5
306-966-2673 (dean's office); 306-966-6164 (fax); 306-966-4050 (admissions office);
306-966-2601 (fax)
Web site: www.usask.ca/medicine

The university began teaching medical students in 1926 when the school of medical sciences opened to provide the first two years of medical training. In 1953, the school became the college of medicine when a four-year term was instituted. The present program requires two years premedical university experience followed by a four-year program in the college of medicine.

Type: public
2011 total enrollment: 238
Clinical facilities: Saskatoon Health Region: Royal University Hospital, St. Paul's Hospital, Saskatoon City Hospital. Regina Qu'Appelle Health Region: Regina General Hospital.

University Officials

President	P. MacKinnon, L.L.B., L.L.M.
Provost and Vice President, Academic	B. Fairbairn, Ph.D.
Vice President (Finance and Resources)	R. Florizone, Ph.D.
Vice Provost	Jim Germida, Ph.D.
Associate Vice President (Financial Services) and Controller	Laura Kennedy, C.A.
Associate Vice President Student and Enrollment Services	D. Hannah, Ph.D.

Medical School Administrative Staff

Dean	W. L. Albritton, M.D.
Associate Dean (Faculty Affairs)	O. A. Olatunbosun, M.D.
Associate Dean (Medical Undergraduate Education)	S. R. Harding, M.D.
Associate Dean (Regina Programs)	G. White, M.D.
Associate Dean (Research)	Louis Qualtiere, Ph.D.
Associate Dean (Physical Therapy and Rehabilitation Sciences)	E. L. Harrison, Ph.D.
Associate Dean (Division of Biomedical Sciences and Graduate Studies)	N. Ovsenek, Ph.D.
Associate Dean (Rural Medical Education)	T. Smith-Windsor, M.D.
Assistant Dean (Undergraduate Education)	G. Linassi, M.B.
Associate Dean (Postgraduate Education)	A. Saxena, M.D.
Associate Dean (Saskatoon)	G. Stoneham, M.D.
Director, School of Physical Therapy	A. Busch, Ph.D.
Director of Admissions	B. Ziola, Ph.D.
Chief Financial Officer and Director of Administration	A. T. Schultz, C.A.
Director of the Physicians' Billing Office	V. Bennett, M.D.
Associate Director (Administration and Finance)	G. Melvin
Assistant Director (Administration and Finance)	C. Brooke
Director of Educational Support and Development	M. D'Eon, Ph.D.
Associate Director (Education Support and Development)	K. Premkumar, Ph.D.
Director of Continuing, Professional Learning	P. Davis, M.D.
Director of Information Technology Unit	J. Costa
Director, Mentoring Programs	G. Mezo-Kricsfalusy
Manager, Research Services	J. Holmstrom
Manager, Human Resources	T. Wray
Administrative Coordinator (Undergraduate)	R. Bourner
Administrative Coordinator (Postgraduate)	D. Spence
Administrative Coordinator (Admissions)	S. Bueckert
Administrative Coordinator (Faculty Affairs)	C. Zorn
Administrative Coordinator (Aboriginal Programs)	Val Arnault-Pelletier
Administrative Coordinator (Educational Support and Development, Community Faculty)	D. Bonnycastle
Administrative Coordinator (Regina Programs)	J. Vogelsang

University of Saskatchewan College of Medicine: SASKATCHEWAN

Administrative Coordinator (Graduate Programs) . . . . A. Zoerb
Administrative Coordinator, Student and Resident Affairs . . . . T. Unger
Administrative Coordinator (Research Groups) . . . . D. Stumborg
Librarian . . . . S. Murphy
Alumni Relations Officer . . . . V. Moore-Wright
Communications Officer (Alumni) . . . . L. Herman
College Development Officer . . . . F. Matiko

Department and Division or Section Chairs

Basic Sciences

Anatomy and Cell Biology . . . . B. Rosser, Ph.D.
Biochemistry . . . . W. Roesler, Ph.D.
Community Health and Epidemiology . . . . N. Muhajarine, Ph.D.
Microbiology and Immunology . . . . P. Bretscher, Ph.D.
Pharmacology . . . . V. Gopal, Ph.D.
Physiology . . . . M. Desautels, Ph.D.

Clinical Sciences

Anaesthesia . . . . D. C. Campbell, M.D.
Family Medicine . . . . A. Danilkewich, M.D.
Medical Imaging . . . . P. Babyn, M.D.
Medicine . . . . V. Hoeppner, M.D.
Obstetrics, Gynecology, and Reproductive Sciences . . . . T. Mainprize, M.D.
Oncology . . . . C. Smith, M.D.
Pathology . . . . J. Blondeau, M.D. (Acting)
Pediatrics . . . . L. Givelichian, M.D. (Acting)
Physical Medicine and Rehabilitation . . . . L. M. Rudachyk, M.D.
Psychiatry . . . . M. Baetz, M.D.
Surgery . . . . A. G. Casson, M.D.

Council of Deans

2012

Council of Deans Administrative Board, 2011-2012

Chair
Claire Pomeroy, M.D., M.B.A.
University of California, Davis, Health System

Chair Elect
Harold Paz, M.D.
Pennsylvania State University College of Medicine

Immediate Past Chair
Philip A. Pizzo, M.D.
Stanford University School of Medicine

Members

Karen Antman, M.D.
Boston University School of Medicine

Paul Raymond Cunningham, M.D., M.B.B.S.
The Brody School of Medicine at East Carolina University

Betty M. Drees, M.D.
University of Missouri-Kansas City School of Medicine

Deborah C. German, M.D.
University of Central Florida College of Medicine

Marsha D. Rappley, M.D.
Michigan State University College of Human Medicine

Paul B. Roth, M.D., M.S., F.A.C.E.P.
University of New Mexico School of Medicine

Benjamin P. Sachs, M.B., B.S., D.P.H., F.A.C.O.G.
Tulane University School of Medicine

Larry J. Shapiro, M.D.
Washington University in St. Louis School of Medicine

Wiley William Souba, Jr., M.D., D.Sc., M.B.A.
Dartmouth Medical School

*AAMC Board of Directors, 2010-2011

Council of Deans

ALABAMA

University of Alabama School of Medicine
Raymond L. Watts, M.D.

University of South Alabama
College of Medicine
Samuel J. Strada, Ph.D.

ARIZONA

University of Arizona College of Medicine
Steve Goldschmid, M.D.

ARKANSAS

University of Arkansas for Medical Sciences College of Medicine
Debra H. Fiser, M.D.

CALIFORNIA

Keck School of Medicine of the University of Southern California
Carmen A. Puliafito, M.D., M.B.A.

Loma Linda University School of Medicine
H. Roger Hadley, M.D.

Stanford University School of Medicine
Philip A. Pizzo, M.D.

University of California, Davis,
School of Medicine
Claire Pomeroy, M.D., M.B.A.

University of California, Irvine,
School of Medicine
Ralph Clayman, M.D.

University of California, Los Angeles
David Geffen School of Medicine
A. Eugene Washington, M.D.

University of California, San Diego
School of Medicine
David A. Brenner, M.D.

University of California, San Francisco,
School of Medicine
Samuel Hawgood, M.B.B.S.

COLORADO

University of Colorado School of Medicine
Richard D. Krugman, M.D.

CONNECTICUT

University of Connecticut School of Medicine
Bruce T. Liang, M.D.

Yale University School of Medicine
Robert J. Alpern, M.D.

DISTRICT OF COLUMBIA

George Washington University
School of Medicine and Health Sciences
Jeffrey S. Akman, M.D.

Georgetown University School of Medicine
Stephen Ray Mitchell, M.D.

Howard University College of Medicine
Mark Johnson, M.D., M.P.H.

FLORIDA

Charles E. Schmidt College of Medicine at Florida Atlantic University
David Bjorkman, M.D.

Florida International University
College of Medicine
John A. Rock, M.D.

Florida State University College of Medicine
John P. Fogarty, M.D.

University of Central Florida
College of Medicine
Deborah C. German, M.D.

University of Florida College of Medicine
Michael L. Good, M.D.

University of Miami Leonard M. Miller
School of Medicine
Pascal J. Goldschmidt, M.D.

USF Health Morsani College of Medicine
Stephen Klasko, M.D., M.B.A.

GEORGIA

Emory University School of Medicine
Thomas J. Lawley, M.D.

Medical College of Georgia at
Georgia Health Sciences University
Peter Buckley, M.D., M.B.B.S.

Mercer University School of Medicine
William F. Bina, III, M.D., M.P.H.

Morehouse School of Medicine
Valerie Montgomery Rice, M.D.

HAWAII

University of Hawaii, John A. Burns
School of Medicine
Jerris R. Hedges, M.D., M.S.

ILLINOIS

Chicago Medical School at Rosalind Franklin University of Medicine & Science
Russell Robertson, M.D.

Loyola University Chicago Stritch
School of Medicine
Linda Brubaker, M.D.

Northwestern University
The Feinberg School of Medicine
Eric G. Neilson, M.D.

Rush Medical College of Rush University Medical
Center
Thomas A. Deutsch, M.D.

Southern Illinois University School of Medicine
J. Kevin Dorsey, M.D., Ph.D.

University of Chicago Division of the Biological
Sciences The Pritzker School of Medicine
Kenneth S. Polonsky, M.D.

University of Illinois College of Medicine
Dimitri T. Azar, M.D., M.B.A.

INDIANA

Indiana University School of Medicine
D. Craig Brater, M.D.

IOWA

University of Iowa Roy J. and Lucille A. Carver
College of Medicine
Paul B. Rothman, M.D.

KANSAS

University of Kansas School of Medicine
Barbara F. Atkinson, M.D.

KENTUCKY

University of Kentucky College of Medicine
Frederick C. de Beer, M.D.

University of Louisville School of Medicine
Edward Halperin, M.D., M.A.

LOUISIANA

Louisiana State University School of Medicine in
New Orleans
Steve Nelson, M.D.

Louisiana State University School of Medicine in
Shreveport
Andrew Chesson, Jr., M.D.

Tulane University School of Medicine
Benjamin P. Sachs, M.B.B.S., D.P.H.

MARYLAND

Johns Hopkins University School of Medicine
Edward D. Miller, Jr., M.D.

Uniformed Services University of the Health Sciences F. Edward Hebert School of Medicine
Larry W. Laughlin, M.D., Ph.D.

University of Maryland School of Medicine
E. Albert Reece, M.D., Ph.D., M.B.A.

MASSACHUSETTS

Boston University School of Medicine
Karen Antman, M.D.

Harvard Medical School
Jeffrey S. Flier, M.D.

Tufts University School of Medicine
Harris A. Berman, M.D.

University of Massachusetts Medical School
Terence R. Flotte, M.D.

MICHIGAN

Michigan State University
College of Human Medicine
Marsha D. Rappley, M.D.

Oakland University William Beaumont
School of Medicine
Robert Folberg, M.D.

University of Michigan Medical School
James O. Woolliscroft, M.D.

Wayne State University School of Medicine
Valerie M. Parisi, M.D., M.P.H., M.B.A.

Council of Deans

MINNESOTA

Mayo Medical School
Keith D. Lindor, M.D.

University of Minnesota Medical School
Aaron L. Friedman, M.D.

MISSISSIPPI

University of Mississippi School of Medicine
James E. Keeton, M.D.

MISSOURI

Saint Louis University School of Medicine
Philip O. Alderson, M.D.

University of Missouri-Columbia
School of Medicine
Robert J. Churchill, M.D.

University of Missouri-Kansas City
School of Medicine
Betty M. Drees, M.D.

Washington University in St. Louis
School of Medicine
Larry J. Shapiro, M.D.

NEBRASKA

Creighton University School of Medicine
Rowen K. Zetterman, M.D.

University of Nebraska College of Medicine
Bradley E. Britigan, M.D.

NEVADA

University of Nevada School of Medicine
Thomas L. Schwenk, M.D.

NEW HAMPSHIRE

Dartmouth Medical School
**Wiley "Chio" Souba, Jr., M.D., D.Sc.,
   M.B.A.**

NEW JERSEY

Cooper Medical School of Rowan University
Paul Katz, M.D.

University of Medicine and Dentistry of
New Jersey-New Jersey Medical School
Robert L. Johnson, M.D.

University of Medicine and Dentistry of New
Jersey-Robert Wood Johnson Medical School
Peter S. Amenta, M.D., Ph.D.

NEW MEXICO

University of New Mexico School of Medicine
Paul B. Roth, M.D., M.S.

NEW YORK

Albany Medical College
Vincent P. Verdile, M.D., M.S.

Albert Einstein College of Medicine of
Yeshiva University
Allen M. Spiegel, M.D.

Columbia University
College of Physicians and Surgeons
Lee Goldman, M.D., M.P.H.

Hofstra North Shore - LIJ School of Medicine
Lawrence G. Smith

Mount Sinai School of Medicine
Dennis S. Charney, M.D.

New York Medical College
Ralph A. O'Connell, M.D.

New York University School of Medicine
Robert T. Grossman, M.D.

State University of New York
Downstate Medical Center College of Medicine
Ian L. Taylor, M.D., M.B.Ch.B., Ph.D.

State University of New York
Upstate Medical University
David B. Duggan, M.D.

The School of Medicine at Stony Brook University
Medical Center
Kenneth Kaushansky, M.D.

University at Buffalo State
University of New York
School of Medicine & Biomedical Sciences
Michael E. Cain, M.D.

University of Rochester
School of Medicine and Dentistry
Mark B. Taubman, M.D.

Weill Cornell Medical College
Laurie H. Glimcher, M.D.

NORTH CAROLINA

Duke University School of Medicine
Nancy C. Andrews, M.D., Ph.D., M.S.

The Brody School of Medicine at
East Carolina University
Paul R. Cunningham, M.D., M.B.B.S.

University of North Carolina at Chapel Hill School
of Medicine
William L. Roper, M.D., M.P.H.

Wake Forest School of Medicine of
Wake Forest Baptist Medical Center
Edward Abraham, M.D.

NORTH DAKOTA

University of North Dakota
School of Medicine and Health Sciences
Joshua Wynne, M.D., M.P.H., M.B.A.

OHIO

Case Western Reserve University
School of Medicine
Pamela B. Davis, M.D., Ph.D.

Northeast Ohio Medical University
Jeffrey Susman, M.D.

Ohio State University College of Medicine
Charles J. Lockwood, M.D.

The University of Toledo College of Medicine
Jeffrey Gold, M.D.

University of Cincinnati College of Medicine
Thomas F. Boat, M.D., M.S.

Wright State University
Boonshoft School of Medicine
Howard M. Part, M.D.

OKLAHOMA

University of Oklahoma College of Medicine
M. Dewayne Andrews, M.D.

OREGON

Oregon Health & Science University
School of Medicine
Mark A. Richardson, M.D., M.Sc.B., M.B.A.

PENNSYLVANIA

The Commonwealth Medical College
Lois M. Nora, M.D., J.D., M.B.A.

Drexel University College of Medicine
Daniel V. Schidlow, M.D.

Jefferson Medical College of
Thomas Jefferson University
Mark L. Tykocinski, M.D.

Pennsylvania State University
College of Medicine
Harold Paz, M.D.

Temple University School of Medicine
Arthur M. Feldman, M.D., Ph.D.

Raymond and Ruth Perelman
School of Medicine at the
University of Pennsylvania
J. Larry Jameson, M.D., Ph.D.

University of Pittsburgh School of Medicine
Arthur S. Levine, M.D.

PUERTO RICO

Ponce School of Medicine and Health Sciences
Joxel Garcia, M.D.

San Juan Bautista School of Medicine
Yocasta Brugal Mena, M.D.

Universidad Central del Caribe
School of Medicine
Jose Ginel Rodriguez, M.D.

University of Puerto Rico School of Medicine
Pedro J. Santiago Borrero, M.D.

RHODE ISLAND

The Warren Alpert Medical School of
Brown University
Edward J. Wing, M.D.

Council of Deans

SOUTH CAROLINA

Medical University of South Carolina
College of Medicine
Etta D. Pisano, M.D.

University of South Carolina
School of Medicine
Richard A. Hoppmann, M.D.

University of South Carolina School of Medicine,
Greenville
Jerry R. Youkey, M.D.

SOUTH DAKOTA

Sanford School of Medicine The University of
South Dakota
Rodney R. Parry, M.D.

TENNESSEE

East Tennessee State University
James H. Quillen College of Medicine
Philip C. Bagnell, M.D.

Meharry Medical College
Charles Mouton, M.D., M.S.

University of Tennessee Health Science Center College of Medicine
David Stern, M.D.

Vanderbilt University School of Medicine
Jeffrey R. Balser, M.D., Ph.D.

TEXAS

Baylor College of Medicine
Paul E. Klotman, M.D.

Texas A&M Health Science Center
College of Medicine
T. Samuel Shomaker, M.D., J.D.

Texas Tech University Health Sciences Center Paul
L. Foster School of Medicine
Jose Manuel de le Rosa, M.D.

Texas Tech University Health Sciences Center
School of Medicine
Steven L. Berk, M.D.

The University of Texas
School of Medicine at San Antonio
Francisco Gonzalez-Scarano, M.D.

University of Texas Medical Branch
School of Medicine
Donald Prough, M.D.

University of Texas Medical School at Houston
Giuseppe N. Colasurdo, M.D.

University of Texas Southwestern Medical Center at
Dallas Southwestern Medical School
J. Gregory Fitz, M.D.

UTAH

University of Utah School of Medicine
Vivian S. Lee, M.D., Ph.D., M.B.A.

VERMONT

University of Vermont College of Medicine
Frederick C. Morin, III, M.D.

VIRGINIA

Eastern Virginia Medical School
Richard Homan, M.D.

University of Virginia School of Medicine
Steven T. Dekosky, M.D.

Virginia Commonwealth University
School of Medicine
Jerome F. Strauss, III, M.D., Ph.D.

Virginia Tech Carilion School of Medicine
Cynda Ann Johnson, M.D., M.B.A.

WASHINGTON

University of Washington School of Medicine
Paul G. Ramsey, M.D.

WEST VIRGINIA

Marshall University
Joan C. Edwards School of Medicine
Robert C. Nerhood, M.D.

West Virginia University School of Medicine
Arthur J. Ross III, M.D., M.B.A.

WISCONSIN

Medical College of Wisconsin
Joseph E. Kerschner, M.D.

University of Wisconsin
School of Medicine and Public Health
Robert N. Golden, M.D.

CANADA

ALBERTA

University of Alberta
Faculty of Medicine and Dentistry
Verna Yiu, M.D.

University of Calgary Faculty of Medicine
Thomas E. Feasby, M.D.

BRITISH COLUMBIA

University of British Columbia
Faculty of Medicine
Gavin C.E. Stuart, M.D.

MANITOBA

University of Manitoba Faculty of Medicine
Brian Postl, M.D.

NEWFOUNDLAND

Memorial University of Newfoundland
Faculty of Medicine
James Rourke, M.D.

NOVA SCOTIA

Dalhousie University Faculty of Medicine
Thomas J. Marrie, M.D.

ONTARIO

McMaster University
Michael G. DeGroote School of Medicine
John G. Kelton, M.D.

Northern Ontario School of Medicine
Roger Strasser, M.D.

University of Ottawa Faculty of Medicine
Jacques Bradwejn, M.D.

Queen's University Faculty of Health Sciences
Richard K. Reznick, M.D., M.Ed.

University of Toronto Faculty of Medicine
Catharine Whiteside, M.D., Ph.D.

The University of Western Ontario - Schulich
School of Medicine & Dentistry
Michael J. Strong, M.D.

QUEBEC

Faculty of Medicine Université Laval
Renald Bergeron, M.D.

McGill University Faculty of Medicine
David Eidelman, M.D.

Universite de Montreal Faculty of Medicine
Hélène Boisjoly, M.D.

Universite de Sherbrooke Faculty of Medicine
Pierre Cossette, M.D.

SASKATCHEWAN

University of Saskatchewan College of Medicine
William L. Albritton, M.D., Ph.D.

Council of Academic Societies

2012

Council of Academic Societies Administrative Board, 2011-2012

Chairperson
Kathleen G. Nelson, M.D.
Academic Pediatric Association
Senior Associate Dean for Faculty Development
University of Alabama School of Medicine

Chairperson-Elect
Rosemarie L. Fisher, M.D.
Association of Program Directors in Internal Medicine
Professor of Medicine Director and
Associate Dean Graduate Medical Education
Yale University School of Medicine

Immediate Past Chair
James M. Crawford, M.D., Ph.D.
Association of Pathology Chairs
Senior Vice President for Laboratory Services
Chair, Department of Pathology and Laboratory Medicine
North Shore-Long Island Jewish Health System

Board Members

Richard deShazo, M.D.
American Academy of Allergy, Asthma and Immunology Training Program Directors
Professor of Medicine and Pediatrics
University Hospitals and Clinics/University of Mississippi Medical Center

Evelyn C. Granieri, M.D., M.P.H., M.S.Ed.
American Geriatrics Society
Chief, Divison of Geriatric Medicine
Columbia University College of Physicians and Surgeons

Aviad Haramati, Ph.D.
International Association of Medical Science Educators
Professor of Physiology and Medicine
Georgetown University School of Medicine

Vincent D. Pellegrini, Jr., M.D.
American Orthopaedic Association
Professor and Chair Department of Orthopaedics
University of Maryland School of Medicine

Thomas E. Smith, Ph.D., M.S.
American Society for Biochemistry and Molecular Biology
Professor Emeritus Department of Biochemistry
Howard University College of Medicine

Thomas E. Strax, M.D.
American Academy of Physical Medicine and Rehabilitation
Professor & Chairman, Dept. of PM&R
University of Medicine and Dentistry of New Jersey-University Hospital

Barbara L. Thompson, M.D.
Association of Departments of Family Medicine
Chair, Department of Family Medicine
University of Texas Medical Branch School of Medicine

Thomas C. Westfall, Ph.D.
Association of Medical School Pharmacology Chairs
Saint Louis University School of Medicine
Chairman, Department of Pharmacological and Physiological Science
Saint Louis University Hospital

LuAnn Wilkerson, Ed.D.
Society of Directors of Research in Medical Education
Senior Associate Dean for Medical Education
University of California, Los Angeles
David Geffen School of Medicine

Council of Academic Societies Representatives, 2011-2012

BASIC SCIENCES

ANATOMY AND CELL BIOLOGY

American Association of Anatomists

Steven M. Hill, Ph.D.
Professor and Chair Dept. of Structural
& Cellulary Biology
Tulane University School of Medicine
1430 Tulane Ave # Sl-49
New Orleans, Louisiana 70112-2632

Association of Anatomy, Cell Biology andNeurobiology Chairpersons

Richard D. Dey, Ph.D., M.S.
Professor and Chair, Dept. Neurobiology
& Anatomy
West Virginia University School of
Medicine
PO Box 9128
Morgantown, West Virginia 26506-9128

Michael T. Shipley, Ph.D.
Chair, Department of Anatomy and
Neurobiology
University of Maryland School of
Medicine
20 Penn Street HSF II Rm. S251
Baltimore, Maryland 21201

BIOCHEMISTRY

American Society for Biochemistry and Molecular Biology

William C. Merrick, Ph.D., M.S.
Professor
Case Western Reserve University School
of Medicine
2689 Colchester Rd
Cleveland Heights, Ohio 44106-3650

Thomas E. Smith, Ph.D., M.S.
Professor Emeritus Department of
Biochemistry
Howard University College of Medicine
3121 Brooklawn Ter
Chevy Chase, Maryland 20815-3937

Association of Medical and Graduate Departments of Biochemistry

Yusuf Awni Hannun, M.D.
Senior Associate Dean, Basic Sciences
Chair, Biochemistry & Molecular Biology
Medical University of South Carolina
College of Medicine
173 Ashley Ave
Rm 501A
Charleston, South Carolina 29425-8908

ENDOCRINOLOGY

Endocrine Society

Melissa Kay Thomas, M.D., Ph.D.
Assistant Professor of Medicine
Harvard Medical School
50 Blossom St
Their 306
Boston, Massachusetts 02114-2605

MICROBIOLOGY

American Society for Microbiology

Kenneth I. Berns, M.D., Ph.D.
Director, Genetics Institute
University of Florida College of
Medicine
1376 Mowry Rd
PO Box 103610
Gainesville, Florida 32610-3610

Terrance G. Cooper, Ph.D.
Van Vleet Professor Department of
Microbiology
University of Tennessee Health Science
Center College of Medicine
858 Madison Ave
Memphis, Tennessee 38103-3409

Association of Medical School Microbiology and Immunology Chairs

Dennis Ohman, Ph.D.
Chair, Department of Microbiology and
Immunology
Virginia Commonwealth University School
of Medicine
PO BOX 980565
Richmond, Virginia 23298-0565

NEUROSCIENCE

Association of Medical School Neuroscience Department Chairs

John H. Byrne, Ph.D., M.A.
Associate Dean for Research Affairs
University of Texas Medical School at
Houston
Dept of Neurobiology & Anatomy
6431 Fannin, MSB 7.046
Houston, Texas 77030-1501

Michael Friedlander, Ph.D.
Senior Dean for Research, Executive
Director, VT Carilion Research Institute
Virginia Tech Carilion School of
Medicine
1906 Belleview Ave SE
Roanoke, Virginia 24014-1838

Society for Neuroscience

Michael Friedlander, Ph.D.
Senior Dean for Research, Executive
Director, VT Carilion Research Institute
Virginia Tech Carilion School of
Medicine
1906 Belleview Ave SE
Roanoke, Virginia 24014-1838

M. Kerry O'Banion, M.D., Ph.D.
Director, Medical Scientist Training
Program; Professor of Neurobiology
& Anatomy
University of Rochester School of
Medicine and Dentistry
601 Elmwood Ave
Box 603
Rochester, New York 14642-0001

PATHOLOGY

Academy of Clinical Laboratory Physicians and Scientists

Steven L. Spitalnik, M.D.
Professor of Pathology and Cell Biology
Columbia University College of Physician
and Surgeons
630 W 168th St
New York, New York 10032-3725

American Society for Investigative Pathology, Inc.

Martha B. Furie, Ph.D.
Professor, Center for Infectious Disease
Stony Brook University
5120 Stony Brook University
Room 248 CMM
Stony Brook, New York 11794-4232

Mark E. Sobel, M.D., Ph.D.
Managing Officer
American Society for Investigative
Pathology, Inc.
9650 Rockville Pike
Bethesda, Maryland 20814-3993

Association of Pathology Chairs, Inc.

James M. Crawford, M.D., Ph.D.
Senior Vice President for Laboratory
Services Chair, Department of Pathology
and Laboratory Medicine
North Shore-Long Island Jewish Health
System
10 Nevada Dr
Lake Success, New York 11042-1114

Donald Karcher, M.D.
Chair, Department of Pathology Director
of Laboratories
George Washington University School of
Medicine and Health Sciences
2300 Eye St NW
Washington, DC 20037

PHARMACOLOGY - BASIC

American Society for Pharmacology and Experimental Therapeutics

Brian M. Cox, Ph.D.
Professor Dept of Pharmacology
Uniformed Services University of the
Health Sciences F. Edward Hebert
School of Medicine
4301 Jones Bridge Rd
Bethesda, Maryland 20814-4799

Gary O'Neal Rankin, Ph.D.
Professor & Chair Dept. of Pharm,
Physio, & Toxicology
Marshall University Joan C. Edwards
School of Medicine
One John Marshall Drive
Huntington, West Virginia 25755

Association of Medical School Pharmacology Chairs

Joseph R. Haywood II, Ph.D., M.S.
Professor and Chair, Dept. Pharm. &
Toxicology
Michigan State University
B440 Life Science Building
East Lansing, Michigan 48824-1317

Thomas C. Westfall, Ph.D.
St Louis University School of Medicine
Chairman, Department of Pharmacological
and Physiological Science
Saint Louis University Hospital
1402 S Grand Blvd
Saint Louis, Missouri 63104-1004

PHYSIOLOGY

American Physiological Society

Michael Levitzky, Ph.D.
Asst. Dean for Basic Science Affairs
Louisiana State University School of
Medicine in New Orleans
1901 Perdido St
New Orleans, Louisiana 70112-1393

Association of Chairs of Departments of Physiology

Luis G. Navar, Ph.D.
Professor and Chairman Dept. of
Physiology
Tulane University School of Medicine
1430 Tulane Ave # Sl-39
New Orleans, Louisiana 70112-2632

R Clinton Webb, Ph.D., M.S.
H. S. Kupperman Chair in Cardiovascular
Disease, Regengs' Professor &
Chairperson, Department of Physiology
Medical College of Georgia at Georgia
Health Sciences University
3832 Honors Way
Martinez, Georgia 30907

CAS Representatives

MULTISPECIALTY

International Association of Medical Science Educators

Aviad Haramati, Ph.D.
Professor of Physiology and Medicine
Georgetown University School of Medicine
3900 Reservoir Rd NW Rm 213 Bsb
Washington, DC 20007-2126

Frazier Stevenson, M.D.
UME Associate Dean
USF Health Morsani College of Medicine
12901 Bruce B Downs Blvd
Tampa, Florida 33612-4799

CLINICAL SCIENCES

ANESTHESIOLOGY

Association of University Anesthesiologists

Lee A. Fleisher, M.D.
Professor and Chair of Anesthesiology
Raymond and Ruth Perelman School of
Medicine at the University of
Pennsylvania
3400 Spruce St
Dulles Bldg 680
Philadelphia, Pennsylvania 19104-4206

Roberta Hines, M.D.
Yale University School of Medicine
333 Cedar Street
New Haven, Connecticut 06520

DERMATOLOGY

American Academy of Dermatology

Amit G. Pandya, M.D.
Professor Dept. of Dermatology
University of Texas Southwestern Medical
Center at Dallas Southwestern Medical
School
5323 Harry Hines Blvd
Dallas, Texas 75390-9190

Erik J. Stratman, M.D.
Department of Dermatology
Marshfield Clinic
1000 N Oak Avenue
Marshfield, Wisconsin 54449-5703

Association of Professors of Dermatology

Maria K. Hordinsky, M.D.
Professor and Chair, Department of
Dermatology
University of Minnesota Medical School
420 Delaware St SE
Box 98 UMHC
Minneapolis, Minnesota 55455-0341

EMERGENCY MEDICINE

Association of Academic Chairs of Emergency Medicine

Mark C. Henry, M.D.
Professor and Chair Department of
Emergency Medicine
The School of Medicine at Stony Brook
University Medical Center
Health Science Center L 4 R 080
Stony Brook, New York 11794-8350

Gabor D. Kelen, M.D.
Professor & Chair Department of
Emergency Medicine
Johns Hopkins University School of
Medicine
1830 E Monument St Ste 6-100
Baltimore, Maryland 21287-0020

Council of Emergency Medicine Residency Directors

Patrick H. Brunett, M.D.
Department of Emergency Medicine
Oregon Health & Science University
3181 SW Sam Jackson Park Rd
CDW EM
Portland, Oregon 97239-3098

Hal Thomas, M.D.
Emergency Medicine Council of Residency
Directors
Oregon Health & Science University
3181 SW Sam Jackson Park Rd
UHN 52
Portland, Oregon 97239-3098

Society for Academic Emergency Medicine

Katherine L. Heilpern, M.D.
Chair, Department of Emergency Medicine
Emory University School of Medicine
531 Asbury Cir Ste N340
Atlanta, Georgia 30322-1006

David P. Sklar, M.D.
Associate Dean
University of New Mexico School of
Medicine
1 University Of New Mexico
MSC 11 6093
Albuquerque, New Mexico 87131-0001

FAMILY MEDICINE

American Academy of Family Physicians

Stanley Kozakowski, M.D.
Director, Division of Medical Education
American Academy of Family Physicians
11400 Tomahawk Creek Pkwy
Division Of Medical Education
Leawood, Kansas 66211-2680

Samuel C. Matheny, M.D., M.P.H.
Assistant Provost, Global Health
Initiatives
University of Kentucky College of
Medicine
K-322 Kentucky Clinic
Lexington, Kentucky 40536-0284

American Academy of Family Physicians Foundation

Stanley Kozakowski, M.D.
Director, Division of Medical Education
American Academy of Family Physicians
11400 Tomahawk Creek Pkwy
Division Of Medical Education
Leawood, Kansas 66211-2680

Samuel C. Matheny, M.D., M.P.H.
Assistant Provost, Global Health
Initiatives
University of Kentucky College of
Medicine
K-322 Kentucky Clinic
Lexington, Kentucky 40536-0284

Association of Departments of Family Medicine

Elizabeth Baxley, M.D.
Family Medicine Department Chair
University of South Carolina School of
Medicine
Dept Fam & Prev Medicine
3209 Colonial Drive
Columbia, South Carolina 29203

Barbara L. Thompson, M.D.
Chair, Department of Family Medicine
University of Texas Medical Branch
School of Medicine
301 University Blvd
Galveston, Texas 77555-1123

Society of Teachers of Family Medicine

Samuel Cullison, M.D.
Swedish Family Medicine Residency
Swedish Medical Center/Cherry Hill
Program
550 16th Ave Ste 400
Seattle, Washington 98122-5636

Catherine Pipas, M.D., M.P.H.
Associate Professor of Community and
Family Medicine
Dartmouth Medical School
46 Centerra Pkwy Ste 330
Lebanon, New Hampshire 03766-1487

Society of Teachers of Family Medicine Foundation

Samuel Cullison, M.D.
Swedish Family Medicine Residency
Swedish Medical Center/Cherry Hill
Program
550 16th Ave Ste 400
Seattle, Washington 98122-5636

Catherine Pipas, M.D., M.P.H.
Associate Professor of Community and
Family Medicine
Dartmouth Medical School
46 Centerra Pkwy Ste 330
Lebanon, New Hampshire 03766-1487

GENERAL SURGERY

American Surgical Association

L D. Britt, M.D., M.P.H.
Chairman, Department of Surgery
Eastern Virginia Medical School
825 Fairfax Ave
PO Box 1980
Norfolk, Virginia 23507-1914

John M. Daly, M.D.
Dean Emeritus and Harry C. Donahoo
Professor of Surgery
Temple University School of Medicine
3401 N Broad Street
Parkinson Pavilion #445
Philadelphia, Pennsylvania 19140-4106

American Surgical Association Foundation

William G. Cioffi Jr., M.D.
Surgeon-in-Chief
Rhode Island Hospital
593 Eddy St
APS 432
Providence, Rhode Island 02903-4923

Linda G. Phillips, M.D.
Senior Assoc Dean for Faculty Affairs
University of Texas Medical Branch
School of Medicine
301 University Boulevard
Office of the Dean of Medicine
Galveston, Texas 77555-0133

Association for Academic Surgery

Anees B. Chagpar, M.D., M.P.H., M.A.
Director, Yale Breast Center
Yale University School of Medicine
310 Cedar Street
P.O. Box 208062
New Haven, Connecticut 06510-3218

Gretchen Purcell Jackson, M.D., Ph.D.
Assistant Professor of Surgery
Vanderbilt University School of Medicine
2200 Childrens Way
7100 Doctors Office Tr
Nashville, Tennessee 37232-0005

CAS Representatives

Association for Surgical Education

Debra A. Darosa, Ph.D., M.A.
Professor of Surgery Vice Chair of
Education
Northwestern University The Feinberg
School of Medicine
3035 Indianwood Road
Wilmette, Illinois 60091

Merril T. Dayton, M.D.
University at Buffalo State University
of New York School of Medicine
& Biomedical Sciences
100 High St
Buffalo, New York 14203-1126

Society of Surgical Chairs

Edward Eugene Cornwell III, M.D.
Professor and Chair, Department of
Surgery
Howard University College of Medicine
2041 Georgia Ave NW Ste 4B02
Washington, DC 20060-0001

Anthony A. Meyer, M.D., Ph.D.
Professor and Chair Department of
Surgery
University of North Carolina at Chapel
Hill School of Medicine
4041 Burnett-Womack Bldg
Campus Box 7050
Chapel Hill, North Carolina 27599

Society of University Surgeons

Vijay Pranjivan Khatri, M.B.Ch.B., F.A.C.S.
Professor of Surgery
University of California, Davis, School
of Medicine
4501 X St Ste 3010
Sacramento, California 95817-2229

Nipun B. Merchant, M.D.
Professor of Surgery and Cancer Biology
Vanderbilt University Medical Center
2220 Pierce Avenue
597 Preston Research Building
Nashville, Tennessee 37232-6860

GENETICS

American College of Medical Genetics

Charles J. Epstein, M.D.
Chair, Department of Pediatrics
University of California, San Francisco,
School of Medicine
PO Box 0748
San Francisco, California 94143-0748

Michael S. Watson, Ph.D.
Executive Director
American College of Medical Genetics
7220 Wisconsin Ave Ste 300
Bethesda, Maryland 20814-4854

American College of Medical Genetics Foundation

Bruce R. Korf, M.D., Ph.D.
Professor and Chair, Department of
Genetics
University of Alabama School of Medicine
720 20th St S # Kaul230
Birmingham, Alabama 35233-2032

Michael S. Watson, Ph.D.
Executive Director
American College of Medical Genetics
7220 Wisconsin Ave Ste 300
Bethesda, Maryland 20814-4854

American Society of Human Genetics

Reed E. Pyeritz, M.D., Ph.D.
Vice-chair
Raymond and Ruth Perelman School of
Medicine at the University of
Pennsylvania
3400 Spruce St
Penn Tower 1115
Philadelphia, Pennsylvania 19104-4206

Association of Professors of Human and Medical Genetics

Robert J. Desnick, M.D., Ph.D.
Dean for Genetic and Genomic Medicine
Mount Sinai School of Medicine
1425 Madison Avenue
Icahn Medical Institute
New York, New York 10029

Louis J. Elsas, M.D.
Professor and Director Center for
Medical Genetics
University of Miami Leonard M. Miller
School of Medicine
PO Box 16820
D820
Miami, Florida 33101-6820

IMMUNOLOGY

American Academy of Allergy, Asthma and Immunology Training Program Directors

Amal H. Assa'ad, M.D.
Associate Professor of Clinical
Pediatrics
Cincinnati Children's Hospital Medical C
Center
3333 Burnet Ave
Cincinnati, Ohio 45229-3039

Richard D. deShazo, M.D.
Professor of Medicine and Pediatrics,
University of Mississippi Medical Center
Host of Southern Remedy
University Hospitals and
Clinics/University of Mississippi
Medical Center
2500 N. State Street
Jackson, Mississippi 39216-4500

INTERNAL MEDICINE

American Gastroenterological Association

David A. Katzka, M.D.
Professor of Medicine Division of GI
Mayo Clinic College of Medicine
200 1st St SW
Rochester, Minnesota 55905-0001

Helen Marie Shields, M.D.
Associate Professor of Medicine Division
of Gastroenterology
Beth Israel Deaconess Medical Center
330 Brookline Ave # Dana501
Boston, Massachusetts 02215-5400

American Society of Hematology

Scott D. Gitlin, M.D.
Associate Professor
University of Michigan Medical School
1500 E Medical Center Dr
C345 Med Inn; Spc 5848
Ann Arbor, Michigan 48109-5848

Elaine A. Muchmore, M.D.
Associate Chief of Staff for Education
Veterans Affairs San Diego Healthcare
System
7037 Via Valverde
La Jolla, California 92037-5645

Association of Professors of Medicine

Victor L. Schuster, M.D.
Chair, Department of Medicine
Albert Einstein College of Medicine of
Yeshiva
1300 Morris Park Ave
1008 Belfer Bldg
Bronx, New York 10461-1900

Association of Program Directors in Internal Medicine

Rosemarie L. Fisher, M.D.
Professor of Medicine Director and
Associate Dean Graduate Medical
Education
Yale University School of Medicine
20 York St # T-236
New Haven, Connecticut 06510-3220

Clerkship Directors in Internal Medicine

Meenakshy K. Aiyer, M.D.
Associate Professor, Department of
Internal Medicine
University of Illinois College of
Medicine-Peoria
530 NE Glen Oak Avenue
SFNB 5680
Peoria, Illinois 61637-4051

Society of General Internal Medicine

Valerie Weber, M.D.
Founding Chair Dept of Medicine
The Commonwealth Medical College
501 Madison Ave Fl 1
Tobin Hall
Scranton, Pennsylvania 18510-2401

MULTISPECIALTY

American Academy of Sleep Medicine

M. Safwan Badr, M.D.
Division Chief, Division of Pulmonary,
Allergy, Critical Care & Sleep Medicine
Wayne State University School of
Medicine
3990 John R St
Detroit, Michigan 48201-2018

Andrew Chesson Jr., M.D.
Dean
Louisiana State University School of
Medicine in Shreveport
1501 Kings Highway
PO Box 33932
Shreveport, Louisiana 71130-3932

American Geriatrics Society

Evelyn C. Granieri, M.D., M.P.H.
Chief, Divison of Geriatric Medicine
Columbia University College of Physician
and Surgeons
5141 Broadway
Allen Pavilion 3 015
New York, New York 10034-1159

American Medical Women's Association Foundation

Lynn C. Epstein, M.D.
Clinical Professor of Psychiatry
Tufts Medical Center
Tufts Medical Center
One Devonshire Place, #3301
Boston, Massachusetts 02109-3567

CAS Representatives

American Sleep Medicine Foundation

M. Safwan Badr, M.D.
Division Chief, Division of Pulmonary,
Allergy, Critical Care & Sleep Medicine
Wayne State University School of
Medicine
3990 John R St
Detroit, Michigan 48201-2018

Andrew Chesson Jr., M.D.
Dean
Louisiana State University School of
Medicine in Shreveport
1501 Kings Highway
PO Box 33932
Shreveport, Louisiana 71130-3932

NEUROLOGY

American Academy of Neurology

Imran I. Ali, M.D.
Associate Dean for Medical Education
Professor of Neurology
The University of Toledo College of
Medicine
3000 Arlington Ave
MS 1195
Toledo, Ohio 43614-2595

American Neurological Association

Richard T. Johnson, M.D.
Department of Neurology
Johns Hopkins University School of
Medicine
600 N Wolfe St
Meyer 6-181
Baltimore, Maryland 21287-0005

David A. Stumpf, M.D., Ph.D.
American Academy of Neurology
1101 Alpine Ln
Woodstock, Illinois 60098-9726

Association of University Professors of Neurology

James J. Corbett, M.D.
Professor
University of Mississippi School of
Medicine
2500 N State St
Jackson, Mississippi 39216-4505

NEUROSURGERY

Society of Neurological Surgeons

Donald Quest, M.D.
Professor of Neurosurgery
New York Presbyterian Hospital
(Columbia Campus)
710 W 168th St
New York, New York 10032-3726

OBSTETRICS AND GYNECOLOGY

American College of Obstetricians and Gynecologists

Sharon T. Phelan, M.D.
Professor of Ob/GYN Department of Ob/Gyn
University of New Mexico School of
Medicine
13429 Desert Hills Pl NE
Albuquerque, New Mexico 87111

Robert J. Sokol, M.D.
Distinguished Prof. Ob/Gyn; Director for
Human Growth and Development
Wayne State University School of
Medicine
275 E Hancock St
Detroit, Michigan 48201-1405

American Society for Reproductive Medicine

Ricardo Azziz, M.D., M.P.H., M.B.A.
Professor, Obstetrics, Gynecology and
Medicine, President, Georgia Health
Sciences U, CEO, MCG Health System
Georgia Health Sciences University
1120 15th St
Augusta, Georgia 30912-0004

Ponjola Coney, M.D.
Sr. Assoc. Dean for Faculty Affairs
Virginia Commonwealth University School
of Medicine
1101 E Marshall St
Sanger Hall rm 1022 Box 980565
Richmond, Virginia 23298-5048

Association of Professors of Gynecology and Obstetrics

Nancy C. Chescheir, M.D.
Professor, Assistant Dean for Academic
Affairs for Special Projects
University of North Carolina at Chapel
Hill School of Medicine
3010 Old Clinic Building
Campus Box 7516
Chapel Hill, North Carolina 27599-7516

Nadine Katz, M.D.
Sr Assoc Dean Students Academic Affrs;
Professor, Clinical Obstetrics and
Gynecology and Women's Health
Albert Einstein College of Medicine of
Yeshiva
1300 Morris Park Avenue
Belfer Educational Center-Suite 210
Bronx, New York 10461

Council of University Chairs of Obstetrics and Gynecology

Raul Artal, M.D.
Professor and Chair
Saint Louis University-Main Campus
6420 Clayton Rd # 290
Saint Louis, Missouri 63117-1811

William Frazier Rayburn, M.D., M.B.A.
Seligman Professor and Chair Department
of Obstetrics and Gynecology
University of New Mexico School of
Medicine
1 University Of New Mexico
MSC 10 5580
Albuquerque, New Mexico 87131-0001

OPHTHALMOLOGY

American Academy of Ophthalmology

Linda Lippa, M.D.
Professor, Dept. of Ophthalmology
University of California, Irvine, School
of Medicine
PO Box 16517
Irvine, California 92623-6517

Association of University Professors of Ophthalmology

Stuart L. Fine, M.D.
Clinical Professor of Ophthalmology
University of Colorado School of
Medicine
42 Wader
Carbondale, Colorado 81623-8603

Robert E. Kalina, M.D.
Professor of Ophthalmology
University of Washington School of
Medicine
325 9th Ave
Box 359608
Seattle, Washington 98104-2499

ORTHOPAEDICS

American Orthopaedic Association

Vincent D. Pellegrini Jr., M.D.
Professor and Chair Department of
Orthopaedics
University of Maryland School of
Medicine
22 S Greene St Ste S11B
Baltimore, Maryland 21201-1544

Eric L. Radin, M.D.
Professor, Orthopedic Surgery
Tufts University School of Medicine
6 School St
Marion, Massachusetts 02738-1514

OTOLARYNGOLOGY

Association of Academic Departments of Otolaryngology - Head and Neck Surgery

Lanny G. Close, M.D.
Professor of Otolaryngology
Association of Academic Departments of
Otolaryngology - Head and Neck Surgery
630 W 168th St
Box 21 PH 11 131 Stem
New York, New York 10032-0021

Scott P. Stringer, M.D., M.S.
Professor/Chair-Department of
Otolaryngology/Comm, Sciences
University of Mississippi School of
Medicine
2500 N State St
Jackson, Mississippi 39216-4500

Society of University Otolaryngologists/Head and Surgeons

Mona M. Abaza, M.D., M.S.
Associate Professor
University of Colorado School of
Medicine
12631 E 17th Ave Ste B205
Aurora, Colorado 80045-2527

PEDIATRICS

Academic Pediatric Association

Kathleen G. Nelson, M.D.
Senior Associate Dean for Faculty
Development
University of Alabama School of Medicine
1530 3rd Ave South, FOT 1207
Birmingham, Alabama 35294

American Pediatric Society

Stephen Berman, M.D.
Director of the Center for Global Health
and Medical Advisor for the Global
Health Institute
University of Colorado School of
Medicine
13123 E 16th Ave # B032
Aurora, Colorado 80045-7106

Richard Lee Bucciarelli, M.D.
Chair, Department of Pediatrics
University of Florida College of
Medicine
P.O Box 100014
Gainesville, Florida 32610-0296

CAS Representatives

Association of Medical School Pediatric Department Chairs

Marianne E. Felice, M.D.
Chair, Department of Pediatrics
University of Massachusetts Medical
School
55 Lake Ave N
Worcester, Massachusetts 01655-0002

Society for Pediatric Research

Leona Cuttler, M.D.
Chief, Pediatric Endrocrinology,
Diabetes & Metab.
Case Western Reserve University School
of Medicine
11100 Euclid Ave Rm 737
Cleveland, Ohio 44106-1716

Thomas P. Green, M.D.
Chair, Dept. of Pediatrics
Children's Memorial Hospital
2300 N Childrens Plz
Chicago, Illinois 60614-3363

PHARMACOLOGY - CLINICAL

American College of Clinical Pharmacology

James F. Burris, M.D.
Director of Geriatrics/Extended Care
Department of Veterans Affairs
4803 Davenport St NW
Washington, DC 20016-4314

Robert W. Piepho, Ph.D.
Dean Emeritus, School of Pharmacy
University of Missouri Kansas
City - School of Pharmacy
2464 Charlotte St
Kansas City, Missouri 64108-2718

American Society for Clinical Pharmacology and Therapeutics

Darrell R. Abernethy, M.D., Ph.D.
American Society for Clinical
Pharmacology and Therapeutics
3740 Thomas Point Rd
Annapolis, Maryland 21403-5009

David W. Nierenberg, M.D.
Sr Assoc Dean, Medical Education Edward
Tulloh Krumm Professor of Medicine
and Pharmacology/Toxicology
Dartmouth Medical School
1 Medical Center Dr
Dhmc 322W Borwell Hb 7506
Lebanon, New Hampshire 03756-1000

PHYSICAL MEDICINE AND REHABILITATION

American Academy of Physical Medicine and Rehabilitation

Martin Grabois, M.D.
Professor and Chairman Department of
Physical Medicine
Baylor College of Medicine
1333 Moursund St
Houston, Texas 77030-3405

Thomas E. Strax, M.D.
Professor & Chairman, Dept. of PM&R
University of Medicine and Dentistry of
New Jersey-New Jersey Medical School
65 James St
Edison, New Jersey 08820-3947

Association of Academic Physiatrists

Joel A. DeLisa, M.D., M.S.
Professor and Chair Dept of Physical
Medicine and Rehab.
University of Medicine and Dentistry of
New Jersey-New Jersey Medical School
30 Bergen St
ADMC 101
Newark, New Jersey 07107-3000

Lawrence R. Robinson, M.D.
Vice Dean for Clinical Affairs and GME
University of Washington School of
Medicine
1959 NE Pacific St
C414 HSC Box 356380
Seattle, Washington 98195-6380

PLASTIC SURGERY

American Association of Plastic Surgeons

Linda G. Phillips, M.D.
Senior Assoc Dean for Faculty Affairs
University of Texas Medical Branch
School of Medicine
301 University Boulevard
Office of the Dean of Medicine
Galveston, Texas 77555-0133

Plastic Surgery Research Council

David W Mathes, M.D.
Department of Plastic Surgery
University of Washington Academic
Medical Center
301 35Th Ave S
Seattle, Washington 98144-2602

PREVENTIVE MEDICINE

Association for Prevention Teaching andResearch

S. Edwards Dismuke, M.D., M.S.P.H
Dean, KU School of Medicine-Wichita Prof
of Preventive Medicine and Internal
Medicine
University of Kansas School of Medicine
1010 N Kansas St
Wichita, Kansas 67214-3199

Lloyd F. Novick, M.D., M.P.H.
Director, Dept. of Public Health
The Brody School of Medicine at East
Carolina University
600 Moye Blvd
Greenville, North Carolina 27834-4300

PSYCHIATRY

American Association of Chairs of Departments of Psychiatry

Jed Gary Magen, D.O., M.S.
Chair, Dept. of Psychiatry
Michigan State University College of
Human Medicine
A222 E Fee Hall
East Lansing, Michigan 48824-1316

Michael J. Vergare, M.D.
Chair, Dept. Psychiatry & Human Behavior
Daniel Liberman Professor
Jefferson Medical College of Thomas
Jefferson University
1020 Walnut St Rm 611
Philadelphia, Pennsylvania 19107-5543

American Association of Directors of Psychiatric Residency Training

Jed Gary Magen, D.O., M.S.
Chair, Dept. of Psychiatry
Michigan State University College of
Human Medicine
A222 E Fee Hall
East Lansing, Michigan 48824-1316

Sidney H. Weissman, M.D.
Professor of Psychiatry
Northwestern University The Feinberg
School of Medicine
625 N Michigan Ave Ste 1910
Chicago, Illinois 60611-3178

American Psychiatric Association

Michael H. Ebert, M.D.
Associate Dean for Veterans Affairs
Yale University School of Medicine
950 Campbell Ave
West Haven, Connecticut 06516-2770

Mark Rapaport, M.D.
Chair, Department of Psychiatry and
Behavioral Sciences
Emory University School of Medicine
101 Woodruff Circle
Suite 4115
Atlanta, Georgia 30322

PSYCHOLOGY

Association of Psychologists in AcademicHealth Centers

Patrick O. Smith, Ph.D.
Associate Dean, Faculty Affairs
University of Mississippi School of
Medicine
2500 N State St
Jackson, Mississippi 39216-4500

RADIOLOGY

Association of University Radiologists

Jocelyn D. Chertoff, M.D., M.S.
Professor of Radiology & OB/GYN, Asst
Dean Clinical Affairs, V Chanc, Dept of
Diagnostic Radiology Dartmouth-Hitchcock
Dartmouth Medical School
1 Medical Center Dr
Lebanon, New Hampshire 03756-0001

Carolyn Meltzer, M.D.
Chair Radiology Dept, Assoc Dean
Research
Emory University School of Medicine
1364 Clifton Rd NE Ste D112
Atlanta, Georgia 30322-1059

Society of Chairs of Academic Radiology Departments

Norman J. Beauchamp Jr., M.D., M.H.S., M.S.P.H
Professor and Chair, Department of
Radiology
University of Washington School of
Medicine
1959 NE Pacific St
Box 357115
Seattle, Washington 98195-0001

THORACIC SURGERY

American Association for Thoracic Surgery

Walter H. Merrill, M.D.
Professor, Department of Surgery
University of Mississippi School of
Medicine
2500 North State Street
Jackson, Mississippi 39216

CAS Representatives

Richard J. Shemin, M.D.
Chief, Div. of Cardiothoracic Surgery
University of California, Los Angeles
David Geffen School of Medicine
10833 Le Conte Ave
62 182 CHS
Los Angeles, California 90095-3075

Graham Education and Research Foundation

Richard J. Shemin, M.D.
Chief, Div. of Cardiothoracic Surgery
University of California, Los Angeles
David Geffen School of Medicine
10833 Le Conte Ave
62 182 CHS
Los Angeles, California 90095-3075

VASCULAR SURGERY

American Vascular Association Foundation

Caron R. Rockman, M.D.
Assistant Professor
New York University Medical Center
530 1st Ave # 6F
New York, New York 10016-6402

Society for Vascular Surgery

Caron R. Rockman, M.D.
Assistant Professor
New York University Medical Center
530 1st Ave # 6F
New York, New York 10016-6402

HEALTH SERVICES RESEARCH

AcademyHealth

Timothy S. Carey, M.D., M.P.H.
Professor of Medicine
University of North Carolina at Chapel
Hill School of Medicine
5039 Old Clinic Building Cb7110
Chapel Hill, North Carolina 27599-0001

Lisa Simpson, M.B., B.Ch, M.P.H., F.A.A.P.
President and CEO
AcademyHealth
1150 17Th St Nw Ste 600
Washington, DC 20036-4647

MULTISPECIALTY

American Academy of Hospice and Palliative Medicine

Robert Arnold, M.D.
Professor of Medicine
University of Pittsburgh School of
Medicine
Montefiore 932 W, 200 Lothrop St
Pittsburgh, Pennsylvania 15213-2582

Susan Dale Block, M.D.
Professor and Chair Dept of Psychosocial
Oncology and Pallative Care
Harvard Medical School
44 Binney Street, SW 411
Dana-Farber Cancer Institute
Boston, Massachusetts 02115

American Headache Society

Alan Finkel, M.D.
Carolina Headache Institute
American Headache Society
103 Market St
Chapel Hill, North Carolina 27516-4071

Noah Rosen, M.D.
Director of Headache Medicine
North Shore- Long Island Jewish Health
System
1554 Northern Blvd Fl 4
Manhasset, New York 11030-3006

American Medical Women's Association

Lynn C. Epstein, M.D.
Clinical Professor of Psychiatry
Tufts Medical Center
Tufts Medical Center
One Devonshire Place, #3301
Boston, Massachusetts 02109-3567

INTERDISCIPLINARY

Academy on Violence and Abuse

F. David Schneider, M.D., M.P.H.
Professor and Chairman of Family and
Community Medicine
Saint Louis University School of
Medicine
1402 S Grand Blvd
Saint Louis, Missouri 63104-1004

Philip Scribano, D.O., M.S.
Medical Director, Safe Place; and
Program Director, Child Abuse Pediatrics
Fellowship Program
Children's Hospital of Philadelphia
NW Bldg, 12th Fl.
34th and Civic Center Blvd
Philadelphia, Pennsylvania 19103

American Society for Bioethics and Humanities

Arthur Derse, M.D., J.D.
Director, Center for Bioethics and
Medical Humanities
Medical College of Wisconsin
2316 East Edgewood Place
Shorewood, Wisconsin 53211

Joseph J. Fins, M.D.
Chief Division of Medical Ethics
Weill Cornell Medical College
435 E 70th St Apt 4J
New York, New York 10021-5339

Association for the Behavioral Sciences and Medical Education

Lynn C. Epstein, M.D.
Clinical Professor of Psychiatry
Tufts Medical Center
Tufts Medical Center
One Devonshire Place, #3301
Boston, Massachusetts 02109-3567

Frederic Hafferty, Ph.D.
Professor
Mayo Clinic College of Medicine
200 First St, SW
Plummer Bldg, 4th Floor, Room 26
Rochester, Minnesota 55905

Association of Academic Health Sciences Libraries

A. James Bothmer, M.L.S., A.H.I.P.
Associate Vice President/Director, HSL
Creighton University School of Medicine
2500 California Plz
Creighton University
Omaha, Nebraska 68178-0001

Deborah Halsted, M.L.S., M.A.
Senior Associate Director of Operations
HAM-TMC Library
Association of Academic Health Sciences
Libraries
Houston Academic Med-TX
Med Ctr Library
Houston, Texas 77030-2809

Society for Academic Continuing Medical Education

Barbara E. Barnes, M.D., M.S.
Associate Dean for CME Associate Vice
Chancellor for Continuing Ed & Industry
Support
University of Pittsburgh School of
Medicine
600 Grant St
US Steel Tower Fl 58
Pittsburgh, Pennsylvania 15219-2702

John R. Kues, Ph.D.
Associate Dean for Continuous
Professional Development
University of Cincinnati College of
Medicine
PO Box 670556
College Of Medicine
Cincinnati, Ohio 45267-0556

Society of Directors of Research in Medical Education

Boyd F. Richards, Ph.D.
Assistant Vice President, Center for
Educational Research and Evaluation
Columbia University College of Physician
and Surgeons
701 W 168th St
LL Rm 10A
New York, New York 10032-3723

LuAnn Wilkerson, Ed.D.
Senior Associate Dean for Medical
Education
University of California, Los Angeles
David Geffen School of Medicine
10833 LeConte Avenue
Suite 60-048 CHS, Box 951722
Los Angeles, California 90095-1722

Council of Teaching Hospitals and Health Systems

2012

Council of Teaching Hospitals and Health Systems Administrative Board, 2011-2012

Officers

Peter L. Slavin, M.D., Chair
President
Massachusetts General Hospital
Boston, MA

Marna P. Borgstrom, M.P.H., Chair Elect
President and Chief Executive Officer
Yale-New Haven Hospital
New Haven, CT

Steven Lipstein, Immediate Past Chair
President and Chief Executive Officer
BJC Healthcare
Saint Louis, MO

Board Members

Gordon Alexander, M.D.
Advisor, AAMC
Children's Hospital Central California
Clovis, CA

Delos M. Cosgrove, M.D.
Chief Executive Officer
Cleveland Clinic Health System
Cleveland, OH

Melinda Estes, M.D., M.B.A.
President & CEO
Saint Luke's Hospital of Kansas City
Kansas City, MO

David Feinberg, M.D.
CEO & IAssoc. Vice Chancellor
UCLA Medical Center
Los Angeles, CA

William Ferniany, Ph.D.
Chief Executive Officer
UAB Health System
University of Alabama at Birmingham
Birmingham, AL

Robert Joseph Laskowski, M.D., M.B.A.
President and Chief Executive Officer
Christiana Care Health Services
Wilmington, DE

Richard J. Liekweg
President
Barnes-Jewish Hospital
Saint Louis, MO

James Mandell, M.D.
President and CEO
Children's Hospital Boston
Boston, MA

Christopher T. Olivia, M.D.
Senior Vice President, Strategic Planning and New
Ventures
West Penn Allegheny Health System
Pittsburgh, PA

Daniel Kalman Podolsky, M.D.
President
UT Southwestern Medical Center
Dallas, TX

Peter F. Rapp
Executive VP and Executive Director
Oregon Health & Science University
Portland, OR

Michael C. Riordan
President/CEO
Greenville Hospital System
Greenville, SC

Steven M. Safyer, M.D.
President/CEO
Montefiore Medical Center
Bronx, NY

Bruce Schroffel
President and CEO
University of Colorado Hospital
Aurora, CO

Irene M. Thompson
President and CEO
University HealthSystem Consortium
Chicago, IL

Larry Warren
Chief Executive Officer
Howard University Hospital
Washington, DC

MEMBER HOSPITALS
UNITED STATES

ALABAMA

Birmingham

Birmingham Veterans Affairs Medical Center
700 South 19th Street
Birmingham, Alabama 35233

Rica Lewis-Payton, Chief Executive Officer, FACHE 205/558-4726
Scott Isaacks, Acting Associate Director, FAAMA
Mary Mitchell, Chief, Fiscal Service 205/933-4486
Susan J. Laing, Ph.D., Associate Chief of Staff for Education 205/933-8701
Donald Cox, Quality Management/Improvement Director 205/933-8101
Affiliation: University of Alabama School of Medicine

UAB Health System University of Alabama at Birmingham
500 22nd Street South
Suite #408
Birmingham, Alabama 35233-0500
Affiliation: University of Alabama School of Medicine

University of Alabama Hospital
619 South 19th Street
Birmingham, Alabama 35249-6505

Michael Waldrum, Chief Executive Officer 205/975-5138
Marybeth Briscoe, Chief Financial Officer 205/975-5413
Eli I. Capilouto, D.M.D., Provost 205/934-4720
Joan Hicks, Chief Information Officer 205/934-4724
W. John Daniel, University Counsel 205/934-3474
Affiliation: UAB Health System University of Alabama at Birmingham;
University of Alabama School of Medicine

Mobile

University of South Alabama Medical Center
2451 Fillingim Street
Mobile, Alabama 36617

Beth Anderson, Administrator 251/471-7110
William Bush, Chief Financial Officer 251/660-5596
Susan Ankersen, Manager of Hospital Information Systems 251/434-3675
Robert A. Kreisberg, M.D., Vice President, Medical Affairs
Dean 251/460-7189
Sharon Ezelle, Director, Quality Assurance 251/471-7394
Affiliation: University of South Alabama College of Medicine

ARIZONA

Phoenix

Banner Good Samaritan Medical Center
1111 East McDowell Road
Phoenix, Arizona 85006

Larry E. Volkmar, Chief Executive Officer 602/239-2716
Jeremy Williams, Chief Financial Officer 602/839-4321
Alan I. Leibowitz, M.D., Chief Academic Officer 602/239-2296
Mike Warden, Senior Vice President Care Management &
  Quality 602/495-6353
David Bixby, Sr. VP/General Counsel 602/495-4130
John Hensing, M.D., Senior Vice President, Medical Affairs 602/747-4477
Anita Hancock, Director, QMS 602/239-6990
Paul Stander, M.D., Chief Medical Officer 602/239-2260
Affiliation: Bannerhealth; University of Arizona College of Medicine

Bannerhealth
1441 North 12th Street
Phoenix, Arizona 85006
Affiliation: University of Arizona College of Medicine

Maricopa Medical Center
2601 East Roosevelt
Phoenix, Arizona 85008

Betsey Bayless, CEO 602/344-5566
Phil Kelly, Interim Chief Information Officer 602/344-8576
Louis Gorman, County Counsel 602/506-8541
Affiliation: Mayo Medical School; University of Arizona College of Medicine

Phoenix Children's Hospital
1919 East Thomas Street
Phoenix, Arizona 85016

Robert Meyer, President and Chief Executive Officer 602/546-0400
Shane Brophy, Chief Financial Officer 602/546-0394
Affiliation: University of Arizona College of Medicine

St. Joseph's Hospital & Medical Center
350 West Thomas Road
Phoenix, Arizona 85013

Linda Hunt, President 602/406-6001
Patty White, R.N., Chief Operating Officer 602/406-3613
John Peters, VP / CFO 602/406-4618
Charles C. Daschbach, M.D., Director, Academic Affairs 602/406-3322
David Furst, Site Director Chief Information Officer 602/406-3034
Matt Stockslager, VP Associate General Counsel General
  Counsel 602/406-5168
Jackie Aragon, Senior Director, Risk Management Quality
  Management/Improvement Director 602/406-6958
Affiliation: Dignity Health; University of Arizona College of Medicine

Members: ARIZONA-ARKANSAS

Tucson

Southern Arizona Veterans Affairs Health Care System
3601 S. 6th Avenue
Tucson, Arizona 85723

Jonathan H. Gardner, Chief Executive Officer 520/629-1821
Spencer Ralston, Chief Operating Officer 520/629-1821
Larry Korn, Financial Manager 520/629-1813
Jayendra H. Shah, M.D., Chief Medical Officer 520/629-1815
Affiliation: University of Arizona College of Medicine

The University of Arizona Medical Center
1501 N. Campbell
Tucson, Arizona 85724

Misty Hansen, Chief Financial Officer 520/694-4091
Shirley Gabriel, Chief Information Officer 520/694-6465
Scott Sahlman, Sr. VP Legal Counsel 520/694-4403
Andreas Theodorou, M.D., Chief Medical Officer 520/626-5485
Kathy Goff, Director Quality and Outcomes Mgmt. 520/694-2635
Affiliation: University of Arizona College of Medicine

ARKANSAS

Little Rock

Arkansas Children's Hospital
800 Marshall Street
Little Rock, Arkansas 72202

Jonathan R. Bates, M.D., Chief Executive Officer/President 501/364-8000
Scott Gordon, Executive Vice President/COO 501/364-1414
Gena Wingfield, Senior Vice President/CFO 501/364-2555
Darrell Leonhardt, Senior Vice President/CIO 501/364-6002
Sherry Furr, Vice President, Legal Affairs 501/364-4862
Bonnie Taylor, M.D., Senior Vice President/Medical
   Director 501/364-1401
Debby Keene, Compliance Officer HIPAA Privacy Officer 501/364-6668
Affiliation: University of Arkansas for Medical Sciences College of Medicine

Central Arkansas Veterans Healthcare System
4300 W. 7th Street
Little Rock, Arkansas 72205

Michael Whinn, Medical Center Director 501/257-1000
Sallie Houser-Hanfelder, Associate Medical Center Director 501/257-5400
William D. White, M.D., Associate Chief of Staff for
   Education 501/257-5300
Jim Hall, Acting Chief Information Officer 501/257-1522
Ronald H. Dooley, Regional Counsel 615/695-4622
Nicholas P. Lang, M.D., Chief Medical Officer 501/686-8111
Jennifer Purdy, Manager Quality Mangement 501/257-5314
Affiliation: University of Arkansas for Medical Sciences College of Medicine

University of Arkansas for Medical Sciences
4301 West Markham Street
Little Rock, Arkansas 72205

Richard A. Pierson, Vice Chancellor for Clinical Programs 501/686-5662
Melissa Fontaine, Chief Operating Officer 501/686-8955
Daniel Riley, Chief Financial Officer 504/686-8496
Kari L. Cassel, Senior Vice President & CIO, Shands
Healthcare CIO, University of Florida Health Sciences
Center 352/273-9675
Mark Haagemier, General Counsel 501/686-7608
Nicholas P. Lang, M.D., Chief Medical Officer 501/686-8111
Sandra Bennett, Director of Quality Management
Barbara Warren, Project Specialist Quality Management
Department
Joseph Jensen, Clerkship Director/Surgery
Affiliation: University of Arkansas for Medical Sciences College of Medicine

CALIFORNIA

Bakersfield

Kern Medical Center
1830 Flower Street
Bakersfield, California 93305

Affiliation: University of California, Irvine, School of Medicine; University of
California, Los Angeles David Geffen School of Medicine; University
of California, San Diego School of Medicine

Duarte

City of Hope National Medical Center
1500 E. Duarte Road
Duarte, California 91010

Michael A. Friedman, President and CEO 626/256-4673
Gary Conner, Chief Financial Officer 626/930-5445
Affiliation: University of California, Los Angeles David Geffen School of
Medicine; University of California, San Diego School of Medicine

La Jolla

Scripps Green Hospital
10666 N. Torrey Pines Road
La Jolla, California 92037

Robin Brown, Administrator 858/554-3174
Linda Hodges, Associate Administrator 858/626-6398
John Armstrong, Regional Fiscal Director 858/626-7600
Stanley D. Freedman, M.D., Chair, Department of Graduate
Medical Education, Emeritus 858/459-5902
Robert Sarnoff, M.D., Chief of Staff 858/554-8862
Miriam Glendon, Director, PI/Risk Management 858/554-3600
Affiliation: Scripps Health; University of California, San Diego School of
Medicine

Members: CALIFORNIA

Loma Linda

Jerry L. Pettis Memorial Veterans Affair Medical Center
11201 Benton Street
Loma Linda, California 92357

Dean R. Stordahl, Director 909/583-6002
John M. Byrne, D.O., Associate Vice President Medical
Affairs for Education 909/583-6004
Shane Elliott, Chief Information Officer 909/583-6042
Jonathan Zirkle, J.D., Attorney, Regional Counsel 909/583-6297
Dwight Evans, M.D., Chief of Staff 909/583-6007
Patricia Zappia, R.N., HealthCare Quality Improvement
Coordinator 909/583-6171

Affiliation: Loma Linda University School of Medicine

Loma Linda University Medical Center
11234 Anderson Street
P.O. Box 2000
Loma Linda, California 92354

Ruthita Fike, Chief Executive Officer 909/558-4308
Kevin Lang, CFO and Treasurer 909/558-7570
Kent Hansen, General Counsel 909/558-2644
Daniel Giang, M.D., Associate Dean/Director of GME 909/558-8479
James Pappas, Vice President, Quality & Patient Safety 909/558-4637

Affiliation: Loma Linda University School of Medicine

Long Beach

Long Beach Memorial Medical Center
2801 Atlantic Avenue
Long Beach, California 90801

Ross Simmonds, Chief Operating Officer 562/933-1116
Michael Nageotte, Executive Director for Medical Education 562/933-2738
J. Scott Joslyn, Senior Vice President/CIO 562/933-9419
Robert E. Siemer, J.D., General Counsel 562/933-9045
S. Gainer Pillsbury, M.D., Medical Director 562/933-1244
Casey Hudson, Executive Director Resource Management 562/933-0017

Affiliation: University of California, Irvine, School of Medicine

Veterans Affairs Long Beach Healthcare System
5901 E. 7th Street
Long Beach, California 90822

Ronald B. Norby, Medical Center Director 562/826-5400
Ada I. Neale, Associate Director 562/826-5401
Charles Feistman, Chief, Resources Health Care Group 562/826-5460
Kathleen Frechen, Acting Chief Academic Officer 562/826-5627
Michael Mitchell, Chief, Information Resource Management 562/826-5457
Sandor Szabo, M.D., Ph.D., Chief of Staff 562/826-5403
Jane Penny, Chief, Quality Management 919/286-6905
Susan Kulvinskas, Acting PI Coordinator 562/826-5419

Affiliation: University of California, Irvine, School of Medicine

Los Angeles

Cedars-Sinai Medical Center
8700 Beverly Boulevard
Los Angeles, California 90048

Thomas M. Priselac, President/CEO 310/423-5711
Mark Gavens, Senior VP/COO 310/423-6211
Edward Prunchunas, Senior Vice President/CFO 310/423-2312
Shlomo Melmed, M.D., Senior Vice President for Academic
    Affairs Director of Burns and Allen 310/423-4691
Darren Dworkin, Chief Information Officer 310/423-6642
Peter E. Braveman, Senior Vice President, Legal Affairs 310/423-5708
Michael L. Langberg, M.D., Senior Vice President, Medical
    Affairs/Chief Medical Officer 310/423-5147
Neil Romanoff, M.D., Vice President for Medical Affairs 310/423-3666
Affiliation: University of California, Los Angeles David Geffen School of
    Medicine

Kaiser Foundation Hospital
4867 Sunset Boulevard
Los Angeles, California 90027

Mark Costa, Chief Executive Officer 323/783-8100
Sanjit Sodhi, Chief Financial Officer 323/783-4868
Donald Marcus, Chief Medical Officer 323/783-4450
Sima Hartounian, Chief Compliance Officer 323/783-7242
Felice Klein, Director, Physician Education 626/405-6473
Susan Holliday, CEO Assistant to Mark Costa 323/783-5992
Affiliation: Kaiser Permanete Foundation Hospitals, Southern California

LAC + USC Medical Center
1200 N. State Street
Los Angeles, California 90033

Peter Delgado, CEO, LAC+USC Healthcare Network 323/409-2800
Steve Matthews, Ph.D., Acting, Chief Operating Officer 323/226-5991
Lawrence Opas, M.D., Associate Dean for GME & DIO 323/226-5721
Affiliation: Keck School of Medicine of the University of Southern California

UCLA Healthcare
10833 Le Conte Avenue
Los Angeles, California 90095
Affiliation: University of California, Los Angeles David Geffen School of
    Medicine

Members: CALIFORNIA

UCLA Medical Center
10833 Le Conte Avenue
Los Angeles, California 90095

David Feinberg, Associate Vice Chancellor and CEO 310/267-9315
Amir Rubin, Chief Operating Officer 310/267-9302
Paul Staton, CFO 310/267-9308
Jane Boubelik, Chief Counsel 310/794-3138
J. Thomas Rosenthal, M.D., Chief Medical Officer 310/267-9310
Theodore Barry, Quality Management/Improvement
    Director

Affiliation: UCLA Healthcare; University of California, Los Angeles David
        Geffen School of Medicine

USC University Hospital
1500 San Pablo Street
Los Angeles, California 90033
Affiliation: Keck School of Medicine of the University of Southern California;
        Tenet Healthcare Corporation

Veterans Affairs Greater Los Angeles Health Care System
11301 Wilshire Boulevard
Los Angeles, California 90073

Donna M. Beiter, Director 310/268-3132
Arthur Friedlander, D.M.D., DLO/ACOS-Education Dept. of
    Veterans Affairs 310/268-3196
Dean C. Norman, M.D., Chief of Staff, Based Services 310/268-3132

Affiliation: Keck School of Medicine of the University of Southern California;
        University of California, Los Angeles David Geffen School of
        Medicine

Orange

University of California, Irvine, Medical Center
101 The City Drive
Orange, California 92868

Terry Belmont, Chief Executive Officer 714/456-6240
Morris J. Fieling, Chief Financial Officer 714/456-6897
Thomas C. Cesario, M.D., Professor of Medicine 949/824-5926
Joy Grosser, Chief Information Officer Information Systems 714/456-5558
Eugene M. Spiritus, M.D., Medical Director 714/456-6844
Mary Owen, Director, Case Management 714/456-8964

Affiliation: University of California, Irvine, School of Medicine

Palo Alto

Veterans Affairs Palo Alto Health Care System
3801 Miranda Avenue
Palo Alto, California 94304
Affiliation: Stanford University School of Medicine

Pasadena

Kaiser Permanente Foundation Hospitals, Southern California
393 East Walnut Street
Pasadena, California 92120
Affiliation: University of California, Los Angeles David Geffen School of
Medicine

Sacramento

University of California, Davis, Health System
2315 Stockton Boulevard
Sacramento, California 95817

Ann Rice, Chief Executive Officer 916/734-0751
Vincent Johnson, Chief Operating Officer 916/703-5470
Claire Pomeroy, M.D., M.B.A., Chief Executive Officer, UC
Davis Health System, Vice Chancellor, Human Health
Sciences, and Dean, S 916/734-3578
Michael N. Minear, Chief Information Officer 916/734-4055
Anna Orlowski, Hospital Counsel 916/734-2288
Allan Siefkin, M.D., Medical Director, UC Davis Medical Ctr 916/734-1166
Marsha Nelson, Manager, CQI & Patient Safety 916/734-2703
Gary Collins, Analyst VII Clinical Quality Improvement &
Patient Safety 916/734-7637
Affiliation: University of California, Davis, School of Medicine

San Diego

Scripps Health
4275 Campus Point Drive
Suite 220
San Diego, California 92121
Affiliation: University of California, San Diego School of Medicine

UCSD Healthcare
200 West Arbor Drive, MC 8986
San Diego, California 92103-8986
Affiliation: University of California, San Diego School of Medicine

University of California, San Diego, Medical Center
200 West Arbor Drive
San Diego, California 92103-8970

Tom McAfee, M.D., Interim Chief Executive Officer & Dean
of Clinical Affairs 619/543-5338
Mona Sonnenshein, Chief Operating Officer
Tom McAfee, M.D., Interim Chief Executive Officer & Dean
of Clinical Affairs 619/543-5338
Edward Babakanian, Director, Information Systems 619/543-6880
Anthony Perez, J.D., Asst VC, HS Affairs 858/822-3855
Angela Scioscia, Executive Ofr Reproductive Medicine 619/543-2699
Andrea Snyder, Director, PIPS 619/543-6475
Affiliation: UCSD Healthcare; University of California, San Diego School of
Medicine

Members: CALIFORNIA

Veterans Affairs San Diego Healthcare System
3350 La Jolla Village Drive
San Diego, California 92161

Gary Rossio, Director 858/552-8585
Debra Dyer, Chief Information Officer 858/552-8585
Eric Lazare, General Counsel 619/400-5240
Jacqueline G. Parthemore, M.D., Chief of Staff 858/552-8585
Janet Tremblay, R.N., Chief, Performance Improvement
   Management 858/552-8585
Affiliation: University of California, San Diego School of Medicine

San Francisco

California Pacific Medical Center
P.O. Box 7999
San Francisco, California 94120

Warren Browner, Vice President, Academic Affairs 415/600-1400
Jack Bailey, Executive Vice President/COO 415/923-3339
John Gates, Chief Financial Officer 415/600-6519
Jerry Padavano, Chief Information Officer 415/750-6405
Affiliation: University of California, San Francisco, School of Medicine

Community Health Network
2789 25th Street
Second Floor
San Francisco, California 94110
Affiliation: University of California, San Francisco, School of Medicine

Dignity Health
185 Berry Street, Suite 300
San Francisco, California 94017
Affiliation: University of Arizona College of Medicine; University of California,
   San Francisco, School of Medicine

San Francisco General Hospital and Medical Center
1001 Potrero Avenue
San Francisco, California 94110

Sue Currin, Chief Executive Officer 415/206-4051
Ken Jensen, Chief Financial Officer 415/206-7848
Philip Hopewell, M.D., Associate Dean 415/206-8509
Robert Brody, M.D., Chief Information Officer 415/206-8267
Kathy Murphy, Legal Counsel 415/206-2380
Affiliation: Community Health Network; University of California, San Francisco,
   School of Medicine

UCSF Medical Center
500 Parnassus Avenue
San Francisco, California 941430296

Larry Lotenero, Chief Information Officer 415/353-4273
Marcia Canning, Chief Campus Counsel 415/476-5003
Ernest Ring, Chief Medical Officer 415/353-2760
Joy Pao, Director, Quality Improvement 415/353-3017
Brigid Ide, Director, Clinical Resource Management 415/353-1989

Affiliation: University of California, San Francisco, School of Medicine

Santa Barbara

Tenet Healthcare Corporation
3820 State Street
Santa Barbara, California 93105

Trevor Fetter, Chief Executive Officer 469/893-6175
Reynold Jennings, Chief Operating Officer 469/893-2790
Bob Smith, SVP, Regional Operations 469/893-2200
W. Randolph Smith, Senior Vice President, Central and
Northeast Divisions 215/255-7408

Affiliation: Creighton University School of Medicine; Drexel University College
of Medicine; Keck School of Medicine of the University of Southern
California; Louisiana State University School of Medicine in New
Orleans

Stanford

Stanford Hospital and Clinics
300 Pasteur Drive
Stanford, California 94305

Martha H. Marsh, President and CEO Hospital and Clinics 650/723-8542
Daniel Morissette, Chief Financial Officer 650/723-3299
Eugene A. Bauer, M.D., President/CEO 650/723-5708
Carolyn Byerly, Chief Information Officer 650/723-3992
Peter Gregory, M.D., Senior Associate Dean for Clinical
Affairs 650/723-9673
Larry Shuer, Chief of Staff 650/725-3038
Mystique Smith-Bentley, Director, Process Excellence 650/723-6363
Kim Pardini Kiely, R.N., Director Quality Improvment &
Patient Safety 650/736-2191

Affiliation: Stanford University School of Medicine

Torrance

Harbor-UCLA Medical Center
1000 W Carson Box 27
P.O. Box 2910
Torrance, California 90509-2910

Jody Nakasuji, Chief Financial Officer 210/222-3004
Darrell Harrington, Associate Medical Director For Medical
Education Chief, Division of General Internal Medicine 310/222-2903
Susan Black, Quality Management/Improvement Director 310/222-2047
Affiliation: University of California, Los Angeles David Geffen School of
Medicine

COLORADO

Denver

Children's Hospital
1056 East 19th Avenue, Box 020
Denver, Colorado 80218

Jim Shmerling, President/CEO 720/777-6040
Jena Hausman, Vice President 612/672-7484
Len Dryer, Chief Financial Officer 720/777-6731
Mary Anne Leach, Chief Information Officer 720/777-1977
John LaCouture, J.D., Chief Legal Officer 720/777-6650
Affiliation: University of Colorado School of Medicine

University of Colorado Hospital
13001 East 17th Place
P.O. Box 6508
Denver, Colorado 80045-0508

Bruce Schroffel, President and CEO 720/848-7833
John Harney, COO 720/848-7814
Anthony Desurio, Vice President & CFO 720/848-7816
Gregory Stiegmann, M.D., Vice President, Clinical Affairs 303/724-2731
Allen W. Staver Esq., Vice President & General Counsel 720/848-7815
Gregory Stiegmann, M.D., Vice President, Clinical Affairs 303/724-2731
Steven P. Ringel, M.D., Vice President & Clinical
Effectiveness 303/724-2188
Affiliation: University of Colorado School of Medicine

Veterans Affairs Eastern Colorado Health Care System
1055 Clermont Street
Denver, Colorado 80220

Lynette Ross, Medical Center Director 303/393-2800
Eliott Vanderstek, Director, Business Office 303/331-5976
Thomas Meyer, M.D., Associate Chief of Staff, Academic
Affiliations 303/393-2880
Leigh Anderson, Chief of Staff 303/393-2820
Jan Kemp, R.N., Acting Quality Management Coordinator 303/393-4650
Affiliation: University of Colorado School of Medicine

CONNECTICUT

Bridgeport

Bridgeport Hospital
267 Grant Street
Bridgeport, Connecticut 06610

William Jennings, Chief Executive Officer 203/384-3478
Hope Juckel Regan, Executive Vice President/COO 203/384-3338
Patrick McCabe, Senior Vice President, Finance 203/384-3775
Karen Anne Hutchinson, M.D., Director, Medical Education 203/384-3446
Mark Tepping, Chief Information Officer 203/384-3619
Bruce M. McDonald, M.D., Senior Vice President, Medical
Affairs 203/384-3717
Michael Ivy, VP Quality Perf. Mgmt & Risk 203/384-3873
Affiliation: Yale University School of Medicine; Yale-New Haven Health System

Danbury

Danbury Hospital
24 Hospital Avenue
Danbury, Connecticut 06810

J. Murphy, President and CEO 203/739-7701
Steven Rosenberg, Chief Finacial Officer 203/739-7000
Gerard D. Robilotti, Executive Vice President 203/797-7414
Peter Courtway, Chief Information Officer 203/730-5200
Michael Eisner, General Counsel, Wiggin & Dana 203/797-7110
Matthew Miller, M.D., Vice President, Medical Affairs 203/797-7966
Dawn Myles, Chief Quality Officer 203/797-7668
Affiliation: New York Medical College; University of Connecticut School of
Medicine; Yale University School of Medicine

Farmington

University of Connecticut Health Center/John Dempsey Hospital
263 Farmington Avenue
Farmington, Connecticut 06030-5355

Michael Summerer, M.D., Hospital Director 860/679-2233
Jim Thornton, Director, John Dempsey Hospital 860/679-2222
John M. Biancamano, Chief Financial Officer 860/679-1145
Peter J. Deckers, M.D., Chief Academic Officer 860/679-2594
Sandra Armstrong, Chief Information Officer 860/679-3855
William N. Kleinman Esq., Assistant Attorney General 860/679-1114
Richard Simon, Chief of Staff 860/679-3533
Affiliation: University of Connecticut School of Medicine

Members: CONNECTICUT

Hartford

Hartford Hospital
80 Seymour Street
P.O. Box 5037
Hartford, Connecticut 06102.5037

Elliott Joseph, President/CEO 860/545-1200
Stephan O'Neill, Chief Information Officer 860/545-3972
Joseph Klimek, Medical Director 860/545-3501
Affiliation: University of Connecticut School of Medicine

Saint Francis Care
114 Woodland Street
Hartford, Connecticut 06105
Affiliation: University of Connecticut School of Medicine

Saint Francis Hospital and Medical Center
114 Woodland Street
Hartford, Connecticut 06105

Christopher M. Dadlez, President and CEO 860/714-5541
Susan Freeman, M.D., Senior Vice President for Medical
Affairs 860/714-4361
David C. Stone, J.D., Director, Legal Services 860/714-4656
Affiliation: Saint Francis Care; University of Connecticut School of Medicine

New Britain

Central Connecticut Health Alliance Inc.
100 Grand Street
New Britain, Connecticut 06050
Affiliation: University of Connecticut School of Medicine

New Haven

Hospital of St. Raphael
1450 Chapel Street
New Haven, Connecticut 06511

David W. Benfer, President & CEO 203/789-3020
Lawrence McMannis, Vice President, Finance & CFO 203/789-3000
Charles E. Riordan, M.D., Vice President, Medical Affairs 203/789-4196
Gary R. Davidson, Chief Information Officer 203/789-5921
J.C. Lubin-Szafranski, Vice President/General Counsel
Corporate Compliance Officer 203/789-3942
Charles E. Riordan, M.D., Vice President, Medical Affairs 203/789-4196
Affiliation: Yale University School of Medicine

Yale-New Haven Health System
789 Howard Avenue
New Haven, Connecticut 06504

Marna P. Borgstrom, President and Chief Executive Officer 203/688-2608
Affiliation: Yale University School of Medicine

Yale-New Haven Hospital

20 York Street
New Haven, Connecticut 06510

Marna P. Borgstrom, President and Chief Executive Officer 203/688-2608
Richard Aquila, Executive Vice President & Chief Operating
    Officer 203/688-2606
Peter Herbert, M.D., Senior Vice President, Medical Affairs 203/688-2604
Mark Andersen, Senior Vice President, Information Services 203/688-2100
William Aseltyne, Vice President, Legal Services 203/688-2291
Peter Herbert, M.D., Senior Vice President, Medical Affairs 203/688-2604
William Crede, M.D., Med Dir/CQI/Co-Director 203/688-2252

Affiliation: Yale University School of Medicine; Yale-New Haven Health System

Norwalk

Norwalk Hospital

34 Maple Street
Norwalk, Connecticut 06856

Geoffrey Cole, Chief Executive Officer 203/852-2211
Daniel Debarba, Vice President of Finance/CFO 203/852-2000
Lynda Nemeth, R.N., Director, Quality Assurance 203/852-2732

Affiliation: Chicago Medical School at Rosalind Franklin University of Medicine
    & Science; Yale University School of Medicine

Stamford

Stamford Health System

P.O. Box 9317
Stamford, Connecticut 06904-9317

Affiliation: Columbia University College of Physicians and Surgeons

Stamford Hospital

Shelburne Road & West Broad Street
P.O. Box 9317
Stamford, Connecticut 06904-9317

Brian G. Grissler, President/CEO 203/325-5555
Kathleen A. Silard, Senior Vice President, Operations 203/325-7505
Noel I. Robin, M.D., Chair, Department of Medicine 203/276-7485

Affiliation: Columbia University College of Physicians and Surgeons; Stamford
    Health System

West Haven

VA Connecticut Health Care System

950 Campbell Avenue
West Haven, Connecticut 06516

Karen Waghorn, Chief Operating Officer 203/937-3889
Jeffrey Lustman, M.D., Associate Chief of Staff 203/937-3827
Joseph Erdos, M.D., Chief Information Officer 203/932-5711
Michael H. Ebert, M.D., Associate Dean for Veterans Affairs 203/937-3825

Affiliation: Yale University School of Medicine

DELAWARE

Newark

Christiana Care Health System
P.O. Box 1668
Newark, Delaware 19899

Robert J. Laskowski, M.D., President and Chief Executive
Officer 302/428-2570
Gary W. Ferguson, M.P.H., Chief Operating Officer 302/733-1321
Thomas Corrigan, Senior VP, Finance/Managed Care and
CFO 302/623-7203
Brian W. Little, M.D., Ph.D., Chief Academic Officer 302/733-1042
Randall Gaboriault, Chief Information Officer 302/327-3628
Brenda K. Pierce, J.D., R.N., Corporate Counsel, Legal
Affairs 302/623-4474
Jim H. Newman, Sr. VP & Executive Director, Value Institute
& CAO 302/733-2071
Sharon Anderson, R.N., Senior VP, PI and Care
Management 302/733-1203
Paula L. Stillman, M.D., Senior VP, Special Projects 302/733-1346
Mario Voli, Cost Analysis Manager 302/623-7230
Michele Campbell, Corp Director, Pt Safety & Accreditation 302/733-4982
Affiliation: Jefferson Medical College of Thomas Jefferson University

Wilmington

Veterans Affairs Medical and Regional Office Center
1601 Kirkwood Highway
Wilmington, Delaware 19805

Charles M. Dorman, Medical Center Director 302/633-5201
David A. Cord, Associate Director for Operations 302/633-5202
Loci Barbanel, Chief Financial Officer 302/633-5432
Scott Viars, Chief of Information Technology 302/633-5450
Enrique Guttin, Chief of Staff 302/633-5203
Affiliation: Jefferson Medical College of Thomas Jefferson University; University
of Maryland School of Medicine

DISTRICT OF COLUMBIA

Washington

Children's National Medical Center
111 Michigan Avenue, N.W.
Washington, District of Columbia 20010

Jody M. Burdell, Vice President & Cheif Operating Officer 202/884-3924
Mark L. Batshaw, M.D., Chief Academic Officer/Chairman
of Pediatrics 202/884-4007
Kelly Styles, Chief Information Officer 202/884-3792
Raymond S. Sczudlo, Vice President & Chief Legal Officer 202/884-4502
Peter Holbrook, M.D., Chief Medical Officer 202/884-3256
Kathleen Chavanu, Director, Performance Improvement and
Case Management 202/884-4750

Affiliation: George Washington University School of Medicine and Health
Sciences

George Washington University Hospital
2131 K Street, N.W.
Washington, District of Columbia 20037

Kim Russo, Interim CEO 202/715-4006
Richard Davis, Chief Financial Officer 202/715-4006
John F. Williams Jr., M.D., Provost and Vice President for
Health Affairs School of Medicine & Health Sciences 202/994-3727
Gretchen Tegethoff, Chief Information Officer 202/207-7298
Matt Kllem, General Counsel 800/347-7750
Frederick Lough, Clinical Director of Cardiac Surgery 202/775-9371

Affiliation: George Washington University School of Medicine and Health
Sciences; Universal Health Services, Inc.

Georgetown University Hospital
3800 Reservoir Road, N.W.
Washington, District of Columbia 20007

Richard Goldberg, M.D., President 202/444-8645
Joyce Johnson, D.N.S., Senior Vice President, Operations 202/444-3000
Paul Warda, Chief Financial Officer 202/444-4724
Sam W. Wiesel, M.D., Chief Academic Officer 202/687-4601
Catherine Szenczy, Chief Information Officer 410/772-6500
Alex Eremia, General Counsel 202/444-1751
Richard Goldberg, M.D., President 202/444-8645
Helen Turner, Director, Quality Improvement and Medical
Staff Affairs 202/444-3161

Affiliation: Georgetown University School of Medicine; MedStar Health

Members: DISTRICT OF COLUMBIA

Howard University Hospital
2041 Georgia Avenue, N.W.
Washington, District of Columbia 20060

Lilian Chukwuma, Chief Financial Officer 202/865-6660
Alem Moges, Interim Director, Management Services Interim
Director, Management Services 202/865-6781
Natasha Mckenzie, Senior Associate General Counsel for
Health Affair 202/806-8650
Thomas E. Gaiter, M.D., Chief Medical Officer 202/865-6696
Mary Decker Staples, Senior Director, Quality Process
Improvement 202/865-6704

Affiliation: Howard University College of Medicine

Universal Health Services, Inc.
901 23rd Street, N.W.
Washington, District of Columbia 20037

Affiliation: George Washington University School of Medicine and Health
Sciences

Washington DC Veterans Affairs Medical Center
50 Irving Street, N.W.
Washington, District of Columbia 20422

Sanford M. Garfunkel, Medical Center Director 202/745-8100
Nancy A. Thompson, Ph.D., Associate Director, VHA Office
of Special Projects 202/745-2200
Richard Pasquale, Chief, Resource Management 202/745-8229
Galen L. Barbour, M.D., Director, Planning, Education and
Performance Improvement Services 202/745-8416
F. Joseph Dagher, M.D., Chief of Staff 202/745-8225

Affiliation: George Washington University School of Medicine and Health
Sciences; Georgetown University School of Medicine

Washington Hospital Center
110 Irving Street, N.W.
Washington, District of Columbia 20010

John Sullivan, President
Dennis Pullin, Chief Operating Officer
Daniel Macksood, Chief Financial Officer 202/877-6147
James Howard, M.D., Vice President for Academic Affairs 202/877-5285
Joseph Brothman, Assistant Vice President, IS
Robert Ryan, General Counsel/CCO MedStar Health 410/772-6833
Janis M. Orlowski, M.D., Senior Vice President/Chief
Medical Officer 202/877-5284
Christina M. Emrich, R.N., Quality Resource Coordinator 202/877-6822
Bonnie Sakallaris, Quality Management/Improvement
Director
Mary-Michael Brown, Director, Outcomes Measurement 202/877-7957

Affiliation: George Washington University School of Medicine and Health
Sciences; Georgetown University School of Medicine; Howard
University College of Medicine; MedStar Health

FLORIDA

Gainesville

North Florida/South Georgia Veterans Health Care System-Malcom Randall VA Medical Center
1601 SW Archer Road
Gainesville, Florida 32608
Affiliation: University of Florida College of Medicine

Shands Healthcare
1600 S.W. Archer Road
P.O. Box 100326
Gainesville, Florida 32610

Timothy M. Goldfarb, Chief Executive Officer 352/733-1500
William Robinson, Sr VP/Treasurer 352/265-0429
Timothy C. Flynn, M.D., Sr Assoc Dean-Clinical Affairs 352/273-7520
Joan Hovhanesian, Sr. VP/Chief Information Officer 352/265-8317
Paul M. Rosenberg, Senior Vice President/General Counsel 352/265-6995
Nicholas J. Cassisi, M.D., Senior Associate Dean for Clinical
Affai 352/265-0429
Debbie Lynn, Director, Quality and Accreditation Shands
Healthcare 352/265-0002
Affiliation: University of Florida College of Medicine

Jacksonville

Shands Jacksonville Medical Center
655 W. 8th Street
Jacksonville, Florida 32209

Jim Burkhart, President & Administrator 904/244-3002
Greg Millard, Chief Operating Officer 904/244-3558
Guy Benrubi, Chief Academic Officer 904/244-3112
Bill Hastede, Director of Information Services 904/244-4846
Charles Caniff, Vice President General Counsel 904/244-4000
David Vukich, Chief Medical Officer & Vice President 904/244-6340
Joni Lourcey, Dir Quality/Risk Managment 904/244-3477
Affiliation: University of Florida College of Medicine

St. Luke's Hospital
4201 Belfort Road
Jacksonville, Florida 32216
Affiliation: Florida State University College of Medicine; Mayo Medical School;
University of Florida College of Medicine

Members: FLORIDA

Miami

Jackson Memorial Hospital
1611 N.W. 12th Avenue
Miami, Florida 33136

Eneida Roldan, M.D., M.P.H., M.B.A., President and CEO 305/585-6754
Steven M. Klein, Executive Vice President/Chief Operating
Officer 305/585-1111
James S. Phillips, Senior Vice President/CIO 305/585-7137
Eugene Shy, Assistant County Attorney 305/585-1313
Alan Livingstone, M.D., Professor & Chairman DeWitt
Daughtry Family Dept. of Surgery 305/585-1284
Affiliation: University of Miami Leonard M. Miller School of Medicine

Miami Veterans Affairs Medical Center
1201 N.W. 16th Street
Miami, Florida 33125

Mary D. Berrocal, Director 305/324-4455
Paul D. Magalian, Associate Director 305/575-3203
Sandra Cole, Chief Financial Officer 305/575-3115
Gwendolyn Findley, Ph.D., Acting Chief, IRMS 305/324-4455
John R. Vara, M.D., Chief of Staff 305/575-3157
Kathleen Coniglio, Chief, QMPI 305/324-4289
Affiliation: University of Miami Leonard M. Miller School of Medicine

Miami Beach

Mount Sinai Medical Center
4300 Alton Road
Miami Beach, Florida 33140

Steven D. Sonenreich, Chief Executive Officer 305/674-2223
Amy Perry, Senior Vice President & Chief Operating Officer 305/674-2520
Alex Mendez, Sr. VP and Chief Financial Officer Officer 305/674-2089
Tom Gilette, Vice President and Chief Information Officer 305/674-5445
Arnold Jaffee, General Counsel 305/674-2444
Kenneth Ratzan, M.D., Director, Medical Services 305/674-2766
M. Joy, Director, Performance Mgmt. 305/674-2484
Affiliation: University of Miami Leonard M. Miller School of Medicine;
University of South Florida College of Medicine

Orlando

Florida Hospital Orlando
601 East Rollins Street
Orlando, Florida 32803

Lars Houmann, President and CEO 407/303-1531
Affiliation: Florida State University

Orlando Health
1414 Kuhl Avenue
MP 56
Orlando, Florida 32806

Sherrie Sitarik, President and CEO	321/841-5111
Bob Miles, Vice President, Financial Planning Budge	321/843-1046
Jay L. Falk, M.D., Chief Academic Medical Officer	407/237-6324
Rick Schooler, Vice President and CIO	321/841-5233
Timothy Bullard, M.D., Chief Medical Officer	321/848-4242
Stephan J. Harr, Senior Vice President	407/481-7256

Affiliation: Florida State University College of Medicine; University of Florida College of Medicine; University of South Florida College of Medicine

St. Petersburg

All Children's Hospital
801 Sixth Street South
St. Petersburg, Florida 33701

Nancy Templin, Chief Financial Officer	727/767-4787
Joel Momberg, Senior Vice President, Marketing and Community Relations	813/892-4193

Affiliation: University of South Florida College of Medicine

Tampa

H. Lee Moffitt Cancer Center and Research Institute
12902 Magnolia Drive
Tampa, Florida 33612
Affiliation: University of South Florida College of Medicine

Tampa General Hospital
P.O. Box 1289
Tampa, Florida 33601

Ronald A. Hytoff, President/CEO	813/844-7662
Deana Nelson, Executive VP Chief Operating Officer	813/844-7135
Steve Short, Exec VP, Finance and Administration	813/844-4805
Sally Houston, Sr. VP and Chief Medical Officer	813/844-7218
Jim Kennedy, Attorney	813/222-8185
Sally Houston, Sr. VP and Chief Medical Officer	813/844-7218
Chuck Bombard, Director of Quality Improvement	813/844-4097
Nelson Vila, Quality Management/Improvement Director	813/844-7952

Affiliation: University of South Florida College of Medicine

Veterans Affairs Medical Center James A. Haley Veterans Hospital
13000 Bruce B. Downs Boulevard
Tampa, Florida 33612

Stephen M. Lucas, Medical Center Director 813/972-7536
Steven W. Young, Associate Director 813/972-7626
Ariel Rodriguez, M.D., Associate Chief of Staff for Education 813/972-7649
Carolyn Clark, Public Affairs Officer 813/979-3645
Thomas E. Bowen, M.D., Chief of Staff 813/972-7537
Janet Webb, Chief, Quality Management 813/972-7695
Affiliation: University of South Florida College of Medicine

GEORGIA

Atlanta

Atlanta Medical Center
303 Parkway Drive, N.E.
Atlanta, Georgia 30312

William T. Moore, Chief Executive Officer 404/265-6155
William Masterton, Chief Operating Officer 404/265-4301
Lisa Napier, Chief Financial Officer 404/265-4857
George Fuhrman, Program Director General Surgery
    Residency 404/265-6420
Maryland McCarty, Director, Information Systems 404/265-6034
Steven L. Saltzman, M.D., Chief Medical Director 404/265-4585
Lea Gardner, Director, Quality/Risk Management 404/265-3762
Affiliation: Medical College of Georgia School of Medicine; Tenet Healthcare
    Corporation

Children's Healthcare of Atlanta
1600 Tullie Circle
Atlanta, Georgia 30329
Affiliation: Emory University School of Medicine

Children's Healthcare of Atlanta (Includes Egleston and Scottish Rite)
1405 Clifton Road, N.E.
Atlanta, Georgia 30322

Donna Hyland, CEO 404/785-9500
Beth Howell, Senior Vice President Academic Medicine 404/785-7526
Ruth Fowler, Senior Vice President/CFO 404/785-7006
Jay E. Berkelhamer, M.D., SVP, Chief Academic Officer 404/785-7007
Affiliation: Children's Healthcare of Atlanta; Emory University School of
    Medicine

Emory Healthcare
1440 Clifton Road, N.E.
Atlanta, Georgia 30722

John T. Fox, President and Chief Executive Officer 404/778-4432
Jimmy Hatcher, Chief Financial Officer 404/686-7529
Dee Cantrell, Chief Information Officer, RN 404/727-3604
Jane Jordan, Deputy General Counsel Chief Health Counsel 404/712-1512
William A. Bornstein, M.D., Chief Quality and Medical
    Officer 404/686-2821
William A. Bornstein, M.D., Chief Quality and Medical
    Officer 404/686-2821
Affiliation: Emory University School of Medicine

Emory University Hospital
1364 Clifton Road, N.E.
Atlanta, Georgia 30322

John T. Fox, President and Chief Executive Officer 404/778-4432
Robert J. Bachman, Chief Operating Officer 404/686-8500
Jimmy Hatcher, Chief Financial Officer 404/686-7529
Dee Cantrell, Chief Information Officer, RN 404/727-3604
Jane Jordan, Deputy General Counsel Chief Health Counsel 404/712-1512
Ira Horowitz, Chief Medical Officer/ Interim Chair
    Department of Gyn Ob 404/686-8500
Affiliation: Emory Healthcare; Emory University School of Medicine

Emory University Hospital Midtown
550 Peachtree Street, N.E.
Atlanta, Georgia 30365-2225

John T. Fox, President and Chief Executive Officer 404/778-4432
Dane Peterson, COO 404/686-2727
Jimmy Hatcher, Chief Financial Officer 404/686-7529
Dee Cantrell, Chief Information Officer, RN 404/727-3604
Jane Jordan, Deputy General Counsel Chief Health Counsel 404/712-1512
Richard Gitomer, Chief Quality Officer 404/686-8578
Affiliation: Emory Healthcare; Emory University School of Medicine

Grady Memorial Hospital-Atlanta, GA
80 Jesse Hill Jr Drive, S.E.
Atlanta, Georgia 30303

Timothy Jefferson, Executive Vice President/COO 404/616-6162
Sue McCarthy, Chief Financial Officer/Vice President 404/616-7104
Timothy Jefferson, Executive Vice President/COO 404/616-6162
Curtis A. Lewis, Senior Vice President for Medical Affairs 404/616-4261
Affiliation: Emory University School of Medicine; Morehouse School of
    Medicine

Members: GEORGIA

Augusta

Augusta Veterans Affairs Medical Center
One Freedom Way
Augusta, Georgia 30904-6285

Ralph R. Angelo, Associate Director 706/823-2225
Walter Hitch, Chief, Fiscal Department 706/733-0188
Elizabeth Northington, Augusta Informatics Manager 706/733-0188
Thomas W. Kiernan, M.D., Chief of Staff 706/733-0188
Ellen W. Harbeson, Quality Management Coordinator 706/733-0188
Affiliation: Medical College of Georgia School of Medicine

MCG Health, Inc.
1120 15th Street
Augusta, Georgia 30912
Affiliation: Medical College of Georgia School of Medicine

Medical College of Georgia Hospital and Clinics
1120 15th Street
Augusta, Georgia 30912

Dennis Romer, Senior Vice President/CFO 706/721-3929
Hal Scott, Vice President/CIO 703/721-9674
Virginia Roddy, General Counsel 706/721-5709
Ralph John Caruana, M.D., Associate Dean for Clinical
 Affairs & Chair of Clinical Sciences 407/266-1051
Peppy McBride, Director of Quality Management 706/721-6221
Affiliation: MCG Health, Inc.; Medical College of Georgia School of Medicine

Decatur

Veterans Affairs Medical Center (Atlanta)
1670 Clairmont Road
Decatur, Georgia 30033

James A. Clark, CEO 404/728-7602
James A. Clark, Chief Operating Officer 404/728-7602
Vince Covington, Acting Chief Financial Officer 404/728-7685
Norberto Fas, Chief Academic Officer 404/321-6111
Antonia Mohamed, Chief Information Officer 404/321-6111
David Bower, M.D., Chief of Staff 404/728-7604
Pat Booher, Quality Improvement Coordinator 404/728-7676
Gladys Felan, Quality Managerment/Improvement Director 404/321-6111
Vickie Heggen, Quality Management Coordinator 404/321-6111
Affiliation: Emory University School of Medicine

Macon

Central Georgia Health Systems
691 Cherry Street
Macon, Georgia 31201
Affiliation: Mercer University School of Medicine

Medical Center of Central Georgia
777 Hemlock Street
P.O. Box 6000
Macon, Georgia 31208-6000

A. Don Faulk, President/CEO 478/633-1450
Michael Gilstrap, Executive Vice President/COO 478/633-1452
Rhonda Perry, Senior Vice President 478/633-1452
Ken Banks, General Counsel 478/633-6980
Steve Barry, PI/RM 478/633-7932

Affiliation: Central Georgia Health Systems

Savannah

Memorial Health University Medical Center
4700 Waters Avenue
Savannah, Georgia 31404

Margaret M.C. Gill, Sr. VP, Operations 912/350-8515
Jeff Treasure, Sr Vice President and CFO 608/782-9480
Edward E. Abrams, D.Ed., Exec Dir & Associate Dean 912/350-8302
Patricia Lavely, Sr. VP Chief Information Officer 912/350-8544
Debra Geiger, Associate Legal Counsel 912/350-8026
Ramon Meguiar, M.D., Sr V.P. & Chief Medical Officer 912/350-9456

Affiliation: Medical College of Georgia School of Medicine; Memorial Health,
Inc.; Mercer University School of Medicine

Memorial Health, Inc.
4700 Waters Avenue
Savannah, Georgia 31404

Affiliation: Medical College of Georgia School of Medicine; Memorial Health,
Inc.; Mercer University School of Medicine

ILLINOIS

Berwyn

MacNeal Hospital
3249 South Oak Park Avenue
Berwyn, Illinois 60402

Brian Lemon, President 708/783-3380
Scott Steiner, Chief Operating Officer 708/783-2997
Mary Elizabeth Cleary, Chief Financial Officer 708/783-5378
Diana Viravec, M.D., Chief Academic Advisor 708/783-3869
Charles Bareis, M.D., Medical Director 708/795-3400

Affiliation: Vanguard Health System

Chicago

Advocate Illinois Masonic Medical Center
836 Wellington Avenue
Chicago, Illinois 60657

Susan Nordstrom Lopez, President 773/296-7081
Jack Gilbert, Vice President Finance & Support Service 773/296-7809
William Werner, M.D., Designated Institutional Officer 773/296-5888
Adem Arslani, Director, Information Systems 773/296-8022
Michael E. Kerns, Vice President, Legal Counsel 630/990-5026
Robert G. Zadylak, M.D., Vice President Medical
Management 773/296-8004
William Werner, M.D., Designated Institutional Officer 773/296-5888

Affiliation: Advocate Health Care; University of Illinois College of Medicine

Children's Memorial Hospital
2300 Children's Plaza
Chicago, Illinois 60614

Patrick Magoon, M.A., President & CEO 773/880-4008
Gordon Bass, Chief Operating Officer 773/880-4010
Paula Noble, Treasurer/CFO 773/880-3978
Sharon M. Unti, M.D., Asst Prof, Res Prog Dir 773/880-4302
Stanley B. Krok, Chief Information Officer 773/880-4939
Donna Wetzler, General Counsel 773/880-3934
Edward Ogata, M.D., Chief Medical Officer 773/880-4012

Affiliation: Northwestern University The Feinberg School of Medicine

Cook County Hospital
1835 West Harrison Street
Chicago, Illinois 60612

Johnny Brown, CEO 312/864-5500
Michael Ayres, Chief Financial Officer 312/864-0908
Mike Sommers, Chief Information Officer 312/864-8060
Bradley Langer, M.D., Interim Medical Director 312/864-5100
Susan Klein, Director, Quality Assurance 312/864-0800

Affiliation: Loyola University Chicago Stritch School of Medicine; University of
Illinois College of Medicine

Mount Sinai Hospital
California & 15th Streets
Chicago, Illinois 60608

Karen Teitelbaum, Chief Executive Officer Executive Vice
President/COO 773/257-5322
Charles Weis, Chief Financial Officer 773/257-6642
Maurice Schwartz, Director 773/257-6971
Peter Ingram, Vice President, Strategy and Information
Systems 773/257-6541
Maurice Schwartz, Director 773/257-6971

Affiliation: Chicago Medical School at Rosalind Franklin University of Medicine
& Science; Sinai Health System

Northwestern Memorial Hospital
251 East Huron Street
Chicago, Illinois 60611

Dean M. Harrison, President/CEO 312/926-3007
Dennis Murphy, Executive Vice President 312/926-0882
Doug Young, Chief Financial Officer 312/926-6953
Charles W. Watts, M.D., Senior Vice President, Medical
Affairs 312/926-4774
Timothy Zoph, Vice President, Information Services 312/926-3040
Rachel Dvorken, Deputy Gernal Counsel 312/926-2236
Lois Huminiak, Clinical Quality Leader 312/926-1069
Cynthia Barnard, Director, Quality Strategies 312/926-4822
Scott A. Kerth, Manager, Clinical Quality Management 312/926-4823
Affiliation: Northwestern University The Feinberg School of Medicine

Rush System for Health
1653 W. Congress Parkway
Chicago, Illinois 60612
Affiliation: Rush Medical College of Rush University Medical Center

Rush University Medical Center
1653 W. Congress Parkway
Chicago, Illinois 60612

Larry J. Goodman, M.D., President and CEO 312/942-7073
Peter W. Butler, Executive VP and Chief Operating Officer 312/942-8801
Tony Davis, Acting Chief Financial Officer 312/942-5600
Thomas A. Deutsch, M.D., Dean, Rush Med College Provost,
Rush University & Sr VP, Medical Affairs 312/942-5567
Luc Van Tran, Senior Vice President/CIO 312/942-3400
Max Brown, VP Legal Affairs/Gen Counsel 312/942-6886
Thomas A. Deutsch, M.D., Dean, Rush Med College Provost,
Rush University & Sr VP, Medical Affairs 312/942-5567
Phil Shaw, Asst. Vice President, Quality Improvement 312/942-7116
Affiliation: Rush Medical College of Rush University Medical Center; Rush
System for Health

Sinai Health System
California Avenue at 15th Street
Chicago, Illinois 60608
Affiliation: Chicago Medical School at Rosalind Franklin University of Medicine
& Science

University of Chicago Hospitals and Health System
5841 South Maryland, MC1114
Chicago, Illinois 60637
Affiliation: University of Chicago Division of the Biological Sciences The
Pritzker School of Medicine; University of Chicago Hospitals and
Health System

University of Chicago Medical Center
5841 South Maryland, MC1114
Chicago, Illinois 60637

Carolyn Wilson, Director of Operations 773/834-1185
Eric Yablonka, Vice President and Chief Information Officer............................... 773/702-9665
Christopher Clardy, Quality Management/Improvement
    Director 773/702-6412

Affiliation: University of Chicago Division of the Biological Sciences The
    Pritzker School of Medicine; University of Chicago Hospitals and
    Health System

University of Illinois at Chicago Medical Center
1740 West Taylor Street
Suite 1400
Chicago, Illinois 60612

John DeNardo, CEO, UIC Healthcare System 312/413-8202
Bernadette Biskup, Chief Operating Officer 312/996-3909
William Devoney, Chief Financial Officer 312/996-3620
William Chamberlin, Chief Medical Officer 312/996-3893
Audrius Polikaitis, CIO 312/996-0660
Thomas Bearrows, University Counsel 312/996-7762
D. Harms, Associate Dean, College of Medicine 312/996-3056
Janet Spunt, Chief Nursing Officer 312/413-9783
Patrick O'Leary, Director, Hospital Finance 312/996-0923
Mary Ortiz, Administrative Assistant 312/413-9446

Veterans Affairs Chicago Health Care System
333 East Huron Street
Chicago, Illinois 60611-3004

Richard Rooney, Acting Associate Director for
    Administration 312/469-2240
Kalpana Mehta, Chief Fiscal Officer 708/202-2480
Howard Loewenstein, Chief, Information Resources
    Management Service 312/569-6511

Affiliation: Northwestern University The Feinberg School of Medicine

Evanston

NorthShore University Health System
1301 Central Street
Evanston, Illinois 60201

Mark R. Neaman, President/CEO 847/570-5005
Jeff Hillebrand, Chief Operating Officer 847/570-5151
Ruric Anderson, M.D., GME Program Director 847/570-2509
Tom Smith, CIO, Information Services 847/982-5420
Janardan D. Khandekar, M.D., Chairman, Dept of Medicine 847/570-2510
Chyna Wilcoxson, Manager, Clinical Decision Support 847/570-1647
Peggy King, R.N., Sr VP, Quality Improvement 847/570-2094
Elizabeth Behrens, Vice President Quality/Performance
    Improvement 847/570-2218

Affiliation: Northwestern University The Feinberg School of Medicine

Hines

Edward Hines, Jr. Hospital Department of Veterans Affairs
P.O. Box 5000
Hines, Illinois 60141

Nathan L. Geraths, Hospital Director 708/202-5625
Jeff Gering, Associate Director 708/202-5637
Kalpana Mehta, Chief Fiscal Officer 708/202-2480
Barbara K. Temeck, M.D., Chief of Staff 708/202-2154
Gordon Brown, Chief, Information Resources Management 708/202-2432
Earl Parsons, Regional Counsel 708/202-2216
Barbara K. Temeck, M.D., Chief of Staff 708/202-2154

Affiliation: Loyola University Chicago Stritch School of Medicine; University of
Illinois College of Medicine

Maywood

Loyola University Health System
2160 South First Avenue
Maywood, Illinois 60153
Affiliation: Loyola University Chicago Stritch School of Medicine

Loyola University Medical Center
2160 South First Avenue
Maywood, Illinois 60153

Michael Scheer, Senior Vice President/CFO 708/216-4252
Arthur J. Krumrey, VP and Chief Information Officer 708/216-8190
William Cannon, Associate Dean, GME 630/216-0371
Anne Porter, VP for Quality and Patient Safety 708/216-5544

Affiliation: Loyola University Chicago Stritch School of Medicine; Loyola
University Health System

Oak Lawn

Advocate Christ Medical Center
4440 West 95th Street
Oak Lawn, Illinois 60453

James H. Skogsbergh, President/CEO 630/572-9393
Robert Pekofske, VP, Finance 708/346-5133
Robert N. Stein, M.D., Vice President, Medical Management 708/346-5007
Ann Sayvetz, General Counsel 630/990-5089
Leticia Losurdo, Manager, Performance Improvement 708/684-3036

Affiliation: Advocate Health Care; University of Illinois College of Medicine

Members: ILLINOIS

Oakbrook

Advocate Health Care
2025 Windsor Drive
Oakbrook, Illinois 60523

James H. Skogsbergh, President/CEO 630/572-9393
Kathy Nelson, Center for Health Information Services Public
Data Consultant 630/990-5082
Tina Esposito, Manager, Business Analytics Center for
Health Information Services 630/990-5658
Don Calcagno Jr., Director, Center for Health Information
Services 630/990-5570

Affiliation: Chicago Medical School at Rosalind Franklin University of Medicine
& Science; University of Chicago Division of the Biological Sciences
The Pritzker School of Medicine; University of Illinois College of
Medicine

Park Ridge

Advocate Lutheran General Hospital
1775 Dempster Street
Park Ridge, Illinois 60068

Julie W. Schaffner, R.N., Chief Operating Officer/Chief
Nurse Executive 847/723-6004
Jim Kelley, Vice President, Finance 847/723-5561
Kris Narasimhan, M.D., Vice President, Medical Management 847/723-3024
Mark Beitzel, Director, Information Systems 847/723-2014
Michael E. Kerns, Vice President, Legal Counsel 630/990-5026
Pam Hyziak, Quality Management/Improvement Director 847/723-7566

Affiliation: Advocate Health Care; Chicago Medical School at Rosalind Franklin
University of Medicine & Science; Midwestern University Chicago
College of Osteopathic Medicine; University of Illinois College of
Medicine

Peoria

OSF HealthCare System
800 N.E. Glen Oak Avenue
Peoria, Illinois 61637
Affiliation: University of Illinois College of Medicine-Peoria

OSF Saint Francis Medical Center
530 N.E. Glen Oak Avenue
Peoria, Illinois 61637

Keith Steffen, Administrator 309/655-2439
Sue Wozniak, Chief Operating Officer Executive Vice
President 309/655-2668
Ken Harbaugh, Chief Financial Officer 309/671-4398
Tim Miller, M.D., Director of Academic and Medical Affairs 309/655-2244
Michael Cruz, President, Quality and Safety Quality
Management/Improvement Director 309/655-6346

Affiliation: OSF HealthCare System; University of Illinois College of Medicine-
Peoria

Springfield

Hospital Sisters Health System
Sangamon Avenue
P.O. Box 19456
Springfield, Illinois 62794-9456
Affiliation: Southern Illinois University School of Medicine

Memorial Health System
701 N. First Street
Springfield, Illinois 62781
Affiliation: Southern Illinois University School of Medicine

Memorial Medical Center
701 North First Street
Springfield, Illinois 62781

Edgar J. Curtis, President and CEO 217/788-3340
Douglas Rahn, Sr. Vice President and COO 217/788-3181
Robert Kay, Senior Vice President/CFO 217/788-3198
Anna Evans, General Counsel VP Internal Audit and
    Compliance 217/788-4311
Mark Weaver, SVP CMO 217/788-3334
Josh Savage, Vice President Quality & Operations 217/788-3685
Affiliation: Memorial Health System; Southern Illinois University School of
    Medicine

St. John's Hospital
800 East Carpenter Street
Springfield, Illinois 62769
Affiliation: Hospital Sisters Health System; Southern Illinois University School
    of Medicine

INDIANA

Indianapolis

Clarian Health
I-65 at 21st Street
P.O. Box 1367
Indianapolis, Indiana 46206

Daniel F. Evans Jr., President/CEO 317/962-5900
Samuel L. Odle, Chief Operating Officer 317/929-8641
Marvin Pember, Executive Vice President/CFO 317/962-3005
Isadore Rivas, Vice President for Finance 317/962-9303
Rich Johnson, VP/CIO 317/962-8796
Norman Tabler, Sr VP/General Counsel 317/962-3306
Richard Graffis, M.D., Executive Vice President and CMO 317/962-8258
Susan McAlister, Director, Nurs Quality and Reg Comp 317/278-6925
Affiliation: Indiana University School of Medicine

Members: INDIANA

Richard L. Roudebush Veterans Affairs Medical Center
1481 W. 10th Street
Indianapolis, Indiana 46202

Thomas Mattice, Associate Medical Center Director 317/554-0128
Paul Pessagno, Chief, Fiscal Service 317/554-0000
Diane Wiesenthal, Ed.D., Chief Education Officer, Education
Service 317/554-0000
John Burke, Chief Information Officer, Information
Management Services 317/554-0000
John Houff, District Counsel 317/226-7876
Kenneth Klotz, M.D., Chief of Staff 317/554-0412
Mary Ann Payne, Chief, Quality Management 317/554-0000
Affiliation: Indiana University School of Medicine

St. Vincent Hospitals and Health Services, Inc.
2001 W. 8th Street
Indianapolis, Indiana 46240

Vincent C. Caponi, Chief Executive Officer 317/338-7080
Robert M. Lubitz, M.D., Director of Medical Education 317/338-6386
Hall Render Killian, Hospital Legal Counsel 317/338-3218
Daniel LeGrand, M.D., President Medical Staff 317/338-2161
Affiliation: Indiana University School of Medicine

Wishard Health Services
1001 West 10th Street
Indianapolis, Indiana 46202

Lisa E. Harris, M.D., Chief Executive Officer and Medical
Director 317/630-7033
Jim N. Hayman, Chief Operating Officer 317/630-6785
Tony Puorro, Interim CFO 317/630-2241
David J. Shaw, Chief Information Officer 317/630-2487
Jessica Barth, Chief Counsel 317/630-6425
Affiliation: Indiana University School of Medicine

Muncie

Clarian Health Partners Inc.
2401 West University Avenue
Muncie, Indiana 47303

Carol Seals, CFO 765/747-3205
Affiliation: Indiana University School of Medicine

Indiana University Health Ball Memorial Hospital
2401 University Avenue
Muncie, Indiana 47303

Michael Haley, President & CEO
Thomas Gardiner, Chief Operating Officer
Thomas Powers, Vice President Information Systems 765/751-5065
Michelle R. Altobella, VP, Office of Legal & Regulatory
Affairs 765/751-5000
Claire Lee, R.N., Director, Quality Management 765/747-4284
Affiliation: Clarian Health Partners Inc.; Indiana University School of Medicine

IOWA

Des Moines

Iowa Health - Des Moines
1200 Pleasant Street
Des Moines, Iowa 50309

William Leaver, President and CEO
Steven R. Stephenson, M.D., Executive VP and Chief
Operating Officer 515/241-6375
Joseph Corfits, Senior VP and CFO 515/241-6507
Douglas B. Dorner, M.D., Senior Vice President Medical
Education and Research 515/241-5901
Sid Ramsey, Vice President, Business Development 515/263-5375
David Burlage, Associate Counsel 515/241-4651
Mark Purtle, VP of Medical Affairs 515/241-5100
Kathie Nessa, Director of Quality 515/263-5448
Affiliation: University of Iowa Roy J. and Lucille A. Carver College of Medicine

Iowa City

Iowa City Veterans Affairs Medical Center
601 Highway 6 West
Iowa City, Iowa 52246

Barry Sharp, Director 319/338-0581
Gary Million, Quality Management Officer 319/338-0581
Terri Schuchard, Chief Financial Officer 319/338-0581
Steve Breese, Chief Academic Officer 319/338-0581
Nancy Johnson, Staff Attorney/Office of Regional Counsel 515/284-4092
Kevin Dellsperger, Director, MD-PhD Program 573/882-7423
Andrea Moen, Quality Management/Improvement Director 319/339-7173
Affiliation: University of Iowa Roy J. and Lucille A. Carver College of Medicine

University of Iowa Hospitals and Clinics
200 Hawkins Drive, 1353 JCP
Iowa City, Iowa 52242

Kenneth Kates, Chief Executive Officer Associate Vice
President-University of Iowa Health 319/356-3155
John H. Staley, Ph.D., Interim COO Senior Associate
Director 319/356-2681
Ken Fisher, Associate Vice President for Finance 319/384-2844
Paul Rothman, Dean, College of Medicine 319/384-4547
Lee T. Carmen, Assoc. Vice President for Information Sys. &
CIO 319/356-4445
William Hesson, Associate Director/ Legal Counsel 319/356-4009
Saradeep Singh, Asst VP Operational Excellence 319/353-7202
Affiliation: University of Iowa Roy J. and Lucille A. Carver College of Medicine

KANSAS

Westwood

University of Kansas Hospital
2330 Shawnee Mission Parkway, Suite 308
Westwood, Kansas 66205

Bob Page-Adams, President and Chief Executive Officer 913/588-1270
Scott Glasrud, Senior Vice President/CFO 913/945-5464
H. William Barkman, M.D., Chief of Staff 913/588-1200
Bob Page-Adams, President and Chief Executive Officer 913/588-1270
Affiliation: University of Kansas School of Medicine

KENTUCKY

Lexington

Lexington Veterans Affairs Medical Center
2250 Leestown Road
Lexington, Kentucky 40511

Forest Farley, Medical Center Director 606/281-3901
DeWayne Hamlin, CEO/Director 208/422-1100
Walter Zawisza, Acting Chief Fiscal Service 859/233-4511
James R. McCormick, M.D., Associate Chief of Staff for
Education 859/281-4914
June Heligrath, Chief Information Management Service 606/281-5985
Daniel Reese, Chief of Staff 606/281-4902
Linda Cranfill, Quality Management and Improvement
Coordinator 606/281-4901
Affiliation: University of Kentucky College of Medicine

University of Kentucky Hospital
800 Rose Street
Lexington, Kentucky 40536

Richard Lofgren, Vice President Clincial Operations 859/323-5220
Sergio Melgar, Chief Financial Officer 859/323-0053
Zed Day, Associate Vice President/UKHC IT 859/257-6771
Ruth Booher, Associate General Counsel 859/323-1161
Paul De Priest, Chief Medical Officer 859/257-6467
Louise White, Quality Management Director 859/323-8062
Affiliation: University of Kentucky College of Medicine

Louisville

Louisville Veterans Affairs Medical Center
800 Zorn Avenue
Louisville, Kentucky 40206

Michael R. Winn, Associate Director 318/424-6088
Babs Roberts, Chief, Fiscal Service 502/287-6256
Stephanie Mayfield, Asssociate Chief of Staff for Education 502/287-6871
Augustine M. Bittner, Chief Information Officer 502/287-6977
David Busse, J.D., District Counsel 502/287-6122
Marylee Rothschild, Acting Chief of Staff 502/287-6200

Affiliation: University of Louisville School of Medicine

U of L Health Care University Hospital
530 S. Jackson Street
Louisville, Kentucky 40202

James Taylor, President/CEO 502/562-4002
Robert Barbier, CFO 502/562-4004
Troy May, CIO, Information Systems 502/562-3637
John Johnson, General Counsel 502/587-3400
Kay Lloyd, Vice President, Operations Improvement 502/562-4584

Affiliation: University of Louisville School of Medicine

LOUISIANA

Baton Rouge

Baton Rouge General Medical Center
3600 Florida Boulevard
Baton Rouge, Louisiana 70806

William Holman, President/CEO 225/387-7767
Edgardo Tenreiro, Executive VP/COO 225/763-4525
Kendall Johnson, Senior Vice President and CFO 225/763-4040
Floyd J. Roberts Jr., M.D., Chief Medical Officer 225/387-7767
Terri McNorton, Chief Information Officer VP, Corporate
    Communications & Marketing 225/237-1604
Kathy Raymond, General Counsel 225/237-1634
Erin Zeringue, Director, Quality & Safety 225/381-6633

Affiliation: General Health System; Louisiana State University School of
    Medicine in New Orleans; Tulane University School of Medicine

General Health System
3600 Florida Boulevard
Baton Rouge, Louisiana 70806

Affiliation: Louisiana State University School of Medicine in New Orleans;
    Tulane University School of Medicine

New Orleans

Medical Center of Louisiana at New Orleans
2021 Perdido Street
New Orleans, Louisiana 70112

Roxane Townsend, Chief Exective Officer 225/485-9815
Colleen Colligan, Chief Financial Officer 504/903-1012
Wayne Wilbright, M.D., Head, Medical Informatics &
Telemedicine 504/903-3985
Michele M. Zembo, M.D., Director of Medical Staff and
GME 504/988-5869

Affiliation: Louisiana State University School of Medicine in New Orleans;
Tulane University School of Medicine

Ochsner Clinic Foundation
1514 Jefferson Highway
New Orleans, Louisiana 70121

Patrick J. Quinlan, M.D., CEO 504/842-4051
Warner Thomas, Executive Vice President Chief Operating
Officer 504/842-4598
Mark Muller, Chief Financial Officer
Scott Posecai, Executive Vice President Chief Financial
Officer 504/842-4097
William W. Pinsky, M.D., EVP and Chief Academic Officer 504/842-6120
Lynn R. Witherspoon, M.D., Vice President Chief
Information Officer 504/842-3400
Cristina Wheat, Counsel, Leg Aff/Risk Mgmt 504/842-4003
Kent Boyer, Quality Management/Improvement Director

Affiliation: Louisiana State University School of Medicine in New Orleans;
Tulane University School of Medicine

Southeast Louisiana Veterans Health Care System
1601 Perdido Street
New Orleans, Louisiana 70112-1262

Julie Catellier, Director 504/565-4830
Jimmy Murphy, Associate Medical Center Director 504/565-4845
Patricia Smith, Chief Financial Officer 504/558-3649
Paul S. Rosenfeld, M.D., Chief of Staff 504/565-4870
Mike Truett, Chief Information Officer 504/565-4881
Andree' Boudreaux, District Counsel 713/383-2784
Julie Catellier, Director 504/565-4830

Affiliation: Louisiana State University School of Medicine in New Orleans;
Tulane University School of Medicine

Touro Infirmary
1401 Foucher Street
New Orleans, Louisiana 70115

Jim Montgomery, President and CEO 504/897-8246
Susan Pitoscia, Chief Operating Officer 504/897-8485
Jeff Lott, Director, Information Services 504/897-8297
Kevin T. Jordan, Director of Medical Affairs ED Medical
    Director 504/897-8392
Bonnie Bicocchi, Director, Quality Assurance 504/897-7524
Michelle Delatte, Director, Quality Assurance & Utilization
    Review 504/897-8779
Affiliation: Louisiana State University School of Medicine in New Orleans;
    Tulane University School of Medicine

Tulane University Hospital & Clinic
1415 Tulane Avenue
New Orleans, Louisiana 70112

Robert Lynch, CEO 504/988-1595
Andre duPlessis, Chief Operating Officer 504/988-1902
Robert Hatcher, Chief Financial Officer 501/988-6606
Sue Rachuig, Director, Information Services 504/988-2884
Tammy Friloux, Associate Vice President 504/988-5410
Affiliation: Tulane University School of Medicine

Shreveport

Overton Brooks Veterans Affairs Medical Center
510 E. Stoner Avenue
Shreveport, Louisiana 71101

George Moore, Medical Center Director 318/424-6037
Kimberly Lane, Fiscal Officer 318/221-8411
John Leavitt, Ph.D., Chief, Education and Training 318/424-6119
Michael Vesta, Chief, Information Resources Management 311/424-6155
Patrick Keen, Staff Attorney 318/424-6196
Lloyd G. Phillips, M.D., Ph.D., Chief of Staff 318/424-6089
Kathryn L. Brooks, Chief, Performance Improvement 318/424-6141
Affiliation: Louisiana State University School of Medicine in Shreveport

MAINE

Portland

Maine Medical Center
22 Bramhall Street
Portland, Maine 04102

Richard W. Petersen, President and CEO 207/662-2491
John Heye, Vice President for Finance 207/662-2654
Barry Bluemenfeld, Chief Information Officer 207/775-7010
Donald E. Quigley, J.D., General Counsel 207/775-7001
Affiliation: University of Vermont College of Medicine

MARYLAND

Baltimore

Franklin Square Hospital
9000 Franklin Square Drive
Baltimore, Maryland 21237

Carl J. Schindelar, President 443/777-7850
Glenn Visbeen, Senior Vice President 443/777-7115
Robert Lally, Chief Financial Officer 443/777-7248
Anthony Sclama, VP, Medical Affairs, DIO 443/777-7298
Patricia Norstrand, Senior Director Department of Quality,
Risk and Safety 443/777-7039
Affiliation: Johns Hopkins University School of Medicine; MedStar Health;
University of Maryland School of Medicine

Johns Hopkins Bayview Medical Center
4940 Eastern Avenue
Baltimore, Maryland 21224

Richard Bennett, Chief Executive Officer 410/550-0781
Carl Francioli, Chief Financial Officer 410/550-0909
David B. Hellmann, M.D., Vice Dean, Bayview Campus 410/550-0516
Stephanie Reel, VP, Management Systems & Info Services 410/735-7333
Joanne E. Pollak, Vice President & General Counsel, JHM 410/614-3322
Dana Anderson, M.D., Medical Director 410/550-2821
Janet M. McIntyre, Director, Quality Management 410/550-7674
Affiliation: Johns Hopkins Health System; Johns Hopkins University School of
Medicine

Johns Hopkins Health System
600 North Wolfe Street
Baltimore, Maryland 21287

Edward D. Miller, M.D., Dean and CEO
Affiliation: Johns Hopkins University School of Medicine

Johns Hopkins Hospital
600 North Wolfe Street
Baltimore, Maryland 21287

Ronald R. Peterson, President 410/955-9540
Judy A. Reitz, Sc.D., Executive Vice President/COO 410/614-2953
Ronald Werthman, Vice President, Finance/Treasurer 410/955-6552
Stephanie Reel, VP, Management Systems & Info Services 410/735-7333
Joanne E. Pollak, Vice President & General Counsel, JHM 410/614-3322
Beryl J. Rosenstein, M.D., Vice President Medical Affairs 410/955-0620
Richard O. Davis, Ph.D., VP, Innovation and Patient Safety 410/955-8311
Affiliation: Johns Hopkins Health System; Johns Hopkins University School of
Medicine

University of Maryland Medical Center
22 South Greene Street
Baltimore, Maryland 21201

Jeffrey A. Rivest, President and Chief Executive Officer 410/328-0313
Herbert Buchanan, Senior Vice President and COO 410/328-3788
Keith D. Persinger, SVP and Chief Financial Officer 410/328-1382
Jon Burns, Chief Information Officer 410/328-6528
Megan Arthur, Sr. Vice President/General Counsel 410/328-1635
Ingrid Connerney, Dr.P.H., R.N., Senior Director, Quality,
   Safety, CE 410/328-7700

Affiliation: University of Maryland Medical System; University of Maryland
   School of Medicine

University of Maryland Medical System
250 W. Pratt Street, Suite 880
Baltimore, Maryland 21201
Affiliation: University of Maryland School of Medicine

Veterans Affairs Maryland Health Care System
10 N. Greene Street
Baltimore, Maryland 21201-1524

Dennis H. Smith, Director, VA Maryland Health Care System
   (VAMHCS) 410/605-7016
Kathy Lockhart, R.N., Associate Director, Operations 410/642-1012
Thomas Scheffler, Chief, Fiscal Service 410/642-2411
Dorothy A. Snow, M.D., Associate Chief of Staff Performance
   Improvement and Education 410/605-7121
Sharon Zielinski, Chief, Information Resource Service 410/605-7083
Frank Giorno, Regional Counsel 410/605-7600
Chuck Swindell, Director, Performance Assessment
   Management Accreditation 410/605-7009

Affiliation: Johns Hopkins University School of Medicine; University of
   Maryland School of Medicine

Bethesda

The National Institutes of Health (NIH) Clinical Center
10 Center Drive, Room 2C146
Bethesda, Maryland 20892-1504

John I. Gallin, M.D., Director, Clinical Center 301/496-4114
Maureen E. Gormley, Chief Operating Officer 301/496-2897
Jon Mckerby, Chief Information Officer
Patricia Kvochak, General Counsel 301/496-6043
David K. Henderson, M.D., Deputy Director for Clinical
   Care 301/496-3515

Affiliation: Georgetown University School of Medicine; Uniformed Services
   University of the Health Sciences F. Edward Hebert School of
   Medicine

Columbia

MedStar Health
5565 Sterret Place-Fifth Floor
Columbia, Maryland 21044

Kenneth A. Samet, Executive Vice President/CEO 410/772-6500
William L. Thomas, M.D., Executive Vice President for
Medical Affairs & CMO 410/772-6544
Michael J. Curran, EVP Chief Financial Officer 410/772-6626
Catherine Szenazy, Chief Information Officer 410/772-6680
Janis Bahner, VP Performance Improvement 410/772-6562

Affiliation: George Washington University School of Medicine and Health
Sciences; Georgetown University School of Medicine; Howard
University College of Medicine; Johns Hopkins University School of
Medicine

Silver Spring

Holy Cross Hospital
1500 Forest Glen Road
Silver Spring, Maryland 20910

Kevin J. Sexton, Chief Executive Officer 301/754-7010
Brooks Sutton, Chief Operating Officer 301/754-7474
Sarah Shulman, Hospital Attorney 301/754-7438
Blair Eig, Vice President, Medical Affairs 301/754-7060

Affiliation: George Washington University School of Medicine and Health
Sciences

MASSACHUSETTS

Boston

Beth Israel Deaconess Medical Center
330 Brookline Avenue
Boston, Massachusetts 02215

Kevin Tabb, Chief Executive Officer 617/667-0270
Eric Buehrens, Chief Operating Officer 617/667-4609
Steven Fischer, Chief Financial Officer 617/667-1961
John D. Halamka, M.D., Chief Information Officer 617/754-8002
Patricia McGovern, General Counsel & SVP Corp/Comm
Affairs 617/667-7323
Kathy Murray, Director of Performance Assessment &
Regulatory Compliance, Health Care Quality 617/632-0396
Kenneth Sands, M.D., Vice President/Healthcare Quality 617/667-1325

Affiliation: CareGroup, Inc.; Harvard Medical School

Boston Medical Center
1 Boston Medical Center Place
Boston, Massachusetts 02118

Kate Walsh, Executive Vice President 671/638-6911
Meg Aranow, Chief Information Officer 617/638-8505
Stephanie Lovell, VP, General Counsel 617/638-7650
Laurie Harrington, Director of Patient Safety & Risk Mgmt. 617/414-1722

Affiliation: Boston University School of Medicine

Brigham and Women's Hospital
75 Francis Street
Boston, Massachusetts 02115

> **Elizabeth Nabel,** Cheif Executive Officer 617/732-5537
> **Michael Reney,** Chief Financial Officer 617/732-7899
> **Sue Schade,** Chief Information Officer 617/525-6050
> **Joan Stoddard,** General Counsel 617/726-4244
> **Anthony Whittemore, M.D.,** Chief Medical Officer 617/732-8515

Affiliation: Harvard Medical School; Partners HealthCare System, Inc.

CareGroup, Inc.
330 Brookline Avenue
Boston, Massachusetts 02215

> **Paul F. Levy,** Chief Executive Officer 617/667-0270

Affiliation: Harvard Medical School

Children's Hospital
300 Longwood Avenue
Boston, Massachusetts 02115

> **James Mandell, M.D.,** President and CEO 617/355-8555
> **Sandra L. Fenwick,** Chief Operating Officer 617/355-7272
> **David Kirschner,** Chief Financial Officer 617/355-6881
> **Orah Platt,** Dean, Academic Affairs 617/355-6347
> **Daniel Nigrin, M.D.,** Acting Vice President, Information
>   Systems 617/355-8977
> **Stuart Novick,** Senior Vice President/General Counsel 617/355-6108
> **John E. Mayer, M.D.,** Special Assistant to the President 617/355-8258
> **Nina A. Rauscher,** Executive Director Program for Patient
>   Safety and Quality 617/355-7742

Affiliation: Harvard Medical School

Faulkner Hospital
1153 Centre Street
Boston, Massachusetts 02130

> **Michael Gustafson,** Chief Executive Officer 617/732-8894
> **Michael Conklin,** Senior Vice President for Finance 617/983-7159
> **Jim Anzeveno,** Director, Information Systems/CIO 617/983-7457

Affiliation: Tufts University School of Medicine

Massachusetts General Hospital
55 Fruit Street
Boston, Massachusetts 02114

> **Peter Slavin,** President 617/724-9300
> **Cindy Aiena,** Chief Financial Officer 617/726-7814
> **Debra Weinstein, M.D.,** Vice President of Graduate Medical
>   Education 617/726-3616
> **James W. Noga,** Chief Information Officer 617/726-7709
> **Christopher Clark,** Legal Counsel and Director, Office for
>   Interactions 617/724-8079
> **Britain Nicholson, M.D.,** Chief Medical Officer 617/726-8283
> **Elizabeth Mort, M.D., M.P.H.,** Assistant in Medicine 617/726-4106
> **Cyrus Hopkins, M.D.,** Office of Quality & Patient Safety 617/726-4304
> **Richard Corder,** Senior Director Service Improvement 617/724-2838

Affiliation: Harvard Medical School; Partners HealthCare System, Inc.

Members: MASSACHUSETTS

Partners HealthCare System, Inc.
800 Bolyston Street
Suite 1150
Boston, Massachusetts 02199

Gary Gottlieb, President 617/732-5537
Thomas P. Glynn, Ph.D., Chief Operating Officer 617/278-1005
Peter Markell, Chief Financial Officer 617/724-4537
George Thibault, M.D., President 212/486-2424
Maureen Goggin, Administrative Director, Office of the
    Chief of Staff 617/278-1028
Linda Shaughnessy, Project Manager, Office of Clinical
    Affairs 781/433-3685

Affiliation: Harvard Medical School

St. Elizabeth's Medical Center of Boston
736 Cambridge Street
Boston, Massachusetts 02135

William Garvin, M.D., Director of Medical Education 617/789-2384
John P. Burke, Chief Information Officer 617/789-2282
Wilson D. Rogers Jr., J.D., Legal Counsel 617/723-1100
H. David Mitcheson, M.D., President, Medical Staff 617/782-1200

Affiliation: Steward Health Care System; Tufts University School of Medicine

Steward Health Care System
500 Boylston Street
Boston, Massachusetts 02116
Affiliation: Tufts University School of Medicine

Tufts Medical Center
750 Washington Street
Boston, Massachusetts 02111

Margaret Vosburgh, Chief Operating Officer 617/636-8700
Kristine Hanscom, Interim Chief Financial Officer 617/636-4242
William Shickolovich, Chief Information Officer 617/636-5899
Jeffrey Weinstein, General Counsel 617/636-2815
David Fairchild, M.D., M.P.H., Chief Medical Officer 617/636-4242

Affiliation: Tufts University School of Medicine

Veterans Affairs Boston Healthcare System
150 S. Huntington Avenue
Boston, Massachusetts 02130

Michael M. Lawson, Director 857/203-6000
Frederick Kanter, M.D., Associate Chief of Staff/ Education 857/364-4141
Richard Wheeler, Chief Information Officer 774/826-2524
Edward Lukey, Regional Counsel 781/687-3600
Michael Charness, Medical Director 857/203-6011
Lynne Cannavo, R.N., Quality Management Manager 508/583-4500

Affiliation: Boston University School of Medicine; Tufts University School of
    Medicine

Brockton

Veterans Affairs Medical Center (West Roxbury/Brockton)
940 Belmont Street
Brockton, Massachusetts 02401

Michael M. Lawson, Director 857/203-6000
Susan MacKenzie, Associate Director 857/203-6001
Joseph Costa, Chief Financial Officer 617/232-9500
Edward Lukey, Regional Counsel 781/687-3600
Michael Charness, Medical Director 857/203-6011

Affiliation: Boston University School of Medicine; Tufts University School of Medicine; University of Massachusetts Medical School

Burlington

Lahey Clinic Medical Center
41 Mall Road
Burlington, Massachusetts 01805

Howard Grant, Chief Executive Officer 781/744-8330
Lynn M. Stofer, Chief Operating Officer 781/744-8623
Timothy O'Connor, Chief Financial Officer 781/744-8134
David J. Schoetz, M.D., Chairman, Department of Medical
Education Professor of Surgery, Tufts University 781/744-8889
Nelson Gagnon, Chief Information Officer 781/744-2922
Donna Cameron, General Counsel 781/744-8408

Affiliation: Harvard Medical School; Tufts University School of Medicine

Cambridge

Cambridge Health Alliance
1496 Cambridge Street
Cambridge, Massachusetts 02139

Patrick Wardell, CEO 617/665-2300

Affiliation: Harvard Medical School

Mount Auburn Hospital
330 Mount Auburn Street
Cambridge, Massachusetts 02138

Jeanette G. Clough, President & CEO 617/499-5700
Nicholas DiIeso, Chief Operating Officer 617/499-5642
Charles J. Hatem, M.D., Director of Medical Education 617/499-5140
Robert Todd, Director of Information Systems 617/599-5606
Leslie A. Joseph, J.D., General Counsel 617/499-5752
Eileen Dillon, R.N., Executive Director, Quality & Safety 617/499-5073

Affiliation: CareGroup, Inc.; Harvard Medical School

Members: MASSACHUSETTS

Pittsfield

Berkshire Medical Center
725 North Street
Pittsfield, Massachusetts 01201

David Phelps, President/CEO 413/447-2743
Helen Downey, COO 413/395-7999
Darlene Rodowicz, Chief Financial Officer 413/447-2994
Henry Tulgan, M.D., Director, Medical Education/Associate
 Dean 413/447-2715
Charles Podesta, Director, Information Services 413/447-2956
John Rogers, Vice President & Coporate Counsel 413/445-9528
Mark Pettus, Chief of Staff
Diane E. Kelly, VP, Quality Management 413/447-2316
Affiliation: University of Massachusetts Medical School

Springfield

Baystate Health System
280 Chestnut Street
Springfield, Massachusetts 01199
Affiliation: Tufts University School of Medicine

Baystate Medical Center
759 Chestnut Street
Springfield, Massachusetts 01199

Mark R. Tolosky, President and Chief Executive Officer 413/794-5890
Trish Hannon, Senior Vice President/COO 413/794-5516
Dennis Chalke, Vice President, Finance, Healthcare
 Operations 413/794-3290
Mark Gorrell, Vice President/CIO 413/794-3230
Loring S. Flint, M.D., Senior Vice President, Medical Affairs 413/794-5612
Janice Fitzgerald, Director, Quality & Medical Management
 Division of Healthcare Quality 413/794-2531
Evan M. Benjamin, M.D., Vice President, Healthcare Quality 413/794-2527
Winthrop Whitcomb, Quality Management/Improvement
 Director
Affiliation: Baystate Health System; Tufts University School of Medicine

Worcester

UMass Memorial Health Care
One Biotech Park
Worcester, Massachusetts 01605

John G. O'Brien, President and CEO 508/334-0100
Wendy Warring, Executive Vice President 508/334-0258
Therese Day, Chief Financial Officer 508/856-2848
Pamela Arora, VP, Chief Information Officer 214/456-6000
Douglas Brown, General Counsel 508/334-0424
Stephen E. Tosi, M.D., Chief Medical Officer 508/334-7746
Affiliation: University of Massachusetts Medical School

MICHIGAN

Ann Arbor

St. Joseph Mercy Hospital
P.O. Box 995
Ann Arbor, Michigan 48106

Garry C. Faja, Chief Executive Officer 734/712-4986
Julie McDonald, COO/Patient Care Services 734/712-2887
Charles Hoffman, VP Financial Services/CFO 734/712-2887
Bruce Deighton, Chief Academic Affairs Officer 734/712-5015
Rolland Mambourg, M.D., Vice President, Physician Services 734/712-7358
Mark E. Cowen, M.D., Medical Director, Quality Institute 734/887-0470
Affiliation: Trinity Health; University of Michigan Medical School; Wayne State
University School of Medicine

University of Michigan Health System
1500 E. Medical Center Drive
Ann Arbor, Michigan 48109
Affiliation: University of Michigan Medical School

University of Michigan Medical Center
1500 E. Medical Center Drive
Ann Arbor, Michigan 48109-0474

Douglas Strong, CEO 734/764-1505
T. A. Denton, COO 734/647-6623
David Morlock, CFO 734/615-0574
Jocelyn DeWitt, Chief Information Officer 734/764-4262
Gloria Hage, General Counsel Health System Attorney 734/764-2178
Deb Guglielmo, Director, Quality Improvement Operations 734/615-5378
Affiliation: University of Michigan Health System; University of Michigan
Medical School

Veterans Affairs Ann Arbor Healthcare System
2215 Fuller Road
Ann Arbor, Michigan 48105

Barbara McLelland, Acting Director 734/845-5258
Karen Ruedel, Chief, Resource Officer 734/845-5700
Mary East, Associate Chief Of Staff For Education 734/761-5382
Marcia Pickard, Acting Chief Information Resource
Management 734/845-5733
Eric Young, M.D., Chief of Staff 734/845-3400
Winifred Verse-Barry, Performance Improvement
Coordinator Quality Management/Improvement Director 734/845-5527
Affiliation: University of Michigan Medical School

Dearborn

Oakwood Healthcare System
One Parklane Boulevard, Suite 1000E
Dearborn, Michigan 48126
Affiliation: University of Michigan Medical School; Wayne State University
School of Medicine

Members: MICHIGAN

Oakwood Hospital and Medical Center
1 Parklane Boulevard
Dearborn, Michigan 48126-4241

Michael Gehab, M.D., Division President 313/553-7125
Ronald Britt, Chief Financial Officer 313/593-7853
Paula Smith, Chief Information Officer 313/724-4506
Mark Lezotte, Corporate Director, Legal Affairs 313/791-1730
Malcolm Henoch, M.D., SVP & Chief Medical Officer 313/253-6009
Sara Atwell, Corporate Director Quality and Care Mgmt 313/791-4620

Affiliation: Oakwood Healthcare System; University of Michigan Medical
School; Wayne State University School of Medicine

Detroit

Detroit Medical Center
3663 Woodward Avenue
Detroit, Michigan 48201-2403

Michael Duggan, CEO 313/745-5192

Affiliation: Wayne State University School of Medicine

Henry Ford Hospital
One Ford Place
Detroit, Michigan 48202

John Popovich, Chief Executive Officer 313/916-8058

Affiliation: Case Western Reserve University School of Medicine; Wayne State
University School of Medicine

John D. Dingell VA Medical Center
4646 John R.
Detroit, Michigan 48201

Pamela J. Reeves, Director 313/576-3234
Leslie Wiggins, Associate Director 313/576-4421
Patricia Kelly, Chief, Finiancial and Budget Service 313/576-1000
Robert C. Johnson, M.B.A., Chief, Business Practice 313/576-3750
Roland Bessette, Regional Counsel 313/471-3644
Basim Dubaybo, Medical Director 313/576-3327
Tarynne Bolden, R.N., Quality Manager 313/576-4644

Affiliation: Wayne State University School of Medicine

Sinai-Grace Hospital
6071 W. Outer Drive
Detroit, Michigan 48235

Conrad L. Mallett Jr., President 313/966-3300
Vernell Williams, Vice President, Operations 313/966-4681
Ken Lipan, Vice President, Finance 313/966-1920
Donald Ragan, Ph.D., Chief Information Officer 313/578-2223
John Haapaniemi, D.O., Chief of Staff 313/966-3224

Affiliation: Detroit Medical Center; Wayne State University School of Medicine

St. John Health System
28000 Dequindre Avenue
Detroit, Michigan 48092-2468
Affiliation: University of Michigan Medical School; Wayne State University
School of Medicine

St. John Hospital and Medical Center
22101 Moross
Detroit, Michigan 48236

Diane Radloff, Executive Vice President 313/343-4000
Tomasine Marx, Chief Financial Officer 586/753-0310
Steven E. Minnick, M.D., Director, Medical Education 313/343-3876
Claudia A. Allen, Chief Information Officer 810/753-1749
Connie Houin, General Counsel 810/753-0461
James Boutrous, M.D., Senior Vice President, Medical Affairs............................... 313/343-3304
Affiliation: Wayne State University School of Medicine

Farmington Hills

Trinity Health
34605 Twelve Mile Road
Farmington Hills, Michigan 48331
Affiliation: University of Michigan Medical School

Flint

Hurley Medical Center
One Hurley Plaza
Flint, Michigan 48502

Patrick Wardell, Cheif Executive Officer 810/257-9237
Kevin Murphy, Chief Financial Officer 810/257-9396
Daniel Coffield, Executive Vice President and Chief
Financial Officer 810/257-9844
Patrick Milostan, Chief Information Officer 810/257-9642
Michael Boucree, M.D., Medical Director 810/257-9544
Chris Surratt, R.N., Director, Quality Management/
Improvement 810/762-6336
Affiliation: Michigan State University College of Human Medicine; University
of Michigan Medical School

McLaren Healthcare Corporation
401 S. Ballenger Highway
Flint, Michigan 48532
Affiliation: Michigan State University College of Human Medicine

Members: MICHIGAN

McLaren Regional Medical Center
401 S. Ballenger Highway
Flint, Michigan 48532

Donald C. Kooy, President/CEO 810/342-2446
Brent Wheeler, Vice President of Ancillary/Support Serv
   Chief Operating Officer 810/342-4407
Rick Wyles, Chief Financial Officer 810/342-2516
Paul M. Romanelli, Ph.D., Director of Medical Education 810/342-2321
Donald C. Kooy, President/CEO 810/342-2446
Richard Sardelli, Director of Legal Affairs/Risk Management 810/342-2427
Edwin H. Gullekson, M.D., VP Medical Affairs 810/342-2450

Affiliation: McLaren Healthcare Corporation; Michigan State University
    College of Human Medicine

Grand Rapids

Spectrum Health
100 Michigan Street, NE
Grand Rapids, Michigan 49503
Affiliation: Michigan State University College of Human Medicine

Spectrum Health, East Campus
1840 Wealthy Street, S.E.
Grand Rapids, Michigan 49506
Affiliation: Spectrum Health

Kalamazoo

Bronson Methodist Hospital
601 John Street
Kalamazoo, Michigan 49007

Frank J. Sardone, President and Chief Executive Officer 269/341-6000
Kenneth Taft, Executive Vice President and Chief Operating
   Officer 269/341-6000
Mary Meitz, Vice President, Chief Financial Officer 269/341-6000
Milton McClurkan Jr., Vice President, Information
   Technology/CIO 269/341-6000
James B. Falahee Jr., J.D., General Counsel 269/341-6000
Jane Janssen, Director 269/341-8539

Affiliation: Michigan State University College of Human Medicine

Lansing

Ingham Regional Medical Center
401 W. Greenlawn Avenue
Lansing, Michigan 48910
Affiliation: Michigan State University College of Human Medicine

Royal Oak

Beaumont Hospital
3601 W. Thirteen Mile Road
Royal Oak, Michigan 48073

Gene Michalski, President and CEO 248/551-0674
Dennis Herrick, Senior Vice President/CFO 248/551-0676
John Musich, Vice President and Director, Medical
Education Designated Institutional Official 248/551-0427
Paul S. Peabody, Vice President/Chief Information Officer 248/597-2800
Thomas McAskin, Vice President and Chief Legal Officer 248/551-0572
Leslie Rocher, Physician-in-Chief, Senior Vice President 248/551-0406
Oltion Chabay, Quality Management/Improvement Director
Samuel Flanders, Sr. V.P. and Chief Quality Officer 248/551-0336
Gloria Seidl, Quality Management/Improvement Director
Wendy Chandler, Director, Outpatient Quality Measures
Corporate Quality 248/551-1507
Paula Levesque, Corporate Director, External Quality
Measures 248/551-0605

Affiliation: Beaumont Hospital System

Beaumont Hospital System
3601 West 13 Mile Road
Royal Oak, Michigan 48073
Affiliation: University of Michigan Medical School; Wayne State University
School of Medicine

MINNESOTA

Bloomington

HealthPartners, Inc.
8100 34th Avenue South
P.O. Box 1309
Bloomington, Minnesota 55440-1309
Affiliation: University of Minnesota Medical School

Minneapolis

Abbott Northwestern Hospital
800 East 28th Street
Minneapolis, Minnesota 55407

Brian Weinreis, Vice President of Finance 612/863-1920
Robert Wieland, VP, Medical Affairs 612/863-4509
Sue Carlson, Director, Quality and Patient Safety 612/863-4875

Affiliation: Allina Hospitals and Clinics; University of Minnesota Medical
School

Allina Hospitals and Clinics
710 East 24th Street
PEI Medical Office Building
Minneapolis, Minnesota 55405
Affiliation: University of Minnesota Medical School

Members: MINNESOTA

Fairview Health Services
2450 Riverside Avenue
Minneapolis, Minnesota 55454
Affiliation: University of Minnesota Medical School

Hennepin County Medical Center
701 Park Avenue South
Minneapolis, Minnesota 55415

Larry Kryzaniak, Chief Financial Officer 612/873-3040
Andy Mitchell, Assistant County Attorney 512/873-3195
Michael Belzer, Medical Director and Chief Medical Officer 612/873-2979
Affiliation: University of Minnesota Medical School

Minneapolis Veterans Affairs Medical Center
One Veterans Drive
Minneapolis, Minnesota 55417

Steven P. Kleinglass, Medical Center Director 612/725-2101
Paul Resel, Chief, Fiscal Service 612/725-2150
Kent Crossley, Associate Chief Of Staff 612/725-2031
Douglas Ball, Chief Information Management Service 612/725-2070
Jack Drucker, Chief of Staff 612/725-2105
Linda B. Duffy, Director, Continuous Improvement and
    Public Relations 612/725-2102
Affiliation: University of Minnesota Medical School

University of Minnesota Medical Center, Fairview
2450 Riverside Avenue
Minneapolis, Minnesota 55454

Steve Hill, Chief Operating Officer 612/273-6575
Terry Carroll, Chief Information Officer 612/672-6641
George Chresand, Sr. Vice President & General Counsel 612/672-6812
James Breitenbucher, Vice President, Medical Affairs 612/273-6086
Susan Noaker, Sr. Director of Quality & Patient Safety 612/273-6992
Affiliation: Fairview Health Services; University of Minnesota Medical School

Rochester

Mayo Health System
Rochester, Minnesota 55901
Affiliation: Florida State University College of Medicine; Mayo Medical School;
    University of Florida College of Medicine

Saint Mary's Hospital
1216 Second Street, S.W.
Rochester, Minnesota 55902

Hugh Smith, Professor of Medicine 507/255-5123
Jeff Korsmo, Chief Operating Officer 507/255-5123
Lee Hecht, Chief Financial Officer
Anthony Windebank, Dean 507/284-3268
Chris Gade, Chair, Division of External Relations 507/284-2430
Sherry L. Hubert, J.D., Legal Counsel 507/284-0787
Affiliation: Mayo Health System; Mayo Medical School

St. Paul

Regions Hospital
640 Jackson Street
St. Paul, Minnesota 55101

Brock Nelson, President and CEO 651/254-2189
Heidi Conrad, Vice President/CFO 651/254-0900
Carl Patow, Assoc. Dean for Academic Affairs University of
  Minnesota Medical School, Exec. Director Health Partne 952/883-7185
Alan Abramson, Senior Vice President/CIO 952/883-7883
Barbara Tretheway, Senior Vice President, General Counsel 952/883-5137
Ken Holmen, M.D., Vice President Medical Affairs 651/254-3691
Timothy Lindquist, R.N., Director, Performance
  Improvement 651/254-3542

Affiliation: HealthPartners, Inc.; University of Minnesota Medical School

MISSISSIPPI

Jackson

G. V. (Sonny) Montgomery Veterans Affairs Medical Center
1500 East Woodrow Wilson Drive
Jackson, Mississippi 39216

Richard J. Baltz, Medical Center Director 601/364-1201
Rebecca Wiley, Chief-Fiscal Service
Joy Willis, Chief Financial Officer 601/364-1289
Kent Kirchner, M.D., Chief of Staff 601/364-1207
Robert Wolak, Chief, Information Resource Management 601/364-1260
Mary E. Barrett, Regional Counsel 601/364-1261
Janet C. Autry, Director, Office of Quality Assessment 601/364-1219

Affiliation: University of Mississippi School of Medicine

Methodist Rehabilitation Center
1350 East Woodrow Wilson Boulevard
Jackson, Mississippi 39216

Mark A. Adams, President/CEO 601/364-3462
Joseph Morette, Executive Vice President & COO
Gary Armstrong, Executive Vice President & CFO
Dobrivoje (Boba) Stokic, M.D., Administrative Director of
  Research 601/364-3314
Gary Armstrong, Executive Vice President & CFO
Tammy Voynik, Vice President, Legal Services 601/364-3360
Samuel Grissom, Medical Director 601/364-3425
Marcia King, Quality Management/Improvement Director 601/364-3359

Affiliation: University of Mississippi School of Medicine

University Hospitals and Clinics/University of Mississippi Medical Center
2500 North State Street
Jackson, Mississippi 39216

Janet Harris, CEO 601/984-1010
Jenny Walker, Director, Finance 601/984-4113
A. Wallace Conerly, M.D., Dean Emeritus 601/984-1010
Robert Jenkins, Staff Attorney 601/984-1776
Margaret Davis, Director of Admissions 601/984-5010
Judy Stump, Director of Performance Improvement 601/984-4100

Affiliation: University of Mississippi School of Medicine

MISSOURI

Columbia

University of Missouri Health Care
One Hospital Drive
Columbia, Missouri 65212

James Ross, Chief Executive Officer 573/884-8738
Kevin Necas, Chief Financial Officer 573/882-1398
Robert J. Churchill, M.D., Hugh E. and Sarah D. Stephenson
Dean 573/884-9080
George Carr, Chief Information Officer BryanLGH Health
System 402/481-3136
William F. Arnet, Counsel 573/882-3211
Kay Davis, Director, Patient Financial Services 573/882-7183

Affiliation: University of Missouri-Columbia School of Medicine

Kansas City

Children's Mercy Hospital
2401 Gillham Road
Kansas City, Missouri 64108

Randall L. O'Donnell, Ph.D., President/CEO 816/234-3650
Jo Stueve, Senior VP, Administrative Services 816/234-3623
Sandra Lawrence, Executive Vice President/CFO 816/234-3205
Joanne Kennedy, M.D., Director, Medical Education 816/234-3371
Jean Ann Breedlove, Chief Information Officer Information
Systems 816/234-3000
Sally Surridge, Vice President/General Counsel 816/234-3653
V. Fred Burry, M.D., Executive Medical Director 816/234-3780

Affiliation: University of Missouri-Kansas City School of Medicine

Saint Luke's Hospital of Kansas City
Wornall Road at Forty-Fourth
Kansas City, Missouri 64111

John Wade, Chief Information Officer 816/932-2514
E. E. Fibuch, M.D., Associate Director, Medical Affairs 816/932-5132

Affiliation: Saint Luke's Shawnee Mission Health System; University of Kansas
School of Medicine; University of Missouri-Kansas City School of
Medicine

Saint Luke's Shawnee Mission Health System
Wornall Road at Forty Fourth
Kansas City, Missouri 64111

Affiliation: University of Kansas School of Medicine; University of Missouri-
Kansas City School of Medicine

Truman Medical Center Hospital Hill
2301 Holmes Street
Kansas City, Missouri 64108

John W. Bluford, Chief Executive Officer 816/404-3500
Catherine Disch, Executive Vice President/Chief Operating
Officer 816/404-3511
Allen Johnson, Chief Financial Officer 816/404-3528
Mark Steele, M.D., Chief Medical Officer Associate Dean 816/404-5300
Mitzi Cardenas, Chief Information Officer 816/404-2141
Lewis Popper, General Counsel 816/404-3625
Mark Steele, M.D., Chief Medical Officer Associate Dean 816/404-5300
Shauna Roberts, Corporate Quality Director 816/404-0226

Affiliation: University of Missouri-Kansas City School of Medicine

Saint Louis

Barnes-Jewish Hospital
One Barnes Jewish Plaza
Saint Louis, Missouri 63110

Richard J. Liekweg, President 314/362-5400
Sharon L. O'Keefe, Vice President and Chief Operating
Officer 314/454-7000
Mark Krieger, VP & Chief Financial Officer
Keith Segraves, Director, Information Systems 314/362-7770
James P. Crane, M.D., Associate Vice Chancellor for Clinical
Affairs/Chief Executive Officer, ... 314/362-6249
Roz Corcoran, Director, Pt. Safety & Clinical PI Patient
Safety and Quality 314/454-8043

Affiliation: BJC HealthCare; Washington University in St. Louis School of
Medicine

St. Louis

BJC HealthCare
4444 Forest Park Avenue
Suite 500
St. Louis, Missouri 63108

Steve Lipstein, President and Chief Executive Officer 314/286-2024
Kevin Roberts, Vice President and CFO 314/286-2002
David A. Weiss, Vice President and Chief Information
Officer 314/286-2008
Michael DeHaven, Senior Vice President and General
Counsel 314/286-2010
Clay Dunagan, M.D., Vice President, Center for Healthcare
Quality and Effectiveness 314/286-2164
Patti Storey, Manager, Clinical Measurement Center for
Healthcare Quality and Effect 314/771-7142

Affiliation: Washington University in St. Louis School of Medicine

Members: MISSOURI-NEBRASKA

Saint Louis University Hospital
3635 Vista at Grand Boulevard
St. Louis, Missouri 63110

Raymond Alvey, Chief Financial Officer 314/577-8005
Dawn Anuszkiewicz, Chief Operating Officer 314/577-8103
Beckie Patrick, Chief Information Officer 314/268-7396
Sue Monaco, Managing Senior Counsel 469/893-2429
Karen B. Webb, M.D., Chief Medical Officer 314/577-8008
Nancy Noedel, Director, Clinical Quality Improvement 314/577-8807

Affiliation: Saint Louis University School of Medicine; Tenet Healthcare
Corporation

St. John's Mercy Medical Center
615 South New Ballas Road
St. Louis, Missouri 63141

Christopher Veremakis, M.D., Chairman, Graduate Medical
Education 314/251-1375
Mark Hutson, Chief Information Officer 314/251-1918
John S. Howard, Director of Legal Services 314/364-3388
Paul Hintze, M.D., Vice President of Medical Affairs 314/251-1955
Mike Moonier, Director, Quality Management 314/569-6544

Affiliation: Saint Louis University School of Medicine; University of Missouri-
Columbia School of Medicine

St. Louis Children's Hospital
One Children's Place
St. Louis, Missouri 63110

Lee Fetter, President 314/454-6000
Doug Vanderslice, Chief Financial Officer 314/454-4275
Gary R. LaBlance, Ph.D., Vice President, Quality Service &
Information Services 314/454-2850

Affiliation: BJC HealthCare; Washington University in St. Louis School of
Medicine

St. Mary's Health Center
6420 Clayton Road
St. Louis, Missouri 63117

Steve Johnson, Interim President 314/768-8075

Affiliation: Saint Louis University School of Medicine

NEBRASKA

Omaha

Creighton University Medical Center
601 North 30th Street
Omaha, Nebraska 68131

Gary Honts, CEO 402/449-5990
Robert Beehler, Chief Operating Officer 402/449-5295
Andrea Heffelfinger, Vice President/Chief Financial Officer 402/449-5371
Stephen J. Lanspa, M.D., Sr. Assc Dean, Academic and
Clinical 402/280-3792

Affiliation: State University of New York Downstate Medical Center College of
Medicine; Tenet Healthcare Corporation

The Nebraska Medical Center
987400 Nebraska Medical Center
Omaha, Nebraska 68198-7400

Glenn A. Fosdick, President/CEO 402/552-3452
Joe B. Graham, Chief Operating Officer 402/552-3485
William Dinsmoor, Chief Financial Officer 402/552-3202
Lianne O. Stevens, Executive Director, Information
Technology 402/552-2480
Stephen B. Smith, Chief Medical Officer 402/552-2290

Affiliation: University of Nebraska College of Medicine

VA Nebraska-Western Iowa Health Care System-Omaha Division
4101 Woolworth Avenue
Omaha, Nebraska 68105

Nancy Gregory, Acting Associate Director 402/346-8800
Kirk Kai, Chief Financial Officer 402/346-8800
William F. Gust, M.D., Associate Chief of Staff, Education 402/346-8800
Kenneth R. Huibregtse, Chief Information Officer 402/346-8800
Paul L. Pullum, St. Louis Regional Counsel Omaha Office 402/346-8800
Rowen K. Zetterman, M.D., Dean, School of Medicine 402/280-2600
Shirley Simons, Chief Quality Officer 402/346-8800

Affiliation: Creighton University School of Medicine

NEW HAMPSHIRE

Lebanon

Dartmouth Hitchcock Alliance
One Medical Center Drive
Lebanon, New Hampshire 03756
Affiliation: Dartmouth Medical School

Dartmouth-Hitchcock Medical Center
One Medical Center Drive
Lebanon, New Hampshire 03756

James Weinstein, CEO 603/650-8779
Daniel Jantzen, COO 603/650-5668
Robin Kilfeather-Mackey, Chief Financial Officer 603/650-5668
Wiley Souba, Vice President of Health Affairs and Dean 603/650-1200
Peter A. Johnson, Chief Information Officer 603/650-8811
Neil F. Castaldo, J.D., General Counsel 603/650-8811
Elissa F. Malcolm, Quality Measurement Analyst Quality &
Patient Safety 603/653-1067
Jennifer Snide, Quality Management/Improvement Director
Scott A. Berry, Senior Director, Clin Population Health 603/650-5540
Polly Campion, Director, Clinical Improvement Director,
Office of Patient Safety 603/653-1056

Affiliation: Dartmouth Hitchcock Alliance; Dartmouth Medical School

NEW JERSEY

Camden

Cooper University Hospital
One Cooper Plaza
Camden, New Jersey 08103

John P. Sheridan, President and Chief Executive Officer 856/968-7481
Jeffrey N. Yarmel, Chief Operating Officer 856/342-2443
Carolyn E. Bekes, M.D., Chief Medical Officer 856/342-2940
John Newsome, Chief Legal Officer 601/984-1738
Raymond Baraldi, Acting Chief Medical Officer 856/968-7397

Affiliation: University of Medicine and Dentistry of New Jersey-Robert Wood
Johnson Medical School

East Orange

Department of Veterans Affairs New Jersey Health Care System
385 Tremont Avenue
East Orange, New Jersey 07018

Kenneth Mizrach, Director 973/676-1000
Tyrone Taylor, Chief, Fiscal Service 973/676-1771
Marilyn A. Miller, Associate Chief of Staff for Education 973/676-1000
Beverly Erhardt, Chief, Information Resources Management
Services 973/676-1000
Max Shemtob, Regional Counsel 973/676-1000
Linda Mowad, Office of Performance Measurement &
Improvement Coordinator 973/676-1000

Affiliation: University of Medicine and Dentistry of New Jersey-New Jersey
Medical School; University of Medicine and Dentistry of New Jersey-
Robert Wood Johnson Medical School

Hackensack

Hackensack University Medical Center
30 Prospect Avenue
Hackensack, New Jersey 07601

Robert Garrett, President/CEO 201/996-2004
Robert Glenning, Sr. VP Finance/CFO 201/996-3371
William Black, M.D., Vice President, Medical Academic
Affairs 201/996-2794
Lex Ferrauiola, Vice President, Information Technology 201/996-3662
Audrey Murphy, Vice President, General Counsel 201/996-3771

Affiliation: University of Medicine and Dentistry of New Jersey-New Jersey
Medical School

Livingston

Saint Barnabas Medical Center
94 Old Short Hills Road
Livingston, New Jersey 07039

John F. Bonamo, M.D., Executive Director 973/322-5502
Barry H. Ostrowsky, Chief Executive Officer 973/322-4092
Patrick Ahearn, Chief Financial Officer/VP of Finance 973/322-2721
Henry Rosenberg, M.D., Director, Department of Medical
Education 973/322-5777
David Mebane, SBHCS Corporate Counsel 973/322-4042
Pamela Micchelli, Director of Standards, Performance
Improvement and Quality 973/322-2614

Affiliation: Mount Sinai School of Medicine; Saint Barnabas Health Care
System

Long Branch

Monmouth Medical Center
300 Second Avenue
Long Branch, New Jersey 07740

Frank Vozos, M.D., Executive Director 732/923-7502
Gerald Tofani, Senior Vice President, Finance 732/923-0180
Joseph Jaegar, Assoc. VP Academics 732/923-6781
Rich Wheatley, Chief Information Officer 732/923-7566
Eric Burkett, Medical Director
Pat Keating, Administrative Director, Performance
Improvement 732/923-6620

Affiliation: Drexel University College of Medicine; Hahnemann University
School of Medicine; Saint Barnabas Health Care System

Morristown

Atlantic Health
475 South Street
P.O. Box 1905
Morristown, New Jersey 07962-1905

Affiliation: Columbia University College of Physicians and Surgeons; Drexel
University College of Medicine; Mount Sinai School of Medicine

Morristown Memorial Hospital
100 Madison Avenue
P.O. Box 1956
Morristown, New Jersey 07962-1956

Joseph A. Trunfio, President & CEO 973/660-3270
Kevin Shanley, Vice President, Finance/CFO 973/660-3166
Don Casey, Vice President for Quality Chief Medical Officer 973/660-3556

Affiliation: Atlantic Health; University of Medicine and Dentistry of New Jersey-
New Jersey Medical School

Neptune

Jersey Shore University Medical Center
1945 Route 33
Neptune, New Jersey 07754

John Gantner, Executive Vice President /CFO Finance 732/751-7520
Rebecca Weber, Director, Information Systems 732/776-4186
Ann Gavzy, Vice President Legal Affairs and General
    Counsel 732/751-7550
Richard Nobile, D.D.S., Medical Staff President 732/776-4250
Lori Christensen, M.D., Chair, Outcomes Management
    Committee 732/776-4747

Affiliation: Meridian Health System; University of Medicine and Dentistry of
    New Jersey-Robert Wood Johnson Medical School

Meridian Health System
Monmouth Shores Corporate Park
1350 Campus Parkway
Neptune, New Jersey 07753

Affiliation: University of Medicine and Dentistry of New Jersey-Robert Wood
    Johnson Medical School

New Brunswick

Robert Wood Johnson Health System
One Robert Wood Johnson Place
New Brunswick, New Jersey 08903

Affiliation: University of Medicine and Dentistry of New Jersey-Robert Wood
    Johnson Medical School

Robert Wood Johnson University Hospital
One Robert Wood Johnson Place
New Brunswick, New Jersey 08903-2601

Stephen K. Jones, President and CEO 732/937-8900
Vincent Jospeh, Executive Vice President 732/937-8910
Robert Irwin, Vice President, Information Systems 732/937-8931
Joshua Bershad, M.D., M.B.A., Interim Chief Medical Officer............................ 732/937-8897

Affiliation: Robert Wood Johnson Health System; University of Medicine and
    Dentistry of New Jersey-Robert Wood Johnson Medical School

Saint Peter's University Hospital
254 Easton Avenue
New Brunswick, New Jersey 08903-0591

Patricia Carroll, President/CEO 732/745-7944
Garrick Stoldt, Senior Vice President, Finance & CFO 732/745-8600

Affiliation: Drexel University College of Medicine

Newark

Newark Beth Israel Medical Center
201 Lyons Avenue
Newark, New Jersey 07112

John A. Brennan, Vice President for Medical Affairs 973/926-7850
Darrell Terry, SVP, Operations Chief Operating Officer 973/926-7851
Joshua Rosenblatt, M.D., Director, Medical Education 973/926-3233
Tom Gregorio, Chief Information Officer 973/926-8002
Dennis Bordan, Vice President, Medical Affairs Medical
Director 973/926-7330
Margo Malaspina, R.N., Director, Quality Management 973/926-7822
Affiliation: Mount Sinai School of Medicine; Saint Barnabas Health Care
System

University of Medicine and Dentistry of New Jersey-University Hospital
150 Bergen Street
Newark, New Jersey 07103

Robin Wittenstein, Chief Operating Officer 973/972-8027
Thomas Daly, Chief Financial Officer 973/972-3721
Robert A. Saporito, Senior Vice President for Academic
Affairs 973/972-3645
Susan Mettlen, Vice President of Information Technology 973/972-3800
Vivian Sanks-King, J.D., Vice President of Legal Management 973/972-4705
Catherine T. Marino, M.D., Medical Director 973/972-0440
Maryann Sakmyster, Director, Quality Assurance &
Performance Improvement 973/972-1353
Affiliation: University of Medicine and Dentistry of New Jersey-New Jersey
Medical School

West Orange

Saint Barnabas Health Care System
95 Old Short Hills Road
West Orange, New Jersey 07052

Mark Pilla, Executive Vice President of Operations 973/322-4069
Affiliation: Drexel University College of Medicine; Hahnemann University
School of Medicine; Mount Sinai School of Medicine

NEW MEXICO

Albuquerque

New Mexico Veterans Affairs Medical Center
1501 San Pedro SE
Albuquerque, New Mexico 87108

George Marnell, Director 505/265-1711
Jerald D. Molnar, Associate Director 505/265-1711
Michael McNeill, Chief, Fiscal Service 505/265-1711
Curtis O. Kapsner, M.D., Associate Director Academic &
Research A 505/265-1711
Renee Lameka, Quality Manager 505/265-1711
Affiliation: University of New Mexico School of Medicine

University of New Mexico Hospital
2211 Lomas Boulevard, N.E.
Albuquerque, New Mexico 87106

> **Stephen W. McKernan,** CEO/Assoc. VP, UNMHSC Clinical
> Operations 505/272-2121
> **Jody Harris,** Chief Financial Officer 505/272-3335
> **Paul B. Roth, M.D., F.A.C.E.P.,** Chancellor for Health
> Sciences and Dean 505/272-2398
> **Ronald Margolis,** Chief Information Officer 505/272-2121
> **Saundra Brown-Savoy,** General Counsel 505/272-2377
> **Robert Bailey,** Medical Director 505/272-2525

Affiliation: University of New Mexico School of Medicine

NEW YORK

Albany

Albany Medical Center Hospital
43 New Scotland Avenue
Albany, New York 12208

> **James J. Barba,** President/CEO/Chairman of the Board 518/262-3830
> **Gary J. Kochem,** Chief Operating Officer 518/262-3028
> **William Hasselbarth,** Executive Vice President/CFO 518/262-8795
> **Vincent P. Verdile, M.D., M.S.,** Dean and Executive VP for
> Health Affairs, Albany Med College 518/262-6008
> **Arthur Gross,** Senior Vice President/CIO Albany Medical
> Center Hospital 518/262-8006
> **Dennis DeLisle,** Vice President Information Technology 518/262-8006
> **Lee R. Hessberg,** Senior Vice President/General Counsel 518/262-3808
> **Melissa Armao,** Senior Application Specialist Quality
> Management 518/262-2797
> **Karen Houston, R.N.,** Director, Quality Management 518/262-3796

Affiliation: Albany Medical College

Albany Veterans Affairs Medical Center
113 Holland Avenue
Albany, New York 12208

> **Douglas C. Erickson,** Associate Director 518/626-6729
> **Jake Fong,** Financial Coach 518/626-7311
> **Martha Farber, M.D.,** Designated Learning Officer 518/626-5844
> **Mullahey Michael,** Prog Mgr. Info. Resource Mgmt. 518/626-6260
> **Kevin Thiemann,** District Counsel Attorney 518/626-6949

Affiliation: Albany Medical College

Binghamton

United Health Services Hospitals
33-57 Harrison Street
Binghamton, New York 13790

Matthew J. Salanger, President/CEO 607/763-6130
John Carrigg, Chief Operating Officer 607/762-2951
Robert Gomulka, Vice President, Finance 607/762-3011
Don Carlin, General Counsel 607/762-3366
Rajesh Dave, M.D., M.B.A., EVP, Chief Medical Officer and
Medical Education 607/763-6690
Affiliation: State University of New York Upstate Medical University

Bronx

Bronx Lebanon Hospital Center
1276 Fulton Avenue
Bronx, New York 10456

Miguel A. Fuentes Jr., President/CEO 718/590-1800
Steven Anderman, Sr VP Operations/COO 718/588-5586
Victor De Marco, Senior Vice President/CFO 718/901-8600
Ivan Durbak, Chief Information Officer 718/579-2636
Fred Miller, General Counsel Garfunkel, Wild & Travis PC 516/393-2250
Milton A. Gumbs, M.D., Associate Dean for Minority Student
Affairs Associate Professor, Dept of Surgery 718/430-3091
Affiliation: Albert Einstein College of Medicine of Yeshiva University

Bronx Veterans Affairs Medical Center
130 West Kingsbridge Road
Bronx, New York 10468

Mary Ann Musumeci, Medical Center Director 718/584-9000
Roger Johnson, Associate Director 631/261-2747
Edward Ronan, Ph.D., Director, Education Program 718/584-9000
Linda Bund, Director, Education & Information Mgmt. 718/584-9000
Max Shemtob, Regional Counsel 973/676-1000
Jack Hirschowitz, M.D., Mb.Bs., Chief of Staff 718/584-9000
Affiliation: Mount Sinai School of Medicine

Jacobi Medical Center
Pelham Parkway S. and Eastchester Road
Bronx, New York 10461

William P. Walsh, Senior Vice President/Executive Director 718/918-8141
Kathy Garramone, CFO 718/918-3677
Diane Carr, Chief Information Officer 718/918-3690
Joseph Skarzynski, M.D., Medical Director 718/918-4606
Anne Iasiello, Associate Executive Director 718/918-5320
Affiliation: Albert Einstein College of Medicine of Yeshiva University; NYC
Health and Hospitals Corporation

Lincoln Medical and Mental Health Center
234 Eugenio Maria de Hostos
Boulevard (149th Street)
Bronx, New York 10451

Iris Jimenez-Hernandez, Senior Vice President 718/963-8101
Victor Bekker, Network CFO 718/579-5788
Suzanne Monique Carter, Chief Information Officer 212/423-7230
Alan Aviles, President 212/788-3321
Melissa Schori, M.D., Medical Director 718/579-5235
Sara Shahim, Senior Associate Executive Director 718/579-4945

Affiliation: NYC Health and Hospitals Corporation; Weill Cornell Medical
College

Montefiore Medical Center
111 East 210 Street
Bronx, New York 10467

Steven M. Safyer, M.D., President/CEO 718/920-2001
Joel Perlman, CFO
Allen M. Spiegel, M.D., Dean 718/430-2801
Jack Wolf, Vice President, Management Information Systems............................... 718/405-4311
Christopher S. Panczner, SVP/General Counsel 718/920-7787
Rohit Bhalla, Medical Director, Quality Management Chief
Quality Officer 718/920-7245

Affiliation: Albert Einstein College of Medicine of Yeshiva University

North Central Bronx
3424 Kossuth Avenue
Bronx, New York 10467

Kathy Garramone, Chief Operating Officer CFO 718/918-3677
Diane Carr, Chief Information Officer 718/918-3690
Joseph Skarzynski, M.D., Medical Director 718/918-4606
Anne Iasiello, Associate Executive Director 718/918-5320

Affiliation: Albert Einstein College of Medicine of Yeshiva University; NYC
Health and Hospitals Corporation

Brooklyn

Brooklyn Hospital Center
121 DeKalb Avenue
Brooklyn, New York 11201

Richard J. Becker, M.D., President and Chief Executive
Officer 718/250-8005
Paul Albertson, Sr. VP Hosp Operations/Ambulatory Care 718/250-8176
Joseph Guarracino, Chief Financial Officer 718/488-3755
Romulo Genato, Institutional Director for GME 718/250-6920
Irene Farrelly, Vice President, Information Systems 718/250-8330
Paul Albertson, Sr. VP Hosp Operations/Ambulatory Care 718/250-8176

Affiliation: New York-Presbyterian Healthcare System; Weill Cornell Medical
College

Coney Island Hospital
2601 Ocean Parkway
Brooklyn, New York 11235

Arthur Wagner, CEO 718/616-4100
Mary Mong, COO
Paul Pandolfini, Chief Financial Officer 718/616-4834
Silvana Desimone, Chief Information Officer 718/616-5340
Laura Battaglia, Quality Management/ Improvement
Director 718/616-5420

Affiliation: NYC Health and Hospitals Corporation; State University of New
York Downstate Medical Center College of Medicine

Kings County Hospital Center
451 Clarkson Avenue
Brooklyn, New York 11203

Antonio Martin, CEO 718/334-4900
George Proctor, Chief Operating Officer Officer 718/245-3919
Julian John, Chief Financial Officer 718/245-2984
Kathie Rones, M.D., Medical Director/Associate Dean 718/245-3921

Affiliation: NYC Health and Hospitals Corporation; State University of New
York Downstate Medical Center College of Medicine

Long Island College Hospital
339 Hicks Street
Brooklyn, New York 11201

Debra D. Carey, Cheif Executive Officer 718/270-4293
John Byne, Chief Operating Officer 718/283-8004
Gerry Dantis, Director of Hospital Finance 718/826-4901
Frank E. Lucente, M.D., Vice Dean, GME 718/270-4188
Marc Milstein, Corp. Chief Information Officer 212/523-8448
Jill Clayton, Hospital Counsel 718/780-2927
Margaret Casey, Director of Admissions 902/494-1847

Affiliation: Continuum Health Partners, Inc.; State University of New York
Downstate Medical Center College of Medicine

Maimonides Medical Center
4802 10th Avenue
Brooklyn, New York 11219

Pamela S. Brier, President 718/283-7025
Mark McDougle, Chief Operating Officer 718/283-8577
Robert Naldi, Senior Vice President/CFO, Finance 718/283-3900
Walter Fahey, Chief Information Officer 718/283-1800
Joyce A. Leahy, Vice President/General Counsel 718/283-7441
Samuel Kopel, M.D., Medical Director 718/283-7088
Sheila Namm, Vice President, ... 718/283-6839

Affiliation: Mount Sinai School of Medicine

Members: NEW YORK

New York Methodist Hospital
506 Sixth Street
Brooklyn, New York 11215

Mark J. Mundy, President/CEO 718/780-3101
Edward Zaidberg, Senior Vice President, Finance 718/780-3031
Stanley Sherbell, M.D., Executive Vice President/Medical
Affairs 718/780-3284
Grethel Marks, Director of Medical Records 718/780-3385
Stanley Sherbell, M.D., Executive Vice President/Medical
Affairs 718/780-3284

Affiliation: New York-Presbyterian Healthcare System; State University of New
York Downstate Medical Center College of Medicine; Weill Cornell
Medical College

SUNY Downstate Medical Center/University Hospital of Brooklyn
445 Lenox Road
Box 75
Brooklyn, New York 11203

Debra D. Carey, Chief Executive Officer 718/270-4293
David J. Conley, Chief Operating Officer 718/270-2403
Gerry Dantis, Director of Hospital Finance 718/826-4901
Ian L. Taylor, M.D., M.B.Ch.B., Ph.D., Sr. VP for Biomedical
Education & Research, Dean of the College of Medicine 718/270-3776
Bert Robles, Interim Chief Information Officer 718/270-2335
Kevin O'Mara, Associate University Counsel 718/270-4762
Michael Lucchesi, M.D., Chief Medical Officer 718/270-2407
Torrance Akinsanya, Sr. Assoc Administrator/Quality Mgmt 718/270-4762

Affiliation: State University of New York Downstate Medical Center College of
Medicine

Veterans Affairs New York Harbor Health Care System-Brooklyn Campus
800 Poly Place
Brooklyn, New York 11209

Affiliation: State University of New York Downstate Medical Center College of
Medicine

Woodhull Medical & Mental Health Center
760 Broadway
Brooklyn, New York 11206

Iris Jimenez-Hernandez, Senior Vice President 718/963-8101
Eve Borzon, Chief Operating Officer 718/963-8004
Milton Nunez, Chief Financial Officer 718/963-8125
Edward Fishkin, Medical Director 718/963-8569
Cynthia Bianchi, Chief Information Officer 718/963-8024
Edward Fishkin, Medical Director 718/963-8569
Melba Talan, Quality Management/Improvement Director 718/963-8548

Affiliation: NYC Health and Hospitals Corporation; State University of New
York Downstate Medical Center College of Medicine

Buffalo

Kaleida Health
100 High Street
Buffalo, New York 14203
Affiliation: University at Buffalo State University of New York School of
Medicine & Biomedical Sciences

Kaleida Health/Buffalo General Hospital
The Buffalo General Hospital
100 High Street
Buffalo, New York 14203

Lawrence Zielinski, President 716/859-5600
Joseph Kissler, Senior Vice President, Finance/CFO 716/859-5600
Cynthia Ann Ambres, M.D., Chief Medical Officer/Executive
Vice President 718/588-6921
Affiliation: Kaleida Health; University at Buffalo State University of New York
School of Medicine & Biomedical Sciences

Roswell Park Cancer Institute
Elm and Carlton Streets
Buffalo, New York 14263

Donald Trump, President and CEO 716/845-8261
Gregory McDonald, Chief Financial Officer
JoAnne Ruh, Vice President of Information Technology 716/845-3033
Michael Sexton, J.D., General Counsel 716/845-8717
Judy Smith, M.D., Medical Director 716/845-7724
Dana Fox-Jenkins, Assistant Vice President Organizational
Performance Improvement 716/845-8921
Affiliation: University at Buffalo State University of New York School of
Medicine & Biomedical Sciences

Veterans Affairs Western New York Healthcare System
3495 Bailey Avenue
Buffalo, New York 14215

Brian Stiller, CEO/Director 612/725-2103
Dennis D. Heberling, Facility Manager 716/862-8526
Royce Calhoun, Business Manager 716/862-8503
Patricia Widzinski, R.N., Facility Education Coordinator 716/862-6085
Margaret Owczarzak, Information Systems Manager 716/862-3254
Affiliation: University at Buffalo State University of New York School of
Medicine & Biomedical Sciences

Cooperstown

Bassett Healthcare
One Atwell Road
Cooperstown, New York 13326
Affiliation: Columbia University College of Physicians and Surgeons; University
of Rochester School of Medicine and Dentistry

Members: NEW YORK

Mary Imogene Bassett Hospital
One Atwell Road
Cooperstown, New York 13326

William F. Streck, M.D., President/CEO 607/547-3100
Bertine C. McKenna, Ph.D., Executive Vice President/COO 607/547-3100
Nicholas Nicoletta, Corporate Vice President/CFO 607/547-3635
James T. Dalton, M.D., Director of Medical Education 607/547-3764
Joseph Diver, VP, Information Services Chief Information
  Officer 607/547-3094
L. Andrew Rauscher, Medical Director 607/547-3779
Ronette Kinzelman, Director, Organizational Quality
  Program 607/547-6609
Susan Jamback, Executive Director, Physician Services 607/547-3070

Affiliation: Bassett Healthcare; Columbia University College of Physicians and
  Surgeons; University of Rochester School of Medicine and Dentistry

Elmhurst

Elmhurst Hospital Center
79-01 Broadway
Elmhurst, New York 11373

Chris D. Constantino, Executive Director 718/334-1638
Julius Wool, Executive Director 718/883-2351
Alfred Marino, Chief Information Officer 718/334-2401

Affiliation: Mount Sinai School of Medicine; NYC Health and Hospitals
  Corporation

Queens Hospital Center
79-01 Broadway
Elmhurst, New York 11373

Julius Wool, Executive Director 718/883-2351
Alfred Marino, Chief Information Officer 718/334-2401
Terry Flexer, Senior Associate Executive Director 718/883-2222

Affiliation: Mount Sinai School of Medicine; NYC Health and Hospitals
  Corporation

Great Neck

North Shore-Long Island Jewish Health System
145 Community Drive
Great Neck, New York 11021

Michael Dowling, President and Chief Executive Officer 516/465-8003
Mark Solazzo, Chief Operating Officer
Robert S. Shapiro, Senior VP Finance/CFO 516/465-8162
David Battinelli, M.D., Senior Associate Dean for Education 516/463-7198
Keith C. Thompson, Sr VP Legal Affairs 516/465-8333
Lawrence G. Smith, M.D., Dean, Executive Vice President &
  Physician-in-Chief 516/463-7202
Abrams Kenneth, Clinical Operations 516/465-8313

Affiliation: Albert Einstein College of Medicine of Yeshiva University; New York
  University School of Medicine; State University of New York
  Downstate Medical Center College of Medicine; The School of
  Medicine at Stony Brook University Medical Center

Manhasset

North Shore University Hospital
300 Community Drive
Manhasset, New York 11030

Susan Somerville, Executive Director
Richard P. McGrail, Vice President,, CIO 516/734-3333
Keith C. Thompson, Sr VP Legal Affairs 516/465-8333
Paul Gitman, M.D., Vice President Medical Affairs 718/470-7606
Yosef Dlugacz, Ph.D., Sr VP, Quality Management 516/465-2686
Affiliation: Albert Einstein College of Medicine of Yeshiva University; New York
University School of Medicine; North Shore-Long Island Jewish
Health System

Melville

Winthrop South Nassau University Health System, Inc.
100 Huntington Quadrangle
Suite 1C14
Melville, New York 11747
Affiliation: The School of Medicine at Stony Brook University Medical Center

Mineola

Winthrop-University Hospital
259 First Street
Mineola, New York 11501

John Collins, President and CEO 516/663-2200
Palmira Cataliotti, Chief Financial Officer Quarterly
Benchmark Report recipient 516/576-5883
John F. Aloia, M.D., Chief Academic Officer 516/663-2442
Nicholas A. Casabona, Director of Information Technology 516/663-2370
Joseph Greensher, M.D., Medical Director 516/663-2288
James Flaherty, VP Administration Associate Administrator 516/663-2940
Affiliation: The School of Medicine at Stony Brook University Medical Center;
Winthrop South Nassau University Health System, Inc.

New Hyde Park

Long Island Jewish Medical Center
270-05 76th Avenue
New Hyde Park, New York 11040

Chantal L. Weinhold, Corporate Compliance Office 516/465-8097
Keith C. Thompson, Sr VP Legal Affairs 516/465-8333
Paul Gitman, M.D., Vice President Medical Affairs 718/470-7606
Yosef Dlugacz, Ph.D., Sr VP, Quality Management 516/465-2686
Affiliation: Albert Einstein College of Medicine of Yeshiva University; North
Shore-Long Island Jewish Health System

Members: NEW YORK

New Rochelle

Sound Shore Health System
16 Gion Place
New Rochelle, New York 10802
Affiliation: New York Medical College

Sound Shore Medical Center of Westchester
16 Guion Place
New Rochelle, New York 10802

John R. Spicer, President/CEO 914/365-3700
Douglas O. Landy, Executive Vice President/COO 914/365-3710
Albert Farina, Chief Financial Officer
Stephen Jesmajian, M.D., Chief Academic Officer 914/365-3680
Barbara J. Cooke, Director, Hospital Information Systems 914/365-4025
Eileen O'Rourke, In-House Labor Counsel 914/365-4815
Jeffrey S. Stier, M.D., Medical Director 914/365-3609
Gwyn Grant, Director Quality Management 914/365-3708
Affiliation: New York Medical College; Sound Shore Health System

New York

Bellevue Hospital Center
27th and First Avenue
New York, New York 10016

Lynda D. Curtis, CEO/Senior Vice President 212/562-4132
Steven Alexander, Deputy Executive Director
Aaron Cohen, CFO 212/562-4372
Robert I. Grossman, M.D., The Saul J. Farber Dean, Chief
Executive Officer, NYU Langone Medical Center 212/263-3269
Don Lee, CIO 212/562-3391
Eric Manheimer, M.D., Medical Director 212/562-4743
Emily Mescon, Quality Management/ Improvement Director 212/562-3718
Affiliation: New York University School of Medicine; NYC Health and Hospitals
Corporation

Beth Israel Medical Center
First Avenue at 16th Street
New York, New York 10003

Richard Freeman, Chief Operating Officer
John Collura, Executive Vice President Chief Financial
Officer 212/636-8468
Harris M. Nagler, M.D., Chief Academic Officer 212/844-8920
Marc Milstein, Corp. Chief Information Officer 212/523-8448
Kathryn C. Meyer, J.D., Senior Vice President, Legal Affairs 212/523-2162
David Bernard, Chief Medical Officer 212/420-2140
Donna Wilson, R.N., Director, Quality Improvement 212/420-4596
Affiliation: Albert Einstein College of Medicine of Yeshiva University;
Continuum Health Partners, Inc.

Continuum Health Partners, Inc.
555 West 57th Street
19th Floor
New York, New York 10019

Stanley Brezenoff, President 212/523-8130
Harris M. Nagler, M.D., Chief Academic Officer 212/844-8920

Affiliation: Albert Einstein College of Medicine of Yeshiva University; Columbia
University College of Physicians and Surgeons; New York University
School of Medicine; State University of New York Downstate
Medical Center College of Medicine

Harlem Hospital Center
506 Lenox Avenue
New York, New York 10037

Denise Soares, CEO 212/523-5582
Stephen Lawrence, Ph.D., Chief Operating Officer 212/939-1398
Rick Walker, Chief Financial Officer 212/939-2027
Gerald E. Thomson, M.D., F.A.C.P., Senior Associate Dean 212/939-1375
Suzanne Monique Carter, Chief Information Officer 212/423-7230
Alan Aviles, President 212/788-3321
Glendon Henry, M.D., Medical Director 212/939-3872
Emma Beveridge, Senior Associate Director, Quality
Management 212/939-1287

Affiliation: Columbia University College of Physicians and Surgeons; NYC
Health and Hospitals Corporation

Hospital for Joint Diseases Orthopaedic Institute
301 East 17th Street
New York, New York 10003

Affiliation: New York University School of Medicine; NYU Langone Medical
Center

Hospital for Special Surgery
535 East 70th Street
New York, New York 10021

Louis A. Shapiro, President and CEO 212/606-1625
Lisa Goldstein, Vice President/COO 212/606-1236
Stacey Malakoff, Chief Financial Officer 212/606-1239
Thomas P. Sculco, M.D., Executive Assistant to the Surgeon-
in-Chief 212/606-1475
John Cox, M.D., Chief Information Officer 212/606-1554
Constance Margolin, Vice President Legal Affairs 212/606-1153
Russell F. Warren, M.D., Surgeon-in-Chief/Medical Director 212/606-1178
Marion Hare, Associate Director, Administration and Quality
Management 212/606-1236

Affiliation: Weill Cornell Medical College

Lenox Hill Healthcare Network
100 East 77th Street
New York, New York 10021

Affiliation: New York University School of Medicine; State University of New
York Downstate Medical Center College of Medicine

Lenox Hill Hospital
100 East 77th Street
New York, New York 10021

Gladys George, President/CEO 212/434-2010
Terence M. O'Brien, Executive Vice President/COO 212/434-2010
Michael Breslin, Vice President, CFO 212/434-2040
Louis Ajamy, Vice President/CIO 212/434-2180
Anthony Antonacci, Medical Director
Terri Gillette, Director of Performance Improvement and
    Patient Safety 212/434-2434
Affiliation: Lenox Hill Healthcare Network; New York University School of
        Medicine; State University of New York Downstate Medical Center
        College of Medicine

Memorial Sloan-Kettering Cancer Center
1275 York Avenue
New York, New York 10021

Craig Thompson, President and CEO 212/639-6561
John R. Gunn, Executive Vice President 212/639-6017
Michael Gutnick, Senior Vice President, Finance 646/227-3413
Patricia Skarulis, Chief Information Officer 646/227-3315
Roger N. Parker, Senior Vice President and General Counsel............................ 212/639-5800
Affiliation: Weill Cornell Medical College

Metropolitan Hospital Center
1901 First Avenue
New York, New York 10029

Meryl Weinberg, Executive Director 212/423-8993
Michael Kaufman, Deputy Executive Director 212/423-8001
Elizabeth Guzman, Chief Financial Officer 212/423-7722
Alan Aviles, President 212/788-3321
Richard K. Stone, M.D., Medical Director 212/423-8131
Affiliation: New York Medical College; NYC Health and Hospitals Corporation

Mount Sinai Hospital
One Gustave L. Levy Place
New York, New York 10029

Wayne Keathley, President & COO 212/241-8888
Donald Scanlon, Chief Financial Officer 212/731-3534
Nathan G. Kase, M.D., Interim CEO/President, Mt. Sinai
    Medical Center/Interim Dean, Mt. Sinai School 212/241-8888
Michael G. MacDonald, Senior Vice President/General
    Counsel 212/263-7291
Ira S. Nash, M.D., Chief Medical Officer; SVP for Medical
    Affairs 212/241-3282
Affiliation: Mount Sinai School of Medicine; NYU Langone Medical Center

New York-Presbyterian Healthcare System
525 East 68th Street
New York, New York 10021

Herbert Pardes, Executive Vice Chair of the Board of
Trustees 212/305-8000
Arthur A. Klein, M.D., Senior Vice President/COO 212/746-3577

Affiliation: Columbia University College of Physicians and Surgeons; State
University of New York Downstate Medical Center College of
Medicine; Weill Cornell Medical College

NewYork-Presbyterian Hospital The University Hospital of Columbia and Cornell
525 East 68th Street
New York, New York 10021

Herbert Pardes, Executive Vice Chair of the Board of
Trustees 212/305-8000
Steven Corwin, M.D., Eexutive VP/Chief Operating Officer 212/746-4068
Phyllis Lantos, Eexutive VP/Chief Financial Officer 212/305-6845
Aurelia Boyer, Vice President 212/585-6427
Maxine Fass Esq., Sr. VP, Chief Legal Officer 212/746-6500
Eliot Lazar, VP and Chief Quality Officer 212/746-0386

Affiliation: Columbia University College of Physicians and Surgeons; New York-
Presbyterian Healthcare System; Weill Cornell Medical College

NYC Health and Hospitals Corporation
125 Worth Street
New York, New York 10013

Alan Aviles, President 212/788-3321

Affiliation: Albert Einstein College of Medicine of Yeshiva University; Columbia
University College of Physicians and Surgeons; Mount Sinai School
of Medicine; New York Medical College

NYU Hospitals Center
550 First Avenue
New York, New York 10016

Robert I. Grossman, M.D., The Saul J. Farber Dean, Chief
Executive Officer, NYU Langone Medical Center 212/263-3269
Bernard Birnbaum, SVP, Vice Dean and Chief of Hosp Oper 212/263-5221
Michael Burke, Corporate Chief Financial Officer 212/263-3092
Steve Abramson, M.D., Vice Dean for Educ, Fac and Acad
Affairs 212/263-8003
Annette Johnson, SVP, Vice Dean and General Counsel 212/263-7921
Robert Press, Chief Medical Officer 212/263-2680

Affiliation: New York University School of Medicine; NYU Langone Medical
Center

NYU Langone Medical Center
550 1st Avenue
New York, New York 10016-6402

Affiliation: Mount Sinai School of Medicine; New York University School of
Medicine

St. Luke's-Roosevelt Hospital Center
1000 Tenth Avenue
New York, New York 10019

Frank Cracolici, President/CEO 212/523-5700
Timothy Day, Executive Vice President Chief Operating
Officer 212/523-8781
John Collura, Executive Vice President Chief Financial
Officer 212/636-8468
Bonnie Sessa, Vice President Chief Information Officer 212/523-8448
Kathryn C. Meyer, J.D., Senior Vice President, Legal Affairs 212/523-2162
Robert Catalano, Senior Vice President Chief Medical
Officer 212/523-4303
Eva Johansson, R.N., Director, Quality Improvement 212/523-2030

Affiliation: Columbia University College of Physicians and Surgeons;
Continuum Health Partners, Inc.

Veterans Affairs New York Harbor Health Care System-New York Campus
423 East 23rd Street
New York, New York 10010

John J. Donnellan Jr., Medical Center Director 718/630-3521
D. Max Lewis, Associate Director 212/686-7500
Daniel Downey, Chief, Fiscal Service 212/686-7500
Peter J. Juliano, Chief, Medical Administration Service 212/686-7500
Michael S. Simberkoff, M.D., Chief of Staff 212/686-7500
Joann Flannery, Special Assistant Director, Quality
Management 212/686-7500

Affiliation: New York University School of Medicine

Northport

Northport Veterans Affairs Medical Center
79 Middleville Road
Northport, New York 11768
Affiliation: The School of Medicine at Stony Brook University Medical Center

Rochester

Strong Health System
601 Elmwood Avenue
Rochester, New York 14642
Affiliation: University of Rochester School of Medicine and Dentistry

Strong Memorial Hospital
601 Elmwood Avenue
Rochester, New York 14642

Steven I. Goldstein, Vice President, Acute Care, Health
System General Director/CEO, Strong Memorial 585/275-7685
Kathleen M. Parrinello, R.N., Senior Director/COO 585/275-4605
Leonard Shute, Sr Dir, Finance/CFO Memorial and
Highland Hospitals 585/275-3033
Richard Irving Burton, M.D., Senior Associate Dean,
Academic Affairs 585/275-2747
Jerome Powell, Director of Information Systems 585/784-6118
Jeanine Arden Ornt, General Counsel, URMC/Strong Health.............................. 585/275-8571
Robert J. Panzer, M.D., Director, OCPE/Chief Quality
Officer 585/273-4438
Affiliation: Strong Health System; University of Rochester School of Medicine
and Dentistry

Staten Island

Staten Island University Hospital
475 Seaview Avenue
Staten Island, New York 10305

Anthony Ferreri, President and CEO 718/226-9034
Donna Proske, Chief Operating Officer Chief Nursing
Executive 718/226-9761
Tom Reca, Chief Financial Officer 718/226-1148
Mark Jarrett, Chief Medical Director 718/226-1944
Arthur Fried, General Counsel 718/226-8262
Mark Jarrett, Chief Medical Director 718/226-1944
Karen Lefkovic, VP Quality Management 718/226-9514
Angela Roccanova, Director of Quality and Risk Management 718/226-6193
Affiliation: North Shore-Long Island Jewish Health System; State University of
New York Downstate Medical Center College of Medicine

Stony Brook

Stony Brook University Hospital
HSC, Level 4, Suite 215
Stony Brook, New York 11794-8410

Steven L. Strongwater, M.D., Former CEO 860/970-7053
Bruce Solomon, Chief Operating Officer 631/444-2840
Dennis Mitchell, Chief Financial Officer 631/444-4100
Norman H. Edelman, M.D., VP, Health Sciences Center/
Dean 631/444-2080
Dennis L. Proul, Chief Information Officer 631/444-7994
Susan Blum, J.D., Associate Counsel 631/444-8250
William H. Greene, M.D., Associate Director of Medical and
Regulatory Affairs 631/444-2721
Affiliation: The School of Medicine at Stony Brook University Medical Center

Syracuse

Syracuse Veterans Affairs Medical Center
800 Irving Avenue
Syracuse, New York 13210

James Cody, Medical Center Director 315/425-4892
Marcia V. Wadsworth, Chief Financial Officer 315/425-4400
Michael W. Valerio, Ph.D., Associate Chief of Staff for
    Education 315/425-4639
James Nichols, Chief Information Services 315/425-4400
David Altieri, Legal Counsel 315/425-4839
Eric Yeager, Quality Management/Improvement Director 315/425-4395
Affiliation: State University of New York Upstate Medical University

University Hospital, SUNY Upstate Medical University
750 E. Adams Street
Syracuse, New York 13210

John B. McCabe, M.D., Chief Executive Officer 315/464-4223
Ann Sedore, Ph.D., Chief Operating Officer 315/464-6138
Stuart Wright, Chief Financial Officer 315/464-6530
Terry Wagner, Chief Information Officer University Hospital 315/464-4252
Patricia Numann, M.D., Medical Director 315/464-4603
Affiliation: State University of New York Upstate Medical University

Valhalla

Westchester Medical Center
Valhalla, New York 10595

Michael D. Israel, President Chief Executive Officer 914/493-7018
Gary Burnicke, Executive Vice President, Business 914/493-2816
John Moustakakis, Chief Information Officer SrVP
    Information Systems 914/493-5019
Julie Switzer, General Counsel Executive Vice President 914/493-5666
Renee Garrick, Medical Director 914/493-8078
Affiliation: New York Medical College

NORTH CAROLINA

Chapel Hill

UNC Health Care System
101 Manning Drive
Chapel Hill, North Carolina 27514
Affiliation: University of North Carolina at Chapel Hill School of Medicine

University of North Carolina Hospitals
101 Manning Drive
Chapel Hill, North Carolina 27514

Gary L. Park, President 919/966-5111
Christopher S. Ellington, Senior Vice President & CFO 919/966-3530
J. P. Kichak, Vice President/CIO University of North
Carolina Hospitals 919/966-2320
Benjamin I. Gilbert, Senior Vice President, Legal Services 919/966-6285
Stanley R. Mandel, M.D., Chief of Staff Emeritus 919/966-4131
Brian Goldstein, Executive Associate Dean for Clinical
Affairs/Chief of Staff 919/966-5112
Larry Mandelkehr, Director, Performance Improvement 919/966-0488
Martha Shackelford, Clinical Compliance Manager
Performance Improvement/Patient Safety

Affiliation: UNC Health Care System; University of North Carolina at Chapel
Hill School of Medicine

Charlotte

Carolinas HealthCare System
1000 Blythe Boulevard
Charlotte, North Carolina 28203
Affiliation: University of North Carolina at Chapel Hill School of Medicine

Carolinas Medical Center
1000 Blythe Boulevard
P.O. Box 32861 (Zip 28232-2861)
Charlotte, North Carolina 28203

Suzanne H. Freeman, R.N., President 704/355-3344
Phyllis Wingate-Jones, Senior Vice President, Operations 704/355-5073
Greg Gombar, EVP Administrative Services, CFO-CHS 704/355-2154
James McDeavitt, M.D., Senior VP, Education & Research 704/355-3146
John J. Knox, Senior VP/Chief Information Officer 704/355-1116
Keith Smith, Senior Vice President & General Counsel 704/355-3858

Affiliation: Carolinas HealthCare System; University of North Carolina at
Chapel Hill School of Medicine

Durham

Duke University Health System
Box 3701
Durham, North Carolina 27710
Affiliation: Duke University School of Medicine

Duke University Hospital
Box 3708
Durham, North Carolina 27710

Kevin Sowers, Interim CEO Chief Operating Officer 919/681-6624
Sabrina Olsen, Chief Financial Officer 919/613-8924
Asif Ahmad, M.D., Chief Information Officer 919/668-0521
Gail Shulby, Compliance Officer 919/681-8176

Affiliation: Duke University Health System; Duke University School of Medicine

Members: NORTH CAROLINA

Durham Veterans Affairs Medical Center
508 Fulton Street
Durham, North Carolina 27705

Ralph Gigliotti, Medical Center Director 919/286-6903
Phyllis Smith, Associate Director 919/286-6904
David Kuboushek, Chief Financial Manager 919/286-6914
Toby Dickerson, Chief, Information Resources Management
John D. Shelburne, M.D., Ph.D., Chief of Staff 919/286-6907
Jane Penny, Chief, Quality Management 919/286-6905
Affiliation: Duke University School of Medicine

Greenville

Pitt County Memorial Hospital
2100 Stantonsburg Road
Greenville, North Carolina 27835

Steven Lawler, President
David S. Hughes, Chief Financial Officer 252/847-7479
Edward L. McFall, Chief Information Officer 252/847-4976
Nancy B. Aycock, General Counsel 252/847-6300
Ernest Larkin, M.D., Chief Medical Officer 252/847-5345
Affiliation: The Brody School of Medicine at East Carolina University;
　　　　　　University Health System of Eastern Carolina, Inc.

University Health System of Eastern Carolina, Inc.
2100 Stantonsburg Road
Greenville, North Carolina 27835
Affiliation: The Brody School of Medicine at East Carolina University

Winston-Salem

North Carolina Baptist Hospital
Medical Center Boulevard
Winston-Salem, North Carolina 27157

Thomas E. Sibert, M.D., Chief Excutive Officer 336/716-6211
William B. Applegate, M.D., M.P.H., M.A.C.P., President 336/716-4424
Ronald H. Small, VP, Quality Outcomes/ Interim VP I.S. 336/713-3406
J. McLain Wallace Jr., Vice President, Legal Affairs 336/716-2817
Patricia L. Adams, M.D., Chief of Professional Services 336/716-9592
Affiliation: Wake Forest University School of Medicine

NORTH DAKOTA

Fargo

MeritCare Hospital
P.O. Box MC
Fargo, North Dakota 58122

Jeff Hass, SVP, Hospital 701/234-6300
Lisa Carlson, CFO 701/234-4811
Bruce Pitts, Associate Dean 701/293-4108
Craig Hewitt, Executive Partner, Information Systems 701/234-6174
Paul Richard, EVP, General Legal Counsel 701/234-6919
Rhonda Ketterling, Chief Medical Officer 701/234-2661
Molly Clark, Director, Clinical Systems Improvement 605/333-7496
Jennifer Wagenaar, Quality Management/Improvement
Director 605/328-7876
Affiliation: University of North Dakota School of Medicine and Health Sciences

OHIO

Akron

Akron General Medical Center
400 Wabash Avenue
Akron, Ohio 44307
Affiliation: Northeastern Ohio Universities Colleges of Medicine and Pharmacy

Children's Hospital Medical Center of Akron
One Perkins Square
Akron, Ohio 44308-1062

William H. Considine, President 330/543-8293
Mark Watson, Chief Operating Officer 330/543-8290
Micheal Trainer, Chief Financial Officer 330/543-8384
Norman Christopher, M.D., Director, Emergency/Trauma
Services 330/379-8452
Chuck Kozak, Chief Information Officer 330/543-4080
Shawn Lyden, Executive VP, Corporate Counsel 330/543-4250
Michael Bird, M.D., M.P.H., Vice President of Medical
Services 330/543-8970
Dorothy Winter, Director of Quality Improvement 330/542-8992
Affiliation: Northeastern Ohio Universities Colleges of Medicine and Pharmacy

Members: OHIO

Summa Health System
525 East Market Street
P.O. Box 2090
Akron, Ohio 44309-2090

Thomas Strauss, President/CEO	330/375-3000
Robert Harrigan, Executive Vice President/COO	330/375-3000
Michael Rutherford, Chief Financial Officer	330/375-3196
Joseph Zarconi, M.D., Vice President, Medical Education and Research	330/375-3106
Charles Ross, M.D., Chief Information Officer/Vice President, Information and Technical	330/996-8544
William Powell, Vice President Legal Services	330/375-3954
Dale Murphy, M.D., Vice President Medical Affairs	330/375-3314
Don Jackovitz, Director, Quality & Resource Management	330/375-3880

Affiliation: Northeastern Ohio Universities Colleges of Medicine and Pharmacy

Cincinnati

Cincinnati Children's Hospital Medical Center
3333 Burnet Avenue
Cincinnati, Ohio 45229-3039

Scott Hamlin, Senior Vice President, Finance	513/636-7454
Elizabeth A. Stautberg, Vice Presdient, General Counsel	513/636-4069
Michael K. Farrell, M.D., Chief of Staff	513/636-6717

Affiliation: University of Cincinnati College of Medicine

Cincinnati Veterans Affairs Medical Center
3200 Vine Street
Cincinnati, Ohio 45220

Linda Smith, M.P.A., Medical Center Director	513/475-6300
David Ninneman, Associate Medical Center Director	513/475-6301
Scott Hamlin, Chief Fiscal Service	513/636-7454
Mary Oden, Assistant Medical Center Director for Education	513/475-6517
Clarence Brooks, Chief, Info Res Mgmt Services	513/475-6314
Mary Garcia, Regional Counselor	937/267-5367
Kathleen Sandlin, Chief Quality Management	513/475-6522

Affiliation: University of Cincinnati College of Medicine

Good Samaritan Hospital
375 Dixmyth Avenue
Cincinnati, Ohio 45220

John Prout, President/CEO	513/569-6141
Claus von Zychlin, Executive Vice President/COO	513/563-6149
Craig Rucker, Chief Financial Officer	513/569-6107
Rick Moore, Vice President Chief Information Officer	513/569-6800
Donna Nienaber, Sr. Vice President, Corporate Counsel	513/569-6062
Larry Johnstal, Director, Clinical Improvement & Medical Staff Administration	513/569-6160

Affiliation: University of Cincinnati College of Medicine

UC Health
3200 Burnet Avenue
Cincinnati, Ohio 45229
Affiliation: University of Cincinnati College of Medicine

University Hospital
234 Goodman Street
Cincinnati, Ohio 45219

Douglas Arvin, Chief Financial Officer
Andrew Filak, Senior Associate Dean for Academic Affairs
and Chair, Department of Medical Education 513/558-7342
Jay Brown, Vice President IS&T 513/585-7109
Gary R. Harris Esq., General Counsel 513/585-6452
Michael Archdeacon, Medical Director 513/558-2978
Kathleen Beal, Director, Quality Management 513/584-5721
Affiliation: UC Health; University of Cincinnati College of Medicine

Cleveland

Cleveland Clinic Health System
9500 Euclid Avenue
Cleveland, Ohio 44195
Affiliation: Case Western Reserve University School of Medicine

Louis Stokes Veterans Affairs Medical Center
10701 East Boulevard
Cleveland, Ohio 44106

Susan Fuehrer, Medical Center Director 216/421-3206
Gene DeAngelas, Chief, Fiscal Service 216/526-3030
Murray Altose, Chief Of Staff (Wp) 216/421-3030
Michael Hickman, Chief, Information Resources 216/838-6096
Peter F. Goyer, M.D., Chief of Staff 216/526-3030
Kimberly Kresevic, Quality Management/Improvement
Director 216/791-3800
Affiliation: Case Western Reserve University School of Medicine

MetroHealth System
2500 MetroHealth Drive
Cleveland, Ohio 44109

Mark Moran, Chief Executive Officer & President 216/778-5700
Jeff Rooney, Interim CFO 216/778-5016
Ben Brouhard, Executive Vice President Chief of Staff 216/778-4900
Vince Miller, Vice Presdient/CIO 216/778-5007
William G. West, General Counsel 216/778-5723
J. Jeffrey Alexander, President of Medical Staff Medical
Center 216/778-4811
Affiliation: Case Western Reserve University School of Medicine; MetroHealth
System

Members: OHIO

University Hospitals Case Medical Center
11100 Euclid Avenue
Cleveland, Ohio 44106-5000

Fred Craig Rothstein, M.D., President 216/844-6217
Sonia Salvino, Interim Vice President Finance 216/844-4916
Jerry Mark Shuck, M.D., D. Sc., Director of GME 216/844-3871
Janet L. Miller, Senior Vice President and General Counsel 216/767-8256
Michael Anderson, Interim Chief Medical Officer Interim
Senior Vice President 216/983-5633

Affiliation: Case Western Reserve University School of Medicine; University
Hospitals HealthSystem

University Hospitals HealthSystem
11100 Euclid Avenue
Cleveland, Ohio 44106-5000

Affiliation: Case Western Reserve University School of Medicine

Columbus

Arthur G. James Cancer Hospital and Richard J. Solove Research Institute
300 West 10th Avenue, Suite 519
Columbus, Ohio 43210

Steven Gabbe, Vice President Center Expansion & Outreach 614/293-5485
Dennis J. Smith, Director of Administration 614/293-3300
Michael Rutherford, Administrator of Financial Services 614/293-3300
Maxine J. Moehring, Director of Information Systems 614/293-3300
Colleen Allen, R.N., M.B.A., Director of Clinical Quality &
Resource Management 614/293-3300

Affiliation: Ohio State University College of Medicine

Grant-Riverside Methodist Hospitals, Grant Medical Center Campus
111 S. Grant Avenue
Columbus, Ohio 43215

Vinson Yates, CEO 614/566-9000
Edsel Cotter, Senior Operations Officer 614/566-9164
Bruce T. Vanderhoff, M.D., Chief Medical Officer 614/544-4416
Fred T. Nobrega, M.D., Vice President, Medical Affairs 614/566-9971

Affiliation: Ohio State University College of Medicine; OhioHealth

Grant-Riverside Methodist Hospitals, Riverside Campus
3535 Olentangy River Road
Columbus, Ohio 43214

Bruce Hagen, President 614/566-3602
Michael Louge, Chief Financial Officer 614/566-4757

Affiliation: Ohio State University College of Medicine; OhioHealth

Nationwide Children's Hospital, Inc.
700 Children's Drive
Columbus, Ohio 43205-2696

Steve Allen, CEO 614/722-2259
Rick Miller, President/CEO 614/722-2259
Tim Robinson, Chief Financial Officer 614/722-5972

Affiliation: Ohio State University College of Medicine

Ohio State University Health System
410 West Tenth Avenue
Columbus, Ohio 43210
Affiliation: Ohio State University College of Medicine

OhioHealth
3555 Olentangy River Road
Columbus, Ohio 43214
David Blom, President 614/544-4412
Affiliation: Ohio State University College of Medicine

Wexner Medical Center at Ohio State University
410 West Tenth Avenue
Columbus, Ohio 43210
Larry A. Anstine, Executive Director 614/293-9700
Eric Kunz, Associate VP Facilities/Materiel Mgt 614/247-8328
Mike Rutherford, Chief Financial Officer 614/292-4060
Hagop Mekhijian, Associate Vice President 614/293-8158
Asif Ahmad, M.D., Chief Information Officer 919/668-0521
Hagop Mekhijian, Associate Vice President 614/293-8158
Susan Moffatt-Bruce, Quality Management/Improvement
Director 650/723-5771
Gail Marsh, Chief Strategy Officer 614/247-8314
Affiliation: Ohio State University College of Medicine; Ohio State University
Health System

Dayton

Children's Medical Center
One Children's Plaza
Dayton, Ohio 45404
David Kinsaul, President/CEO 937/641-3445
David Miller, Vice President/CFO 937/641-3000
Elizabeth Fredette, CIO/Director/Information Services 937/641-5975
Thomas F. Murphy, M.D., Vice President, Medical Affairs 937/641-5871
Carol Wise, Director Quality Resource Mgmt 937/641-3000
Affiliation: Wright State University Boonshoft School of Medicine

Dayton Veterans Affairs Medical Center
4100 West Third Street
Dayton, Ohio 45428
Guy Richardson, Medical Center Director 937/262-2114
Terry E. Taylor, F.A.C.H.E., Associate Director 937/262-2166
Lawrence Andrews, Chief, Fiscal Service 937/268-6511
Ronald Beaulieu, ACOS of Education 937/268-6511
Susan M. Sherer, Chief, Information Officer 937/262-2104
Melissa Miller, Staff Attorney 937/268-6511
Steven M. Cohen, M.D., Chief of Staff 937/262-2106
Lisa Durham, R.N., Chief, Quality Management Service 937/268-6511
Affiliation: Ohio State University College of Medicine; Wright State University
Boonshoft School of Medicine

Members: OHIO

Miami Valley Hospital
One Wyoming Street
Dayton, Ohio 45409

Mary H. Boosalis, President & CEO 937/208-2701
Bobbie Gerhart, Chief Operating Officer 937/208-2701
Scott Shelton, Chief Financial Officer 937/208-8000
Molly Hall, Vice President and Chief Academic Officer 937/208-2518
Nikkie Clancy, Chief Information Officer
Dale Creech, General Counsel
Gary Lollier, Medical Director 937/208-2239
Tim Collins, Vice President, Quality Management 937/208-6047
Affiliation: Wright State University Boonshoft School of Medicine

Independence

Cleveland Clinic Foundation
6801 Brecksville Road, RK45
Independence, Ohio 44131

Delos M. Cosgrove, M.D., Chief Executive Officer 216/570-9507
Steven Glass, Chief Fianancial Officer 216/444-2575
Eric Topol, M.D., Dean, Scripps School of Medicine,
    Director of Translational Science & CAO, Scripps Health 858/554-5707
C. Martin Harris, M.D., Chief Information Officer 216/444-4246
David W. Rowan, General Counsel 216/444-2340
J. Michael Henderson, Director, Quality Insititute 216/445-0318
Affiliation: Case Western Reserve University School of Medicine; Cleveland
    Clinic Health System

Kettering

Kettering Medical Center
3535 Southern Boulevard
Kettering, Ohio 45429

Brett Spenst, Chief Financial Officer 937/395-8520
Charles Scriven, Chief Academic Officer 937/395-8618
Frank Engler, Manager, Community Affairs & Institutional
    Advancement 937/395-8866
Gregory Wise, VP, Medical Affairs 937/395-8658
Stephen House, M.D., Director, Clinical Management 937/395-8856
Affiliation: Loma Linda University School of Medicine; Wright State University
    Boonshoft School of Medicine

Toledo

University of Toledo Medical Center
3000 Arlington Avenue
Toledo, Ohio 43614

Jeffrey Gold, Chancellor and Exec Vice President of
Biosciences & Health Affairs, Dean of the College of
Medicine & Life Sciences 419/383-4243
Mark Chastang, VP & Executive Director, UT Medical Ctr 419/383-3407
Scott Scarborough, Senior VP for Finance & Administration 419/383-6866
Godfrey Ovwigho, VP for Information Technology/CIO 419/530-3955
Lauri Cooper, Senior General Counsel 419/383-4577
Ronald A. McGinnis, Medical Director 419/383-3520
Norine Wasielewski, Admn. Quality & Clinical Safety 419/383-3968
Affiliation: The University of Toledo College of Medicine

Youngstown

Northside Medical Center
500 Gypsy Lane
Youngstown, Ohio 44501

Charles Neumann, CEO 330/841-3551
Roxia B. Boykin, R.N., Executive Vice President & COO 330/884-5858
Chuck Lane, Chief Financial Officer 901/516-2193
Mark Kishel, Chief Medical Officer 330/884-5089
Tim Roe, Chief Information Officer 330/884-1365
Eugene Mowed, M.D., Director of Medical Ecucation 330/884-3951
Affiliation: Northeastern Ohio Universities Colleges of Medicine and Pharmacy;
ValleyCare Health System of Ohio

St. Elizabeth Health Center
1044 Belmont Avenue
P.O. Box 1790
Youngstown, Ohio 44501
Affiliation: Northeastern Ohio Universities Colleges of Medicine and Pharmacy

ValleyCare Health System of Ohio
3530 Belmont Avenue
Youngstown, Ohio 44505
Affiliation: Northeastern Ohio Universities Colleges of Medicine and Pharmacy

OKLAHOMA

Oklahoma City

Oklahoma City Veterans Affairs Medical Center
921 N.E. 13th Street
Oklahoma City, Oklahoma 73104

David Wood, Medical Center Director 405/456-1000
Anne Kreutzer, Associate Director 405/456-5134
Haze McDougal, Chief Fiscal Service 405/456-1807
Steven R. Orwig, M.D., Associate Chief of Staff for
Education 405/456-3319
Stephanie Darr, Staff Attorney 405/456-5177
D. Robert McCaffree, M.D., Chief of Staff, Associate Dean,
College of Medicine 405/456-5135
Donna DeLise, Director, Quality Management 405/456-5194
Affiliation: University of Oklahoma College of Medicine

OU Medical Center
P.O. Box 26307
1200 Everett Drive, Everett Tower
Oklahoma City, Oklahoma 73104

Cole C. Eslyn, President and Chief Executive Officer 405/271-5911
Becki Benoit, Chief Operating Officer, Adult Services 405/271-5911
Jim Watson, Chief Financial Officer 405/271-5911
Larry Forsyth, Director, Information Systems 405/271-5559
Curt Steinhart, CMO/ Assistant Dean for Medical Affairs
Professor of Pediatrics, OU SOM 405/271-5911
Kathy Jost, Quality Management-Improvement Director 405/271-6310
Affiliation: University of Oklahoma College of Medicine

OREGON

Portland

Oregon Health & Science University
3181 S.W. Sam Jackson Park Road
Portland, Oregon 97239-3098

Peter F. Rapp, Executive VP and Executive Director 503/494-4036
Cynthia M. Grueber, Chief Operating Officer 503/494-1450
Lawrence Furnstahl, Chief Financial Officer
Diana Gernhart, Chief Financial Officer 503/494-1283
Lesley M. Hallick, Ph.D., Vice President/Provost 503/494-4460
Bridget Haggerty, CIO 503/494-7752
Steve Stadum, General Counsel 503/494-5222
Christine Slusarenko, Director, Quality Management 503/494-6459
Affiliation: Oregon Health & Science University School of Medicine

Portland Veterans Affairs Medical Center

P.O. Box 1034
Portland, Oregon 97207

David Stockwell, Deputy Director/Admin and Finance 503/721-1014
Susan Heublein, Finance Services 503/273-5278
David Douglas, AD for Information Management 503/220-8262
Rex Cray, Regional Counsel 503/326-2441
Nancy Kraft, Acting Chief, Quality & Performance Serv 503/220-8262

Affiliation: Oregon Health & Science University School of Medicine

PENNSYLVANIA

Allentown

Lehigh Valley Hospital

P.O. Box 7017
17th & Chew Streets
Allentown, Pennsylvania 18105

Ronald Swinfard, President and CEO 610/402-7505
Louis L. Liebhaber, Chief Operating Officer 610/402-7516
Joseph Felkner, Sr. Vice President & CFO 610/402-7501
Harry F. Lukens, Sr VP Information Services/CIO 610/402-1406
Glenn Guanowsky, Legal Counsel 610/402-2776
Anthony Ardire, Quality Management/Improvement Director
Marlene Ritter, Director, Quality Services
Robert Murphy, Senior VP, Quality and Care Management 610/402-1770

Affiliation: Drexel University College of Medicine; Pennsylvania State University
College of Medicine

Bethlehem

St. Luke's Hospital

801 Ostrum Street
Bethlehem, Pennsylvania 18015

Richard A. Anderson, President & CEO 610/954-4000
Thomas Lichten Walner, Senior Vice President, Finance 610/954-3100
Joel C. Rosenfeld, M.D., Chief Academic Officer 610/954-2540
Cynthia Jones, Chief Information Officer 610/954-3331
Seymour Traub, Vice President/General Counsel 610/954-4114
Charles D. Saunders, M.D., Senior Vice President Medical
and Academic Affairs 610/954-4654
Donna Sabol, Assistant Vice President Network Performance
Improvement 610/954-4102

Affiliation: Philadelphia College of Osteopathic Medicine; Temple University
School of Medicine; University of Pennsylvania School of Medicine

Members: PENNSYLVANIA

Danville

Geisinger Health System
100 N. Academy Avenue
Danville, Pennsylvania 17822

Glenn D. Steele Jr., M.D., Ph.D., President/CEO 570/271-6168
Frank J. Trembulak, Executive Vice President/COO 570/271-6467
Kevin Brennan, Vice President, Finance 570/271-6211
Linda M. Famiglio, M.D., Chief Academic Officer Academic
 Affairs Associate Dean, Temple University SOM 570/271-6114
Kristen Beech, General Counsel
Albert Bothe Jr., M.D., Chief Quality Officer 570/271-7200
Affiliation: Temple University School of Medicine

Erie

Hamot Medical Center
201 State Street
Erie, Pennsylvania 16550

John T. Malone, President/CEO 814/877-2431
V. James Fiorenzo, Chief Operating Officer 814/877-6588
Steve Danch, CFO 814/877-6162
Richard W. Long, M.D., Chief Medical Officer/DME 814/877-3080
Joseph Butler, Chief Information Officer 814/877-2432
Affiliation: Drexel University College of Medicine

Harrisburg

Pinnacle Health Hospitals
P.O. Box 8700
Harrisburg, Pennsylvania 17105-8700

Michael Young, Chief Executive Officer 717/231-8200
William Pugh, Chief Financial Officer 717/231-8245

Hershey

The Milton S. Hershey Medical Center
500 University Drive
P.O. Box 850
Hershey, Pennsylvania 17033

Harold L. Paz, M.D., M.S., CEO, SVP for Health Affairs,
 Dean COM, Penn State Univ. 717/531-8323
Kevin J. Haley, Director of Finance Chief Financial Officer 717/531-6614
Kenneth Blythe, Chief Information Officer 717/531-1083
R. Mark Faulkner Esq., General Counsel 814/238-4926
Michael R. Weitekamp, M.D., Professor of Medicine 717/531-8803
Affiliation: Pennsylvania State University College of Medicine

Latrobe

Latrobe Area Hospital
121 West Second Avenue
Latrobe, Pennsylvania 15650
Affiliation: Jefferson Medical College of Thomas Jefferson University

Philadelphia

Albert Einstein Medical Center (Albert Einstein Healthcare Network)
5501 Old York Road
Philadelphia, Pennsylvania 19141

Barry R. Freedman, President and CEO 215/456-7010
A. Susan Bernini, Chief Operating Officer 215/456-6010
Douglas McGee, Chief Academic Officer & ACGME DIO 215/456-7056
Kenneth D. Levitan, Chief Information Officer 215/456-8131
Penny Rezet Esq., General Counsel 215/456-7993
Richard Greenberg, M.D., President Medical Staff 215/457-4444
Jeffrey Cohn, M.D., Chief Quality Officer 215/456-8914
Affiliation: Jefferson Medical College of Thomas Jefferson University

Children's Hospital of Philadelphia
34th and Civic Center Boulevard
Philadelphia, Pennsylvania 19104

Steven M. Altschuler, M.D., President and Chief Executive
  Officer 267/426-6142
Madeline Bell, Executive Vice President COO 267/426-6981
Thomas Todorow, Sr. Vice President, Finance 267/426-6957
Bryan Wolf, SVP and Chief Information Officer 215/590-2869
Bonnie S. Brier, J.D., Senior Vice President, General
  Counsel Secretary of the University 212/998-4095
James Steven, M.D., Sr Vice President for Medical Affairs,
  CMO and PSO 267/426-6149
Affiliation: University of Pennsylvania School of Medicine

Fox Chase Cancer Center
333 Cottman Avenue
Philadelphia, Pennsylvania 19111

Michael Seiden, President 215/728-2849
Joseph Hediger, Chief Financial Officer 215/728-6900
J. Beck, Chief Academic Officer 215/214-1490
Robert F. Ozols, M.D., Chief Clinical Officer, Emeritus 215/728-2673
Delinda Pendleton, R.N., Director, Quality Management &
  Infection Control 215/728-2660
Affiliation: Temple University School of Medicine

Hospital of the University of Pennsylvania
3400 Spruce Street
Philadelphia, Pennsylvania 19104

Ralph W. Muller, Chief Executive Officer 215/662-2203
Garry L. Scheib, Chief Operating Officer 215/662-3227
Diane Corrigan, CFO
Arthur H. Rubenstein, M.B.B.Ch., Division of Endocrinology,
Diabetes and Metabolism 215/898-6796
Lee J. Dobkin, Chief Counsel, UPHS 215/746-5220
Bernett L. Johnson Jr., M.D., Senior Medical Officer, HUP 215/662-6153
Patrick J. Brennan, M.D., Chief Medical Officer and Senior
Vice President 215/615-0668
Affiliation: University of Pennsylvania Health System; University of Pennsylvania
School of Medicine

Philadelphia Veterans Affairs Medical Center
3900 Woodland Avenue
Philadelphia, Pennsylvania 19104

Margaret O'Shea Caplan, Chief Operating Officer 215/823-5858
Graciela McDaniel, Chief Financial Officer
Laura Veet, M.D., Director of Women's Health Education 202/461-1070
Jose Lopez, Regional Counsel 215/823-7811
Martin F. Heyworth, M.D., Chief of Staff 215/823-5859
Linda Aumiller, Quality Management Director 215/823-6372
Affiliation: University of Pennsylvania School of Medicine

St. Christopher's Hospital for Children
Erie Avenue at Front Street
Philadelphia, Pennsylvania 19134-1095

Caroyn Jackson, Chief Executive Officer 212/427-8881
Jeff Snyder, Chief Operating Officer 215/427-5146
Gil Cottle, Chief Financial Officer 215/427-8901
Daniel V. Schidlow, M.D., Interim Dean 215/762-3500
Maureen Fee, Chief Medical Officer 215/427-8872
Affiliation: Drexel University College of Medicine; Tenet Healthcare
Corporation

Temple University Health System
Broad and Ontario Streets
Philadelphia, Pennsylvania 19140
Affiliation: Temple University School of Medicine

Temple University Hospital
Broad and Ontario Streets
Philadelphia, Pennsylvania 19140

Sandy Gomberg, Interim Chief Executive Officer 215/707-6036
Edward Chabalowski, Chief Financial Officer
Arthur Papacostas, Ph.D., Chief Information Officer 215/707-5828
Beth C. Koob, J.D., Chief Counsel 215/707-5605
Susan L. Freeman, Chief Medical Officer 215/707-0766
Affiliation: Temple University Health System; Temple University School of
Medicine

Tenet Health System, Hahnemann University Hospital

Broad and Vine Streets-MS #300
Philadelphia, Pennsylvania 19102

Michael P. Halter, CEO 215/762-7167
James Burke, COO 215/762-7000
Brian Rielly, Chief Financial Officer 215/762-3180
Tom Nataloni, Regional Director, Information Services 215/762-7000
Barbara Zurzolo, Senoir Managing Counsel 215/255-7413
George Amrom, M.D., Vice President of Medical Affairs 215/762-3209
Joann Lucas, Quality Improvement Director 215/762-4783

Affiliation: Drexel University College of Medicine; Tenet Healthcare
Corporation

Thomas Jefferson University Hospital

11th and Walnut Streets
Philadelphia, Pennsylvania 19107

Thomas J. Lewis, President/CEO 215/955-1397
David McQuaid, Executive VP, COO 215/955-4164
Neil Lubarsky, Sr. VP/CFO 215/955-9993
Stephen Tranquillo, Chief Information Officer 215/955-2790
Stacey Meadows, J.D., Vice President and General Counsel 215/955-0765
Geno Merli, SVP for Clincal Affairs and CMO 215/955-8433
Rachel Sorokin, Interim CMO 215/955-0733

Affiliation: Jefferson Health System; Jefferson Medical College of Thomas
Jefferson University

University of Pennsylvania Health System

3400 Spruce Street
Philadelphia, Pennsylvania 19104
Affiliation: University of Pennsylvania School of Medicine

Pittsburgh

Allegheny General Hospital

420 East North Avenue, Suite 420
Pittsburgh, Pennsylvania 15212

Keith Ghezzi, Interim President/CEO 412/359-8588
Duke Rupert, Interim Chief Operating Officer 412/359-3595
Edwrad Rober, Vice President/Finance 412/359-8550
Tony Farah, Acting Chief Medical Officer 412/359-6583
John Foley, VP/CIO 412/359-1793
Judith Hlafscak, Senior Legal Counsel 412/330-2521
Sharon Kiely, Vice Chair of Clinical Affairs 412/359-8811

Affiliation: Drexel University College of Medicine; West Penn Allegheny Health
System

Members: PENNSYLVANIA

Magee-Womens Hospital
300 Halket Street
Pittsburgh, Pennsylvania 15213

Leslie C. Davis, President 412/641-4010
Ketul Patel, Vice President Operations 412/641-8746
Eileen Simmons, Chief Financial Officer 412/641-1815
W. Allen Hogge, M.D., Chief Academic Officer 412/647-4168
Louis Baverso, Chief Information Officer 412/641-1165
Dennis English, Vice President Medical Affairs 412/641-4119
Jeannine Konzier, Quality Management/Improvement
    Director
Affiliation: University of Pittsburgh School of Medicine

Mercy Hospital of Pittsburgh
1400 Locust Street
Pittsburgh, Pennsylvania 15219

William Cook, President 412/232-8111
Jack Gaenzle, Senior Vice President and Chief Financial
    Officer 412/232-7107
Irving Freeman, Ph.D., Vice President
Stephen D. Adams, Vice President, IT, & CIO 412/232-7544
Rebecca C. O'Connor, J.D., General Counsel 412/232-7977
JoAnn V. Narduzzi, M.D., Vice President, Academic Affairs 412/232-7601
Mary Menegazzi, Director, Quality/Clinical Applications 412/232-8371
Affiliation: Jefferson Medical College of Thomas Jefferson University;
        Pittsburgh Mercy Health System, Inc.

Pittsburgh Mercy Health System, Inc.
1400 Locust Street
Pittsburgh, Pennsylvania 15219
Affiliation: Jefferson Medical College of Thomas Jefferson University

UPMC
200 Lothrop Street
Pittsburgh, Pennsylvania 15213
Affiliation: University of Pittsburgh School of Medicine

UPMC Presbyterian Shadyside
200 Lothrop Street
Pittsburgh, Pennsylvania 15213

John Innocenti, President 412/647-5286
Mark Sevco, Chief Operating Officer 412/623-1514
Eileen Simmons, Chief Financial Officer 412/641-1815
W. Dennis Zerega, Ed.D., Vice President, Office of Graduate
    Medical Education 412/647-6340
Jim Venturella, Chief Information Officer 412/802-0091
Richard L. Simmons, M.D., Medical Director 412/648-1823
Lyda Dye, Director, Clinical Information & Program 412/647-9276
Jill Larkin, Quality Management/Improvement Director 412/647-8271
Affiliation: University of Pittsburgh School of Medicine; UPMC

Veterans Affairs Pittsburgh Healthcare System
University Drive
Pittsburgh, Pennsylvania 15240

Robert Callahan, Associate Director for Site Operations
James Baker, Chief Fiscal Officer 412/822-1055
Mary Lou Zemaitis, Director of Education 412/365-5723
Angelo Baiocchi, Vice President, Information Management 412/688-6476
Rajiv Jain, Chief of Staff
Barbara Reichbaum, R.N., Quality & Performance
Management Coord. 412/784-3777
Affiliation: University of Pittsburgh School of Medicine

West Penn Allegheny Health System
4800 Friendship Avenue
Pittsburgh, Pennsylvania 15224

Christopher Olivia, Senior Vice President, Strategic Planning
and New Ventures 412/544-5660
David Kiehn, CFO
Affiliation: Drexel University College of Medicine; Temple University School of
Medicine; University of Pittsburgh School of Medicine

Western Pennsylvania Hospital
4800 Friendship Avenue
Pittsburgh, Pennsylvania 15224

Edward M. Klaman, President and CEO 412/578-5335
Pamela Gallagher, Chief Financial Officer
Elliot Goldberg, M.D., Director Medical Education Vice
Chairman Dept. of Medicine 412/578-6929
Marian R. Block, M.D., Chief Quality Officer 412/578-7227
Affiliation: Temple University School of Medicine; University of Pittsburgh
School of Medicine; West Penn Allegheny Health System

Radnor

Jefferson Health System
259 Radnor Chester Road, Suite 290
Radnor, Pennsylvania 19087-5261
Affiliation: Jefferson Medical College of Thomas Jefferson University

Springfield

Crozer-Keystone Health System
Healthplex Pavilion II
100 W. Sproul Road
Springfield, Pennsylvania 19064
Affiliation: Temple University School of Medicine

Members: PENNSYLVANIA

Upland

Crozer-Chester Medical Center
One Medical Center Boulevard
Upland, Pennsylvania 19013

Joan K. Richards, President 610/338-8278
Joseph H. Saunders, Vice President, Operations 610/447-2000
Philip Ryan, Chief Financial Officer 610/338-8278
Marc Edelman, Vice President, Quality Improvement and
    Utilization Management 610/447-2380
Affiliation: Crozer-Keystone Health System; Temple University School of
    Medicine

Wynnewood

Lankenau Hospital
100 Lancaster Avenue
Wynnewood, Pennsylvania 19096

Phil Robinson, President and CEO 484/476-2000
Robert Kauffman, VP Finance and Budget 610/526-8482
Karen Thomas, Sr. VP and Chief Information Officer 610/993-2322
Affiliation: Jefferson Medical College of Thomas Jefferson University; Main
    Line Health

Main Line Health
100 Lancaster Avenue
Wynnewood, Pennsylvania 19096

John Lynch, CEO 610/526-5010
Michael Buongiorno, CFO 610/526-8281
Affiliation: Jefferson Medical College of Thomas Jefferson University

York

Wellspan Health
45 Monument Road
Suite 200
York, Pennsylvania 17405

Affiliation: Pennsylvania State University College of Medicine; University of
    Maryland School of Medicine; University of Pennsylvania School of
    Medicine

York Hospital
YH-1001 S. George Street
York, Pennsylvania 17403

Raymond Rosen, Vice President, Operations 717/851-2122
Michael O'Connor, Senior Vice President, Finance 717/851-2123
Richard Sloan, Chief Academic Officer 717/851-2026
R. Hal Baker, M.D., Chief Information Officer 717/812-7850
Glen D. Moffett, Vice President/General Counsel 717/851-2165
Peter M. Hartmann, M.D., Vice President, Medical Affairs 717/851-2224
Affiliation: Pennsylvania State University College of Medicine; University of
    Maryland School of Medicine; University of Pennsylvania School of
    Medicine; Wellspan Health

PUERTO RICO

San Juan

San Juan Veterans Affairs Medical Center
10 Casia Street
San Juan, Puerto Rico 00921-3201

Evelyn Ramos, Acting Associate Director 787/641-7582
Ricardo Ochoa, Financial Manager 787/641-7582
Michela Zbogar, Network Director 727/319-1126
David Kitterman, Chief, Health Administration and
Informatics Service 787/641-2974
John (Jack) Thompson, General Counsel 787/641-7582
Sandra C. Gracia-Lopez, Chief of Staff 787/641-7582
Lavell Velez, Quality Manager 787/641-7582
Affiliation: Ponce School of Medicine and Health Sciences; University of
Puerto Rico School of Medicine

RHODE ISLAND

Pawtucket

Memorial Hospital of Rhode Island
111 Brewster Street
Pawtucket, Rhode Island 02860

Shelley MacDonald, R.N., Senior Vice President,
Operations/Chief of Nursing 401/729-2341
Michael Ryan, Sr. VP, Finance 401/729-2260
Elizabeth Girard, Senior Vice President, Administration 401/729-2130
Raymond Ortelt, Director, Information Services 401/729-2993
Affiliation: The Warren Alpert Medical School of Brown University

Providence

Care New England Health System
45 Willard Avenue
Providence, Rhode Island 02905
Affiliation: The Warren Alpert Medical School of Brown University

Lifespan, Inc.
Coro Building
167 Point Street
Providence, Rhode Island 02903

George A. Vecchione, President/CEO 401/444-6699
Mamie Wakefield, SR. VP of Finance 401/444-7093
Arthur A. Klein, Sr. VP Chief Physician Officer 401/444-9990
Carole M. Cotter, Senior Vice President/CIO 401/444-6404
Kenneth E. Arnold, Senior Vice President/General Counsel 401/444-6627
Mary R. Cooper, VP, Quality 401/444-2221
Affiliation: The Warren Alpert Medical School of Brown University; Tufts
University School of Medicine

Members: RHODE ISLAND

Miriam Hospital
164 Summit Avenue
Providence, Rhode Island 02906

Timothy Babineau, President CEO 401/444-5131
Mamie Wakefield, Senior VP of Finance 401/444-7093
Carole M. Cotter, Senior Vice President/CIO 401/444-6404
Kenneth E. Arnold, Senior Vice President/General Counsel 401/444-6627
Diana Wantoch, Director, Quality Management 401/793-2015
Affiliation: Lifespan, Inc.; The Warren Alpert Medical School of Brown
    University

Rhode Island Hospital
593 Eddy Street
Providence, Rhode Island 02903

Timothy Babineau, President CEO 401/444-5131
Mamie Wakefield, Senior VP of Finance 401/444-7093
Carole M. Cotter, Senior Vice President/CIO 401/444-6404
Kenneth E. Arnold, Senior Vice President/General Counsel 401/444-6627
Affiliation: Lifespan, Inc.; The Warren Alpert Medical School of Brown
    University; Tufts University School of Medicine

Roger Williams Hospital
825 Chalkstone Avenue
Providence, Rhode Island 02908

Addy Kane, Senior Vice President, CFO 401/456-2476
Alan B. Weitberg, M.D., Chairman, Department of Medicine 401/456-2070
Susan Cerrone Abely, Vice President, CIO 401/456-6750
Kimberly A. O'connell, Vice President and General Counsel 401/456-2498
Thomas DeNucci, M.D., President, Medical Staff 401/456-2000
Kathleen Perry, Quality & Materials Management Director 401/456-2390
Nancy Fogarty, Director of Quality 401/456-2043
Affiliation: Boston University School of Medicine

Women and Infants Hospital of Rhode Island
101 Dudley Street
Providence, Rhode Island 02905

Constance A. Howes, Chief Executive Officer 401/274-1100
Dick Argys, Chief Operating Officer
Debra Paul, Vice President for Fianance 401/274-1122
Joanna Cain, Chair of Obstetrics and Gynecology Chief
    Academic Officer 401/274-1122
Cedric Priebe, VP, Information Services 401/921-2711
Thomas R. Courage Esq., Vice President/General Counsel 401/274-1100
Denise Henry, Directory, Quality Management 401/274-1122
Affiliation: Care New England Health System; The Warren Alpert Medical
    School of Brown University

SOUTH CAROLINA

Charleston

Medical University of South Carolina Medical Center
169 Ashley Avenue
Charleston, South Carolina 29425

W. Stuart Smith, Chief Executive Officer 843/792-2000
Lisa Montgomery, Admin for Financial Services 843/792-4775
David J. Northrup, Director, Healthcare Computing Services 843/792-6675
Annette Drachman, Director, Legal Affairs 843/792-3864
John E. Heffner, M.D., Executive Medical Director 843/792-9537
Christopher Rees, Quality Director 843/792-0855
Affiliation: Medical University of South Carolina College of Medicine

Ralph H. Johnson Veterans Affairs Medical Center
109 Bee Street
Charleston, South Carolina 29401

John E. Barilich, Director 843/789-7200
Nancy P. Campbell, M.S.W., Associate Director 843/789-7500
Cassandra Helfer, Cheif Financial Officer 843/789-6362
Joseph John, ACOS for Education 843/789-7942
Michael R. Cortright, Chief Information Officer 843/789-7167
Florence N. Hutchison, M.D., Chief of Staff 843/577-5011
Shirley Cooper, M.S.N., R.N., Quality Management
Coordinator 843/789-7303
Affiliation: Medical University of South Carolina College of Medicine

Columbia

Palmetto Health
1301 Taylor Street, Suite 9A
P.O. Box 2266
Columbia, South Carolina 29202

Charles D. Beaman, President/CEO 803/296-5042
John Singlering, Chief Operating Officer 803/434-2819
Paul Duane, Chief Financial Officer 803/296-2112
James I. Raymond, M.D., Chief Medical Officer 803/296-2152
Michelle Edwards, Interim Chief Information Officer 803/434-4949
Howard West, Senior Vice President/General Counsel 803/296-2100
Fran King, Director of Clinical Effectiveness 803/434-3122
Affiliation: Palmetto Health Alliance; University of South Carolina School of
Medicine

Palmetto Health Alliance
P.O. Box 2266
Columbia, South Carolina 29202-2266
Affiliation: University of South Carolina School of Medicine

Members: SOUTH CAROLINA-SOUTH DAKOTA

Greenville

Greenville Hospital System
300 E. McBeen Avenue, Suite 300
Accounts Payable
Greenville, South Carolina 29601

Michael C. Riordan, President/CEO 864/455-7978
Gregory J. Rusnak, Chief Operating Officer 864/455-6146
Skip Morris, Interim Chief Financial Officer
Jerry R. Youkey, M.D., Founding Dean 864/455-7880
Doran A. Dunaway, Vice President, Information Services 864/455-4707
Joe Blake, VP, Legal Affairs & General Counsel 864/455-6146
Thomas W. Diller, M.D., VP, Clinical Effectiveness & Quality 864/455-7880
Affiliation: Medical University of South Carolina College of Medicine;
University of South Carolina School of Medicine

SOUTH DAKOTA

Sioux Falls

Avera McKennan Hospital and University
800 East 21st Street
Sioux Falls, South Dakota 57105-1096

David Kapaska, Reginal President
Julie Norton, Senior Vice President of Finance 605/322-7818
Matthew J. Michels, Legal Counsel 605/322-7013
Mary Leedom, Medical Support Services Director 605/322-7975
Affiliation: Sanford School of Medicine The University of South Dakota

Sanford USD Medical Center
1305 West 18th Street
Sioux Falls, South Dakota 57117-5039

Kelby K. Krabbenhoft, President/CEO 605/333-6574
Randy Bury, Chief Administrative Officer 605/333-7177
Michelle Bruhn, Chief Financial Officer 605/333-6450
David Rossing, Senior VP Sioux Valley Clinic 605/328-6943
Arlyn Broekhuis, Director of Information Systems 605/333-7329
Kim Patrick, Corporate Counsel 605/357-2904
Ken Aspaas, Chief Medical Officer 605/333-6426
Mona Hohman, Director of Compliance/Privacy Officer 605/328-6714
Jenn Wagenaar, Quality Management Coordinator 605/328-7876
Affiliation: Sanford School of Medicine The University of South Dakota; Sioux
Valley Hospitals and Health System

Sioux Valley Hospitals and Health System
1305 West 18th Street
Sioux Falls, South Dakota 57105
Affiliation: Sanford School of Medicine The University of South Dakota

TENNESSEE

Chattanooga

Erlanger Health System
975 East Third Street
Chattanooga, Tennessee 37403
Affiliation: University of Tennessee College of Medicine Chattanooga

Erlanger Medical Center - Baroness Campus
975 East Third Street
Chattanooga, Tennessee 37403
James Brexler, President/CEO 423/778-6110
Britt Tabor, CFO 423/778-7729
Affiliation: Erlanger Health System

Johnson City

Johnson City Medical Center Hospital, Inc.
400 North State of Franklin Road
Johnson City, Tennessee 37604
Brad Nurkin, President/CEO
Candace Jennings, Vice President/COO Washington County
Operations 423/431-1061
Marvin Eichorn, Senior Vice President/CFO 423/461-1017
Richard Eshbach, Chief Information Officer/VP 423/610-6104
Affiliation: East Tennessee State University James H. Quillen College of
Medicine; Mountain States Health Alliance

Mountain States Health Alliance
701 N. State of Franklin Road, Suite 1
Johnson City, Tennessee 37604
Affiliation: East Tennessee State University James H. Quillen College of
Medicine

Knoxville

University of Tennessee Medical Center
1924 Alcoa Highway
Knoxville, Tennessee 37920
Joseph R. Landsman Jr., President and Chief Executive
Officer 865/305-9430
Thomas Fisher, Chief Financial Officer 865/305-6097
Affiliation: University of Tennessee Health Science Center College of Medicine

Members: TENNESSEE

Memphis

Methodist Healthcare-University Hospital
1265 Union Avenue
Memphis, Tennessee 38104

Kevin Spiegel, Chief Executive Officer 901/516-2600
Chris McLean, Chief Financial Officer 901/516-7000
Affiliation: University of Tennessee Health Science Center College of Medicine

Regional Medical Center at Memphis
877 Jefferson Avenue
Memphis, Tennessee 38103

Reginald Wood, President and Chief Executive Officer 901/545-8498
Peggie Allen, Chief Financial Officer 901/545-7676
Jim Leonard, Chief Information Officer 901/545-8628
Monica Wharton, Vice President, Corporate Legal 901/545-8223
Jack McCue, Sr VP Clinical Affairs/CMO 901/575-7676
Jason Fogg, VP, Healthcare Excellence 901/545-6972
Affiliation: University of Tennessee Health Science Center College of Medicine

Veterans Affairs Medical Center, Memphis, Tennessee
1030 Jefferson Avenue
Memphis, Tennessee 38104

Patricia O. Pittman, Medical Center Director 901/577-7200
Patrick Coney, Chief, Fiscal Service 901/523-8990
James B. Lewis, Associate Chief of Staff 901/577-7207
Jenny Pangle, Chief Information Officer 901/577-7209
Tammy Kennedy, Regional Counsel General Counsel 615/695-4633
Margarethe Hagemann, M.D. 901/577-7202
Affiliation: University of Tennessee Health Science Center College of Medicine

Nashville

Vanderbilt University Medical Center
1161 21st Avenue, South
Nashville, Tennessee 37232-2102

David R. Posch, Chief Executive Officer 615/343-5013
Warren E. Beck, Director, Finance, Chief Financial Officer 615/322-0084
Nicholas Zeppos, Chancellor 615/322-1813
William W. Stead, M.D., Associate Vice Chancellor 615/936-1424
Julia Caldwell Morris, Associate General Counsel 615/936-0323
Wright Pinson, M.D., Deputy Vice Chancellor for Health
Affairs 615/343-9324
Affiliation: Vanderbilt University School of Medicine

Vanguard Health System
20 Burton Hills Boulevard
Suite 100
Nashville, Tennessee 37215
Affiliation: University of Chicago Division of the Biological Sciences The
Pritzker School of Medicine

Veterans Affairs Tennessee Valley Health Care System
1310 24th Avenue South
Nashville, Tennessee 37212

Juan Marales, Chief Executive Officer 615/327-5332
Emma Metcalf, Chief Operating Officer 615/225-4900
Jim Hayes, Chief Financial Officer 615/225-4520
Sam Sells, Acting Associate Staff For Education 615/321-4751
Bernice G. Burchfield, Chief, Information Resources
  Management 615/456-9909
Tammy Kennedy, Regional Counsel General Counsel 615/695-4633
Kathy Burnham, Acting Chief, Nursing Services 615/893-1360
Affiliation: Meharry Medical College; Vanderbilt University School of Medicine

TEXAS

Dallas

Baylor University Medical Center
3500 Gaston Avenue
Dallas, Texas 75246

John McWhorter, President 214/820-4140
Frederick Savelsbergh, Vice President, Finance/Hospital
  Financial Officer 214/820-1913
Brad Gahm, Interim-General Counsel 214/820-3924
David J. Ballard, M.D., Ph.D., Senior Vice President
  Healthcare Research & Improvement 214/820-7986
Irving Prengler, Vice President of Medical Affairs 214/820-7772
Affiliation: University of Texas Southwestern Medical Center at Dallas
  Southwestern Medical School

Children's Medical Center of Dallas
1935 Motor Street
Dallas, Texas 75235

Christopher J. Durovich, President/CEO 214/456-7890
Nancy Templin, Senior Vice President 214/456-2960
Pamela Arora, VP, Chief Information Officer 214/456-6000
Anne Long, J.D., VP, Legal Affairs 214/456-2099
Julio Perez Fontan, M.D., Medical Director 214/648-9635
Affiliation: University of Texas Southwestern Medical Center at Dallas
  Southwestern Medical School

Dallas County Hospital District, Parkland Health & Hospital System
5201 Harry Hines Boulevard
Dallas, Texas 75235

Ron J. Anderson, M.D., President/CEO 214/590-8076
Samuel Lee Ross Jr., M.D., Chief Medical Officer
John Dragovits, Chief Financial Officer 214/590-8097
Les Clonch, Senior Vice President/CIO 214/590-4786
Tom L. Cox, Director of Legal Affairs 214/590-4575
Kirk A. Calhoun, M.D., President 903/877-7750
Affiliation: University of Texas Southwestern Medical Center at Dallas
  Southwestern Medical School

Members: TEXAS

Methodist Dallas Medical Center
1441 N. Beckley Avenue
Dallas, Texas 75203

Stephen Mansfield, Chief Executive Officer 214/947-8181
Michael Schaefer, Executive Vice President/CFO 214/947-4510
Pamela G. McNutt, Senior Vice President/CIO 214/947-4530
Mickey Price, Senior Vice President-Legal Affairs 214/947-4515
Virginia Davis, Vice President 214/947-2524

Affiliation: University of Texas Southwestern Medical Center at Dallas
Southwestern Medical School

UT Southwestern Medical Center
5151 Harry Hines Boulevard
Dallas, Texas 75235

Daniel Podolsky, M.D., President 214/648-2508
Kirk A. Kirksey, VP for Information Resources 214/648-6252
Leah A. Hurley, J.D., Vice President for Legal Affairs 214/648-7986

Affiliation: University of Texas Southwestern Medical Center at Dallas
Southwestern Medical School

Galveston

University of Texas Medical Branch Hospitals at Galveston
301 University Boulevard
Galveston, Texas 77555

Donna Sollenberger, Executive Vice President/CEO 409/772-6116

Affiliation: University of Texas Medical Branch School of Medicine

Houston

Harris County Hospital District
2525 Holly Hall
P.O. Box 66769
Houston, Texas 77054

David S. Lopez, Chief Executive Officer 713/873-2300
George Masi, Chief Operating Officer 713/873-2300
Michael Norby, Chief Financial Officer 713/566-6790
Tim Tindle, Chief Information Officer 713/566-6034
Mercedes Leal, Div Chief Harris Co Attny Off 713/566-6550
Wayne J. Riley, M.D., M.P.H., President and Chief Executive
Officer 615/327-6904
Constance Ferguson, Director, Quality Assurance 713/566-6413

Affiliation: Baylor College of Medicine; University of Texas Medical School at
Houston

Memorial Hermann Healthcare System
6411 Fannin
Houston, Texas 77030

Craig Cordola, Chief Executive Officer 713/704-3700
David F. Bradshaw, Chief Information Officer 713/776-4042
Randy Gleason, General Counsel 713/704-4000
Craig Cordola, Chief Executive Officer 713/704-3700

Affiliation: University of Texas Medical School at Houston

Methodist Health Care System
6565 Fannin Street
Houston, Texas 77030
Affiliation: Weill Cornell Medical College

Methodist Hospital
6565 Fannin Street
Houston, Texas 77030
Marc Boom, M.D., CEO 713/441-2671
H. Dirk Sostman, M.D., EVP and Chief Medical Officer 713/441-3455
Ramon Cantu, J.D., Executive VP, Chief Legal Officer 713/441-3182
Affiliation: Methodist Health Care System; Weill Cornell Medical College

Michael E. DeBakey Veterans Affairs Medical Center
2002 Holcombe Boulevard
Houston, Texas 77030
Affiliation: Baylor College of Medicine

St. Luke's Episcopal Health System
P.O. Box 20269
Houston, Texas 77225
Affiliation: Baylor College of Medicine; University of Texas Medical School at
Houston

St. Luke's Episcopal Hospital
6720 Bertner
Houston, Texas 77030
Margaret M. Van Bree, Ph.D., CEO 832/355-8081
Steve Pickett, Chief Financial Officer 832/355-8701
Ann Thielke, R.N., J.D., Vice President, Senior Legal
Counsel 832/355-3403
Angela A. Shippy, Vice President, Medical Affairs 832/355-4614
Mark LaRocco, Ph.D., Vice President, Patient Safety Officer 832/355-6340
Affiliation: Baylor College of Medicine; St. Luke's Episcopal Health System;
University of Texas Medical School at Houston

Texas Children's Hospital
6621 Fannin
Houston, Texas 77030
Mark A. Wallace, President/CEO 832/824-1160
Benjamin Melson, CFO/Executive VP 832/825-1120
Affiliation: Baylor College of Medicine

Members: TEXAS

University of Texas M. D. Anderson Cancer Center
1515 Holcombe Boulevard
Houston, Texas 77030

John Mendelsohn, M.D., President 713/792-6000
Leon J. Leach, Executive Vice President 713/745-1076
Dwain Morris, VP and CFO 713/794-5162
Raymond DuBois, Chief Academic Officer 713/745-4495
Lynn Vogel, VP & Chief Information Officer 713/745-7960
Matt Masek, VP & Chief Legal Officer 713/745-6633
Thomas W. Burke, M.D., EVP & Physician-In-Chief 713/745-3825

Affiliation: Baylor College of Medicine; The University of Texas School of
Medicine at San Antonio; University of Texas Medical Branch;
University of Texas Medical School at Houston

Lubbock

University Medical Center Health System
602 Indiana Avenue
Lubbock, Texas 79415

David Allison, Chief Executive Officer 806/775-8517
Mark Funderburk, Chief Operating Officer 806/775-8511
Jeff Dane, Chief Financial Officer 806/775-8505
Bill Eubanks, Vice President and CIO 806/775-9055
Lois Wischkaemper, Legal Counsel 806/761-0995
Vernon Farthing, M.D., Vice President of Medical Staff
Affairs 806/762-8461
Nancy Nava, Director of Performance Improvement 806/775-9266

Affiliation: Texas Tech University Health Sciences Center School of Medicine;
University Medical Center Health System

Odessa

Medical Center Hospital
500 W. 4th Street
Odessa, Texas 79760

William Webster, Chief Executive Officer 432/640-2404
Robert Abernethy, Chief Financial Officer
Gary Barnes, Chief Information Officer
Bruce Becker, Chief Medical Officer 432/640-1059
Sherrill Rhodes, Director of Performance Improvement 432/640-1175

Affiliation: Texas Tech University Health Sciences Center School of Medicine

San Antonio

University Health System
4502 Medical Drive
San Antonio, Texas 78229

George B. Hernandez Jr., President/CEO 210/358-2000
Peggy Deming, Executive Vice President/CFO 210/358-2101
Bill Phillips, Vice President Chief Information Officer 210/358-4300
Karen McMurry, Vice President, Legal Services/Risk MNGT 210/358-2005
Michelle Ingram, Director of Quality/Improvement Services 210/358-2278
Affiliation: The University of Texas School of Medicine at San Antonio

Veterans Affairs South Texas Health Care System
7400 Merton Minter Boulevard
San Antonio, Texas 78229

Marie Weldon, Director 210/617-5140
I. Rachal, Chief, Fiscal Service 210/617-5124
Raymond Chung, M.D., Chief of Staff (11) 602/222-6489
Simon Willett, Chief, Office of Information Technology 210/617-5126
Richard Bauer, M.D., Chief of Staff 210/617-5176
Gary Anziani, Chief, Quality Management 210/617-5300
Affiliation: The University of Texas School of Medicine at San Antonio

Temple

Central Texas Veterans Health Care System
1901 Veterans Memorial Drive
Temple, Texas 76504

Thomas C. Smith, Director 254/743-0013
Affiliation: Texas A&M Health Science Center College of Medicine

Scott and White Memorial Hospital
2401 South 31st Street
Temple, Texas 76508

Robert Wilton Pryor, M.D., President and CEO 254/724-1912
Dennis Laraway, Chief Financial Officer 254/724-4482
Donald Wesson, Vice Dean-Temple Campus 254/724-2368
William McCombs, Chief Information Officer 254/724-7439
Jimmy Carroll, J.D., General Counsel 254/724-2543
Stephen Sibbitt, Hospital Medical Director 254/724-6583
Affiliation: Texas A&M Health Science Center College of Medicine

UTAH

Salt Lake City

University of Utah Health System
50 North Medical Drive
Salt Lake City, Utah 84132
Affiliation: University of Utah School of Medicine

Members: UTAH-VERMONT

University of Utah Hospital
50 North Medical Drive
Salt Lake City, Utah 84132

David Entwistle, Chief Executive Officer	801/587-3572
Quinn McKenna, Chief Operating Officer	801/581-2377
Gordon Crabtree, Chief Financial Officer	801/581-7164
A. Lorris Betz, M.D., Ph.D., Interim President	801/581-5701
Jim Turnbull, Chief Information Officer	801/587-6016
Thomas Miller, Chief Medical Officer	801/581-2482
Carol Hadlock, Quality Management/Improvement Director	801/587-3793

Affiliation: University of Utah Health System; University of Utah School of Medicine

VERMONT

Burlington

Fletcher Allen Health Care
111 Colchester Avenue (Burgess 1)
Burlington, Vermont 05401

Angeline Marano, COO	802/847-5040
Roger Deshares, Chief Financial Officer	802/847-7527
Frederick C. Morin III, M.D., Dean	802/656-2156
Chuck Podesta, Chief Technology Officer Chief Information Officer	802/847-8484
Spencer Knapp, General Counsel	
Norman Ward, M.D., Vice President Medical Affairs	

Affiliation: University of Vermont College of Medicine

White River Junction

White River Junction VA Medical Center
215 North Main Street
White River Junction, Vermont 05009

Robert M. Walton, Director	802/291-6206
Joan Wilmot, CFO	802/295-9363
Matthew Rafus, Chief, OI&T	802/295-9363
Neil Nulty, J.D., Regional Counsel Attorney	802/296-5116
Joanne Puckett, R.N., E.D.M., Quality Manager	802/295-9363

Affiliation: Dartmouth Medical School; University of Vermont College of Medicine

446

VIRGINIA

Charlottesville

University of Virginia Medical Center
Jefferson Park Avenue
Charlottesville, Virginia 22908

R. Edward Howell, VP/CEO 434/243-9308
Larry Fitzgerald, Chief Financial Officer 434/924-5426
Arthur Garson Jr., M.D., Director, Center for Health Policy;
University Professor and Professor of Public Health
Sciences 434/924-8419
Barbara Baldwin, GIR Steering Committee 804/360-9689
Sally Nan Barber, Director of State and Federal Government
Relations 434/243-5920
Stacy Crowell, Director, Quality & Performance
Improvement 434/924-5120
Affiliation: University of Virginia School of Medicine

Falls Church

INOVA Fairfax Hospital
3300 Gallows Road
Falls Church, Virginia 22046

Rubin Pasternak, CEO 703/776-3332
Rod Huebbers, COO 703/776-4391
Ron Ewald, Chief Financial Officer 703/776-2711
Russell Seneca, Chief Academic Officer 703/776-3563
Joseph Hallal, Medical Director 703/560-7919
Terry Sher, Director Quality Leadership 703/776-2741
Affiliation: George Washington University School of Medicine and Health
Sciences; Georgetown University School of Medicine; INOVA
Health System

INOVA Health System
3300 Gallows Road
Falls Church, Virginia 22046

Affiliation: George Washington University School of Medicine and Health
Sciences; Georgetown University School of Medicine; Virginia
Commonwealth University School of Medicine

Richmond

Hunter Holmes McGuire Veterans Affairs Medical Center
1201 Broad Rock Boulevard
Richmond, Virginia 23249

Michael B. Phaup, Medical Center Director 804/675-5500
Charles E. Sepich, C.H.E., CEO/Director 210/617-5141
Thomas Vergne, Chief, Fiscal Service 804/675-5004
Katherine Gianola, M.D., Chief Information Officer 804/675-5000
Judy L. Brannen, M.D., Clinical Director, Undergraduate
and Graduate Medical Education 804/675-5481
Rose Polatty, Interim, Chief of Quality Management 804/675-5000
Affiliation: Virginia Commonwealth University School of Medicine

Members: VIRGINIA

Medical College of Virginia Hospitals
P.O. Box 980510
Richmond, Virginia 23298

John F. Duval, Chief Excutive Officer 804/828-0938
Linda Pearson, Senior VP of Finance 804/828-7076
Carl F. Gattuso, Senior Vice President Chief Information
Officer 804/828-4638
Jean F. Reed, J.D., General Counsel 804/828-9010
Ron Clark, M.D., Chief Medical Officer, Clinical 804/828-4654
Affiliation: Virginia Commonwealth University School of Medicine

Roanoke

Carilion Medical Center
1906 Belleview Avenue
Roanoke, Virginia 24014

Nancy Howell Agee, Chief Executive Officer 540/981-8844
Donald Lorton, Chief Financial Operator 540/985-5125
Daniel Harrington, DIO, Carilion Clinic GME 540/521-6605
Daniel Barchie, Chief Information Officer 540/224-1568
Briggs Andrews, SVP, Legal Services 540/224-5063
Mark Werner, Chief Medical Officer 540/981-9407
Carolyn Chrisman, VP, Quality Interaction and Improvement.............................. 540/981-8384
Affiliation: University of Virginia School of Medicine

Salem

Salem Veterans Affairs Medical Center
1970 Roanoke Boulevard
Salem, Virginia 24153

Carolyn Adams, Associatiate Medical Director 540/983-1046
Richard Schroeder, Chief, Resources Support Service 540/982-2463
Maureen F. McCarthy, M.D., Associate Chief of Staff/
Education 540/982-2463
John R. Miller, Chief, Information Management Service 540/982-2463
Kathleen K. Oddo, Regional Counsel 540/857-2162
Carol S. Carlson, Quality Manager 540/982-2463
Affiliation: Edward Via Virginia College of Osteopathic Medicine; University of
Virginia School of Medicine; Virginia Tech Carilion School of
Medicine

WASHINGTON

Seattle

Children's Hospital and Regional Medical Center
4800 Sand Point Way, N.E.
Seattle, Washington 98105

Thomas N. Hansen, M.D., Chief Executive Officer 206/987-2001
Patrick J. Hagan, President and COO 206/526-2003
Kelly Wallace, SVP and Chief Financial Officer 206/987-2003
F. Bruder Stapleton, M.D., Professor and Chair Department
of Pediatrics 206/987-2150
Drexel DeFord, SVP and Chief Information Officer 206/987-2012
Jeffrey M. Sconyers, J.D., Senior Vice President and General
Counsel 206/987-2044
David Fisher, M.D., SVP and Medical Director 206/987-2005
Cara Bailey, VP Continuous Performance Improvement 206/526-2012
Affiliation: University of Washington School of Medicine

Harborview Medical Center University of Washington Hospitals
325 Ninth Avenue, #359717
Seattle, Washington 98104

Eileen Whalen, Executive Director 206/744-3036
Johnese Spisso, Chief Health System Officer 206/685-5020
Lori Mitchell, Chief Financial Officer 206/744-9703
Tom M. Martin, Director of UW Medicine 206/543-3155
Kristin Miles, General Counsel 206/543-4150
J. Goss, Acting Medical Director/Acting Associate Dean 206/744-3134
Affiliation: University of Washington School of Medicine; UW Medicine

University of Washington Medical Center
1959 N.E. Pacific Street, Box 356429
Seattle, Washington 98195-6151

Stephen Zieniewicz, Executive Director 206/598-6364
Mike Vanderlinde, Director Gov. Financial Relations &
Reimbursement 206/744-9701
Preston Simmons, Senior Operating Officer 206/598-6301
Paul Ishizuka, Chief Financial Officer 206/598-6305
James S. Fine, M.D., M.S., Chief Information Officer, UW
Medicine, ITS Chair of Department of Laboratory
Medicine 206/598-6151
Dina Yunker, Assistant Attorney General 206/543-4150
Thomas O. Staiger, Medical Center 206/598-5807
Julie Duncan, Director, Quality Assessment and Improvement 206/598-6168
Wendy Wilkins-Russell, Medicaid Relationship Director 206/598-4446
Affiliation: University of Washington School of Medicine; UW Medicine

Members: WASHINGTON-WEST VIRGINIA

UW Medicine
1959 N.E. Pacific Street, Box 356151
Seattle, Washington 98195

Paul G. Ramsey, M.D., CEO, UW Medicine, Exec VP for
Medical Affairs Dean of the SOM 206/543-7718
Johnese Spisso, Chief Health System Officer 206/685-5020
Bruce Ferguson, (Retired) Vice Pres Medical Affairs. - CFO 206/685-7129

Affiliation: University of Washington School of Medicine

Veterans Affairs Puget Sound Health Care System
1660 South Columbian Way
Seattle, Washington 98108-1597

DeAnn R. Dietrich, Deputy Director 206/764-2299
Kenneth Hudson, Chief Financial Officer 206/764-2666
Phillip G. Rakestraw, Ph.D., Executive Director Center for
Education & Development 206/764-2596
Glen Zwinger, Service Line Manager Information Systems
Service 206/764-2221
Gordon Starkebaum, Chief of Staff 206/764-2260
Robin S. Cook, Director, Quality Improvement 206/764-2650

Affiliation: University of Washington School of Medicine

WEST VIRGINIA

Charleston

CAMC Health System
501 Morris Street
P.O. Box 1547
Charleston, West Virginia 25326
Affiliation: West Virginia University School of Medicine

Charleston Area Medical Center
501 Morris Street
P.O. Box 1547
Charleston, West Virginia 25326

David L. Ramsey, President/CEO 304/348-7627
Glenn Crotty, Executive Vice President/COO 304/348-7438
Larry Hudson, Executive Vice President/CFO 304/388-7629
Lynn Pettry Brookshire, Vice President for Information
Services 304/348-9705
Marshall McMullen, General Counsel 304/348-6710
Elizabeth Spangler, Chief Medical Officer 304/388-7177

Affiliation: CAMC Health System; West Virginia University School of Medicine

Fairmont

West Virginia United Health System
1000 Technology Drive, Suite 2320
Fairmont, West Virginia 26554
Affiliation: West Virginia University School of Medicine

Morgantown

West Virginia University Hospitals, Inc.
1 Medical Center Drive
Morgantown, West Virginia 26506

Bruce McClymonds, President 304/598-4355

Mary Jo Shahan, Interim Vice President, Finance Chief
Financial Officer 304/598-4554

Rich King, Interim Vice President, Information Technology
Chief Information Officer 304/598-4133

Michael Sirott, General Counsel 304/598-4070

Affiliation: West Virginia United Health System; West Virginia University
School of Medicine

WISCONSIN

LaCrosse

Gundersen Lutheran Health Care System
1910 South Avenue
LaCrosse, Wisconsin 54601
Affiliation: University of Wisconsin School of Medicine and Public Health

Lutheran Hospital-LaCrosse
1900 South Avenue
LaCrosse, Wisconsin 54601

Jeffrey E. Thompson, Chief Executive Officer 608/782-7300

David Chestnut, M.D., Chief Academic Officer 608/782-7300

Debra Rislow, R.N., M.B.A., Chief Information Officer 608/782-7300

Daniel Lilly, General Counsel 608/782-7300

Jean Krause, Chief Quality Officer 608/782-7300

Affiliation: Gundersen Lutheran Health Care System; University of Wisconsin
School of Medicine and Public Health

Madison

University of Wisconsin Hospital and Clinics
600 Highland Avenue
Madison, Wisconsin 53792

Donna Katen-Bahensky, President & CEO 608/263-8991

Michael Buhl, SVP, Chief Financial Officer 608/263-7877

Mike Sauk, VP, Information Technology 608/263-9004

Carl J. Getto, M.D., Executive Vice President and CMO
Associate Dean for Hospital Affairs 901/545-7888

Sue Sanford-Ring, Director, Quality and Patient Safety 608/203-4623

Judy Wanless, Quality Management/Improvement Director 608/203-4618

Affiliation: University of Wisconsin School of Medicine and Public Health

Members: WISCONSIN

Milwaukee

Aurora Health Care
3000 W. Montana Street
Milwaukee, Wisconsin 53215

Nick Turkal, President/CEO 414/647-3130

Affiliation: Medical College of Wisconsin; University of Wisconsin School of
Medicine and Public Health

Children's Hospital of Wisconsin
9000 West Wisconsin Avenue
Milwaukee, Wisconsin 53226

Peggy Troy, CEO 414/266-6125
Cinthia Christensen, Executive Vice President/COO 414/266-3010
Weldon Gage, Treasurer/CFO 414/266-6220
Michael L. Jones, M.B.A., Chief Information Officer 414/266-6412
Sheila Reynolds, Corporate Vice President/General Counsel 414/266-3469
Robert Miller, M.D., Vice President, Medical Affairs 414/266-3002

Affiliation: Medical College of Wisconsin

Froedtert Hospital and Health System
9200 West Wisconsin Avenue
Milwaukee, Wisconsin 53226

William D. Petasnick, President 414/805-2606
Catherine J. Buck, Executive Vice President Chief Operating
Officer 414/259-2915
Catherine Mode Eastham, J.D., Vice President & General
Counsel 414/805-2994
Andrew J. Norton, M.D., SVP & CMO 414/805-3060
Kerri Danninger, Quality Management/Improvement
Director 414/805-5052
Karen L. Carlson, Director, Quality Management 414/805-5051

Affiliation: Medical College of Wisconsin

Sinai Samaritan Medical Center,
945 N. 12th Street
P.O. Box 342
Milwaukee, Wisconsin 53201-0342

George Hinton, Chief Executive Officer 414/219-7293
David Eager, Chief Financial Officer 414/219-1607
Jack Steinman, Vice President Information Services 414/345-3400
Diane Beaudry, Director, Quality Management 414/649-7152

Affiliation: Aurora Health Care; Medical College of Wisconsin; University of
Wisconsin School of Medicine and Public Health

St. Luke's Medical Center
2900 W. Oklahoma Avenue
Milwaukee, Wisconsin 53215

Mary O'Brien, Vice President and Chief Administrative
  Officer 414/647-3000
David Eager, Chief Financial Officer 414/219-1607
Linda S. Hotchkiss, M.D., Vice President Medical Affairs 414/219-7340
Philip Loftus, Chief Information Officer

Affiliation: Aurora Health Care; University of Wisconsin School of Medicine
  and Public Health

CORRESPONDING MEMBER HOSPITALS

CALIFORNIA

Martinez

Veterans Affairs Northern California Health Care System
150 Muir Road
Martinez, California 94553

Brian O'Neil, Director 916/843-9058
Lawrence H. Carroll, Associate Director/East Bay Division 925/372-2015
Alice M. Defriese, Ph.D., Associate Chief of Staff for
Education 916/843-7334
Elizabeth Blohm, Chief, Benefits & Data Management Svc. 925/370-4558
Lucille W. Swanson, Medical Director 925/372-2010
Affiliation: University of California, Davis, School of Medicine

San Jose

Santa Clara Valley Health and Hospital Systems
751 South Bascom Avenue
San Jose, California 95128

Robin Roche, Acting Director 408/885-4004
Kim Roberts, Chief Financial Officer 408/885-6868
David Kerns, M.D., Chief Medical Officer 408/885-4001
Robert Feldman, Chief Information Officer 408/885-5356
Dolly Goel, M.D., Medical Director 408/885-5105
Carolyn Brown, Director, Performance and Outcomes Mgmt. 408/885-5105
Affiliation: Stanford University School of Medicine

COLORADO

Denver

National Jewish Health
1400 Jackson Street
Denver, Colorado 80206

Michael Salem, President & CEO 303/398-1031
Ron Berge, Chief Operating Officer 303/398-1601
Christine Forkner, Comptroller/CFO 303/398-1005
Greg Downey, M.D., Chief Academic Officer 303/398-1436
Jim Harbin, Director, Information Systems 303/398-1950
Gary Cott, M.D., EVP Medical and Clinical Serv 303/398-1084
Affiliation: University of Colorado School of Medicine

CONNECTICUT

Greenwich

Greenwich Hospital
Five Perryridge Road
Greenwich, Connecticut 06830-4697

Frank A. Corvino, President/CEO 203/863-3900
Quinton Friesen, Chief Operating Officer 203/863-3905
Eugene Colucci, Chief Financial Officer 203/863-3006
Marvin Lipschutz, Chief Quality Officer Chief Academic
  Officer 203/863-3986
James Weeks, Chief Information Officer 203/863-3422
Deborah Hodys, General Counsel General Counsel 203/863-3950
Charles B. Seelig, M.D., Medical Director 203/863-3913
Sue Migliardi, Quality Management/Director Quality
  Management/ Improvement Director 203/863-3337
Affiliation: Yale University School of Medicine; Yale-New Haven Health System

IDAHO

Boise

Boise Veterans Affairs Medical Center
500 W. Fort Street
Boise, Idaho 83702
Affiliation: University of Washington School of Medicine

ILLINOIS

Chicago

Rehabilitation Institute of Chicago
345 East Superior Street
Suite 1507
Chicago, Illinois 60611

Joanne C. Smith, M.D., Senior Vice President and Chief
  Operating Officer 312/238-0838
Peggy Kirk, Senior Vice President for Clinical Operations
  Chief Operating Officer 312/238-3305
Ed Case, Chief Financial Officer 312/238-7625
Elliot J. Roth, M.D., Senior Vice President/Medical Director 312/238-4864
Tim McKula, VP IS and CIO Chief Information Officer 312/238-5195
Nancy E. Paridy, J.D., Senior Vice President/General
  Counsel & GRR General Counsel 312/238-6208
Affiliation: Northwestern University The Feinberg School of Medicine

North Chicago

Veterans Affairs Chicago Health Care System
3001 Green Bay Road
North Chicago, Illinois 60064

Saint Singh, Associate Chief Of Staff 847/578-3700
Brad Nystrom, Chief, Informatics 847/578-3815
Tariq Hassan, Chief of Staff 847/578-3701

Affiliation: Chicago Medical School at Rosalind Franklin University of Medicine
& Science

MASSACHUSETTS

Boston

Dana-Farber Cancer Institute
44 Binney Street
Boston, Massachusetts 02115

Edward J. Benz Jr., M.D., President & CEO 617/632-4266
Janet E. Porter, Ph.D., Executive VP & COO 617/632-4602
Dorothy Puhy, Executive VP/CFO 617/632-5244
Jeffrey R. Kessler, Vice President Information Services 617/632-3316
Richard Boskey, General Counsel 617/632-3606
Lawrence Shulman, M.D., Senior VP for Medical Affairs
Chief Medical Officer 617/632-2277
Maureen Connor, R.N., Director for Quality Improvement
Interim Director 617/632-4263

Affiliation: Harvard Medical School

TEXAS

Tyler

University of Texas Health Center at Tyler
11937 U.S. Highway 271
Tyler, Texas 75708

Kirk A. Calhoun, M.D., President 903/877-7750
Robert L. Marshall, Chief Operating Officer 903/877-7750
Vernon Moore, Chief Business and Finance Officer 903/877-2831
John Yoder, Chief Information Officer 903/877-7443

Affiliation: University of Texas Southwestern Medical Center at Dallas
Southwestern Medical School

WEST VIRGINIA

Huntington

Cabell Huntington Hospital
1340 Hal Greer Boulevard
Huntington, West Virginia 25701

Brent A. Marsteller, Executive Director 304/526-2052
Robert Hickman, Vice President, Administration 304/526-2052
David Ward, Senior Vice President/CFO 304/526-2052
Paul English Smith, J.D., General Counsel Legal Services and
  Risk Management 304/526-2057
Hoyt J. Burdick, M.D., VP Medical Affairs 304/526-2064
Valerie Smith, Director, Quality and Resource Management 304/526-2396
Affiliation: Marshall University Joan C. Edwards School of Medicine

Steering Committees of AAMC Groups

2012

Steering Committees of AAMC Groups

Chief Medical Officers Group (CMOG) Steering Committee

Chair
Laura L. Forese, M.D., M.P.H.
New York-Presbyterian Hospital
The University Hospital of Columbia
and Cornell

Chair-Elect
Jonathon D. Truwit, M.D., B.S.E
University of Virginia School of Medicine

Past Chair
Carl J. Getto, M.D.
Regional Medical Center at Memphis

Members

Richard G. Adams, M.D.
Howard University Hospital

Wendy W. Brown, M.D., M.P.H.
Veterans Affairs Chicago Health Care System

Stephanie Lynne Hall, M.D.
LAC + USC Medical Center

Malcolm Henoch, M.D., M.B.A.
Oakwood Healthcare, Inc.

Janis M. Orlowski, M.D.
Washington Hospital Center

Andreas Theodorou, M.D.
University Medical Center

Government Relations Representatives (GRR) Steering Committee

Chair
John Erwin
Conference of Boston Teaching Hospitals

Chair-Elect
Robert H. Blaine, M.A.
Washington University in St. Louis

Past Chair
Robert Vann Acuff, Ph.D.
East Tennessee State University
James H. Quillen College of Medicine

Members

Ryan Adesnik
Stanford University School of Medicine

Mark D. Bowen
University of Nebraska Medical Center

Lynne L Davis Boyle
OHSU Medical Group

Mary Edwards
Fairview Health Services

John Engelen
Emory University School of Medicine

Joshua P. Farrelman
University of Rochester

Peter M. Grollman
Children's Hospital of Philadelphia

Nancy Hardt, M.D.
University of Florida
College of Medicine

Thomas W. Prewitt, M.D.
University of Mississippi School of Medicine

Gina Petredis
Cleveland Clinic Fdn-Oh

Paul Takayama
University of California, San Francisco,
School of Medicine

Gary S. Young
Cooper University Hospital

Steering Committees

Group on Business Affairs (GBA) Steering Committee

Chair
Marcia Cohen, M.B.A.
Stanford University School of Medicine

Chair-Elect
Arnim Dontes
University of Texas Southwestern Medical Center at Dallas Southwestern Medical School

Members

Lisa Abbott
Weill Cornell Medical College

Mary W. Brown
Tulane University School of Medicine

Ronaldo G. Espiritu
University of California, San Diego School of Medicine

Harrold G. McDermott, M.B.A.
University of Alabama School of Medicine

Katherine L. Peck, M.B.A.
University of Florida College of Medicine

Barbara Schroeder, M.S.
Emory University School of Medicine

Cameron W. Slocum, M.B.A.
University of Texas Medical Branch School of Medicine

Group on Diversity and Inclusion (GDI) Steering Committee

Chair
David Acosta, M.D., FAAFP
University of Washington School of Medicine

Chair-Elect
Leon McDougle, M.D., M.P.H.
Ohio State University College of Medicine

Past Chair
Maria Soto-Greene, M.D.
University of Medicine and Dentistry of New Jersey-New Jersey Medical School

Members

Juan Amador
AAMC

Edward J. Callahan, Ph.D.
University of California, Davis, School of Medicine

Andre Lemont Churchwell, M.D.
Vanderbilt University School of Medicine

Deborah W. Davis
Virginia Commonwealth University

Jose Manuel de la Rosa, M.D.
Texas Tech University Health Sciences Center Paul L. Foster School of Medicine

Clarence Lam, M.D., M.P.H.
Johns Hopkins Bloomberg School of Public Health

Karen A. Lewis, M.S.
Meharry Medical College

Francis Lu, M.D.
University of California, Davis, School of Medicine

J. Lloyd Michener, M.D.
Duke University School of Medicine

Ann-Christine Nyquist, M.D., M.S.P.H
University of Colorado School of Medicine

Anthony R. Rodriguez, M.D.
Drexel University College of Medicine

Susan B. Wilson, Ph.D., M.B.A
University of Missouri-Kansas City School of Medicine

Group on Educational Affairs (GEA) Steering Committee

Chair
Karen Szauter, M.D.
University of Texas Medical Branch
School of Medicine - Galveston

Chair-Elect
Brian Mavis, Ph.D.
Michigan State University
College of Human Medicine

Northeast Region Chair
Lee Ann Manchul, M.D.
University of Toronto Faculty of Medicine, Princess
Margaret Hospital

Central Region Chair
Anne Gunderson, Ed.D., G.N.P.
University of Cincinnati College of Medicine

Southern Region Chair
Gary C. Rosenfeld, Ph.D.
The University of Texas
Medical School at Houston

Western Region Chair
Kevin H. Souza, M.S.
University of California, San Francisco
School of Medicine

Council of Deans Liaison
Lois Margaret Nora, M.D., J.D., M.P.H.
The Commonwealth Medical College

OSR Liaison to GEA
Ronnie Zeidan
Medical College of Georgia at
Georgia Health Sciences University

ORR Liaison to GEA
Jonathan Amiel, M.D.
Columbia University
College of Physicians and Surgeons

Research In Medical Education (RIME)
Section Leader
Summers Kalishman, Ph.D.
University of New Mexico
School of Medicine

Undergraduate Medical Education (UGME) Section
Leader
Elizabeth Nelson, M.D.
Baylor College of Medicine

Graduate Medical Education (GME)

Chair
Jamie Padmore
MedStar Health

CGEA Representative
Monica L. Lypson, M.D., M.P.H.E.
University of Michigan Medical School

NEGEA Representative
Frederick Schiavone, Ph.D.
Stony Brook University School of Medicine

SGEA Representative
Carol Thrush, Ed.D.
University of Arkansas for Medical Sciences
College of Medicine

WGEA Representative
Sandrijn van Schaik, M.D., Ph.D.
University of California, San Francisco,
School of Medicine

Continuing Medical Education (CME)

Chair
Barbara E. Barnes, M.D., M.S.
University of Pittsburgh School of Medicine

Chair-Elect
Morris J. Blachman, Ph.D.
University of South Carolina
School of Medicine

Past Chair
John R. Kues, Ph.D.
University of Cincinnati College of Medicine

Members

Shayla Woodson
AAMC

Kenneth E. Wolf, Ph.D.
UCLA/Drew Medical Education Program

Robert Morrow, M.D.
Albert Einstein College of Medicine of
Yeshiva University

David Davis, M.D.
AAMC

Ginny A. Jacobs, M.Ed., M.L.S.
University of Minnesota Medical School

Bonnie M. Miller, M.D.
Vanderbilt University School of Medicine

Carol Goddard
AAMC

Steering Committees

Group on Faculty Affairs (GFA) Steering Committee

Chair
Mary M. Moran, M.D.
Drexel University College of Medicine

Chair-Elect
Luanne E. Thorndyke, M.D.
University of Massachusetts Medical School

Past Chair
Jeannette M. Shorey, II, M.D.
University of Arkansas for Medical Sciences College of Medicine

Members

Steven M. Block, M.B. B.C.H.
Wake Forest University School of Medicine

James Mackinnon Crawford, M.D., Ph.D.
North Shore-Long Island Jewish Health System

Laura Fentem, M.Ed.
University of Oklahoma Health Sciences Center

Lois J. Geist, M.D.
University of Iowa Roy J. and Lucille A. Carver College of Medicine

Leslie A. Morrison, M.D.
University of New Mexico School of Medicine

Kathleen G. Nelson, M.D.
University of Alabama School of Medicine

Karen D. Novielli, M.D.
Jefferson Medical College of Thomas Jefferson University

James Neutens, Ph.D.
University of Tennessee Medical Center

Vivian Reznik, M.D., M.P.H.
University of California, San Diego School of Medicine

Roberta E. Sonnino, M.D., F.A.C.S., F.A.A.P.
Wayne State University School of Medicine

Henry W. Strobel, Ph.D.
University of Texas Medical School at Houston

Valerie N. Williams, Ph.D., M.P.A.
University of Oklahoma College of Medicine

James Wyss, M.D.
University of Medicine and Dentistry of New Jersey-New Jersey Medical School

Group on Faculty Practice (GFP) Steering Committee

Chair
Scott Hofferber
University of Missouri-Columbia School of Medicine

Chair-Elect
Craig Henry Syrop, M.D.
University of Iowa Roy J. and Lucille A. Carver College of Medicine

Past Chair
Paul A. Taheri, M.D., M.B.A.
Fletcher Allen Health Care

Members

Lisa Anastos
University of Chicago Medical Center

Dayle Benson, M.H.A.
University of Utah School of Medicine

Bruce M. Elliott, M.D.
Medical University of South Carolina College of Medicine

Greg Pauly
Massachusetts General Hospital

James John Potyraj, M.S., M.H.A.
Virginia Commonwealth University School of Medicine

Lawrence Leviticus Sanders, Jr., M.D., M.B.A.
Grady Memorial Hospital-Atlanta, GA

Harold Paz, M.D.
Pennsylvania State University College of Medicine

Group on Graduate Research, Education, and Training (GREAT) Steering Committee

Chair
Wayne T. McCormack, Ph.D.
University of Florida College of Medicine

Chair-Elect
Michael F. Verderame, Ph.D.
Pennsylvania State University
College of Medicine

Past Chair
Nancy Street, Ph.D.
University of Texas
Southwestern Medical Center at Dallas Southwestern Medical School

Members

Myles Akabas, M.D., Ph.D.
Albert Einstein College of Medicine of
Yeshiva University

Mary Brenan Bradley, M.L.A.
Washington University in St. Louis
School of Medicine

Victoria Freedman, Ph.D.
Albert Einstein College of Medicine of
Yeshiva University

Alison Hall, Ph.D.
Case Western Reserve University
School of Medicine

Lisa Kozlowski, Ph.D.
Jefferson Medical College of
Thomas Jefferson University

Charlotte Kuh, Ph.D.
No inst affil specified

Maria De Fatima Lima, Ph.D.
Meharry Medical College

Robinna G. Lorenz, M.D., Ph.D.
University of Alabama School of Medicine

Claire Pomeroy, M.D., M.B.A.
University of California, Davis, Health System

Richard F. Rest, Ph.D.
Drexel University College of Medicine

Naomi Rosenberg, Ph.D.
Tufts University School of Medicine

Rodney Ulane, Ph.D.
National Institutes of Health

Jamboor K. Vishwanatha, Ph.D.
University of North Texas-Hlth Sci Ctr at
Ft Worth

Thomas C. Westfall, Ph.D.
Saint Louis University Hospital

Keith D. Wilkinson, Ph.D.
Emory University School of Medicine

Steering Committees

Group on Information Resources (GIR) Steering Committee

Chair
Jill Jemison
University of Vermont College of Medicine

Chair-Elect
Barbara Baldwin
University of Virginia Medical Center

Past Chair
Brett A. Kirkpatrick, M.L.S.
University of Texas Medical Branch
School of Medicine

Members

Bridget Barnes
Oregon Health & Science University
School of Medicine

Ted Hanss
University of Michigan Medical School

Ron N. Price, Jr.
Loyola University Chicago
Stritch School of Medicine

Kevin H. Souza, M.S.
University of California, San Francisco,
School of Medicine

Gretchen Tegethoff
George Washington University Hospital

Group on Institutional Advancement (GIA) Steering Committee

Chair
Chad B. Ruback, M.S.Ed., M.B.A.
University of Iowa Roy J. and Lucille A. Carver
College of Medicine

Chair-Elect
Joni Westerhouse
Washington University in St. Louis
School of Medicine

Past Chair
Dale Tate
UCLA Medical Center

Members

Jill Austin, M.B.A.
Vanderbilt University School of Medicine

David Bruce Anderson, M.B.A.
University of North Carolina at Chapel Hill School
of Medicine

Martha Kelly Bates, M.F.A.
Chicago Medical School at Rosalind Franklin University of Medicine & Science

Barry J. Collins, M.B.A.
University of Virginia Medical Alumni Association
& Medical School Foundation

Patricia Comey
Drexel University College of Medicine

Brenda Maceo
University of Southern California

Elizabeth Rigby
Partners HealthCare System, Inc.

Larry Schafer
Weill Cornell Medical College

Steven R. Singer, M.P.A.
Dana-Farber Cancer Institute

Shawn M. Vogen, Ph.D.
Loyola University of Chicago

Group on Institutional Planning (GIP) Steering Committee

Chair
Rhonice Burnett
Johns Hopkins University School of Medicine

Chair-Elect
Angie Souza
University of Arizona College of Medicine

Members

Pam Bounelis, Ph.D.
University of Alabama School of Medicine

Walter L. Douglas
University of Medicine and Dentistry of New Jersey-New Jersey Medical School

Donna K. Gissen
University of Louisville School of Medicine

Rama Iyengar
Mount Sinai School of Medicine

Sean Ossont, M.B.A., M.H.A.
University of Rochester
School of Medicine and Dentistry

Linda Reimann
Washington University in St. Louis
School of Medicine

Lynette Stewart Seebohm
University of Utah School of Medicine

Group on Regional Medical Campuses (GRMC) Steering Committee

Chair
Craig Cheifetz, M.D.
Virginia Commonwealth University
School of Medicine

Membership Chair
Geoffrey W. Payne, Ph.D.
University of British Columbia
Faculty of Medicine

Members

Linda Boyd, D.O.
Georgia Health Sciences University

James C. Norton, Ph.D.
University of Kentucky College of Medicine

Leonel Vela, M.D., M.P.H.
The University of Texas
School of Medicine at San Antonio

Steering Committees

Group on Research Advancement and Development (GRAND) Steering Committee

Chair
Robert P. Kimberly, M.D.
University of Alabama School of Medicine

Chair-Elect
Lars F. Berglund, M.D., Ph.D.
University of California, Davis,
School of Medicine

Past Chair
Richard John Bookman, Ph.D.
University of Miami Leonard M. Miller
School of Medicine

Members

Alison M. J. Buchan, Ph.D.
University of British Columbia
Faculty of Medicine

Curt Civin, M.D.
University of Maryland School of Medicine

Lawrence E. Cornett, Ph.D.
University of Arkansas for Medical Sciences College of Medicine

Peter John Arwyn Davies, M.D., Ph.D.
University of Texas Medical School at Houston

Brian Herman, Ph.D.
The University of Texas
School of Medicine at San Antonio

Robert A. Rizza, M.D.
Mayo Medical School

Sally A. Shumaker, Ph.D., M.A.
Wake Forest University School of Medicine

Group on Resident Affairs (GRA) Steering Committee

Chair
Mark C. Wilson, M.D., M.P.H.
University of Iowa Roy J. and Lucille A. Carver
College of Medicine

Chair-Elect
Monica L. Lypson, M.D., M.P.H.E.
University of Michigan-Ann Arbor

Past Chair
Marilane Brookes Bond, Ed.D., M.B.A.
Emory University School of Medicine

Members

Kathryn Andolsek, M.D., M.P.H.
Duke University Hospital

Miriam Elizabeth Bar-on, M.D.
University of Nevada School of Medicine

Donald W. Brady, M.D.
Vanderbilt University School of Medicine

James A. Clardy, M.D.
University of Arkansas for Medical Sciences College of Medicine

Ann M. Dohn, M.A.
Stanford Hospital and Clinics

Sara Jo Grethlein, M.D., F.A.C.P.
Bassett Healthcare

Susan E. Kirk, M.D.
University of Virginia School of Medicine

Jill A. Moormeier, M.D., M.P.H.
University of Missouri-Kansas City
School of Medicine

Carole Lowman Pillinger, M.D.
William Jennings Bryan Dorn Veterans Admin.
Hospital

Joel C. Rosenfeld, M.D., M.Ed.
St. Luke's Hospital

Frederick Schiavone, M.D.
The School of Medicine at Stony Brook University
Medical Center

Sunny G. Yoder
AAMC

Group on Student Affairs (GSA) Steering Committee

Chair
Patricia A. Barrier, M.D., M.P.H.
Mayo Clinic College of Medicine

Chair-Elect
W. Scott Schroth, M.D., M.P.H.
George Washington University
School of Medicine and Health Sciences

Past Chair
Maureen Garrity, Ph.D.
University of Colorado School of Medicine

Members

Adam Aponte, M.D.
Hofstra North Shore - LIJ School of Medicine

Steven L. Berk, M.D.
Texas Tech University Health Sciences Center
School of Medicine

Rachel Margaret Ann Brown, M.D.
University of Missouri-Columbia
School of Medicine

Steven T. Case, Ph.D., M.S.
University of Mississippi School of Medicine

Robert D. Coughlin
Harvard Medical School

Marc J. Kahn, M.D., M.B.A.
Tulane University School of Medicine

Michael Gerard Kavan, Ph.D.
Creighton University School of Medicine

James Kerwin, M.D.
University of Arizona College of Medicine

Thomas Wayne Koenig, M.D.
Johns Hopkins University School of Medicine

Karen A. Lewis, M.S.
Meharry Medical College

Vickie Lindsey
AAMC

Chris Meiers, Ph.D.
University of Kansas School of Medicine

Lori Provost
Muhlenberg College

Steven Carl Specter, Ph.D.
USF Health Morsani College of Medicine

Jonathan F. Thomas
University of Kentucky College of Medicine

Geoffrey Young, Ph.D.
AAMC

Group on Women in Medicine and Science Coordinating Committee

Chair
Jocelyn D. Chertoff, M.D., M.S.
Dartmouth Medical School

Chair-Elect
Rebecca Rainer Pauly, M.D.
University of Florida College of Medicine

Past Chair
J. Renee Navarro, M.D.
University of California, San Francisco,
School of Medicine

Members

Emily Abdoler, B.A.
University of Michigan Medical School

Archana Chatterjee, M.D., Ph.D.
Creighton University School of Medicine

Elizabeth Coakley, M.A.
AAMC

Betty M. Drees, M.D.
University of Missouri-Kansas City
School of Medicine

Lynn Kathryn Gordon, M.D., Ph.D.
University of California, Los Angeles
David Geffen School of Medicine

Lauren Jolliff
AAMC

Elisabeth Kunkel, M.D.
Jefferson Medical College of
Thomas Jefferson University

Marisa Oishi, M.D., M.P.H.
Brooklyn Hospital Center

Susan Kasper Pingleton, M.D.
University of Kansas Medical Center

Angela Sharkey, M.D.
Saint Louis University School of Medicine

Elizabeth Travis, Ph.D.
University of Texas
M. D. Anderson Cancer Center

Organization of Student Representatives

2012

Organization of Student Representatives Administrative Board, 2011-2012

Chair
Joe Thomas
University of Kentucky College of Medicine

Chair-Elect
Ronnie Zeidan
Medical College of Georgia at Georgia Health Sciences University

Past Chair
David Friedlander
Vanderbilt University School of Medicine

Regional Chairs

Central
Reem Nubani
Southern Illinois University School of Medicine

Northeast
Judith Wilbur
University of Massachusetts Medical School

Southern
Anne Porter
University of Texas Health Sciences Center at San Antonio

Western
Dawn Pruett
Oregon Health & Science University School of Medicine

Delegates

Communications
Colleen Kays
Columbia University College of Physicians & Surgeons

Community & Diversity
Utibe Essien
Albert Einstein College of Medicine of Yeshiva University

Legislative Affairs
Bill Teeter
Tulane University School of Medicine

Medical Education
Meghan Crawley
University at Buffalo SUNY School of Medicine & Biomedical Sciences

Student Affairs
Mariya Kalashnikova
Keck School of Medicine of the University of Southern California

Ex-Officio

Katie Spina
Boston University School of Medicine

Organization of Resident Representatives

2012

Chair
Jonathan M. Amiel, M.D.
Columbia University College of Physicians and Surgeons

Chair-Elect
Brenessa Lindeman, M.D.
Johns Hopkins University School of Medicine

Immediate Past Chair
Justin Matthew Weis, M.D.
University of Rochester Medical Center

Members

William Edwards Bynum, IV, M.D.
Uniformed Services University of the Health Sciences
F. Edward Hebert School of Medicine

Brenessa Lindeman, M.D.
Johns Hopkins University

Dawn Marie Emick, M.D.
Duke University School of Medicine

Joe Hall
Medical College of Georgia at Georgia Health Sciences University

Brandon Kellie, M.D.
Case Western Reserve University School of Medicine

Debra Regier, M.D. Ph.D.
Children's National Medical Center

Other Members

2012

Distinguished Service Members

Distinguished Service Membership in the Association of American Medical Colleges recognizes significant contributions to the association. Distinguished Service Members are elected by vote upon recommendation.

Council of Deans

William G. Anlyan
Harry N. Beaty
Steven C. Beering
A. Lorris Betz
Stuart Bondurant
L. Thompson Bowles
William T. Butler
David R. Challoner
D. Kay Clawson
Jordan J. Cohen
Robert M. Daugherty Jr.
William B. Deal
Haile T. Debas

Robert J. Glaser
James A. Hallock
Jeffrey L. Houpt
William N. Hubbard
John J. Hutton
Richard Janeway
Robert P. Kelch
Julius Krevans
Richard D. Krugman
Philip R. Lee
William H. Luginbuhl
Stanley Olson

William Peck
Deborah E. Powell
E. Albert Reece
Ralph Snyderman
Robert D. Sparks
Edward J. Stemmler
Robert C. Talley
Robert L. Van Citters
Andrew G. Wallace
Donald E. Wilson
Emery A. Wilson
I. Dodd Wilson

Council of Academic Societies

Diana S. Beattie
Kenneth I. Berns
Alfred Jay Bollet
Rita M. Charon
Sam L. Clark Jr.
Carmine D. Clemente
Terrance G. Cooper
Joe D. Coulter
William H. Dantzler

Joel DeLisa
Robert J. Desnick
N. Eckhert
Robert E. Forster II
Michael Friedlander
Paul J. Friedman
Myron Genel
Robert L. Hill

Randall K. Holmes
Robert O. Kelley
Frank G. Moody
Hiram C. Polk
George F. Sheldon
William B. Weil Jr.
Virginia V. Weldon
Frank C. Wilson Jr.

Council of Teaching Hospitals and Health Systems

Theresa A. Bischoff
J. Robert Buchanan
Frank A. Butler
John W. Colloton
David D'Eramo
Spencer Foreman
Harvey A. Holzberg

R. Edward Howell
Michael M. E. Johns
William B. Kerr
Paul L. McCarthy
Ralph W. Muller
Herbert Pardes
Thomas M. Priselac

Mitchell T. Rabkin
Barbara L. Schuster
Elliot J. Sussman
Samuel O. Thier
Irvin G. Wilmot
Daniel H. Winship

Emeritus

Emeritus Membership in the Association of American Medical Colleges was established in 1958 to recognize those individuals who had reached retirement age or had become emeritus members of their faculty and who, prior to retirement, had been active in the affairs of the association. According to guidelines established by the association, Emeritus Members must be judged to have given outstanding service to the association through membership on its Councils, Committees, or Task Forces. Emeritus Members are elected by vote.

Shelley A. Bader, Ed. D. (2010)
DeWitt C. Baldwin Jr., M.D. (1983)
Robert S. Blacklow, M.D. (2003)
Arnold L. Brown Jr., M.D.(1991)
Stebbins B. Chandor, M.D. (2004)
John D. Chase, M.D. (1983)
Robert M. D'Alessandri, M.D. (2005)
Walter J. Daly, M.D. (1996)
W. Dale Dauphinee, M.D. (2007)
Thomas D. Dublin, M.D. (1986)
William E. Easterling Jr., M.D. (1995)
John W. Eckstein, M.D. (1991)
Ronald G. Evens, M.D. (2007)
Bernard J. Fogel, M.D. (1996)
Robert E. Frank (1991)
Earl J. Frederick (1992)
Daniel H. Funkenstein, M.D. (1983)
James R. Gay, M.D. (1986)
Irma E. Goertzen (2004)
David S. Greer, M.D. (1992)
Arthur P. Grollman, M.D., Ph.D. (2001)
E. Nigel Harris, M.D. (2005)
James W. Haviland, M.D. (1976)
Treuman Katz (2007)

Thomas C. King, M.D. (1995)
David Korn, M.D. (2008)
John K. Lattimer, M.D., D.Sc. (1981)
Donlin M. Long, M.D., Ph.D. (2001)
Ruy V. Lourenco, M.D., Ph.D. (2000)
Robert U. Massey, M.D. (1987)
Betty H. Mawardi, Ph.D. (1985)
Layton McCurdy, M.D. (2000)
Glenn R. Mitchell (1995)
Woodrow W. Morris, M.D. (1984)
Gerald S. Moss, M.D. (2005)
Richard H. Moy, M.D. (1993)
Eric B. Munson (2004)
Leonard M. Napolitano, Ph.D. (1994)
Malcom Randall (2000)
Morton I. Rapoport, M.D. (2003)
Seymour L. Romney, M.D. (1987)
Richard S. Ross, M.D. (1992)
Antonio Scarpa, M.D., Ph.D. (2010)
Irene M. Thompson (2007)
Gail L. Warden (2004)
Larry Warren (2006)
David S. Weiner (2003)
Donald Weston, M.D. (1991)

Index

2012

Index

Index

Index

Index

Index

Index

Index

Index

Index

Index

Index

Index

Index

Index

Index

Index

Index

Index

Index

Index

Index

Index

Index

Index

Index

Index

Index

L

Index

Index

Index

M

Index

Index

Index

Index

Index

Index

Index

536

Index

Index

Index

Index

Index

Index

Index

Index

Index

Index

Index

V

Index

Index

Index